WITHDRAWN
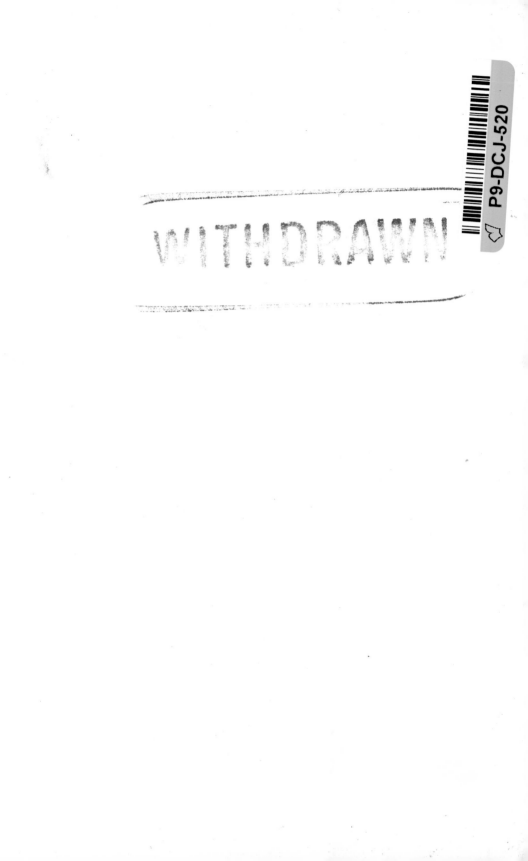

ORIGINS AND DEVELOPMENT OF SCHIZOPHRENIA

ORIGINS and DEVELOPMENT of SCHIZOPHRENIA

ADVANCES IN EXPERIMENTAL PSYCHOPATHOLOGY

Edited by
MARK F. LENZENWEGER
ROBERT H. DWORKIN

AMERICAN PSYCHOLOGICAL ASSOCIATION
WASHINGTON DC

Hillsborough Community College LRC

Copyright © 1998 by the American Psychological Association. All rights reserved. Except as permitted under the United States Copyright Act of 1976, no part of this publication may be reproduced or distributed in any form or by any means, or stored in a database or retrieval system, without the prior written permission of the publisher.

Published by
American Psychological Association
750 First Street, NE
Washington, DC 20002

Copies may be ordered from
APA Order Department
P.O. Box 92984
Washington, DC 20090–2984

In the United Kingdom, Europe, Africa, and the Middle East, copies may be ordered from American Psychological Association
3 Henrietta Street, Covent Garden
London WC2E 8LU, England

Typeset in Minion by EPS Group Inc., Easton, MD

Printer: Data Reproductions Corp., Auburn Hills, MI
Jacket designer: Berg Design, Albany, NY
Technical/production editor: Amy J. Clarke

Library of Congress Cataloging-in-Publication Data
Origins and development of schizophrenia : advances in experimental
 psychopathology / edited by Mark F. Lenzenweger and Robert H. Dworkin.
   p. cm.
 Includes bibliographical references and indexes.
   ISBN 1–55798–497–2 (cloth : alk. paper)
   1. Schizophrenia—Etiology. I. Lenzenweger, Mark F. II. Dworkin, Robert H.
 RC514.075 1998
 616.89′82071—dc21   97-52362
 for Library of Congress   CIP

British Library Cataloging-in-Publication Data
A CIP record is available from the British Library.

Printed in the United States of America
First edition

To the memory of
David Rosenthal, PhD, David Shakow, PhD, and Joseph Zubin, PhD,
the founders of experimental psychopathology—mentors
and models for many.

APA Science Volumes

Attribution and Social Interaction: The Legacy of Edward E. Jones

Best Methods for the Analysis of Change: Recent Advances, Unanswered Questions, Future Directions

Cardiovascular Reactivity to Psychological Stress and Disease

The Challenge in Mathematics and Science Education: Psychology's Response

Changing Employment Relations: Behavioral and Social Perspectives

Children Exposed to Marital Violence: Theory, Research, and Applied Issues

Cognition: Conceptual and Methodological Issues

Cognitive Bases of Musical Communication

Conceptualization and Measurement of Organism–Environment Interaction

Converging Operations in the Study of Visual Selective Attention

Creative Thought: An Investigation of Conceptual Structures and Processes

Developmental Psychoacoustics

Diversity in Work Teams: Research Paradigms for a Changing Workplace

Emotion and Culture: Empirical Studies of Mutual Influence

Emotion, Disclosure, and Health

Evolving Explanations of Development: Ecological Approaches to Organism–Environment Systems

Examining Lives in Context: Perspectives on the Ecology of Human Development

Global Prospects for Education: Development, Culture, and Schooling

Hostility, Coping, and Health

Measuring Patient Changes in Mood, Anxiety, and Personality Disorders: Toward a Core Battery

Occasion Setting: Associative Learning and Cognition in Animals

Organ Donation and Transplantation: Psychological and Behavioral Factors

Origins and Development of Schizophrenia: Advances in Experimental Psychopathology

The Perception of Structure

Perspectives on Socially Shared Cognition

Psychological Testing of Hispanics

Psychology of Women's Health: Progress and Challenges in Research and Application

Researching Community Psychology: Issues of Theory and Methods

The Rising Curve: Long-Term Gains in IQ and Related Measures

Sleep and Cognition

Sleep Onset: Normal and Abnormal Processes

Stereotype Accuracy: Toward Appreciating Group Differences

Stereotyped Movements: Brain and Behavior Relationships

Studying Lives Through Time: Personality and Development

The Suggestibility of Children's Recollections: Implications for Eyewitness Testimony

Taste, Experience, and Feeding: Development and Learning

Temperament: Individual Differences at the Interface of Biology and Behavior

Through the Looking Glass: Issues of Psychological Well-Being in Captive Nonhuman Primates

Uniting Psychology and Biology: Integrative Perspectives on Human Development

Viewing Psychology as a Whole: The Integrative Science of William N. Dember

APA expects to publish volumes on the following conference topics:

Computational Modeling of Behavioral Processes in Organizations

Dissonance Theory 40 Years Later: A Revival With Revisions and Controversies

Marital and Family Therapy Outcome and Process Research

Models of Gender and Gender Differences: Then and Now
Psychosocial Interventions for Cancer

As part of its continuing and expanding commitment to enhance the dissemination of scientific psychological knowledge, the Science Directorate of the APA established a Scientific Conferences Program. A series of volumes resulting from these conferences is produced jointly by the Science Directorate and the Office of Communications. A call for proposals is issued twice annually by the Scientific Directorate, which, collaboratively with the APA Board of Scientific Affairs, evaluates the proposals and selects several conferences for funding. This important effort has resulted in an exceptional series of meetings and scholarly volumes, each of which has contributed to the dissemination of research and dialogue in these topical areas.

The APA Science Directorate's conferences funding program has supported 47 conferences since its inception in 1988. To date, 40 volumes resulting from conferences have been published.

WILLIAM C. HOWELL, PHD
Executive Director

VIRGINIA E. HOLT
Assistant Executive Director

Contents

List of Contributors   xv

Prologue: The Origins and Development of
Schizophrenia   xix
Mark F. Lenzenweger and Robert H. Dworkin

Part One: Models of Liability and Etiology

1   Genotypes, Genes, Genesis, and Pathogenesis in
Schizophrenia   5
Irving I. Gottesman and Steven O. Moldin

2   A Two-Hit Working Model of the Etiology of
Schizophrenia   27
Sarnoff A. Mednick, Jennifer B. Watson, Matti Huttunen,
Tyrone D. Cannon, Heikki Katila, Ricardo Machon,
Birgitte Mednick, Meggin Hollister, Josef Parnas,
Fini Schulsinger, Nina Sajaniemi, Peter Voldsgaard,
Reijo Pyhala, Dan Gutkind, and Xueyi Wang

3   Genetic and Perinatal Influences in the Etiology of
Schizophrenia: A Neurodevelopmental Model   67
Tyrone D. Cannon

4   Schizotypy and Schizotypic Psychopathology: Mapping
an Alternative Expression of Schizophrenia Liability   93
Mark F. Lenzenweger

5   Regulation of Information Flow in the Nucleus
Accumbens: A Model for the Pathophysiology of
Schizophrenia   123
Anthony A. Grace and Holly Moore

Part Two: Neurocognitive Processes

6   How Are Deficits in Motion Perception Related to
    Eye-Tracking Dysfunction in Schizophrenia?   161
    Philip S. Holzman, Yue Chen, Ken Nakayama,
    Deborah L. Levy, and Steven Matthysse

7   Disinhibition in Antisaccade Performance in
    Schizophrenia   185
    Deborah L. Levy, Nancy R. Mendell,
    Christian A. LaVancher, Joanna Brownstein,
    Olga Krastoshevsky, Laurie Teraspulsky,
    Kimberly S. McManus, Yungtai Lo, Rebecca Bloom,
    Steven Matthysse, and Philip S. Holzman

8   Lateralization, Memory, and Language in
    Schizophrenia: Some Facts and an Artifact   211
    Brendan A. Maher and Theo C. Manschreck

9   Neural Mechanisms Underlying Hallucinations in
    Schizophrenia: The Role of Abnormal Fronto-Temporal
    Interactions   235
    Emily Stern and David A. Silbersweig

10 The Role of Cognitive Psychology in Guiding Research
    on Cognitive Deficits in Schizophrenia:
    A Process-Oriented Approach   247
    Raymond A. Knight and Steven M. Silverstein

Part Three: Approaches to Vulnerability

11 Neurocognitive Vulnerability Factors for Schizophrenia:
    Convergence Across Genetic Risk Studies and
    Longitudinal Trait–State Studies   299
    Keith H. Nuechterlein, Robert F. Asarnow,
    Kenneth L. Subotnik, David L. Fogelson, Joseph Ventura,
    Richard D. Torquato, and Michael E. Dawson

12 Backward-Masking Performance in Schizophrenia   329
    Michael F. Green and Keith H. Nuechterlein

13 High-Risk Research in Schizophrenia: New Strategies,
    New Designs   349
    Barbara A. Cornblatt, Michael Obuchowski,
    Alyson Andreasen, and Christopher Smith

14 Affective Expression and Affective Experience in
    Schizophrenia   385
    Robert H. Dworkin, Harriet Oster, Scott C. Clark, and
    Stephanie R. White

Part Four: Developmental Processes, Course, and Outcome

15 Prediction From Longitudinal Assessments of
    High-Risk Children   427
    L. Erlenmeyer-Kimling, Simone A. Roberts, Donald Rock,
    Ulla Hildoff Adamo, Barbara Maminski Shapiro, and
    Sky Pape

16 Expressed Emotion and the Pathogenesis of Relapse
    in Schizophrenia   447
    Jill M. Hooley and Jordan B. Hiller

17 Developmental Changes in the Behavioral Expression
    of Vulnerability for Schizophrenia   469
    Elaine F. Walker, Kym M. Baum, and Donald Diforio

    Epilogue: Comments on the Origins and Development
    of Schizophrenia   493
    Richard R. J. Lewine

Author Index   505
Subject Index   533
About the Editors   557

Contributors

Ulla Hildoff Adamo, MA, New York State Psychiatric Institute,
New York, NY

Alyson Andreasen, BA, Long Island Jewish-Hillside Hospital Medical
Center, Glen Oaks, NY

Robert F. Asarnow, PhD, University of California, Los Angeles

Kym M. Baum, MA, Emory University

Rebecca Bloom, BA, University of Nottingham, England

Joanna Brownstein, BA, McLean Hospital, Belmont, MA

Tyrone D. Cannon, PhD, University of Pennsylvania

Yue Chen, PhD, Harvard University

Scott C. Clark, MD, Columbia University

Barbara A. Cornblatt, PhD, Long Island Jewish-Hillside Hospital
Medical Center, Glen Oaks, NY

Michael E. Dawson, PhD, University of Southern California

Donald Diforio, MA, Emory University

Robert H. Dworkin, PhD, University of Rochester

L. Erlenmeyer-Kimling, PhD, DSc (hon), Columbia University and
New York State Psychiatric Institute, New York, NY

David L. Fogelson, MD, University of California, Los Angeles

Irving I. Gottesman, PhD, University of Virginia

Anthony A. Grace, PhD, University of Pittsburgh

Michael F. Green, PhD, University of California, Los Angeles, and
West Los Angeles VA Medical Center

Dan Gutkind, BA, University of Southern California

Jordan B. Hiller, MA, Harvard University

Meggin Hollister, PhD, University of Pennsylvania

Philip S. Holzman, Harvard University and McLean Hospital,
Belmont, MA

Jill M. Hooley, DPhil, Harvard University

Matti Huttunen, MD, University of Southern California

Heikki Katila, MD, University of Helsinki, Finland

Raymond A. Knight, PhD, Brandeis University

Olga Krastoshevsky, McLean Hospital, Belmont, MA

Christian A. LaVancher, BA, McLean Hospital, Belmont, MA

Mark F. Lenzenweger, PhD, Cornell University and Cornell University
    Medical College

Deborah L. Levy, PhD, Harvard University Medical School and
    McLean Hospital, Belmont, MA

Richard R. J. Lewine, PhD, Emory University School of Medicine

Yungtai Lo, MA, State University of New York at Stony Brook

Ricardo Machon, PhD, Loyola–Marymount University

Brendan A. Maher, PhD, Harvard University

Theo C. Manschreck, MD, Harvard University Medical School

Steven Matthysse, PhD, Harvard University Medical School and
    McLean Hospital, Belmont, MA

Kimberly S. McManus, MA, McLean Hospital, Belmont, MA

Birgitte Mednick, PhD, University of Southern California

Sarnoff A. Mednick, PhD, DrMed, University of Southern California

Nancy R. Mendell, PhD, State University of New York at Stony Brook

Steven O. Moldin, PhD, National Institute of Mental Health,
    Rockville, MD

Holly Moore, PhD, University of Pittsburgh

Ken Nakayama, PhD, Harvard University

Keith H. Nuechterlein, PhD, University of California, Los Angeles

Michael Obuchowski, PhD, Long Island Jewish-Hillside Hospital
    Medical Center, Glen Oaks, NY

Harriet Oster, PhD, New York University

Sky Pape, BFA, New York State Psychiatric Institute, New York, NY

Josef Parnas, MD, Copenhagen Health Service, Copenhagen,
    Denmark

Reijo Pyhala, PhD, National Public Health Institute, Helsinki, Finland

Simone A. Roberts, BA, New York State Psychiatric Institute, New York, NY

Donald Rock, PhD, Educational Testing Service, Princeton, NJ

Nina Sajaniemi, MS, University of Helsinki, Finland

Fini Schulsinger, MD, DrMed, Copenhagen Health Service, Copenhagen, Denmark

Barbara Maminski Shapiro, BA, New York State Psychiatric Institute, New York, NY

David A. Silbersweig, MD, Cornell University Medical College

Steven M. Silverstein, PhD, University of Rochester Medical Center

Christopher Smith, BA, Long Island Jewish-Hillside Hospital Medical Center, Glen Oaks, NY

Emily Stern, MD, Cornell University Medical College

Kenneth L. Subotnik, PhD, University of California, Los Angeles

Laurie Teraspulsky, PhD, McLean Hospital, Belmont, MA

Richard D. Torquato, MA, University of California, Los Angeles

Joseph Ventura, PhD, University of California, Los Angeles

Peter Voldsgaard, MD, Copenhagen Health Service, Copenhagen, Denmark

Elaine F. Walker, PhD, Emory University

Xueyi Wang, MD, Kailuan Mental Hospital, Tangshan, China

Jennifer B. Watson, MA, University of Southern California

Stephanie R. White, BA, Goucher College

Prologue:
The Origins and Development of Schizophrenia

Mark F. Lenzenweger and Robert H. Dworkin

Schizophrenia, the most devastating form of psychopathology known, continues to elude those scientists seeking to definitively illuminate its pathogenesis. Affecting almost 1% (Gottesman, 1991) of the U.S. population alone, this disorder costs the country in excess of $70 billion annually (Wyatt, Henter, Leary, & Taylor, 1995) in direct care and aftercare costs as well as lost earnings. Despite its elusive nature, great strides have been made during the past decade by experimental psychopathologists seeking to understand the basic processes known to be dysfunctional in schizophrenia across a variety of substantive domains and levels of analysis (e.g., psychophysiologic, affect and emotion, cognition and memory, neurobiology, and genetics). The rapid advance in our knowledge of this disorder has been fostered by developments in theory (e.g., latent liability, neurodevelopmental, and schizotypy models), an enhanced understanding of cognition and emotion systems in relation to brain functioning, and significant diagnostic improvements (e.g., *Diagnostic and Statistical Manual of Mental Disorders* criteria and the multidimensional symptom model) as well as by technological innovations (e.g., neuroimaging, linkage analysis, quantitative trait loci). Moreover, the cohorts of individuals "at risk" for schizophrenia, followed longitudinally by the major "high-risk" studies begun in the 1960s and 1970s, have traversed much of the risk period for the illness, and those conducting the high-risk investigations are now examining schizophrenia spectrum outcomes.

The history of schizophrenia research is marked by a variety of vicissitudes that very nearly have no parallel in research on other forms of psychopathology. Early observers of the illness, such as Kraepelin (1919/1971) and Bleuler (1950), emphasized the value of careful phenomenologic description, the utility of longitudinal observation, and the possible role of genetic factors in the etiology of the illness. However, through the 1930s, 1940s, and 1950s, largely because of the fascination of many American psychiatrists and psychologists with psychoanalytic theory and methods as well as models stressing social causation of psychopathology, theory and research in schizophrenia were often characterized by a focus on the environment and various psychosocial forces. This focus on environmental influences was frequently guided by an implicit assumption that such factors were causally related to the etiology and development of schizophrenia.

During this period, research efforts directed at an explication of cognition and emotion in schizophrenia, determination of the relevance of genetic influences to etiology, or consideration of brain-based models of pathology were forced to swim upstream against a strong current. Moreover, at this time, the importance of phenomenology and diagnosis was considerably diminished, as it did not fit well with the prevailing zeitgeist. However, beginning in the early 1960s, the "rediscovery" of the value of careful description and diagnosis increased the field's responsiveness to the application of methods from the experimental psychology laboratory and to questions regarding cognition, emotion, and brain–behavior relations as well as to the fruitful integration of the behavioral genetic and neurobiology vantage points. Hence, schizophrenia research began to move forward once again. The synergy generated by this confluence of scientific perspectives has yielded considerable new knowledge in recent years as well as opened a variety of novel and fascinating areas for future schizophrenia research.

We believe that the most important advances in recent schizophrenia research have come from those scientists working across multiple domains and levels of analysis simultaneously. This volume, therefore, contains chapters written by those researchers who have been working in at least two of the following areas in schizophrenia research: (a) affect and emotion; (b) high-risk research and developmental processes; (c) genetics of complex behaviors; (d) cognitive neuroscience, neuroimaging, and psychophysiology; and (e) theoretical models of liability and pathogenesis. This volume represents a forum in which these scientists could present and develop further their theoretical and methodological approaches to research in schizophrenia. We anticipated that all of our contributors would share their views on the future directions of schizophrenia research and, more important, direct their thoughts and speculations, informed by models and data, to address the fundamental question of *How does schizophrenia emerge and develop?* In short, we hoped to hear from each of our contributors their latest thoughts on the mechanisms through which the pathology in schizophrenia operates to affect thought, emotion, behavior, and, of course, brain functioning. We present this volume so others can examine these various models, position statements, critiques, and proposals for current and ongoing experimental psychopathology-based approaches to the pathogenesis of schizophrenia.

There are three themes that reverberate throughout this volume, each to a different degree for each of the chapters, and they provide the context in which these may be read by psychologists, psychiatrists, and any researcher with an active interest in schizophrenia. Those three themes are the experimental psychopathology perspective, integration and consolidation, and a forward-looking vantage point. The experimental psychopathology perspective emphasizes the leverage provided by the use of rigorous laboratory-based approaches in gaining an understanding of the fundamental nature of schizophrenia. Experimental psychopathology has always sought to move beyond a mere description of schizophrenia and enumeration of the various associated features of the illness. Using many of the tools and strategies of experimental psychology, it has emphasized a methodologic approach advocating a systematic probing and illumination of processes and mechanisms thought to be central to the development of schizophrenia, the articulation of data-based models that attempt to integrate across levels of analysis, and—perhaps above all else—the utility of the laboratory as well as reliable and valid measurement in pursuing these aims. The focus of the experimental psychopathologist and the goal of the endeavor, even in instances where one might be concerned with a distal feature of the illness (e.g., symptoms, signs), has been the illumination of those proximal factors driving the process or outcome of interest.

The second theme influencing the chapters in this volume concerns integration and consolidation. In many respects, knowledge generated by the experimental psychopathology perspective has been growing for the past 30 years, and many share an enthusiasm that suggests that the field has made genuine progress in understanding the nature of schizophrenia. Many processes involved in the illness (or assumptions about those processes) can now be reliably pointed to as established fact, whereas 20 years ago these same features were open to sometimes vociferous debate. For example, consider the debates of the 1960s and early 1970s regarding the role of genetic influences in the disorder or the notion that somehow the brain was intimately involved in this illness. We know now that the "schizophrenogenic mother" is more of a myth than otherwise and that the secrets of the DNA code responsible, in part, for susceptibility to schizophrenia await discovery. We know now that disorders of attention, thought, and emotion in the illness derive from dysfunction or dysregulation of underlying brain circuitry, both structural and neurobiological, rather than from being caught in a psychological "double bind." Our contributors, each in their own areas, have sought to organize the knowledge relevant to the questions that intrigue them in a manner that shows us where the field is and what is known. Finally, each of the chapters, to varying extents, points the way for future research, noting questions that need to be answered, methodological and theoretical issues that require resolution, and, in some cases, formal proposals for moving forward. In this manner, the chapters offer succinct efforts at taking stock as well as research-based blueprints for the future.

This volume is organized into four major parts with a concluding postscript. Part 1 concerns models of liability and etiology. In the first chapter, Gottesman and Moldin review the classic as well as contemporary evidence implicating a substantial role for genetic influences in the etiology of schizophrenia. They explore the attractive potential of contemporary research methods in genetics, particularly quantitative trait loci strategies that unify molecular and quantitative genetic approaches, and optimistically predict the identification of probable susceptibility loci for schizophrenia within the coming years. In the next chapter, Mednick et al. document an extensive series of studies that has led them to hypothesize a "two-hit" model of schizophrenia. In their model, which carefully integrates genetic and environmental influences, they propose that a genetically determined liability for the illness in interaction with birth or delivery complications will give rise to schizophrenia. Cannon proposes a neurodevelopmental model of schizophrenia that seeks to place perinatal hypoxia in a salient triggering role in relation to a genetic predisposition. Weighing the evidence for a neurodevelopmental model, which Cannon notes remains necessarily circumstantial, he integrates findings that speak not only to schizophrenia but also to other phenotypic manifestations of schizophrenia liability. Lenzenweger, in the next chapter, proposes that schizotypic psychopathology must be regarded as a valid form of expression for schizophrenia liability. Integrating a wide range of studies that cover family history, laboratory indexes, clinical phenomenology, delimitation from other disorders, and follow-up, he suggests that an extension of the schizophrenia phenotype is warranted. Finally, in the last chapter in Part 1, Grace and Moore systematically develop a neurobiological model that speaks to the important role the nucleus accumbens may play in regulating information flow in the brain and how dysregulation in this system may give rise to some features of schizophrenia. Eschewing simplistic single neurotransmitter conceptualizations of the neurobiological dysfunction in schizophrenia, Grace and Moore present an integrative model that incorporates the influences of other neurotransmitter systems, notably the glutamatergic system, in relation to the dopaminergic dysfunction known to be central to the illness.

Part 2 of this volume concerns neurocognitive processes in schizophrenia and, more specifically, several fine-grained discussions of the experimental exploration of these processes. The contributors to this section have given special attention to matters methodological in the examination of neurocognitive processes in schizophrenia. In their chapter, Holzman—the pioneering figure in the scientific study of eye tracking dysfunction (ETD) in schizophrenia—et al. describe the further dissection of this important deviation in the oculomotor system. These investigators have sought to delve deeper into the nature of ETD and, informed by the most recent developments in vision science, they discuss the role of motion perception in relation to ETD. Levy et al., in the next chapter, carefully examine the hypothesized process of disinhibition in relation to performance on the antisaccade task, a measure gaining considerable attention in the experimental psychopathology literature as a possible marker for schizophrenia liability. Levy et al. demonstrate the value of systematic experimentation in decomposing antisaccade performance into its constituent components. Maher and Manschreck, in their chapter, take up the issue of lateralization in schizophrenia and discuss their approach to both its assessment and meaning in relation to other features of schizophrenia, such as language and time of day during which laboratory assessments occur. Maher and Manschreck urge caution in the interpretation of laboratory data that are collected at differing times across the day, a position worthy of attention in future laboratory studies. Stern and Silbersweig describe the considerable utility of positron emission tomography in schizophrenia, particularly as it is related to core features of the illness. Their research represents a model for linking a technologically advanced procedure with a meaningful symptom of schizophrenia, namely hallucinations. Finally, Knight and Silverstein provide a comprehensive overview of the role of cognitive psychology models in research directed at probing cognitive processes in schizophrenia. These investigators discuss a "process-oriented" approach to cognitive research that runs counter to more traditional "task-oriented" and newer "task decomposition" laboratory approaches to cognition in schizophrenia.

In Part 3 of this volume, various approaches to vulnerability are examined in detail. Here, our contributors emphasize disturbances in cognitive and affective processes as markers of vulnerability and seek to place them within a variety of broader theoretical frameworks for the pathogenesis of schizophrenia. Nuechterlein et al. propose that vulnerability factors may be subdivided into stable versus mediating vulnerability factors. According to their approach to vulnerability, the mediating vulnerability factor lies between the traditional stable vulnerability and state markers, and the mediating factors may reveal causal influences more closely positioned to schizophrenia symptom formation and exacerbation. Green and Nuechterlein, in the next chapter, discuss emerging evidence suggesting that deficits detected on a backward masking task may in fact be usefully considered as a valid marker of schizophrenia vulnerability. In their chapter, Cornblatt et al. examine the contributions of the traditional high-risk research design in schizophrenia and highlight the need to develop novel at-risk strategies, suggesting that further refinements may better inform primary prevention efforts. The advantages of an "at-risk sibling design" are reviewed, and Cornblatt et al. present data supportive of this approach to vulnerability detection. Dworkin et al. explore the long-standing and vexing questions regarding experience versus expression of affect in schizophrenia. These investigators highlight the need to weigh the role of neuromotor dysfunction in the study of affective experience and expression in schizophrenia as well as the utility of constructs that emphasize anhedonia and analgesia.

Part 4 of this volume concerns developmental processes, course, and outcome in schizophrenia. The three contributions highlight the challenges of isolating those factors predictive of schizophrenia onset versus those that may serve a maintaining or relapse-triggering role. Erlenmeyer-Kimling et al. summarize what is known regarding those variables that might predict the development of schizophrenia on the basis of the results from the New York High-Risk Project. These investigators report a pattern of findings that strongly implicates the utility of cognitive measures, particularly those tapping verbal working memory components of cognition, in identifying susceptibility for schizophrenia. Hooley and Hiller, in the next chapter, provide an incisive examination of the construct of expressed emotion (EE) in relation to relapse in schizophrenia. They go considerably beyond, however, a mere consideration of the EE–relapse association and propose an approach for examining the developmental–causal process whereby EE exerts its powerful relapse-triggering or symptom-maintaining function. Walker et al. discuss the role of cortisol, the glucocorticoid that has recently been the focus of investigation in many other behavioral traits and disorders, in schizophrenia by relating it to the well-established stress–dopamine association. Walker et al. propose that hypercortisolemia may be related to the exacerbation of schizophrenia symptoms within a developmental framework.

This volume ends with a cautionary postscript by R. R. J. Lewine. In his chapter, Lewine urges caution in the rush of experimental psychopathologists to embrace new technologies for use in laboratory experimentation (e.g., neuroimaging). Albeit in the role of a collegial critic, he takes various trends in contemporary schizophrenia research to task. His criticisms will surely be shared by some and offer food for thought for all involved in schizophrenia research.

In the 18 chapters composing this volume, we see the contributions that research carried out from an experimental psychopathology perspective has made in our understanding of schizophrenia. Although the number of contributors for any volume must be necessarily limited, we believe that nearly all investigators of schizophrenia will find perspectives in this volume consistent with their efforts. Moreover, it is our hope that, in light of our commitment to experimental psychopathology, this volume will serve as a benchmark for current schizophrenia research in the experimental psychopathology tradition. At various junctures in the history of schizophrenia research, a general stock taking of the field has occurred. In 1967, *The Origins of Schizophrenia* (Romano, 1967) appeared, followed quickly by Rosenthal and Kety's (1968) *The Transmission of Schizophrenia*. In the late 1970s, Wynne, Cromwell, and Matthysse (1978) published the important volume, *The Nature of Schizophrenia: New Approaches to Research and Treatment*. The 1980s saw the appearance of *Controversies in Schizophrenia: Changes and Constancies* (Alpert, 1985), and high-risk research was summarized as of the mid-1980s in *Children at Risk for Schizophrenia: A Longitudinal Perspective* (Watt, Anthony, Wynne, & Rolf, 1984). Our greatest hope for this volume is that some of its chapters will serve as a foundation for future research in the way that these volumes have provided the foundation for current research in schizophrenia.

Finally, as a word about the dedication of this volume, David Rosenthal, David Shakow, and Joseph Zubin each made landmark contributions to our understanding of schizophrenia. However, in many ways, one of their most important contributions was as role models and mentors for many of those investigators now working within an experimental psychopathology approach to schizophrenia. Each of these scholars saw the value of the laboratory and systematic research strategies in efforts to reveal the secrets of schizophrenia. For many of us, the research tradition and legacy created by these three giants continues to guide, encourage, and inspire our work in schizophrenia.

REFERENCES

Alpert, M. (Ed.). (1985). *Controversies in schizophrenia: Changes and constancies.* New York: Guilford Press.

Bleuler, E. (1950). *Dementia praecox or the group of schizophrenias* (J. Zinkin, Trans.). New York: International Universities Press.

Gottesman, I. I. (1991). *Schizophrenia genesis: The origins of madness.* New York: Freeman.

Kraepelin, E. (1971). *Dementia praecox and paraphrenia* (R. M. Barclay, Trans.; G. M. Robertson, Ed.). Huntington, NY: Krieger. (Original work published 1909–1913, original translation of selected portions published 1919)

Romano, J. (Ed.). (1967). *The origins of schizophrenia.* Amsterdam: Excerpta Medica Foundation.

Rosenthal, D., & Kety, S. S. (Eds.). (1968). *The transmission of schizophrenia.* Oxford, England: Pergamon Press.

Watt, N. F., Anthony, E. J., Wynne, L. C., & Rolf, J. E. (1984). *Children at risk for schizophrenia: A longitudinal perspective.* Cambridge, England: Cambridge University Press.

Wyatt, R. J., Henter, I., Leary, M. C., & Taylor, E. (1995). An economic evaluation of schizophrenia—1991. *Social Psychiatry and Psychiatric Epidemiology, 30,* 196–205.

Wynne, L. C., Cromwell, R. L., & Matthysse, S. (Eds.). (1978). *The nature of schizophrenia: New approaches to research and treatment.* New York: Wiley.

ORIGINS AND DEVELOPMENT OF SCHIZOPHRENIA

PART ONE

Models of Liability
and Etiology

Genotypes, Genes, Genesis, and Pathogenesis in Schizophrenia

Irving I. Gottesman and Steven O. Moldin

Both the etiological heterogeneity and the clinical (onset, course, outcome) heterogeneity of schizophrenia with its recognized spectrum variations "conspire" to present schizophreniologists with a complex disease. The resultant complexities have resulted in slower than necessary progress, as they are often not recognized when scientists work only in their areas of expertise with insufficient efforts to keep their eyes on the "big picture." A hierarchical and epigenetic approach to understanding and using the complexities involved is outlined by cloning and mutating a model proposed for "traversing the biological complexity" (Sing, Zerba, & Reilly, 1994, p. 6; also see Sing, Haviland, & Reilly, 1996) observed in coronary artery disease. The theoretical and conceptual explanations of the model to follow assure the validity and the convergence of findings from family, twin, and adoption studies (Gottesman, 1994).

The stages in the hierarchy involve distal causes such as genes and genotypes, endophenotypes (Gottesman & Shields, 1972) such as com-

---

The views expressed here are the personal opinions of the authors and should not be taken to infer agreement or endorsement by the National Institutes of Health or the federal government.

promised brain functioning and anatomy and their neuropsychological indicators (e.g., Lenzenweger, chapter 4; Stern & Silbersweig, chapter 9; and Walker, chapter 17, all in this volume), and proximal causes such as biological and psychosocial stressors, both inter- and intrafamilial. The onomatopoeic words in the title cannot be interchanged with one another and are juxtaposed to compel their correct usage in the context provided below. All of the contributors to this volume on schizophrenia are "correct" to different degrees at different stages of the epigenesis of the processes predisposing to the development of schizophrenia. Emergent properties at each stage of the hierarchy as a probable consequence of nonlinear interactions of relevant contributors (Sing et al., 1996; Strohman, 1997; Woolf, 1997) confound efforts at prediction for groups of schizophrenia patients, as do individual differences in background factors on which the major factors above are imposed. Even identical twins discordant for schizophrenia after many years of follow-up produce offspring who, followed up into adulthood, have very similar and high risks for developing schizophrenia themselves (Gottesman & Bertelsen, 1989). Thus, a "normal" identical twin, despite having the necessary genotype, will not express the genotype but will transmit it with equal dispositional power to his or her offspring as that of the affected proband.

For multifactorial disorders with variable ages of onset and with variable degrees of ontogenetic expression, single gene models for the most distal causes are not adequate. Progress in the search for quantitative trait loci is introduced here. Previous efforts to sketch big pictures that go beyond narrow domains of expertise, such as those of Meehl (1990), Gottesman and Shields (1972), and Nuechterlein et al. (chapter 11, this volume), each partially correct, are reexamined in the light of the model put forward for coronary artery disease and its endpoints. We are in agreement with Katschnig's (1987) sobering observation that

> although "boxologies" may be criticized—since boxes connected with arrows do not explain anything— . . . they draw attention to factors other than those which are a specific researcher's interest. Vulnerability [diathesis × stressor] models . . . bring those [researchers] in very different fields closer together. (p. 354)

It is difficult to model multifactorial diseases that are relatively common in the human species and have an appreciable genetic component. It may well be that the solution is to put forward a "market basket" of complementary models (Gottesman, 1993, 1994; McGue & Gottesman, 1989; Moldin & Gottesman, 1997, in press), which, in the aggregate, do a good job of accounting for the empirical data produced by schizophreniologists, regardless of their "union cards." Such a solution would not necessarily lead to anarchic chaos and running off in all directions at once, so long as it is constrained by independently replicated empirical facts from each of the contributing disciplines and scientists.

BACKGROUND

Schizophrenia, which afflicts about 2 million adults in the United States and has an estimated total yearly cost of over $70 billion (Wyatt, Henter, Leary, & Taylor, 1995), is clearly a major public health concern. Family, twin, and adoption studies conducted over the last 30 years have provided very strong evidence that both genes and environment play a role in the complex etiology of schizophrenia (cf. Gottesman, 1991; Kendler & Diehl, 1995). In this chapter, we approach schizophrenia in regard to some of the newer developments in genetics and genetic epidemiology that may not be so familiar to psychosocially oriented researchers. Our discussion serves as a bridge between past work and current directions for the next decade or more of intensive genetic research on schizophrenia.

Although the majority (>80%) of individuals who are a first-degree relative of someone with schizophrenia do not themselves develop schizophrenia, data from over 40 family studies spanning 7 decades of research consistently show that risks to different classes of relatives of affected individuals are many times greater than the general population risk (Gottesman, 1991). Risk varies as a function of the degree of genetic relatedness to an affected individual, with the highest (48%) being to the monozygotic (MZ) cotwin of an affected individual—MZ twins share 100% of their genes in common.

The median MZ concordance rate (46%) for schizophrenia is approximately three times the corresponding dizygotic (DZ) concordance rate (14%) in six twin studies published in the last 25 years (Prescott & Gottesman, 1993). The newest report from Finland (Cannon et al., this volume) is in complete agreement with the earlier findings. This MZ:DZ ratio of over 3:1 strongly implicates genetic factors, and the MZ concordance rate of significantly less than 100% implicates the role of nongenetic factors.

Model fitting using schizophrenia twin data from recent studies yielded a heritability of 0.89, with no contribution from the common environment (McGuffin, Asherson, Owen, & Farmer, 1994). A model of somewhat lower heritability (0.74), also without contribution from the common environment, provides the best statistical fit to the transmission of definite schizophrenia in an earlier analysis of twin and family data (McGue, Gottesman, & Rao, 1983). Nongenetic factors that influence risk to schizophrenia are thus likely to be nonshared environmental effects (i.e., systematic or nonsystematic, idiosyncratic environmental events).

A polygenic (multilocus) model has been consistently supported— and a sufficient single major gene model has been consistently excluded—in the quantitative analysis of actual and simulated schizophrenia family data (Gottesman & Shields, 1967; McGue & Gottesman, 1989; Moldin, 1994; O'Rourke, Gottesman, Suarez, Rice, & Reich, 1982; Rao, Morton, Gottesman, & Lew, 1981). Risk ratios for classes of relatives of schizophrenia probands in pooled Western European twin and family studies were consistent with the influence of two or three major loci in interaction (Risch, 1990). These empirical observations are congruent with a multilocus model for schizophrenia proposed 30 years ago (Gottesman & Shields, 1967).

In summary, it is clear that one or more single major loci do not account for a large proportion of the familial aggregation of schizophrenia. The number of susceptibility loci, the disease risk conferred by each locus, and the degree of interlocus interaction all remain unknown.

GENE–ENVIRONMENT INTERACTION

Environmental effects that contribute to liability to schizophrenia across contemporary cultures include nonspecific stressors, obstetrical complications, and illicit drug abuse (Gottesman, 1991). However, the predictive power of any one of these factors for a schizophrenia phenotype (i.e., the probability of developing schizophrenia given the exposure to one of these factors) is low.

The Finnish Adoptive Study of Schizophrenia found evidence for gene–environment interaction, with the implicated genetic agents acting to control sensitivity to the environment (Tienari et al., 1994). Communication deviance in adoptive parents inferred from projective test results—a nonspecific environmental factor found in many families—in conjunction with high genetic risk was associated with increased risk to developing schizophrenia.

Data on gene–environment interactions in schizophrenia have been provided from studies of African Caribbean individuals who immigrated to the United Kingdom. Sugarman and Craufurd (1994) found that the parents of African Caribbean and White schizophrenia patients had approximately similarly increased risks for developing the disorder (i.e., genetic predisposition is an important risk factor for schizophrenia in the African Caribbean community); however, the siblings of second-generation African Caribbean probands who were born in the United Kingdom were at significantly greater risk than any other relative group (i.e., environmental risk factors more common in the African Caribbean immigrant community were operative).

Hutchinson et al. (1996) replicated this result and found that although morbid risks of schizophrenia were similar for parents and siblings of White and first-generation African Caribbean patients, the morbid risk of siblings of second-generation African Caribbean psychotic probands was seven times that of their White counterparts. The rate of schizophrenia among African Caribbeans in their native environment was within the ranges reported in World Health Organization studies and was markedly lower than the high rates among second-generation African Caribbeans in London (Bhugra et al., 1996). Genetic susceptibility in combination with increased environmental risk factors specific to this population were likely responsible for an excess of schizophrenia in this immigrant population. Possible candidate environmental risk factors include prenatal rubella infection, cannabis abuse (culturally sanctioned marijuana habits), psychosocial factors like failed assimilation, or other environmental factors common only to a particular birth cohort (Hutchinson et al., 1996).

A large-scale path analytic study for schizophrenia involving a longitudinal assessment of twins and a careful assessment of highly regarded environmental risk factors, as conducted by Kendler et al. (1995) for major depression, has not yet been done. Such a study may permit discrimination between two models: an additive one versus one specifying genetic control of sensitivity to the environment (Kendler & Eaves, 1986; Kendler et al., 1995). In the additive model, increases in risk associated with exposure to environmental risk factors are similar for individuals with low- and high-risk genotypes; in other words, environmental and genetic risk factors operate independently. In a model that specifies genetic control of sensitivity to the environment, increases in liability associated with exposure to environmental effects is greater for those with high-risk genotypes; thus, genes alter one's individual sensitivity to the schizophrenia-inducing effects of particular environmental factors. The interaction of genetic liability and environmental factors (stressful life events) in major depression was best explained by the latter model in a large population-based sample of female twins (Kendler et al., 1995). Such a model will probably permit a more accurate understanding of the etiology of schizophrenia in which genetic and environmental risk factors interact in complex ways.

LINKAGE STUDIES

Although the single locus model as an explanation for the familial aggregation of schizophrenia has failed repeatedly (McGue & Gottesman, 1989; O'Rourke et al., 1982), investigators lacking experience with the genetics of complex traits have persisted in conducting traditional linkage studies under single locus model assumptions.[1] Evidence consistent with single locus inheritance was provided by a single report of linkage

---

[1] Portions of this section and the next on association are drawn from Moldin and Gottesman (1997), where the topics are covered in more detail.

using DNA polymorphisms on chromosome 5 for schizophrenia in a sample of British and Icelandic pedigrees (Sherrington et al., 1988). However, numerous nonreplications of this finding have been published; the combined reanalysis of numerous data sets by McGuffin et al. (1990), among them the original report (Sherrington et al., 1988), excluded a susceptibility locus from the implicated region of chromosome 5. Analyses of additional chromosome 5 microsatellite markers in a new sample of British and Icelandic families by one of the original investigators led to an exclusion of the entire region implicated on chromosome 5, and it is now clear that the original linkage report was probably a false-positive result (Gurling & Sharma, 1994).

In the genetic investigation of complex diseases using many markers to detect linkage, a very stringent standard must be adopted for the assertion of linkage to guarantee a high likelihood that the conclusion will be replicated by other investigators. To infer linkage to a given chromosomal region, we must compare the odds in favor of the hypothesis of linkage versus the odds in favor of the hypothesis of no linkage. The odds ratio is expressed as the likelihood, or probability, of these events; the common logarithm of this likelihood ratio is the definition of the *lod score*. In studies of classical Mendelian diseases, where the mode of familial transmission is known to be that of a dominant or a recessive locus, the lod score criterion for reporting linkage is 3. The nominal significance level (p value) of a lod score of 3 when testing a single marker in large samples is .0001 (Ott, 1991). This means that there is a probability of .0001 of encountering a lod of 3 or larger under the null hypothesis of no linkage. A lod of 3 can also be expressed in terms of an odds ratio; that is, a lod of 3 means that the observed data are 1,000 times more likely to arise under a specified hypothesis of linkage than under the null hypothesis of no linkage. The lod score and p value obtained in a sample depend on whether there is a linkage, the information content of the marker, and properties of the sample (e.g., size and number of affected individuals; cf. Ott, 1991).

Continuing improvements in genetic technologies, including the availability of 16,000 human genes and some 450,000 short copy DNA fragments as markers (see www.ncbi.nlm.nih.gov/science96/), now permit systematic screening of the entire human genome as a strategy for the identification of susceptibility genes with small effects that influence risk to complex traits including coronary artery disease, schizophrenia, and diabetes. Increasing the number of markers being tested requires an adjustment to the lod score of 3, which is used when testing a single marker, to prevent inflation of Type I errors. Lander and Kruglyak (1995) proposed a superego set of guidelines to interpret linkage results for complex diseases. They distinguished the nominal significance level, which is the probability of encountering a linkage statistic (in this case, the lod score) of a given magnitude at one specific locus, from the genomewide significance level, which is the probability that one would encounter such a deviation somewhere in an entire scan of the human genome. A given lod score has a corresponding nominal p value and a genomewide p value.

Lander and Kruglyak (1995) proposed that linkage evidence be evaluated on the basis of genomewide p values, even when they have not yet been conducted within the study being reported, and be classified as "suggestive," "significant," or "highly significant." Significant linkage evidence that is obtained in a second independent sample (with a less stringent nominal p value of only .01) is considered "confirmed." Suggestive linkage reports often result from chance findings and too often turn out to be wrong but are worth reporting as tentative findings at this stage of our ignorance. Etiological heterogeneity is a double-edged weapon to be used sparingly in the defense of nonreplicated results. Although genomewide significance values are important, interpretation of linkage reports can also be facilitated through the use of simulations of genotype information on the sample to determine the probability of obtaining a false-positive result (cf. Weeks, Lehner, Squires-Wheeler, Kaufmann, & Ott, 1990).

Table 1 presents a summary of recent linkage studies in schizophrenia; only published peer-reviewed reports of positive evidence for linkage to defined chromosomal regions are listed. A more comprehensive review and critique is provided elsewhere (Moldin & Gottesman, 1997). Such results are considered here in the light of the criteria

Table 1

Recently Reported Chromosomal Regions for Schizophrenia by Linkage Analysis

Region	Reference
3p	Pulver et al. (1995)
5q	Schwab et al. (1997), Straub et al. (1997)
6p	Antonarakis et al. (1995), Moises et al. (1995), Schizophrenia Linkage Collaborative Group for Chromosomes 3, 6 and 8 (1996), Schwab et al. (1995), Straub et al. (1995), Wang et al. (1995).
8p	Kendler et al. (1996), Pulver et al. (1995), Schizophrenia Linkage Collaborative Group for Chromosomes 3, 6 and 8 (1996)
9p	Moises et al. (1995)
20p	Moises et al. (1995)
22q	Coon et al. (1994), Gill et al. (1996), Lasseter et al. (1995), Polymeropoulos et al. (1994), Pulver et al. (1994), Vallada et al. (1995).

Note. p = short arm of the chromosome; q = long arm of the chromosome. From "Genes, Experience, and Chance in Schizophrenia: Positioning for the 21st Century," by S. O. Moldin and I. I. Gottesman, 1997, *Schizophrenia Bulletin, 23,* p. 550.

suggested by Lander and Kruglyak (1995); only those meeting criteria for suggestive or significant linkage evidence are considered in detail.

The widely heralded results for chromosome 6 reported by Wang et al. (1995) for Irish schizophrenia pedigrees is the strongest evidence thus far for linkage in schizophrenia (genomewide $p > .03$). However, correction for testing across multiple diagnostic and transmission models increased the p value to between .05 and .07. With the addition of 79 new pedigrees from the same western Irish population for a total of 265—which would be expected to increase linkage evidence—a new team of investigators reported somewhat diminished evidence (Straub et al., 1995); a genomewide p of about .13 was obtained, without adjustment for testing across multiple diagnostic and transmission models. Suggestive evidence for linkage to chromosome 6 was found by

Schwab et al. (1995) with 78 German affected sibling pairs. Analyses of 713 families from around the world, contributed by 14 research groups, failed to show more than suggestive evidence of linkage to this short arm of chromosome 6 region (Schizophrenia Linkage Collaborative Group for Chromosomes 3, 6 and 8, 1996).

Nonreplications of chromosome 6 linkage have also been reported (Garner et al., 1996; Gurling et al., 1995; Mowry et al., 1995; Riley, Rajagopalan, Mogudi-Carter, Jenkins, & Williamson, 1996). An additional concern is that the markers implicated by the studies reporting suggestive evidence (Schwab et al., 1995; Straub et al., 1995; Wang et al., 1995) lie within a very large chromosomal region, perhaps 30 centimorgans long, that contains hundreds of genes. Wang et al. (1996) found evidence for linkage disequilibrium between schizophrenia and a gene on chromosome 6 that causes spinocerebellar ataxia Type 1 (SCA1). The authors did not state how many other genes were examined, making it difficult to interpret the statistical meaning of their finding; if valid, these results would substantially narrow the candidate disease gene region on chromosome 6.

Suggestive evidence for linkage to chromosome 8 was found in two studies (Kendler et al., 1996; Pulver et al., 1995); less than suggestive evidence would be obtained if the parametric analyses conducted by Kendler et al. were corrected for the testing of multiple transmission and disease models. Analyses conducted in the collaborative sample of 713 families also resulted in suggestive evidence for linkage to a susceptibility locus on chromosome 8 (Schizophrenia Linkage Collaborative, 1996). Exclusion of the families in which the linkage was initially reported (Pulver et al., 1995), but not of Kendler et al.'s families, resulted in suggestive linkage evidence in the remaining subset. At least one study failed to find linkage to this region (Moises et al., 1995). The evidence for susceptibility loci on other chromosomes is less compelling.

Briefly, the strongest linkage evidence so far supports the existence of schizophrenia susceptibility loci on chromosomes 6 and 8; however, the magnitude of the statistical evidence and the existence of nonreplication demonstrate that these are not yet confirmed and convincing findings. The inability to obtain more compelling evidence may result from one of the following: (a) genes on chromosomes 6 and 8 confer susceptibility to schizophrenia, but they have such a small relative effect on disease risk that a very large sample is required for their detection (the failure to obtain such evidence in a large collaborative analysis of multiple data sets reflects a loss of power attributable to methodological differences in diagnosis, ascertainment, or genotyping across studies); (b) genes on 6 and 8 confer susceptibility to schizophrenia in a small proportion of families, perhaps 15–30% (failures to replicate reflect the confounding effects of genetic heterogeneity); or (c) the reported positive results are due to chance. Unfortunately, these three explanations are currently indistinguishable. Reported linkages to other chromosomes (3, 5, 9, 20, 22) are less compelling than those discussed for 6 and 8.

ASSOCIATION STUDIES

Association studies offer a different strategy than linkage studies for finding susceptibility genes. The most likely explanations for disease–marker associations are a disease locus is physically very close to the marker studied, the marker interacts with a second locus that contributes to disease susceptibility, or the marker itself is involved in disease risk. The hope is that rather than implicating a chromosomal region (as in linkage analysis), a specific gene involved in disease susceptibility can be identified. The traditional method (a population-based association study) involves contrasting the frequency of a marker in patients versus controls. As discussed by others (Crowe, 1993; Gelernter, Goldman, & Risch, 1993; Kidd, 1993), this particular type of association study that does not use pairs of relatives offers little hope for unambiguous results in the genetic analysis of mental disorders; major problems include the difficulties in choosing the proper controls and in determining the appropriate statistical significance level while maintaining an acceptably low false-positive rate.

However, the use of association studies for detection of genes through linkage disequilibrium mapping is extremely important. An alternative method is the family-based association tests (Spielman,

15

McGinnis, & Ewens, 1993) termed TDT (transmission disequilibrium tests), in which the two parents of the affected individual (actually, the nontransmitted parental alleles) serve as controls. Risch and Merikangas (1996) recommended using this approach on a large scale to search for associations across the entire genome in future studies. They argue that successful detection of genes for complex diseases may occur with large-scale association analysis of all 50,000–100,000 human genes (currently, more than 16,000 are identified [see www.ncbi.nlm.nih.gov]); however, the technology to permit this has not yet been developed.

NON-MENDELIZING GENETIC INFLUENCES

Even when combined with linkage and association studies, traditional behavior–genetic analysis of genetic variability using family, twin, and adoption studies is not the whole story of genes and behavior. An important aspect of genetic influence that is not encompassed by these designs comes from nonpolymorphic (only one allelic form in the population) genes. Nonpolymorphic genes presumably specify the fundamental blueprint for the species. They do not contribute to individual variability, but they are transmitted through Mendelian principles. However, there are genetic sources of variability that are not transmitted through the standard Mendelian principles and thus not captured by behavior–genetic designs. One list of such mechanisms includes mitochondrial inheritance, gonadal mosaicism, imprinting (wherein a gene's expression is modulated on the basis of whether it is transmitted from the father or the mother), and progressive or dynamic amplification (Morton, 1993).

The mechanism of progressive amplification has deservedly received attention over the past 5 years. Fragile X disorder (de Vries et al., 1997; Simonoff, Bolton, & Rutter, 1996; Sutherland & Mulley, 1996), a leading cause of mental retardation, exemplifies the pattern of progressive amplification through pedigrees. A CGG trinucleotide in an untranslated segment of the FMR-1 gene on the X chromosome is normally repeated less than 50 times. When the gene mutates, these unstable CGG repeats are amplified, resulting in hundreds or even thousands of copies. The premutations are expanded to full mutations (termed *triplet repeats*) only when transmitted by the mother. Fathers with the premutation have normal daughters who may be at risk to pass on the disorder.

The implications of triplet repeat mutations for psychopathology may be substantial, but this area of research applied to schizophrenia is still very much in its infancy. Huntington's disease follows the same pattern of inheritance (Huntington's Disease Collaborative Research Group, 1993). The extent of the amplified region (a CAG repeat) is associated with age of onset, with earlier onset cases having longer repeated regions. It is noteworthy that a few Huntington's disease patients may have had expansions of less than 35 CAG repeats, and some individuals with 36–39 repeats may not develop the disease (Nance, 1996); clearly, stochastic processes and epistasis need to be considered for such a "simple" disease, just as they must be for schizophrenia. Early onset cases are more likely to be those with the at-risk allele transmitted from their father, an apparent example of genomic imprinting. These associations of molecular processes with age of onset illustrate the need to incorporate developmental aspects of both genetics and psychopathology into schizophrenia research strategies.

Recent empirical results and theorizing suggest the plausibility of a variability in degree of homozygosity as a source of genetic variability for psychopathology. A key construct in this line of theorizing and research is *developmental instability*. Indicators of developmental instability include some types of minor physical anomalies and fluctuating asymmetries such as deviations from symmetry in bilateral physical characteristics, for example, fingerprints, and brain structures. Among others, Markow and Gottesman (1989, 1993) and Yeo and Gangestad (1993) have documented associations between developmental instability—likely during the prenatal period—and psychopathology, including schizophrenia and some childhood disorders. These authors suggested that genetic heterozygosity leads to multiple forms of proteins, and these multiple forms may confer on the organism a better ability to adapt to changing metabolic demands resulting from changing environmental demands. Conversely, genetic homozygosity would reduce the organism's metabolic buffering and thus render it susceptible to insult from environmental perturbations (Woolf, 1997).

The degree of genetic homozygosity is, of course, a function of the state of paired alleles, manifested only when the zygote is formed. Thus, homozygosity is not transmitted from parent to offspring and is not detectable as a genetic effect in traditional twin, family, or adoption studies. Effects of genetic homozygosity would be misidentified as environmental variance in parent–offspring analyses and as nonadditive genetic variance in twin studies. These brief considerations of non-Mendelizing genetic effects caution researchers not to become paradigm bound if they wish to discover the panorama of genetic influences on schizophrenia.

THE NEAR FUTURE FOR GENETIC RESEARCH IN SCHIZOPHRENIA

Considerable advances have been made in the investigation of genetic aspects of schizophrenia at both the level of genetic epidemiology and the levels of molecular genetics. The vast area of pathogenesis, informed by genetics, has only been scratched. The new findings that are available have been greeted with a healthy tempered skepticism, appropriate for science. The pace of reporting new findings means that almost all have still not been scrutinized. The fact that gene regions so far identified do not map onto known functional genes with a preferred status as "candidate genes" (i.e., related to central nervous system functioning or to neurotransmitter-related genes suggested by the pharmacological treatments for the disease) adds to the skepticism.

We speculate that progress will be made on many fronts, not just the molecular genetic one, and that the areas will fertilize and inform each other. Psychopathology researchers could profitably imitate advances made in research on heart disease, diabetes, and cancer. We can imagine a process analogous to the assembling of a space platform in orbit around the Earth—self-contained and essential elements could be developed from advances in neuroanatomy, developmental biology, neurochemistry, virology, and the study of cell connections and cell death—and all of the elements could be joined to the genetic one to form the whole general system that works to tell researchers, eventually, what schizophrenia is all about. Teams are already trying to confirm the reported linkages and are beginning to sequence the regions that have been suggested in a "brute force" effort to find genes and their mutations. Within 2–5 years, a number of the actual genes may be identified and cloned; not until then may a large proportion of scientists believe that something important has really happened in this field— statistical evidence is indirect, and cloning some responsible functional genes is the "smoking gun" researchers all want to find.

Next, we expect to come the figuring out of the neurodevelopmental pathways and interactions of the genes with their internal and external environments, perhaps taking 5 more years. It will be important to pursue research on the nervous systems of inbred mice, even though they do not get schizophrenia, to determine the effects of human genes transplanted into them. Then, over a subsequent 10-year period, the pharmaceutical industry may develop the drugs in a rational, as opposed to the traditional empirical, game plan. This sequence of speculations need not proceed one step at a time; each of the stages can commence as the information develops. Although this progress toward the alleviation of the suffering of the mentally ill goes on, society could be forced to contend with a number of ethical and moral issues. Through the foresight of some of our best minds, some 5% of the genome budget has been set aside to study and to deal with anticipated ethical issues (see ethical, legal, and social issues at www.ornl.gov/hgmis/resource/elsi.html) connected to genetic privacy, health insurance, marriage, and abortion. Model laws for genetic privacy have already been passed in some states, and bills are pending in both the U.S. Senate and the U.S. House of Representatives to guarantee relief (Rothenberg et al., 1997).

Barriers to further progress include the need to balance proprietary secrecy to protect profits against the immediate needs of society to relieve consumers and their families from their burdens. Encouraging the necessary collaboration of teams around the world also requires a balance between narcissistic and economic self-interest versus the pride in group achievement of a clear social good. Clearly, there is plenty of work left to do.

REFERENCES

Antonarakis, S. E., Blouin, J. L., Pulver, A. E., Wolyniec, P., Lasseter, V. K., Nestadt, G., Kasch, L., Babb, R., Kazazian, H. H., & Dombroski, B. (1995). Schizophrenia susceptibility and chromosome 6p24-22. *Nature Genetics, 11,* 235–236.

Bhugra, D., Hilwig, M., Hossein, B., Marceau, H., Neehall, J., Leff, J., Mallett, R., & Der, G. (1996). First-contact incidence rates of schizophrenia in Trinidad and one year follow-up. *British Journal of Psychiatry, 169,* 587–592.

Coon, H., Holik, J., Hoff, M., Reimherr, F., Wender, P., Myles-Worsley, M., Waldo, M., Freedman, R., & Byerley, W. (1994). Analysis of chromosome 22 markers in nine schizophrenia pedigrees. *American Journal of Medical Genetics, 54,* 72–79.

Crowe, R. R. (1993). Candidate genes in psychiatry: An epidemiological perspective. *American Journal of Medical Genetics, 48,* 74–77.

de Vries, B. B., van den Ouweland, A. M., Mohkamsing, S., Duivenvoorden, H. J., Mol., E., Gelsema, K., van Rijn, M., Halley, D. J., Sandkuijl, L. A., Oostra, B. A., Tibben, A., & Niermeijer, M. F. (1997). Screening and diagnosis for the fragile X syndrome among the mentally retarded: An epidemiological and psychological survey. Collaborative Fragile X Syndrome Group. *American Journal of Human Genetics, 61,* 660–667.

Garner, C., Kelly, M., Cardon, L., Joslyn, G., Carey, A., LeDuc, C., Lichter, J., Harris, T., Loftus, J., Shields, G., Comazzi, M., Vita, A., Smith, A. M., Dann, J., Crow, T. J., & DeLisi, L. E. (1996). Linkage analyses of schizophrenia to chromosome 6p24-22: An attempt to replicate. *American Journal of Medical Genetics, 67,* 595–610.

Gelernter, J., Goldman, D., & Risch, N. J. (1993). The A1 allele at the D_2 dopamine receptor gene and alcoholism: A reappraisal. *Journal of the American Medical Association, 269,* 1673–1677.

Gill, M., Vallada, H., Collier, D., Sham, P., Holmans, P., Murray, R., McGuffin, P., Nanko, S., Owen, M., Antonarakis, S., Housman, D., Kazazian, H., Nestadt, G., Pulver, A. E., Straub, R. E., MacLean, C. J., Walsh, D., Kendler, K. S., DeLisi, L., Polymeropoulos, M., Coon, H., Byerley, W., Lofthouse, R., Gershon, E., Goldin, L., Crow, T., Freedman, R., Laurent, C., Boodeau-Pean, S., d'Amato, T., Jay, M., Campion, D., Mallet, J., Wildenauer, D. B., Lerer, B., Albus, M., Ackenheil, M., Ebstein, R. P., Hallmayer, J., Maier, W., Gurling, H., Curtis, D., Kalsi, G., Brynjolfsson, J., Sigmundson, T., Petursson, H., Blackwood, D., Muir, W., St. Clair, D., He, L., Maguire, S., Moises, H. W., Hwu, H.-G., Yang, L., Wiese, C., Tao, L., Liu, X., Kristbjarnarson, H., Levinson, D. F., Mowry, B. J., Donis-Keller, H., Hayward, N. K., Crowe, R. R., Silverman, J. M., Nancarrow, D. J., & Read, C. M. (1996). A combined analysis of D22S278 marker alleles in affected sib-pairs: Support for a susceptibility locus for schizophrenia at chromosome 22q12. *American Journal of Medical Genetics, 67,* 40–45.

Gottesman, I. I. (1991). *Schizophrenia genesis: The origins of madness.* New York: Freeman.

Gottesman, I. I. (1993). Origins of schizophrenia: Past as prologue. In R. Plomin & G. E. McClearn (Eds.), *Nature, nurture, and psychology* (pp. 231–244). Washington, DC: American Psychological Association.

Gottesman, I. I. (1994). Schizophrenia epigenesis: Past, present, and future. *Acta Psychiatrica Scandinavica, 384*(Suppl.), 26–33.

Gottesman, I. I., & Bertelsen, A. (1989). Confirming unexpressed genotypes for schizophrenia: Risks in the offspring of Fischer's Danish identical and fraternal discordant twins. *Archives of General Psychiatry, 46,* 867–872.

Gottesman, I. I., & Shields, J. (1967). A polygenic theory of schizophrenia. *Proceedings of the National Academy of Sciences of the USA, 58,* 199–205.

Gottesman, I. I., & Shields, J. (1972). *Schizophrenia and genetics: A twin study vantage point.* New York: Academic Press.

Gurling, H., Kalsi, G., Chen, A. H.-S., Green, M., Butler, R., Read, T., Murphy, P., Curtis, D., Sharma, T., & Petursson, H. (1995). Schizophrenia susceptibility and chromosome 6p24–22. *Nature Genetics, 11,* 234–235.

Gurling, H., & Sharma, T. (1994). Genetic linkage analysis and clinical approaches to the resolution of heterogeneity in the schizophrenias. In E. S. Gershon & C. R. Cloninger (Eds.), *Genetic approaches to mental disorders* (pp. 231–251). Washington, DC: American Psychiatric Association.

Huntington's Disease Collaborative Research Group. (1993). A novel gene containing a trinucleotide repeat that is expanded and unstable on Huntington's disease chromosomes. *Cell, 72,* 971–983.

Hutchinson, G., Takei, N., Fahy, T. A., Bhugra, D., Gilvarry, C., Moran, P., Mallett, R., Sham, P., Leff, J., & Murray, R. M. (1996). Morbid risk of schizophrenia in first-degree relatives of White and African-Caribbean patients with psychosis. *British Journal of Psychiatry, 169,* 776–780.

Katschnig, H. (1987). Vulnerability and trigger models/rehabilitation: Discussion. In H. Häfner, W. F. Gattaz, & W. Janzarik (Eds.), *Search for the causes of schizophrenia* (pp. 353–358). Berlin, Germany: Springer-Verlag.

Kendler, K. S., & Diehl, S. R. (1995). Schizophrenia: Genetics. In H. I. Kaplan & B. J. Sadock (Eds.), *Comprehensive textbook of psychiatry, VI* (6th ed., pp. 942–957). Baltimore: Williams & Wilkins.

Kendler, K. S., & Eaves, L. J. (1986). Models for the joint effect of genotype and environment on liability to psychiatric illness. *American Journal of Psychiatry, 143,* 279–289.

Kendler, K. S., Kessler, R. C., Walters, E. E., MacLean, C., Neale, M. C., Heath, A. C., & Eaves, L. J. (1995). Stressful life events, genetic liability, and onset of an episode of major depression in women. *American Journal of Psychiatry, 152,* 833–842.

Kendler, K. S., MacLean, C. J., O'Neill, A., Burke, J., Murphy, B., Duke, F., Shinkwin, R., Easter, S. M., Webb, B. T., Zhang, J., Walsh, D., & Straub, R. E. (1996). Evidence for a schizophrenia vulnerability locus on chromosome 8p in the Irish Study of High-Density Schizophrenia Families. *American Journal of Psychiatry, 153,* 1534–1540.

Kidd, K. K. (1993). Associations of disease with genetic markers: Deja vu all over again. *American Journal of Medical Genetics, 48,* 71–73.

Lander, E., & Kruglyak, L. (1995). Genetic dissection of complex traits: Guidelines for interpreting and reporting linkage results. *Nature Genetics, 11,* 241–247.

Lasseter, V. K., Pulver, A. E., Wolyniec, P. S., Nestadt, G., Meyers, D., Karayiorgou, M., Housman, D., Antonarakis, S., Kazazian, H., & Kasch, L. (1995). Follow-up report of potential linkage for schizophrenia on chromosome 22q: Part 3. *American Journal of Medical Genetics, 60,* 172–173.

Markow, T. A., & Gottesman, I. I. (1989). Dermatoglyphic fluctuating asymmetry in psychotic twins. *Psychiatry Research, 29,* 37–44.

Markow, T. A., & Gottesman, I. I. (1993). Behavioral phenodeviance: A Lerneresque conjecture. *Genetica, 89,* 297–305.

McGue, M., & Gottesman, I. I. (1989). Genetic linkage in schizophrenia: Perspectives from genetic epidemiology. *Schizophrenia Bulletin, 15,* 453–464.

McGue, M., Gottesman, I. I., & Rao, D. C. (1983). The transmission of schizophrenia under a multifactorial threshold model. *American Journal of Human Genetics, 35,* 1161–1178.

McGuffin, P., Asherson, P., Owen, M., & Farmer, A. (1994). The strength of the genetic effect: Is there room for an environmental influence in the aetiology of schizophrenia? *British Journal of Psychiatry, 164,* 593–599.

McGuffin, P., Sargeant, M., Hetti, G., Tidmarsh, S., Whatley, S., & Marchbanks, R. M. (1990). Exclusion of a schizophrenia susceptibility gene from the chromosome 5q11-q13 region. New data and a reanalysis of previous reports. *American Journal of Human Genetics, 47,* 524–535.

Meehl, P. E. (1990). Toward an integrated theory of schizotaxia, schizotypy, and schizophrenia. *Journal of Personality Disorders, 4,* 1–99.

Moises, H. W., Yang, L., Kristbjarnarson, H., Wiese, C., Byerley, W., Macciardi, F., Arolt, V., Blackwood, D., Liu, X., Sjogren, B., Aschauer, H. N., Hwu, H.-G., Jang, K., Livesley, W. J., Kennedy, J. L., Zoega, T., Ivarsson, O., Bui, M.-T., Yu, M.-H., Havsteen, B., Commenges, D., Weissenbach, J., Schwinger, E., Gottesman, I. I., Pakstis, A. J., Wetterberg, L., Kidd, K. K., & Helgason, T. (1995). An international two-stage genome-wide search for schizophrenia susceptibility genes. *Nature Genetics, 11,* 321–324.

Moldin, S. O. (1994). Indicators of liability to schizophrenia: Perspectives from genetic epidemiology. *Schizophrenia Bulletin, 20,* 169–184.

Moldin, S. O., & Gottesman, I. I. (1997). Genes, experience, and chance in schizophrenia: Positioning for the 21st century. *Schizophrenia Bulletin, 23,* 547–561.

Moldin, S. O., & Gottesman, I. I. (in press). Population genetic methods in psychiatry. In H. I. Kaplan & B. J. Sadock (Eds.), *Comprehensive textbook of psychiatry* (Vol. 7). Baltimore: Williams & Wilkins.

Morton, N. E. (1993). Genetic epidemiology. *Annual Review of Genetics, 27,* 523–538.

Mowry, B. J., Nancarrow, D. J., Lennon, D. P., Sandkuijl, L. A., Crowe, R. R., Silverman, J. M., Mohs, R. C., Siever, L. J., Endicott, J., & Sharpe, L. (1995). Schizophrenia susceptibility and chromosome 6p24-22. *Nature Genetics, 11,* 233–234.

Nance, M. A. (1996). Invited editorial—Huntington disease: Another chapter rewritten. *American Journal of Human Genetics, 59,* 1–6.

O'Rourke, D. H., Gottesman, I. I., Suarez, B. K., Rice, J. P., & Reich, T. (1982). Refutation of the general single locus model for the etiology of schizophrenia. *American Journal of Human Genetics, 34,* 630–649.

Ott, J. (1991). *Analysis of human genetic linkage* (rev. ed.). Baltimore: John Hopkins University Press.

Polymeropoulos, M. H., Coon, H., Byerley, W., Gershon, E. S., Goldin, L., Crow, T. J., Rubenstein, J., Hoff, M., Holik, J., & Smith, A. M. (1994). Search for a schizophrenia susceptibility locus on human chromosome 22. *American Journal of Medical Genetics, 54,* 93–99.

Prescott, C. A., & Gottesman, I. I. (1993). Genetically mediated vulnerability to schizophrenia. *Psychiatric Clinics of North America, 16,* 245–267.

Pulver, A. E., Karayiorgou, M., Wolyniec, P. S., Lasseter, V. K., Kasch, L., Nestadt, G., Antonarakis, S., Housman, D., Kazazian, H. H., & Meyers, D. (1994). Sequential strategy to identify a susceptibility gene for schizophrenia: Report of potential linkage on chromosome 22q12-q13.1: Part 1. *American Journal of Medical Genetics, 54,* 36–43.

Pulver, A. E., Lasseter, V. K., Kasch, L., Wolyniec, P., Nestadt, G., Blouin, J. L., Kimberland, M., Babb, R., Vourlis, S., & Chen, H. (1995). Schizophrenia: A genome scan targets chromosomes 3p and 8p as potential sites of susceptibility genes. *American Journal of Medical Genetics, 60,* 252–260.

Rao, D. C., Morton, N. E., Gottesman, I. I., & Lew, R. (1981). Path analysis of qualitative data on pairs of relatives: Application to schizophrenia. *Human Heredity, 31,* 325–333.

Riley, B. P., Rajagopalan, S., Mogudi-Carter, M., Jenkins, T., & Williamson, R. (1996). No evidence for linkage of chromosome 6p markers to schizophrenia in Southern African Bantu-speaking families. *Psychiatric Genetics, 6,* 41–49.

Risch, N. J. (1990). Linkage strategies for genetically complex traits: I. Multilocus models. *American Journal of Human Genetics, 46,* 222–228.

Risch, N. J., & Merikangas, K. (1996). The future of genetic studies of complex human diseases. *Science, 273,* 1516–1517.

Rothenberg, K., Fuller, B., Rothstein, M., Duster, T., Kahn, M. J. E., Cunningham, R., Fine, B., Hudson, K., King, M.-C., Murphy, P., Swergold, G., &

Collins, F. (1997). Genetic information and the workplace: Legislative ap proaches and policy challenges. *Science, 275,* 1755–1757.

Schizophrenia Linkage Collaborative Group for Chromosomes 3, 6 and 8. (1996). Additional support for schizophrenia linkage on chromosomes 6 and 8: A multicenter study. *American Journal of Medical Genetics, 67,* 580–594.

Schwab, S. G., Albus, M., Hallmayer, J., Honig, S., Borrmann, M., Lichtermann, D., Ebstein, R. P., Ackenheil, M., Lerer, B., & Risch, N. (1995). Evaluation of a susceptibility gene for schizophrenia on chromosome 6p by multi-point affected sib-pair linkage analysis. *Nature Genetics, 11,* 325–327.

Schwab, S. G., Eckstein, G. N., Hallmayer, J., Lerer, B., Albus, M., Borrmann, M., Lichtermann, D., Ertl, M. A., Maier, W., & Wildenauer, D. B. (1997). Evidence suggestive of a locus on chromosome 5q31 contributing to susceptibility for schizophrenia in German and Israeli families by multipoint affected sib-pair linkage analysis. *Molecular Psychiatry, 2,* 156–160.

Sherrington, R., Brynjolfsson, J., Petursson, H., Potter, M., Dudleston, K., Barraclough, B., Wasmuth, J., Dobbs, M., & Gurling, H. M. D. (1988). Localization of a susceptibility locus for schizophrenia on chromosome 5. *Nature, 336,* 164–167.

Simonoff, E., Bolton, P., & Rutter, M. (1996). Mental retardation: Genetic findings, clinical implications and research agenda. *Journal of Child Psychology and Psychiatry, 37,* 259–280.

Sing, C. F., Haviland, M. B., & Reilly, S. L. (1996). Genetic architecture of common multifactorial diseases. In *Ciba Foundation Symposium 197: Variation in the human genome* (pp. 211–232). Chichester, UK: Wiley.

Sing, C. F., Zerba, K. E., & Reilly, S. L. (1994). Traversing the biological complexity in the hierarchy between genome and CAD endpoints in the population at large. *Clinical Genetics, 46,* 6–14.

Spielman, R. S., McGinnis, R. E., & Ewens, W. J. (1993). Transmission test for linkage disequilibrium: The insulin gene region and insulin-dependent diabetes mellitus (IDDM). *American Journal of Human Genetics, 52,* 506–516.

Straub, R. E., MacLean, C. J., O'Neill, F. A., Burke, J., Murphy, B., Duke, F., Shinkwin, R., Webb, B. T., Zhang, J., Walsh, D., & Kendler, K. S. (1995). A potential vulnerability locus for schizophrenia on chromosome 6p24-22: Evidence for genetic heterogeneity. *Nature Genetics, 11,* 287–293.

Straub, R. E., MacLean, C. J., O'Neill, F. A., Walsh, D., & Kendler, K. S. (1997). Support for a possible schizophrenia vulnerability locus in region 5q22-31 in Irish families. *Molecular Psychiatry, 2,* 148–155.

Strohman, R. C. (1997). The coming Kuhnian revolution in biology. *Nature Biotechnology, 15,* 194–200.

Sugarman, P. A., & Craufurd, D. (1994). Schizophrenia in the Afro-Caribbean community. *British Journal of Psychiatry, 164,* 474–480.

Sutherland, G. R., & Mulley, J. C. (1996). Fragile X syndrome and fragile XE mental retardation. *Prenatal Diagnosis, 16,* 1199–1211.

Tienari, P., Wynne, L. C., Moring, J., Lahti, I., Naarala, M., Sorri, A., Wahlberg, K. E., Saarento, O., Kaleva, M., & Laksy, K. (1994). The Finnish Adoption Study of Schizophrenia. Implications for family research. *British Journal of Psychiatry, 164,* 20–26.

Vallada, H. P., Gill, M., Sham, P., Lim, L. C., Nanko, S., Asherson, P., Murray, R. M., McGuffin, P., Owen, M., & Collier, D. (1995). Linkage studies on chromosome 22 in familial schizophrenia. *American Journal of Medical Genetics, 60,* 139–146.

Wang, S., Detera-Wadleigh, S., Coon, H., Sun, C.-E., Goldin, L. R., Duffy, D. L., Byerley, W. F., Gershon, E. S., & Diehl, S. R. (1996). Evidence of linkage disequilibrium between schizophrenia and the SCA1 CAG repeat on chromosome 6p23. *American Journal of Human Genetics, 59,* 731–736.

Wang, S., Sun, C. E., Walczak, C. A., Ziegle, J. S., Kipps, B. R., Goldin, L. R., & Diehl, S. R. (1995). Evidence for a susceptibility locus for schizophrenia on chromosome 6pter-p22. *Nature Genetics, 10,* 41–46.

Weeks, D. E., Lehner, T., Squires-Wheeler, E., Kaufmann, C. A., & Ott, J. (1990). Measuring the inflation of the lod score due to its maximization over model parameter values in human linkage analysis. *Genetic Epidemiology, 7,* 237–243.

Woolf, C. (1997). Does the genotype for schizophrenia often remain unexpressed because of canalization and stochastic events during development? *Psychological Medicine, 27,* 659–668.

Wyatt, R. J., Henter, I., Leary, M. C., & Taylor, E. (1995). An economic evaluation of schizophrenia—1991. *Social Psychiatry and Psychiatric Epidemiology, 30,* 196–205.

Yeo, R. A., & Gangestad, S. W. (1993). Developmental origins of variation in human hand preference. *Genetica, 89,* 281–296.

2

A Two-Hit Working Model of the Etiology of Schizophrenia

Sarnoff A. Mednick, Jennifer B. Watson,
Matti Huttunen, Tyrone D. Cannon, Heikki Katila,
Ricardo Machon, Birgitte Mednick, Meggin Hollister,
Josef Parnas, Fini Schulsinger, Nina Sajaniemi,
Peter Voldsgaard, Reijo Pyhala, Dan Gutkind,
and Xueyi Wang

We propose a "two-hit model" to explain the basis of schizophrenia. This model was shaped by the findings of four major longitudinal projects: the Copenhagen High-Risk Project, the Fetal Viral Infection Project, the Danish Birth Cohort, and the Copenhagen and Helsinki Habituation Projects. First, an outline of the two-hit model is presented, followed by a discussion of findings from the four projects. The chapter ends with a hypothesis and discussion of the trauma associated with an earthquake in China.

The working model of the first hit includes the following:

1. The first hit stems from a genetic liability for schizophrenia. This genetic liability consists of a preprogrammed disruption of fetal neural development during a period of gestation critical for schizophrenia.

2. This disruption can be partially mimicked by *adventitious teratogenic* factors that coincide with the critical neural development period for schizophrenia. An example of an adventitious teratogen is a maternal influenza infection in the 2nd trimester.

3. Although it is clear that a teratogen may be serious enough to kill the

fetus, in many cases the effect of the genetic disruption may be more serious and extensive than the effect of an adventitious teratogen.

4. The first hit (genetic or teratogen) creates a vulnerability for schizophrenic decompensation. If the individual's perinatal and childhood experiences are free of severe stress, he or she will exhibit adult behavior that approximates the *Diagnostic and Statistical Manual of Mental Disorders* (4th ed. [*DSM-IV*]; American Psychiatric Association [APA], 1994) diagnosis of schizotypal or paranoid personality disorder.

The working model of the second hit includes the following:

5. The second hit can take the form of delivery complications (DCs) or nonoptimal early child rearing. The nature of the second hit helps determine the psychopathological course of illness.

6. For those made vulnerable by the first hit, DCs may damage periventricular brain regions (associated with the autonomic nervous system's excitatory functioning), which may contribute to severe reductions in emotional responding and expression (Cannon et al., 1988; Cannon, Mednick, & Parnas, 1990a). This DC-related damage may increase risk for schizophrenia with predominantly negative symptoms.

7. Those made vulnerable by the first hit who did not suffer severe DCs may experience decompensation if they encounter severe stresses during early childhood. For such individuals who have responsive autonomic nervous systems, the stress may cause them to decompensate with predominantly positive symptom schizophrenia.

8. Those with DCs that lead to periventricular damage will have increased risk for predominantly negative symptoms, regardless of the presence or absence of childhood stressors.

PROJECT 1: THE 1962 COPENHAGEN HIGH-RISK PROJECT

The 1962 Copenhagen High-Risk Project was developed in 1950s in response to the difficulties in examining the etiology of schizophrenia by comparing hospitalized schizophrenia patients with normal controls.

The high-risk project research design provides a method for investigating premorbid risk factors that relate to the development of schizophrenia and other psychotic illnesses. In a high-risk design, the offspring of the schizophrenic parents are then followed longitudinally with assessments of the at-risk children continuing into adulthood. The purpose of the project was to examine children before they suffered the consequences of schizophrenia and to attempt to identify premorbid factors that distinguish future schizophrenia patients. These premorbid distinguishing characteristics may contribute to the development of a better understanding of etiology.

Research Design and Methods

The original 1962 Copenhagen High-Risk Project examined 207 children with schizophrenic mothers and 104 control participants. We first examined them extensively when they were (on average) 15.1 years of age. The purpose of the project was to examine children before they suffered the consequences of schizophrenia and to attempt to identify premorbid factors that distinguish future schizophrenia patients. These premorbid distinguishing characteristics may contribute to the development of a better understanding of etiology.

Diagnostic Methods

Psychiatric functioning was appraised in 1972–1974 when the patients were a mean age of 25 years and again in 1986–1989 when the patients were a mean age of 39 years. The diagnostic procedure in 1972–1974 included two structured interviews, each of which allowed the interviewer to arrive at a diagnosis: the Present State Examination (PSE; Wing, Cooper, & Sartorius, 1974) and the Current and Past Psychopathology Scales (Endicott & Spitzer, 1972). The psychopathological data from this assessment were later converted into *DSM-III-R* (3rd ed. rev.; APA, 1987) diagnoses (Parnas et al., 1993). The procedure in 1986–1989 included an administration of the Schedule for Affective Disorders and Schizophrenia–Lifetime Version (Spitzer & Endicott, 1977), the PSE, the PSE lifetime ratings of psychotic symptoms, the PSE syndrome checklist for current and lifetime psychopathology, the

Scale for the Assessment of Positive Symptoms (Andreasen, 1983b), the Scale for the Assessment of Negative Symptoms (Andreasen, 1983a), and the Personality Disorder Examination (Loranger, Susman, Oldman, & Russakoff, 1985). Excluding those who died or emigrated, more than 90% of the sample originally seen in 1962 was assessed in this manner. In addition, the entire sample was screened in the national psychiatric register.

Information, thus collected, was used to determine Axis I and II *DSM-III-R* diagnoses for each individual at each assessment. An independent analysis of the interview data yielded a high rate of agreement with the original diagnoses (κs = .90–.95). A lifetime *DSM-III-R* diagnosis was determined (Parnas et al., 1993).

CT Scan Procedures

A total of 126 high-risk and 77 low-risk patients underwent computerized tomography (CT) scanning as part of the 1986–1989 assessment. Patients scanned were representative of the original sample with respect to age, gender, risk status, lifetime psychiatric diagnosis, and history of perinatal complications. Scans were performed on a CT scanner (Somaton DRG, Siemens, Iselin, NJ) at Hvidovre Hospital in Copenhagen (Denmark). An average of 13 slices was taken parallel to the supraorbitomedial line, each with a thickness of 8 mm and no overlap. Images were processed on a 256 × 256 matrix.

A semiautomated computer algorithm was used to obtain volumetric, area, and linear measurements of the cerebral spinal fluid (CSF) spaces in the region of the ventricles and cortical sulci (both overall and for the frontal interhemispheric fissure and the right and left sylvian fissures separately), which were then expressed as percentages of (total or hemispheric) brain volume, area, and width, respectively. All measurements were then standardized to the same metric (i.e., $M = 5$, $SD = 1$).

DCs Score

Most births in Denmark are attended by midwives who complete a standardized form concerning the course of the delivery as well as the pre- and postnatal conditions of the mother and newborn. The information available in the protocols is considered by Danish obstetricians to be accurate but not necessarily exhaustive; some complications may have occurred but were not reported (especially milder complications). Protocols were obtained for 166 high-risk patients.

In our working model, DCs represent one type of second hit. The complications included in the DC index are as follows (each complication contributes one point to the total score): abnormal fetal position, premature rupture of membranes, vaginal explorations, stimulants, asphyxia, pelvic contractions during delivery, bleeding during delivery, uterine inertia, artificial help (e.g., forceps, Caesarean section), low to low–normal birth weight, and prolonged labor. Previous work has indicated that low to low–normal birth weight and prolonged labor times are associated with a heightened risk of perinatal hypoxia (reduction of oxygen supply to the fetus during the birth process) and intraventricular hemorrhaging (Brann, 1985), both of which may lead to necrosis of cells and enlargement of the ventricular system. For this reason, birth weights in the bottom quartile of the distribution (less than 3,100 g) and labor times in the upper quartile of the distribution (greater than 17 hr) were each scored as one complication; 46 patients had no complications, 55 had one complication, and 65 had two or more complications.

High-Risk Project, Hypothesis 1

For the High-Risk Project, our first hypothesis stipulates that genetic risk for schizophrenia will increase vulnerability to environmental trauma (second hit). We propose that as level of genetic risk increases, DCs will be associated with a multiplicative increase in anomalies of the brain.

Background

A fetus with 2nd-trimester developmental handicaps (first hit) then faces birth. It is possible that the resultant neural anomalies, vascular brain developmental anomalies, or both produce a special vulnerability of the high-risk fetus to DCs. This may make the high-risk fetus especially vulnerable to the stress of a difficult birth and may increase risk for bleeding in the ventricles, anoxia (lack of oxygen), and damage to periventricular tissue.

The results of two pilot studies (Cannon & Mednick, 1989; Cannon et al., 1993), based on the 15 schizophrenia patients identified in 1972, support the hypotheses derived from the working model. In 1986–1989, we completed a diagnostic assessment of the 1962 high-risk sample and ascertained 31 schizophrenia patients in the high-risk group. Cannon and Mednick were able to test the working model more decisively with this larger group of schizophrenia patients. The second article (Cannon et al., 1993) following this latest assessment examines the hypothesized interaction between genetic predisposition and DCs. These researchers used a cohort analytic study of 60, 72, and 25 individuals with zero, one, or two parents, respectively, who were affected with schizophrenia-spectrum disorders. They were examined in 1986–1989 with psychiatric interviews and CT scans.

Results

There were significant linear increases in CSF–brain ratios in the sulcal regions of the cerebral cortex as a function of level of genetic risk (see Figure 1). Individuals with two affected parents evidenced greater cortical sulcal enlargement than did individuals with one affected parent. In turn, individuals with one affected parent evidenced greater cortical sulcal enlargement than did individuals with no affected parents. In addition, genetic risk for schizophrenia and DCs were found to interact in the prediction of the subcortical (i.e., ventricular) CSF–brain ratio. The effect of DCs was greater among those with two schizophrenic (or schizophrenia-spectrum) parents compared with those with one affected parent and greater among those with one affected parent compared with those of normal parents. These effects were significant after controlling for the effects of age, gender, substance abuse, and history of organic brain syndromes and head injuries.

Discussion

We interpret the cortical anomalies as resulting from the genetic first hit (disruptions in fetal neural development) and the subcortical, ventricular abnormalities having resulted from a second hit, DCs.

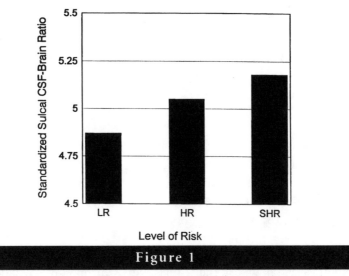

Figure 1

Genetic risk for schizophrenia and average sulcul CSF–brain ratio. CSF = cerebral spinal fluid; LR = low risk; HR = high risk; SHR = schizophrenic high risk.

High-Risk Project, Hypothesis 2

These findings led us to hypothesize that schizophrenia patients and individuals with genetically related conditions (e.g., schizotypals) would share the cortical anomalies (relative sulcal enlargement) whereas only schizophrenia patients (not schizotypal patients) would evidence the ventricular enlargement.

Background

There is a consistent body of evidence indicating a genetic relationship between schizophrenia and schizotypal personality disorder (SPD). In view of this, one would expect to find similar distributions of (genetically related) cortical brain abnormalities among individuals with SPD and schizophrenia. We predicted that among offspring of schizophrenic parents, those who develop schizophrenia or SPD will evidence an equivalent degree of cortical sulcal enlargement and that both groups will evidence greater cortical sulcal enlargement than high-risk individuals with nonspectrum psychiatric disorders and no disorders and low-risk individuals with and without psychiatric disorders. In addition, we predicted that high-risk individuals with schizophrenia will evidence a greater degree of ventricular enlargement than high-risk individuals with SPD, nonspectrum psychiatric disorders, and no disorders and low-risk individuals with and those without psychiatric disorders.

Methods

We used the cohort analytic study of the following six groups: high-risk patients: (1) 17 with schizophrenia, (2) 31 with SPD, (3) 33 with nonspectrum psychiatric disorder, and (4) 45 with no psychiatric disorder; low-risk patients: (5) 31 with nonspectrum psychiatric disorders of all types and (6) 46 with no psychiatric disorders.

Results

As hypothesized, high-risk individuals with schizophrenia or with SPD evidenced equivalent degrees of cortical sulcal enlargement; both groups evidenced significantly greater sulcal enlargement than did high-risk individuals with non-schizophrenia-spectrum disorders and no disorders and low-risk individuals with and those without psychiatric disorder (see Figure 2). High-risk individuals with schizophrenia evidenced significantly greater ventricular enlargement than all the other groups. The enlarged ventricles–schizophrenia findings relate mainly to predominantly negative symptom schizophrenia.

We conclude that among high-risk offspring, cortical abnormalities (because of neural developmental failures related to level of genetic risk) are expressed equally across the schizophrenia spectrum (SPDs and schizophrenia patients). Subcortical abnormalities are more pronounced and specific to schizophrenia. Above, we indicated that an important source of these subcortical abnormalities was DCs among those who have suffered the first hit. Cannon et al. (1994) have reported earlier that there were low levels of DCs among SPD patients.

Discussion

Individuals with the diagnosis of SPD and those with the diagnosis of schizophrenia share the experience of the first hit that results in cortical anomalies. Patients with SPD may not be schizophrenic because they

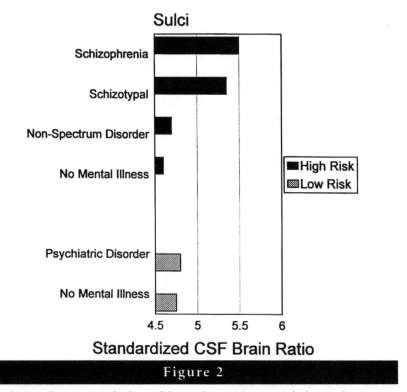

Figure 2

Psychiatric diagnoses in high- and low-risk participants: Sulcal CSF–brain ratio. CSF = cerebral spinal fluid.

are fortunate enough to avoid postpregnancy stressors, such as DCs or unstable families. Those who have experienced the first hit and suffer DCs evidence widened ventricles. In this study, we have only considered the genetic source of the first hit. In discussing Project 2, the Fetal Viral Infection Project, we examine the interaction of the influenza teratogen with DCs.

High-Risk Project, Hypothesis 3

We hypothesize that for those who have suffered a (genetic) first hit and have not suffered severe DCs, the risk of schizophrenia will be increased if they are exposed to unstable rearing circumstances. Unstable rearing circumstances will not increase risk for schizophrenia among low-risk individuals.

Background

We have supported this hypothesis in the context of the 1962 high-risk study (Cannon, Mednick, & Parnas, 1990b; Walker, Cudeck, Mednick, & Schulsinger, 1981) with the initial group of 15 schizophrenia patients. We have now completed a study of family rearing and 1989 outcomes, with 31 schizophrenia patients from the high-risk group.

Methods

From birth to age 15 years, we have coded, month by month, the rearing history of the participants of the 1962 High-Risk Project, indicating whether the child was with his or her biological mother, biological father, or both; foster reared in a family with no psychiatric illness; or reared in a public care institution for normal children.

Results

We replicated earlier results: Among high-risk participants, rates of adult schizophrenia are highest for those reared in a public care institution, lower for those raised by a schizophrenic parent, and lowest for those raised in a normal foster family (Gutkind et al., 1998). These findings are especially significant for those placed in institutions before the age of 3 years. All of these differences are statistically significant (Gutkind et al., 1998). Rearing circumstances, however, do not relate to risk of schizophrenia in the low-risk group.

PROJECT 2: FETAL VIRAL INFECTION

The Fetal Viral Infection Project focuses on the first hit of the working model, the disruption of fetal neural development. The Fetal Viral Project was based on the hypothesis that a teratogenic disturbance in fetal brain development during the 2nd trimester of gestation may increase the risk for some forms of schizophrenia.

Early Studies of Teratogenicity

In the 19th century, it became clear that exogenous chemical and physical conditions could adversely affect the embryonic development of many species. Studies were conducted, however, only on species whose fertilization and development took place outside the mother (echinoderms [e.g., sea urchins], amphibians, and fish). Mammalian embryos, whose fertilization and development were better protected and took place at an almost constant temperature, were held to be relatively impervious to external challenge.

Malformations of newborn mammals were, nevertheless, observed. With the mammalian fetus so well protected, it was thought that malformations must be due to genetic factors. This was the view until the 1930s when Hale (1933) reported a litter of 11 piglets born without eyeballs. The parents had normal eyes and were previously (and subsequently) able to produce offspring with normal eyes. Hale traced this deficit to a diet lacking in Vitamin A during the ill-fated pregnancy. Warkany (1965)—who is considered by many to be the father of mammalian teratology—conducted a systematic series of studies on the effects of riboflavin deficiency on the skeletal development of the fetal rat. Because the effects of riboflavin deficiency have a gradual onset and termination, Warkany developed a method to determine critical periods during gestation of sensitivity to the exposure. He administered galactoflavin, which quickly acts to inhibit many actions of riboflavin. The galactoflavin produced the equivalent of a riboflavin deficiency of rapid onset. When the galactoflavin was removed, the riboflavin rapidly resumed its normal potency. This methodological innovation permitted Warkany to determine with some precision the specific fetal anomalies associated with exposure during specific stages of gestation. This issue of the "sharpness" (Warkany's term) of the methodological tool is relevant to the purpose of this research. An influenza epidemic has a limited duration and therefore can be a relatively sharp methodological tool (relative to teratogens, e.g., smoking or marital stress). In this research, we were interested in learning whether a maternal influenza infection during a specific portion of the gestational period is associated with adult schizophrenia (McClure, 1995).

Maternal Exposure to Infection

Mednick, Machon, Huttunen, and Bonnet (1988) reported an elevated rate of schizophrenia among Helsinki residents exposed to the 1957 influenza epidemic during their 2nd trimester of gestation. These results for the 1957 epidemic have been replicated in independent studies completed in a number of international settings (Adams, Kendell, Hare, & Munk-Jorgensen, 1993; Fahy, Jones, Sham, Takei, & Murray, 1993; Kendell & Kemp, 1989; Kunugi, Takei, & Nanko, 1994; Machon & Mednick, 1994; Mednick, Machon, Huttunen, & Barr, 1990; O'Callaghan, Sham, Takei, Glover, & Murray, 1991; Waddington, 1992; Welham, McGrath, & Pemberton, 1993). Several of the reports are specific to Month 6 of gestation (Barr, Mednick, & Munk-Jorgensen, 1990; Kendell & Kemp, 1989; Kunugi et al., 1994; O'Callaghan et al., 1991; Sham et al., 1992). All of these successful replications used approximately the same methodology as the original Helsinki study. There have been four failures to replicate these findings (Bowler & Torrey, 1990; Crow, Done, & Johnstone, 1991; Selten & Slaets, 1994; Susser, Lin, Brown, Lumey, & Erlenmeyer-Kimling, 1994). We should point out that in none of these studies was any direct evidence of an actual maternal infection demonstrated.

Multiepidemic Studies

In Denmark, studying over 7,500 schizophrenia patients we noted that over a period of 40 years and across a series of influenza epidemics, significantly increased numbers of schizophrenia patients were born 4 months after periods with unusually high population levels of influenza infection (Barr et al., 1990). In other words, if there was an unusually virulent influenza epidemic during an individual's 6th month of gestation, that individual had a significantly elevated risk of adult schizophrenia. This finding has also been replicated in five multiepidemic studies (Barr et al., 1990; Morris et al., 1994; Sham et al., 1992; Takei et al., 1994; Welham et al., 1993).

Importance of Viral Studies

The viral-epidemiological studies are important for two reasons. First, they implicate a neural developmental disturbance in the etiology of at least some forms of schizophrenia. Second, the delimited duration of the influenza epidemic makes it possible to estimate the period of gestation critical for schizophrenia. Viral infections must account for only a fraction of the cases of schizophrenia; genetic factors and other teratogens, of course, also play a role. An influenza infection occurring at a critical period of neural development may partially mimic or exacerbate the genetic effect.

Discussion

There are nonreplications, but on the whole, however, the replications of the Helsinki 1957 epidemic findings and the multiepidemic findings support the hypothesis that a 2nd-trimester maternal influenza infection increases risk for adult schizophrenia in the offspring.

Fetal Viral Infection, Hypothesis 1

All of the studies described above examined only the exposure of the mother to the viral epidemic. We hypothesize that a greater proportion of mothers of schizophrenia patients exposed during the 2nd trimester will have suffered an antenatal, clinic-documented influenza infection than mothers of schizophrenia patients exposed in the 1st trimester, 3rd trimester, or both.

Background

In all of the earlier studies, the increased risk of infection was measured by the overlap of the 2nd trimester of gestation with the height of the influenza epidemic. There is no evidence that any of the women actually suffered a viral infection. It was deemed important to anchor the findings by demonstrating prospectively obtained, documented evidence of an actual infection.

Methods

In anticipation of the 1957 influenza pandemic, the health authorities of Finland requested that the obstetrical nurses in maternity clinics be alert to record influenza infections in pregnant women. Because Finnish women visit these maternity clinics an average of 13 times during the pregnancy, the reports of the obstetrical nurses were made in close temporal proximity to the time of the infection. We checked schizophrenia patients whose 2nd trimester of gestation occurred during the height of the epidemic to determine whether their mothers had an antenatal clinic record of a documented influenza infection.

Results

We found that of the Helsinki schizophrenia patients whose 2nd trimester of gestation overlapped the height of the epidemic, 86.7% had an antenatal clinic record of a 2nd-trimester, maternal, upper respiratory infection during the 1957 pandemic. Only 20% of those exposed in the 1st or 3rd trimesters had an antenatal clinic record of a maternal infection (the population rate of infection in Helsinki during the epidemic was 20%; Machon & Mednick, 1994). It must be recalled that a certain number of the 1957 birth cohort would have become adult schizophrenia patients without the epidemic. Thus, we are hypothesizing that the maternal influenza results in an increase in number of schizophrenia patients among individuals whose mothers suffered an influenza infection in the 2nd trimester. It follows, therefore, that all of the excess of 2nd-trimester schizophrenia patients should have experienced a maternal 2nd-trimester infection. This seems to be close to what we observed (Machon & Mednick, 1994).

Fetal Viral Infection, Hypothesis 2

We propose that schizophrenia patients exposed to a 2nd-trimester teratogen will evidence a pattern of clinical symptoms distinctly different from the symptoms of schizophrenia patients not exposed to the 2nd trimester teratogen or who were exposed in the 1st or 3rd trimester.

Background

As reported below, we found no interaction between genetic predisposition and the teratogen, maternal influenza. This suggests that these etiological factors are associated with different subtypes of schizophrenia.

Methods

We examined the patients of the Helsinki schizophrenia study (Mednick & Silverton, 1988) to determine if the 2nd-trimester schizophrenia patients evidenced a distinctive pattern of symptoms. The patients were interviewed and hospital records were coded for 172 symptoms. We subjected symptoms ratings to factor analysis and found eight symptom factors. We compared the factor scores for each of these eight factors in the 2nd-trimester schizophrenia patients with those of control groups.

Results

The 2nd-trimester schizophrenia patients were significantly elevated on three of the factors related to paranoid traits: suspiciousness, delusions of reference, and delusions of jealousy (Machon & Mednick, 1994). These data appear to indicate that teratogen-related schizophrenia patients evidence a disorder dominated by suspicion and paranoid symptoms.

Fetal Viral Infection, Hypothesis 3

For this hypothesis, we propose that teratogenic agents (e.g., a 2nd-trimester maternal influenza infection) will interact with genetic risk to increase risk for schizophrenia patients. Thus, a 2nd-trimester maternal influenza should be strongly associated with adult schizophrenia patients among individuals with elevated genetic predisposition for schizophrenia.

Background

Only a small number of fetuses exposed to maternal influenza in the 2nd trimester actually become schizophrenia patients. Perhaps the maternal influenza only increases risk for adult schizophrenia in fetuses already made vulnerable by genetic predisposition.

Methods

To test this hypothesis, we asked whether the strength of the 2nd-trimester effect increases as a function of increasing genetic predisposition for schizophrenia. We first tested this hypothesis in the context of a data set, which was constructed by selecting all schizophrenia patients in Finland and then identifying their first-degree relatives. From these families, we selected all those born in the 9 months after the 1957 influenza epidemic and divided them into three groups on the basis of the trimester of gestation during which they were exposed to the epidemic. Each of these three trimester groups were further divided into three subgroups (high, medium, and low) on the basis of the percentage of their first-degree relatives who were diagnosed as schizophrenic. A comparison of these groups permitted us to assess the strength of the 2nd-trimester effect in groups at varying levels of genetic risk for schizophrenia.

Results

The hypothesis was not supported. As genetic risk increased (from low to high) the strength of the 2nd-trimester influenza effect decreased significantly.

Methodological Problem

The index case was the family member exposed to the 1957 epidemic during gestation. We arrived at degree of genetic risk for this individual by computing percentage of first-degree relatives diagnosed as schizophrenic. Under some conditions, this criterion of risk may be flawed. Let us take an extreme example; consider two probands, each with two first-degree relatives. Suppose that in Case 1 the two relatives are the parents of the proband, whereas in Case 2 the two relatives are siblings of the proband (with the parents missing). The parents of Case 1 may be 50 years of age and will have gone through a major part of their risk period for the onset of schizophrenia. The two siblings of Case 2, however, may be 14 and 15 years old. Clearly, we must make a determination of degree of familial risk that is not biased by the age of the family members assessed. To do this, we must supplement information on the percentage of affected first-degree relatives with information on the number and ages of the parents and siblings of the index case. Although we did not have this information for the total nation of Finland, we did have a comparable data set limited to certain urban areas of Finland that does have information on the number of parents and siblings and their ages. This data set permits us to compute the genetic risk of the index case, taking into account the period of risk exposure (ages) of the family members.

Calculating Low-Risk Rates

In the data set that includes all of Finland, we included only families that contain at least one schizophrenia patient. The index family member was born in the 9 months following the 1957 epidemic. We defined degree of genetic risk to the index case by the percentage of the other members of the family with schizophrenia. For this data set, however, we do not have families in which (a) a child (without schizophrenia) was born in the postepidemic period and (b) there are no schizophrenia patients among the other members of the family. This latter group is needed to calculate the rate of schizophrenia among index cases who have no first-degree relatives with schizophrenia (low-risk group).

Above, we have described an urban Finnish population that identified all Finns born in these affected urban areas after the 1957 epidemic and also identified their families, without regard to the mental health status of family members. That is, this data set includes all families who resided in these urban areas with an index case born during this period, including families without a schizophrenic family member. These urban areas include 21.4% of the children born in Finland in the 9 months following the 1957 epidemic (13,448 children). This urban data set permits us to calculate the percentage of index cases with zero schizophrenic, first-degree relatives.

Genetic Predisposition

We defined three levels of genetic predisposition for the index participant born in the 9 months following the 1957 influenza epidemic. Low-risk participants had no first-degree family members with schizophrenia (0%). Medium-risk patients had 24% (range = 14–35%) of their first-degree family members with schizophrenia. High-risk patients had 46% (range = 36–62%) of their first-degree family members with schizophrenia.

Teratogenic Risk

Teratogenic risk was defined as relatively high for those exposed to the 1957 epidemic in their 2nd trimester of gestation. Teratogenic risk was defined as relatively low for those exposed to the 1957 epidemic during their 1st or 3rd trimesters of gestation.

Results

We compared the strength of the 2nd-trimester effect among those at low-, medium-, and high-familial predisposition to schizophrenia. The highest rate of schizophrenia occurred in those exposed in the 2nd trimester and who had no first-degree relatives with schizophrenia. For these individuals at low-genetic risk, the 2nd-trimester-exposed group had a significantly higher rate of schizophrenia than the rate for those exposed in the 1st and 3rd trimesters, $\chi2(1, N = 13.448) = 10.42, p < .001$. Among those at medium- or high-genetic risk, the 2nd-trimester-exposed patients did not evidence significantly elevated rates of schizophrenia.

These patients were screened in the registers for schizophrenia diagnoses in 1992. As noted above, a potential confound in the analyses is the possibility that the first-degree relatives of the 2nd-trimester-exposed patients differ in age (and therefore period of risk) from the first-degree relatives of the 1st- and 3rd-trimester patients. This would reduce the equivalence of the 3 trimesters in level of genetic risk. We calculated the percentage of parents among first-degree relatives of the index cases (e.g., if an index case has two parents and four siblings, then 33% of his or her first-degree relatives are parents). Across the trimesters and levels of genetic risk, there was little variation in the percentage of first-degree relatives who were parents (0.7–40.3%). We also calculated the mean years of birth of the parents and the siblings of the index cases for each trimester of exposure and for each level of genetic risk. The average year of birth of the parents varied very little across these groups (February 1928–March 1928); the average year of birth of the siblings also varied very little (February 1956–September 1956). These data suggest that the significant difference in rates of schizophrenia among those at low-genetic risk, as a function of trimester of exposure, cannot be ascribed to differences in the years of risk exposure of each proband's family.

One interpretation of the data suggests that those with a high-genetic predisposition for schizophrenia already have exceeded a threshold of 2nd-trimester-neural disruption; as expressed, the 2nd-trimester influenza infection seems not to add further schizophrenia-relevant brain-development disruption. This result was not predicted but must be seriously considered because it is based on a substantial population of urban residents.

Fetal Viral Infection, Hypothesis 4

We hypothesize that the maternal-influenza-based disturbance in development will produce brain changes, which may be detected by an MRI examination. Using the CT scan findings from the 1962 hisk-risk study that noted cortical anomalies especially related to level of genetic predisposition, we further hypothesize that the virus-associated anomalies will mainly be found in cortical structures.

Methods

To test this hypothesis, in cooperation with Huttunen, Cannon, and Standardskjold, in Helsinki, Denmark, we have collected MRI data from the Helsinki-born schizophrenia patients whose mothers suffered an influenza infection in their 2nd trimester of gestation during the 1957 epidemic. They were born February 15–May 14, 1958. For controls, we examined schizophrenia patients and normal controls born in Helsinki in 1955 (a year with a low rate of influenza infections). We decided that if we detected anatomical changes in those exposed in the 2nd trimester, we would also examine schizophrenia patients exposed to the 1957 epidemic in their 1st or 3rd trimester of gestation.

Currently, we have analyzed the MRI data for 19 2nd-trimester-exposed schizophrenia patients, 66 schizophrenia patients, 54 siblings without schizophrenia of schizophrenic parents, and 35 normal controls, all born in Helsinki in 1955.

Results

Preliminary comparisons of sulcal and ventricular CSF–brain volume ratios for the right and left hemispheres among 19 viral (1957–1958) schizophrenia patients and 66 control schizophrenia patients present an interesting pattern. (All controls were born in 1955.) Compared with the nonviral schizophrenia patients, the viral schizophrenia patients showed a significant increase in the sulcal CSF–brain ratio in the left hemisphere, F)2, 59) = 5.86, $p < .005$. Viral-exposed schizophrenia patients also showed a nonsignificant increase in the right hemisphere. In contrast, there were no significant differences between these groups in the ventricular CSF–brain ratio.

Discussion

These results suggest that viral schizophrenia patients are characterized by specific brain abnormalities that differ at least quantitatively from those seen in non-viral-exposed schizophrenia patients. The scoring of the MRIs will soon be completed. This will provide us with an opportunity to identify specific cortical areas affected by the 3rd-trimester influenza.

The Timing of the Genetic or Teratogenic Disturbance

1. As was pointed out above, in Helsinki and Copenhagen it was demonstrated that a maternal influenza infection in the 2nd trimester of gestation can increase a fetus's risk for adult schizophrenia (Barr et al., 1990; Mednick et al., 1988).
2. Using the same methodology and population, in Helsinki Machon, Mednick, and Huttunen (1997) also found that a 2nd-trimester maternal influenza infection is associated with increased risk for adult major affective disorder.
3. We have tried to learn what factor may determine whether schizophrenia or affective disorder will be the negative adult outcome associated with a 2nd-trimester maternal influenza infection.
4. The precise times of the overlap of the maternal influenza infection and the stage of gestation were plotted for patients with schizophrenia and those with affective disorder. The distributions revealed that whereas about half of the schizophrenia patients suffered a maternal infection in the 6th month of gestation, this was true for only 10% of the affective disorder cases. The majority of those with affective disorder suffered a maternal infection in the 5th month of gestation.
5. The Finnish Criminal Register provided us with the conviction

records of all the Helsinki population born in the 9 months after the 1957 influenza pandemic. We noted no relationship between property crime and period of gestation of exposure to the 1957 pandemic. Convictions for violent crimes were, however, significantly associated with exposure to the 1957 epidemic during the 2nd trimester of gestation. There was a tendency for violent offenders to have been exposed at the cusp of the 6th and 7th months of gestation.

Comment

We interpret these data as follows: The maternal influenza infection acted as a teratogenic disturbance that disrupted the development of the fetal brain. But to increase risk for schizophrenia, it must be true that this disruption (a) occurs during a period (or periods) of rapid development of specific brain regions and that (b) a deficit in these specific brain regions plays a significant role in increasing risk of adult schizophrenia. Periods of rapid development are periods of special vulnerability for brain areas. A teratogen or a genetically programmed disruption of development during this vulnerable period will have exaggerated effects on the specific brain regions undergoing rapid growth at that time. For example, if a failure of development of a subarea of the prefrontal cortex or thalamus is a risk factor for schizophrenia, then one period of vulnerability might comprise those days of gestation during which the prefrontal cortex, thalamus, or both are most rapidly developing. We propose that there exists a period (or periods) of fetal brain development during which a disturbance may increase risk specifically for schizophrenia. If the genetic or teratogenic developmental disruption strikes at a different gestational period, some other brain area will very likely be undergoing rapid development; the risk for schizophrenia will not be increased. If a deficit in this other brain region is important in the etiology of another mental disorder, then the risk for that disorder will be increased.

During fetal development, every area, system, and circuit of the brain has its growth spurts. If the area does not fully develop in those assigned periods, the developing brain does not backtrack to compensate; the area is left with a deficit. Genetic expression moves on to develop the next scheduled area. The failure of adequate development of a brain area may produce adaptive reassignment of function. But very likely such adaptation comes at a cost.

The development of the fruit fly, *Drosophila melanogaster,* provides an instructive model of this hypothesis. The effect of teratogens on *Drosophila* development has been an intense subject of study since 1947 by Gloor. The most commonly studied teratogen has been heat shock; one example of heat shock is exposure of a *Drosophila* larva to a temperature of 40.8° Celsius for 35 min (Schlesinger, Ashburner, & Tissieres, 1982). The term *heat shock* is now used also to refer to other types of teratogens, such as chemical exposures or stress. Heat shock has been tested systematically with *Drosophila.* Different structural anomalies have been observed with heat shock exposure at different stages of development. Distortions of development are observed, which resemble mutant gene defects, and are termed *phenocopies.* As might be expected, the offspring of these phenocopy *Drosophila* develop normally. These phenocopies are the "results of interruption of gene expression at critical periods in development when there are rapid changes in gene expression" (Petersen & Mitchell, 1982, p. 345). Heat shock stops RNA and protein synthesis.

When the heat shock teratogen is presented, cell activity is dominated by heat shock proteins; normal gene expression is put on hold. When the danger to the cell is past, the genes begin to express normally again. There is, however, an internal timing process that informs the cell which part of the *Drosophila* is scheduled next for rapid development. Thus, 37 hr into the pupal stage, the wings are scheduled for rapid development (see Figure 3). This wing development must be completed in the next 4 hr because at Hour 41 the head begins rapid development and the development of the wings ceases or is very severely diminished.

The genes are expressed on a specific schedule and do not return to a previous cycle of expression in an organ to remedy developmental errors. If the heat shock teratogen is presented between Hour 37 and Hour 41, the development of the wings is disturbed and they develop

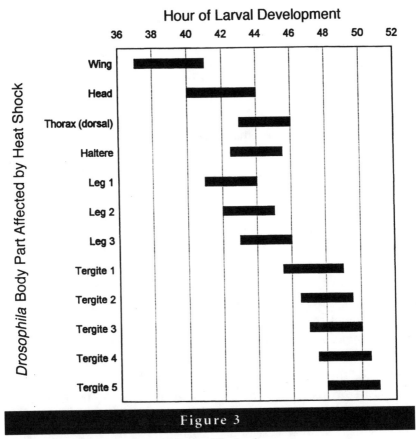

Figure 3

Timing of heat shock by hour of *Drosophila* development.

abnormally or not at all. Whatever element of the *Drosophila* (e.g., wings, legs) that should have undergone rapid development during the teratogen-induced interruption suffers incomplete or abnormal development.

Heat shock is not the only teratogen that has been tested using the *Drosophila* model. In the original study by Gloor (1947), ether was also found to be an effective teratogen. Many other chemical teratogens (e.g., alcohol) have been tested and found to yield equivalent effects. The terms *heat shock* and *heat-shock proteins* are used also for teratogens other than heat. The heat-shock-protein response to survival stress is well conserved among organisms. It may be seen in yeast as well as human cells.

The relevance of this model to human brain development and to the action of teratogens is clear. In response to a teratogen (e.g., a maternal influenza infection, severe stress, maternal alcohol or tobacco consumption), cells assume a defensive stance. Heat-shock proteins dominate cell behavior; normal gene expression is put on hold. At the time that the teratogen strikes if an element of the prefrontal cortex or thalamus is scheduled for rapid development, that development will suffer a deficit. When the influence of the teratogen dissipates, normal gene expression once again dominates development. The expression of temporally appropriate genes, however, skips the development of the element interrupted by the teratogen (in our example, the specific element of the prefrontal cortex, thalamus, or both) and moves on to the next brain area scheduled for rapid development. As in Figure 3, if we simply substitute a list of brain areas for the different elements of the *Drosophila* and change the time scale, we can see the relevance of the *Drosophila* model to human brain development.

It is well known that there is a specific sequence of organ development in the fetus. In the 1st trimester, the effect of a teratogen is dependent on its timing. In a well-known example, thalidomide is effective as a teratogen during 1 week in the 1st trimester. Barker (1994) suggested that nutritional deprivation early in the pregnancy may increase risk for lung deficits; poor nutrition late in the pregnancy may damage liver growth. We propose that the same principle is true for the development of the brain in the latter part of gestation. The timing of a teratogen determines which brain areas may fail to develop fully; the functional characteristics of these flawed brain areas may play a predispositional role in a variety of human outcomes. In concert with other teratogenic events, genetic factors, and postnatal environmental events, these teratogenic disturbances can predispose an individual to a major mental or behavioral disorder. Alternatively the teratogen may play a predispositional role in shaping the specific characteristics of the cognitive ability, the personality, and the temperament of an adult.

We propose the development of a paradigm that encourages the study of the long-term developmental consequences associated with the timing and severity of teratogenic disturbances.

PROJECT 3: DANISH BIRTH COHORT PROJECT

Between 1959 and 1961, several Danish investigators conducted an intensive perinatal study of the 9,125 consecutive deliveries at the University Hospital in Copenhagen. All aspects of the pregnancies and deliveries were recorded, including the Rhesus (Rh) compatibility of the mother and infant.

Background

The placental barrier probably bars the influenza virus from directly affecting the fetus. Thus, what is the mechanism that creates this developmental disturbance in the 2nd trimester? One possible mechanism might involve maternal autoantibodies, or alloantibodies. The autoantibodies elicited by the influenza virus may cross the placental barrier and disrupt fetal neurodevelopment by acting on fetal brain tissue antigens (Laing, Knight, Wright, & Irving, 1995). Evidence from animal studies shows that maternal autoantibodies can interfere with fetal brain development (Rick, Gregson, Adinolphi, & Liebowitz, 1981).

The Danish Birth Cohort presented us with the opportunity to test whether maternal antibodies, transmitted through the placenta due to Rh incompatibility, could possibly be associated with an increased risk for schizophrenia (Hollister, Laing, & Mednick, 1996). Hollister et al. conducted a study to examine the hypothesis that Rh incompatibility would increase risk for adult schizophrenia.

Danish Birth Cohort Project, Hypothesis 1

For this project, we propose that the rate of schizophrenia will be higher among Rh-incompatible fetuses compared with Rh-compatible fetuses. Rh incompatibility consists of the mother being Rh negative and the infant being Rh positive.

51

Methods

The participants of the birth cohort ($N = 1,867$, all the male participants in the cohort whose blood was typed), born in Copenhagen in 1959–1961, were a part of a larger perinatal cohort. All the details of the blood typing and treatment were recorded by senior obstetrical and pediatric scientists at the time of pregnancy and delivery. We studied only male participants because Rh-incompatibility-related hemolytic disease of the fetus and newborn most commonly affects them.

The 1,867 participants were separated into two groups: the Rh-incompatible group ($n = 535$) and the Rh-compatible group ($n = 1,332$). We checked these 1,867 participants in the Danish Psychiatric Register of the Institute for Psychiatric Demography in Aarhus, Denmark, in 1992, when the participants were 31–33 years of age. This permitted us to compare the Rh-compatible and -incompatible participants for rates of hospital-diagnosed schizophrenia.

Results

The rate of schizophrenia was significantly higher among the Rh-incompatible participants (2.1%) than among the Rh-compatible participants (0.8%). Hemolytic disease results when mothers produce autoantibodies at the time of delivery of the first Rh-incompatible child (occasionally this is associated with a miscarriage or abortion). Once the mother is immunized, hemolytic disease in the second- or later-born fetus and newborn can result from lysis of fetal erythrocytes by transplacentally acquired maternal erythrocyte alloantibodies. Thus, the first-born Rh-incompatible child is usually spared; the later-born children are at high risk of hemolytic disease, which may result in death or neurological damage.

We observed that the rate of schizophrenia increased as a function of increasing birth order. Second- and later born Rh-incompatible male offspring were significantly more likely to develop schizophrenia (2.6%) than second- or later born Rh-compatible male offspring (0.8%). A logistic regression was conducted to control for the possible confounding influences of marital status, age of mother, number of pregnancies, and stage of gestation; the differences remained significant. The rate of schizophrenia among first-born Rh-incompatible male participants (1.1%) was not significantly different from that of first-born Rh-compatible male participants (0.7%). The rate of no other psychiatric illness was elevated (including affective psychoses, organic psychoses, and paranoid psychoses); the results seem specific for schizophrenia.

Discussion

How might Rh incompatibility increase risk for adult schizophrenia? First, it is not unlikely to have led to hemolytic disease of the fetus and newborn. This condition can result in chronic fetal hypoxia, resulting from hemolysis, and can have serious effects on neural development. Mednick (1970) noted earlier that hypoxia is very likely to be at the basis of the elevation in obstetrical complications among schizophrenia patients, as did others (McNeil, 1988). Ben Ari (1992) and Mednick also noted specifically the vulnerability of the hippocampus to hypoxia. Neuropathology studies have implicated hippocampal abnormality in schizophrenia patients (Jeste & Lohr, 1989). Migration of neurons into the hippocampus is highly active in the 2nd trimester, at which time the transfer of maternal antibodies to the fetus is underway (Adinolphi, 1985).

Another possible link of Rh incompatibility with schizophrenia is the fact that hemolytic disease often leads to hyperbilirubinemia (excessive concentrations of bilirubin in the blood, which may lead to jaundice), which can damage the basal ganglia and the hippocampus. Although the number of cases of schizophrenia in the Hollister et al. (1996) study is rather small, it is of interest that number of hospitalizations and average stay in a hospital suggest that the Rh-incompatible schizophrenia patients are less severely ill than the Rh-compatible schizophrenia patients. Perhaps the Rh-compatible schizophrenia patients have a higher rate of genetically predisposed conditions. The incompatible schizophrenia patients also have a higher rate (not statistically significant) of paranoid schizophrenia. Machon and Mednick (1994) noted that 2nd-trimester-influenza schizophrenia patients tend to be less severely ill and to evidence paranoid subtypes.

53

In presenting these data, we certainly do not wish to suggest that a large proportion of schizophrenia patients can be explained by Rh incompatibility. Since the mid-1960s, in fact, prophylactic treatments prevent hemolytic disease associated with Rh incompatibility. Instead, these findings provide evidence for a possible mechanism (maternal autoantibodies acting on fetal brain tissue antigens) to help us understand the influenza infection findings.

PROJECT 4: THE COPENHAGEN AND HELSINKI HABITUATION PROJECTS

Background

One important question the influenza studies raise is What effect does the 2nd-trimester infection have on brain functioning that later increases risk for schizophrenia? We have suggested that the maternal influenza infection disrupts fetal neural migration, positioning, connecting, and pruning. Failures in such processes should produce defects in the form of cognitive deficits, which with appropriate techniques might be evident and measurable in infant behavior. To examine this question, we identified new samples of women who suffered an influenza infection during the 2nd trimester and examined the cognitive functioning of their infants at 6 months of age.

We chose to examine visual attention habituation. Measures of infant habituation of visual attention are generally interpreted as reflecting preverbal, cognitive processes critical for the later intellectual development of the child. Tests of infant habituation of attention are excellent predictors of later intellectual development (Slater, 1995), school readiness, and IQs. In brief, infants who show fast habituation of attention show evidence of an intact, well-developed brain; slow habituators may show evidence of flawed brain development.

The Copenhagan Habituation Project Hypothesis

For the Copenhagen project, our hypothesis stipulates that a 2nd-trimester maternal influenza infection will increase risk for failures in neural development in the fetus. Furthermore, we propose that such failures of development will produce deficits in cognitive ability, which may be detected by testing habituation at 6 months of age.

Methods

We first identified a group of Danish women who, during a mild influenza epidemic in Copenhagen, had suffered an influenza infection during their pregnancy. We examined habituation in the 6-month-old infants of these women (and controls). The Danish pediatrician who conducted the habituation testing was unaware of whether (and when, if the case) the mother suffered an infection. The pediatrician examined 203 infants, 147 mothers reported no infection during their pregnancy, 39 reported an influenza infection during either the 1st or 3rd trimester, and 17 suffered an influenza infection during the 2nd trimester of gestation. (The reports were made in the obstetrical clinic at the time of the infection.)

For the habituation testing, we had the 6-month-old infant sit on the mother's lap in a dark cubicle. A picture of a smiling woman was projected at a distance of 18 in. (45.72 cm) from the infant. Each time the infant fixated on this picture, we recorded the length of time of the fixation. When the infant fixated on two consecutive looks for 50% (or less) of the duration of the previously longest fixation, the session for that stimulus was closed. The procedure was repeated with a simple geometric figure. The measure has been shown to have excellent reliability in the literature as well as in this study. The most appropriate index of habituation suggested by the literature is the infant's total looking time.

Results

Infants whose mothers did not have an infection evidenced habituation at about the same rate as those whose mothers reported an infection in the 1st or 3rd trimester. Infants whose mothers reported an infection during the 2nd trimester evidenced significantly longer total looking times (poorer habituation) than did the other infant groups (see Figure 4).

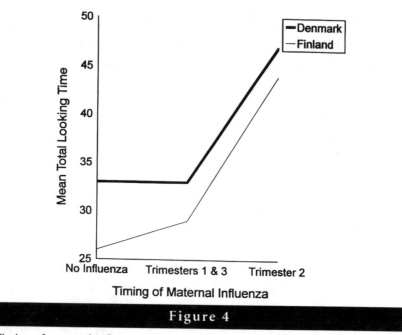

Figure 4

Timing of maternal influenza infection and infant habituation. Mean total looking time is by the second.

The Helsinki Habituation Project Hypothesis

For the Helsinki project, our hypothesis stipulates that a 2nd-trimester maternal influenza infection will increase risk for failures in neural development in the fetus. In addition, we propose that such failures of development will produce deficits in cognitive ability, which may be detected by testing habituation at 6 months of age (a replication of the Copenhagen Habituation Project).

Methods

During the winter of 1993–1994 in Helsinki, we recognized that the city was in the early stages of a moderately severe influenza epidemic. Women at two large obstetrical clinics in Helsinki were asked to report on infections during each visit to the obstetric clinic. Serological analyses were completed. A child clinical psychologist tested 83 six-month-old infants in Helsinki. She did not know whether, or when, the women had suffered from the infection. We began the study in Helsinki too late to detect 3rd-trimester infections; therefore, only those infants who were exposed during the 1st and 2nd trimesters were studied.

Results

In our analyses of the habituation data, we only included infants whose mothers had titre levels of 1.6 and above (in immune response), indicating significantly raised levels of influenza A/Finland/292/93M (H3N2) antibodies. The infants whose mothers had a serology-confirmed influenza infection during the 2nd trimester (especially in the 6th month of gestation) evidenced significant deficits in habituation of visual attention.

The Copenhagen habituation findings were replicated. Maternal reports of 2nd-trimester influenza infection were associated with deficits in habituation of visual attention in the 6-month-old infant. Infants whose mothers had no viral infection (by maternal report and serology) or whose infection occurred in the 1st trimester evidenced normal habituation (see Figure 4).

Discussion of the Copenhagen and Helsinki Habituation Projects

Six-month-old infants whose mothers suffered an influenza infection during their 2nd trimester evidenced impaired habituation to visual stimuli. Longitudinal studies indicate that 4- to 6-month-old infants who evidence poor habituation tend to manifest failures in cognitive tasks in later childhood. Venables (1997) reported that 3-year-olds whose mothers were exposed in the 2nd trimester to the Mauritius, 1968, Type A influenza epidemic evidenced poor habituation of a skin conductance response. Significantly, habituation has been shown to be defective among adolescents with an elevated genetic predisposition for schizophrenia (Hollister, Mednick, Brennan, & Cannon, 1994). We hypothesize that the maternal influenza partially mimics this genetic predisposition and, for this reason, is associated with habituation deficits. Schizophrenia patients consistently evidence failures in habituation (Braff & Saccuzzo, 1985). Brain areas involved in visual habituation (the medio-dorsal nucleus of the thalamus, the dorsolateral prefrontal cortex, and the brain stem; Adler et al., 1982; Karson et al., 1991) may have suffered a failure of development associated with the maternal influenza infection during the 2nd trimester. These areas have been found to evidence deficits in neuropathology studies of schizophrenia patients (Akbarian, Bunney, et al., 1993; Akbarian, Vinuela, et al., 1993).

AUXILIARY PROJECT: CHINA EARTHQUAKE

In 1976, a severe earthquake (7.8 on the Richter Scale) struck Tangshan, China, resulting in 655,000 deaths, thousands of injuries, and widespread destruction of houses and basic services. However, the catastrophic event may serve as a natural experiment. We propose the general hypothesis that the earthquake induced extreme and severe psychological and physical stress, which, in turn, produced physiological responses to the pregnant Tangshan women and served to disturb the neural and hormonal development of their fetuses.

Background

Mednick et al. (1988) have noted an apparent window of vulnerability in fetal brain development that includes the 2nd trimester of gestation. Barr et al. (1990) and others (Kendell & Kemp, 1989; Kunugi et al., 1994; O'Callaghan et al., 1991; Sham et al., 1992) have reported a significant 6-month effect. It was a purpose of the Tangshan study to attempt to further narrow this window of vulnerability within the 6th month of gestation. We discussed above some limitations of this study in narrowing the vulnerability window. Huttunen and Niskanen (1973) have presented evidence that the shock of being informed of a husband's death when a wife is in the 2nd trimester of her pregnancy will increase risk of psychosis in the offspring. We wish to extend these findings by studying the effects of a severe earthquake as a stressor.

China Earthquake Project Hypothesis

We hypothesize that the stress of a severe earthquake occurring during the 2nd trimester of gestation will disrupt neural development by producing deficits in cognitive functioning, thus increasing the risk for schizophrenia and schizophrenia-spectrum conditions. We hypothesize that for women who were in their 6th month of pregnancy during the severe earthquake in Tangshan, this extremely severe stress produced physiological responses that disturbed the neural development of their fetuses.

Methods

We have just completed examining a population of 19-year-olds who, while in utero, were exposed to the severe Tangshan earthquake (1976, 7.8 on the Richter Scale). All pregnant women in Tangshan, at all stages of gestation, experienced the earthquake. We intend to determine whether the stage of gestation at the time of the fetal exposure to the earthquake is related to an increase in schizophrenia-spectrum conditions, brain anomalies, and neurointegrative deficits. To the benefit of the population and the research (except for the 1st day), aftershocks occurred at a distance from Tangshan (60 km) and were deep in the earth (17 km), minimizing the effects of these aftershocks on the population and the research.

We examined 606 youths (exposed to the earthquake in 1976 at some time during their gestation) using a variety of cognitive and personality tests. We collected the same data from those born the year after the earthquake (1977). These 606 controls were tested 1 year after the index participants were examined. Thus, both groups were the same age at the time of testing.

Results (Preliminary)

Preliminary results for the Raven Progressive Matrices have been examined. We have compared independent individuals who were exposed to the earthquake in the 3rd and 6th months with controls born the same months 1 year later (not-earthquake exposed). There is no difference in Raven scores between the control participants and those exposed in the 3rd month of gestation; however, those exposed to the earthquake in the 6th month evidenced significantly reduced Raven scores in comparison with controls. These results are consistent with our findings in habituation of 6-month-old infants exposed to influenza in the 6th month of gestation.

CONCLUSION

We proposed a two-hit working model of the etiology of schizophrenia. The first hit causes a 2nd-trimester disruption in the development of the brain. This disruption may be genetically programmed or due to an adventitious teratogen (e.g., a maternal influenza infection). The genetically programmed and the teratogenic developmental disruption (first hit) interferes with fetal brain development in brain areas undergoing rapid development. If the disruption occurs during a critical period for the development of schizophrenia-relevant brain areas, then the first hit will increase risk of adult schizophrenia. Comparisons of brain-imaging findings for those with an elevated genetic risk for schizophrenia and those who suffered a maternal 2nd-trimester influenza infection revealed similar patterns of deficits in cortical structure.

The second hit consists of an environmental stress. We investigated two types of second hits, DCs and unstable rearing conditions. In genetically vulnerable infants, DCs are associated with widened ventricles. The same DCs in those not at genetic risk are not associated with ventriculomegaly. Those made vulnerable by the first hit (who do not experience DCs) may be at increased risk to suffer decompensation if they encounter severe stresses in early childhood. The stress of institutional care in the first 3 years of life is especially associated with increased risk for schizophrenia.

We also demonstrated severe infant and adolescent cognitive deficits associated with a disruption of development caused by a 2nd-trimester maternal influenza infection or maternal exposure to a severe earthquake during the 6th month of gestation. We propose that exposure as a fetus to a maternal influenza or a severe prenatal stress may cause vasoconstriction of the placenta, which, in turn, results in deleterious effects on the fetus's developing brain structures.

REFERENCES

Adams, W., Kendell, R. E., Hare, E. H., & Munk-Jorgensen, P. (1993). Epidemiological evidence that maternal influenza contributes to the etiology of schizophrenia: An analysis of Scottish, English, and Danish data. *British Journal of Psychiatry, 163*, 522–534.

Adinolphi, M. (1985). The development of the human blood-CSF-brain barrier. *Developmental and Medical Child Neurolology, 27*, 532–537.

Adler, L. E., Pachtman, E., Franks, R., Pecevich, M., Waldo, M. D., & Freedman, R. (1982). Neuropsycholgoical evidence for a defect in neuronal mechanisms involved in sensory gating in schizophrenia. *Biological Psychiatry, 17*, 639–654.

Akbarian, S., Bunney, W. E., Jr., Potkin, S. G., Wigal, S. B., Hagman, J. O., Sandman, C. A., & Jones, E. G. (1993). Altered distribution of nicotinamide-adenine dinucleotide phosphate-diaphorase cells in frontal lobe of schizophrenics implies disturbances of cortical development. *Archives of General Psychiatry, 50*, 169–177.

Akbarian, S., Vinuela, A., Kim, J. J., Potkin, S. G., Bunney, W. E., Jr., & Jones, E. G. (1993). Distorted distribution of nicotinamide-adenine dinucleotide phosphate-diaphorase neurons in temporal lobe of schizophrenics implies anomalous cortical development. *Archives of General Psychiatry, 50*, 178–187.

American Psychiatric Association. (1987). *Diagnostic and statistical manual of mental disorders* (3rd ed., rev.). Washington, DC: Author.

American Psychiatric Association. (1994). *Diagnostic and statistical manual of mental disorders* (4th ed.). Washington, DC: Author.

Andreasen, N. C. (1983a). *The Scale for the Assessment of Negative Symptoms (SANS).* Iowa City: University of Iowa.

Andreasen, N. C. (1983b). *The Scale for the Assessment of Positive Symptoms (SAPS).* Iowa City: University of Iowa.

Barker, D. J. P. (1994). *Mothers, babies and disease in later life.* London: British Medical Journal.

Barr, C. E., Mednick, S. A., & Munk-Jorgensen, P. (1990). Exposure to influenza epidemics during gestation and adult schizophrenia: A 40-year study. *Archives of General Psychiatry, 47*, 869–874.

Ben Ari, Y. (1992). Effects of anoxia and aglycemia of the adult and immature hippocampus. *Biology of the Neonate, 62*, 225–230.

Bowler, A. E., & Torrey, E. F. (1990). Influenza and schizophrenia: Helsinki and Edinburgh. *Archives of General Psychiatry, 47*, 876–877.

Braff, D. L., & Saccuzzo, D. P. (1985). The time course of information-processing deficits in schizophrenia. *American Journal of Psychiatry, 142*, 170–174.

Brann, A. W. (1985). Factors during neonatal life that influence brain disorders. In J. D. Freeman (Ed.), *Prenatal and perinatal factors associated with brain disorders* (pp. 263–358). Washington, DC: National Institutes of Health.

Cannon, T. D., Fuhrmann, M., Mednick, S. A., Machon, R. A., Parnas, J., & Schulsinger, F. (1988). Third ventricle enlargement and reduced electrodermal responsiveness. *Psychophysiology, 25,* 153–156.

Cannon, T. D., & Mednick, S. A. (1989). Genentic and perinatal determinants of structural brain deficits in schizophrenia. *Archives of General Psychiatry, 46,* 883–889.

Cannon, T. D., Mednick, S. A., & Parnas, J. (1990a). Antecedents of predominantly negative- and predominantly positive-symptom schizophrenia in a high-risk population. *Archives of General Psychiatry, 47,* 622–632.

Cannon, T. D., Mednick, S. A., & Parnas, J. (1990b). Two pathways to schizophrenia in children at risk. In L. Robins & M. Rutter (Eds.), *Straight and devious pathways from childhood to adulthood* (pp. 328–350). Cambridge, England: Cambridge University Press.

Cannon, T. D., Mednick, S. A., Parnas, J., Schulsinger, F., Praestholm, J., & Vestergaard, A. (1993). Developmental brain abnormalities in the offspring of schizophrenic mothers: I. Contributions of genetic and perinatal factors. *Archives of General Psychiatry, 50,* 551–564.

Cannon, T. D., Mednick, S. A., Parnas, J., Schulsinger, F., Praestholm, J., & Vestergaard, A. (1994). Developmental brain abnormalities in the offspring of schizophrenic mothers: II. Structural brain characteristics of schizophrenia and schizotypal personality disorder. *Archives of General Psychiatry, 51,* 955–962.

Crow, T. J., Done, D. J., & Johnstone, E. C. (1991). Schizophrenia and influenza. *Lancet, 338,* 116–117.

Endicott, J., & Spitzer, R. (1972). Current and Past Psychopathology Scales (CAPPS). *Archives of General Psychiatry, 27,* 678–687.

Fahy, T. A., Jones, P. B., Sham, P. C., Takei, N., & Murray, R. M. (1993). Schizophrenia in Afro-Caribbeans in the UK following prenatal exposure to the 1957 A2 influenza pandemic. *Schizophrenia Research, 6,* 98–99.

Gloor, H. (1947). Versuche mit aether an *Drosophila* [Research with ether in *Drosophila*]. *Revue Suisse Zoologique, 54,* 637–712.

Gutkind, D., Mednick, B., Cannon, T., Parnas, J., Schulsinger, F., & Mednick,

S. A. (1998). *Parental absence and schizophrenia—A 27-year follow-up of the Copenhagen high-risk cohort.* Manuscript submitted for publication.

Hale, F. (1933). Pigs born without eye balls. *Journal of Heredity, 24,* 105–106.

Hollister, J. M., Laing, P., & Mednick, S. A. (1996). Rhesus incompatibility as a risk factor for schizophrenia in male adults. *Archives of General Psychiatry, 53,* 19–24.

Hollister, J. M., Mednick, S. A., Brennan, P., & Cannon, T. D. (1994). Impaired autonomic nervous system habituation in those at genetic risk for schizophrenia. *Archives of General Psychiatry, 51,* 552–558.

Huttunen, M. O., & Niskanen, P. (1973). Prenatal loss of father and psychiatric disorders. *Archives of General Psychiatry, 35,* 429–431.

Jeste, D. V., & Lohr, J. B. (1989). Hippocampal pathologic findings in schizophrenia. *Archives of General Psychiatry, 46,* 1019–1024.

Karson, C. N., Garcia-Rill, E., Beidermann, J. A., Mrak, R. E., Husain, M. M., & Skinner, R. D. (1991). The brain stem reticular formation in schizophrenia. *Psychiatry Research, 40,* 31–48.

Kendell, R. E., & Kemp, I. W. (1989). Maternal influenza in the etiology of schizophrenia. *Archives of General Psychiatry, 46,* 878–882.

Kunugi, H., Takei, N., & Nanko, S. (1994). Head circumference at birth and schizophrenia. *British Journal of Psychiatry, 161,* 274–275.

Laing, P., Knight, J. G., Wright, P., & Irving, W. L. (1995). Disruption of fetal brain development by maternal antibodies as an etiological factor in schizophrenia. In S. A. Mednick & J. M. Hollister (Eds.), *Neural development in schizophrenia: Theory and research* (pp. 215–246). New York: Plenum Press.

Loranger, A. W., Susman, V. L., Oldham, J. M., & Russakoff, L. M. (1985). *Personality Disorder Examination: A structured interview for making diagnosis of* DSM-III-R *personality disorders.* White Plains, NY: Cornell Medical College.

Machon, R. A., & Mednick, S. A. (1994). Adult schizophrenia and early neurodevelopmental disturbances. In A. Zamacola, I. Ribera-Jullien, & B. Hassan-Govroff (Eds.), *Confrontations psychiatriques: Epidemiologie et psychiatrie* [*Psychiatric confrontations: Epidemiology and psychiatry*] (No. 35, pp. 189–215). Paris, France: Specia Rhone-Poulenc Rorer.

Machon, R. A., Mednick, S. A., & Huttunen, M. O. (1997). Adult major affective disorder following prenatal exposure to an influenza epidemic. *Archives of General Psychiatry, 54,* 322–325.

McClure, W. O. (1995). Fetal development and schizophrenia: Historical observations from teratology. In S. A. Mednick & J. M. Hollister (Eds.), *Neural development in schizophrenia: Theory and research* (pp. 13–26). New York: Plenum Press.

McNeil, T. F. (1988). Obstetric factors and perinatal injuries. In M. T. Tsuang & J. C. Simpson (Eds.), *Handbook of schizophrenia* (pp. 319–344). Amsterdam: Elsevier.

Mednick, S. A. (1970). Breakdown in individuals at high risk for schizophrenia: Possible predispositional perinatal factors. *Mental Hygiene, 54,* 50–63.

Mednick, S. A., Machon, R. A., Huttunen, M. O., & Barr, C. E. (1990). Influenza and schizophrenia: Helsinki vs Edinburgh. *Archives of General Psychiatry, 47,* 875–876.

Mednick, S. A., Machon, R. A., Huttunen, M. O., & Bonnet, D. (1988). Adult schizophrenia following prenatal exposure to an influenza epidemic. *Archives of General Psychiatry, 45,* 189–192.

Mednick, S. A., & Silverton, L. (1988). High-risk studies of the etiology of schizophrenia. In M. T. Tsuang & J. C. Simpson (Eds.), *Handbook of schizophrenia. Vol. 3: Nosology, epidemiology and genetics* (pp. 543–562). Amsterdam: Elsevier Science.

Morris, M., Cotter, D., Takei, N., Walsh, D., Larkin, C., Waddington, J. L., & O'Callaghan, E. (1994). An association between schizophrenic births and influenza deaths in Ireland in the years 1921–1971. *Schizophrenia Research, 9,* 137.

O'Callaghan, E., Sham, P., Takei, N., Glover, G., & Murray, R. (1991). Schizophrenia after prenatal exposure to 1957 A2 influenza epidemic. *Lancet, 337,* 1248–1250.

Parnas, J., Cannon, T. D., Jacobsen, B., Schulsinger, H., Schulsinger, F., & Mednick, S. A. (1993). Lifetime *DSM-III-R* diagnostic outcomes in the offspring of schizophrenic mothers: Results from the Copenhagen high-risk study. *Archives of General Psychiatry, 50,* 707–714.

Petersen, N. S., & Mitchell, H. K. (1982). Effects of heat shock on gene expression during development: Induction and prevention of the multihair phenocopy. In M. J. Schlesinger, M. Ashburner, & A. Tissieres (Eds.), *Heat shock from bacteria to man* (pp. 345–352). Cold Spring Harbor, ME: Cold Spring Harbor Laboratory.

Rick, J. T., Gregson, A., Adinolphi, M., & Liebowitz, S. (1981). The behavior of immature and mature rats exposed prenatally to anti-glioside antibodies. *Journal of Neuroimmunology, 1,* 413–419.

Schlesinger, M. J., Ashburner, M., & Tissieres, A. (1982). *Heat shock from bacteria to man.* Cold Spring Harbor, ME: Cold Spring Harbor Laboratory.

Selten, J. P., & Slaets, J. P. (1994). Evidence against maternal influenza as a risk factor for schizophrenia. *British Journal of Psychiatry, 164,* 674–676.

Sham, P. C., O'Callaghan, E., Takei, N., Murray, G. K., Hare, H., & Murray, R. M. (1992). Schizophrenia following pre-natal exposure to influenza epidemics between 1939 and 1960. *British Journal of Psychiatry, 160,* 461–466.

Slater, A. (1995). Individual differences in infancy and later IQ. *Journal of Child Psychology and Psychiatry, 36,* 69–112.

Spitzer, R. L., & Endicott, J. (1977). *Schedule for Affective Disorders and Schizophrenia–Lifetime version* (3rd ed.). New York: New York State Psychiatric Institute.

Susser, E., Lin, S. P., Brown, A. S., Lumey, L. H., & Erlenmeyer-Kimling, L. (1994). No relation between risk of schizophrenia and prenatal exposure to influenza in Holland. *American Journal of Psychiatry, 151,* 922–924.

Takei, N., Sham, P., O'Callaghan, E., Murray, G. K., Glover, G., & Murray, R. M. (1994). Prenatal exposure to influenza and the development of schizophrenia: Is the effect confined to females? *American Journal of Psychiatry, 151,* 117–119.

Venables, P. (1997). Maternal exposure to influenza and cold in pregnancy and electrodermal activity in offspring: The Mauritius Study. *Psychophysiology, 4,* 427–435.

Waddington, J. L. (1992, June). *Schizophrenia after the 1957 influenza epidemic in Ireland.* Paper presented at the meeting of the Royal Society of Psychiatry, Dublin, Ireland.

Walker, E. F., Cudeck, R., Mednick, S. A., & Schulsinger, F. (1981). The effect of parental absence and institutionalization on the development of clinical symptoms in high-risk children. *Acta Psychiatricia Scandinavica, 63,* 95–109.

Warkany, J. (1965). Development of experimental mammalian teratology. In
. J. G. Wilson & J. Warkany (Eds.), *Teratology: Principles and techniques* (pp.
1–20). Chicago: University of Chicago Press.

Welham, J. L., McGrath, J. J., & Pemberton, M. R. (1993). Schizophrenia: Birth-
rates and three Australian epidemics. *Schizophrenia Research, 9*, 142.

Wing, J. K., Cooper, J. E., & Sartorius, N. (1974). *The measurement and classification of psychiatric syndromes.* Cambridge, England: Cambridge University Press.

3

Genetic and Perinatal Influences in the Etiology of Schizophrenia: A Neurodevelopmental Model

Tyrone D. Cannon

In Kraepelin's (1919) original formulation, schizophrenia was viewed as a deteriorating brain disease, similar in natural history to Alzheimer's disease but with onset in early adult life. Despite clinical observations that cognitive deterioration was not present in every case (Bleuler, 1911/1950), the Kraepelinian analogy to dementing disorders has persisted in the consciousness of clinicians and researchers for much of this century. In fact, when the first studies examining the brains of living patients using computed tomography first appeared in 1976, the evidence of gross enlargement of the cerebral ventricles in these patients was interpreted as an anatomical "signature" of a dementing process in the schizophrenic psychoses (Johnstone, Crow, Frith, Husband, & Kreel, 1976; Johnstone et al., 1978).

In the past decade, this view has been radically altered by advances along several lines of inquiry that point to a prenatal–perinatal origin of at least some of the brain abnormalities in schizophrenia. First, numerous prospective studies have found associations between prenatal and perinatal complications (e.g., fetal hypoxia [oxygen deprivation]) and an increased risk for schizophrenia later in life, indicating that obstetric events expected to have an adverse impact on the developing fetal brain could play a role in the etiology of schizophrenia. Second, postmortem neuropathology studies have found evidence of heterotopic displacement of neurons in the hippocampal formation, frontal and temporal cortexes, and other regions, which imply disturbances of brain development in utero. Third, in vivo imaging studies have observed gross neuroanatomical changes (e.g., ventricular enlargement, reduced volumes of frontal and temperolimbic structures) in young, never-treated patients in their first episodes of psychosis and have in general failed to detect evidence of progressive deterioration in such neuropathological markers with increasing length of illness. In addition, structural and functional abnormalities of the brain similar to those seen in schizophrenia have also been observed in some of the unaffected first-degree relatives of schizophrenia patients, suggesting that such abnormalities may be mediated in part by genetic predisposition to the disorder. Finally, prospective studies of high-risk samples (e.g., offspring of schizophrenic parents) and representative birth cohorts have demonstrated that future schizophrenia patients show evidence of neuromotor impairment and cognitive dysfunction during infancy and childhood, suggesting that the neuropathological features predisposing to the disorder are present from birth.

This chapter provides an overview of the empirical research in each of these four fields, elucidating the strengths and weaknesses of the case for viewing schizophrenia as a "neurodevelopmental" condition, sketching the rudiments of a model for understanding neurodevelopmental processes in the genesis and epigenesis of the disorder, and suggesting avenues of future work that could help to solve remaining points of ambiguity.

OBSTETRIC COMPLICATIONS

Serious obstetric complications (OCs) are more frequent in the histories of adult schizophrenia patients than of normal controls (McNeil, 1988). Two questions of major importance in this area are whether more than one neurally disruptive mechanism is involved and whether obstetric influences are sufficient to produce schizophrenia in the absence of a genetic predisposition, act additively or interactively with genetic factors in increasing liability to the disorder, or are themselves a consequence of genetic predisposition.

Fetal Hypoxia

In regard to the first question, McNeil's (1988) review of the OC literature appearing prior to 1988 concluded that of the different types of OCs found to be associated with schizophrenia, labor and delivery complications (LDCs), particularly perinatal hypoxia, have the most robust association. A recent examination of the studies conducted since that review, in which objective birth records were used in comparing rates of LDCs among schizophrenia patients and a variety of different comparison groups (e.g., unaffected siblings, psychiatric controls, normal controls), arrived at the same conclusions (Cannon, 1997). Notably, about 20–30% of the schizophrenia patients ascertained from unselected birth cohorts have a history of hypoxia-associated LDCs, as compared with a base rate of 5–10% in the general population (Buka, Tsuang, & Lipsitt, 1993; McNeil, 1988).

Markers of fetal hypoxia and other OCs have recently been examined in relation to risk for schizophrenia in the Philadelphia cohort of the National Collaborative Perinatal Project (Cannon, Hollister, Bearden, & Hadley, 1997). The participants were 9,236 individuals born to 6,753 mothers from 1959 to 1966 in two innercity hospital obstetric wards. The gestations and births were monitored prospectively with standard research protocols. Psychiatric diagnoses were ascertained by treatment contacts in adulthood with local mental health facilities. In the overall cohort, the odds of schizophrenia increased linearly, whereas the odds of being an unaffected sibling of a schizophrenia patient decreased linearly, with an increasing number of hypoxia-associated OCs. This effect was also present when modeling odds of schizophrenia within families. There was no relationship between these OCs and other psychiatric disorders, and there were no associations between other (prenatal or perinatal) complications and schizophrenia.

Fetal oxygen deprivation may thus represent the primary mechanism in the chain of events leading from hypoxia-associated OCs to perinatal brain damage and later schizophrenia. However, because the vast majority of individuals so exposed do not become schizophrenic (Buka et al., 1993; Cannon, Hollister, et al., 1997; Done et al., 1991), if fetal hypoxia does play a causal role, its influence must depend on other predispositional factors. Because OCs are associated with schizophrenia within families and occur less frequently in unaffected siblings of schizophrenia patients than in low-risk controls (Cannon, 1997), their influence on risk appears to depend on rather than covary with genetic predisposition. In support of this view, Cannon et al. (1993) have observed a greater effect of perinatal hypoxia exposure on neuroimaging measures of structural brain pathology with increasing degree of genetic background for schizophrenia. A genetic factor in schizophrenia may thus confer a heightened susceptibility to the pathogenic effects of fetal oxygen deprivation.

Implications

Together, these findings have three broad-ranging implications. First, it may be possible to prevent schizophrenia in some genetically at-risk individuals with careful prenatal and perinatal monitoring and early intervention. Claims that the incidence of schizophrenia has declined from the pre- to post-WW2 period in developed nations, with the accompanying improvement in obstetric care, are consistent with this notion (see Warner, 1995, for a review); but such claims are based on analyses of hospital admissions, and practices relating to which have also changed during this period. Second, a search for candidate genes that mediate the brain's vulnerability to hypoxic-ischemic neuronal injury appears warranted. The list of such candidates is likely to be relatively long, but prominent suspects might be located within the glutamatergic N-methyl-D-asparate receptor system, as overstimulation of such receptors represents an early event in the sequence leading from hypoxia to neuronal death (Choi & Rothman, 1990). Third, because the proportion of the schizophrenic population with a history of perinatal hypoxia is quite high (i.e., 20–30%), it is possible that hypoxia-associated LDCs represent the single most important environmental contributor to liability.

NEUROPATHOLOGY STUDIES

Nature and Distribution of Findings

Postmortem analysis of brain tissue from individuals diagnosed with schizophrenia while alive offers the unique opportunity to investigate markers of neurodevelopmental versus neurodegenerative changes at the molecular and cellular levels. One approach to this issue is to compare cellular markers of neurodegenerative disease in schizophrenia patients and normal controls with that seen in patients with known neurodegenerative conditions. When this has been done, senile plaques and neurofibrillary tangles, which are present in considerable numbers in the brains of patients with Alzheimer's disease, have not been found to be elevated in schizophrenia patients (Arnold, Franz, & Trojanowski, 1994).

Moreover, a number of neuropathology studies have reported evidence of cellular positioning disturbances in schizophrenia patients consistent with prenatal disturbances of cell migration. These findings include reduced thickness of the granule cell layer of the dentate gyrus (McLardy, 1974), abnormally oriented pyramidal cells in the hippocampus (Conrad, Abebe, Austin, Forsythe, & Scheibel, 1991; Jeste & Lohr, 1989; Kovelman & Scheibel, 1984; Scheibel & Kovelman, 1981), and abnormal distributions and arrangements of cells in the prefrontal cortex (Akbarian, Bunney, et al., 1993; Benes, 1987; Benes, Davidson, & Bird, 1986; Benes, McSparren, Bird, San Giovanni, & Vincent, 1991), entorhinal cortex (Arnold, Hyman, Van Hoesen, & Damasio, 1991; Beckmann & Jakob, 1991; Casanova, Stevens, & Kleinman, 1990; Falkai, Bogerts, Roberts, & Crow, 1988; Jakob & Beckmann, 1986), and temporal cortex (Akbarian, Vinuela, et al., 1993). Such findings are consistent with prenatal influences because in humans, neuronal proliferation, migration, and positioning are almost entirely complete by birth. Notably, findings consistent with prenatal structural ectopias (cellular positioning errors) have also been observed in known neurodevelopmental conditions such as dyslexia (Hynd & Semrud-Clikeman, 1989) and some hereditary forms of epilepsy (Huttenlocher, Taravath, & Mojtahedi, 1994).

Altered cell densities and gray matter volumes have also been observed in these same brain regions (Benes et al., 1986; Benes, Sorensen,
& Bird, 1991; Bogerts et al., 1990; Bogerts, Meertz, & Schonfeldt-Bausch,
1985; Brown et al., 1986; Falkai & Bogerts, 1986; Falkai, Bogerts, &
Rozumek, 1988; Heckers, Heinsen, Geiger, & Beckmann, 1991) as well
as in the mediodorsal thalamic nucleus, nucleus accumbens (Pakkenberg, 1990, 1992a, 1992b), and basal ganglia (Heckers, Heinsen, Heinsen, & Beckmann, 1991). These findings are predominantly consistent
with fewer than normal numbers of neurons in the affected locations,
although increases in neuron counts have been reported in some locations (i.e., basal ganglia) in a few of the studies (Dagg, Booth, Mc-
Laughlin, & Dolan, 1994; Heckers, Heinsen, Heinsen, et al., 1991;
Selemon, Rajkowska, & Goldman-Rakic, 1993).

Altered cell densities and gray matter volumes are less clearly associated with prenatal developmental disturbances than are findings of
abnormal cell positioning. Neurodevelopmental processes that could account for such findings include disturbances of cell proliferation during
gestation, excessive neuronal elimination later in life, or cell death resulting from a teratogenic insult to the brain in utero. Of course, such
findings may also be explained by a neurodegenerative process active
in adulthood. In this case, however, one would expect to see substantial
glial scarring in the regions showing reduced neuron counts. Although
qualitative evidence of gliosis has been reported in a few studies, all
quantitative studies comparing numbers of glia and astrocytes between
schizophrenic and control brains have failed to detect significant differences in these markers of neuronal atrophy (reviewed in Falkai &
Bogerts, 1995).

Implications

Autopsy studies thus provide compelling yet circumstantial evidence of
disturbances of brain development in schizophrenia. There are, however, a number of limitations of this work that bear mentioning. First,
at present, there is no direct evidence that the cytoarchitectural changes
reviewed above participate in the development or maintenance of
schizophrenic symptoms. The regional distribution of these changes is

certainly consistent with current models of the neural systems thought to be involved (Cannon, 1996), but researchers simply do not yet know what the effect of an abnormally positioned pyramidal cell in the hippocampal formation might have in terms of higher order processes, extending from the level of neurotransmission in a single cell to the level of clinical symptomatology.

Second, although some of the findings of autopsy studies are clearly consistent with a prenatal origin (i.e., abnormalities of cell position), it is not yet known whether these findings share an etiologic factor in common with the more gross neuroanatomical changes that can be assayed in living patients (e.g., ventricular enlargement and reduced regional gray matter volumes). Furthermore, even if the structural abnormalities predisposing to schizophrenia originate during brain development, such damage could have secondary neurodegenerative effects later in life. Indeed, involvement of neurodevelopmental and neurodegenerative changes in schizophrenia are not mutually exclusive; both types of processes could be present in the same case and could apply to differing degrees in different cases.

Third, because autopsy studies typically examine a small series of brains from patients whose family, birth, and developmental histories are unknown, they are not well suited to address questions concerning the prevalence of neuropathological changes in the schizophrenic population, the sources of such changes, or their implications for the developmental trajectories of individuals predisposed to the disorder. To address these questions, researchers need to examine measures of brain structure and function in large groups of individuals on whom relevant historical data are available or can be collected.

STRUCTURAL BRAIN-IMAGING STUDIES

Nature and Distribution of Findings

The initial finding of ventricular enlargement in schizophrenia patients (Johnstone et al., 1976, 1978) has now been replicated in over 100 studies, with a smaller number of studies also reporting enlargement of the invaginations of the cortical surface (reviewed in Cannon, 1991; and Gur & Pearlson, 1993). Such findings are general, nonspecific markers of cerebral compromise and appear in numerous other neuropsychiatric conditions, including alcoholism and Alzheimer's disease. In studies using magnetic resonance imaging—which has greater spatial and contrast resolution than computed tomography and permits quantitation of specific gray matter volumes—the most consistently replicated findings are volume reductions in limbic structures (including hippocampus and amygdala), thalamus, and temporal cortex, with inconsistent evidence of volume reductions in the frontal cortex. Some studies report increases in volume in the basal ganglia (reviewed in Gur & Pearlson, 1993). Also of interest is a general trend for markers of pathology to be more pronounced in the left compared with the right hemisphere, although right-hemisphere changes are also present (e.g., Shenton et al., 1992).

Lack of Progression

The evidence of cerebrospinal fluid space enlargement and reduced regional gray matter volumes in schizophrenia could reflect neurodevelopmental changes, neurodegenerative changes, or both. If such abnormalities were at least partly neurodevelopmental in origin, one would expect to see evidence of them early in life among individuals who develop the condition as adults. No such prospective neuroimaging studies have examined structural brain abnormalities in preschizophrenia patients, but ventricular enlargement and reduced temporal lobe volumes have been observed in young, never-treated, and recent-onset cases, indicating that they are present at least as early as the beginning stages of the illness (Cannon, 1991).

In known neurodegenerative conditions such as Alzheimer's disease, gross structural changes in the brain show a marked tendency to progress (i.e., increase in severity) the longer the disease process has been active. It is thus notable that the majority of neuroimaging studies of schizophrenia patients have failed to detect significant correlations between structural neuropathological indicators, such as ventricular enlargement and increasing duration of illness (reviewed in Cannon,

1991). The few studies that have found such correlations did not control for variance related to aging. This is an important omission because there is an increase in cell death (and compensatory ventricular enlargement) with normal aging, a process that accelerates exponentially after the 5th decade of life (Barron, Jacobs, & Kinkel, 1976). When age-related variance has been controlled (i.e., with statistical regression techniques), any tendencies for ventricular volume to correlate with duration of illness have been removed (e.g., Andreasen, Olsen, Dennert, & Smith, 1982; Mathew et al., 1985). Furthermore, in a meta-analytic review of the structural neuroimaging literature appearing prior to 1990, there was no relationship between effect size for ventricular enlargement (i.e., the standardized difference between the schizophrenia and control groups for measures of ventricular size) and the mean duration of illness in the patient groups, after accounting for age (Raz & Raz, 1990).

Although the evidence of a lack of progression from cross-sectional studies is consistent, a stronger basis for examining this issue would be provided by follow-up neuroimaging studies of the same patients over time. Only a handful of such studies have appeared, with the majority failing to detect a difference in the rate of tissue loss between schizophrenia and control groups over a period of 1–8 years (Degreef et al., 1992; DeLisi et al., 1991, 1992; Hoffman, Ballard, Turner, & Casey, 1991; Nasrallah, Olsen, McCalley-Whitters, Chapman, & Jacoby, 1986; Pilowsky, Juliano, Bigelow, & Weinberger, 1988; Sponheim, Iacono, & Beiser, 1991; Vita, Sacchetti, Valvassori, & Cazzullo, 1988). However, a few studies have reported evidence consistent with progressive tissue loss in schizophrenia patients (DeLisi et al., 1995; Kemali, Maj, Galderisi, Milici, & Dalvati, 1989; Woods et al., 1990). It thus appears possible that there is a progressive deterioration in neuroanatomical markers of schizophrenia in at least a subgroup of patients. As we have seen, such deterioration would not rule out a primary neurodevelopmental process because disturbances of cell proliferation and migration can result in excessive cell elimination later in life due to a lack of appropriate connectivity (and other secondary processes). Nevertheless, that there may be deterioration in such markers in adult life suggests that disturbances of brain development may not explain the entirety of the longitudinal course of this disorder.

Appearance in Unaffected Relatives

Genetic epidemiologic studies have demonstrated conclusively that schizophrenia is a substantially heritable disorder. Estimates of the degree of heritability on the basis of concordance rates in twins are on the order of 80%, and the increased risk to biological relatives is independent of sharing a rearing environment with an affected relative (Cannon et al., 1998; Kendler & Diehl, 1993). Biological relatives of schizophrenia patients are also at increased risk for a variety of subpsychotic symptoms (e.g., suspiciousness, magical thinking, perceptual aberrations, social anxiety, and withdrawal), which are summarized in the diagnostic category of schizotypal personality disorder (Kendler & Diehl, 1993). Despite these interesting leads, thus far there have been only a few positive reports linking DNA polymorphisms to the expression of schizophrenia in pedigrees, and all of the positive reports have either failed to replicate or remain to be tested in independent samples (O'Donovan & Owen, 1996). These efforts have been hindered in part by a lack of knowledge of the mode of inheritance, by the possibility that different genes may contribute to different forms of the illness (i.e., genetic heterogeneity), and by an inability to detect nonpenetrant carriers of the predisposing genes (Diehl & Kendler, 1989; Weeks, Lehner, Squires-Wheeler, Kaufmann, & Ott, 1990). The existence of individuals who carry a genotype that predisposes them to schizophrenia but who do not manifest the disorder phenotypically is indicated by the equivalent morbid risks for the disorder among offspring of discordant monozygotic twins (Fischer, 1971; Gottesman & Bertelsen, 1989) and by the fact that the genetic contribution to liability is substantially higher than the 5–10% recurrence risk among first-degree relatives of schizophrenia probands (Cannon et al., 1998). These considerations have led several investigators to search for biological or behavioral characteristics that mark the presence or degree of genotypic risk for the disorder. Such *endophenotypic* indicators (Gottesman, McGuffin, & Farmer, 1987) are likely to be closer to the mechanism of gene action than the clinical phenotype and, as such, are likely to be more sensitive to underlying genetic variation in pedigrees than clinical diagnostic categories.

If some of the neuroanatomical deficits in schizophrenia represent such endophenotypic indicators, many first-degree relatives of schizophrenia patients should thus show some degree of the same deficits when compared with appropriate controls. Weinberger, DeLisi, Neophytides, and Wyatt (1981) found that consistent with this notion, both schizophrenia patients and their healthy siblings had significantly larger ventricles than normal controls, suggesting a familial–genetic component to increased ventricular size in schizophrenia. Reveley, Reveley, Clifford, and Murray (1982) found a similar pattern of results in a study of seven monozygotic twin pairs discordant for schizophrenia, but the differences between the healthy cotwins of schizophrenia patients and the normal control twins, while moderately large effect size (0.8), failed to reach statistical significance. DeLisi et al. (1986) studied 34 affected and unaffected individuals from 11 different families and found a significant association between ventricular size and schizophrenia within families, even after the contributions of several environmental sources of brain pathology were partialed out.

In a study of adult offspring of schizophrenic parents and normal controls in Denmark, Cannon et al. (1993) found that measures of sulcal and ventricular enlargement increased in a stepwise, linear fashion, with an increasing level of genetic risk for schizophrenia (i.e., none, one, or both parents affected with schizophrenia spectrum disorders). In addition, a portion of the extent of ventricular enlargement was predicted by the interaction of degree of genetic risk for schizophrenia with OCs. Among individuals without a history of OCs, ventricular volume tended to increase linearly with the number of parents affected, but this pattern was significantly more pronounced in those with a history of OCs. Notably, there was no difference in ventricular volume as a function of OCs among the low-risk controls, indicating that some degree of genetic risk was required to observe the effect. In addition, high-risk patients with schizotypal personality disorder did not differ from those with no mental illness in their rate of OCs

(Parnas et al., 1982) and, along with the latter, had significantly smaller ventricular volumes than the schizophrenia patients (Cannon et al., 1994).

Proportion of Schizophrenia Population With Structural Abnormalities

It is important to note that all studies have observed considerable over-lap (i.e., on the order of 50%) between the patient and control samples on these neuroanatomical markers. Whereas this pattern could reflect subgroup differences within the schizophrenic population when patients are compared with appropriate biological controls (i.e., their unaffected cotwins and siblings), a substantially higher percentage (i.e., 80–100%) have been found to show deviance on these measures (reviewed in Cannon & Marco, 1994). The use of within-family controls has the major advantage of minimizing the background of random genetic variation in neuroanatomical traits. Twin studies indicate that this genetic variation between unrelated individuals is likely to account for a large share of the overlap between the patient and control distributions on many of these measures (Cannon & Marco, 1994; Reveley et al., 1982).

Within-family analysis also appears to provide a more sensitive basis for investigating neural systems that may be relatively more severely impaired in schizophrenia. In the one published twin study that compared regional neuroanatomical measures in patients with their healthy cotwins against a background of generalized deficit, the medial temporal lobe was relatively more severely affected (i.e., the effect size for volume reduction of the hippocampus was two to three times greater than for the other regions examined; Suddath, Christison, Torrey, Casanova, & Weinberger, 1990). We have recently reported similar findings in a sample of sibling pairs from Denmark, in which patients were found to show a 100–300% increase in cerebrospinal fluid volume compared with their own unaffected siblings, and the degree of difference was significantly more pronounced in the left compared with the right hemisphere (Eyler Zorrilla et al., 1997).

Implications

Neuroimaging studies of adult schizophrenia patients have thus found robust evidence of structural abnormalities of the brain in these patients. Notably, nearly all schizophrenia patients, even those without exposure to neuroleptics, show evidence of these abnormalities when compared with their unaffected siblings and cotwins. Whether ventricular enlargement and reduced regional gray matter volumes precede the diagnosis of schizophrenia remains unclear. It is notable, however, that many of these abnormalities have been seen in young cases in their first episodes of psychosis as well as in some of the unaffected first-degree relatives of schizophrenia patients, suggesting that such abnormalities are at least partially reflective of an underlying (i.e., established prior to onset) vulnerability to schizophrenia. There is also preliminary evidence that genetic factors and OCs may interact in producing some of the structural brain abnormalities characteristic of this disorder.

However, some studies have found evidence consistent with deterioration in some of these markers during the adult course of illness. It will be necessary to conduct follow-up neuroimaging studies on large, well-characterized patient and sibling groups to determine whether signs of neurodegeneration are present in all cases or are confined to a particular subgroup. It is important to emphasize, however, that because insults to the brain in utero can affect the viability of neurons in the adult brain, if deterioration in these markers does occur in at least a subgroup of schizophrenia patients it would not rule out a primary neurodevelopmental cause of the brain pathology in these cases. Progress on this issue awaits the results of longitudinal neuroimaging follow-up examinations on large groups of patients whose birth and developmental histories were studied prospectively.

Given that many of the structural brain deficits observed in schizophrenia patients are also seen in some of their healthy relatives, additional factors are required to explain why some of these individuals manifest the disorder phenotypically and others do not. One possibility is that those cases with schizophrenia have a greater number of genes in a predisposing configuration, in which case, schizophrenia patients should manifest endophenotypic markers to a greater degree than genetically predisposed individuals without schizophrenia. Another, not mutually exclusive, possibility is that schizophrenia patients are uniquely characterized by an environmental risk exposure that magnifies the degree of brain dysfunction above that associated with the disorder's genetic basis. The evidence reviewed above is consistent with both of these models as deficits are nearly always greater in patients than in their own unaffected relatives. Other work indicates that at least some of the increase in anatomical and functional abnormalities of the brain in schizophrenia patients compared with their relatives is mediated by a history of OCs that appear to be unique to schizophrenia patients (Cannon et al., 1993; Cannon, Kaprio, Lönnqvist, Huttunen, & Koskenvuo, 1998).

PROSPECTIVE STUDIES OF COGNITIVE AND NEUROMOTOR FUNCTIONING

High-Risk Studies

Prospective studies of neurobehavioral functioning in preschizophrenia patients and in individuals at elevated genetic risk for schizophrenia also point to a developmental origin of the brain abnormalities in this disorder. Numerous studies have found that offspring of schizophrenic parents show delayed motor development during infancy and perform more poorly on neuropsychological tests than offspring of normal parents in childhood (reviewed in Erlenmeyer-Kimling & Cornblatt, 1987; Walker, 1994). In the few such studies that also obtained information on birth history, cognitive deviance was either greater in or limited to those high-risk offspring with a history of OCs. Because the participants were assessed before any showed overt signs of psychosis, these studies have the advantage of ruling out factors secondary to the illness or treatment as explanations of the impairments. However, a few of the samples in these studies have passed through the period of risk for onset of schizophrenia, and those that have contain only a handful of target outcomes. Thus, presently, there is limited information on the degree to which early cognitive deviance predicts schizophrenia in such samples. It also remains to be demonstrated whether any predictive relationships generalize to the total population of schizophrenia patients, only 5–10% of whom have schizophrenic parents.

Cohort Studies

In a recent prospective study of a large, unselected birth cohort, risk for an adult diagnosis of schizophrenia was found to increase linearly across decreasing tertiles of the distributions of general intellectual functioning at 11 and 15 years of age (Jones, Rodgers, Murray, & Marmot, 1994). This pattern suggests that most preschizophrenia patients are below their expected level of functioning at these ages. That is, if only a subgroup of such cases were cognitively impaired, risk should be elevated among individuals in the lowest tertile of the distribution but should not differ between individuals in the upper tertiles.

We recently replicated and extended the findings just summarized in the Philadelphia cohort of the National Collaborative Perinatal Project (Cannon, Bearden, Hollister, & Hadley, 1997). In the overall cohort, the odds of schizophrenia and of being an unaffected sibling of a schizophrenia patient both increased linearly across decreasing levels of cognitive functioning at 4 and 7 years of age. Within families, preschizophrenia patients had lower test scores than their unaffected siblings at age 7 but not at age 4; this disparity was related to a history of perinatal hypoxia in the preschizophrenia patients. Nonverbal but not verbal deficits at age 7 predicted other psychotic disorders and neurotic disorders. Cognitive deficits are thus evident in preschizophrenia patients as early as age 4. The distribution of functioning in these cases is unimodally shifted downward, suggesting that most fail to reach their expected level of cognitive attainment during childhood. Unaffected siblings show qualitatively similar deficits, suggesting that childhood cognitive dysfunction marks genetic predisposition to the disorder. Perinatal hypoxia may magnify this dysfunction in increasing risk for phenotypic schizophrenia.

Neurodevelopment and Adult Onset

That there is evidence of disturbed brain functioning in infants and children destined to become schizophrenic in adulthood implies that the initiating events for this pathology occurred before or around the time of birth. However, onset of the formal diagnostic symptoms and signs of schizophrenia is quite rare before late adolescence and early adulthood. The latency between the gestational events hypothesized to create a predisposition to schizophrenia and onset of symptoms later in life poses perhaps the most difficult issue for a neurodevelopmental model to explain.

There are at least five potential neurodevelopmental explanations for this phenomenon, all of which remain to be tested empirically. First, Weinberger (1987) proposed a model by which a lesion developed during gestation or birth might remain dormant from a psychiatric symptom perspective until the brain systems needed to express the most complex forms of human cognition and behavior fully mature in early adult life. This argument is aided by evidence that some of the neural systems likely critical for the expression of schizophrenic symptoms (particularly prefrontal cortical areas) are the latest to reach maturity in humans. Second, although some of the neuropathological changes in schizophrenia may have a prenatal–perinatal origin, developmental changes occurring during late adolescence and early adulthood (e.g., cell elimination) may potentiate the expression of schizophrenic symptoms (Feinberg, 1982; Keshavan, Anderson, & Pettegrew, 1994). Third, hormonal changes during adolescence might interact with a preexisting brain lesion to potentiate behavioral expressions that are not possible (or less likely) in prepubertal individuals. Fourth, stress and other factors arising during postnatal social development could help to trigger the onset of psychotic symptomatology in individuals with developmentally acquired vulnerabilities. Fifth, neurodevelopmental disturbances could be critical in establishing a vulnerability to schizophrenia, but very slow-progressing degenerative changes might then accrue, reaching a threshold for expression of psychotic symptoms in early adulthood. These five models are not mutually exclusive, and each appears to represent at least a biologically plausible explanation for the latency of onset of schizophrenia if neurodevelopmental factors are involved.

CONCLUSIONS

In the past decade, there has been considerable progress in researchers' understanding of the origins of schizophrenia and of the roles of structural and functional pathology of the brain in its etiology and pathophysiology. Contrary to the classical view of schizophrenia as a form of dementia, it is becoming increasingly apparent that the neurobiological foundations of this disorder are established at least in part during the development of the brain. Numerous well-designed population and cohort studies have observed associations between OCs, particularly perinatal hypoxia, and an increased risk for phenotypic schizophrenia as well as a greater severity of its neuropathological features, particularly in individuals at elevated genetic risk for the disorder. Many of the cytopathological findings observed in autopsy studies of schizophrenia patients are consistent with a gestational origin, and glial scarring and other markers of neurodegenerative disease are noticeably absent in these patients. Neuroimaging studies of adult patients have found that against a background of generalized cerebral deficit, impairments in frontal and medial temporal lobe systems and their interconnections are prominent markers of this illness, which are likely to play key roles in the formation and maintenance of its characteristic symptoms. Furthermore, many of the structural and functional deficits observed in schizophrenia patients also appear to a lesser extent in some of their unaffected first-degree relatives, indicating that these neuropathological markers are mediated in part by genetic predisposition to the disorder. In addition, prospective high-risk and cohort studies have found that motor and cognitive deficits are present during infancy and childhood—long before the first appearance of formal diagnostic symptoms and signs of schizophrenia.

It must be emphasized that no study has directly linked a molecular or cellular event during the development of the brain to the etiology of schizophrenia. Thus, the case for viewing schizophrenia as a neurodevelopmental disorder still rests entirely on circumstantial evidence. At the same time, it would seem highly unlikely that these diverse lines of inquiry would agree in pointing to an involvement of neurodevelopmental disturbances in schizophrenia if such factors were not contributory. This conclusion in no way rules out the possibility that Kraepelin (1919) was accurate in hypothesizing neurodegenerative features in at least some cases. However, if a "dementia-like" deterioration of the brain does occur in schizophrenia, it is very unlike that in known dementing disorders, in that markers of neuronal atrophy are not prominent and the rate of tissue loss is so slight as not to be detectable in most studies. It would thus seem more appropriate to view schizophrenia as fundamentally an inherited disorder of brain development, whose expression and underlying pathophysiology are moderated by neuropathic insults in utero and, possibly, secondary neuronal changes during the adult course of the illness.

REFERENCES

Akbarian, S., Bunney, W. E., Jr., Potkin, S. G., Wigal, S. B., Hagman, J. O., Sandman, E. A., & Jones, E. G. (1993). Altered distribution of nicotinamide-adenine dinucleotide phosphate-diaphorase cell in frontal lobe of schizophrenics implies disturbances in cortical development. *Archives of General Psychiatry, 50,* 169–177.

Akbarian, S., Vinuela, A., Kim, J. J., Potkin, S., Bunney, W. E., Jr., & Jones, E. G. (1993). Distorted distribution of nicotinamide-adenine dinucliotide phosphate-diaphorase neurons in temporal lobe of schizophrenics implies anomalous cortical development. *Archives of General Psychiatry, 50,* 178–187.

Andreasen, N. C., Olsen, S. A., Dennert, J. W., & Smith, M. R. (1982). Ventricular enlargement in schizophrenia: Relationship to positive and negative symptoms. *Archives of General Psychiatry, 139,* 297–302.

Arnold, S. E., Franz, B. R., & Trojanowski, J. Q. (1994). Elderly patients with schizophrenia exhibit infrequent neurodegenerative lesions. *Neurobiology of Aging, 15,* 299–303.

Arnold, S. E., Hyman, B. T., Van Hoesen, G. W., & Damasio, A. R. (1991).

Some cytoarchitectural abnormalities of the entorhinal cortex in schizophrenia. *Archives of General Psychiatry, 48,* 625–632.

Barron, S. A., Jacobs, L., & Kinkel, W. R. (1976). Changes in size of normal lateral ventricles during aging determined by computerized tomography. *Neurology, 26,* 1011–1013.

Beckmann, H., & Jakob, H. (1991). Prenatal disturbances of nerve cell migration in the entorhinal region: A common vulnerability factor in functional psychoses? *Journal of Neural Transmission, 84,* 155–164.

Benes, F. M. (1987). An analysis of the arrangement of neurons in the cingulate cortex of schizophrenic patients. *Archives of General Psychiatry, 44,* 608–616.

Benes, F. M., Davidson, B., & Bird, E. D. (1986). Quantitative cytoarchitectural studies of the cerebral cortex of schizophrenics. *Archives of General Psychiatry, 43,* 31–35.

Benes, F. M., McSparren, J., Bird, E. D., San Giovanni, J. P., & Vincent, S. L. (1991). Deficits in small interneurons in prefrontal and cingulate cortices of schizophrenic and schizoaffective patients. *Archives of General Psychiatry, 48,* 996–1001.

Benes, F. M., Sorensen, I., & Bird, E. D. (1991). Reduced neuronal size in posterior hippocampus of schizophrenic patients. *Schizophrenia Bulletin, 17,* 597–608.

Bleuler, E. (1911). *Dementia praecox or the group of schizophrenias.* New York: International University Press. (Reprinted in 1950)

Bogerts, B., Falkai, P., Haupts, M., Greve, B., Ernst, S. T., Tapernon-Franz, U., & Heinzmann, U. (1990). Postmortem volume measurements of limbic systems and basal ganglia structures in chronic schizophrenics: Initial results from a new brain collection. *Schizophrenia Research, 3,* 295–301.

Bogerts, B., Meertz, E., & Schonfeldt-Bausch, R. (1985). Basal ganglia and limbic system pathology in schizophrenia: A morphometric study of brain volume and shrinkage. *Archives of General Psychiatry, 42,* 784–791.

Brown, R., Colter, N., Corsellis, J. A. N., Crow, T. J., Frith, C. D., Jagoe, R., Johnstone, E. C., & Marsh, L. (1986). Postmortem evidence of structural brain changes in schizophrenia: Differences in brain weight, temporal horn area and parahippocampal gyrus compared with affective disorder. *Archives of General Psychiatry, 43,* 36–42.

Buka, S. L., Tsuang, M. T., & Lipsitt, L. P. (1993). Pregnancy/delivery complications and psychiatric diagnosis: A prospective study. *Archives of General Psychiatry, 50,* 151–156.

Cannon, T. D. (1991). Genetic and perinatal sources of structural brain abnormalities in schizophrenia. In S. A. Mednick, T. D. Cannon, C. E. Barr, & M. Lyon (Eds.), *Fetal neural development and adult schizophrenia* (pp. 174–198). Cambridge, England: Cambridge University Press.

Cannon, T. D. (1996). Abnormalities of brain structure and function in schizophrenia: Implications for etiology and pathophysiology. *Annals of Medicine, 28,* 533–539.

Cannon, T. D. (1997). On the nature and mechanisms of obstetric influences in schizophrenia: A review and synthesis of epidemiologic studies. *International Review of Psychiatry, 9,* 387–397.

Cannon, T. D., Bearden, C. E., Hollister, J. M., & Hadley, T. (1997). A prospective cohort study of childhood cognitive deficits as precursors of schizophrenia. *Schizophrenia Research, 24,* 99–100.

Cannon, T. D., Hollister, J. M., Bearden, C. E., & Hadley, T. (1997). A prospective cohort study of genetic and perinatal influences in schizophrenia. *Schizophrenia Research, 24,* 248.

Cannon, T. D., Kaprio, J., Lönnqvist, J., Huttunen, M., & Koskenvuo, M. (1998). The genetic epidemiology of schizophrenia in a Finnish twin cohort: A population-based modeling study. *Archives of General Psychiatry, 55,* 67–74.

Cannon, T. D., & Marco, E. (1994). Structural brain abnormalities as indicators of vulnerability to schizophrenia. *Schizophrenia Bulletin, 20,* 89–102.

Cannon, T. D., Mednick, S., Parnas, J., Schulsinger, F., Praestholm, J., & Vestergaard, A. (1993). Developmental brain abnormalities in the offspring of schizophrenic mothers: I. Contributions of genetic and perinatal factors. *Archives of General Psychiatry, 50,* 551–564.

Cannon, T. D., Mednick, S. A., Schulsinger, F., Parnas, J., Praestholm, J., & Vestergaard, A. (1994). Developmental brain abnormalities in the offspring of schizophrenic mothers: II. Structural brain characteristics of schizophrenia and schizotypal personality disorder. *Archives of General Psychiatry, 51,* 955–962.

Casanova, M. F., Stevens, J. R., & Kleinman, J. E. (1990). Astrocytosis in the molecular layer of the dentate gyrus: A study in Alzheimer's disease and schizophrenia. *Psychiatry Research, 35,* 149–166.

Choi, D. W., & Rothman, S. M. (1990). The role of glutamate neurotoxicity in hypoxic-ischemic neuronal death. *Annual Review of Neuroscience, 13,* 171–182.

Conrad, A. J., Abebe, T., Austin, R., Forsythe, S., & Scheibel, A. B. (1991). Hippocampal pyramidal cell disarray in schizophrenia as a bilateral phenomenon. *Archives of General Psychiatry, 48,* 413–417.

Dagg, B. M., Booth, J. D., McLaughlin, J. E., & Dolan, R. J. (1994). A morphometric study of the cingulate cortex in mood disorder and schizophrenia. *Schizophrenia Research, 11,* 137.

Degreef, S. R., Ashtari, M., Bogerts, B., Bilder, R. M., Jody, D. N., Alvir, J. M., & Lieberman, J. A. (1992). Volumes of ventricular system subdivisions measured from magnetic resonance images in first-episode schizophrenic patients. *Archives of General Psychiatry, 49,* 531–537.

DeLisi, L. E., Goldin, L. R., Hamovit, J. R., Maxwell, E., Kurtz, D., & Gershon, E. S. (1986). A family study of the association of increased ventricular size with schizophrenia. *Archives of General Psychiatry, 43,* 148–153.

DeLisi, L. E., Hoff, A. L., Schwartz, J. E., Shields, G. W., Halthore, S. N., Gupta, S. M., Henn, F. A., & Anand, A. K. (1991). Brain morphology in first-episode schizophrenic-like psychotic patients: A quantitative magnetic resonance imaging study. *Biological Psychiatry, 29,* 159–175.

DeLisi, L. E., Stritzke, P., Riordan, H., Holan, V., Boccio, A., Kushner, M., McClelland, J., Van Eyl, O., & Anand, A. (1992). The timing of brain morphological changes in schizophrenia and their relationship to clinical outcome. *Biological Psychiatry, 31,* 241–254.

DeLisi, L. E., Tew, W., Xie, S., Hoff, A. L., Sakuma, M., Kushner, M., Lee, G., Shedlack, K., Smith, A. M., & Grimson, R. (1995). A prospective follow-up study of brain morphology and cognition in first-episode schizophrenic patients: Preliminary findings. *Biological Psychiatry, 38,* 349–360.

Diehl, S. R., & Kendler, K. S. (1989). Strategies for linkage studies of schizophrenia: Pedigrees, DNA markers, and statistical analyses. *Schizophrenia Bulletin, 15,* 403–419.

Done, D. J., Johnstone, E. C., Frith, C. D., Golding, J., Shepherd, P. M., & Crow, T. J. (1991). Complications of pregnancy and delivery in relation to psychosis in adult life: Data from the British Perinatal Mortality Survey sample. *British Medical Journal, 302,* 1576–1580.

Erlenmeyer-Kimling, L., & Cornblatt, B. (1987). High-risk research in schizophrenia: A summary of what has been learned. *Journal of Psychiatric Research, 21,* 401–411.

Eyler Zorrilla, L. T., Cannon, T. D., Kronenberg, S., Mednick, S. A., Parnas, J., Praestholm, J., & Vestergaard, A. (1997). Structural brain abnormalities in discordant offspring of schizophrenic mothers. *Biological Psychiatry, 42,* 1080–1086.

Falkai, P., & Bogerts, B. (1986). Cell loss in the hippocampus of schizophrenics. *European Archives of Psychiatry and Neurological Science, 106,* 505–517.

Falkai, P., & Bogerts, B. (1995). The neuropathology of schizophrenia. In S. R. Hirsch & D. R. Weinberger (Eds.), *Schizophrenia* (pp. 275–292). Cambridge, MA: Blackwell Science.

Falkai, P., Bogerts, B., Roberts, G. W., & Crow, T. J. (1988). Measurement of the alpha-cell-migration in the entorhinal region: A marker for developmental disturbances in schizophrenia? *Schizophrenia Research, 1,* 157–158.

Falkai, P., Bogerts, B., & Rozumek, M. (1988). Cell loss and volume reduction in the entorhinal cortex of schizophrenics. *Biological Psychiatry, 24,* 515–521.

Feinberg, I. (1982). Schizophrenia: Caused by a fault in programmed synaptic elimination during adolescence? *Journal of Psychiatry Research, 17,* 319–330.

Fischer, M. (1971). Psychoses in the offspring of schizophrenic monozygotic twins and their normal co-twins. *British Journal of Psychiatry, 118,* 43–52.

Gottesman, I. I., & Bertelsen, A. (1989). Confirming unexpressed genotypes for schizophrenia: Risks in the offspring of Fischer's Danish identical and fraternal discordant twins. *Archives of General Psychiatry, 46,* 867–872.

Gottesman, I. I., McGuffin, P., & Farmer, A. E. (1987). Clinical genetics as clues to the "real" genetics of schizophrenia (A decade of modest gains while playing for time). *Schizophrenia Bulletin, 13,* 23–47.

Gur, R. E., & Pearlson, G. D. (1993). Neuroimaging in schizophrenia research. *Schizophrenia Bulletin, 19,* 337–353.

Heckers, S., Heinsen, H., Geiger, B., & Beckmann, H. (1991). Hippocampal neuron number in schizophrenia: A stereological study. *Archives of General Psychiatry, 48,* 1002–1008.

Heckers, S., Heinsen, H., Heinsen, Y., & Beckmann, H. (1991). Cortex, white matter, and basal ganglia in schizophrenia: A volumetric postmortem study. *Biological Psychiatry, 29,* 556–566.

Hoffman, W. F., Ballard, L., Turner, E. H., & Casey, D. E. (1991). Three year follow-up of older schizophrenics: Extrapyramidal syndromes, psychiatric symptoms, and ventricular brain ratio. *Biological Psychiatry, 30,* 913–926.

Huttenlocher, P. R., Taravath, S., & Mojtahedi, S. (1994). Periventricular heterotopia and epilepsy. *Neurology, 44,* 51–55.

Hynd, G. W., & Semrud-Clikeman, M. (1989). Dyslexia and brain morphology. *Psychological Bulletin, 106,* 447–482.

Jakob, J., & Beckmann, H. (1986). Prenatal developmental disturbances in the limbic allocortex in schizophrenics. *Journal of Neural Transmission, 65,* 303–326.

Jeste, D. V., & Lohr, J. B. (1989). Hippocampal pathologic findings in schizophrenia: A morphometric study. *Archives of General Psychiatry, 46,* 1019–1024.

Johnstone, E. C., Crow, T. J., Frith, C. D., Husband, J., & Kreel, L. (1976). Cerebral ventricular size and cognitive impairment in chronic schizophrenia. *Lancet, i,* 924–926.

Johnstone, E. C., Crow, T. J., Frith, C. D., Stevens, M., Kreel, L., & Husband, J. (1978). The dementia of dementia praecox. *Acta Psychiatrica Scandinavica, 57,* 305–324.

Jones, P., Rodgers, B., Murray, R., & Marmot, M. (1994). Child developmental risk factors for adult schizophrenia in the British 1946 birth cohort. *Lancet, 344,* 1398–1402.

Kemali, D., Maj, M., Galderisi, S., Milici, N., & Dalvati, A. (1989). Ventricle-to-brain ratio in schizophrenia: A controlled follow-up study. *Biological Psychiatry, 26,* 753–756.

Kendler, K. S., & Diehl, S. R. (1993). The genetics of schizophrenia: A current, genetic-epidemiologic perspective. *Schizophrenia Bulletin, 19,* 261–285.

Keshavan, M. S., Anderson, S., & Pettegrew, J. W. (1994). Is schizophrenia due to excessive synaptic pruning in the prefrontal cortex? The Feinberg hypothesis revisited. *Journal of Psychiatric Research, 28,* 239–265.

Kovelman, J. A., & Scheibel, A. B. (1984). A neurohistological correlate of schizophrenia. *Biological Psychiatry, 19,* 1601–1621.

Kraepelin, E. (1919). *Dementia praecox and paraphrenia.* Edinburgh, Scotland: Livingston.

Mathew, R. J., Partain, C. L., Rakash, R., Kulkarni, M. V., Logan, T. P., & Wilson, W. H. (1985). A study of the septum pellucidum and corpus callosum in schizophrenia with MR imaging. *Acta Psychiatrica Scandinavica, 72,* 414–421.

McLardy, T. (1974). Hippocampal zinc and structural deficits in brains from chronic alcoholics and some schizophrenics. *Journal of Orthomolecular Psychiatry, 4,* 32–36.

McNeil, T. F. (1988). Obstetric factors and perinatal injuries. In M. T. Tsuang & J. C. Simpson (Eds.), *Handbook of schizophrenia. Vol. 3: Nosology, epidemiology and genetics* (pp. 319–343). Amsterdam: Elsevier Science.

Nasrallah, H. A., Olsen, S. C., McCalley-Whitters, M., Chapman, S., & Jacoby, C. G. (1986). Cerebral ventricular enlargement in schizophrenia. *Archives of General Psychiatry, 43,* 157–159.

O'Donovan, M. C., & Owen, M. J. (1996). The molecular genetics of schizophrenia. *Annals of Medicine, 28,* 541–546.

Pakkenberg, B. (1990). Pronounced reduction of total neuron number in mediodorsal thalamic nucleus and nucleus accumbens in schizophrenics. *Archives of General Psychiatry, 47,* 1023–1028.

Pakkenberg, B. (1992a). Stereological quantitation of human brains from normal and schizophrenic individuals. *Acta Psychiatrica Scandinavica, 137*(Suppl.), 20–33.

Pakkenberg, B. (1992b). The volume of the mediodorsal thalamic nucleus in treated and untreated schizophrenics. *Schizophrenia Research, 7,* 95–100.

Parnas, J., Schulsinger, F., Teasdale, T. W., Schulsinger, H., Feldman, P. M., & Mednick, S. A. (1982). Perinatal complications and clinical outcome within the schizophrenia spectrum. *British Journal of Psychiatry, 140,* 416–420.

Pillowsky, B., Juliano, D. M., Bigelow, L. B., & Weinberger, D. R. (1988). Stability of CT scan findings in schizophrenia: Results of an 8 year follow-up study. *Journal of Neurology, Neurosurgery and Psychiatry, 51,* 209–213.

Raz, S., & Raz, N. (1990). Structural brain abnormalities in the major psychoses: A quantitative review of the evidence from computerized imaging. *Psychological Bulletin, 108,* 93–108.

Reveley, A. M., Reveley, M. A., Clifford, C. A., & Murray, R. M. (1982). Cerebral ventricular size in twins discordant for schizophrenia. *Lancet, 1,* 540–541.

Scheibel, A. B., & Kovelman, J. A. (1981). Disorientation of the hippocampal pyramidal cell and its process in the schizophrenic patient. *Biological Psychiatry, 16,* 101–102.

Selemon, L. D., Rajkowska, G., & Goldman-Rakic, P. S. (1993). A morphometric analysis of the prefrontal areas 9 and 46 in the schizophrenic and normal human brain. *Schizophrenia Research, 9,* 151.

Shenton, M. E., Kikinis, R., Jolesz, R. A., Pollack, S. D., LeMay, M., Wible, C. G., Hokama, H., Martin, J., Metcalf, D., Coleman, M., & McCarley, R. W. (1992). Left-lateralized temporal lobe abnormalities and their relationship to thought disorder: A computerized, quantitative MRI study. *New England Journal of Medicine, 327,* 604–612.

Sponheim, S. R., Iacono, W. G., & Beiser, M. (1991). Stability of ventricular size after the onset of psychosis in schizophrenia. *Psychiatry Resonance Neuroimaging, 40,* 21–29.

Suddath, R. L., Christison, G. W., Torrey, E. F., Casanova, M. F., & Weinberger, D. R. (1990). Anatomical abnormalities in the brains of monozygotic twins discordant for schizophrenia. *New England Journal of Medicine, 322,* 789–794.

Vita, A., Sacchetti, E., Valvassori, G., & Cazzullo, C. L. (1988). Brain morphology in schizophrenia: A 2 to 5 year CT scan follow-up study. *Acta Psychiatrica Scandinavica, 78,* 618–621.

Walker, E. F. (1994). Developmentally moderated expressions of the neuropathology underlying schizophrenia. *Schizophrenia Bulletin, 20,* 453–480.

Warner, R. (1995). Time trends in schizophrenia: Changes in obstetric risk factors with industrialization. *Schizophrenia Bulletin, 21,* 483–500.

Weeks, D. E., Lehner, T., Squires-Wheeler, E., Kaufmann, C., & Ott, J. (1990). Measuring the inflation of the lod score due to its maximization over model parameter values in human linkage analysis. *Genetic Epidemiology, 7,* 237–243.

Weinberger, D. R. (1987). Implications of normal brain development for the pathogenesis of schizophrenia. *Archives of General Psychiatry, 44,* 660–669.

Weinberger, D. R., DeLisi, L. E., Neophytides, A. N., & Wyatt, R. J. (1981). Familial aspects of CT scan abnormalities in chronic schizophrenic patients. *Psychiatric Research, 4,* 65–71.

Woods, B. T., Yurgelun-Todd, D., Benes, F. M., Frankenburg, F. R., Pope, H. G., & McSparren, J. (1990). Progressive ventricular enlargement in schizophrenia: Comparison to bipolar affective disorder and correlation with clinical course. *Biological Psychiatry, 27,* 341–352.

4

Schizotypy and Schizotypic Psychopathology: Mapping an Alternative Expression of Schizophrenia Liability

Mark F. Lenzenweger

In the discipline of experimental psychopathology, it has not been an uncommon experience for one to hear of the rather extreme expansion the concept *schizophrenia* underwent through the 1940s into the 1960s. Anecdotes are often told by long-term observers of the field that some psychologists and psychiatrists, during that time, actually believed that nearly every living person had a "psychotic core" and could conceivably develop schizophrenia if the conditions were toxic enough for the person. In a certain sense, this expansion diminished the clinical and research utility of the schizophrenia diagnosis to a rather nominal level and practically rendered useless the notion of an underlying liability for the disease. However, as many know, neo-Krapelinean notions reemerged in the definition and study of psychopathology during the

I wish to acknowledge my colleagues who have collaborated with me on the various studies summarized in this chapter, namely, Michael Coleman, Barbara A. Cornblatt, Philip S. Holzman, Lauren Korfine, Deborah Levy, Armand W. Loranger, Steven Matthysse, Gillian O'Driscoll, and Sohee Park. I also gratefully acknowledge the numerous consultations and words of advice from Paul E. Meehl and Leslie J. Yonce in connection with the taxometric analyses summarized here. I express my appreciation to Jack D. Barchas for his support of my work and laboratory. Finally, I thank the many able and energetic undergraduate research assistants whom I had the privilege to work with in my laboratory while they were at Cornell University.

1970s; largely in response to research findings (e.g., US–UK Cross National Project; Cooper et al., 1972), contemporary diagnostic criteria and standards for schizophrenia came to reflect a sensibly narrow and rational stance. But what of the notion of an *underlying liability* for schizophrenia? Can it manifest itself somehow without going on to reveal itself as the full-blown clinical condition of schizophrenia? If schizophrenia liability could express itself in alternative form, what would it look like? These questions have served as guideposts in the work my coworkers and I have conducted over the past 10 years in my laboratory on schizotypic psychopathology, which I suggest must now be viewed unambiguously as an alternative expression of schizophrenia liability. In this chapter, I first present the historical development of the schizotypic model and then present a series of studies that demonstrate the links between schizotypy and the liability of schizophrenia.

EARLY OBSERVATIONS AND A HEURISTIC MODEL

It should come as no surprise that both Kraepelin (1909–1913/1971 and Bleuler (1911/1950), given their keen observational skills, conjectured that it might be possible for schizophrenia to manifest itself in an alternative manner. For example, Kraepelin (1909–1913/1971) noted

> in the families attacked there comes under observation with relative frequency besides dementia praecox a series of other anomalies, especially manic-depressive insanity and eccentric personalities . . . the latter are probably for the most part to be regarded as "latent schizophrenias" and therefore essentially the same as the principal malady. (p. 234)

Bleuler (1911/1950) suggested that

> there is also a latent schizophrenia, and I am convinced that this is the most frequent form, although admittedly these people hardly ever come for treatment . . . . In this form we see *in nuce*

all the symptoms which are present in the manifest types of the disease. (p. 239)

Both Kraepelin and Bleuler based their observations on experiences they had had with continuing contact with the relatives of their schizophrenia patients. Thus, the theoretical foundation for a view of schizophrenia liability that can manifest itself in varying fashion was set in place nearly 100 years ago. This foundation, however, was built largely on descriptive observations of the biological relatives of individuals affected with schizophrenia or on the clinical presentation of "schizophrenia-like," but nonpsychotic, patients that presented to office practitioners of psychotherapy; it essentially remained so constructed until the early 1980s (Kendler, 1985).

With the exception of the renowned Danish Adoption Study (Kety, Rosenthal, Wender, & Schulsinger, 1968), which found elevated rates of "borderline" or "latent" schizophrenia in the biological relatives of schizophrenia adoptees, there was little empirical laboratory evidence that linked schizotypic states to a liability for schizophrenia prior to the early 1980s. More systematic exploration of the relations between schizotypic disorders and schizophrenia began with the introduction of the diagnostic criteria for schizotypal personality disorder [SPD] in the *Diagnostic and Statistical Manual of Mental Disorders* (3rd ed. [*DSM-III*]; American Psychiatric Association [APA], 1980). These criteria were derived, in part, from the diagnostic framework used by Kety et al. (Spitzer, Endicott, & Gibbon, 1979). There is evidence to suggest that persons that would have been diagnosed with schizophrenia according to *DSM-II* (2nd ed.; APA, 1968) were probably diagnosed, to some extent, as schizotypal according to the *DSM-III* nomenclature (Loranger, 1990). In addition to a lack of empirical evidence linking schizotypic psychopathology to schizophrenia at this time, there was little by way of a unified model to guide laboratory investigations in this area prior to the 1960s. Fortunately, one particularly influential model of the relations between a hypothetical latent liability for schizophrenia and its possible variable manifest expressions was proposed, namely, the model proposed by psychologist P. E. Meehl (1962, 1990). This model has stimulated considerable research from the experimental psychopathology vantage point—an influence that can be detected in other chapters in this volume.

In a brief overview, Meehl (1962, 1990) theorized that diagnosable schizophrenia is the complex developmental result of a major genetic factor relatively specific for schizophrenia interacting with other genetically determined *potentiators* (e.g., anxiety, hedonic potential, social introversion) and environmental stressors. He hypothesized in 1962, long before the emergence of the neurosciences—as researchers think of them today—that the genetic influence for schizophrenia codes for a functional central nervous system synaptic control aberration he termed *hypokrisia*, which results in *schizotaxia* or extensive "synaptic slippage" throughout the brain. Through social learning experiences, essentially all schizotaxic individuals develop *schizotypy*, a personality organization that harbors the latent liability for schizophrenia (cf. Meehl, 1990, p. 35). As a personality organization, schizotypy cannot be observed directly per se, however, this latent personality organization gives rise to schizotypic psychological and behavioral manifestations (Meehl, 1964), such as subtle thought disorder, and is reflected in deviance on laboratory measures (e.g., eye-tracking dysfunction, sustained attention deficits). Individuals with schizotypy at the latent level are called *schizotypes*. According to Meehl's model, schizotypic individuals (although not necessarily diagnosable as *DSM-IV* [4th ed.; APA, 1994] SPD) clinically exhibit cognitive slippage, interpersonal aversiveness, pan-anxiety, and mild depression. The majority of such individuals remain only schizotypic throughout the life span, whereas a subset go on to develop diagnosable schizophrenia. The seminal conjectures of Meehl have been variously amended, revised, and expanded by a variety of contemporary workers over the past 35 years; however, his model can be credited with having spawned a vast number of experimental and otherwise empirical investigations of schizophrenia. His model has served as a valuable heuristic for studies linking schizotypic psychopathology to a liability for schizophrenia in many laboratories.

A slightly amended version of Meehl's (1964) model can be found in Figure 1. It is important to review several features of the model, the

Schizotypy and Schizophrenia: A Developmental Model

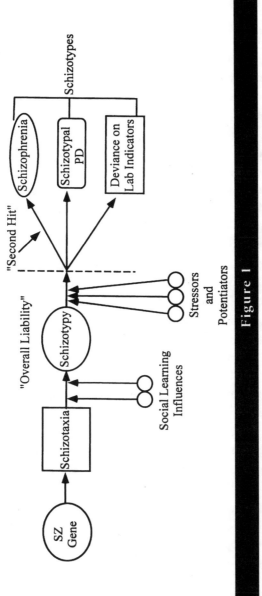

Figure 1

Schematic view of the relations among schizotypy, stressors, and potentiators in the determination of various outcomes such as schizophrenia (SZ), schizotypic psychopathology, and deviance on laboratory indicators. The broken vertical line depicts the plane of observation. Schizotypy represents a latent liability for schizophrenia. Overall liability refers to the product of schizotypy, social learning influences, potentiators, and stressors. Note that all persons carrying schizotypy are by definition schizotypes, regardless of clinical outcomes (the right side of the figure). PD = personality disorder. From Figure 1 of "Toward an Integrated Theory of Schizotaxia, Schizotypy, and Schizophrenia," by P. E. Meehl, 1990, *Journal of Personality Disorders, 4,* p. 27. Copyright 1990 by Guilford Press: New York. Adapted, in part, with permission.

meaning of which are not always fully appreciated in the schizotypy research literature. To begin, schizotypy refers to a latent construct that cannot be observed directly (i.e., with the unaided naked eye). Only manifestations of schizotypy can be discerned (e.g., as schizophrenia, SPD, or deviance on a laboratory measure of relevance to schizophrenia [e.g., eye-tracking dysfunction, impaired sustained attention]); therefore, one can only speak of schizotypy indicators. This feature of the model is depicted as the broken vertical line in Figure 1, which signifies the plane of observation (below the line is the latent level, above the line the observable level). Second, although all individuals (excluding phenocopies) who develop diagnosable schizophrenia are by definition schizotypes, not all schizotypes go on to develop schizophrenia; it is precisely this feature of the model that highlights the latent liability conceptualization. It is worth noting, as well, that the model does not require schizophrenia cases to have been diagnosably schizotypal (e.g., DSM-IV SPD) prior to the development of psychosis. Finally, in this amended depiction of Meehl's model, an interacting factor designated as a "second hit" is included to hold out the possibility that an exogenous agent (e.g., viral infection during pregnancy, noisome working conditions) of some importance may help to trigger the development of clinical schizophrenia in an individual carrying the liability.

In this model, the schizotype per se is viewed as a person who expresses a variant of a genuine liability for schizophrenia. The study of schizotypic psychopathology, therefore, does not involve the study of an analogue of the clinical illness or some hypothetical ersatz schizophrenia, although this point is not always fully appreciated in literature reviews (e.g., Sher & Trull, 1996). I have consistently argued that schizotypic individuals represent a variant in the expression of schizophrenia liability and that as such, schizotypic psychopathology is likely to be an especially useful unit of analysis in the study of schizophrenia. This is so because (a) schizotypic psychopathology is characterized by the absence of third-variable confounds (e.g., medication, institutionalization, deterioration effects) and (b) inclusion of the schizotypic disorders in a variety of inquiries, particularly genetic strategies, enhances the power of such investigations.

THE SCHIZOTYPE: DESCRIPTION
AND DETECTION

For the remainder of this chapter, I describe a series of studies that were designed to empirically evaluate the fundamental theoretical conjecture that links schizotypic psychopathology to a liability for schizophrenia. Schizotypes, for the purposes of this discussion, can be thought of as displaying many of the signs and symptoms of *DSM-IV* SPD (see APA, 1994, pp. 641–645), however the *DSM* SPD criteria set should not be considered an exhaustive listing of schizotypic phenomena (cf. Meehl's, 1964, Checklist for Schizotypic Signs or Kendler, Lieberman, & Walsh's, 1989, Structured Interview for Schizotypy). Moreover, as I have argued elsewhere (Lenzenweger, 1993), it may in fact be the case that even other Axis II personality disorder diagnostic criteria, as defined by the *DSM*, bear a valid connection to schizotypy, the latent liability for schizophrenia.

In attempting to assemble schizotypes for study in any laboratory investigation, one is faced with the fact that the vast majority of schizotypic persons probably do not ever report for treatment at hospitals, clinics, or research institutes (a reality that echoes Bleuler's, 1911/1950, observations; cf. Loranger, 1990). Those who do present may in fact be somewhat atypical in that they may be experiencing increased depression, heightened suicidality, or other circumstances not directly reflective of their liability for schizophrenia, complicating factors that may limit the generalizability of findings derived from studies using hospital samples (Lenzenweger & Korfine, 1992b). This raises the question about how best to locate schizotypes for study. The three methods, which are not mutually exclusive in terms of implementation, are the (a) clinical, (b) familial–biological, and (c) psychometric–laboratory index approaches. The clinical approach implied in psychiatric diagnostic schemes involves, obviously, the use of explicit diagnostic criteria to identify either SPD or paranoid personality disorder (e.g., *DSM-IV*). Limitations of the clinical approach include the reality that most schizotypes probably never present at clinics and that the *DSM* constructs of SPD and paranoid personality disorder may miss important aspects of schizotypy.

Second, one could be concerned with the biological relatives of schizophrenia patients and speak of "genotypic" schizotypes. Although many first-degree relatives of schizophrenia patients will not evidence their underlying genetic predisposition to the illness through schizotypic symptomatology (and fewer still will have schizophrenia), they are, as a group, at increased statistical risk for schizophrenia and can be spoken of as schizotypes. Some relatives of schizophrenia patients will, indeed, display schizotypic symptomatology (e.g., Kendler et al., 1993). It is essential to note that not all biological relatives of schizophrenia patients will carry the liability for the illness (Hanson, Gottesman, & Meehl, 1977), therefore this approach to defining schizotypes yields an admixture of at-risk versus not-at-risk individuals.

Third, the psychometric–laboratory index approach involves the use of reliable and valid psychometric (or laboratory) measures of schizotypy to detect schizotypic psychopathology, as defined by quantitative deviance on such measures. In the psychometric variant, scales designed to assess various schizotypic manifestations serve to define and measure the schizotypy construct; schizotypic status may be defined by deviance on one or more of such measures. The psychometric approach has been discussed and reviewed recently (see Chapman, Chapman, & Kwapil, 1995; Edell, 1995; and Lenzenweger, 1994). A limitation of both psychometrically assessed schizotypy and clinically identified conditions (e.g., SPD) is that neither is likely to be perfectly related to an underlying schizotypy construct; therefore, they should both be considered fallible approaches to the measurement of true schizotypy.

BRIDGING SCHIZOTYPIC PSYCHOPATHOLOGY, SCHIZOPHRENIA, AND SCHIZOTYPY: EMPIRICAL STUDIES

Body Image and Perceptual Aberrations in Schizotypy

In theoretical discussions of schizotypy, a great deal of importance has been attached to body image and perceptual distortions in schizotypy, as defined by both Rado (1953, 1960) and Meehl (1990). Rado described body-image distortions and the perceptual anomalies thought to characterize the psychological experience of the schizotype. Meehl identified body-image aberrations as a schizotypic sign in his 1964 manual, providing rich descriptions of the clinical manifestations of such phenomena (pp. 24–27). Furthermore, Meehl (1990) referred to body-image distortions several times in his revised theory of schizotypy (see pp. 9, 19, and 23). Perceptual and body-image distortions as phenomenologic manifestations of a liability for (or expression of) schizophrenia (and other psychoses) have a long history in descriptive psychopathology (Chapman, Chapman, & Raulin, 1978).

Loren Chapman, Jean Chapman, and M. L. Raulin (1978) developed the Perceptual Aberration Scale (PAS) to operationalize the rich clinical observations of body-image distortion and perceptual aberrations abounding in the schizophrenia literature (e.g., Meehl, 1964). The PAS is a 35-item true–false self-report measure of disturbances and distortions in perceptions of body image as well as other objects. Item content and the details of the PAS's construction can be found elsewhere (see Chapman & Chapman, 1985; Chapman et al., 1978).

The PAS has served as the primary psychometric index of schizotypy used in my laboratory studies. Subjects were selected for inclusion in the following studies on the basis of demonstrated deviance (or relative lack thereof) on the PAS. My coworkers and I typically use an epidemiological method for screening potential subjects for study through the systematic location of a large number of subjects using a door-to-door, face-to-face method of screen distribution and collection. With this method, we were able to determine response rates to the screening request, avoid the test-taking attitudes so common in the screening of undergraduate students in large class settings, and capitalize on the human contextual factors in soliciting research participation. The response rates for such screenings typically exceeded 80%. Schizotypes for the laboratory studies were selected from those scoring 2 σ or more above the overall sample mean; normal controls were selected randomly from the pool of individuals scoring no higher than .5 σ above the mean. This measurement methodology was used to collect a pool of subjects for some of the studies discussed below.

An Empirical Bridging Strategy

In an effort to illuminate the areas of convergence between the realms of schizotypic pathology and schizophrenia, I adopted an empirical bridging strategy that derives from the original validation strategy advocated by Robins and Guze (1970; cf. Cronbach & Meehl, 1955). This approach involves examining the psychometrically identified schizotype from a variety of vantage points, specifically (a) family history, (b) clinical phenomenology, (c) laboratory tests, (d) delimitation from other disorders (conditions), and (e) a follow-up study. These vantage points can be embodied in a series of questions, each of which I have attempted to address with a focal study.

Does Schizophrenia Appear Among the Biological Relatives of Schizotypes?

In a study carried out at the New York Hospital, Lenzenweger and Loranger (1989a) examined the lifetime expectancy (morbid risk) of treated schizophrenia, unipolar depression, and bipolar disorder in the biological first-degree relatives of 101 nonpsychotic psychiatric patients (probands), classified as either "schizotypy positive" or "schizotypy negative" according to the PAS. The relatives of schizotypy-positive probands were significantly more likely to have been treated for schizophrenia than the relatives of schizotypy-negative probands (3.75% vs. 0.00%, $z = 2.559$, $p < .005$, one-tailed); the morbid risk for treated unipolar depression or bipolar disorder among the relatives of the two proband groups did not differ.

Berenbaum and McGrew (1993) reported that PAS deviance is familial, which is consistent with the Lenzenweger and Loranger (1989a) results. Of related interest, Battaglia et al. (1991) found in a study of the relatives of schizotypal patients that recurrent illusions (akin to perceptual aberrations) were found in every schizotypal patient with a personality disorder and a positive family history of schizophrenia.

Do Psychometrically Identified Schizotypes Reveal Clinically Significant Schizotypic Symptoms?

Using the same patient sample as described in the previous section, I was able to determine whether deviance on the PAS was associated with

clinically significant psychopathology, specifically schizotypic psychopathology. Given that the modal schizotype is most likely to reveal any
number of the symptoms defined in the *DSM* system for SPD as well
as high levels of anxiety, I hypothesized that patients with elevations on
the PAS would be characterized by increased SPD phenomenology and
anxiety. Using the Personality Disorder Examination (PDE; 1985 version) for the Axis II assessments, Lenzenweger and Loranger (1989b)
found that elevations on the PAS were indeed most closely associated
with SPD symptoms and clinically assessed anxiety. Others have found
that nonclinical subjects, identified as schizotypic through application
of the psychometric approach, also reveal schizotypic and psychotic-
like phenomenology (cf. Chapman & Chapman, 1995; Chapman, Edell,
& Chapman, 1980; and Edell, 1995).

Do Schizotypes Display Deviance on Laboratory Measures Comparable With That Seen Among Schizophrenia Patients?

My coworkers and I have carried out a number of investigations designed to determine if psychometrically identified schizotypes display
deviance on laboratory tasks on which actual schizophrenia patients are
known to perform poorly. The laboratory studies in schizotypy were all
carried out at Cornell University (Ithaca, NY). Subject selection for
these studies followed the procedure noted above, with schizotypic subjects drawn from a large pool of randomly ascertained participants.

In examining the performance of schizotypes on laboratory tasks
relevant to schizophrenia, my coworkers and I sought to move beyond
descriptive discussions of schizotypic phenomenology, which typically
focus on schizotypic features as diluted schizophrenia signs and symptoms. We sought to examine the very neurocognitive processes that have
been the focus of extensive research in recent years in schizophrenia,
namely, sustained attention (Cornblatt & Keilp, 1994), executive functioning (Weinberger, Berman, & Zec, 1986), working memory (Park &
Holzman, 1992), eye tracking (Levy, Holzman, Matthysse, & Mendell,
1993), thought disorder (Johnston & Holzman, 1979), attentional inhibition (Beech, Powell, McWilliam, & Claridge, 1989), and antisaccade
performance (Fukushima, Fukushima, Chiba, & Tanaka, 1988). Stated
simply, if the schizotype represents an alternative expression of

schizophrenia liability as conjectured, then one should be able to find abnormalities in neurocognitive functioning comparable in nature, although perhaps less severe, with those seen in the performance of persons with schizophrenia.

Sustained attentional functioning and MMPI deviance. The first study in this series examined sustained attention in a group of schizotypes ($n = 32$) versus normal controls ($n = 43$) using the low a priori signal probability, high-processing load Continuous Performance Test (CPT), developed by Cornblatt and colleagues (Cornblatt, Lenzenweger, & Erlenmeyer-Kimling, 1989; Cornblatt, Risch, Faris, Friedman, & Erlenmeyer-Kimling, 1988). On the CPT-IP (Identical Pairs version), the schizotypic subjects revealed a lower d' than did normal controls, $t(73) = 1.72$, $p < .05$, with an effect size (Cohen's d) of .40 (Lenzenweger, Cornblatt, & Putnick, 1991). The lower d' for the schizotypes was due largely to fewer correct detections (or "hits") on the CPT.

Replication of the Lenzenweger et al. (1991) results, using the same measure of sustained attention, has been reported by Obiols, Garcia-Domingo, de Trincheria, and Domenech (1993). Grove et al. (1991) have also reported a significant association between high PAS scores and poor sustained attention performance among the first-degree biological relatives of individuals with diagnosed schizophrenia. This pattern of findings, comparable with modal high-risk findings, is consistent with results obtained in a study of schizophrenia patients (Cornblatt et al., 1989) and with previous attentional studies of children at risk for schizophrenia (Cornblatt & Erlenmeyer-Kimling, 1985; Nuechterlein & Dawson, 1984) that support a global sustained attention deficit related to the schizophrenia diathesis. Overall, these data provide convergent evidence suggesting that information-processing deficits observed in schizophrenia individuals as well as children at risk for schizophrenia are present among psychometrically defined schizotypes.

The subjects in this study also completed the Minnesota Multiphasic Personality Inventory (MMPI) as part of the laboratory procedures. PAS-identified schizotypic subjects, as a group, displayed an average MMPI profile consistent with that from individuals with actual schizotypic features, whereas the control subjects did not (Lenzenweger,

1991). A multivariate profile analysis, moreover, revealed that the schizotypic group's MMPI profile differed significantly in shape from the control group's profile, suggesting the possible demarcation of a typological difference between the groups. Finally, schizophrenia-related MMPI high point codes were found five times more frequently among the schizotypic group (71.9%) as contrasted with the control group (13.6%; $z = 5.16$, $p < .00001$; Lenzenweger, 1991). These MMPI data suggest that the PAS-identified schizotypic group, although nonpsychotic, displayed evidence of schizophrenia-related deviance on a well-known standard measure of psychopathology and personality.

Executive functioning: Performance on the Wisconsin Card Sorting Test. In another study, my coworkers and I sought to examine the performance of psychometrically identified schizotypes on the Wisconsin Card Sorting Test (WCST). Considerable recent attention has been focused on difficulties in abstract reasoning and novel problem solving in schizophrenia patients (Gold & Harvey, 1993), processes that are hypothesized to be mediated by the prefrontal cortex. Moreover, evidence has been presented that some schizophrenic symptoms may reflect a dysfunctional frontal system (e.g., Goldman-Rakic, 1991; Levin 1984a, 1984b; Weinberger et al., 1986). Much of this research has used the WCST as a measure of abstraction ability and executive functioning.

In this study, Lenzenweger and Korfine (1991, 1994) contrasted the WCST performance for 23 schizotypes versus 28 normal controls. Consistent with the general trend in the schizophrenia research literature, the schizotypes achieved fewer categories than the controls at the level of a trend ($z = 1.42$, $p < .10$), with an effect size of .34. However, of considerable interest, we observed that the schizotypes more frequently failed to maintain set during the WCST relative to controls ($z = 2.16$, $p < .02$), with an effect size of .60. This suggests that although the schizotypes did not reveal massively impaired performance (i.e., categories achieved), they did display a marked propensity to lose the sorting principle throughout the WCST, possibly suggestive of lower levels of inhibition or increased distractibility. This particular finding, that is, increased failures to maintain a set among the schizotypes, was subsequently replicated in an additional study using the WCST (Park, Holzman, & Lenzenweger, 1995).

Examination of schizotypic patients on multiple laboratory tasks: The Cornell–Harvard Schizotypy Study. During the late 1980s and into the early 1990s, data from other laboratories began to emerge that also addressed the neurocognitive functioning of schizotypes. Especially striking about those studies, not unlike the ones from Cornell, was that nearly all of them were univariate in nature. That is, the modal study in schizotypy research typically examines one aspect of cognitive or psychophysiologic performance, usually involving one laboratory task. An effort was therefore made to remedy this situation by undertaking a relatively large collaborative study that joined the energies of my laboratory at Cornell with those of the Psychology Research Laboratory, directed by Philip S. Holzman at Harvard and McLean Hospital (Belmont, NY). In this study, we sought to examine multiple processes in the same schizotypic and control subjects.

In this study, we carefully examined PAS-defined schizotypic ($n = 31$) and normal control ($n = 26$) subjects on tasks (or with procedures) assessing executive functioning (WCST), spatial working memory (delayed response task), antisaccade performance, spatial negative priming, thought disorder (Thought Disorder Index), and eye tracking. The results of univariate contrasts are contained in Table 1. As can be seen from the table, the schizotypic subjects revealed increased failures to maintain a set on the WCST (Park et al., 1995), poorer spatial working memory on the delayed response task (Park et al., 1995), increased levels of antisaccade errors (particularly of a perseverative nature; O'Driscoll, Lenzenweger, & Holzman, 1997), increased levels of thought disorder (Coleman, Levy, Lenzenweger, & Holzman, 1996), poorer negative priming performance (Park, Lenzenweger, Püschel, & Holzman, 1996), and worse smooth pursuit eye-tracking quality (O'Driscoll et al., 1997) relative to controls. This general pattern of findings suggests that schizotypic individuals, as a group, may possess subtle frontally mediated deficits manifested through disinhibition, poor attention, and perseverative tendencies. We emphasize, however, that we have not tried to localize these deficits to specific brain areas, given that the tasks used

Table 1
Cornell–Harvard Schizotypy Study: Laboratory Task Performance for Schizotypic and Normal Controls

Task	SZT			Control				
	M	SD	n	M	SD	n	p	d
WCST FMS	1.11	1.49	28	0.48	0.67	23	.05	.54
Delayed response (%)	90.00	8.00	28	93.00	5.00	23	.05	.49
Antisaccade (% correct)	94.00	6.70	31	98.00	2.40	24	.02	.79
Antisaccade (perseveration error)	9.50	10.20	31	2.20	3.80	24	.002	.95
TD-TDI	8.83	15.30	30	3.65	4.97	26	.05	.46
TD-TDI sum	7.27	10.52	30	3.00	3.32	26	.02	.55
Eye tracking	1.99	0.73	28	2.42	0.79	23	.02	.57
Negative priming (%)	-1.47	6.42	30	-4.40	6.66	25	.05	.45

Note. *n*s for the various tasks differ because of missing data. All statistical tests were evaluated using one-tailed procedures given the model-guided a priori unidirectional hypotheses under consideration. SZT = schizotypic subjects; WCST FMS = Wisconsin Card Sorting Test Failures to Maintain a Set; TD = thought disorder; TDI = Thought Disorder Index; TDI sum = total number of thought disordered responses; eye tracking = smooth pursuit eye-tracking performance; *d* = Cohen's *d* (effect size).

were complex, in and of themselves, and the systems subserving the processes tapped by the tasks were also complex and interrelated. For example, whereas sustained attentional performance necessarily involves frontally mediated processes related to decision criteria, detection of the actual signals may reflect the activity of midbrain areas. Performance on this task may be tapping, at a minimum, two different dopaminergic systems (cf. Grace, 1991; Grace & Moore, chapter 5, this volume). Each of the findings in this collaborative study has been discussed in detail in the original research reports, and the interested reader is referred to them for details.

The results of this study struck me as rather remarkable in at least two ways. First, the schizotypes, as a group, performed significantly worse than the controls on all of the laboratory tasks. This consistency, at the level of group means, across the battery of tasks confirms what prior univariate findings had only been able to hint at; namely, schizotypes reveal multiple deficits on tasks relevant to schizophrenia. This study, however, enjoyed the methodological feature of examining the same subjects on multiple tasks, which enabled us to carefully dissect individual differences across the tasks. Second, through an analysis of a deviance index sensitive to individual differences, we discovered that not all schizotypes were deviant on all laboratory tasks. In fact, less than 20% of the schizotypic subjects were deviant, as referenced against the normal controls, on three or more of the laboratory tasks simultaneously. This feature of the performance of the schizotypic subjects highlights the utility of examining multiple processes in the same subjects and, more or less, confirms that heterogeneity in performance deficits is likely to characterize the schizotype in a manner comparable with that seen among schizophrenia patients. Current work in my laboratory is seeking to further specify the latent structure of schizotypy through the use of this data set from both a traditional multivariate approach as well as a latent trait model—informed Bayesian analysis (cf. Matthysse, 1993).

The influence of mental state factors on laboratory findings. In this context, it is worth noting that none of the laboratory findings discussed above were the simple by-product of an anxious mental state, dysphoric mental state, or both. In all of the foregoing analyses across all studies, state anxiety, trait anxiety, and depression were taken into account through appropriate control procedures and in no instance was a finding vitiated through the removal of the effect of these mental state variables. It is worth noting that the schizotypes, as a group, tended to have higher levels of anxiety, depression, or both relative to controls in all of the studies; however, those mental state factors did not appear to drive the relations between schizotypy status and any given laboratory index.

What Is the Latent Structure of Schizotypy?
Quantitative Versus Qualitative

Research on the delimitation of schizotypic psychopathology from other disorders could proceed along two lines. First, one could assess the delimitation of schizotypic pathology from other phenotypic disorders, namely, the relative discreteness of individual disorders. This particular issue concerns the relative internal coherence of a disorder and, hopefully, a lack of excessive overlap (or comorbidity because of phenomenologic commonalties in diagnostic criteria) with other conditions. The prototypic study in this area is the Spitzer et al. (1979) investigation, which essentially established the criteria for the *DSM*'s SPD diagnosis (see Siever, Bernstein, & Silverman, 1991, for a review of this type of study). A second approach to the issue of delimitation concerns delimitation at the latent level with a focus on the detection of the possible existence of qualitative discontinuities separating a given class of persons from others. With respect to schizotypy, particularly as conceived in Meehl's (1962, 1990) model, my work has focused exclusively on the issue of delimitation at the latent level.

On the latent structure of schizotypy. Assuming that schizotypy, as conceptualized by Meehl (1962, 1990), represents a defensible latent liability construct (i.e., not visible to the unaided naked eye) and the potential research utility of valid schizotypy indexes is evident, a basic question about the fundamental structure of schizotypy remains: Is it continuous (i.e., dimensional) or is it truly discontinuous (or qualitative) in nature? For example, at the level of the gene, both Meehl's model and the latent trait model (Holzman et al., 1988; Matthysse, Holzman, & Lange, 1986) suggest the existence of a qualitative discontinuity, whereas the polygenic multifactorial threshold model (Gottesman, 1991) predicts a continuous distribution of levels of liability. Clarification of the structure of schizotypy may help to resolve ambiguous issues that remain in discussions concerning appropriate genetic models for schizophrenia; such information may aid in planning future studies in this area. Nearly all investigations of the structure of schizophrenia liability conducted to date have relied exclusively on fully expressed, diagnosable schizophrenia (see Gottesman, 1991), and the results of these studies have left the question of liability structure unresolved. Moreover, one surely cannot reason with confidence that a unimodal distribution of phenotypic schizotypic traits supports the existence of a continuum of liability (e.g., Kendler et al., 1991). In recent years, however, it has been proposed that a possible "expansion" of the schizophrenia phenotype to include other schizophrenia-related phenomena, such as eye-tracking dysfunction (Holzman et al., 1988), might be helpful in efforts to illuminate the latent structure of liability in schizophrenia. As suggested by the foregoing studies, I have pursued an approach, complementary to the "extended phenotype" proposal, through the application of a psychometric approach to the detection of schizotypy (see Lenzenweger, 1993) and subsequent laboratory studies. An important step in this research program has involved a systematic study of the latent structure of the PAS, which has served as the primary tool in schizotypic study subject selection. This work has been guided by the theoretical model suggested by Meehl (which has been extended, amended, and revised by others), which holds that the schizotype is a "type" of individual, differing from others in quality, not merely degree.

Taxometric exploration of the latent structure of schizotypy. My coworkers and I have explored the latent structure of schizotypy through application of Meehl's (1973, 1992; Meehl & Golden, 1982; Meehl & Yonce, 1996) MAXCOV procedure to the covariance structure of scores on the PAS. Our samples have been randomly ascertained from nonclinical university populations and have been purged of invalid responders and those with suspect test-taking attitudes. Using the

MAXCOV procedure, Lenzenweger and Korfine (1992a; Korfine & Lenzenweger, 1995) have found evidence that suggests that the latent structure of schizotypy, as assessed by the PAS, is taxonic (i.e., qualitative) in nature and, moreover, that the base rate of the schizotypy taxon is approximately 5–10%. The taxon base rate figure is relatively consistent with the conjecture by Meehl (1990) that schizotypes can be found in the general population at a rate of 10%. In my work, I have also conducted a variety of control analyses that have served to check the MAXCOV procedure and ensure that the technique does not generate spurious evidence of taxonicity. Korfine and Lenzenweger (1995) have demonstrated that (a) MAXCOV detects a latent continuum when one is hypothesized to exist, (b) MAXCOV analyses based on dichotomous data do not automatically generate taxonic results, and (c) item endorsement frequencies do not correspond to taxon base rate estimates (i.e., my base rate estimates are not a reflection of endorsement frequencies). Finally, in my recent work (Lenzenweger, 1998) MAXCOV analysis applied to three continuous measures of schizotypy revealed results that were highly consistent with my coworkers and my prior research in this area. These data, taken in aggregate, although they do not unambiguously confirm that the structure of schizotypy is qualitative, are clearly consistent with such a conjecture. This suggests that schizotypic psychopathology is discontinuous in its latent structure and this raises interesting possibilities for future genetic research in this area. With respect to delimitation, the results of the MAXCOV analyses suggest that the PAS identifies a class of individuals who appear relatively distinct from others. More important, individuals who score deviantly high on the PAS and are likely to be schizotypy taxon members display a pattern of performance deficits, family history correlates, and clinical symptomatology that is clearly consistent with an underlying liability for schizophrenia.

These results also raised an especially interesting theoretical problem with respect to process-oriented approaches to the study of schizophrenia. In short, if the schizotype differs qualitatively from other persons in possessing a liability for schizophrenia that has a taxonic structure, is it theoretically defensible to assume cognitive and emotional processes are structured comparably across normal control subjects and schizotypes? The process approach to the study of psychopathology implicitly assumes continuity in the form and structure of, say, a cognitive process, and presumably differences in a process across normative and pathological populations represent quantitative variation. But what if normative and pathological populations were qualitatively different? Would it not conceivably be the case that one must begin investigations in this area with the affection status of the individual (or group) as the primary determinant of the direction one ought to take in the design of investigations? This issue clearly requires greater analytic exploration but may prove useful in the long term with respect to a methodological approach to schizophrenia.

What Is the Status of Schizotypes at Long-Term Follow-Up?

At the present time, my coworkers and I do not have clinical outcome–follow-up data on our schizotypic and control subjects. We do, however, plan to conduct a series of careful follow-up examinations, using both clinical measures and laboratory indexes, as each of the study samples approaches a point in time 10 years after their initial assessment. We are unaware of any other long-term follow-ups of psychometrically identified schizotypic subjects that will have used *both* psychometric and laboratory measures as predictors of clinical status at follow-up examinations. The utility of laboratory measures in predicting clinical status at follow-up has been demonstrated by the long-term follow-up study by Cornblatt, Lenzenweger, Dworkin, and Erlenmeyer-Kimling (1992), in which childhood attentional dysfunction predicted diagnosable schizotypic psychopathology nearly 20 years later. In this study, the laboratory measure provided a refined source of information over and above the affection status (e.g., schizophrenia) of the subjects' parents. It is our hope that a combination of psychometrically defined schizotypy and laboratory measure performance will provide a sharper probe of clinical outcome over the developmental course of our subjects. We view our intended follow-up studies as building on the landmark follow-up study of psychometrically identified schizotypes (or "psychosis-prone" subjects) completed recently by Chapman, Chapman, Kwapil, Eckblad, and Zinser (1994).

THE SCHIZOTYPE AS A VALID EXTENSION OF THE SCHIZOPHRENIA PHENOTYPE

The overall pattern of findings (see Exhibit 1) that have emerged from my laboratory suggests that psychometrically identified schizotypes (identified with the PAS) reveal a pattern of familial illness, laboratory performance, and clinical phenomenology that is strikingly consistent with what is seen in the case of actual schizophrenia. Although the magnitude of deficits observed on the various laboratory measures and psychological tests used do not reach the level of deficit displayed by actual schizophrenia patients, the direction and pattern of the findings among the schizotypes on these tasks is more similar to schizophrenia-related deviance than otherwise, and obtained effect sizes have been persuasive. Moreover, to address the most skeptical views, perhaps, were psychometrically identified schizotypy to have genuinely nothing to do with the construct schizotypy hypothesized to underlie schizophrenia,

---

Exhibit 1

Summary of Schizophrenia-Related Features Found Among Psychometrically Identified Schizotypes

- Increased morbid risk for schizophrenia in biological relatives
- Impaired sustained attention
- Impaired spatial working memory
- Impaired antisaccade performance
- Impaired smooth pursuit eye-tracking performance
- Decreased negative priming effect (increased disinhibition)
- Impaired executive functioning and increased loss of set
- Increased clinically significant schizotypic psychopathology
- Schizophrenia related MMPI deviance
- Increased levels of thought disorder
- Taxonic latent structure delimiting a schizotypy class

Note. MMPI = Minnesota Multiphasic Personality Inventory.

---

then the pattern of findings observed in our studies of schizotypy (Exhibit 1) would be a rather remarkable coincidence.

My theoretical position based on the overall pattern of results, as one might expect, is quite different from the "coincidence" viewpoint. The data collected appear to strongly suggest that the psychometrically identified schizotype most probably represents an alternative expression of the same schizotypy that underlies schizophrenia (see Figure 1). This is not to say that the PAS is the "royal road" to schizotypy but merely that individuals identified by deviance on that scale appear to represent a class of individuals who may also carry the latent liability for schizophrenia. Moreover, I do not expect that all of my schizotypes will decompensate into clinical schizophrenia over the life course, as consistent with Meehl's model; some may go on to psychosis, some may appear merely as schizotypic (perhaps even diagnosable as SPD by *DSM-IV* criteria), and some may remain relatively compensated and be schizotypic only in the sense of revealing subtle deviances on laboratory measures across the life span. It is conceivable that some genuine schizotypes may move quietly through the life span showing virtually no evidence, symptomatologic or otherwise, of their underlying liability (cf. Gottesman & Bertelsen, 1989).

CONCLUSION

I argue that these data strongly support a model that holds that schizophrenia liability can express itself in alternative forms and that the psychometric schizotype is such a variant of schizophrenia liability, so to speak. Furthermore, I do not suggest that all persons carry "a little bit of schizotypy"—akin to the outdated notions of the "psychotic core" that eroded the utility of the liability concept 40–50 years ago— but rather I suggest that only a certain proportion of the population carries schizotypy (perhaps 5–10%), a class or taxon of carriers to be more precise. The methodologic implication of this theoretical approach is that the schizotype should be included in many analyses as an extension of the schizophrenia phenotype, a rational and data-driven extension of the phenotype. Inclusion of the schizotype in an extended phenotype of schizophrenia liability, for example, (a) enhances the power of genetic investigations of schizophrenia (see Holzman, 1994, and Matthysse & Parnas, 1992, for comparable points regarding other psychological probes, e.g., eye-tracking dysfunction) and (b) may provide a useful "high fidelity" window into schizophrenia liability uncontaminated by third-variable confounds (e.g., medication effects, institutionalization, deterioration). I strongly advocate further study of the schizotype from multiple experimental psychopathology vantage points as well as other perspectives (e.g., genetics, neurobiology; e.g., Grace & Moore, chapter 5, this volume).

REFERENCES

American Psychiatric Association. (1968). *Diagnostic and statistical manual of mental disorders* (2nd ed.). Washington, DC: Author.

American Psychiatric Association. (1980). *Diagnostic and statistical manual of mental disorders* (3rd ed.). Washington, DC: Author.

American Psychiatric Association. (1994). *Diagnostic and statistical manual of mental disorders* (4th ed.). Washington, DC: Author.

Battaglia, M., Gasperini, M., Sciuto, G., Scherillo, P., Diaferia, G., & Bellodi, L. (1991). Psychiatric disorders in the families of schizotypal subjects. *Schizophrenia Bulletin, 17,* 659–668.

Beech, A. R., Powell, T., McWilliam, J., & Claridge, G. S. (1989). Evidence of reduced 'cognitive inhibition' in schizophrenia. *British Journal of Clinical Psychology, 28,* 109–116.

Berenbaum, H., & McGrew, J. (1993). Familial resemblance of schizotypic traits. *Psychological Medicine, 23,* 327–333.

Bleuler, E. (1950). *Dementia praecox or the group of schizophrenias.* (J. Zinkin, Trans.). New York: International Universities Press. (Original work published 1911)

Chapman, L. J., & Chapman, J. P. (1985). Psychosis proneness. In M. Alpert (Ed.), *Controversies in schizophrenia: Changes and constancies* (pp. 157–172). New York: Guilford Press.

Chapman, J. P., Chapman, L. J., & Kwapil, T. R. (1995). Scales for the measurement of schizotypy. In A. Raine, T. Lencz, & S. Mednick, (Eds.),

Schizotypal personality (pp. 79–106). New York: Cambridge University Press.

Chapman, L. J., Chapman, J. P., Kwapil, T. R., Eckblad, M., & Zinser, M. C. (1994). Putatively psychosis-prone subjects 10 years later. *Journal of Abnormal Psychology, 103,* 171–183.

Chapman, L. J., Chapman, J. P., & Raulin, M. L. (1978). Body-image aberration in schizophrenia. *Journal of Abnormal Psychology, 87,* 399–407.

Chapman, L. J., Edell, W. S., & Chapman, J. P. (1980). Physical anhedonia, perceptual aberration, and psychosis proneness. *Schizophrenia Bulletin, 6,* 639–653.

Coleman, M. J., Levy, D. L., Lenzenweger, M. F., & Holzman, P. S. (1996). Thought disorder, perceptual aberrations, and schizotypy. *Journal of Abnormal Psychology, 105,* 469–473.

Cooper, J. E., Kendell, R. E., Gurland, B. J., Sharpe, L., Copeland, J. R. M., & Simon, R. (1972). *Psychiatric diagnosis in New York and London: A comparative study of mental hospital admissions.* New York: Oxford University Press.

Cornblatt, B. A., & Erlenmeyer-Kimling, L. (1985). Global attentional deviance as a marker of risk for schizophrenia: Specificity and predictive validity. *Journal of Abnormal Psychology, 94,* 470–486.

Cornblatt, B. A., & Keilp, J. G. (1994). Impaired attention, genetics, and the pathophysiology of schizophrenia. *Schizophrenia Bulletin, 20,* 31–46.

Cornblatt, B. A., Lenzenweger, M. F., Dworkin, R. H., & Erlenmeyer-Kimling, L. (1992). Childhood attentional dysfunction predicts social isolation in adults at risk for schizophrenia. *British Journal of Psychiatry, 161*(Suppl. 18), 59–68.

Cornblatt, B. A., Lenzenweger, M. F., & Erlenmeyer-Kimling, L. (1989). The Continuous Performance Test, Identical Pairs Version: II. Contrasting attentional profiles in schizophrenic and depressed patients. *Psychiatry Research, 29,* 65–85.

Cornblatt, B. A., Risch, N. J., Faris, G., Friedman, D., & Erlenmeyer-Kimling, L. (1988). The Continuous Performance Test, Identical Pairs Version (CPT-IP): I. New findings about sustained attention in normal families. *Psychiatry Research, 26,* 223–238.

Cronbach, L. J., & Meehl, P. E. (1955). Construct validity in psychological tests. *Psychological Bulletin, 52,* 281–302.

Edell, W. S. (1995). The psychometric measurement of schizotypy using the Wisconsin scales of psychosis-proneness. In G. A. Miller (Ed.), *The behavioral high-risk paradigm in psychopathology* (pp. 3–46). New York: Springer-Verlag.

Fukushima, J., Fukushima, K., Chiba, T., & Tanaka, S. (1988). Disturbances of voluntary control of saccadic eye movements in schizophrenic patients. *Biological Psychiatry, 23,* 670–677.

Gold, J. M., & Harvey, P. D. (1993). Cognitive deficits in schizophrenia. *Psychiatric Clinics of North America, 16,* 295–312.

Goldman-Rakic, P. S. (1991). Prefrontal cortical dysfunction in schizophrenia: The relevance of working memory. In B. Carroll (Ed.), *Psychopathology and the brain* (pp. 1–23). Raven Press: New York.

Gottesman, I. I. (1991). *Schizophrenia genesis: The origins of madness.* New York: Freeman.

Gottesman, I. I., & Bertelsen, A. (1989). Confirming unexpressed genotypes for schizophrenia: Risks in the offspring of Fischer's Danish identical and fraternal discordant twins. *Archives of General Psychiatry, 46,* 867–872.

Grace, A. A. (1991). Phasic versus tonic dopamine release and the modulation of dopamine system responsivity: A hypothesis for the etiology of schizophrenia. *Neuroscience, 41,* 1–24.

Grove, W. M., Lebow, B. S., Clementz, B. A., Cerri, A., Medus, C., & Iacono, W. G. (1991). Familial prevalence and coaggregation of schizotypy indicators: A multitrait family study. *Journal of Abnormal Psychology, 100,* 115–121.

Hanson, D. R., Gottesman, I. I., & Meehl, P. E. (1977). Genetic theories and the validation of psychiatric diagnosis: Implications for the study of children of schizophrenics. *Journal of Abnormal Psychology, 86,* 575–588.

Holzman, P. S. (1994). The role of psychological probes in genetic studies of schizophrenia. *Schizophrenia Research, 13,* 1–9.

Holzman, P. S., Kringlen, E., Matthysse, S., Flanagan, S. D., Lipton, R. B., Cramer, G., Levin, S., Lange, K., & Levy, D. L. (1988). A single dominant gene can account for eye tracking dysfunctions and schizophrenia in offspring of discordant twins. *Archives of General Psychiatry, 45,* 641–647.

Johnston, M. H., & Holzman, P. S. (1979). *Assessing schizophrenic thinking.* San Francisco: Jossey-Bass.

Kendler, K. S. (1985). Diagnostic approaches to schizotypal personality disorder: A historical perspective. *Schizophrenia Bulletin, 11,* 538–553.

Kendler, K. S., Lieberman, J. A., & Walsh, D. (1989). The Structured Interview for Schizotypy (SIS): A preliminary report. *Schizophrenia Bulletin, 15,* 559–571.

Kendler, K. S., McGuire, M., Gruenberg, A. M., O'Hare, A., Spellman, M., & Walsh, D. (1993). The Roscommon Family Study: III. Schizophrenia-related personality disorders in relatives. *Archives of General Psychiatry, 50,* 781–788.

Kendler, K. S., Ochs, A. L., Gorman, A. M., Hewitt, J. K., Ross, D. E., & Mirsky, A. F. (1991). The structure of schizotypy: A pilot multitrait twin study. *Psychiatry Research, 36,* 19–36.

Kety, S. S., Rosenthal, D., Wender, P. H., & Schulsinger, F. (1968). The types and prevalence of mental illness in the biological and adoptive families of adopted schizophrenics. *Journal of Psychiatric Research, 6,* 345–362.

Korfine, L., & Lenzenweger, M. F. (1995). The taxonicity of schizotypy: A replication. *Journal of Abnormal Psychology, 104,* 26–31.

Kraepelin, E. (1971). *Dementia praecox and paraphrenia* (R. M. Barclay, Trans.; G. M. Robertson, Ed.). Huntington, NY: Krieger. (Original work published 1909–1913)

Lenzenweger, M. F. (1991). Confirming schizotypic personality configurations in hypothetically psychosis-prone university students. *Psychiatry Research, 37,* 81–96.

Lenzenweger, M. F. (1993). Explorations in schizotypy and the psychometric high-risk paradigm. In L. J. Chapman, J. P. Chapman, & D. Fowles (Eds.), *Progress in experimental personality and psychopathology research* (No. 16, pp. 66–116). New York: Springer.

Lenzenweger, M. F. (1994). The psychometric high-risk paradigm, perceptual aberrations, and schizotypy: An update. *Schizophrenia Bulletin, 20,* 121–135.

Lenzenweger, M. F. (1998). *Deeper into the schizotypy taxon: On the robust nature of MAXCOV analysis.* Manuscript submitted for publication, Cornell University.

Lenzenweger, M. F., Cornblatt, B. A., & Putnick, M. E. (1991). Schizotypy and sustained attention. *Journal of Abnormal Psychology, 100,* 84–89.

Lenzenweger, M. F., & Korfine, L. (1991, December). *Schizotypy and Wisconsin Card Sorting Test performance.* Paper presented at the sixth annual meeting of the Society for Research in Psychopathology, Harvard University, Cambridge, MA.

Lenzenweger, M. F., & Korfine, L. (1992a). Confirming the latent structure and base rate of schizotypy: A taxometric analysis. *Journal of Abnormal Psychology, 101,* 567–571.

Lenzenweger, M. F., & Korfine, L. (1992b). Identifying schizophrenia-related personality disorder features in a nonclinical population using a psychometric approach. *Journal of Personality Disorders, 6,* 264–274.

Lenzenweger, M. F., & Korfine, L. (1994). Perceptual aberrations, schizotypy and the Wisconsin Card Sorting Test. *Schizophrenia Bulletin, 20,* 345–357.

Lenzenweger, M. F., & Loranger, A. W. (1989a). Detection of familial schizophrenia using a psychometric measure of schizotypy. *Archives of General Psychiatry, 46,* 902–907.

Lenzenweger, M. F., & Loranger, A. W. (1989b). Psychosis proneness and clinical psychopathology: Examination of the correlates of schizotypy. *Journal of Abnormal Psychology, 98,* 3–8.

Levin, S. (1984a). Frontal lobe dysfunctions in schizophrenia—I. Eye movement impairments. *Journal of Psychiatric Research, 18,* 27–55.

Levin, S. (1984b). Frontal lobe dysfunctions in schizophrenia—II. Impairments of psychological brain functions. *Journal of Psychiatric Research, 18,* 57–72.

Levy, D. L., Holzman, P. S., Matthysse, S., & Mendell, R. (1993). Eye tracking dysfunction and schizophrenia: A critical perspective. *Schizophrenia Bulletin, 19,* 461–536.

Loranger, A. (1990). The impact of *DSM-III* on diagnostic practice in a university hospital: A comparison of *DSM-II* and *DSM-III* in 10,914 patients. *Archives of General Psychiatry, 47,* 672–675.

Matthysse, S. (1993). Genetics and the problem of causality in abnormal psychology. In P. B. Sutker & H. E. Adams (Eds.), *Comprehensive handbook of psychopathology* (pp. 178–186). New York: Springer-Verlag.

Matthysse, S., Holzman, P. S., & Lange, K. (1986). The genetic transmission of schizophrenia: Application of Mendelian latent structure analysis to eye tracking dysfunctions in schizophrenia and affective disorder. *Journal of Psychiatric Research, 20,* 57–67.

Matthysse, S., & Parnas, J. (1992). Extending the phenotype of schizophrenia: Implications for linkage analysis. *Journal of Psychiatric Research, 26,* 329–344.

Meehl, P. E. (1962). Schizotaxia, schizotypy, schizophrenia. *American Psychologist, 17,* 827–838.

Meehl, P. E. (1964). *Manual for use with Checklist of Schizotypic Signs.* Minneapolis: University of Minnesota.

Meehl, P. E. (1973). MAXCOV–HITMAX: A taxonomic search method for loose genetic syndromes. In P. E. Meehl (Ed.), *Psychodiagnosis: Selected papers* (pp. 200–224). Minneapolis: University of Minnesota Press.

Meehl, P. E. (1990). Toward an integrated theory of schizotaxia, schizotypy, and schizophrenia. *Journal of Personality Disorders, 4,* 1–99.

Meehl, P. E. (1992). Factors and taxa, traits and types, differences of degree and differences in kind. *Journal of Personality, 60,* 117–174.

Meehl, P. E., & Golden, R. R. (1982). Taxometric methods. In P. C. Kendall & J. N. Butcher, (Eds.), *Handbook of research methods in clinical psychology* (pp. 127–181). New York: Wiley.

Meehl, P. E., & Yonce, L. J. (1996). Taxometric analysis: II. Detecting taxonicity using covariance of two quantitative indicators in successive intervals of a third indicator (MAXCOV procedure). *Psychological Reports, 78,* 1091–1227.

Nuechterlein, K. H., & Dawson, M. (1984). Information processing and attentional functioning in the developmental course of schizophrenic disorders. *Schizophrenia Bulletin, 10,* 160–203.

Obiols, J. E., Garcia-Domingo, M., de Trincheria, I., & Domenech, E. (1993). Psychometric schizotypy and sustained attention in young males. *Personality and Individual Differences, 14,* 381–384.

O'Driscoll, G., Lenzenweger, M. F., & Holzman, P. S. (1997). *Antisaccade and smooth pursuit eye-tracking performance in relation to schizotypy.* Manuscript submitted for publication.

Park, S., & Holzman, P. S. (1992). Schizophrenics show working memory deficits. *Archives General Psychiatry, 49,* 975–982.

Park, S., Holzman, P. S., & Lenzenweger, M. F. (1995). Individual differences in working memory in relation to schizotypy. *Journal of Abnormal Psychology, 104,* 355–363.

Park, S., Lenzenweger, M. F., Püschel, J., & Holzman, P. S. (1996). Attentional inhibition in schizophrenia and schizotypy: A spatial negative priming study. *Cognitive Neuropsychiatry, 1,* 125–149.

Rado, S. (1953). Dynamics and classification of disordered behavior. *American Journal of Psychiatry, 110,* 406–416.

Rado, S. (1960). Theory and therapy: The theory of schizotypal organization and its application to the treatment of decompensated schizotypal behavior. In S. C. Scher & H. R. Davis (Eds.), *The outpatient treatment of schizophrenia* (pp. 87–101). New York: Grune & Stratton.

Robins, E., & Guze, S. (1970). Establishment of diagnostic validity in psychiatric illness: Its application to schizophrenia. *American Journal of Psychiatry, 126,* 983–987.

Sher, K. J., & Trull, T. J. (1996). Methodological issues in psychopathology research. *Annual Review of Psychology, 47,* 371–400.

Siever, L. J., Bernstein, D. P., & Silverman, J. M. (1991). Schizotypal personality disorder: A review of its current status. *Journal of Personality Disorder, 5,* 178–193.

Spitzer, R. L., Endicott, J., & Gibbon, M. (1979). Crossing the border into borderline personality and borderline schizophrenia: The development of criteria. *Archives of General Psychiatry, 36,* 17–24.

Weinberger, D. R., Berman, K. F., & Zec, R. F. (1986). Physiologic dysfunction of dorsolateral prefrontal cortex in schizophrenics: I. Regional cerebral blood flow evidence. *Archives of General Psychiatry, 43,* 114–124.

5

Regulation of Information Flow in the Nucleus Accumbens: A Model for the Pathophysiology of Schizophrenia

Anthony A. Grace and Holly Moore

Schizophrenia is among the most devastating of the neuropsychiatric disorders with regard to its impact on patients and their families and, as such, has been subject to a most intensive interdisciplinary series of investigations. Nonetheless, the pathophysiology of this disorder has resisted definition. Initial investigations focused on the neurotransmitter dopamine (DA) and its effects on structures within the limbic system. This orientation was based on correlative pharmacological data substantiating a role for DA in schizophrenia, including the propensity of indirect DA agonists such as L-DOPA and amphetamine to mimic some aspects of this disorder in normal humans (Angrist, 1994; Connell, 1958), and the finding that all antipsychotic drugs characterized to date are antagonists at DA receptors (D_2 family; A. Carlsson & Lindqvist, 1963; Peroutka & Snyder, 1980; Seeman, 1992). However, convincing evidence for a primary site of pathology within the DA system has not been found (Bachus & Kleinman, 1996; Sedvall & Farde, 1995). Indeed, closer examination of the original data implicating DA as a primary factor in schizophrenia has revealed inadequacies. For example, animal studies indicate that psychosis is induced in normal subjects by amphetamine at doses that produce a dramatic increase in release of DA within the brain (e.g., Hertel et al., 1995; Sharp, Zetterstrom, Ljungberg, & Ungerstedt, 1987; for a review, see Kuczenski & Segal, 1994); however, despite massive efforts, little evidence exists to substantiate an increase in DA levels or release within the brains of schizophrenia patients (Sedvall & Farde, 1995; van Kammen, Peters, & van Kammen, 1986). Furthermore, although the psychotic symptomatology associated with amphetamine can be rapidly reversed by acute administration of a DA receptor blocking drug (Schuckit, 1989), antipsychotic drugs do not achieve maximal therapeutic efficacy in schizophrenia patients until administered repeatedly for weeks or longer (Johnstone, Crow, Frith, Carney, & Price, 1978). This clinical course of antipsychotic drug administration would not be expected if the mechanism of therapeutic action were based primarily on receptor blockade. Thus, one would expect that a drug whose primary mode of action involved blockade of DA receptors would exert its maximal pharmacological actions when administered acutely, with the development of tolerance as the system compensated for the diminished DA receptor stimulation. In contrast, antipsychotic drugs require repeated administration to achieve a therapeutic level of action, and their antipsychotic efficacy does not typically exhibit tolerance even with long-term administration (Palmstierna & Wistedt, 1987). Therefore, although it is clear that the DA system plays a role in the expression of schizophrenic symptomatology, it seems that the primary pathological factor lies elsewhere in the central nervous system.

More recently, investigators have amassed evidence suggestive of a frontal lobe pathology in schizophrenia patients, including a reduction in indexes of activity in the dorsolateral aspect of the prefrontal cortex (PFC; i.e., Berman, Zec, Weinberger, 1986; Bogerts, 1993; Buchsbaum et al., 1992; Liddle et al., 1992), particularly in those patients with prominent deficit syndrome (Andreasen et al., 1995; Tamminga et al., 1992). Moreover, lesions of the PFC in adult humans produce a syndrome that shares some characteristics with the deficit state (or negative symptoms) of schizophrenia (Nasrallah, Fowlerm, & Judd, 1981). Indeed, a failure to activate the PFC (Berman et al., 1986) appears to correlate with the poor performance exhibited by schizophrenia patients on specific tasks that have been shown to require an intact frontal cortex (e.g., the Wisconsin Card Sorting Test task; Fey, 1951; for a review, see Goldberg & Gold, 1995). Nonetheless, despite this functional evidence, anatomical disturbances of the PFC that would appear to be of sufficient magnitude to disrupt behavior are not commonly observed in schizophrenia patients (Shapiro, 1993; Weinberger & Lipska, 1995). The majority of pathological changes reported in schizophrenia have been found in cortical (including PFC) and basal forebrain regions related to the limbic system. An involvement of the amygdala was advanced by studies of schizophrenia patients showing reductions in the metabolic rate of limbic-related cortical areas that connect reciprocally with the amygdala (Tamminga et al., 1992) as well as morphological alterations within the amygdala itself (i.e., Breier et al., 1992; Reynolds, 1992; Rossi et al., 1994). Disturbances in neurotransmission in the amygdala and the related anterior cingulate cortex are believed to relate to particular symptoms of schizophrenia, such as blunted affect, inability to interpret and respond in social situations, and attentional deficits (Andreasen et al., 1995; Kirkpatrick & Buchanan, 1990; Reynolds, 1992; Tamminga et al., 1992). Indeed, these symptoms resemble the effects of amygdala lesions in nonhuman primates as well as the behavioral deficits in humans with lesions of the anterior cingulate cortex, which is reciprocally connected with the amygdala (Devinsky, Morrell, & Vogt, 1995; Tamminga et al., 1992). Although most of the evidence regarding the amygdala points to its possible role in the expression of negative symptoms in schizophrenia, a compelling set of data indicate that there are changes in the hippocampus and parahippocampal and entorhinal cortexes that relate to a possible etiology of schizophrenia. This includes reports of preferential decreases in volume (Bogerts, Meertz, & Schonfeldt-Bausch, 1985; Breier et al., 1992) and abnormal activation (assessed by cerebral blood flow or glucose utilization; Liddle et al., 1992) in the temporal lobe region containing the hippocampus. These changes are particularly apparent in the afflicted cohort of twins discordant for schizophrenia (Suddath, Christison, Torrey, Casanova, & Weinberger, 1990; Weinberger, Berman, Suddath, & Torrey, 1992), with both the structural and the functional (i.e., glucose utilization or blood flow) abnormalities corre-

125

lated with the severity of positive symptoms (Bogerts et al., 1985; Liddle et al., 1992). Also reported in the hippocamal, parahippocampal, or entorhinal cortexes of schizophrenia patients are a variety of changes at the cellular level, including disordered cellular organization (i.e., Altshuler, Conrad, Kovelman, & Scheibel, 1987; Arnold, Hyman, Van Hoesen, & Damasio, 1991), decreased numbers of neurons (Akbarian et al., 1993; Arnold et al., 1995; Maier, Ron, Barker, & Tofts, 1995), and decreases in cytoskeletal or synaptic proteins (Arnold, Lee, Gur, & Trojanowski, 1991; Eastwood, Burnet, & Harrison, 1995). These changes have been interpreted as reflecting abnormal development of the temporal cortex (Akbarian et al., 1993; Altshuler et al., 1987; Arnold, Hyman, et al., 1991; Arnold, Lee, et al., 1991; Eastwood et al., 1995). On the basis of evidence for a possible primary pathology in these temporal limbic areas in schizophrenia, our studies have focused on the nature of the functional interdependence among the PFC, amygdala, and hippocampus in the mammalian brain by examining synaptic interactions in the *nucleus accumbens*. This is a region in which inputs from these cortical structures converge and overlap with the mesolimbic DA system and from which projections can influence higher cognitive processing through a thalamocortical network that ultimately modulates the PFC. In this chapter, we first review the importance of the nucleus accumbens to schizophrenia as revealed by basic research in this area. We then discuss the possible effects of disruptions of cortical development on this system as they relate to neurodevelopmental theories of schizophrenia.

RELEVANCE OF THE NUCLEUS ACCUMBENS TO SCHIZOPHRENIA

The striatum is functionally subdivided into regions based on the source of its inputs and the anatomical locus of the thalamocortical regions it influences. The dorsal striatum is involved primarily in the integration of sensorimotor information, with anterior striatal regions likely to be involved in the planning of complex, learned motor acts (Alexander, DeLong, & Strick, 1986). All sensory and motor areas of the neocortex project topographically to the dorsal striatum (caudate-putamen), wherein cortically derived signals are integrated under the modulatory influence of the nigrostriatal DA system. Projections from the dorsal striatum make up two related loops that through the globus pallidus and a related area of the substantia nigra, regulate motor thalamus and, ultimately, motor planning and execution areas in the frontal cortex. The role of this system in motor control is demonstrated by the impact of pathological changes in these systems, such as the dancelike choreoathetotic movements produced by excitotoxic degeneration of the striatum in Huntington's disease and the tremor and akinesia associated with degeneration of the nigrostriatal DA innervation in Parkinson's disease.

The ventral regions of the striatum, however, appear to mediate more basic locomotor and appetitive behaviors driven by the affective state of the organism, behaviors previously associated with functions of the limbic system (Heimer & Alheid, 1991; Mogenson, Jones, & Yim, 1984). The medial portion of the ventral striatum, the nucleus accumbens, receives excitatory inputs almost exclusively from limbic-related structures, including the hippocampus, amygdala, limbic thalamus, and prelimbic and infralimbic cortices (see Figure 1; Groenewegen et al., 1991). As such, the nucleus accumbens, along with its distinct DA input, has a demonstrated involvement in reward learning, drug addiction, and affective processes (Altman et al., 1996; Robbins, Cador, Taylor, & Everitt, 1989). It has also attracted the attention of researchers interested in the biological bases of psychiatric disorders, including schizophrenia, for a number of reasons. Anatomically, the accumbens receives afferent input from each of the cortical regions linked with schizophrenia, including the PFC (Sesack, Deutch, Roth, & Bunney, 1989), archicortex (hippocampus; Christie, James, & Beart, 1987; Kelley & Domesick, 1982), and the cortical-like basolateral amygdala (Christie et al., 1987; McDonald, 1991). In addition, the accumbens receives a massive dopaminergic input from the limbic-associated ventral tegmental cell group (Voorn, Jorritsma-Byham, Van Dijk, & Buijs, 1986). In turn, the nucleus accumbens provides input to regions such as the ventral pallidum, which influences several limbic-related thalamocortical circuits (Heimer & Alheid, 1991). A major target of the accumbens-ventral pallidal system is the mediodorsal nucleus of the thalamus (Lavin & Grace,

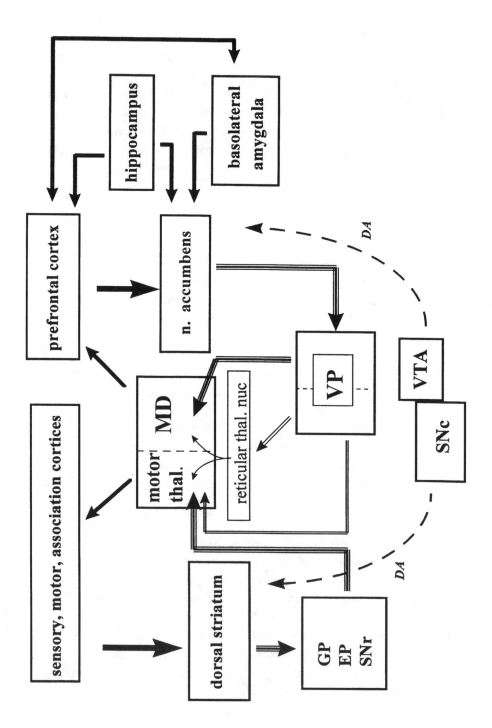

Figure 1

A schematic diagram of the dorsal extrapyramidal and ventral limbic cortical-basal ganglia circuits. Excitatory (glutamatergic), inhibitory (GABAergic), and dopaminergic pathways are indicated by solid, vertically hatched, and dotted lines, respectively. The dorsal circuit (left) consists of projections from sensory cortices to the dorsal striatum, which, in turn, projects to areas in the globus pallidus (GP), entopeduncular nucleus (EP; analogous to the internal GP in humans), and substantia nigra pars reticulata (SNr). The GP, EP, and SNr send GABAergic inputs to the motor thalamus (motor thal.), which, in turn, sends excitatory inputs to the cortex. The dorsal circuit receives dopaminergic inputs from the substantia nigra pars compacta (SNc). The ventral pathway, shown on the right, consists of excitatory projections from the prefrontal cortex, hippocampus, and amygdala to the nucleus accumbens (n. accumbens), which sends inputs to the ventral pallidum (VP). The VP provides a major projection to the mediodorsal (MD) and minor projections to the reticular and motor thalamic nuclei (O'Donnell et al., 1997). The ventral circuit is modulated by dopaminergic inputs from the ventral tegmental area (VTA). The ventral pathway, acting through the limbic modulation of PFC, nucleus accumbens, and mediodorsal thalamus, regulates motor output that is guided by the relationships among the internal (i.e., emotion or motivation) state of the animal, external sensory signals, and internal representations associated with these signals. DA = dopamine; reticular thal. nuc = reticular thalamus nuclei.

1994; O'Donnell, Lavin, Enquist, Grace, & Card, 1997; Young, Alheid, & Heimer, 1984), which is the thalamic region that provides the major regulatory control over the center of highest (i.e., most evolved) cognitive function of the brain, the PFC (Ray & Price, 1992; Uylings & van Eden, 1990). The mediodorsal thalamus also modulates the basolateral amygdala and nucleus accumbens through relays in the midline thalamic nuclei (Amaral, Price, Pitkanen, & Carmichael, 1992). Changes within each of the structures of the ventral circuit shown in Figure 1 have been observed with varying degrees of severity and coexpression in the brains of schizophrenia patients (Andreasen et al., 1995, 1996; Bogerts, 1993; Pakkenberg, 1990; Tamminga et al., 1992), providing compelling evidence for the involvement of this circuit in the pathogenesis of the disease. Moreover, numerous studies have identified a host of changes that occur within a subregion of the nucleus accumbens, known as the "shell," and emerge following repeated administration of antipsychotic drugs, including the induction of immediate early genes (i.e., Merchant et al., 1994), expression of peptide messenger RNA (i.e., Jaber, Tison, Fournier, & Bloch, 1994), and intercellular dye coupling (O'Donnell & Grace, 1995a; Onn & Grace, 1995). The delayed onset of these alterations during antipsychotic drug treatment is believed to reflect potential sites of therapeutic action because it corresponds to the delayed onset of therapeutic efficacy of these drugs when administered to schizophrenia patients (Johnstone et al., 1978).

AFFERENT INPUTS TO THE NUCLEUS ACCUMBENS AND THEIR FUNCTIONAL INTERACTIONS

To develop a model of how a dysfunction in one or more regions of the limbic cortical-basal ganglia circuit (Figure 1) could contribute to the pathophysiology of schizophrenia, we focused our efforts on examining interactions among these circuits in the normal system. We approached this problem by using electrophysiological recordings from identified neurons in the rat brain because (a) all structures of this circuit are present in this subject and (b) we can readily use more direct and well-controlled procedures in this subject to investigate the cellular bases of systems interactions. Therefore, although our studies focus on a disease state that is, arguably, uniquely human, these animal studies provide information that is generally applicable to our understanding of these systems, even as they are further elaborated in the human organism. By using in vivo extracellular and intracellular recordings combined with anatomical and tract-tracing techniques, we have examined in detail the activity of neurons in the nucleus accumbens, their drive by excitatory afferents, the pharmacology of regulation by the DA system, and their influence on output pathways that control thalamocortical function.

The primary cell type in the nucleus accumbens is the medium spiny neuron (Meredith, Pennartz, & Groenewegen, 1993). This cell received this designation due to its moderate soma size (i.e., approximately 20–30 micrometers) and its modest dendritic field (i.e., 200–300 micrometers). Nonetheless, each of these neurons receives massive numbers of excitatory inputs. On the basis of numbers obtained in the dorsal striatum, it is estimated that each of these neurons receives approximately 5,000 excitatory inputs from cortical structures, in addition to receiving 4,500–8,000 inputs from DA terminals (Doucet, Descarries, & Garcia, 1986). Therefore, these cells integrate a massive amount of information from cortical structures. Our investigations show that electrical stimulation of the afferent fibers arising from the PFC, the cortical-like region of the amygdala, and the hippocampus produce excitatory postsynaptic potentials (EPSPs) in accumbens neurons (O'Donnell & Grace, 1995b). These EPSPs, which are brief, small-amplitude, graded membrane depolarizations in accumbens neurons, are typically not adequate in themselves to cause the cell to fire action potentials. However, each of these excitatory inputs appears to exert a unique type of excitatory influence over the accumbens neurons.

In the intact rat, neurons in the nucleus accumbens are constantly bombarded with spontaneously occurring EPSPs, driven predominantly by PFC afferents. These EPSPs are present in neurons that are not firing spontaneously due to the presence of a very hyperpolarized membrane potential. In contrast, a small population of accumbens neurons have a more depolarized membrane potential, enabling them to fire tonically.

However, approximately 60% of the neurons in the accumbens exhibit unique patterns of alternation in their membrane potential that potently modulates spike firing. In these cells, the hyperpolarized, non-firing membrane potential is interrupted by large-amplitude, long-duration, plateau-like depolarizations on which spike firing is generated (Figures 2 and 3). This alternation is a true bimodal distribution in membrane depolarization and cell excitability, in that there is little or no transition between the two states, one at the nonfiring, hyperpolarized state and one at the depolarized level at which the cells fire action potentials (Figures 2 and 3). Indeed, the presence of these depolarizing plateaus is the primary determinant of whether the EPSPs produced in an accumbens cell will lead to the firing of an action potential and transfer of information on to other brain systems that receive inputs from the accumbens (O'Donnell & Grace, 1995b, in press; O'Donnell et al., 1997).

Because of the importance of these plateau depolarizations in controlling activity of accumbens neurons, we performed a series of studies aimed at ascertaining their origin. We found that altering the membrane potential of the cell by current injection, although it potently affected the ability of the cell to discharge action potentials, did not alter the pattern or frequency of these depolarizing events. This suggests that the potentials were not generated by an intrinsic membrane property of the accumbens cell itself but more likely were produced by the influence of afferent inputs. The response that most closely resembled these depolarization plateaus occurred directly following stimulation of the fornix (Figure 2), which supplies input from the subiculum of the hippocampus. The involvement of the hippocampus in generating these plateau depolarizations was confirmed in studies showing that a transection of the fornix eliminated biphasic cell firing in the accumbens and, moreover, that application of lidocaine to the fornix (but not adjacent structures) produced a reversible inactivation of the depolarizing plateaus characteristic of the biphasically active accumbens cells (Figure 3; O'Donnell & Grace, 1995b). From this evidence, it appears that activity within the subiculum of the hippocampus is responsible for the spontaneous generation of plateau membrane depolarizations in ac-

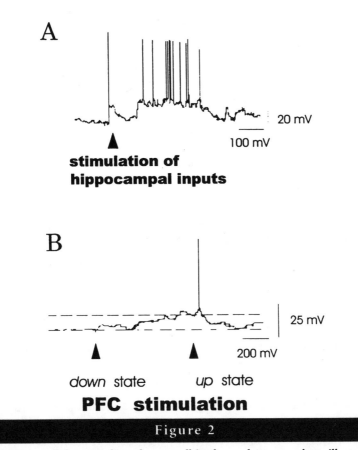

A

20 mV

100 mV

**stimulation of
hippocampal inputs**

B

25 mV

200 mV

down state   *up* state

PFC stimulation

Figure 2

In vivo intracellular recordings from a cell in the nucleus accumbens illustrate the role of the hippocampally driven bistable state in the responsivity of the neuron. (A) Electrical stimulation of the hippocampal input to the accumbens (arrowhead) triggers a short-latency depolarization, which is followed by a prolonged plateau depolarization on which the cell generates spike activity. (B) In contrast, stimulation of the prefrontal cortex (PFC) input to accumbens cells produces a qualitatively different response that depends on the state of the neuron. When the accumbens cell is in the down (hyperpolarized) state, PFC stimulation (left arrowhead) elicits only an excitatory postsynaptic potential that is not sufficient to result in an action potential. However, when the neuron is in the up (depolarized) state, the same amplitude of PFC stimulation (right arrowhead) evokes an action potential, thus allowing information to flow through the accumbens to the ventral pallidum and thalamus.

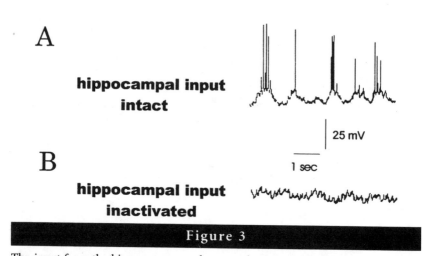

A

**hippocampal input
intact**

| 25 mV

B

**hippocampal input
inactivated**

1 sec

Figure 3

The input from the hippocampus to the accumbens is required for the accumbens neurons to exhibit their biphasic activity. (A) In the intact system, the membrane potential of accumbens neurons spontaneously shifts from a more negative, hyperpolarized state to a depolarized state in which it generates spikes activity. (B) In contrast, when the hippocampal input is inactivated by application of the local anesthetic lidocaine, the accumbens cell is seen to remain in the hyperpolarized state; no depolarization plateaus, spike firing, or transmission of information through the accumbens occurs under these conditions.

cumbens neurons. It is interesting to note that the temporal pattern of the biphasic membrane shifts in accumbens cells corresponds roughly to the frequency of activity rhythms occurring in the entorhinal cortex–hippocampal circuit in the rat (Iijima et al., 1996), further pointing to a relationship between information processing in the hippocampus and changes in excitability in neurons in the accumbens.

HIPPOCAMPAL MODULATION OF PFC
THROUGHPUT IN THE ACCUMBENS

The studies described above demonstrate that the input from the subiculum of the hippocampus to the nucleus accumbens was primarily responsible for permitting spontaneous spike discharge in this structure. However, this input appears to play a more substantial role when one considers its interactions with other inputs to this region. As illustrated previously, stimulation of the PFC produces excitation in the form of an EPSP within accumbens neurons. However, by itself, the excitatory signal provided to accumbens neurons from the PFC does not appear to be sufficiently powerful: Even when a large proportion of these inputs are stimulated to discharge, they can rarely induce a nonactive (hyperpolarized) accumbens neuron to fire an action potential; instead, this stimulation is more likely to elicit only a subthreshold EPSP. However, the net effect of the PFC input on the accumbens neuron appears to depend on the state of the membrane potential. Thus, stimulation of prefrontal inputs in a biphasic cell during the period when it is in a hyperpolarized state produces only a subthreshold EPSP. In contrast, stimulation of the prefrontal afferents when the accumbens cell is exhibiting a plateau membrane depolarization readily evokes spike discharge, followed immediately by a cessation of the plateau potential and a return to the hyperpolarized, nonfiring state. In a similar manner, a plateau depolarization produced by stimulation of the hippocampal inputs enables a normally subthreshold input from the PFC to evoke spike discharge in an accumbens neuron. As a result, activity within the hippocampal–accumbens afferent is required for the PFC input to cause action potential firing in the accumbens cell; whereas in the absence of hippocampal input, the PFC afferent cannot influence the nucleus accumbens cells or their projection sites. In this way, the hippocampus controls information flow through the accumbens by controlling the temporal window within which particular accumbens neurons are in the depolarized state and capable of firing spikes and passing information on to their targets (O'Donnell & Grace, in press).

FUNCTIONAL IMPLICATIONS OF HIPPOCAMPAL GATING IN THE ACCUMBENS

This regulatory control of nucleus accumbens neurons by the hippocampus has important functional implications with regard to normal brain function as well as to schizophrenia. Contextual learning, requiring the formation of associations among multiple cues, is correlated with neuronal activity in the hippocampus (Salzmann, Vidyasagar, &

Creutzfeldt, 1993) and is abolished by lesions of the hippocampus (Phillips & LeDoux, 1992). For example, lesions of the ventral subiculum disrupt the conditioning of fear to a context, such as a chamber with multiple cues, but leave intact the ability to condition fear to individual stimuli (Phillips & LeDoux, 1992); similarly, neurons in the posterior hippocampus respond more reliably to context during learning than to discrete stimuli (Salzmann et al., 1993). Given the devastating effects of hippocampal damage to learning and memory in humans (Squire, 1987), it is likely that the hippocampus and its connections with the nucleus accumbens are necessary for the ability to use memories of relationships between stimuli (contextual memory) to evaluate the present set of stimuli occurring within a particular environmental context and to choose the most effective response strategy from a multitude of possibilities. In contrast, the PFC, interpreted from its position as the most anterior of the precentral (i.e., motor-related) cortices, could be the region in which the multitude of potentially effective behavioral response patterns are generated. By supplying the nucleus accumbens with a context-dependent bias based on set and experience, the hippocampus may be positioned to ultimately influence the selection of a response by facilitating within the nucleus accumbens only the neuronal responses to the prefrontal behavioral commands that are congruent with the current context. As the context shifts, the hippocampal inputs activate a different set of neurons congruent with the new context.

This model system is consistent with some of the observations made in schizophrenia patients. Studies using a variety of paradigms have shown that schizophrenia patients have a deficit in context-dependent associative processes (Hemsley, 1994; Rizzo, Danion, Van Der Linden, & Grange, 1996; Silverstein et al., 1996; van den Bosch, 1995). Furthermore, as outlined previously, schizophrenia patients exhibit deficits in tasks that require PFC involvement, such as the Wisconsin Card Sorting Test. In this task, schizophrenia patients fail to show activation of the PFC when faced with the need to switch strategies (i.e., Berman et al., 1986; Kawasaki et al., 1993; Weinberger et al., 1992); indeed, studies have shown that schizophrenia patients tend to show a concurrent overactivation of the temporal lobe during performance of this task (Weinberger et al., 1992). Our findings may provide a neurophysiological explanation for these results. Thus, in the normal individual, the need to switch strategies is encoded by the hippocampus and the requirement for alteration in strategies is communicated through the subiculum to the nucleus accumbens by means of activation of a new set of neurons. In addition, the cortex is driven to provide a number of additional potential response patterns representing alternate specific solutions to the paradigm. Following activation of the "correct" (i.e., most congruent with the new context) PFC afferent input to the accumbens, hippocampal activity is rapidly restored to baseline (a process that we assume is too rapid to register as an alteration in metabolic activity), while the PFC settles into the "program" for the chosen strategy. If correct, this program can then be reinforced by hippocampal gating of activity within the PFC–accumbens-ventral pallidal-mediodorsal thalamic–PFC loop (see Figure 1). In contrast, we propose that in the schizophrenia patient, there is a failure of the hippocampus to provide context-dependent information to the accumbens. Because this prevents the system from "overriding" the currently selected strategy, the schizophrenia patient shows perseverative behavior, the hippocampal input is not deactivated (which results in maintained increased metabolism in the hippocampus), and the new contextually congruent motor program in the PFC–accumbens-ventral pallidal-mediodorsal thalamic–PFC loop fails to be executed. In this way, disruption of the hippocampal input to the accumbens could contribute to the role of hypofrontality in the perseverative behaviors characteristic of schizophrenia (Goldberg, Weinberger, Berman, Pliskin, & Podd, 1987).

THE AMYGDALA EXERTS A QUALITATIVELY DIFFERENT GATING INFLUENCE OVER INFORMATION FLOW IN THE ACCUMBENS

In addition to the inputs received from the hippocampus and the PFC, neurons in the nucleus accumbens also receive excitatory transmission from afferents that originate in the amygdala (see above). In recent studies, we have found that stimulation of the amygdala can also pro-

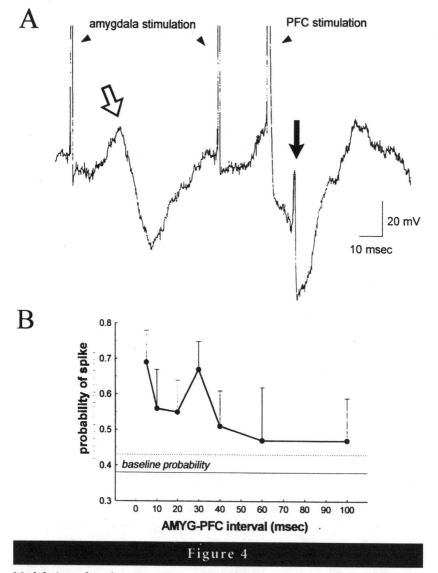

Figure 4

Modulation of nucleus accumbens (NAC) neuronal activity by inputs from the amygdala (AMYG). (A) The extracellular recording trace of an accumbens neuron that fired action potentials in response to stimulation of the prefrontal cortex (PFC) in about 30% of the trials. Stimulation of the amygdalar inputs produces slow potentials (open arrow), which may reflect excitatory synaptic activity in the NAC. When electrical stimulation of the PFC input is applied within 40 ms following

C

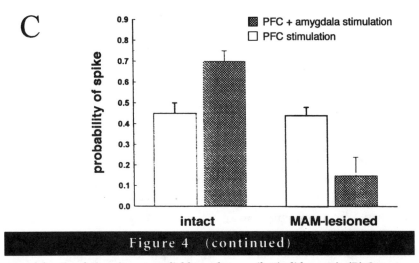

Figure 4 (continued)

amygdala stimulation, it more reliably evokes a spike (solid arrow). (B) Summary of the interaction between amygdala stimulation and PFC-driven spike activity in NAC neurons. The probability of a PFC-evoked spike was significantly increased if the PFC stimulation occurred within 40 ms of the amygdala stimulation. (C) In contrast to normal rats, in adult rats exposed to the mitotoxin methylazoxy-methanol acetate (MAM) early in development, NAC neurons exhibited altered responses to stimulation of their excitatory afferents. In intact animals, amygdala stimulation significantly increased the probability of a PFC-evoked spike (left bars). In MAM-treated rats, this facilitation was abolished, and a trend for an inhibition of PFC-evoked firing was observed (right bars).

vide a gating influence over PFC activity in the nucleus accumbens. However, in this case, the nature of the interaction is different from that observed with the hippocampus. Thus, rather than providing re-petitive, long-duration depolarizing plateaus as the gating signal, stim-ulation of the amygdala will only facilitate prefrontal-evoked spiking if it precedes PFC stimulation by less than 40 ms (Figure 4; Moore & Grace, 1996). As a consequence, the amygdalar input appears to provide more of an event-related gating instead of a more general context-dependent gating, as we proposed for the hippocampal influence. How would such an input be predicted to affect this system? It is evident from numerous studies that the amygdala is involved in affective re-sponses and may mediate the subjective emotional experience of exter-nal stimuli (Aggleton, 1992; Everitt & Robbins, 1992; LeDoux, 1995). Perhaps this provides a means by which potent emotionally charged stimuli that have immediate relevance for the survival of the organism can override an otherwise context-limited response system. This shift in the modulation of PFC-accumbens throughput would accompany the direct outputs from the amygdala to basal forebrain, hypothalamic, and brainstem autonomic and motor centers that would immediately initiate a "fight or flight" response to the perceived threat (Figure 5). For example, one could imagine a case where an individual is engrossed in categorizing butterflies in the field (context) when a bear appears on the scene (affect-generating stimulus). It would be important for such specific stimuli to override the context-dependent gating that would otherwise place ineffective constraints on the response. In this way, the subject could "break out" of the context-limited response profile set up by the hippocampus to allow an amygdala-driven emotional override of response selection to escape a dangerous situation (Figure 5).

PSYCHOTOMIMETIC DRUG ACTIONS IN A NEUROPHYSIOLOGICAL MODEL OF SCHIZOPHRENIA

Although studies using amphetamine have provided evidence suggestive of an involvement of DA in schizophrenia, it is clear that the psycho-pathological change induced by DA agonists is not a precise replica of the schizophrenia patient. Thus, amphetamine psychosis is typically limited to mimicking a paranoid type of psychosis (Angrist, 1994). Moreover, amphetamine appears to exacerbate only the positive (i.e., delusions, hallucinations) symptoms (Angrist, Rotrosen, & Gershon, 1980). Indeed, some have argued that this drug may actually improve cognitive deficits and some negative symptoms in patients that have their positive symptoms under adequate control by antipsychotic drugs (i.e., Daniel et al., 1991; van Kammen & Boronow, 1988). In contrast, the dissociative anesthetic phencyclidine (phenyl-cyclohexyl-piperidine [PCP]) in many respects appears to be a more accurate pharmacological mimic of the schizophrenic disorder. Thus, PCP administration to "normal" humans has been reported to be capable of inducing a broad array of schizophrenia-like symptoms, including positive symptoms, negative

140

symptoms, and disorganizational–formal thought disorder conditions (Luby, Gottlieb, Cohen, Rosenbaum, & Domino, 1962). Perhaps more significant is the manner by which PCP affects schizophrenia patients. Thus, whereas PCP induces a psychotomimetic state in normal humans for hours, when given to schizophrenia patients it causes a psychotic state that is maintained for weeks. Moreover, the condition induced in schizophrenia patients is reported to be one that accurately reflects the symptom profile for that individual patient; that is, it replicates the subtype of schizophrenia as well as the mix of positive and negative symptoms to such an extent that the patient is reported to be unable to distinguish it from a relapse (Javitt & Zukin, 1991; Luby et al., 1962).

A consideration of the pharmacology of PCP may reveal why this drug accurately mimics schizophrenia, in particular, why it is uniquely potent in schizophrenia patients. At psychotomimetic doses, PCP has been classified as a negative allosteric modulator of the n-methyl-D-aspartate(NMDA)-gated channel (Javitt & Zukin, 1991). This means that PCP enters the ion channel activated by stimulation of the NMDA subtype of glutamate receptors, thereby inhibiting ion flow through the channel. In this way, PCP down-modulates glutamatergic processes. In our studies, we found that systemic administration of PCP to a rat had a selective influence on accumbens cell activity; that is, it potently decreased both the amplitude and the frequency of hippocampally driven plateau depolarizations (O'Donnell & Grace, 1997). Therefore, PCP appears to produce an attenuation of hippocampal gating that is analogous to what we proposed to occur in the schizophrenia patient. However, perhaps more significant for schizophrenia is that PCP is a "trapped" channel blocker (Honey, Miljovic, & MacDonald, 1985). As such, it is sufficiently compact, so that once it enters the NMDA channel, the channel pore is capable of "closing" behind the molecule, thereby trapping it inside the channel. In this state, PCP cannot leave the channel unless the channel is again opened by glutamate stimulation. In a human with normal glutamatergic activity, this process should be readily reversible. However, in the schizophrenia patient, in which it has been proposed that a subset of glutamatergic afferents may be hypoactive (M. Carlsson & Carlsson, 1990; Grace, 1991), PCP would have potent and prolonged

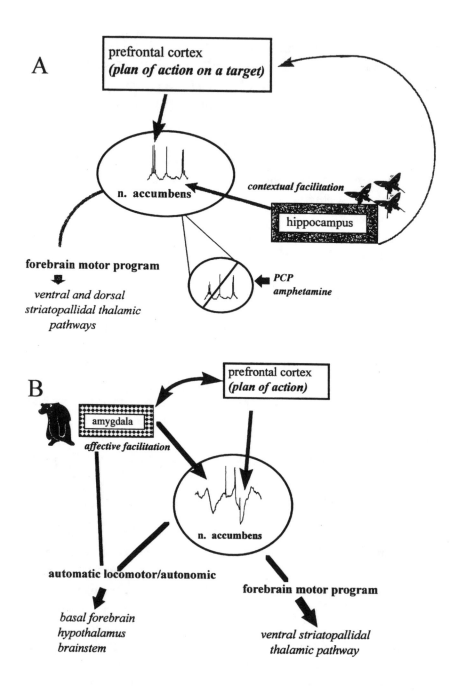

actions specifically at those glutamatergic synapses that have pathologically low levels of excitatory stimulation. Indeed, this may be the mechanism through which PCP can specifically mimic the type of schizophrenic psychopathology present in an individual patient; that is, it would have its most potent inhibitory actions at precisely those synapses that receive inadequate glutamatergic stimulation.

How do the DA-related psychotomimetics fit into this story? One possibility is that the net effect of DA stimulation is at least roughly analogous (but perhaps less selective) to the PCP model, that is, an attenuation of corticoaccumbens throughput. Indeed, we have found that the afferent input to the accumbens arising from the PFC is potently modulated by DA. Thus, administration of low doses of the D_2 DA agonist quinpirole inhibits the ability of the PFC to excite accumbens neurons (O'Donnell & Grace, 1994). Moreover, this inhibition appears to be tonic in nature; that is, it does not require activation of the DA neurons themselves to exert this influence. Thus, the DA system provides a background level of suppression of accumbens cell drive from the PFC.

It is possible that at least some of the psychotic symptoms derived from PCP and amphetamine relate to their common actions on PFC

Figure 5

(*Opposite page*) A schematic representation of how limbic inputs to the nucleus accumbens (n. accumbens) may function when information is processed in a context-dependent condition (A) and when this is interrupted by an emotionally charged event (B). In the context-driven example (A), the individual is limiting his or her information processing to the stimuli that are within a defined context (e.g., butterfly classification). Accordingly, the multiple potential response patterns generated by the prefrontal cortex (e.g., "look at that monarch butterfly," "smell those pretty flowers," "listen to the waterfall in the distance") are filtered according to the present context (i.e., "follow that monarch butterfly"). This context is transferred by the hippocampal input to the nucleus accumbens, which then allows only butterfly-related information to pass on to the thalamus. In contrast, when an emotionally charged, life-threatening stimulus appears (i.e., a bear), the amygdala input is capable of overriding the hippocampally mediated context-limited signaling through the nucleus accumbens to facilitate inputs specifically required to respond to the threat. PCP = phenyl-cyclohexyl-piperidine.

throughput in the accumbens. Thus, PCP can attenuate activation of accumbens neurons by inhibiting hippocampal gating of the PFC. In a similar manner, DA agonists can also attenuate this throughput, in this case, by presynaptically inhibiting PFC stimulation of the accumbens neurons (i.e., O'Donnell & Grace, 1994). Indeed, the two processes may act in concert to yield the complete schizophrenia profile, particularly if one takes developmental issues into account (see also O'Donnell & Grace, in press).

SYNAPTIC PLASTICITY AND THE IMPACT OF NEONATAL HIPPOCAMPAL LESIONS ON LIMBIC SYSTEM FUNCTION IN THE HUMAN ADULT

A new direction of research into the etiology of schizophrenia has attempted to incorporate developmental factors into its etiology. It has been known for some time that schizophrenia is genetically linked; however, even identical twins (who should have identical genetic makeup) only show an approximate 50% concordance for schizophrenia (Torrey, 1992). This implies that it is a genetic load working in concert with "something else" that determines whether an individual develops schizophrenia. Evidence from epidemiological studies has shown that the incidence of schizophrenia among an at-risk population is increased significantly if the mother is afflicted with certain types of influenza during the second trimester of her pregnancy (see references in Weinberger & Lipska, 1995). This has led investigators to explore the potential impact of developmentally induced deficits on the limbic system function. Recent studies by Weinberger and colleagues have suggested that unlike loss of hippocampal function in the adult animal, there may be a unique link between hippocampal pathology early in development and schizophrenia. Thus, although lesions of the ventral hippocampus in adults fail to produce substantial alterations in limbic system-mediated behaviors, if the lesion is performed neonatally, a characteristic behavioral disruption emerges when the rats are tested as adults (Lipska, Jaskiw, & Weinberger, 1993). This deficit is characterized by hyperlocomotion and increased responsiveness to stress and amphetamine and therefore mimics the effects produced by PFC lesions in adult rats (Braun et al., 1993). What is the relationship between a neonatal lesion of the hippocampus and the emergence of dysfunction in the corticoaccumbens DA system in adults? It is unlikely that the deficits themselves are due to the hippocampal pathology because the loss of this structure in the adult fails to similarly affect DA-mediated behaviors. One possibility is that damage to the hippocampus in the neonate triggers a compensatory response in systems in which its input is required for normal function. Indeed, several studies have shown that glutamatergic transmission is required for several types of long-term plastic changes in DA system function (Emmi, Rajabi, & Stewart, 1996; Kalivas, 1995). Furthermore, if this reorganization persists beyond adolescence, the structural changes will become permanent.

The evidence reviewed thus far indicates that lesions of the ventral hippocampus in neonatal but not adult rats leads to changes in DA regulation of limbic system-mediated behaviors in adult animals. One possible explanation for these findings is that the homeostatic compensations produced neonatally in response to hippocampal damage are not an attempt to restore functions mediated by the ventral hippocampus directly but instead are directed toward compensating for the loss of its regulatory influence over other systems. We have provided evidence that within the accumbens the ventral hippocampus potently modulates PFC excitation of accumbens neurons, thereby gating PFC information throughput within this structure. Given this context, one could imagine that damage to this hippocampal gating mechanism would result in an alteration in the other "arm" of this intersection to compensate for this loss of regulation. We propose that this involves changes in the relationship between the corticoaccumbens glutamatergic input and its modulation by DA. As cited earlier, there is substantial evidence that glutamatergic systems exert potent regulatory control over the induction of long-term compensatory changes in the DA system. Thus, it is possible that neonatal damage to the hippocampus results in a reorganization within the corticoaccumbens system and its regulation by DA to compensate for this loss of gating.

DEVELOPMENTAL DISRUPTION MAY ALTER THE BALANCE BETWEEN HIPPOCAMPAL- AND AMYGDALA-REGULATED INFORMATION FLOW

We have recently begun studies using a novel technique for producing developmental disruption of limbic circuit formation by arresting the division and migration of neurons during the period at which the hippocampal projection cells are migrating into their laminar arrangement. Treatment of pregnant dams at prenatal Day 15 with the antimitotic agent methylazoxymethanol acetate (MAM) has been shown to result in lower numbers of projection cells in the temporal cortex, with a dose-dependent disruption in the organization and morphology of the remaining cells (Dambska, Haddad, Kozlowski, Lee, & Shek, 1982; Moore & Grace, 1997). This is consistent with observations made in schizophrenia patient brains (see above) and, as observed in schizophrenia, this loss and disruption of cells is not accompanied by the reactive gliosis or vacuoles characteristic of necrosis (Roberts, 1990). Moreover, rats with this treatment show cognitive deficits analogous to those observed in schizophrenia patients (Hemsley, 1994; Mohammed et al., 1986). Taken together, we consider these neuroanatomical and behavioral effects of prenatal MAM administration be a more accurate approximation of the type of developmental pathology that has been postulated to give rise to schizophrenia in humans (see Akbarian et al., 1993; Arnold et al., 1995; Arnold, Hyman, et al., 1991).

In our preliminary results, we found that rats exposed to MAM prenatally exhibited a unique disruption of PFC gating in the accumbens. Thus, whereas the hippocampus provided a profound gating influence over the PFC input to the accumbens in normal rats, in the MAM-treated animals this effect was absent. Moreover, amygdala stimulation exerted two unique effects in the MAM animals: (a) Amygdala stimulation alone reliably triggered spike discharge in the majority of accumbens neurons and (b) amygdala stimulation actually suppressed the response of accumbens cells to PFC stimulation (Figure 4; Moore & Grace, 1997). One implication of this study is that the developmental disruption not only attenuates hippocampal-mediated, context-dependent gating in the accumbens, it may actually replace it with a primarily affect-dependent gating process mediated by the amygdala. If such a condition exists in the schizophrenic brain, one potential consequence would be that the afflicted individual would fail to use context and experience to select an appropriate response among those proposed by the PFC; instead the patient would produce an amygdala-driven response based solely on the affective nature of the stimulus. Perhaps this could explain why schizophrenia patients often report that they are flooded with emotional stimuli over which they have little control and which appear to guide their inappropriate behavioral responses.

CONCLUSION

Our electrophysiological studies have shown that the cortical inputs from the PFC, hippocampus, and basolateral amygdala to the nucleus accumbens have unique excitatory effects on accumbens cells. More important, the hippocampal and amygdalar inputs gate PFC inputs, facilitating the responses of the accumbens cell to stimulation by its PFC inputs. This evidence is consistent with the idea that the hippocampus selectively permits the PFC activation of accumbens cells on the basis of context, while the amygdalar inputs facilitate PFC signals on the basis of the emotional valence of events (Figure 5). Further studies have indicated that the reduction of hippocampal gating of PFC signals through either a decrease in glutamatergic transmission by PCP or an increase in dopaminergic transmission by amphetamine within the nucleus accumbens may be an important mechanism underlying PCP and amphetamine-induced psychoses. Finally, our preliminary evidence from a rodent model of schizophrenia indicates that developmental disruption of cells in the hippocampus can lead to profound changes in hippocampal and amygdalar gating of PFC-accumbens transmission, which may, in part, underlie the release of behavior from context and the driving of behavior by perceived emotional significance of individual stimuli in the schizophrenia patient.

REFERENCES

Aggleton, J. P. (1992). The functional effects of amygdala lesions in humans: A comparison with findings from monkeys. In J. P. Aggleton (Ed.), *The amygdala* (pp. 485–504). New York: Wiley-Liss.

Akbarian, S., Vinuela, A., Kim, J. J., Potkin, S. G., Bunney, W. E., Jr., & Jones, E. G. (1993). Distorted distribution of nicotinamide-adenine dinucleotide phosphate-diaphorase neurons in temporal lobe of schizophrenics implies anomalous cortical development. *Archives of General Psychiatry, 50*, 178–187.

Alexander, G. E., DeLong, M. R., & Strick, P. L. (1986). Parallel organization of functionally segregated circuits linking basal ganglia and cortex. *Annual Review of Neuroscience, 9*, 357–381.

Altman, J., Everitt, B. J., Glautier, S., Markou, A., Nutt, D., Oretti, R., Phillips, G. D., & Robbins, T. W. (1996). The biological, social and clinical bases of drug addiction: Commentary and debate. *Psychopharmacology, 125*, 285–345.

Altshuler, L. L., Conrad, A., Kovelman, J. A., & Scheibel, A. (1987). Hippocampal pyramidal cell orientation in schizophrenia. A controlled neurohistologic study of the Yakovlev collection. *Archives of General Psychiatry, 44*, 1094–1098.

Amaral, D. G., Price, J. L., Pitkanen, A., & Carmichael, S. T. (1992). Anatomical organization of the primate amygdaloid complex. In J. Aggleton (Ed.), *The amygdala* (pp. 1–66). New York: Wiley-Liss.

Andreasen, N. C., O'Leary, D. S., Cizadlo, T., Arndt, S., Rezai, K., Ponto, L. L. B., Watkins, G. L., & Hichwa, R. D. (1996). Schizophrenia and cognitive dysmetria: A positron-emission tomography study of dysfunctional prefrontal-thalamic-cerebellar circuitry. *Proceedings of the National Academy of Sciences, 93*, 9985–9990.

Andreasen, N. C., Swayze, V., O'Leary, D. S., Nopoulos, P., Cizadlo, T., Harris, G., Arndt, S., & Flaum, M. (1995). Abnormalities in midline attentional circuitry in schizophrenia: Evidence from magnetic resonance and positron emission tomography. *European Neuropsychopharmacology, 5*(Suppl.), 37–41.

Angrist, B. (1994). Amphetamine psychosis: Clinical variations of the syndrome. In A. K. Cho & D. S. Segal (Eds.), *Amphetamine and its analogues* (pp. 387–414). San Diego, CA: Academic Press.

Angrist, B. M., Rotrosen, J., & Gershon, S. (1980). Differential effects of amphetamine and neuroleptics on negative vs. positive symptoms in schizophrenia. *Psychopharmacology, 72,* 17–19.

Arnold, S. E., Franz, B. R., Gur, R. C., Gur, R. E., Shapiro, R. M., Moberg, P. J., & Trojanowski, J. Q. (1995). Smaller neuron size in schizophrenia in hippocampal subfields that mediate cortical–hippocampal interactions. *American Journal of Psychiatry, 152,* 738–748.

Arnold, S. E., Hyman, B. T., Van Hoesen, G. W., & Damasio, A. R. (1991). Some cytoarchitectural abnormalities of the entorhinal cortex in schizophrenia. *Archives of General Psychiatry, 48,* 625-632.

Arnold, S. E., Lee, V. M., Gur, R. E., & Trojanowski, J. Q. (1991). Abnormal expression of two microtubule-associated proteins (MAP2 and MAP5) in specific subfields of the hippocampal formation in schizophrenia. *Proceedings of the National Academy of Sciences, 88,* 10850–10854.

Bachus, S. E., & Kleinman, J. E. (1996). The neuropathology of schizophrenia. *Journal of Clinical Psychiatry, 57*(Suppl.), 72–83.

Berman, K. F., Zec, R. F., & Weinberger, D. R. (1986). Physiologic dysfunction of dorsolateral prefrontal cortex in schizophrenia. II. Role of neuroleptic treatment, attention, and mental effort. *Archives of General Psychiatry, 43,* 126–135.

Bogerts, B. (1993). Recent advances in the neuropathology of schizophrenia. *Schizophrenia Bulletin, 19,* 431–439.

Bogerts, B., Meertz, E., & Schonfeldt-Bausch, R. (1985). Basal ganglia and limbic system pathology in schizophrenia: A morphometric study of brain volume and shrinkage. *Archives of General Psychiatry, 42,* 784–791.

Braun, A. R., Jaskiw, G. E., Vladar, K., Sexton, R. H., Kolachana, B. S., & Weinberger, D. R. (1993). Effects of ibotenic acid lesion of the medial prefrontal cortex on dopamine agonist-related behaviors in the rat. *Pharmacology Biochemistry and Behavior, 46,* 51–60.

Breier, A., Buchanan, R. W., Elkashef, A., Munson, R. C., Kirkpatrick, B. S., Gellad, R. (1992). Brain morphology and schizophrenia: A magnetic resonance imaging study of limbic, prefrontal cortex, and caudate structures. *Archives of General Psychiatry, 49,* 921–926.

Buchsbaum, M. S., Haier, R. J., Potkin, S. G., Nuechterlein, K., Bracha, H. S., Katz, M., Lohr, J., Wu, J., Lottenberg, S., Jerabek, P. A., Trenary, M., Tafalla, R., Reynolds, C., & Bunney, W. E., Jr. (1992). Frontostriatal disorder of cerebral metabolism in never-medicated schizophrenics. *Archives of General Psychiatry, 49,* 935–942.

Carlsson, A., & Lindqvist, M. (1963). Effect of chlorpromazine or haloperidol on formation of 3-methoxytyramine and normetanephrine in mouse brain. *Acta Pharmacolica et Toxicologica, 20,* 140–144.

Carlsson, M., & Carlsson, A. (1990). Interactions between glutamatergic and monoaminergic systems within the basal ganglia—Implications for schizophrenia and Parkinson's disease. *Trends in Neurosciences, 13,* 272–276.

Christie, M. J., James, L. B., & Beart, P. M. (1987). An excitant amino acid projection from the medial prefrontal cortex to the anterior part of nucleus accumbens in the rat. *Journal of Neurochemistry, 45,* 477–482.

Connell, P. H. (1958). *Amphetamine psychosis.* London: Chapman & Hall.

Dambska, M., Haddad, R., Kozlowski, P. B., Lee, M. H., & Shek, J. (1982). Telencephalic cytoarchitectonics in the brains of rats with graded degrees of micrencephaly. *Acta Neuropathologica, 58,* 203–209.

Daniel, D. G., Weinberger, D. R., Jones, D. W., Zigun, J. R., Coppola, R., Handel, S., Bigelow, L. B., Goldberg, T. E., Berman, K. F., & Kleinman, J. E. (1991). The effect of amphetamine on regional cerebral blood flow during cognitive activation in schizophrenia. *Journal of Neuroscience, 11,* 1907–1917.

Devinsky, O., Morrell, M. J., & Vogt, B. A. (1995). Contributions of anterior cingulate cortex to behaviour. *Brain, 118,* 279–306.

Doucet, G., Descarries, L., & Garcia, S. (1986). Quantification of the dopamine innervation in adult rat neostriatum. *Neuroscience, 19,* 427–445.

Eastwood, S. L., Burnet, P. W., & Harrison, P. J. (1995). Altered synaptophysin expression as a marker of synaptic pathology in schizophrenia. *Neuroscience, 66,* 309–319.

Emmi, A., Rajabi, H., & Stewart, J. (1996). Behavioral and neurochemical recovery from partial 6-hydroxydopamine lesions of the substantia nigra is blocked by daily treatment with glutamate receptor antagonists MK-801 and CPP. *Journal of Neuroscience, 16,* 5216–5224.

Everitt, B. J., & Robbins, T. W. (1992). Amygdala-ventral striatal interactions and reward-related processes. In J. P. Aggleton (Ed.), *The amygdala* (pp. 401–430). New York: Wiley-Liss.

Fey, E. T. (1951). The performance of young schizophrenics and young normals on the Wisconsin Card Sorting Test. *Journal of Consulting Psychology, 15,* 311–319.

Goldberg, T. E., & Gold, J. M. (1995). Neurocognitive functioning in patients with schizophrenia: An overview. In F. E. Bloom & D. J. Kupfer (Eds.), *Psychopharmacology: The fourth generation of progress* (pp. 1245–1258). New York: Raven Press.

Goldberg, T. E., Weinberger, D. R., Berman, K. F., Pliskin, N. H., & Podd, M. H. (1987). Further evidence for dementia of the prefrontal type in schizophrenia? A controlled study of teaching the Wisconsin Card Sorting Test. *Archives of General Psychiatry, 44,* 1008–1014.

Grace, A. A. (1991). Phasic versus tonic dopamine release and the modulation of dopamine responsivity: A hypothesis for the etiology of schizophrenia. *Neuroscience, 41,* 1–24.

Groenewegen, H. J., Berendse, H. W., Meredith, G. E., Haber, S. N., Voorn, P., Wolters, J. G., & Lohmann, A. H. M. (1991). Functional anatomy of the ventral, limbic system-innervated striatum. In P. Willner & J. Scheel-Kruger (Eds.), *The mesolimbic dopamine system: From motivation to action* (pp. 19–60). Chichester, England: Wiley.

Heimer, L., & Alheid, G. F. (1991). Piecing together the puzzle of basal forebrain anatomy. In T. C. Napier, P. C. Kalivas, & I. Hanin (Eds.), *The basal forebrain: Anatomy to function* (pp. 1–42). New York: Plenum.

Hemsley, D. R. (1994). A cognitive model for schizophrenia and its possible neural basis. *Acta Psychiatrica Scandinavica, 90*(Suppl.), 80–86.

Hertel, P., Mathe, J. M., Nomikos, G. G., Iurlo, M., Mathe, A. A., & Svensson, T. H. (1995). Effects of d-amphetamine and phencyclidine on behavior and extracellular concentrations of neurotensin and dopamine in the ventral striatum and the medial prefrontal cortex of the rat. *Behavioural Brain Research, 72,* 103–114.

Honey, C. R., Miljovic, Z., & MacDonald, J. F. (1985). Ketamine and phencyclidine cause a voltage-dependent block of responses to L-aspartic acid. *Neuroscience Letters, 61,* 135–139.

Iijima, T., Witter, M. P., Ichikawa, M., Tominaga, T., Kajiwara, R., & Matsumoto,

G. (1996, May 24). Entorhinal–hippocampal interactions revealed by real-time imaging. *Science, 272,* 1176–1179.

Jaber, M., Tison, F., Fournier, M. C., & Bloch, B. (1994). Differential influence of haloperidol and sulpiride on dopamine receptors and peptide mRNA levels in the rat striatum and pituitary. *Molecular Brain Research, 23,* 14–20.

Javitt, D. C., & Zukin, S. R. (1991). Recent advances in the phencyclidine model of schizophrenia. *American Journal of Psychiatry, 148,* 1301–1308.

Johnstone, E. C., Crow, T. J., Frith, C. D., Carney, M. W. P., & Price, J. S. (1978). Mechanism of the antipsychotic effect in the treatment of acute schizophrenia. *Lancet, 1,* 848–851.

Kalivas, P. W. (1995). Interactions between dopamine and excitatory amino acids in behavioral sensitization to psychostimulants. *Drug & Alcohol Dependence, 37,* 95–100.

Kawasaki, Y., Maeda, Y., Suzuki, M., Urata, K., Higashima, M., Kiba, K., Yamaguchi, N., Matsuda, H., & Hisada, K. (1993). SPECT analysis of regional cerebral blood flow changes in patients with schizophrenia during the Wisconsin Card Sorting Test. *Schizophrenia Research, 10,* 109–116.

Kelley, A. E., & Domesick, V. B. (1982). The distribution of the projection from the hippocampal formation to the nucleus accumbens in the rat: An anterograde- and retrograde-horseradish peroxidase study. *Neuroscience, 7,* 2321–2335.

Kirkpatrick, B., & Buchanan, R. W. (1990). The neural basis of the deficit syndrome of schizophrenia. *Journal of Nervous and Mental Disease, 178,* 545–555.

Kuczenski, R., & Segal, D. S. (1994). Neurochemistry of amphetamine. In A. K. Cho & D. S. Segal (Eds.), *Amphetamine and its analogs* (pp. 81–114). San Diego, CA: Academic Press.

Lavin, A., & Grace, A. A. (1994). Modulation of dorsal thalamic cell activity by the ventral pallidum: Its role in the regulation of thalamocortical activity by the basal ganglia. *Synapse, 18,* 104–127.

LeDoux, J. E. (1995). Emotion: Clues from the brain. *Annual Review of Neuroscience, 46,* 209–236.

Liddle, P. F., Friston, K. J., Frith, C. D., Hirsch, S. R., Jones, T., & Frackowiak,

R. S. (1992). Patterns of cerebral blood flow in schizophrenia. *British Journal of Psychiatry, 160,* 179–186.

Lipska, B. K., Jaskiw, G. E., & Weinberger, D. R. (1993). Postpubertal emergence of hyperresponsiveness to stress and to amphetamine after neonatal excitotoxic hippocampal damage: A potential animal model of schizophrenia. *Neuropsychopharmacology, 9,* 67–75.

Luby, E. D., Gottlieb, J. S., Cohen, B. D., Rosenbaum, G., & Domino, E. F. (1962). Model psychoses and schizophrenia. *American Journal of Psychiatry, 119,* 61–67.

Maier, M., Ron, M. A., Barker, G. J., & Tofts, P. S. (1995). Proton magnetic resonance spectroscopy: An in vivo method of estimating hippocampal neuronal depletion in schizophrenia. *Psychological Medicine, 25,* 1201–1209.

McDonald, A. J. (1991). Organization of amygdaloid projections to the prefrontal cortex and associated striatum in the rat. *Neuroscience, 44,* 1–14.

Merchant, K. M., Dobie, D. J., Filloux, F. M., Totzke, M., Aravagiri, M., & Dorsa, D. M. (1994). Effects of chronic haloperidol and clozapine treatment on neurotensin and c-fos mRNA in rat neostriatal subregions. *Journal of Pharmacology and Experimental Therapeutics, 271,* 460–471.

Meredith, G., Pennartz, C., & Groenewegen, H. J. (1993). The cellular framework for chemical signalling in the nucleus accumbens. *Progress in Brain Research, 99,* 3–24.

Mogenson, G., Jones, D. L., & Yim, C. Y. (1984). From motivation to action: Functional interface between the limbic system and the motor system. *Progress in Neurobiology, 14,* 69–97.

Mohammed, A. K., Jonsson, G., Sundstrom, E., Minor, B. G., Soderberg, U., & Archer T. (1986). Selective attention and place navigation in rats treated prenatally with methylazoxymethanol. *Brain Research, 395,* 145–155.

Moore, H., & Grace, A. A. (1996). Interactions between amygdala and prefrontal cortical afferents to the nucleus accumbens and their modulation by dopamine receptor activation. *Society for Neuroscience Abstracts, 22,* 1088.

Moore, H. M., & Grace, A. A. (1997). Anatomical changes in limbic structures produced by methylazoxymethanol acetate (MAM) during brain development are associated with changes in physiological interactions among afferents to the nucleus accumbens. *Society for Neuroscience Abstracts, 23,* 2378.

Nasrallah, H. A., Fowlerm, R. C., & Judd, L. L. (1981). Schizophrenia-like illness following head injury. *Psychosomatics, 22,* 359–361.

O'Donnell, P., & Grace, A. A. (1994). Tonic D_2-mediated attenuation of cortical excitation in nucleus accumbens neurons recorded in vitro. *Brain Research, 634,* 105–112.

O'Donnell, P., & Grace, A. A. (1995a). Different effects of subchronic clozapine and haloperidol on dye coupling between neurons in the rat striatal complex. *Neuroscience, 66,* 763–767.

O'Donnell, P., & Grace, A. A. (1995b). Synaptic interactions among excitatory afferents to nucleus accumbens neurons: Hippocampal gating of prefrontal cortical input. *Journal of Neuroscience, 15,* 3622–3639.

O'Donnell, P., & Grace, A. A. (1997). PCP decreases the up state of bistable accumbens neurons. *Society for Neuroscience Abstracts, 23,* 1282.

O'Donnell, P., & Grace, A. A. (in press). Dysfunctions in multiple interrelated systems as the neurobiological bases of schizophrenic symptom clusters. *Schizophrenia Bulletin.*

O'Donnell, P., Lavin, A., Enquist, L. W., Grace, A., & Card, J. P. (1997). Interconnected parallel circuits between rat nucleus accumbens and thalamus revealed by retrograde transsynaptic transport of pseudorabies virus. *Journal of Neuroscience, 17,* 2143–2167.

Onn, S.-P., & Grace, A. A. (1995). Repeated treatment with haloperidol and clozapine exerts differential effects on dye coupling between neurons in subregions of striatum and nucleus accumbens. *Journal of Neuroscience, 15,* 7024–7036.

Pakkenberg, B. (1990). Pronounced reduction of total neuron number in mediodorsal thalamic nucleus and nucleus accumbens in schizophrenics. *Archives of General Psychiatry, 47,* 1023–1028.

Palmstierna, T., & Wistedt, B. (1987). Absence of acquired tolerance to neuroleptics in schizophrenic patients. *American Journal of Psychiatry, 144,* 1084–1085.

Peroutka, S. J., & Snyder, S. H. (1980). Relationship of neuroleptic drug effects at brain dopamine, serotonin, alpha-adrenergic, and histamine receptors to clinical potency. *American Journal of Psychiatry, 137,* 1518–1522.

Phillips, R. G., & LeDoux, J. E. (1992). Differential contribution of amygdala and hippocampus to cued and contextual fear conditioning. *Behavioral Neuroscience, 106,* 274–285.

Ray, J. P., & Price, J. L. (1992). The organization of the thalamocortical connections of the mediodorsal thalamic nucleus in the rat, related to the ventral forebrain–prefrontal cortex topography. *Journal of Comparative Neurology, 323,* 167–197.

Reynolds, G. (1992). The amygdala and the neurochemistry of schizophrenia. In J. P. Aggleton (Ed.), *The amygdala* (pp. 561–574). New York: Wiley-Liss.

Rizzo, L., Danion, J.-M., Van Der Linden, M., & Grange, D. (1996). Impairment of memory for spatial context in schizophrenia. *Neuropsychology, 10,* 376–384.

Robbins, T. W., Cador, M., Taylor, J. R., & Everitt, B. J. (1989). Limbic–striatal interactions in reward-related processes. *Neuroscience and Biobehavioral Reviews, 13,* 155–162.

Roberts, G. W. (1990). Schizophrenia: The cellular biology of a functional psychosis. *Trends in Neurosciences, 13,* 207–211.

Rossi, A., Stratta, P., Mancini, F., Gallucci, M., Mattei, P., Core, L., Di Michele, V., & Casacchia, M. (1994). Magnetic resonance imaging findings of amygdala-anterior hippocampus shrinkage in male patients with schizophrenia. *Psychiatry Research, 52,* 43–53.

Salzmann, E., Vidyasagar, T. R., & Creutzfeldt, O. D. (1993). Functional comparison of neuronal properties in the primate posterior hippocampus and parahippocampus (area TF/TH) during different behavioural paradigms involving memory and selective attention. *Behavioural Brain Research, 53,* 133–149.

Schuckit, M. A. (1989). *Drug and alcohol abuse: A clinical guide to diagnosis and treatment* (3rd ed.). New York: Plenum Medical.

Sedvall, G., & Farde, L. (1995). Chemical brain anatomy in schizophrenia. *Lancet, 346,* 743–749.

Seeman, P. (1992). Dopamine receptor sequences: Therapeutic levels of neuroleptics occupy D_2 receptors, clozapine occupies D_4. *Neuropsychopharmacology, 7,* 261–284.

Sesack, S. R., Deutch, A. Y., Roth, R. H., & Bunney, B. S. (1989). Topographical organization of the efferent projections of the medial prefrontal cortex in the rat: An anterograde tract-tracing study with phaseolus vulgaris leucoagglutinin. *Journal of Comparative Neurology, 290,* 213–242.

Shapiro, R. M. (1993). Regional neuropathology in schizophrenia: Where are we? Where are we going? *Schizophrenia Research, 10,* 187–239.

Sharp, T., Zetterstrom, T., Ljungberg, T., & Ungerstedt, U. (1987). A direct comparison of amphetamine-induced behaviours and regional brain dopamine release in the rat using intracerebral dialysis. *Brain Research, 401,* 322–330.

Silverstein, S. M., Knight, R. A., Schwarzkopf, S. B., West, L. L., Osborn, L. M., & Kamin, D. (1996). Stimulus configuration and context effects in perceptual organization in schizophrenia. *Journal of Abnormal Psychology, 105,* 410–420.

Squire, L. (1987). *Memory and brain.* New York: Oxford University Press.

Suddath, R. L., Christison, G. W., Torrey, E. F., Casanova, M. F., & Weinberger, D. R. (1990). Anatomical abnormalities in the brains of monozygotic twins discordant for schizophrenia. *New England Journal of Medicine, 322,* 789–794.

Tamminga, C. A., Thaker, G. K., Buchanan, R., Kirkpatrick, B., Alphs, L. D., Chase, T. N., & Carpenter, W. T. (1992). Limbic system abnormalities identified in schizophrenia using positron emission tomography with fluorodeoxyglucose and neocortical alterations with deficit syndrome. *Archives of General Psychiatry, 49,* 522–530.

Torrey, E. F. (1992). Are we overestimating the genetic contribution to schizophrenia? *Schizophrenia Bulletin, 18,* 159–170.

Uylings, H. B., & van Eden, C. G. (1990). Qualitative and quantitative comparison of the prefrontal cortex in rat and in primates, including humans. *Progress in Brain Research, 85,* 31–62.

van den Bosch, R. (1995). Context and cognition in schizophrenia. In J. A. Den Boer, H. G. M. Westenberg, & H. M. van Praag (Eds.), *Advances in the neurobiology of schizophrenia* (pp. 343–366). Chichester, England: Wiley.

van Kammen, D. P., & Boronow, J. J. (1988). Dextro-amphetamine diminishes negative symptoms in schizophrenia. *International Clinical Psychopharmacology, 3,* 111–121.

van Kammen, D. P., Peters, J., & van Kammen, W. B. (1986). Cerebrospinal fluid studies of monoamine metabolism in schizophrenia. *Psychiatric Clinics of North America, 9,* 81–97.

Voorn, P., Jorritsma-Byham, B., Van Dijk, C., & Buijs, R. M. (1986). The dopaminergic innervation of the ventral striatum in the rat: A light- and electron-microscopical study with antibodies against dopamine. *Journal of Comparative Neurology, 251,* 84–99.

Weinberger, D. R., Berman, K. F., Suddath, R., & Torrey, E. F. (1992). Evidence of dysfunction of a prefrontal-limbic network in schizophrenia: A magnetic resonance imaging and regional cerebral blood flow study of discordant monozygotic twins. *American Journal of Psychiatry, 149,* 890–897.

Weinberger, D. R., & Lipska, B. K. (1995). Cortical maldevelopment, antipsychotic drugs, and schizophrenia: A search for common ground. *Schizophrenia Research, 16,* 87–110.

Young, W. S., III, Alheid, F. G., & Heimer, L. (1984). The ventral pallidal projection to the mediodorsal thalamus: A study with fluorescent retrograde tracers and immunohistofluorescence. *Journal of Neuroscience, 4,* 1626–1638.

PART TWO

Neurocognitive Processes

6

How Are Deficits in Motion Perception Related to Eye-Tracking Dysfunction in Schizophrenia?

Philip S. Holzman, Yue Chen, Ken Nakayama,
Deborah L. Levy, and Steven Matthysse

In 1973, Holzman, Proctor, and Hughes published a short article reporting that schizophrenia patients showed an abnormality in following a smoothly moving target with their eyes. Subsequent reports showed that the same abnormality occurred in about 40% of the first-degree relatives of schizophrenia patients; that the phenomenon was not a function of neuroleptic drug treatment, measurement artifact, population characteristics, or inattention; and that performance remained stable over time, even when measurements were separated by several years (Iacono & Lykken, 1981; Levy, Lipton, Holzman, & Davis, 1983). Several replications of the essential findings quickly appeared, the earliest being those of Iacono and Lykken (1979) and Shagass, Amadeo, and Overton (1974). Reviews, appearing periodically during the intervening 25 years, have recounted the many replications of the basic phenomenon, the most recent by Levy, Holzman, Matthysse, and Mendell (1993). In this chapter, we explore the nature of this abnormality and trace one of its components to a disorder in speed discrimination. After a brief description of the attributes of smooth pursuit eye move-

This work was supported by National Institute of Mental Health Grants MH 31154, MH 31340, MH 49487, MH 44866, and MH 01021, by a grant from the Roy A. Hunt Foundation, and by a Scottish Rite Schizophrenia Fund research grant.

ments, we review some representative studies that explore the abnormalities in those eye movements in schizophrenia patients. We then trace the origin of a specific aspect of smooth pursuit dysfunction in schizophrenia to relatively insensitive velocity discrimination.

The phenomenon of abnormal pursuit in schizophrenia was at first puzzling simply because there was no obvious connection between an impairment in eye tracking and schizophrenia. This riddle became more perplexing when our laboratory conducted two studies of monozygotic and dizygotic twins discordant for clinical schizophrenia that showed a pattern of twin concordance for eye-tracking dysfunction (ETD) that fit a model of dominant inheritance, in spite of the twins being discordant for the clinical features of schizophrenia; the studies found essentially a 2:1 ratio in concordance for ETD (Holzman, Kringlen, Levy, & Haberman, 1980; Holzman et al., 1977). Whatever the pathophysiology of ETD, it appeared that it was genetically transmitted. Additional studies established that lithium carbonate could produce ETD in patients with bipolar disorders, producing an elevated rate of ETD in this clinical group. The familial aggregation of ETD, however, was restricted to the relatives of schizophrenia patients (Holzman, O'Brian, & Waternaux, 1991; Levy et al., 1985). The normal population prevalence seems to be at about 8% (Levy et al., 1983).

SMOOTH PURSUIT EYE MOVEMENTS

A brief digression is necessary to describe some characteristics about normal smooth pursuit eye movements (SPEM). Figure 1 schematically represents a target, say a small spot of light, which is at first stationary and then begins to move slowly to the right. In an unimpaired SPEM, there is a latency of about 120 ms before the eye begins to move and accelerate in speed in the direction of the target. After about 200 ms, the person becomes aware that the target is not on the fovea and a *saccadic,* or rapid eye movement, swiftly places the eye on the target, after which eye velocity matches target velocity. If after a few seconds the target moves abruptly back to its starting point, the eye, nevertheless, continues to follow the target's trajectory for about 200 ms—the approximate latency for a saccadic eye movement—even though the

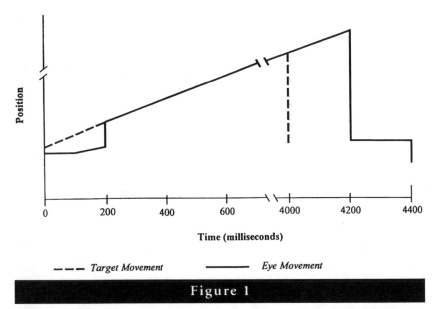

Position (y-axis)

Time (milliseconds) (x-axis)

0   200   400   600   4000   4200   4400

— — — *Target Movement*   ———— *Eye Movement*

Figure 1

Schematic representation of smooth pursuit eye movements. Target trajectory is indicated by the dotted line, eye movement by the solid line; 120 ms after the onset of the target movement, the eye begins an accelerated smooth pursuit. To match fovea and target, a saccadic eye movement is generated at about 200 ms. In normal smooth pursuit, eye and target velocity are matched. The diagram shows a return of the target to its origin after 4000 ms. After a 200-ms delay in the eye movement, a saccadic eye movement is generated, which falls short of the target, necessitating another refoveating saccade 200 ms later.

target has changed its path. The eye then makes a corrective saccade to refoveate the target, but the saccade fails to place the fovea on the target because the saccade matches the extent of the target's jump. Two hundred milliseconds later a corrective saccade refoveates the target.

A SEARCH FOR THE ROOTS OF ETD

The difference between qualitatively normal eye tracking and ETD (Figure 2) is quickly grasped by the viewer, although it is not possible to specify what the defect is without quantifying the main features of performance. Several investigators proposed that the essence of ETD was low steady-state, or *closed-loop*, gain and excessive numbers of sac-

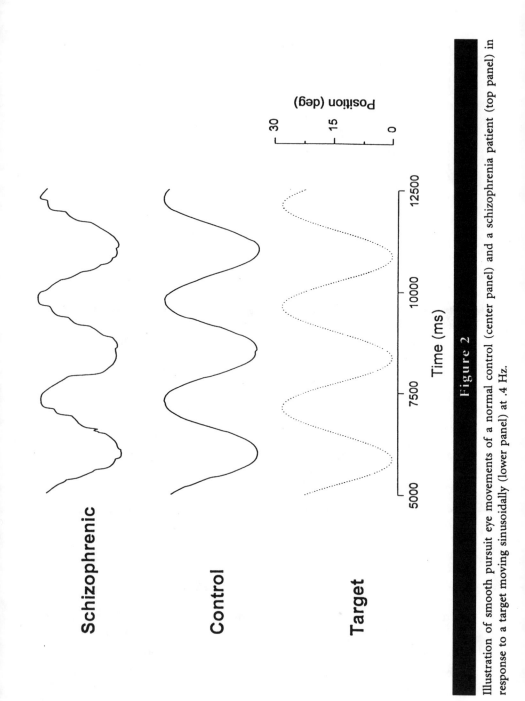

Figure 2

Illustration of smooth pursuit eye movements of a normal control (center panel) and a schizophrenia patient (top panel) in response to a target moving sinusoidally (lower panel) at .4 Hz.

cadic eye movements that are principally corrective (e.g., Abel, Fried-man, Jesberger, Malki, & Meltzer, 1991; Abel & Ziegler, 1988). Closed-loop gain is a measure of eye speed; it is computed as the ratio of eye velocity to target velocity. A gain of 1.0 indicates a perfect match between the speed of the target and the speed of the eye. This pattern of low gain with increased rates of catch-up saccades is found in a variety of central nervous system conditions, such as supranuclear palsy, Parkinson's disease, and hemispheric lesions (Leigh & Zee, 1991). Other investigators proposed that intrusive saccades, such as anticipatory saccades and square wave jerks, are characteristic of schizophrenia patients. Although measures such as closed-loop gain and saccade frequency are relevant, their usefulness has been limited because the statistical methods used to document their relevance ignore the well-known heterogeneity of schizophrenia patients with respect to eye tracking. Because schizophrenia patients comprise a mixture of two groups—those with qualitatively normal eye tracking and those with ETD—the results of comparisons of schizophrenia patients as a single group with normal controls are inherently unstable. Whether schizophrenia patients differ from normal controls depends on the proportion of patients with ETD. Therefore, when comparing the eye tracking of schizophrenia patients as a group with the eye tracking of normal controls, it is necessary to compare the several parameters of eye-tracking performance of schizophrenia patients with ETD and those with normal eye tracking and then compare both groups with normal controls (Levy et al., 1993).

Another parameter of eye tracking is *open-loop* gain, which is a measure of the extent to which a person responds to a perception of movement without benefit of any feedback from a response or from a detection of a position change in the target. Levin et al. (1988), using the search-coil method for recording eye movements, was able to detect a severe impairment in open-loop gain in schizophrenia patients. Although only five patients were involved, there was no overlap between the patients and a control group. Open-loop gain refers to the acceleration of the eye 120 ms after a pursuit target beings to move; it is best measured using a "step-ramp" target, first introduced by Rashbass (1961). Figure 3 shows a step-ramp target. The target first steps a few

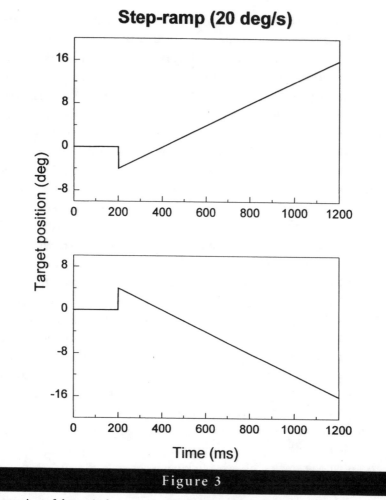

Step-ramp (20 deg/s)

Figure 3

Illustration of the typical step-ramp (Rashbass, 1961) target. The target is stationary before it steps a few degrees either to the right (top panel) or left (lower panel), after which it begins immediately to move smoothly in the direction opposite to that of the step and crosses the midline within 200 ms.

degrees in one direction and then begins to move smoothly in the opposite direction, recrossing the zero line in 200 ms or a bit less. By having the target recross the midline in less than 200 ms (the latency of a saccade), Rashbass was able to eliminate the early initial saccade that accompanies SPEM (see Figure 1), demonstrating that the pursuit and saccadic systems were independent.

Many studies have shown that the characteristics of saccadic eye movements to a stationary target, such as latency, accuracy, and the relation of these parameters to each other, were normal in schizophrenia patients (e.g., Iacono, Tuason, & Johnson, 1981; Levin, Holzman, Rothenberg, & Lipton, 1981; Levin, Jones, Stark, Merrin, & Holzman, 1982). But a few studies, however, reported that saccades to moving targets fell short of the target, that is, were hypometric.

Some attempts to identify the essential abnormality in ETD in schizophrenia patients have relied on extrapolations from extirpation studies in lower primates and on reasoning from the effects of other central nervous system diseases. These attempts—reasoning by analogy—have not been particularly illuminating. Other attempts have relied on new imaging techniques. For example, a positron emission tomography study by Gillian O'Driscoll et al. (in press) identified several areas that show selective increases in regional cerebral blood flow during smooth pursuit, compared with saccadic eye movements. These include dorsomedial cuneus (Area V3A)—the human analogue of the middle temporal–medial superior temporal (MT–MST) areas, the striate cortex, and a region in the dorsal intraparietal (IP) sulcus as well as Area 9 in the superior frontal gyrus (O'Driscoll et al., in press). A complex network is clearly involved in generating normal SPEM. Therefore, the search for a special area or a special group of cells that is the seat of SPEM, and consequently harbors the secret of ETD, is quixotic.

The distinguished British neurologist, John Hughlings Jackson (1835–1911), formulated principles for the functional organization of the brain, which even today are unsurpassed. Following Jackson's model, we suggest that SPEM, like most complex psychological functions, is organized in a vertical manner in the central nervous system, with multiple representations: first at the level of the brain stem or lower, next at a sensory cortical level, and last at the highest level, that of the frontal cortex. Multiple and redundant representations of functions are the rule in the nervous system. The more complex the behavior, the more parts of the brain are involved. For the most part, brain–behavior relations rely on networks, systems, and subsystems rather than single loci. Furthermore, there is more than one way to accomplish approximately the same behavior, and therefore several subsystems may be activated at the same time, in parallel, when one responds to a behavioral intention or demand. Thus, impairment of any one section of a system affects the behavior regulated by that system and results in a reorganization of the system. We can, however, seek a localized site for the simplest of the functions—like the perception of color or of movement—that are involved in a complex behavior like SPEM.

THE FOCUS ON MOTION DISCRIMINATION

Our recent attempts to probe into the nature of ETD in schizophrenia patients have focused on motion perception. We could, of course, have focused on the motor component of SPEM, but for several reasons we realized that the perceptual aspects of SPEM were the more strategic starting places that would lead to the uncovering of a key abnormality. First, we recognized that the slow eye movements of schizophrenia patients are normal if the oculomotor system is stimulated vestibularly or through the brain stem (Lipton, Levin, & Holzman, 1980). For example, in the smooth phase of a vestibularly driven nystagmus, another slow eye movement, schizophrenia patients show none of the characteristics ETD when stimulated by the requirement to follow a moving target (Levy, Holzman, & Proctor, 1978). Full-field optokinetic nystagmus, another vestibularly driven behavior, is also normal in contrast to partial-field optokinetic nystagmus, which shows the characteristics of ETD (Latham, Holzman, Manschreck, & Tole, 1981). Thus, there is no reason to believe that the motor components of SPEM or of saccadic eye movements, for that matter, are impaired in schizophrenia patients.

The investigation of the perception of motion presents a challenge with respect to where to begin and what methods to use. Over 20 areas of the extrastriate visual cortex have been identified as playing a major role in the visual experience of monkeys. Some of these make contributions to the detection of color, others to form. At least two of these areas in extrastriate regions play an important role in the processing of moving stimuli: the area MT and the MST area. Both MT and MST respond vigorously when pursuit eye movements are executed, and lesions of MT temporarily impair the capacity to detect motion. The MT area has a high number of cells that respond to objects moving in one direction and other cells that respond to movement in another direction. Several independent studies have shown that the pursuit system responds to the velocity of a target in a manner similar to the response of cells known to be involved in visual motion processing in areas MT and MST (Movshon, Lisberger, & Krauzlist, 1990; Newsome & Pare, 1988; Newsome, Wurtz, Dursteler, & Mikami, 1985).

We decided to measure the speed discrimination of schizophrenia patients for two reasons: (a) There are specific motion sensitive areas in the brain and (b) at least one of the quantitative parameters of ETD involves a poor match between the speed of the eye and of the target. The time honored method of psychophysics presented us with the opportunity to measure not only the motion discrimination thresholds of our participants but also other aspects of visual experience that involve very similar judgments and, therefore, serve as control or comparison measurements. One way to assess motion perception is to examine how much contrast is needed to perform a specific motion task. We know, for example, that when there is an abnormality in the processing of visual signals, such as detection of motion, direction of motion, or slant orientation, the task requires much higher contrast to be performed accurately—if it can be performed at all (Nakayama, 1985; Pasternak, 1987; Pasternak & Merrigan, 1994; Plant & Nakayama, 1993; Watson, Barlow, & Robson, 1983). It is true, of course, with many visual functions. For example, when one needs to read very small type, one requires more brightness than if the type were large. Thus, contrast sensitivity provides a common measurement for assessing the functional integrity of motion and other visual-processing tasks.

We measured the contrast sensitivities for a (a) velocity discrimination, (b) detection of contrast, (c) detection of the direction of slant (orientation), and (d) detection of direction of motion. Figure 4 illus-

1. Velocity Discrimination

Which one moves faster?

2. Detection

Which one contains gratings?

3. Orientation Discrimination

Do gratings tilt to the right?

4. Direction Discrimination

Do gratings move to the right?

Figure 4

Diagrammatic representation of the four motion perception tasks: (a) detection of velocity differences between two moving gratings by recognizing which is moving faster, (b) detection of contrast differences by asking which circle contains the grating, (c) detection of orientation by asking which grating tilts to the right, and (d) detection of motion by asking which grating moves to the right. Differences between schizophrenia patients and normals were reliably obtained for detecting differences in velocity.

trates the four tasks that made up our set of motion discrimination studies. We performed two studies. The first study was part of the doctoral dissertation of German Palafox (1993), conducted in our laboratory and in the Vision Sciences Laboratory of Harvard. Palafox tested 19 schizophrenia patients and 15 control participants. The patients were recruited from a private mental hospital in the Boston (MA) area. Diagnoses were made according to *The Diagnostic and Statistical Manual of Mental Disorders* (3rd ed., rev. [*DSM-III-R*]; American Psychiatric Association, 1987) criteria, as determined from a chart review supplemented by information from the Structured Clinical Interview for *DSM-III-R* (patient version; SCID-P; Spitzer, Williams, Gibbon, & First, 1990), performed by trained interviewers. The normal control participants were experienced in making psychophysical judgments and, therefore, represented a very specialized group. The details of the psychophysical method are presented in Palafox's dissertation and in Chen et al. (in press).

The normal control participants in this first study had very low thresholds; that is, they required comparatively little contrast for all of the visual tasks and were significantly better than the schizophrenia patients at making the psychophysical judgments, although the differences were not dramatic. This superiority no doubt reflected the experience the control participants had in making these judgments. On the tasks that called for speed discriminations, however, the groups diverged most dramatically. As it became more difficult to judge which of the two gratings was moving faster (i.e., when the differences in speed were relatively small), the patients required 2–3 log units more contrast to make those judgments accurately. Figure 5 shows this result.

We repeated this experiment with another group of 15 schizophrenia patients and another control group of 19 participants who, this time, were as unpracticed in making psychophysical judgments as were the patients. All patients had been discharged from the hospital at least 6 months prior to the testing and were in various states of remission at the time of the study. Diagnoses were based on a standardized interview (SCID) and a review of all hospital records conducted by trained interviewers who were unaware of the nature of the study. Nor-

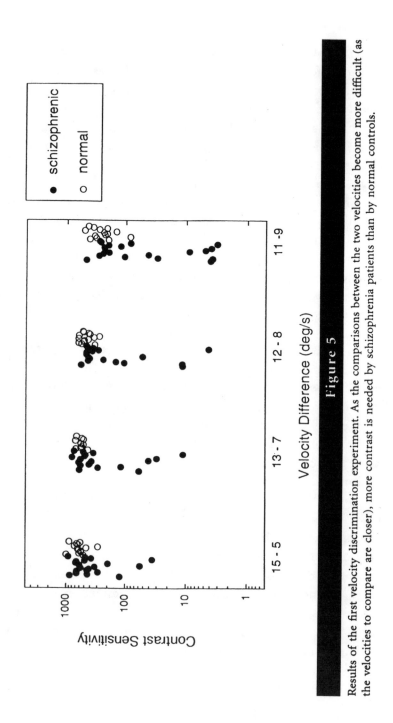

Figure 5

Results of the first velocity discrimination experiment. As the comparisons between the two velocities become more difficult (as the velocities to compare are closer), more contrast is needed by schizophrenia patients than by normal controls.

mal control participants were also interviewed with the SCID. None of the controls met *DSM-III-R* criteria for any psychotic disorder.

In this second study (Chen et al., in press), essentially identical to the first, the patients differed from the control participants only on the most difficult speed discrimination tasks, which were presented around two frequencies: 10°/s and 20°/s. The groups did not differ with respect to contrast discrimination and orientation discrimination. Figure 6 shows these results.

To determine the stability of the thresholds, we retested four schizophrenia patients and four normal control participants on all of the tasks in the second study. The retesting took place over a 2-month period after the first testing. The results showed highly reliable thresholds on all of the tests: contrast detection, orientation discrimination, and speed discrimination. All of the participants maintained a stable threshold level, indicating that the judgment of speed discrimination is stable over time. The finding in the two experiments that speed discrimination is impaired in schizophrenia patients and that this impairment is characteristic of the person has validity.

We were now ready to examine the relation between these stable differences in velocity discrimination and the SPEM performances of the patients.

RELATION OF MOTION DISCRIMINATION TO ETD

The 15 schizophrenia and 19 normal participants were tested on a battery of SPEM tasks, which included several variations in target presentation. For this study, we analyzed responses to two of these targets, a sine wave and a step-ramp target. The target was a small circle of light that transcribed 1.25° of visual angle and was displayed 22 in. (55.88 cm) in front of the person.

For the trials using a sine wave target, the circle of light oscillated horizontally at .4 Hz, with an amplitude of $\pm$ 12°. The peak velocity of this target was about 30°/s. Two 30-s trials were administered to each person.

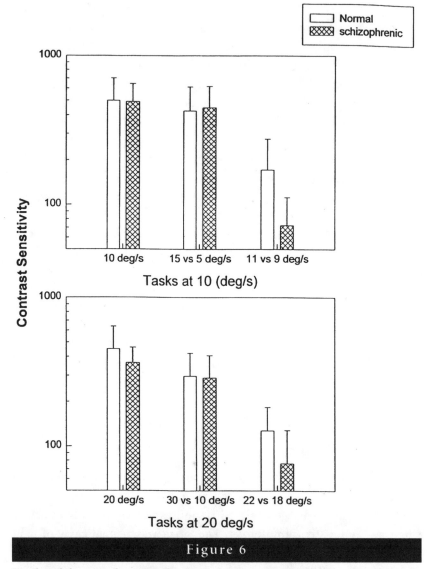

Figure 6

Results of the second motion discrimination experiment. The first comparison in each panel shows that contrast sensitivity does not differ between the schizophrenia patients and the controls. At speeds that differ widely (15°/s vs. 5°/s and 30°/s vs. 10°/s), the patients perform as well as the normal controls. At velocities that are closer together (11°/s vs. 9°/s and 22°/s vs. 18°/s), however, significantly more contrast is required by the patients to see the velocity differences.

For the step-ramp targets, the target first stepped either to the right or to the left a specified amount, in accordance with Rashbass's (1961) computations for eliminating the initial saccade (actually 1°, 2°, and 4° for the 5°, 10°, and 20°/s targets). After the step, the target moved horizontally at a constant speed of 5°, 10°, or 20°/s in the direction opposite to that of the step. The ramp component for each trial began 200 ms after the initial step. Direction and speed were randomized, so that the trials were unpredictable, which was in contrast to the sine wave trials whose trajectory was predictable. Three sets of eight trials were administered, so that each target in each direction was administered four times.

All participants and patients were fitted with spectacle frames on which were mounted photodiodes that project infrared light and sensors that receive the reflections of that infrared light from the eyes. This position information was fed into a computer, where it was amplified and digitized and then saved for later analysis. The sampling rate was 1 ms. The testing was preceded by calibration runs, which were repeated at several points during the testing. All participants and patients viewed the target on a computer monitor, with their head immobilized by a custom-fitted bite bar.

Relation of Motion Detection Sensitivity to Onset of Pursuit

Open-loop gain, as we indicated above, is a measure of the observer's response to the perception of the moving target before there is any feedback from the movement of the eye itself. It is assessed from a measurement of eye acceleration during the first 120 ms after the target begins to move (the second derivative of the eye position during that period). In normal responses, the eye starts to accelerate, trying to match eye velocity to target velocity. The magnitude of the acceleration varies linearly with the speed of the target (up to a certain speed); as expected, in our study, the mean open-loop gain values for all participants increased as the target velocity increased from 5°/s to 10°/s to 20°/s. As can be seen from Figure 7, the initial accelerations increased in a linear manner for the normal control group. For the schizophrenia

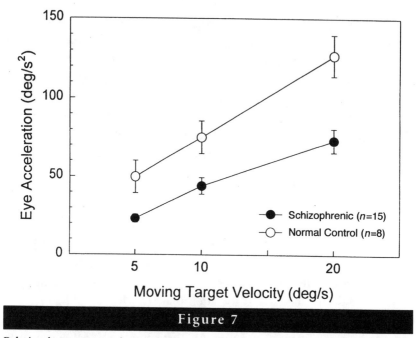

Figure 7

Relation between open-loop gain (acceleration of the eye 120 ms after target move-ment) and target velocity in schizophrenia patients and normal control partici-pants. Initial acceleration is significantly lower in schizophrenia patients at all target speeds—a difference that increases with increasing target speed.

patients, however, the initial acceleration of the eye is strikingly low for all three target speeds. The patients and control participants differed from each other at all of the target ramp speeds, although the differ-ences were greatest at the fastest ramp speed of 20°/s. These data are consistent with previous findings with respect to open-loop gain (e.g., Levin et al., 1988; see also Clementz & McDowell, 1994).

We computed the correlations between initial acceleration at 120 ms following the onset of target movement (open-loop gain) and speed discrimination thresholds. These correlations are highly significant, in-dicating that initial acceleration of pursuit movements for the step-ramp targets was related to speed discrimination sensitivity. For ex-ample, at the moderate ramp speeds of 10°/s and motion discrimination around the 10°/s baseline, the correlation between speed discrimination and open-loop gain was .70. These relations are described in more detail in Chen et al. (in press).

Figure 8 illustrates the open-loop gain tracings of a schizophrenia patient and a normal control. The control participant tracing shows a gradual increase in velocity after the target has begun its ramp trajectory, depicted by the quadratic slope. The patient tracing, in contrast, shows no such acceleration of eye movement; the eye does not move. After about 200 ms, there is a saccadic eye movement that refoveates the target, indicating that the patient detected movement of the target much later than the normal control did and then responded to the target's position change rather than to its initial movement. Thus, the normal control participant began eye movement smoothly about 120 ms after the target began to move. The schizophrenia patients, however, began their eye movements with a saccade 200 ms after the target moved or with a smooth pursuit movement with very low acceleration.

Relation of Motion Detection Sensitivity to Maintenance of Pursuit

We examined the relation of the velocity discrimination thresholds to three measures of maintenance of pursuit, that is, to the integrity of SPEM after the pursuit response had begun. The measures were peak steady-state gain, saccade frequency, and a qualitative rating of ETD on a 5-point scale. All of these parameters were assessed from the pursuit of the .4 Hz sine wave.

Peak steady-state gain was measured by computing the ratio of the velocity of the eye to the velocity of the target when the target was at or near its maximum speed, after first discarding from the computation all saccades, blinks, and artifacts. We determined that the mean peak gain scores of the schizophrenia patients with qualitative ratings of ETD was .73 ($\pm$ .07), compared with .80 ($\pm$ .04) for the normal group. This difference was statistically significant. Peak steady-state gain scores were significantly related to velocity discrimination thresholds: For gratings moving at 10°/s, the correlation was .53; for gratings moving at 20°/s, the correlation was .32. The former correlation coefficient is signifi-

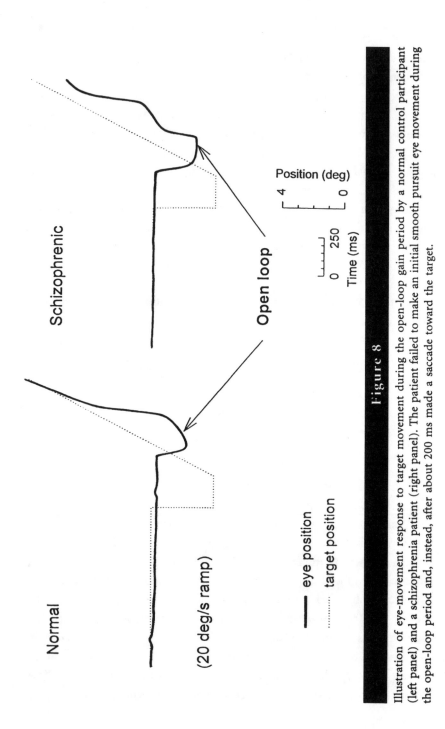

Figure 8

Illustration of eye-movement response to target movement during the open-loop gain period by a normal control participant (left panel) and a schizophrenia patient (right panel). The patient failed to make an initial smooth pursuit eye movement during the open-loop period and, instead, after about 200 ms made a saccade toward the target.

cantly different from 0; the latter is not, undoubtedly because of insufficient power. Thus, patients with lower peak steady-state pursuit gain had elevated speed discrimination thresholds.

With respect to saccade frequency, schizophrenia patients differed from the normal controls, in that the patients produced significantly more saccades during SPEM than did the normal controls. The correlation between number of saccades during SPEM and speed sensitivity thresholds, however, was not significant.

Seven of the 15 schizophrenia patients manifested ETD, which is within the prevalence reported for other groups of schizophrenia patients (Levy et al., 1993). None of the correlations between speed discrimination thresholds and qualitative ratings, however, was significantly different from zero.

It therefore appears that the qualitative ratings of SPEM and saccade frequency are unrelated to the sensitivity of detection of differences in velocity. When sustained pursuit was measured by a purer measure of eye speed, steady-state gain (or peak gain), however, there was a significant relation between speed discrimination thresholds and SPEM maintenance.

CONCLUSION

Our data show a strong relation between impairments in speed discrimination and those parameters of SPEM that include speed measurements. Thus, peak gain and open-loop gain are significantly related to the psychophysically measured contrast thresholds for speed discrimination. Contrast sensitivity per se and orientation sensitivity, however, are not. Other measures of integrity of SPEM that have been used in studies of schizophrenia patients that have shown themselves to be predictive of the presence of schizophrenia or family membership in which there is a schizophrenia patient, such as the qualitative score, were unrelated to speed discrimination. Clearly, the qualitative score, a complex measure, includes more than gain assessments. It includes the extent to which the eye is on the target and may be off the target by events other than slower eye speed. It also includes extraretinal events not taken into account in the measures of gain.

To understand the relations between speed discrimination to SPEM in schizophrenia, we must take note of the fact that the processing of visual stimuli is carried out in many different areas of the visual system. These separate areas contribute unique qualities to the sensory experience, such as the perception of form, slant, color, and movement (Ungerleider & Mishkin, 1982; Wurtz, Komatsu, Yamasaki, & Dursteler, 1990; Zeki, 1974). We also know that areas MT and MST play a principal role in the adaptive control of eye movements, including SPEM, both at the onset of pursuit and the maintenance of pursuit. There is also evidence that these areas are not the sole contributors to motion processing.

Our studies suggest strongly that areas MT and MST are implicated in the ETD of schizophrenia patients. But this relationship is not the complete explanation of the ETD found in schizophrenia patients and their relatives. Imaging studies in coordination with further psychological parsing of the pursuit task can help to explain more of the process involved in the eye-tracking patterns in schizophrenia patients.

REFERENCES

Abel, L. A., Friedman, L., Jesberger, J. A., Malki, A., & Meltzer, H. Y. (1991). Quantitative assessment of smooth pursuit gain and catch-up saccades in schizophrenia and affective disorders. *Biological Psychiatry, 29,* 1063–1072.

Abel, L. A., & Ziegler, A. (1988). Smooth pursuit eye movements in schizophrenics: What constitutes quantitative assessment? *Biological Psychiatry, 24,* 747–761.

American Psychiatric Association. (1987). *Diagnostic and statistical manual of mental disorders* (3rd ed., rev.). Washington, DC: Author.

Chen, Y., Palafox, G., Nakayama, K., Levy, D. L., Matthysse, S., & Holzman, P. S. (in press). Motion perception in schizophrenia. *Archives of General Psychology.*

Clementz, B. A., & McDowell, J. E. (1994). Smooth pursuit in schizophrenia: Abnormalities of open- and closed-loop responses. *Psychophysiology, 31,* 79–86.

Holzman, P. S., Kringlen, E., Levy, D. L., & Haberman, S. (1980). Deviant eye tracking in twins discordant for psychosis. *Archives of General Psychiatry, 37,* 627–631.

Holzman, P. S., Kringlen, E., Levy, D. L., Proctor, L. R., Haberman, S., & Yasillo, N. J. (1977). Abnormal pursuit eye movement in schizophrenia: Evidence for a genetic marker. *Archives of General Psychiatry, 34,* 802–805.

Holzman, P. S., O'Brian, C., & Waternaux, C. (1991). Effects of lithium treatment on eye movements. *Biological Psychiatry, 29,* 1001–1015.

Holzman, P. S., Proctor, L. R., & Hughes, D. W. (1973, July 13). Eye tracking in schizophrenia. *Science, 181,* 179–181.

Iacono, W. G., & Lykken, D. T. (1979). Eye tracking and psychopathology: New procedures applied to a sample of normal monozygotic twins. *Archives of General Psychiatry, 36,* 1361–1369.

Iacono, W. G., & Lykken, D. T. (1981). 2 year retest stability of eye tracking performance and comparison of electrooculographic and infra-red recording techniques: Evidence of EEG in the electro-oculogram. *Psychophysiology, 18,* 49–55.

Iacono, W. G., Tuason, V. B., & Johnson, R. A. (1981). Dissociation of smooth pursuit and saccadic eye tracking in remitted schizophrenics. *Archives of General Psychiatry, 38,* 991–996.

Latham, C., Holzman, P. S., Manschreck, T., & Tole, J. (1981). Optokinetic nystagmus and pursuit eye movements in schizophrenia. *Archives of General Psychiatry, 38,* 997–1003.

Leigh, R. J., & Zee, D. S. (1991). *The neurology of eye movements* (2nd ed.) Philadelphia: Davis.

Levin, S., Holzman, P. S., Rothenberg, S. J., & Lipton, R. B. (1981). Saccadic eye movements in psychotic patients. *Psychiatry Research, 5,* 47–58.

Levin, S., Jones, A., Stark, L., Merrin, E. L., & Holzman, P. S. (1982). Saccadic eye movements of schizophrenic patients measured by reflected light technique. *Biological Psychiatry, 17,* 1277–1287.

Levin, S., Luebke, A., Zee, D., Haines, T., Robinson, D. R., & Holzman, P. S. (1988). Smooth pursuit eye movements in schizophrenics: Quantitative measurements with the search-coil technique. *Journal of Psychiatric Research, 22,* 195–206.

Levy, D. L., Dorus, E., Shaughnessy, R., Yasillo, N. J. Pandy, G. N., Janicak, P. G., Gibbons, R. D., Gaviria, M., & Davis, J. M. (1985). Pharmacologic evidence for specificity of pursuit dysfunction to schizophrenia: Lithium carbonate associated abnormal pursuit. *Archives of General Psychiatry, 42,* 335–341.

Levy, D. L., Holzman, P. S., Matthysse, S., & Mendell, N. R. (1993). Eye tracking and schizophrenia: A critical perspective. *Schizophrenia Bulletin, 19,* 461–536.

Levy, D. L., Holzman, P. S., & Proctor, L. R. (1978). Vestibular responses in schizophrenia. *Archives of General Psychiatry, 35,* 972–981.

Levy, D. L., Lajonchere, C., Dorogusker, B., Zitner, R., Tartaglini, A., Lieberman, J. A., Szymanski, S., Lee, S., & Mendell, N. (1998). *Eye-tracking dysfunction in schizophrenia: I. Quantitative characterization in first-episode patients.* Manuscript submitted for publication, McLean Hospital, Belmont, MA.

Levy, D. L., Lipton, R. B., Holzman, P. S., & Davis, J. M. (1983). Eye tracking dysfunction unrelated to clinical state and treatment with haloperidol. *Biological Psychiatry, 18,* 813–819.

Lipton, R. B., Levin, S., & Holzman, P. S. (1980). Horizontal and vertical smooth pursuit eye movements: The oculocephalic reflex and the functional psychoses. *Psychiatry Research, 3,* 193–203.

Movshon, A., Lisberger, S. G., & Krauzlist, R. G. (1990). Visual motion signals supporting smooth pursuit eye movements. In *Cold Spring Harbor Symposia on Quantitative Biology* (Vol. 55, pp. 707–716). Cold Spring Harbor, NY: Cold Spring Harbor Laboratory.

Nakayama, K. (1985). Biological image motion processing: A review. *Vision Research, 25,* 625–660.

Newsome, W. T., & Pare, E. B. (1988). A selective impairment of motion perception following lesions of the middle temporal visual area (MT). *Journal of Neuroscience, 8,* 2201–2211.

Newsome, W. T., Wurtz, R. H., Dursteler, M. R., & Mikami, A. (1985). Deficits in visual motion processing following ibotenic acid lesions of the middle temporal visual area of the Macaque monkey. *Journal of Neuroscience, 5,* 825–840.

O'Driscoll, G. A., Strakowski, S. M., Alpert, N. M., Matthysse, S. W., Rauch, S. L., Levy, D. L., & Holzman, P. S. (in press). A comparative study of smooth pursuit and saccadic eye movements in humans using positron emission tomography. *Biological Psychiatry.*

Palafox, G. P. (1993). *Possible origins of the smooth pursuit deficit in schizophrenia:' Motion processing in schizophrenic patients and normal controls.* Unpublished doctoral dissertation, Harvard University, Cambridge, MA.

Pasternak, T. (1987). Discrimination of differences in velocity and flicker rate depends on directionally selective mechanisms. *Vision Research, 30,* 625–660.

Pasternak, T., & Merrigan, W. H. (1994). Motion perception following lesions of the superior temporal sulcus in the monkey. *Cerebral Cortex, 4,* 247–259.

Plant, G. T., & Nakayama, K. (1993). The characteristics of residual motion perception in the hemifield contralateral to lateral occipital lesions in humans. *Brain, 116,* 1336–1345.

Rashbass, C. (1961). The relationship between saccadic and smooth tracking eye movements. *Journal of Physiology, 159,* 326–338.

Shagass, C., Amadeo, M., & Overton, D. (1974). Eye-tracking performance in psychiatric patients. *Biological Psychiatry, 9,* 245–260.

Spitzer, R., Williams, J., Gibbon, M., & First, M. (1990). *Structured Clinical Interview for* DSM-III-R: *Patient version* (SCID-P, version 1.0). Washington, DC: American Psychiatric Press.

Ungerleider, L. F., & Mishkin, M. (1982). Two cortical visual systems. In D. J. Ingel, M. A. Gooddale, & R. J. W. Mansfield (Eds.), *Analysis of visual behavior* (pp. 549–586). Cambridge, MA: MIT Press.

Watson, A. B., Barlow, H. B., & Robson, J. G. (1983, March 6). What does the eye see best? *Nature, 302,* 419–422.

Wurtz, R. H., Komatsu, H., Yamasaki, D. S. G., & Dursteler, M. R. (1990). Cortical visual motion processing for oculomotor control. In B. Cohen & I. Bodis-Wollner (Eds.), *Vision and brain* (pp. 211–231). New York: Raven Press.

Zeki, S. M. (1974). Functional organization of a visual area in the posterior bank of the superior temporal sulcus of the rhesus monkey. *Journal of Physiology, 236,* 549–573.

7

Disinhibition in Antisaccade Performance in Schizophrenia

Deborah L. Levy, Nancy R. Mendell,
Christian A. LaVancher, Joanna Brownstein,
Olga Krastoshevsky, Laurie Teraspulsky,
Kimberly S. McManus, Yungtai Lo, Rebecca Bloom,
Steven Matthysse, and Philip S. Holzman

In this chapter, we present an experimental application of behavioral parsing: decomposing the components of performance of a complex task to understand more about the process underlying performance differences between schizophrenia patients and normal controls. Our focus is on an antisaccade task. The chapter begins with a brief presentation of background materials about the kinds of eye-movement tasks that are relevant to the experimental design and a summary of findings in the literature. Schizophrenia patients make more errors on an antisaccade task than do normal controls. We interpret the performance differences between schizophrenia patients and normal controls reported in the literature as follows: Schizophrenia patients have increased difficulty inhibiting *prepotent* (overlearned and automatic) responses. This hypothesis is tested by parsing one series of task designed to progressively enhance inhibition of prepotent responses (antisaccades) and another series of task designed to progressively enhance disinhibition of prepotent responses (reflexive saccades). We found that reflexive saccade errors in

This study was supported in part by National Institute of Mental Health Grants RO1 MH49487, RO1 MH31340, P01 MH31154, and KO5 MH01021.

schizophrenia patients can be normalized to those of controls when they have adequate time to inhibit prepotent responding. We interpret the need for more time as an indication of weakened inhibition of prepotent responding in patients relative to controls.

REVIEW OF THE LITERATURE ON
EYE-MOVEMENT TASKS

In reflexive saccade tasks, participants are required to make a fast eye movement to a target that jumps from one location to another. Figure 1 illustrates correct performance on a reflexive saccade task. In anti-saccade tasks, participants are instructed not to follow a target to its new location, that is, to look to the opposite periphery. If a centrally located target jumps to the left, for example, the participant's task is to look to the right but without first making a reflexive glance at the target

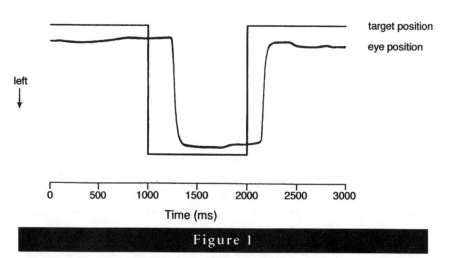

Figure 1

Correct performance of a reflexive saccade task. Latency = 243 ms. Although data from a normal control are used in all of the examples, the same phenomenon could be identically illustrated with data from a schizophrenia patient.

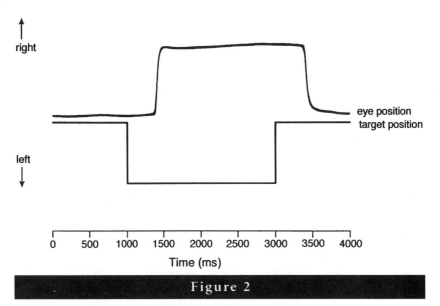

Figure 2

Correct performance of an antisaccade task. Latency = 381 ms.

on the left. The eye movement to the right is an *antisaccade*. Correct performance on an antisaccade task is illustrated in Figure 2. The most commonly used measure of antisaccade performance is the frequency of reflexive saccade errors—making a reflexive glance toward the target at its new location, instead of looking to the opposite periphery. Figure 3 illustrates this error as well as its immediate correction, which, as we discuss below, is typical of both schizophrenia patients and normal controls whenever they make errors.

The normal range for reflexive saccade latency is 200 ms ± 25–50 ms (Leigh & Zee, 1991). The reflexive saccade latencies of schizophrenia patients generally fall within this range (Clementz, McDowell, & Zisook, 1994; Couch & Fox, 1934; Crawford, Haegar, Kennard, Reveley, & Henderson, 1995a, 1995b; Diefendorf & Dodge, 1908; Done & Frith, 1989; Fukushima et al., 1988; Fukushima, Fukushima, Miyasaka, & Yamashita, 1994; Fukushima, Fukushima, Morita, & Yamashita, 1990; Fukushima, Morita, et al., 1990; Iacono, Tuason, & Johnson, 1981; Levin, Holzman, Rothenberg, & Lipton, 1981; Levin, Jones, Stark, Merrin, & Holzman 1982; Levy et al., 1997; Mackert & Flechtner, 1989; Mather & Putchat,

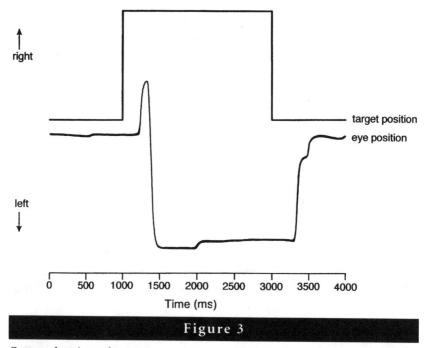

right

left

target position
eye position

Time (ms)

Figure 3

Corrected antisaccade error.

1983; Thaker, Nguyen, & Tamminga, 1989; Yee et al., 1987). The finding of normal reflexive saccade latency in schizophrenia patients indicates that speed of response is not slowed when the task is to look toward a target that appears unpredictably in one's periphery.

Schizophrenia patients also consistently show a higher rate of reflexive saccades when performing an antisaccade task compared with normal controls (Clementz et al., 1994; Crawford et al., 1995a, 1995b; Fukushima et al., 1988, 1994; Fukushima, Fukushima, et al., 1990; Fukushima, Morita, et al., 1990; Levy et al., 1997; Rosse, Schwartz, Kim, & Deutsch, 1993; Sereno & Holzman, 1995; Thaker et al., 1989). Instead of looking in the direction opposite that of the peripheral target, they look toward the peripheral target more often than normal controls do. Both normal controls and schizophrenia patients spontaneously correct almost all reflexive saccade errors: After making an incorrect reflexive saccade toward the target, they immediately make an antisaccade to the opposite periphery (see Figure 3). Data on other features of performance, such as whether the latency of antisaccades is significantly slower in schizophrenia patients than in other participants, are less consistent. In some studies (Clementz et al., 1994; Crawford et al., 1995b; Levy et al., 1997), no group differences in antisaccade latency have been found, but Fukushima and colleagues (Fukushima et al., 1988, 1994; Fukushima, Fukushima, et al., 1990; Fukushima, Morita, et al., 1990) reported that the latency of antisaccades was significantly slower in schizophrenia patients than in other groups. The specificity of these findings to schizophrenia among psychopathological populations is supported by data showing that patients with affective and anxiety disorders do not differ from normal controls in frequency of reflexive saccade errors (Clementz et al., 1994; Crawford et al., 1995a, 1995b). Neuroleptic drug treatment does not account for the differences between schizophrenia patients and normal controls (Crawford et al., 1995a). Abnormal performance by relatives of schizophrenia patients has also been reported, but the specifics of the finding are inconsistent across studies and have not been uniformly confirmed. Clementz et al. found an elevated rate of reflexive saccade errors in relatives of schizophrenia patients but no slowing of antisaccade latency. Thaker, Cassady, Adami, Moran, and Ross (1996) observed slower antisaccade latency but no increase in errors. Levy et al. found no difference between siblings of schizophrenia patients and siblings of normal controls in either latency or error rate.

INTERPRETATION OF THE LITERATURE AND RATIONALE FOR THE PARSING STRATEGY

The usual rationale for examining antisaccade performance in schizophrenia patients emphasizes its potential value in terms of neuroanatomical localization. Patients with lesions involving the dorsolateral–mesial frontal lobes (Guitton, Buchtel, & Douglas, 1985) as well as patients with other central nervous system diseases (e.g., Alzheimer's disease, Huntington's disease, progressive supranuclear palsy) make an increased number of reflexive saccade errors on antisaccade tasks

(Fletcher & Sharpe, 1986; Lasker, Zee, Hain, Folstein, & Singer, 1987; Leigh, Newman, Folstein, Lasker, & Jensen, 1983; Pierrot-Deseilligny, Rivaud, Gaymard, & Agid, 1991; Pierrot-Deseilligny, Rivaud, Pillon, Fournier, & Agid, 1989). The positive findings in schizophrenia patients have typically been interpreted to implicate frontal lobe dysfunction (Clementz et al., 1994; Crawford et al., 1995a, 1995b; Fukushima et al., 1988, 1994; Fukushima, Fukushima, et al., 1990; Fukushima, Morita, et al., 1990; Rosse et al., 1993; Sereno & Holzman, 1995; Thaker et al., 1989). As was discussed elsewhere (Levy, 1996; Levy et al., 1997), however, the essential characteristics of the antisaccade performance decrement shown by patients with dorsolateral–mesial frontal lesions (Guitton et al., 1985)—inability to generate an antisaccade, production of hypometric antisaccades, failure to correct reflexive saccade errors— have never been described in schizophrenia patients.

The contrasting cognitive demands of the two kinds of saccade tasks—reflexive saccades to a novel stimulus and antisaccades away from a novel stimulus—provide a clue about the process underlying increased reflexive saccade errors. In the usual reflexive saccade task, the unpredicted appearance of a visual target provokes a reflexive eye movement toward that target. This response is prepotent and is adaptive because it places the new object on the fovea, where it is seen in the sharpest detail. The antisaccade task, however, requires the participant to look away from a novel target, which moves the target off the fovea, pitting the automatic reflex to look at the target against the instruction to inhibit this reflex. Inhibiting the prepotent response tendency to look at the target and compelling oneself to look away from the target are effortful and difficult. The typical error rate in normal participants is about 25%. Latencies of antisaccades in all participants are markedly slowed (a difference of 83–113 ms) compared with those of reflexive saccades (Levy et al., 1997), and even extensive practice does not make antisaccade latency equal to reflexive saccade latency (Hallett, 1978).

Two lines of evidence support the inference that the poorer performance of schizophrenia patients on an antisaccade task reflects disproportionate difficulty inhibiting prepotent responses. First, perseverative errors on the Wisconsin Card Sorting Test (WCST) and the Stroop effect are significantly correlated with frequency of reflexive saccade errors (Crawford et al., 1996; Levy et al., 1997). The common process that seems to be implicated by the significant association among these variables is inhibition of dominant responses. The number of categories achieved on the WCST, which does not require inhibition of competing response tendencies, in contrast, is not significantly correlated with frequency of reflexive saccade errors (Crawford et al., 1996; Levy et al., 1997).

Second, schizophrenia patients who make many errors (>40%) on an antisaccade task—failing to inhibit a reflexive saccade toward a novel stimulus when they should only look away from it—also make significantly faster reflexive saccades—those directed toward a target—than do schizophrenia patients whose antisaccade error rate falls within the normal range (Crawford et al., 1996). This combination of findings in the same individuals—increased reflexive saccade errors on an antisaccade task and faster reflexive saccades—suggests that difficulty inhibiting prepotent responses under conditions that call for inhibition is associated with a corresponding increase of disinhibition of prepotent responses under conditions that promote disinhibition.

One condition designed to facilitate the initiation of prepotent responses is the "gap" paradigm. Introducing a brief temporal delay between the offset of one target and the onset of another allows attention to be disengaged from one stimulus before encountering the next one, thereby reducing reflexive saccade latency compared with simultaneous offset (no gap) of a central target and onset of a peripheral one (Ross & Ross, 1980; Saslow, 1967). Disengaging attention from one stimulus enhances readiness to engage the next one, resulting in faster latencies in responding to subsequent stimuli. Using such a gap paradigm, Sereno and Holzman (1993) found that the gap produced a significantly larger reduction in reflexive saccade latency in schizophrenia patients than in normal controls compared with a no-gap condition. Sereno and Holzman interpreted the disproportionately faster responses of the patients in the gap condition as an indication that attention may be more easily disengaged in schizophrenia patients than in normal controls. The larger gap-induced reduction in reflexive saccade latency in the schizophrenia patients is consistent with the interpretation that the prepotent response, in this case, to make a reflexive saccade to a novel target, is more disinhibited in schizophrenia patients than in normal controls, as a result of which it is faster.

To understand more about the process underlying the increased reflexive saccade error rate shown by schizophrenia patients, we adopted a strategy of behavioral parsing. This approach has been used to identify the functional correlates of behavior (McCarthy, Blamire, Rothman, Gruetter, & Shulman, 1993; Petersen, Fox, Posner, Mintun, & Raichle, 1989; Posner, Petersen, Fox, & Raichle, 1988) as well as to clarify the time course of successive stages of information-processing disturbances (Green, Nuechterlein, & Mintz, 1994), and it has been proposed as a way of identifying single gene effects (Matthysse, 1996). Holzman (1994) has described this approach as one of *successive parsing*: decomposing the components of a complex behavior in such a way that each successive condition includes all features of the previous condition as well as a single additional operation that distinguishes it from the prior one. Each condition serves as a control for the next one, allowing the cognitive operation, motor operation, or both required for the one new behavior to be isolated.

Such a parsing strategy is essential for isolating which of the behaviors required to perform the antisaccade task correctly are compromised because the task is behaviorally complex. It has cognitive, visual, memory, and motor components and involves several discrete operations: (a) detecting and fixating on a central target, (b) detecting a peripheral target, (c) remembering the approximate location (left or right) of the peripheral target, (d) inhibiting a reflexive saccade to the target, and (e) executing a saccade to an unmarked location in the periphery opposite of the target.

EXPERIMENTAL METHODS

Task Description

Antisaccade Tasks

For this study, we adapted a well-known series of reflexive saccade paradigms to the antisaccade task, varying one feature of the task at a time. We used three antisaccade paradigms, a gap condition, a no-gap/no-overlap condition, and an overlap condition. This series of conditions progressively facilitates inhibition of the prepotent response to look at the peripheral target rather than away from it, as successful performance requires. The antisaccade task requires inhibition of prepotent responses. In light of our interpretation of the existing literature that the increased frequency of reflexive saccade errors on an antisaccade task in schizophrenia patients reflects increased difficulty inhibiting the prepotent response, we expected that errors would decline as inhibition was progressively facilitated.

In all conditions, the participants were instructed to fixate on a target located straight ahead until it turned off, at which time they were to look as quickly as possible in the direction opposite to that of a peripheral target (i.e., look to the left if the target appeared on the right). After a specific time interval, the center target reappeared and the participant was instructed to refixate on it, signaling the beginning of the next trial. The tasks were administered in the order in which they were described. Antisaccade tasks were administered prior to reflexive saccade tasks to minimize "set" effects on the error score (i.e., performing a reflexive saccade task requires looking at the target, which is the prepotent response in all participants but is an error on the antisaccade task) and to prevent fatigue from interfering with efficiency on the harder (i.e., antisaccade) tasks.

Of the three experimental paradigms used, described below, the one that would be expected to facilitate inhibition of a prepotent response the least in an antisaccade task is the gap condition. In the gap condition, a central target was illuminated for 2,000 ms (2 s) and turned off 150 ms before the appearance of a peripheral target. The peripheral target remained on for 2,000 ms (see Figure 4). Participants received a minimum of 3 practice cycles to ensure that they understood the task. The test trial consisted of 16 cycles.

The no-gap/no-overlap condition fell midway between the gap and overlap conditions; it was expected to facilitate inhibition of the prepotent response to look at the peripheral target more than the gap condition but less than the overlap condition. In the no-gap/no-overlap

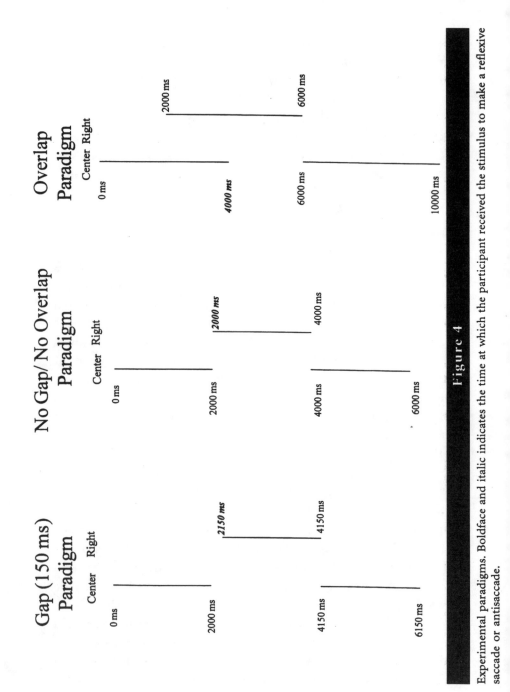

Figure 4

Experimental paradigms. Boldface and italic indicates the time at which the participant received the stimulus to make a reflexive saccade or antisaccade.

194

condition, the peripheral target turned on simultaneously with the off-set of the central target (see Figure 4). Two versions of the no-gap/no-overlap condition were presented. The two conditions differed only in the length of time the central and peripheral targets were illuminated. In the first condition, the central target remained illuminated for 2,000 ms and the peripheral target remained on for 2,000 ms. In the second, the central target remained illuminated for 1,000 ms (1 s) and the peripheral target remained on for 1,000 ms. Participants received a minimum of 3 practice cycles to ensure that they understood each task. The test trial consisted of 16 cycles for the 2,000-ms condition and 32 cycles for the 1,000-ms condition. By comparing the two no-gap/no-overlap conditions, we could assess the effects on performance of making the task faster. The effect of the gap—having the central fixation point turned off before the peripheral target appeared—can be examined by comparing performance in the gap condition with performance in the no-gap/no-overlap condition.

Of the three experimental paradigms, the one that we expected to facilitate inhibition of the prepotent response to look at the peripheral target the most was the overlap condition. In the overlap condition, the peripheral target was illuminated (i.e., "overlapped") for a fixed time period, while the central target was simultaneously displayed (see Figure 4). As with the other antisaccade tasks, the participants were instructed to fixate a target located straight ahead until it turned off, at which time they were to look as quickly as possible in the direction opposite to that of a peripheral target. Two versions of the overlap condition were presented. In the first overlap condition, the central and peripheral targets overlapped for 2,000 ms. The central target remained illuminated for a total of 4,000 ms. After 2,000 ms, the peripheral target was illuminated and remained on for 4,000 ms. Two thousand milliseconds after the peripheral target came on, the central target turned off, signaling the participant to look in the direction opposite that of the peripheral target. In the second condition, the central and peripheral targets overlapped for 1,000 ms. The central target remained illuminated for a total of 2,000 ms. After 1,000 ms, the peripheral target was illuminated and remained on for 3,000 ms.

One thousand milliseconds after the peripheral target came on, the central target turned off, signaling the participants to look in the direction opposite that of the peripheral target. Participants received a minimum of 3 practice cycles to ensure that they understood the task. The test trials consisted of 10 cycles for the 2,000-ms overlap condition and 16 cycles for the 1,000-ms overlap condition. The effect of overlap can be assessed by comparing each overlap condition with the no-gap/no-overlap condition. The effect of the length of the overlap can be assessed by comparing the two overlap conditions with each other.

Reflexive Saccade Tasks

The identical gap paradigm was also used as a reflexive saccade task. Two no-gap/no-overlap tasks were administered. These two conditions differed from each other only in the length of time the center target was illuminated before the peripheral target appeared. In one condition, the center target was illuminated for 2,000 ms and the peripheral target was illuminated for 2,000 ms. In the second condition, the center target was illuminated for 1,000 ms and the peripheral target was illuminated for 2,000 ms. The participants were instructed to look as quickly as possible at the peripheral light. The effects on performance of shortening the fixation interval preceding the appearance of the peripheral target can be assessed by comparing the two no-gap/no-overlap conditions. In both the reflexive saccade and antisaccade tasks, the peripheral target appeared on the left or right quasirandomly and each direction was presented an equal number of times.

Method of Eye-Movement Recording

Horizontal eye movements were recorded in a darkened room using infrared reflectometry. Head movement was prevented by a custom bite bar made of a participant's dental impression. Eye position was calibrated in 3° intervals to ±10.5°. Stimuli were presented on a color monitor positioned 22 in. (55.88 cm) in front of the participants. Data were collected and analyzed using customized software.

Dependent Measures

The following dependent measures were assessed: (1) *saccade latency*— the interval between the target's appearance at its peripheral location and the beginning of the saccadic eye-movement response—for (a) the first saccade following target displacement during the reflexive saccade task and (b) correct antisaccades; (2) a percent error score (number of reflexive saccade errors ÷ number of valid cycles on the antisaccade tasks); and (3) a percent corrected errors score (number of corrected reflexive saccade errors ÷ total number of reflexive saccades on the antisaccade tasks). A reflexive saccade toward the peripheral target followed by a correct antisaccade before the target returned to center was considered a corrected error (see Figure 3).

Participants

The tasks described above were administered to 18 outpatients who met *DSM-III-R* (American Psychiatric Association, 1987) criteria for schizophrenia or schizoaffective disorder and 18 normal controls. The average duration of illness of the patients was 12.2 years ($SD = 7.6$ years), and their average score on the Brief Psychiatric Rating Scale (Overall & Gorham, 1962) was 39.3 ($SD = 9.6$), indicating symptoms of moderate severity at the time of testing. Normal controls were recruited through the Department of Internal Medicine at a local medical center. None of the controls had ever been psychotic, and none met criteria for any Axis II schizophrenia spectrum personality disorder. All participants were between 18 and 55 years old and had no diagnosed central nervous system disease, no substance abuse or dependence within 5 years, and an estimated verbal IQ greater than 70, based on the vocabulary subtest of the Wechsler Adult Intelligence Scale–Revised (Wechsler, 1981).

A significantly smaller proportion of the schizophrenia group was women than in the normal control group (22.2% vs. 41.7%). The two groups did not differ in age (schizophrenia patients: 34.5 ± 7.9 years; normal controls: 33.6 ± 11.9 years) or estimated verbal IQ scores (schizophrenia patients: 107.5 ± 10.3; normal controls: 105.6 ± 11.99).

None of these variables was significantly related to the oculomotor measures.

Thirteen schizophrenia patients were taking antipsychotic drugs. The median dose of antipsychotic medication was 250 mg in chlorpromazine equivalents. Twelve of these 13 patients were also receiving antianxiety, antidepressant, antiparkinsonian, or antimanic medication or some combination of these medications. One patient was receiving no psychotropic medications at the time of testing. Three patients were receiving psychotropic drugs other than antipsychotics (antianxiety medication only, antidepressant medication only, antianxiety and antidepressant medication). Two controls were taking antidepressant medication.

The Structured Clinical Interview for *DSM-III-R*–Patient Edition (Spitzer, Williams, Gibbon, & First, 1990) was administered to all participants by trained interviewers. Nonpatients also received the Structured Interview for Schizotypal Symptoms (Kendler, 1989). Axis I syndromes and Axis II schizophrenia spectrum personality disorders meeting *DSM-III-R* criteria were assigned, on the basis of a consensus of four clinicians who reviewed the interview material, a narrative summarizing the interview and records of previous psychiatric hospitalizations. Interviews and the diagnostic assessments as well as eye-movement testing and analysis were performed without knowledge of group membership.

Statistical Methods

Group differences in antisaccade and reflexive saccade latency were analyzed using two-way repeated measures analysis of variance (ANOVA). The percent error scores and percent corrected error scores were not normally distributed. Therefore, the raw scores for each of these variables were converted to their ranks, and two-way ANOVAs were performed on the ranks. The baseline antisaccade task was the 2,000-ms no-gap/no-overlap condition. The baseline reflexive saccade task involved 2,000-ms intervals between all target positions. Effects of altering task parameters were assessed using *t* tests for paired data (latency) or the Wilcoxon Signed-Rank Test (percent error).

RESULTS

Reflexive Saccade Tasks

Data for the latency of the several reflexive saccade tasks are presented graphically in Figure 5. Schizophrenia patients had significantly faster latencies than normal controls on the three reflexive saccade tasks, $F(1, 66) = 26.3$, $p = .0001$, averaging 20.3 ms quicker. Task also had significant effects on latency, $F(2, 66) = 40.85$, $p = .0001$, but there was no interaction between group and task, $F(2, 66) = 0.87$, $p = .42$, indicating that the magnitude of the difference between groups was the same for each task. In both groups, reflexive saccade latency was slowest when 2,000 ms of fixation preceded the appearance of the peripheral target. Reducing the period of fixation prior to the appearance of the peripheral target to 1,000 ms resulted in significantly faster reflexive saccades,

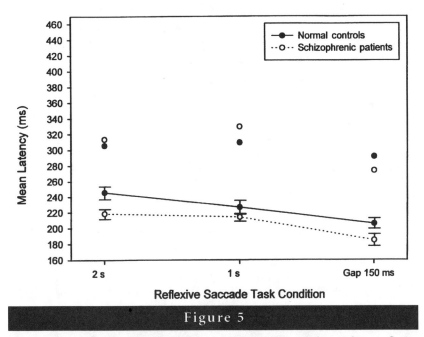

Figure 5

Mean latency of schizophrenia patients and normal controls on three reflexive saccade tasks. Unconnected circles show mean latency of each group on antisaccade tasks using the same paradigm.

$t(34) = -2.31$, $p = .03$. Imposition of the 150-ms gap between offset of the center fixation target and illumination of the peripheral target produced the fastest reflexive saccades, and the change in latency was statistically significant, $t(34) = -10.89$, $p = .0001$.

Antisaccade Tasks

Data for latency and percent error scores from the several antisaccade tasks are presented in Figures 6 and 7, respectively. Lengthening the fixation period in the no-gap/no-overlap conditions did not significantly affect antisaccade latency in either group, normal controls: $t(16) = -0.45$, $p = .66$; schizophrenia patients: $t(17) = -1.19$, $p = .25$, or percent error scores among the normal controls ($T = -17.00$, $p = .35$). Schizophrenia patients, however, made significantly more errors when the fixation period was 2,000 ms than 1,000 ms, $T = 42.50$, $p = .04$. The gap condition made antisaccade latency faster by 12.7% in the

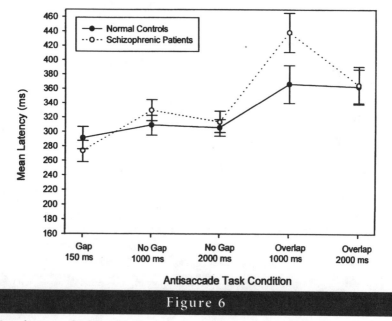

Figure 6

Mean latency of schizophrenia patients and normal controls on five antisaccade tasks.

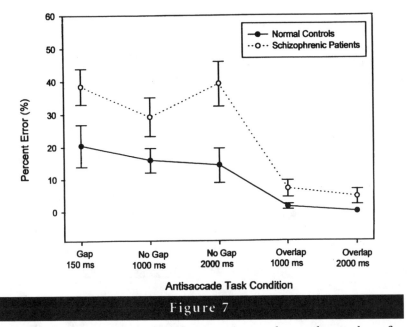

Figure 7

Mean percent error score of schizophrenia patients and normal controls on five antisaccade tasks.

patients, $t(17) = 5.45$, $p = .0001$, and by 4.7% in the controls, $t(16) = 1.83$, $p = .09$. Percent error scores did not change in either group (normal controls: $T = -22.50$, $p = .17$; schizophrenia patients: $T = 1.50$, $p = .96$).

Both overlap conditions produced a speed–accuracy tradeoff in all participants—antisaccade latencies were the slowest and errors were reduced to very low levels in both overlap conditions. The longer overlap also resulted in the lowest error rate in both groups. In the patients, percent error scores dropped from a baseline level of 39.3% to 7.1% in the 1,000-ms overlap condition ($T = 68.00$, $p = .00003$) and to 4.6% in the 2,000-ms overlap conditions ($T = 68.00$, $p = .00003$). In the controls, percent errors dropped from a baseline level of 14.4% to 1.5% in the 1,000-ms condition ($T = 27.50$, $p = .002$) and to 0.0% in the 2,000-ms overlap conditions ($T = 27.50$, $p = .002$). Latency showed a corresponding slowing in both overlap conditions. In the 1,000-ms overlap condition, responses slowed by 39.8% in the patients, $t(16) =$ -4.63, $p = .0003$, and by 19.8% in the controls, $t(16) = -3.01$, $p =$ .008. In the 2,000-ms overlap condition, responses slowed by 16.6% in the patients, $t(16) = -2.38$, $p = .03$, and by 18.7% in the controls, $t(16)$ $= -3.02$, $p = .008$.

To achieve a reduction in errors comparable with that of the controls in the shorter overlap condition, the patients had to slow down their responses twice as much as the controls. This pattern is reflected in significant Group × Task interactions for both latency of antisaccades, $F(4, 130) = 2.74$, $p = .03$, and for percent error score, $F(4, 128)$ $= 2.64$, $p = .04$. Whereas the length of the overlap had a meager effect (1.1%) on the magnitude of the slowing of antisaccade latency in the controls, $t(16) = 0.15$, $p = .88$, latencies were slowed 20% more following the shorter overlap than following the longer overlap in the patients, $t(16) = 2.622$, $p = .02$.

There were no group, $F(1, 66) = 0.34$, $p = .56$, task, $F(4, 66) =$ 0.62, $p = .64$, or Group × Task interaction, $F(3, 66) = 0.56$, $p = .64$, effects on percent corrected errors. In the nonoverlap conditions, which yielded the highest reflexive saccade error rates in all groups, virtually all errors were corrected (error correction averaged 92.4–100.0% in the normal controls and 94.1–97.3% in the schizophrenia patients).

DISCUSSION

Many of the features of the performance of schizophrenia patients on the reflexive saccade and antisaccade tasks were similar to those of normal controls. When task conditions fostered disinhibition, both groups performed faster; when task conditions enhanced inhibition, both groups performed slower. Schizophrenia patients were, however, predisposed to disinhibited responding, in that compared with the controls, their reflexive saccades were significantly faster. The schizophrenia patients made significantly more reflexive saccade errors on all variations of the antisaccade task except when the experimental paradigm facilitated inhibition of peremptory responses, as in the overlap conditions. The normal controls' accuracy on the antisaccade task also benefited when inhibition of dominant responses was maximized; that is, in the overlap conditions, their responses slowed and they made fewer errors. Only the patients, however, were sensitive to the amount of time available to inhibit responding.

The series of antisaccade tasks progressively enhanced inhibition of prepotent responses in both groups. In the gap condition of the antisaccade series, which inhibits prepotent responses the least, all participants performed the fastest. The 150-ms gap provided the time both to disengage attention from the central fixation target and to prepare to make the appropriate eye-movement response when the peripheral target appeared. In contrast, both the no-gap/no-overlap and the overlap conditions inhibited disengagement from the central target, slowing down initiation of an antisaccade. Latency was faster for all participants in the no-gap/no-overlap condition than in the overlap conditions because the simultaneous offset of the central light and appearance of the peripheral target allowed disengagement from the central target to begin as soon as the peripheral target appeared. Disengagement was maximally inhibited in the overlap conditions, which yielded the slowest responses, because attention remained fixed on the central target, even after the peripheral target appeared during the overlap period.

In contrast to the gap condition, which improved speed of response but not error rate, the overlap condition produced a speed–accuracy tradeoff by all participants: Regardless of the length of the overlap, performance was slower and more accurate than during the no-gap/no-overlap or gap conditions. Both groups were susceptible to the speed–accuracy tradeoff imposed by an overlap. Schizophrenia patients, however, were susceptible to the length of the overlap. When the overlap was shorter, 1,000 ms, disproportionately greater slowing was required for the patients to achieve a reduction in errors comparable with that of the controls. However, when the overlap was twice as long, slowing was equivalent in both groups.

When schizophrenia patients were given the time to inhibit a prepotent response, as they were in both overlap conditions, antisaccade errors were normalized, regardless of the duration of the overlap interval. Errors were also reduced and responses were also slowed in the controls, but the magnitude of the effect of the short overlap condition (1,000 ms) on both dependent measures was significantly greater in the patients compared with the longer overlap condition (2,000 ms). The overlap postponed disengagement from the central target, which, in turn, inhibited the triggering of the dominant response to look at the peripheral target instead of looking away from it. The 1,000-ms overlap period was too short for the patients to inhibit a prepotent reflexive saccade and to prepare to initiate an antisaccade, but the 2,000-ms overlap did give them enough preparatory time. Thus, schizophrenia patients were able to inhibit prepotent responses, but they needed more than 1,000 ms, whereas 1,000 ms were adequate for the normal controls. We interpret the greater dependence of the patients on time to disengage—or to inhibit responding—as indicators of difficulty inhibiting peremptory responding.

A similar pattern was observed on the series of reflexive saccade tasks, which incrementally disinhibited prepotent responses. In both groups, latency was longest in the condition that was the most inhibitory (the 2,000-ms no-gap/no-overlap condition) and shortest in the condition (gap) that facilitated prepotent responses the most. This pattern is expectable when one considers the cognitive demands of the three tasks in this series. When the fixation period prior to offset of the central target and onset of the peripheral target was longer (i.e., 2,000 ms), the hold on attention was greater; thus, it took longer to override the inhibitory effect of the delay period and to make a reflexive saccade. In the shorter waiting period (i.e., 1,000 ms), the hold on attention and the magnitude of the inhibitory effect of the fixation period were less strong, decreasing the time it took to disengage and then to make a reflexive saccade. In the gap condition, attention had already disengaged from the central target before the stimulus to make a reflexive saccade appeared. The absence of inhibition in the gap condition induced a state of readiness to respond, and reflexive saccade latencies were the fastest, as shown in studies of express saccades (Fischer & Breitmeyer, 1987).

Just as schizophrenia patients seemed to benefit disproportionately more than the normal controls from conditions that facilitated inhibition of peremptory responses, they also showed more response facilitation under conditions that potentiated disinhibition. Schizophrenia patients performed significantly faster than normal controls on all the reflexive saccade tasks, which inherently potentiate disinhibited responses—some conditions (e.g., the gap) more so than others did. Although the gap effect was not large enough to produce a statistically significant Group × Task interaction for the reflexive saccade tasks, the direction of our results is consistent with Sereno and Holzman's (1993) finding that maximizing disinhibition has a significantly larger effect on patients than on controls. Sereno and Holzman found that the gap reduced reflexive saccade latency by 8.1% in patients and 3.2% in controls. They used an 800-ms no-gap/no-overlap condition to compare with the gap condition. Our reflexive saccade condition that was most comparable with theirs was the 1,000-ms no-gap/no-overlap condition, which also produced a larger (although not statistically significant) reduction in reflexive saccade latency in the patients (13.7%) than in the controls (9.4%). Compared with the longer (2,000 ms) no-gap/no-overlap condition, the gap condition produced an equivalent reduction in reflexive saccade latency in controls (16.4%) and in patients (15.6%). The less inhibitory (i.e., shorter) no-gap/no-overlap condition had a smaller inhibitory effect on schizophrenia patients than on normal controls, and the more inhibitory (i.e., longer) no-gap/no-overlap condition had an equivalent effect on the two groups. Thus, on the reflexive saccade tasks as well as on the antisaccade tasks when patients were given more time to inhibit prepotent responding, their responses slowed by as much as those of the normal controls; but when they had less time, they slowed by much less.

Yet, even when inhibition was maximized on the reflexive saccade tasks (2,000-ms no-gap/no-overlap), patients never responded as slowly as the controls. As with the overlap conditions of the antisaccade task, sensitivity to the time available to inhibit prepotent responses distinguished the patients from the controls. In both the antisaccade and reflexive saccade paradigms, 2,000 ms was long enough in both paradigms to induce comparable inhibition and 1,000 ms was too short for the patients. The difference between 1,000 and 2,000 ms is rather small; but in this instance, it was long enough to maximize differences in response inhibition between patients and controls. It is likely that further refinement of the tasks would allow researchers to establish more precisely what the critical time interval is that mediates response inhibition differences between schizophrenia patients and normal controls.

Several features of the design of our study may account for why we did not obtain a statistically significantly larger effect of the gap in patients than in controls, as Sereno and Holzman (1993) did. We used a gap interval of 150 ms to minimize anticipatory responding, as did Sereno and Holzman. However, a gap interval of 200–300 ms produces the largest reduction in reflexive saccade latency (Ross & Ross, 1980; Saslow, 1967). Had the gap been longer than 150 ms, we may have obtained a larger effect. Similarly, a longer gap in the antisaccade task may have resulted in a statistically significant reduction in latency and a statistically significant increase in errors. We also used fewer trials (16) than Sereno and Holzman did (40), which reduced our power to detect significant differences.

CONCLUSION

In the usual antisaccade paradigm (the no-gap/no-overlap conditions), schizophrenia patients typically respond as quickly as normal participants, but they make about twice as many reflexive saccade errors. It is possible to normalize their error rate, going from a baseline of 39.3% in the standard paradigm to a low of 4.6%, simply by increasing the time available to inhibit a reflexive glance and prepare to make an antisaccade by 1,000 ms. Schizophrenia patients need more time to inhibit prepotent responses, and they respond faster when responses are disinhibited, suggesting a dysregulation of inhibitory controls. Because many investigators have implicated the frontal lobes in the antisaccade performance of schizophrenia patients, it seems to us that it would now be appropriate to determine whether similar parsing strategies are capable of normalizing performance in patients with focal frontal pathology.

REFERENCES

American Psychiatric Association. (1987). *Diagnostic and statistical manual of mental disorders* (3rd ed., rev.). Washington, DC: American Psychiatric Association.

Clementz, B. A., McDowell, J. E., & Zisook, S. (1994). Saccadic system functioning among schizophrenia patients and their first-degree relatives. *Journal of Abnormal Psychology, 103,* 277–287.

Couch, F. H., & Fox, J. C. (1934). Photographic study of ocular movements in mental disease. *Archives of Neurology and Psychiatry, 34,* 556–578.

Crawford, T. J., Haegar, B., Kennard, C., Reveley, M. A., & Henderson, L. (1995a). Saccadic abnormalities in psychotic patients. I. Neuroleptic-free psychotic patients. *Psychological Medicine, 25,* 461–471.

Crawford, T. J., Haegar, B., Kennard, C., Reveley, M. A., & Henderson, L. (1995b). Saccadic abnormalities in psychotic patients. II. The role of neuroleptic treatment. *Psychological Medicine, 25,* 473–483.

Crawford, T. J., Puri, B. K., Nijran, K., Jones, B., Kennard, C., & Lewis, S. W. (1996). Abnormal saccadic distractibility in patients with schizophrenia: A ^{99m}Tc-HMPAO SPET study. *Psychological Medicine, 26,* 265–277.

Diefendorf, A. R., & Dodge, R. (1908). An experimental study of the ocular reactions of the insane from photographic records. *Brain, 31,* 451–489.

Done, D. J., & Frith, C. D. (1989). Automatic and strategic volitional saccadic eye movements in psychotic patients. *European Archives of Psychiatry and Neurological Science, 239,* 27–32.

Fischer, B., & Breitmeyer, B. (1987). Mechanisms of visual attention revealed by saccadic eye movements. *Neuropsychologia, 25,* 73–83.

Fletcher, W. A., & Sharpe, J. A. (1986). Saccadic eye movement dysfunction in Alzheimer's disease. *Annals of Neurology, 20,* 464–471.

Fukushima, J., Fukushima, K., Chiba, T., Tanaka, S., Yamashita, I., & Kato, M. (1988). Disturbances of voluntary control of saccadic eye movements in schizophrenic patients. *Biological Psychiatry, 23,* 670–677.

Fukushima, J., Fukushima, K., Miyasaka, K., & Yamashita, I. (1994). Voluntary control of saccadic eye movement in patients with frontal cortical lesions and parkinsonian patients in comparison with that in schizophrenics. *Biological Psychiatry, 36,* 21–30.

Fukushima, J., Fukushima, K., Morita, N., & Yamashita, I. (1990). Further analysis of the control of voluntary saccadic eye movements in schizophrenic patients. *Biological Psychiatry, 28,* 943–958.

Fukushima, J., Morita, N., Fukushima, K., Chiba, T., Tanaka, S., & Yamashita, I. (1990). Voluntary control of saccadic eye movements in patients with schizophrenic and affective disorders. *Journal of Psychiatric Research, 24,* 9–24.

Green, M. F., Nuechterlein, K. H., & Mintz, J. (1994). Backward masking in schizophrenia and mania: I. Specifying a mechanism. *Archives of General Psychiatry, 51,* 939–944.

Guitton, D., Buchtel, H. A., & Douglas, R. M. (1985). Frontal lobe lesions in man cause difficulties in suppressing reflexive glances and in generating goal-directed saccades. *Experimental Brain Research, 58,* 455–472.

Hallett, P. E. (1978). Primary and secondary saccades to goals defined by instructions. *Vision Research, 18,* 1279–1296.

Holzman, P. S. (1994). Parsing cognition: The power of psychology paradigms. *Archives of General Psychiatry, 51,* 952–954.

Iacono, W. G., Tuason, V. B., & Johnson, R. A. (1981). Dissociation of smooth pursuit and saccadic eye tracking in remitted schizophrenics: An ocular reaction time task that schizophrenics perform well. *Archives of General Psychiatry, 38,* 991–996.

Kendler, K. S. (1989). *Structured Interview for Schizotypal Symptoms* (Version 1.5). Richmond: Virginia Medical College, Department of Psychiatry.

Lasker, A. G., Zee, D. S., Hain, T. C., Folstein, S. E., & Singer, H. S. (1987). Saccades in Huntington's disease: Initiation defects and distractibility. *Neurology, 37,* 364–370.

Leigh, R. J., Newman, S. A., Folstein, S. E., Lasker, A. G., & Jensen, B. A. (1983). Abnormal ocular motor control in Huntington's disease. *Neurology, 33,* 1268–1275.

Leigh, R. J., & Zee, D. S. (1991). *The neurology of eye movements.* Philadelphia: F. A. Davis.

Levin, S., Holzman, P. S., Rothenberg, S. J., & Lipton, R. B. (1981). Saccadic eye movements in psychotic patients. *Psychiatry Research, 5,* 47–58.

Levin, S., Jones, A., Stark, L., Merrin, E. L., & Holzman, P. S. (1982). Saccadic eye movements of schizophrenic patients measured by reflected light technique. *Biological Psychiatry, 17,* 1277–1287.

Levy, D. (1996). Location, location, location: The pathway from behavior to brain locus in schizophrenia. In S. Matthysse, D. L. Levy, J. Kagan, & F. M. Benes (Eds.), *Psychopathology: The evolving science of mental disorder* (pp. 100–126). New York: Cambridge University Press.

Levy, D. L., Mendell, N. R., Bloom, R., LaVancher, C. A., Lo, Y., Brownstein, J., Yurgelun-Todd, D., Matthysse, S., & Holzman, P. S. (1997). *Antisaccades in schizophrenic patients: Experimental confirmation and theoretical reassessment.* Manuscript submitted for publication, McLean Hospital, Harvard Medical School.

Mackert, A., & Flechtner, M. (1989). Saccadic reaction times in acute and remitted schizophrenics. *European Archives of Psychiatry and Neurological Science, 239,* 33–38.

Mather, J. A., & Putchat, C. (1983). Motor control of schizophrenics. I. Oculomotor control of schizophrenics: A deficit in sensory processing, not strictly in motor control. *Journal of Psychiatric Research, 17,* 343–360.

Matthysse, S. (1996). The *Drosophila* eye and the genetics of schizophrenia. In S. Matthysse, D. L. Levy, J. Kagan, & F. M. Benes (Eds.), *Psychopathology: The evolving science of mental disorder* (pp. 557–580). New York: Cambridge University Press.

McCarthy, G., Blamire, A. M., Rothman, D. L., Gruetter, R., & Shulman, R. G. (1993). Echo-planar magnetic resonance imaging studies of frontal cortex activation during word generation in humans. *Proceedings of the National Academy of Sciences, 90,* 4952–4956.

Overall, J. E., & Gorham, D. R. (1962). The Brief Psychiatric Rating Scale. *Psychological Reports, 10,* 799–812.

Petersen, S. E., Fox, P. T., Posner, M. I., Mintun, M., & Raichle, M. E. (1989). Positron emission tomographic studies of the processing of single words. *Journal of Cognitive Neuroscience, 1,* 153–170.

Pierrot-Deseilligny, C., Rivaud, S., Gaymard, B., & Agid, Y. (1991). Cortical control of visually-guided saccades. *Brain, 114,* 1473–1485.

Pierrot-Deseilligny, C., Rivaud, S., Pillon, B., Fournier, E., & Agid, Y. (1989). Lateral visually-guided saccades in progressive nuclear palsy. *Brain, 112,* 471–487.

Posner, M. I., Petersen, S. E., Fox, P. T., & Raichle, M. E. (1988). Localization of cognitive functions in the human brain. *Science, 240,* 1627–1631.

Ross, L. E., & Ross S. M. (1980). Saccade latency and warning signals: Stimulus onset, offset, and change as warning events. *Perception and Psychophysics, 27*, 251–257.

Rosse, R. B., Schwartz, B. L., Kim, S. Y., & Deutsch, S. I. (1993). Correlation between antisaccade and Wisconsin Card Sorting Test performance in schizophrenia. *American Journal of Psychiatry, 150*, 333–335.

Saslow, K. (1967). Effects of components of displacement step stimuli upon latency of saccadic eye movements. *Journal of the Optical Society of America, 57*, 1024–1029.

Sereno, A. B., & Holzman, P. S. (1993). Express saccades and smooth pursuit eye movement function in schizophrenic, affective disorder, and normal subjects. *Journal of Cognitive Neuroscience, 5*, 303–316.

Sereno, A. B., & Holzman, P. S. (1995). Antisaccades and smooth pursuit eye movements in schizophrenia. *Biological Psychiatry, 37*, 394–401.

Spitzer, R., Williams, J., Gibbon, M., & First, M. (1990). *Structured Clinical Interview for DSM-III-R–Patient edition* (Version 1.0). Washington, DC: American Psychiatric Association.

Thaker, G. K., Cassady, S., Adami, H., Moran, M., & Ross, D. E. (1996). Eye movements in spectrum personality disorders: Comparison of community subjects and relatives of schizophrenic patients. *American Journal of Psychiatry, 153*, 362–368.

Thaker, G. K., Nguyen, J. A., & Tamminga, C. A. (1989). Increased saccadic distractibility in tardive dyskinesia: Functional evidence for subcortical GABA dysfunction. *Biological Psychiatry, 25*, 49–59.

Wechsler, D. (1981). *Manual for the Adult Intelligence Scale–Revised.* New York: The Psychological Corporation.

Yee, R. D., Baloh, R. W., Marder, S. R., Levy, D. L., Sakala, S. M., & Honrubia, V. (1987). Eye movements in schizophrenia. *Investigative Ophthalmology and Visual Science, 28*, 366–374.

8

Lateralization, Memory, and Language in Schizophrenia: Some Facts and an Artifact

Brendan A. Maher and Theo C. Manschreck

A nomalous lateralization has been a focus of interest in research into the pathology of schizophrenia for some time. The empirical literature is substantial and cannot be summarized adequately here (see useful reviews by Goldberg and Seidman, 1991, and Gruzelier, 1991). However, the consistent tenor of early empirical studies has been that schizophrenia patients show more left or mixed lateralization in a variety of task situations than do nonschizophrenia patients or samples of the normal population. The anomalies include disparities between laterality of hand and eye dominance (e.g., Gur, 1977), lateralization of skin-conductance responses to auditory stimuli (Gruzelier & Venables, 1972), visual-field dominance (Heilman & Valenstein, 1979) as well as in general hand preference. In the years since these studies were reported, there have been replications and failures to

The findings reported in this chapter are the result of the work done in our laboratory of experimental psychopathology first at the New Hampshire Hospital (Concord, NH) and later at the Corrigan Mental Center (Fall River, MA) and the laboratory of Brendan Maher at Harvard University. Throughout, this work has been done with the collaboration or assistance of Crystal Blyler, Deborah Redmond, Scott Beaudette, Monica Chu, Tatiana Sitnikova, and Steven Candela.

replicate—a matter that appears to be explained in some part by differences in the criteria used to define lateralization and in the response measures used to detect the effects of lateralization.

A key distinction in the assessment of laterality is between measures of preference and measures of performance. Hand preference has been a long-standing basis for distinguishing between left and right lateralization of handedness, with hand preference in writing having special prominence. Preference measurement can be found in such instruments as the Edinburgh Inventory (Oldfield, 1971) and the Annett Scale (Annett, 1967). Simple preference items inevitably constrain the participants' responses to a series of dichotomies of right versus left. Thus, the hand used for drawing is either left or right, regardless of whether the quality of the drawing varies with the use of the preferred versus nonpreferred hand. When multi-item preference measures are used, the distribution of laterality takes the form of a J curve, with most people showing a clear preponderance of right preferences, a smaller proportion showing a left preponderance, and very few showing equal mixtures of right and left preferences. A typical distribution of this kind is shown in Figure 1. The data come from the Annett Scale scores of 112 normal adults tested in our laboratory.

Not surprisingly, the general picture that emerges is that people are mostly either right-handed or left-handed, with a small number in the ambidextrous range. This, in turn, has directed attention to the examination of the simple dichotomy of left-handed versus right-handed patients within the schizophrenic diagnostic group. Studies using the preference method look at the relationship of lateralization to certain components of the syndromes of schizophrenia. Lishman and McMeekan (1976) reported that left-handedness was significantly more common in schizoaffective patients than in either schizophrenic or control groups. Luchins, Weinberger, and Wyatt (1979) reported lower total time in a hospital in left-handed than in right-handed patients, with no differences in age of onset or length of illness. These findings suggest that left-handed patients include a subtype of relatively mild schizophrenia and that differences in the reported inci-

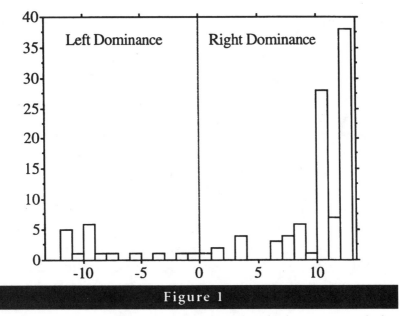

Distribution of net laterality (right–left preference totals) from Annett Scale data ($N = 112$).

dence of left-handedness in various studies simply reflect the presence of different proportions of this subtype.

Recent studies have investigated the relationship of hand preference to a range of performance samples of schizophrenia patients. The first study (Manoach, Maher, & Manschreck, 1988) found that left-handed writing preference differentiated thought-disordered (TD) from non-thought-disordered (NTD) schizophrenia patients. TD was assessed with the Schedule of Affective Disorders and Schizophrenia (SADS; Spitzer & Endicott, 1977). Left-handed schizophrenia patients showed significantly higher scores on the subscales of Derailment, Understand-ability, Poverty of Information, and a marginally significant difference on Illogical Thinking. These findings were supported by a later study (Manoach, 1994).

A previous investigation (Maher, Manschreck, & Rucklos, 1980) had established that schizophrenia patients with high TD scores performed significantly less well than NTD patients on a measure of immediate recall in a series of word lists that provided an increasing approximation to normal sentence structure; this measure was based on work by Miller and Selfridge (1950) and is described in detail below. The findings of these two studies point to the parallel conclusions that (a) in schizophrenia patients left-handedness is associated with TD and (b) TD is associated with poorer performance on context-aided verbal recall. This led Manschreck, Maher, Redmond, Miller, and Beaudette (1996) to examine the relationship of all three variables in another study. Here, the findings were that in schizophrenia patients, left-handedness was associated with both TD and poorer performance on context-aided immediate recall for verbal material.

Although the findings were clear and significant, we recognized certain limitations in the measures and in the implicit assumption that left-handedness in the normal population was not associated with anomalies of cognition. Accordingly, we turned to the measurement of lateral performance, rather than preference, because the use of preference measures has been a limiting factor in the sensitivity with which the correlates of anomalous lateralization might be assessed.

In response to this, Brendan Maher developed a relatively simple method for measuring performance differences in a manual task. We wanted to use a task in which there were minimal demands on the patients' understanding of instructions or on prior learned skills and one that would be brief, portable, and plausibly culture free. We finally selected the task of drawing simple lines free hand. This method was presented by Blyler, Maher, Manschreck, and Fenton (1997) and is described below. Previous attempts to develop measures based on line drawings have been reported (e.g., Shimoyama et al., 1990), but none appear to have been used to determine lateralization. After reviewing this method, we focus on how lateralization, when measured by performance assessments, affects the quality of memory outcomes in normal participants. The outcomes of these studies and the importance of time of day (TOD) measurement is revealed and is then applied to schizophrenia patients and their memory and language functioning.

MEASUREMENT OF PERFORMANCE BY LINE DRAWING

The participant is asked to draw a straight line from one bottom corner of a 2-in. (5.08 cm) square to the upper corner obliquely opposite. A straight line of 45° would be a perfect response. The participant draws four such lines in sequence, two with each hand. One from bottom left to upper right and the other from bottom right to upper left. Each of the resulting four lines is scanned with a flat-bed optical scanner into a computer graphic format (e.g., PICT). The resulting graphic is then digitized into a series of 135–140 X,Y pairs. These pairs provide the data for a first-order linear regression, for which the resulting root mean square (RMS) residual constitutes the error score. A perfectly straight line would, of course, produce zero error. From the whole procedure, four RMS scores are obtained. These provide the basis for assessing performance asymmetries, the main derived score consisting of the total of the two RMS for the right hand, subtracted from the total for the left hand, and divided by the total of all four. This gives relative laterality of error as a percentage of total error, thereby compensating for overall differences in line-drawing ability as such. Left relative laterality scores have a negative sign (more error with the right hand that with the left), whereas right relative laterality scores have a positive sign. For purposes of certain analyses, we compute absolute laterality, which is the same as relative laterality, with all values given a positive sign.

The distribution of laterality obtained from normal participants (those described in Figure 1) is shown in Figure 2. The distribution is approximately binomial, although the range extends to higher values on the right than the left. The correlation between the Annett Scale and the performance measure in this sample is $+.48$, $p \geq .0001$. Although related, the two methods of assessment share only a modest common variance, almost certainly in part because of a constriction of range leading to floor and ceiling effects in the preference measure—constraints absent in the performance measure. We can see this when we split the data set by the simple dichotomy of which hand is used in writing. The means on the two measures appear as follows. Annett: right hand $= +10.20$; left hand $= -4.80$; line drawing: right hand $=$

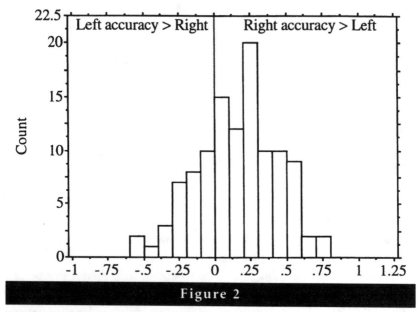

Figure 2

Distribution of net laterality in a performance task (left–right errors) on the line-drawing task from normal control data ($N = 112$).

+.19; left hand = −.14. The pile up of right-handed participants at the ceiling of the preference measure was striking.

DIFFERENCES IN PREFERENCE VERSUS PERFORMANCE OUTCOMES ON MEASURES OF LATERALITY

The fact that different measures give us different patterns of quantitative results is unimportant, unless we find that one of the measures is more sensitive than the other to relationships with other variables. With this in mind, we first examined the correlation between laterality and context-aided memory—a relationship already found by Manschreck et al. (1996) in schizophrenia patients.

This question is of more than methodological interest. It is possible that left lateralization in normal individuals is associated with some subclinical cognitive anomalies that cannot be easily detected with relatively insensitive preference measures but might be evident when performance measures are used. The published literature so far available does not include any systematic studies of this question.

The Task

We used the context-aided verbal recall measure called the Miller–Selfridge (M-S) Test, which consists of four word lists that vary from a completely random sequence without syntactic or semantic structure to lists that increasingly resemble a normal sentence; the lists increase from no context to greater degrees of context (Miller & Selfridge, 1950). Each list consists of 20 equal-frequency words. Participants are asked to write down all the words that they can recall immediately after hearing a recording of a list. The zero-order list (MS1) is composed of high-frequency, randomly selected words so that context does not aid recall. The first-order list (MS2) is constructed by an individual who writes a sentence from a single high-frequency word. The word following the given word in the individual's sentence is added on to the list and then given to another person who constructs a sentence from it. This process is repeated until the first-order word list consists of 20 words. The second- and third-order lists (MS3 and MS4) are created in the same fashion, except that individuals are asked to create a sentence from a sequential word pair for the second-order list and from a sequence of three words for the third-order list. The participants in our experiment produced the following lists (see Exhibit 1).

Measurement

The total score for each list was the total number of words correctly recalled out of 20. An overall context memory score (MS234) was computed by summing the scores from each context-aided list (i.e., MS2 + MS3 + MS4). This improves the reliability of the assessment of context-aided performance. To measure the gain in performance when the individual participant goes from the rote condition to the context-aided condition, we computed an additional derived score by subtracting the score on the rote list, MS1, from the score on MS4, the list with the

	Exhibit 1		
	Word List		
MS1	MS2	MS3	MS4
open	tea	sun	family
everything	realizing	was	was
its	most	nice	large
low	so	dormitory	dark
late	the	is	animal
horse	together	I	came
hard	home	like	roaring
play	and	chocolate	down
lie	for	cake	the
important	were	but	middle
pass	wanted	I	of
fill	to	think	my
hear	concert	that	friends
know	I	book	love
however	posted	is	books
person	he	he	passionately
on	her	wants	every
great	it	to	kiss
go	the	school	is
fear	walked	there	fine

maximum degree of context. Measures of primacy and middle and recency recall scores were computed for the first list with no context (MS1) and for the last list with the highest degree of context (MS4). The primacy score was the fraction of correctly recalled words from the first 5 words of the list, the middle score was the fraction of correctly recalled words from the middle 10 words, and the recency score was the fraction of correctly recalled words from the last 5 words of the list.

Results

Schizophrenia patients showed significant impairment in the ability to show increased recall with increased control but did not differ markedly from controls in their recall of the first list. The degree of impairment in schizophrenia patients was greater not only if they used the left hand for writing but also was (a) negatively proportionate to the ratio of dorso-lateral frontal area to whole brain volume in these patients (Maher, Manschreck, Woods, Yurgelun-Todd, & Tsuang, 1995) and (b) more impaired in TD than NTD patients (Maher et al., 1980). In all of these comparisons, the first list, MS1, did not differentiate between comparisons groups and was not correlated with proportional frontal dorso-lateral brain volume. The other lists did differentiate in increasing relationship to the degree of context built into the list.

We administered this memory measure to 40 members of the sample of 112 normal participants described above. The relationship of preference laterality to memory performance was not significant. The correlation coefficient with Net Laterality on the Annett Scale and MS4 − MS1 was $r = -.195$, $P = .2276$; with MS234, the coefficient was $r = +.048$, $p = .768$. In short, there is nothing in these data to suggest that anomalous or left-dominant laterality is related to memory impairment in the normal population. Turning to the performance measure, we found coefficients as follows: Relative Laterality and MS4 − MS1, $r = .43$, $p = .008$; MS234, $r = .47$, $p = .008$.

This finding opened up another question: Does the correlation reflect a steadily increasing improvement as we move from very left lateral to very right lateral, or is it somewhat curvilinear, with the worst performances being of individuals who have minimum laterality? We tested this first by fitting a second-order polynomial regression to the data. The effect in both cases was to slightly increase the magnitudes of the coefficient, while slightly reducing the level of significance (which remained significant, however). Extreme left lateralization values were, as we have seen, less frequent and of lower magnitude than extreme right values, which created a curve that was both shallow and asymmetrical. The principle of parsimony prevailed in favor of the simple first-order linear fit. We then approached the question by calculating the absolute laterality, that is, laterality as a departure from zero with all signs positive. The coefficients were essentially unchanged. In short, it appears that the key variable is clear lateralization (whether right or left dominance does not seem to matter too much) versus little lateralization, or *ambidominance*.

Artifacts: The Noon Slump

The implication of these data from memory impairment in poorly lateralized normal participants seemed sufficiently important, so we examined the data for the presence of possible artifacts that might account for the results. Within the sample of 40 normal controls already mentioned was included a sample of 29 participants whom had taken more extensive laboratory measures, permitting us to identify possible artifacts not present in the larger data set. These individuals had no history of mental illness, were drawn from the Cambridge–Boston area, and were paid for their participation in a series of language and motor tasks that included the M-S test. Eleven were women, and 18 were men; the mean age was 41.7 years (23–62 years); and mean education was 15.4 years (11–22 years). Fifteen were self-reported right-handers, and 11 were self-reported left-handers. Prior to the test, 17 reported having consumed some form of caffeine that day. The participants were tested within a time schedule that ran from 0800 to 1800.

Possible artifacts included gender, hand preference, and TOD. Analysis of variance revealed no significant association between recall (total of all MS lists) and gender, $N = 29$, $F(1, 27) = 1.23$, $p = .27$, or hand-preference, $N = 29$, $F(1, 27) = .023$, $p = .74$. We also examined the possibility that gender, hand preference, and TOD might be inadvertently confounded. No significant associations were found between any of these variables.

Unlike a preference measure, a performance measure is likely to be affected by any of the variables that affect performance of a task, such as general alertness or arousal, attentional focusing, motivation, fatigue, and so forth. Research suggests that the immediate recall of learning done in the morning is superior to that done in the afternoon or evening, whereas long-term recall of material originally learned in the afternoon appears better than that learned in the morning. Short- and long-term memory has also been linked to diurnal variations in plasma hormone levels as well as to basal arousal (Davis, 1987).

The effects of TOD differences concerning immediate and long-term memory performance have generally been interpreted with respect to circadian arousal effects on the learning process. Millar, Styles, and Wastell (1980) have demonstrated that retrieval latency in a long-term semantic classification task varies as a function of TOD, concluding that there is an association between an improvement in retrieval efficiency and the purported increase in arousal during the day. Other factors, such as whether a participant is a morning or night type, have been investigated. Anderson (1991) has demonstrated that performance on verbal recall tasks may vary with individual differences in circadian rhythm. Hence, many factors must be taken into account when investigating the effect of TOD on memory.

These studies generally assume that TOD effects will be linear across the day and that the evening will be better than the morning or vice versa, depending on the kind of task and the kind of individual who is performing the task. In our analysis of these effects, a different and consistent pattern emerged.

Our 29 normal participants had been scheduled to fit their individual availability; we did not have TOD in mind as a systematic variable and would have found it difficult to do so at that point. However, we examined the regression of the measures of performance laterality and of memory on TOD. In both cases, the calculation of a simple linear regression on the data sets produced nonsignificant coefficients. In the case of MS234, $r = .014$ and $p = .94$. However, visual inspection of this scattergram for memory performance suggests that the period of 1100–1300 appears to define the boundaries of a midday slump. We therefore fitted a second-order polynomial to the data, with the results presented in Figure 3.

Before pursuing the components of this curve, we turned to a sample of 52 psychiatric patients on whom we had also begun to gather TOD data to see if the same phenomenon appeared. The curve is presented in Figure 4. As is evident, it closely resembles Figure 3. These

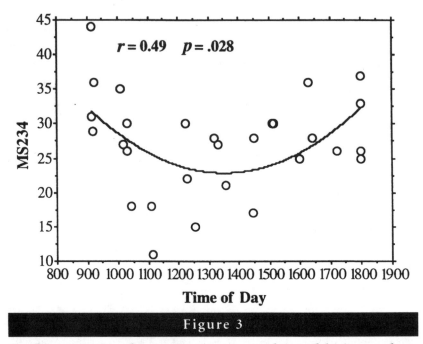

$r = 0.49$ $p = .028$

Time of Day

Figure 3

Curvilinear regression of context memory scores and time of day in normal participants ($n = 29$, $r = .49$, $p = .028$).

patients were of various diagnoses. Separation by diagnosis resulted in samples too small to analyze with any confidence. Such analyses are in progress as we accumulate a larger database.

Turning to the separate components of the memory measure in normal controls, we looked at the polynomial regressions for each list separately, bearing in mind that MS1 had no approximation to sentence structure and that the other three lists did in increasing amounts. The coefficients were as follows: MS1: $r = .32$, $p = .224$; MS2: $r = .25$, $p = .43$; MS3: $r = .46$, $p = .043$; MS4: $r = .56$, $p = .007$. It is clear that MS1 and MS2 show little or no TOD effect but that with increasing context, MS3 and MS4 do reflect the effect. This is consistent with previous findings that suggest that the processing and retrieval of context-aided material differs from that for role unrelated material (Maher & Skovengaard, 1988; Miller & Selfridge, 1950; Sharma & Sen, 1977). For the

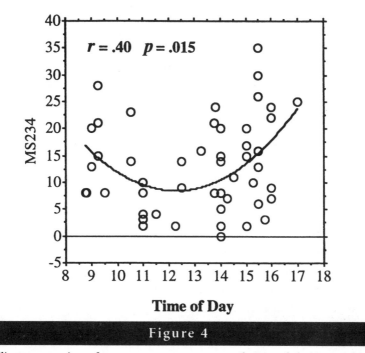

Figure 4

Curvilinear regression of context memory scores and time of day in psychiatric patients ($n = 52$, $r = .40$, $p = .015$).

derived score, the following results were found: MS3 + MS4 − MS1, $r = .58$, $p = .005$. The essence of these findings is that TOD had an effect on context-aided verbal-recall memory but no demonstrable effect on simple recall of a context-free word list.

At this point, the question arose as to whether the correlation between laterality and memory might be an artifact of combined poorer performance on both measures when given during the midday hours. In our previous studies and in all the studies that we have located in the literature, we could find no instance in which TOD had been examined in relation to correlations between separate variables; we could not therefore rule it out as a serious contributor to what might at base be a spurious correlation.

As a preliminary approach to this, we computed the correlations in both normal participants and in various samples of patients, excluding the data obtained between 1100 and 1300. For the normal participants, the correlations between absolute laterality and MS4 − MS1 and MS234 and between relative laterality and these two measures ranged from +.13 to +.19, all four nonsignificant. In short, within the available data, when TOD had been eliminated, there was no evidence that performance laterality in normal participants was associated with context memory performance. When we included the midday data, the comparable correlations had r ranging from .52 to .70, all significant. In short, the inclusion of the midday data creates a spurious correlation by virtue of the fact that performance on both measures is depressed by the TOD effect. This artifact is troubling. It suggests that unless TOD effects are analyzed in studies in which they have not been systematically randomized by assignment, an investigator might be misled into concluding that two response systems are related by a basic underlying traitlike process, unaware that the effect is due to a situational variable that affects performance generally.

LATERALITY AND MEMORY IN SCHIZOPHRENIA

TOD Study

We now turn to the question of possible associations between lateralization and memory in schizophrenia patients when midday effects have been eliminated. Our sample of 35 schizophrenia patients was obtained from the Corrigan Mental Health Center (Fall River, RI) and the Slater Hospital (Providence, RI). All had uncomplicated diagnoses of schizophrenia. The demographic data are as follows: age $M = 33.7$ (19−64), length of illness $M = 29.5$ years (2−47 years), education $M = 12.3$ years (3−20), ratio of men:women = 19/16. When we eliminated the midday TOD effect, we found that a simple first-order linear regression of MS4 − MS1 on absolute laterality produced a significant coefficient of +0.41, $p = .01$. The scattergram is presented in Figure 5.

Here, the correlation between laterality and context memory is not an artifact of TOD. When we restored the midday data to the analysis, the correlation increased to +.50, indicating that the patient sample

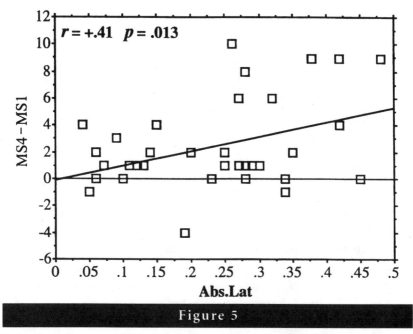

Figure 5

Regression of context-aided gain (MS4 − MS1) in a schizophrenia sample ($n =$ 35, $r = .41$, $p = .013$) with the effect of midday testing eliminated. Abs.Lat = absolute laterality.

was susceptible to TOD effects but that these do not account for the more basic correlation between laterality and context-aided memory.

Discussion

The general tenor of these conclusions is that performance laterality and recall in context-aided verbal memory are vulnerable to TOD effects in both normal and psychiatric samples. A midday slump accounts for the bulk of the effect in normal participants. When these effects were eliminated, there was no evidence of significant association between performance lateralization and memory in the normal population. Although the same midday slump effect is evident in schizophrenia (and other psychiatric) patients, elimination of the midday data does not eliminate the relationship between performance lateralization in schizophrenia patients. This relationship is positive, with a greater lateral dominance in performance associated with a greater gain from context in verbal recall.

Previous studies (Manoach, 1984; Manoach et al., 1988; Manschreck et al., 1996) have implicated left-handedness in the occurrence of both TD and failure to exhibit context-aided gain in verbal memory. The present data suggest that left- versus right-hand preference may not be important but that left-hand preference is associated with relatively poorer lateralization than is right-handed preference. In short, left-hand preference may be a surrogate variable for low absolute lateralization, at least in schizophrenia patients but not in normal controls. We could test this by a simple analysis of hand preference and absolute laterality values in schizophrenia patients in our database. We found that 58% of our left-hand preference schizophrenia patients obtained absolute laterality values between 0.00 and 0.14, while only 17% of right-hand preference patients fell in that range. When we turned to normal controls, we found that there was relatively little difference between the mean performance laterality of right-handed and left-handed individuals. In both cases, approximately 32% fell into the 0.0−0.14 range. This suggests that left-handedness is an indicator of atypically poor lateralization of performance only in schizophrenia patients, not in the general population. By inference, we might speculate that the origins of left-handedness in schizophrenia differ from those in the general population. This hypothesis has been advanced (see Coren, 1996, for a review of relevant literature) that organic damage in early life creates a subtype of pathologically left-handed individuals who would otherwise have been right-handed. The presumptive damage is assumed to be also involved in the broader pathology that gives rise to the spectrum of schizophrenic symptoms later in life.

However, organic damage is not the only possible path to anomalies in hemispheric dominance. Crow and his colleagues (e.g., Crow, 1995; Crow, Colter, Frith, Johnstone, & Owens, 1989; Crow, Done, & Sacker, 1996) have proposed that anomalies of hemispheric dominance are present in many schizophrenia patients on the basis of a genetic developmental disorder. According to this hypothesis, the 2nd decade of life is normally marked by the activation of neurodevelopmental processes that reach completion in early adulthood, with a clear dominance of one hemisphere (usually, but not always, the left hemisphere). In the proposed genetic developmental disorder underlying schizophrenia, the normal emergence of clear dominance of one hemisphere is not achieved. The effects of this only become grossly apparent in late adolescence, which is when the contrast between the behavior of the incipient schizophrenia patient and that of his or her normal peers becomes increasingly obvious. This hypothesis includes the suggestion that the putative genetic disorder is sex linked, with the male population being more vulnerable. As the anomaly affects the normal dominance of the left hemisphere, language function is particularly affected and assumes a central position in the clinical manifestations of the disorder (De Lisi et al., 1997).

Although the clinical manifestations of schizophrenia arising on this basis become most evident in adolescence, the failure to develop asymmetry may have effects beginning in the 9th and 10th year of life. These effects are less noticeable at that age—a circumstance that gives rise to the impression that the underlying pathological processes do not occur until adolescence. The hypothesis further proposes that the greater the severity of the disorder (i.e., the more complete the failure of the development of hemispheric asymmetry), the earlier the onset of schizophrenia. Emerging from this is a model of one kind of early onset schizophrenia characterized by poor development of hemispheric asymmetry, with a predominance of male patients, more mixed-handedness in preference, more ambilaterality in performance, and marked frequency of language disorder.

Studies of lateralization (by preference or performance) that demonstrate that schizophrenia patients are more often left-handed or mixed-handed than are members of the normal population are consistent with the possibility both that this reflects a genetic developmental pathology and that it reflects early exogenous brain damage. In short, both hypotheses—early brain damage and genetic developmental pathology—may be true for some patients but not for others. The exogenous and endogenous origins of poor lateralization may constitute one dichotomy within the heterogeneous complexity of schizophrenia.

LATERALITY AND LANGUAGE IN SCHIZOPHRENIA

Oral Description Study

In keeping with the previous suggestion, we might expect that poorly lateralized left-handed schizophrenia patients might show a different pattern of symptoms than that shown by well-lateralized patients of either hand preference. Accordingly, we looked at the relationship of performance lateralization in schizophrenia patients to various measures of language utterance. These measures had been obtained from schizophrenia patients asked to provide an oral description of Pieter Breughel's *The Wedding Feast*, which we have used extensively to obtain a record of language utterance to a standard stimulus under free-response conditions. With samples of left-handed ($n = 19$) and right-handed ($n = 82$), the correlations between absolute lateralization and language variables are shown in Table 1.

The central theme of the findings is clear; poor performance later-

Table 1

Correlations Between Absolute Performance Lateralization and Repetition in Language in Schizophrenia Patients by Hand Preference

Variable	Left-handed ($n = 19$)		Right-handed ($n = 82$)	
	Correlation	Significance	Correlation	Significance
Repeated word types (%)	−.605	.02	.009	.97
Repeated words (%)	−.460	.05	.160	.13
No. of phrase repetitions	−.430	.06	.009	.97
Type: Token ratio	.310	.18	.040	.65

Note. Correlations are with absolute lateralization and each variable.

alization in left-handed schizophrenia patients is associated with significantly greater repetitiousness in language. The same relationship is not found in right-handed schizophrenia patients. These findings are in line with a previously reported association between repetitiousness and rated TD in schizophrenia patients (Maher, Manschreck, Hoover, & Weisstein, 1987).

Discussion

With due recognition of the dangers of causative interpretation in correlational research and of the many uncontrolled factors that may influence patient performance, we suggest that our data are consistent with the hypothesis that a subset of schizophrenia patients are characterized by left-handed preference coupled with poor performance lateralization and that these patients are likely to exhibit (a) difficulty in the effective use of context in immediate verbal recall and (b) repetitiousness in language utterance at the level of words or phrases—a repetitiousness that affects clinical ratings of TD. Poor performance lateralization in right-handed preference schizophrenia patients is associated with this pattern of impaired capacity from context-aided memory in verbal recall, not with repetitious language.

Some investigators have suggested that attentional factors play a differential role in the control of precise motor performance in left-handers compared with right-handers (e.g., Peters, 1987). Peters used a task in which participants were required to tap twice as fast with one hand as with the other at a rate that they created. Right-handed participants performed more accurately when the faster rate was made with the right hand than with the left hand. Left-handers did not show this asymmetry. He suggested that the difference lies in the focusing of attention required in any motoric task and that attention is normally focused on the performance by the preferred hand, to the detriment of performance by the nonpreferred hand, when both hands are involved in a dual manual task. Left-handers however perform equally well with both hands in such tasks, stimulating the suggestion that the phenomena of ambilateral dominance in left-handed participants arises not necessarily from differential dominance of motor programming but from differential capacity to confine the focus attention on the nominally preferred left hand. This is a speculative proposal and is in need of more convincing empirical support. However, it does provide an interesting possible basis for the relationships so commonly found in schizophrenia between impaired motor performance and anomalous language.

We also note that TOD may be a very significant artifact affecting information processing by both patients and normal controls—significant enough to require analysis of its effects as a standard part of data presentation in psychopathology research. It creates the real possibility that uncorrelated variables will appear associated by virtue of the occurrence of low performance on the relevant tasks when both are performed at a disadvantageous TOD. The possibility also exists that the hours of availability of normal controls and of patients may themselves differ in ways that make TOD an unrecognized confounding variable —with obvious consequences for the meaning of differences in group performance.

CONCLUSIONS

On the basis of the data that we have obtained in our laboratories and have reported here, certain conclusions appear warranted. The first of these is that in schizophrenia patients, there appear to be significant associations with hand lateralization and performance in short-term recall of verbal material and with repetitiousness in language utterance. Clearly, the detailed unraveling of the neuropsychological basis for these associations is a very complex task. Our data to this point do not warrant any extended speculations.

A second conclusion is that the TOD at which behavior occurs is an important potential confound in studies in which participants are engaged in tasks that place some demand on attention, motivation, and general arousal. As the literature indicates, this has been adequately documented by other investigators in studies of normal participants. Our data here make it clear that the same effect can be seen in the performance of schizophrenia patients. A real possibility exists that the

availability of time slots for the testing of patients and control participants may differ, especially when the controls are constrained by their
work schedules. When this leads to unnoticed confounds between TOD
and participant group status, it is possible that spurious differences (or
spuriously large differences) between the performance of patients and
controls will be found or that real differences will be minimized or
obscured. In our investigations, we now routinely record the TOD as a
systematic variable in all studies in which it might be relevant. The
same caution also needs perhaps to be observed in research involving
demands on the attention of the investigator, as in the case of the
application of ratings to samples of behavior.

REFERENCES

Anderson, M. J. (1991). Individual differences in the effect of time of day on
long-term memory access. *American Journal of Psychology, 104,* 241–255.

Annett, M. (1967). The binomial distribution of right, mixed, and left-handedness. *Quarterly Journal of Experimental Psychology, 19,* 327–333.

Blyler, C. R., Maher, B. A., Manschreck, T. C., & Fenton, W. S. (1997). Line
drawing as a possible measure of lateralized motor performance in schizophrenia. *Schizophrenia Research, 26,* 15–23.

Coren, S. (1996). Pathological causes and consequences of left-handedness. In
D. Elliott & E. A. Roy (Eds.), *Manual asymmetries in motor performance*
(pp. 83–98). Boca Raton, FL: CRC Press.

Crow, T. J. (1995). The relationship between morphologic and genetic findings
in schizophrenia. In R. Fog, J. Gerlach, & R. Hemmingsen (Eds.), *Schizophrenia: Alfred Benzon Symposium* (pp. 15–25). Copenhagen, Denmark:
Munksgaard.

Crow, T. J., Colter, N., Frith, C. D., Johnstone, E. C., & Owens, D. G. C. (1989).
Developmental arrest of cerebral asymmetries in early onset schizophrenia.
Psychiatry Research, 29, 247–253.

Crow, T. J., Done, D. J., & Sacker, A. (1996). Cerebral lateralization is delayed
in children who later develop schizophrenia. *Schizophrenia Research, 22,*
181–185.

Davis, Z. T. (1987). The effect of time of day of instruction on eighth-grade students' English and mathematics achievement. *High School Journal, 71,* 78–80.

De Lisi, L. E., Sakuma, M., Kushner, M., Finer, D. L., Hoff, A. L., & Crow, T. J. (1997). Anomalous cerebral asymmetry and language processing in schizophrenia. *Schizophrenia Bulletin, 23,* 255–271.

Goldberg, E., & Seidman, L. J. (1991). Higher cortical functions in normals and in schizophrenia: A selective review. In S. R. Steinhauer, J. H. Gruzelier, & J. Zubin (Eds.), *Handbook of schizophrenia. Vol. 5: Neuropsychology, psychophysiology, and information processing* (pp. 553–597). Amsterdam: Elsevier.

Gruzelier, J. H. (1991). Hemispheric imbalance: Syndromes of schizophrenia, premorbid personality, and neurodevelopmental influences. In S. R. Steinhauer, J. H. Gruzelier, & J. Zubin (Eds.), *Handbook of schizophrenia: Vol. 5. Neuropsychology, psychophysiology, and information processing* (pp. 599–650). Amsterdam: Elsevier.

Gruzelier, J. H., & Venables, P. H. (1972). Skin conductance orienting activity in a heterogenous sample of schizophrenics. *Journal of Nervous and Mental Diseases, 155,* 277–287.

Gur, R. E. (1977). Motoric laterality imbalance in schizophrenia. *Archives of General Psychiatry, 34,* 33–37.

Heilman, K., & Valenstein, E. (1979). Mechanisms underlying hemispatial neglect. *Archives of Neurology, 5,* 166–170.

Lishman, W. A., & McMeekan, E. R. L. (1976). Hand preference patterns in psychiatric illness. *British Journal of Psychiatry, 129,* 158–166.

Luchins, D. J., Weinberger, D. R., & Wyatt, R. J. (1979). Anomalous lateralization associated with a milder form of schizophrenia. *American Journal of Psychiatry, 136,* 1598–1599.

Maher, B. A., Manschreck, T. C., Hoover, T. M., & Weisstein, C. C. (1987). Thought disorder and measured features of language production in schizophrenia. In P. Harvey & E. Walker (Eds.), *Positive and negative symptoms in psychosis: Description, research and future directions* (pp. 195–215). Hillsdale, NJ: Erlbaum.

Maher, B. A., Manschreck, T. C., & Rucklos, M. E. (1980). Contextual constraint and the recall of verbal material in schizophrenia: The effect of thought disorder. *British Journal of Psychiatry, 137,* 69–73.

Maher, B. A., Manschreck, T. C., Woods, B. T., Yurgelun-Todd, D. A., & Tsuang, M. T. (1995). Frontal brain volume and context effects in short-term recall in schizophrenia. *Biological Psychiatry, 37,* 144–150.

Maher, B. A., & Skovengaard, J. (1988). Contextual constraint: A Danish replication of Miller–Selfridge with methodological improvements. *Scandinavian Journal of Psychology, 29,* 194–199.

Manoach, D. S. (1994). Handedness is related to formal thought disorder in schizophrenia. *Journal of Clinical and Experimental Neuropsychology, 16,* 2–14.

Manoach, D. S., Maher, B. A., & Manschreck, T. C. (1988). Left-handedness and thought-disorder in the schizophrenias. *Journal of Abnormal Psychology, 97,* 97–99.

Manschreck, T. C., Maher, B. A., Redmond, D. A., Miller, C., & Beaudette, S. M. (1996). Laterality, memory, and thought disorder in schizophrenia. *Neuropsychiatry, Neuropsychology, and Behavioral Neurology, 9,* 1–7.

Miller, G., & Selfridge, J. (1950). Verbal context and the recall of meaningful material. *American Journal of Psychology, 63,* 176–185.

Millar, K., Styles, B. C., & Wastell, D. G. (1980). Time of day and retrieval from long-term memory. *British Journal of Psychology, 71,* 407–414.

Oldfield, R. C. (1971). The assessment and analysis of handedness: The Edinburgh Inventory. *Neuropsychologia, 9,* 97–114.

Peters, M. (1987). A nontrivial motor performance difference between right-handers and left-handers: Attention as an intervening variable in the expression of handedness. *Canadian Journal of Psychology, 41,* 91–99.

Sharma, N. K., & Sen, A. (1977). Effect of verbal context on communication in Hindi. *Indian Journal of Psychology, 7,* 240–249.

Shimoyama, I., Ninchoji, T., Uemura, K., Nishizawa, S., Yokoyama, T., & Ryu, H. (1990). Line-drawing test across ages. *Perceptual and Motor Skills, 71,* 955–959.

Spitzer, R., & Endicott, J. (1977). *Schedule for affective disorders and schizophrenia.* New York: Biometrics Research.

9

Neural Mechanisms Underlying Hallucinations in Schizophrenia: The Role of Abnormal Fronto-Temporal Interactions

Emily Stern and David Silbersweig

Hallucinations are a prominent and debilitating psychotic symptom of schizophrenia. They usually take the form of voices talking to or about the patient, often in a derogatory fashion. With increased severity of illness, other modalities, such as visual and tactile, may be involved. Up to 75% of patients experience such involuntary percepts in the absence of external stimuli at some point in their illness (Wing, Cooper, & Sartorius, 1974). A striking feature of hallucinations in schizophrenia, in contrast to those accompanying structural neurological disorders, is that they often have affective, conceptual, and behavioral relevance for the patient. Patients become emotionally involved with their hallucinations, incorporate them into delusional belief systems, and may even act on them.

Given the predominantly auditory-linguistic form of schizophrenic hallucinations, as well as the loss of reality testing associated with them, superior temporal and prefrontal abnormalities might be postulated. When considering the role that such neuroanatomical areas might play, one must consider not only the information-processing characteristics of individual subregions but also their pattern of afferent (incoming) and efferent (outgoing) connections. This is consistent with the trend in behavioral neuroscience over the past decade of emphasizing the distributed (rather than purely localized) nature of the neural substrates of behavior (Mesulam, 1990). More recently, the neuropsychological and neurophysiological importance of interactions among the regions making up these parallel distributed systems has also been recognized (Friston, Frith, Fletcher, Liddle, & Frackowiak, 1996).

Rapidly advancing functional neuroimaging technologies when combined with careful study design provide a means of localizing and characterizing neuronal activity associated with human mental states. Positron emission tomography (PET) is a particularly well-developed method of assessing systems-level activity. The use of water (H_2O) or carbon dioxide (CO_2), radiolabeled with a short half-life isotope of oxygen (^{15}O), allows multiple, repeated sampling of brain–mental states in a single study session. These PET radiotracer techniques work by measuring the regional cerebral blood flow changes coupled to local synaptic activity. With high-sensitivity 3-dimensional scanning, specific psychological or psychiatric activation paradigms, and appropriate univariate and multivariate image analysis techniques, statistically significant results can be obtained with single subjects or with groups (Frackowiak & Friston, 1994).

We and our colleagues have performed a series of PET studies focusing on the problem of hallucinations in schizophrenia. These studies use new ^{15}O activation methodologies that extend previous single photon emission computed tomograph and PET approaches (reviewed elsewhere, see Silbersweig & Stern, 1996) to this problem. Here, we discuss our studies in the context of fronto–temporal interactions and their implications for symptom formation. The studies converge on the psychopathophysiological issues, starting with a consideration of schizophrenia as an overall diagnostic syndrome, progressing to an assessment of trait characteristics that predispose to hallucinations in schizophrenia, and ending with an analysis of the specific hallucinating state in schizophrenia. The syndrome and trait studies use a top-down approach—starting with some of the neuropsychological processes thought to be disrupted, scanning normal subjects and patients during appropriately designed activation and control tasks that isolate those processes, and contrasting the brain images associated with those tasks to localize symptomatically relevant dissociations in brain activity. In contrast, the state study uses a bottom-up approach—directly mapping the neural substrates of the symptom and interpreting the results in light of behavioral neuroscientific principles. These investigational strategies are complementary and may inform one another (Silbersweig & Stern, 1996). The design and pertinent results of each study are outlined below, followed by a discussion of the pathophysiological implications of abnormal activity in and interactions between frontal and temporal regions.

PET STUDIES

Words are generated by patients with schizophrenia during auditory-verbal hallucinations, even if the patients attribute them to another source. Word generation therefore involves a set of neuropsychological functions of relevance to the linguistic aspects of typical schizophrenic hallucinations. Eighteen chronic, medicated patients with schizophrenia (divided into three groups of six, on the basis of verbal fluency performance) and six age, sex, premorbid IQ-matched normal control subjects were studied with a paced word-generation, PET-activation paradigm (Frith et al., 1995). The activation task involved generating words starting with a given letter. One letter was presented aurally every 5 s. A given letter was repeated 10 times unless the individual failed to generate an appropriate word, in which case a new letter was presented. The sensory–motor control task involved the presentation of the same type of stimuli, but the subject was instructed to merely repeat the letter aloud (thereby controlling for auditory input and speech output). Images from each condition were processed and analyzed (contrasted) with statistical parametric mapping (SPM) techniques.

In the word-generation condition versus the control condition, normal subjects activated a distributed cortical–subcortical system, including the left dorso-lateral prefrontal cortex, anterior cingulate, and thalamus. Areas of relatively decreased activity for this comparison included the superior temporal cortices (left greater than right). Patients with schizophrenia, regardless of task performance, were able to activate the frontal regions. However, these patients did not show decreased activity in the superior (and, to a lesser extent, middle) temporal cortices. In fact, with a canonical variates analysis (capable of identifying distributed patterns of neural activity accounting for the experimentally induced variance), the patients showed increased activity in these temporal regions.

Instead of examining the overall syndrome of schizophrenia, the next study focused on the symptom trait—the predisposition to hallucinate. The neuropsychological tasks used in this study probed the processes of inner speech and auditory-verbal imagery. Covert speech has been implicated in schizophrenic hallucinations, given the possible disruption of normal linguistic thought processes and the variable finding of subvocal speech (detected with throat microphones) in some hallucinating patients that matched the reported content of their "voices" (Gould, 1949). Auditory-verbal mental imagery is another important process to consider. Like hallucinations, imagery represents perception in the absence of external stimuli; but unlike hallucinations (which are involuntary), it is under voluntary control.

Three groups of six subjects each were studied in this experiment —patients with schizophrenia and a history of hallucinations (trait positive but not currently hallucinating), patients with schizophrenia and no history of hallucinations (trait negative, patient controls), and normal controls (McGuire et al., 1995; McGuire, Silbersweig, Wright, et al., 1996). All groups were matched for age and premorbid IQ. Patients were also matched for illness duration and neuroleptic dose (in chlorpromazine equivalents). Three tasks were performed in a counterbalanced order (to counteract time and order effects). The contrast of Task 2 versus Task 1 isolated inner (silent) speech, whereas the contrast of Task 3 versus Task 2 isolated auditory-verbal imagery.

In this experiment, there was no difference in the functional neuroanatomy of inner speech (including Broca's area) between the schizophrenia patients with a predisposition to hallucinate and the control groups. There was, however, a difference in the auditory-verbal imagery condition. Whereas normal and patient controls showed increased activity in bilateral rostral supplementary motor cortex (in the superior medial frontal lobe) and left middle temporal gyrus, schizophrenia patients with a hallucination trait actually showed decreased activity in these regions.

To map the neural substrates of hallucinations in a direct bottom-up fashion, we developed and validated new techniques of PET image acquisition and analysis (Silbersweig et al., 1993, 1994). The increased sensitivity and temporal discrimination of these methods allowed the study of such transient, randomly occurring symptoms in a naturalistic manner. Five patients with schizophrenia and classic auditory-verbal hallucinations despite medication and one drug naive patient with both visual and auditory-linguistic hallucinations were studied (Silbersweig et al., 1995).

In the patient with visual and auditory-verbal hallucinations, prominent activity was detected in visual and auditory-linguistic association cortices and in posterior cingulate, parahippocampal/mesotemporal, and temporal pole (para)limbic regions as well as in the striatum. The neocortical and posterior cingulate activity was greater in the dominant hemisphere, whereas the mesotemporal and subcortical activity was greater in the nondominant hemisphere. In particular, brain areas positively correlated with hallucinations included left posterior superior temporal gyrus (Wernicke's area), left posterior cingulate gyrus, right striatum, and visual and auditory association cortices. In contrast, brain areas in which activity was negatively correlated with hallucinations included right superior temporal gyrus, right posterior cingulate gyrus, left striatum, bilateral prefrontal cortices, and primary visual and auditory cortices (Silbersweig et al., 1996). The regions of activation common to the group of five patients with auditory-verbal hallucinations were deep (para)limbic and subcortical structures, including the hippocampus, parahippocampal gyrus, anterior cingulate gyrus, thalamus, and ventral striatum. There were no prominent frontal activations in these group analyses.

DISCUSSION

The studies described above demonstrate abnormal fronto-temporal activity and *functional connectivity* (the temporal correlations between spatially remote neurophysiological events; Friston et al., 1996) in schizophrenia in general and in association with hallucinations in particular. These findings contribute to a growing awareness of such abnormalities in schizophrenia (Friston & Frith, 1995; Weinberger, Aloia, Goldberg, & Berman, 1994) and recall the origin of the disorder's name ("split mind"). The mechanisms underlying such aberrant activity are likely to include abnormal mesolimbic dopaminergic modulation (Csernansky, Murphy, & Faustman, 1991) and an abnormal balance between excitation and inhibition in local neuronal circuits (Benes, Vincent, Alsterberg, Bird, & San Giovanni, 1992; Olney & Farber, 1995).

One of the consequences of abnormal functional connectivity is a failure of corollary discharge, or reafferent signaling. Corollary discharge is the process by which information about an intended action is transferred via direct or indirect connections from the efferent region planning or producing the action to an afferent region, which would receive sensory stimulation or feedback as a result of the action. A disruption of this process in schizophrenia, as suggested by Frith (1987, 1996), could result in symptom formation when information about an intended action is not properly monitored or interpreted (as a result of faulty interactions between frontal behavioral regions and posterior perceptual regions). For instance, delusions of control (or passivity) could result when a self-generated movement is not associated with a sense of volition and/or is mistakenly believed to arise from another source, or both. In the case of hallucinations, self-generated verbally mediated thoughts may similarly be misinterpreted as arising from another source.

The "articulatory/phonological loop" working memory system (Baddeley, 1992), localized to the left lateral frontal and temporoparietal regions (Paulesu, Frith, & Frackowiak, 1993), is involved in the "online" processing of such verbally mediated and monitored thought. Another way to conceive of the contribution of abnormal functional connectivity to symptom formation (in the context of working memory deficits in schizophrenia; Goldman-Rakic, 1994) would therefore be as a failure to transfer and update information between the frontal and the temporoparietal components of the loop. This would result in a fragmentation of the stream of auditory-linguistic conscious experience—a possible contributor to hallucinations.

In the word generation experiment, there was a lack of the normal correlation between left dorso-lateral prefrontal activity and superior temporal activity when patients with schizophrenia generated words (there were temporal increases instead of normal decreases in the setting of dorso-lateral prefrontal increases). Although this finding is not specific to patients with hallucinations, it may represent a predisposing factor in light of the theories of symptom formation mentioned above. The dorso-lateral prefrontal cortex is involved in generating volitional behavior (Frith, Friston, Liddle, & Frackowiak, 1991; including speech), and superior temporal cortex is involved in monitoring language (including self-generated speech; McGuire, Silbersweig, & Frith, 1996). Similarly, the inner speech/auditory-verbal imagery experiment demonstrated a failure of normal activation of rostral supplementary motor cortex and left middle temporal cortex in schizophrenia patients with a trait for hallucinations. This medial frontal–middle temporal abnormality may be a more specific predisposing factor for hallucinations, signifying a failure of volitional/preparatory control and semantic/source monitoring of verbally mediated thought (McGuire et al., 1995).

More direct evidence of abnormal frontal and temporal activity was obtained from the bottom-up PET experiments in which patients were imaged in the hallucinating state. These studies showed prominent temporal activations in the setting of an absence of, or even decrease in, prefrontal activity. The subject analyzed individually had activations in lateral (superior and middle) temporal regions, partially overlapping with regions in which decreases were noted in the top-down, nonhallucinating studies. Whereas the bottom-up studies are more specific to the problem of hallucinations than the top-down studies, it is possible to reconcile these results by postulating that regional abnormal balances of excitation–inhibition result in phasic increases in brain activity in these areas, superimposed on tonic decreased activity. This would not be similar to the temporal pattern in seizure foci of patients with epilepsy.

The lateral temporal findings are interesting in light of the auditory-linguistic functions of these regions. Certainly, normal subjects show activations in these areas during exposure to external auditory-linguistic stimuli (outside voices) of the sort reported by hallucinating schizophrenia patients (Silbersweig et al., 1993). Some of the specific sensory content of hallucinations may therefore be determined by such localized aberrant activity. From a mechanistic point of view, however, the medial temporal activations may be even more important. This is because they are so prominent in hallucinating patients yet absent when control subjects listen to or imagine voices. These hippocampal–parahippocampal regions are highly interconnected with other limbic-paralimbic structures as well as association cortices (Pandya & Yeterian, 1985), are involved in the recall or generation of sensory and semantic representations (Schacter, Alpert, Savage, Rauch, & Albert, 1996), and have abnormal morphology (Marsh, Suddath, Higgins, & Weinberger, 1994) and function (Friston, Liddle, Frith, Hirsch, & Frackowiak, 1992; Liddle et al., 1992) associated with psychopathology in schizophrenia. Such structures, together with interrelated thalamic and ventral striatal circuits (which, although not emphasized here, are also likely to play a central pathophysiologic role; Silbersweig & Stern, 1996), may therefore be in a position to trigger the symptomatic events.

All of this appears to occur in the setting of a relative lack of pre-frontal activity (although some frontal activations were present in individual patients). Given the executive role of prefrontal structures as de-scribed above, this hypofrontal–hypertemporal pattern may underlie the lack of reality testing often exhibited by psychotic hallucinating patients.

Finally, preliminary analyses of the single subject activations suggest that hallucinations are associated with more widespread abnormal pat-terns of interregional correlations, including negative rather than pos-itive right-to-left temporal correlations (Silbersweig et al., 1996). This may result in a lack of balance and integration of linguistic and paralinguistic components of verbal thought.

CONCLUSION

We have presented a number of related PET activation studies— focusing with increasing specificity on the diagnosis of schizophrenia, the trait of hallucinations, and the hallucinating state—in which abnormalities in lateral and medial frontal activity as well as lateral and medial temporal activity were noted. Possible mechanisms associated with the pathogenesis of hallucinations were discussed in the context of the neuropsychological functions of and functional connectivity among these interconnected brain regions. Clearly, additional studies are needed to replicate, clarify, and extend the findings mentioned here. More extensive multivariate analyses will also help to address the crucial issue of the interactions, or correlations in activity, among brain regions during hallucinations. In addition, the increased temporal resolution of functional magnetic resonance imaging and magnetoencephalographic methods will be important in determining the spatiotemporal sequence associated with the triggering and spread of abnormal distributed activity underlying symptom formation. Finally, the information gained through functional neuroimaging research must be integrated with relevant findings in cognitive neuropsychological and basic neuroscientific studies to arrive at a comprehensive understanding of the problem of hallucinations in schizophrenia. It is our hope that such an understanding will not only provide insight into this fascinating and devastating neuropsychological phenomenon but also provide a foundation for more targeted, biologically based diagnostic and therapeutic strategies.

REFERENCES

Baddeley, A. (1992). Working memory. *Science, 255*, 556–559.

Benes, F. M., Vincent, S. L., Alsterberg, G., Bird, E. D., & San Giovanni, J. P. (1992). Increased GABAA receptor binding in superficial layers of cingulate cortex in schizophrenics. *Journal of Neuroscience, 12*(3), 924–929.

Csernansky, J. G., Murphy, G. M., & Faustman, W. O. (1991). Limbic/mesolimbic connections and the pathogenesis of schizophrenia. *Biological Psychiatry, 30*(4), 383–400.

Frackowiak, R. S., & Friston, K. J. (1994). Functional neuroanatomy of the human brain: Positron emission tomography—A new neuroanatomical technique. *Journal of Anatomy, 184*(Pt. 2), 211–225.

Friston, K. J., & Frith, C. D. (1995). Schizophrenia: A disconnection syndrome? *Clinical Neuroscience, 3*(2), 89–97.

Friston, K. J., Frith, C. D., Fletcher, P., Liddle, P. F., & Frackowiak, R. S. (1996). Functional topography: Multidimensional scaling and functional connectivity in the brain. *Cerebral Cortex, 6*(2), 156–164.

Friston, K. J., Liddle, P. F., Frith, C. D., Hirsch, S. R., & Frackowiak, R. S. (1992). The left medial temporal region and schizophrenia. A PET study. *Brain 115*(Pt. 2), 367–382.

Frith, C. D. (1987). The positive and negative symptoms of schizophrenia reflect impairments in the perception and initiation of action. *Psychological Medicine, 17*(3), 631–648.

Frith, C. (1996). Neuropsychology of schizophrenia, What are the implications of intellectual and experiential abnormalities for the neurobiology of schizophrenia? *British Medical Bulletin, 52*(3), 618–626.

Frith, C. D., Friston, K. J., Herold, S., Silbersweig, D., Fletcher, P., Cahill, C., Dolan, R. J., Frackowiak, R. S., & Liddle, P. F. (1995). Regional brain activity in chronic schizophrenic patients during the performance of a verbal fluency task. *British Journal of Psychiatry, 167*(3), 343–349.

Frith, C. D., Friston, K., Liddle, P. F., & Frackowiak, R. S. (1991). Willed action and the prefrontal cortex in man: A study with PET. *Proceedings of the Royal Society of London B Biological Science, 244*(1311), 241–246.

Goldman-Rakic, P. S. (1994). Working memory dysfunction in schizophrenia. *Journal of Neuropsychiatry and Clinical Neuroscience, 6*(4), 348–357.

Gould, L. N. (1949). Auditory hallucinations and subvocal speech. *Journal of Nervous and Mental Disease, 109,* 418–427.

Liddle, P. F., Friston, K. J., Frith, C. D., Hirsch, S. R., Jones, T., & Frackowiak, R. S. (1992). Patterns of cerebral blood flow in schizophrenia. *British Journal of Psychiatry, 160,* 179–186.

Marsh, L., Suddath, R. L., Higgins, N., & Weinberger, D. R. (1994). Medial temporal lobe structures in schizophrenia: Relationship of size to duration of illness. *Schizophrenia Research 11*(3), 225–238.

McGuire, P. K., Silbersweig, D. A., & Frith, C. D. (1996). Functional neuroanatomy of verbal self-monitoring. *Brain, 119*(Pt. 3), 907–917.

McGuire, P. K., Silbersweig, D. A., Wright, I., Murray, R. M., David, A. S., Frackowiak, R. S., & Frith, C. D. (1995). Abnormal monitoring of inner speech: A physiological basis for auditory hallucinations. *Lancet, 346,* 596–600.

McGuire, P. K., Silbersweig, D. A., Wright, I., Murray, R. M., Frackowiak, R. S., & Frith, C. D. (1996). The neural correlates of inner speech and auditory verbal imagery in schizophrenia: Relationship to auditory verbal hallucinations. *British Journal of Psychiatry, 169*(2), 148–159.

Mesulam, M. M. (1990). Large-scale neurocognitive networks and distributed processing for attention, language, and memory. *Annals of Neurology, 28* (5), 597–613.

Olney, J. W., & Farber, N. B. (1995). Glutamate receptor dysfunction and schizophrenia. *Archives of General Psychiatry, 52*, 998–1007.

Pandya, D. N., & Yeterian, E. H. (1985). Architecture and connections of cortical association areas. In A. Peters & E. G. Jones (Eds.), *Cerebral cortex* (Vol. 4, pp. 3–61). New York: Plenum.

Paulesu, E., Frith, C. D., & Frackowiak, R. S. (1993). The neural correlates of the verbal component of working memory. *Nature, 326*, 342–345.

Schacter, D. L., Alpert, N. M., Savage, C. R., Rauch, S. L., & Albert, M. S. (1996). Conscious recollection and the human hippocampal formation: Evidence from positron emission tomography. *Proceedings of the National Academy of Sciences USA, 93*(1), 321–325.

Silbersweig, D., & Stern, E. (1996). Functional neuroimaging of hallucinations in schizophrenia: Toward an integration of bottom-up and top-down approaches. *Molecular Psychiatry, 1*, 367–375.

Silbersweig, D. A., Stern, E., Frith, C., Cahill, C., Holmes, A., Grootoonk, S., Seaward, J., McKenna, P., Chua, S. E., Schnorr, L., Jones, T., & Frackowiak, R. S. J. (1995). A functional neuroanatomy of hallucinations in schizophrenia. *Nature, 378*, 176–179.

Silbersweig, D. A., Stern, E., Frith, C. D., Cahill, C., Schnorr, L., Grootoonk, S., Spinks, T., Clark, J., Frackowiak, R., & Jones, T. (1993). Detection of thirty-second cognitive activations in single subjects with positron emission tomography: A new low-dose $H_2(^{15})O$ regional cerebral blood flow three-dimensional imaging technique. *Journal of Cerebral Blood Flow and Metabolism, 13*(4), 617–629.

Silbersweig, D. A., Stern, E., Frith, C., Schnorr, L., Cahill, C., Jones, T., & Frackowiak, R. S. J. (1996). *Disordered brain functional connectivity during hallucinations in a schizophrenic patient.* Paper presented at the 51st annual meeting of the Society of Biological Psychiatry, New York.

245

Silbersweig, D. A., Stern, E., Schnorr, L., Frith, C. D., Ashburner, J., Cahill, C., Frackowiak, R. S., & Jones, T. (1994). Imaging transient, randomly occurring neuropsychological events in single subjects with positron emission tomography: An event-related count rate correlational analysis. *Journal of Cerebral Blood Flow and Metabolism, 14*(5), 771–782.

Weinberger, D. R., Aloia, M. S., Goldberg, T. E., & Berman, K. F. (1994). The frontal lobes and schizophrenia. *Journal of Neuropsychiatry and Clinical Neuroscience, 6*(4), 419–427.

Wing, J. K., Cooper, J. E., & Sartorius, N. (1974). *Measurement and classification of psychiatric symptoms.* Cambridge, England: Cambridge University Press.

10

The Role of Cognitive Psychology in Guiding Research on Cognitive Deficits in Schizophrenia: A Process-Oriented Approach

Raymond A. Knight and Steven M. Silverstein

Specifying the nature of cognitive deficits in schizophrenia can provide an important, and heretofore lacking, theoretical framework for integrating the important domains of neurobiology, cognition, and symptomatology into unified models. The attempt to specify the processes underlying these cognitive deficiencies, however, has proven to be one of the most elusive tasks in psychopathology. In this chapter, we identify and illustrate the major stumbling blocks that have impeded progress in this research. We argue that a process-oriented strategy is a powerful solution to the methodological dilemmas encountered in studying these cognitive deficits. Using research from our laboratories, we illustrate some of the cumulative knowledge toward process specification that this strategy has yielded. Finally, we discuss how the process-oriented approach can contribute to the study of the macrobehavior and symptoms of schizophrenia and how it may be applied to other areas of schizophrenia research.

IMPEDIMENTS TO PROGRESS IN PROCESS SPECIFICATION

All research on schizophrenia has been plagued by a vast number of confounding variables that compromise studies and make straightforward interpretations of results difficult (e.g., varying drug regimes, institutionalization, poor motivation). In addition to these, cognitive studies suffer from their own specific set of difficulties that are often still poorly understood and controlled. The most pervasive and least well-addressed problem in cognitive studies has been the tendency for schizophrenia patients to show inferior performance on a variety of cognitive and perceptual tasks (e.g., Killian, Holzman, Davis, & Gibbons, 1984). Because of this tendency, when schizophrenia patients are shown to be deficient on any single task, little insight into their specific cognitive capabilities is achieved. To address this problem, researchers have proposed a "differential deficit" strategy, in which performance on two dependent measures is compared. It was argued that schizophrenia patients could be inferred to have a "specific deficit" if they could be shown to have a relatively greater deficiency than normal controls on only one task. This strategy was shown, however, to have a fatal flaw because differential performance on two tasks could occur simply as a function of the unequal discriminating power of the tasks chosen (Chapman & Chapman, 1978). That is, more reliable and therefore theoretically more discriminating tasks might produce group differences that are absent when less discriminating tasks are used. Chapman and Chapman (1973, 1978) argued that to remedy this problem, researchers must make experimental tasks equivalent in both difficulty and reliability.

Although, Chapman and Chapman (1973, 1978) identified and described a critical problem in cognitive research on schizophrenia patients, their solution to this problem neglected important issues of process specification and did not provide a viable strategy for researchers interested in applying cognitive models to study schizophrenia patients' processing deficiencies. Most important, they did not address the question of construct validation, or what Embretson (1983) called *construct representation*, when one is focusing on task variability rather than on individual variability. Ensuring that tasks are equally reliable and difficult does not guarantee that such tasks are measuring homogeneous constructs. With Chapman and Chapman's solution, it would be impossible to determine which process would be responsible for any differences that might emerge if a task tapped multiple processes. Moreover, matching tasks on psychometric characteristics, particularly difficulty level, often has unacceptable consequences for the process-oriented researcher. Frequently, matching can only be achieved at the expense of confounding the hypothetical processes being compared (Knight, 1984). In many information-processing and cognitive paradigms, difficulty level varies across conditions as factors such as stimulus exposure duration, stimulus brightness, and target–distractor similarity are manipulated to test specific hypotheses about underlying cognitive mechanisms. Matching on difficulty in these paradigms unmatches on process. Thus, requiring matched tasks eliminates many powerful analytic tools from the process-oriented researcher's arsenal. Even for the task-oriented researcher, however, Chapman and Chapman's solution is suboptimal. Nicewander and Price's (1983) demonstration of several instances in which reliability and discriminatory power are independent seriously questions Chapman and Chapman's basic assumption that matching on reliability guarantees equal discriminatory power. Consequently, for these and other reasons, a process-oriented strategy is proposed to address the general deficit problem (Knight, 1984).

THE PROCESS-ORIENTED STRATEGY

Description

The process-oriented strategy (Knight, 1984, 1987, 1992, 1993) makes use of well-established models from cognitive psychology to predict specific theory-driven patterns of performance within and across tasks that will occur under conditions of adequate and inadequate functioning of specific stages of processing. Although the approach initially assumes that the models generated to explain the cognitive performance of normal participants are applicable to the cognitive performance and deficiencies of schizophrenia patients, the validity of this assumption is either corroborated or disconfirmed by the ability of the models to

predict schizophrenia patients' performance. It is the pattern of performance, not the performance on any one condition or task, that is important. This approach treats the general deficit as an alternate model
and uses paradigms in which one or more specific deficit and general
deficit predictions are not confounded. Analogous to Meehl's (1978)
consistency tests, a model must pass all the tests (i.e., accurately predict
the pattern of performance across conditions and tasks) to be validated,
and paradigms are selected so that each model predicts a distinguishable
pattern of results. The strategy depends directly on the explicit delineation and testing of specific theoretical models and works best when
opposing models are pitted against each other and against the most
likely predictions of a general deficit explanation. Consequently, the
process-oriented approach encourages integration across multiple paradigms and aims at high explanatory power (universality) by requiring
the prediction of performance on multiple, maximally different tasks
(Popper, 1959).

Distinguishing the Process-Oriented Strategy From Other Research Approaches

The process-oriented strategy is easily differentiated from the task-
oriented approach that it was proposed to replace (see Knight, 1984).
It is critical, however, to distinguish the process-oriented strategy from
other strategies that have either used recent cognitive paradigms to
study schizophrenia patients' cognitive deficiencies or have attempted
to isolate critical components of discriminating tasks. Two general alternative approaches can be identified. The first strategy selects paradigms that have been extensively tested in the cognitive research with
normal samples and administers these tasks to schizophrenia patients
and normal controls. This strategy does not, however, embed the chosen
tasks in a detailed theoretical model of the proposed deficiencies of
schizophrenia patients' cognitive processing. Researchers who simply
select potentially informative tasks tend neither to adapt these cognitive
tasks to minimize the problems of schizophrenia patients' general cognitive inefficiencies nor to design the experimental and control condi-

tions to ensure that the pattern of results predicted for a hypothetical specific deficit are not confounded with the obvious predictions of a general deficit model. The second strategy, which has been referred to as a *task decomposition* strategy, studies a task that has consistently been successfully used to discriminate schizophrenia patients from normal controls. This strategy attempts to decompose the target task into its constituent parts and determine which component is most problematic for schizophrenia patients. This strategy is illustrated in research reported elsewhere in this book (see Green & Nuechterlein, chapter 12; and Holzman, chapter 6). We distinguish the process-oriented approach from each of these two strategies in turn.

An example of the first strategy highlights some of the serious interpretative flaws that can accompany its application. In a' tone-discrimination study designed to assess echoic memory functioning in schizophrenia, Javitt, Strous, Grochowski, Ritter, and Cowan (1997) found that when two tones were presented sequentially with no delay between them, schizophrenia patients appeared unimpaired; but when a brief delay was introduced, schizophrenia patients were found deficient in both easy and difficult tone discrimination conditions. Unfortunately, the no-delay condition clearly had a ceiling effect, and these same results would be predicted by a general deficit model (i.e., discrimination occurred only in the delay tasks that potentially had more adequate discriminatory power; see Chapman & Chapman, 1973, 1978).

In an attempt to remedy this problem, Javitt et al. (1997) introduced a more discriminating no-delay task in which the difference between tone frequencies (Δf) was manipulated. In this task, discrimination between schizophrenia patients and normal controls emerged only in moderately difficult Δf conditions. No discrimination was evident at the easiest (ceiling effect) or most difficult (floor effect) Δf conditions. Once again, these results are perfectly confounded with the a priori predictions of a general deficit model, which would posit that schizophrenia patients' general cognitive deficiencies tend to produce discrimination on tasks that assess moderate difficulty levels. Consequently, no conclusions about the nature of schizophrenia patients' specific cognitive–perceptual deficits can be inferred from these results. It is instructive to note that when 5% Δf represented a ceiling effect in the first paradigm, no difference between normal controls and schizophrenia patients emerged; but when the experimental method was changed so that this same percentage of Δf represented a moderate difficulty level, differences in performance emerged. Thus, whether a particular Δf discriminated was a function of its difficulty level within the experimental paradigm rather than its absolute Δf, suggesting that discrimination covaried with the artifacts of the task rather than with a specific deficiency. Unfortunately, such confounding of specific deficit and general deficit predictions is a common problem in many studies by researchers who select interesting cognitive tasks but do not create experimental designs that take into account schizophrenia patients' global performance deficits.

The second group of strategies, the task decomposition strategies, which attempt to break a discriminating task into its component parts, can be plagued by this same inappropriate selection of dependent measures. Whether schizophrenia patients show a performance deficit on any particular task tested as a subcomponent of the original task may simply be a function of the discriminatory power of the subtask. If researchers do not implement some method of addressing this problem, their conclusions about what aspect of the target task is most deficient in schizophrenia patients may be driven by the psychometric artifacts of the tasks they have chosen rather than by any specific deficiencies in the schizophrenia patients' cognitive capacities. In applying this strategy, it is possible, of course, that the decomposition could be embedded in cognitive theory and appropriate controls could be instituted to address problems of general performance deficiencies (see Green & Nuechterlein, chapter 12, this volume). Then, the strategy becomes a specific, more circumscribed application of the more general process-oriented approach described below. Its major limitation is that by definition it does not aim to predict performance across multiple paradigms. It shares with the process-oriented approach the focus on underlying cognitive processes that are embedded in a cognitive theory of task performance. Moreover, it does not, as do other task decomposition strategies, simply dissect a task by an analysis of apparent performance demands on component parts of the task without consideration of either cognitive theory or the differential discriminatory power of component tasks.

Successful implementation of the process-oriented strategy requires several critical steps. First, the deficit theory must be sufficiently specific, so that it predicts a priori a pattern of performance (within and across tasks) that would occur if the theory was correct. Second, this predicted specific deficit pattern must not be confounded with the predictions of a general deficit model. Third, paradigms must typically be adapted for administration to schizophrenia patients to minimize problems of motivation, fatigue, and interpersonal aversion and must focus the task on the key components of the proposed deficiency. A critical first step here is to demonstrate that all control groups exhibit performance indicative of normal functioning with the adapted version of the task. It is quite problematic to interpret schizophrenia patients' performance on a particular paradigm when they are compared with normal controls who have not shown adequate functioning of the studied process because some change in the adapted task alters the performance of normal controls from what is expected by the theory. The failure of controls to achieve the predicted pattern of results in an adapted task is unfortunately one of the frequent downfalls of what might otherwise be well-designed studies. Fourth, tasks should be designed so that schizophrenia patients can convincingly demonstrate the adequacy of their performance on conditions that assess intact processes (see Knight, 1984). Such inclusion allows discrimination between specific and generalized deficit aspects of performance. Fifth, the best implementation of the strategy usually involves a study design that tests competing models of the performance deficit, because corroboration is strengthened when it is demonstrated against the backdrop of disconfirmation of an opposing theory.

It has been speculated that the process-oriented strategy's dependence on the current state of cognitive psychology constitutes a serious limitation of the strategy (see Knight, 1984). It is conceivable that current formulations of a deficit theory could become obsolete in the light of the development of new, more comprehensive, and better validated theories of cognitive processing. Thus far, however, such fears have been unfounded. We illustrate that more advanced models have not invalidated previous research on cognitive deficiencies but rather have provided new and enriched perspectives from which previous results can be reinterpreted and new hypotheses can be generated and tested.

Specification Progress Using the Process-Oriented Strategy

There is a growing body of research in which the process-oriented strategy has been applied (reviewed earlier in Knight, 1984, 1992, 1993). Below, we illustrate the application of this strategy in our work, summarize the progress made by using this strategy, and indicate the future directions of our specification research. We focus on more recent studies and summarize only the most pivotal of earlier studies.

Testing the Original Sperling Iconic Imagery Model

Our process-oriented search for the early information-processing dysfunctions in schizophrenia began with a study that suggested that the first visual stage of image processing might be deficient in patients with histories of poor premorbid social functioning (Knight, Sherer, & Shapiro, 1977). In all of the research from our laboratories, we have divided schizophrenia patients into subgroups on the basis of their premorbid social functioning, which was determined by ratings in Farina, Garmezy, and Barry's (1963) adaptation of the Phillips (1953) scale. Whereas good premorbid patients demonstrate adequate levels of premorbid social functioning and have frequently been married, their poor premorbid counterparts have few friends, poor dating histories, and are rarely in a long-term relationship.

Using an adaptation of Sperling's (1960) partial report technique, we found that poor premorbid schizophrenia patients did not benefit from a visual cue that focused attention on a portion of a letter matrix and allowed normal controls and good premorbid schizophrenia patients to enhance their reporting of the cued letters. These data suggested that poor premorbid schizophrenia patients might be deficient in the first visual perceptual moment, called *the iconic image* by Neisser (1967). In the first formulation of this stage, Sperling hypothesized that iconic memory constituted a large, veridical reverberation of the stimulus that decayed completely within the 1st second after stimulus offset.

Other research conducted at the same time using another paradigm, backward masking (Saccuzzo, Hirt, & Spencer, 1974), suggested a similar locus to explain schizophrenia patients' early information-processing deficiencies. In the typical backward-masking paradigms used in schizophrenia research, a masking stimulus (a patterned but meaningless stimulus configuration of equal intensity to or greater intensity than the target) is presented at various durations after the offset of a target stimulus. When the masking stimulus is presented at short intervals after target offset, performance is at chance levels. As the interstimulus interval (ISI) increases, performance improves, until it finally equals the no-mask level. This is what has been termed a *Type A masking function* (Breitmeyer, 1984). For schizophrenia patients, especially those with more chronic histories and poorer prognosis, such masks interfered at ISIs between 150 and 250 ms, considerably exceeding the interfering ISIs for control groups (Balogh & Merritt, 1987).

At this time, the extant models of early information processing suggested that there were a multitude of processing deficiencies that could account for the inferior performance of poor premorbid schizophrenia patients on these partial report and masking tasks. These included either inadequacies in the formation or decay of iconic memory or deficiencies in any one of several transfer functions from iconic to subsequent storage. The process-oriented approach dictates that researchers seek paradigms that allow them to systematically test each of these processing deficiencies, controlling for general processing deficits. Two groups of researchers (Knight, Sherer, Putchat, & Carter, 1978; Spaulding et al., 1980) implemented this approach. They both used a stimulus integration technique (Eriksen & Collins, 1967, 1968) that allowed them to assess the decay of the icon, independent both of subsequent transfer problems and of general cognitive deficiencies. They found that the decay of schizophrenia patients' icons was intact. Their results suggested that transfer problems are a more likely locus of schizophrenia patients' processing deficit.

Discriminating Sensory Store From STVM

Advances started in the mid-1970s on the understanding of the stages of early processing led us to reconceptualize schizophrenia patient's deficits, explained some discrepancies we had found in the stimulus integration studies cited above (see Knight, 1984), and provided paradigms to further specify the parameters of the cognitive deficiencies in schizophrenia. It became clear that a model that allowed for two early processing stages instead of one better accounted for results in the first 600 ms of visual processing. Converging evidence (Cowan, 1988; Loftus, Hanna, & Lester, 1988; Long, 1980; W. A. Phillips, 1974; Potter, 1976) suggested two early processing stages for visual stimuli: Stage 1, a brief (approximately 100 ms) stage consisting of a large capacity veridical sensory store in which perceptual information is processed, and Stage 2, a subsequent limited capacity store, called short-term visual memory (STVM) by Phillips, which is highly efficient for another 500 ms and can persist longer. STVM is hypothesized to involve the allocation of conceptual resources to the perceptual representation that is the output of the first stage (Loftus et al., 1988). Moreover, the consolidation of information that takes place in STVM is considered a prerequisite for long-term storage. Stimulus identification is possible with Stage 1 perceptual processing, but Stage 2 cognitive processing is necessary for subsequent recognition (Loftus et al., 1988; Potter, 1976). Whereas elements in Stage 1, sensory store, are quickly identified and processed in parallel, elements in Stage 2, STVM, are transferred sequentially, one element at a time, to subsequent stages (Kroll & Hershenson, 1980; W. A. Phillips, 1974; Rosen & Hershenson, 1983).

Spaulding et al.'s (1980) clear finding that schizophrenia patients' sensory store, like that of all control groups, decayed within 100 ms suggested that the masking stimulus, which disrupted their processing of a target at ISIs of 150 to 250 ms, has to interfere with their STVM, not their already decayed sensory store. This suggested, of course, that a deficit in STVM might explain both schizophrenia patients' partial report and backward-masking deficiencies. The differential masking effects of meaningful and meaningless masks on STVM processing provided a method to test this hypothesis further (Knight, Elliott, & Freedman, 1985). In normal participants, it had been established that only a cognitive meaningful mask, not a meaningless pattern mask, interfered with the processing of information in STVM (Potter, 1976).

Therefore, we (Knight et al., 1985) created a picture memory masking paradigm, adapted from Hulme and Merikle's (1976), in which we presented colored, naturalistic scenes as target pictures, followed at various stimulus onset asynchronies (SOA, the time between target and mask onset) with either a random-noise mask (a dense matrix, randomly filled with dark and light dots), pattern masks (random arrays of colored shapes), or cognitive masks (photographs of real-world scenes; Potter, 1976). We tested the hypothesis that only a cognitive picture mask would reduce processing in STVM for control groups but both cognitive and pattern masks would yield equal, prolonged masking functions in STVM for poor premorbid schizophrenia patients, corroborating the hypothesis that STVM in schizophrenia patients is excessively susceptible to interference. Consistent with expectations, masking functions of the groups did not differ when a random noise mask was used as a baseline control. Normal participants, nonschizophrenia psychotic patients, and good premorbid schizophrenia patients experienced no masking in STVM when a pattern mask was used but evidenced significant masking effects in STVM when a cognitive picture mask was presented. Only the poor premorbid schizophrenia patients experienced equal disruption of target processing when either a patterned or a cognitive mask was used at 300 ms SOA, as is consistent with the predictions for a deficient STVM.

This paradigm serves as a good example of the process-oriented approach's strategies and how it manages to finesse the general deficit problem. The study was designed so that different processing deficit models predicted specific, distinguishable patterns of performance across conditions. Control groups all performed in accord with the predictions of the cognitive model. The study included conditions in which poor premorbid schizophrenia patients were predicted to and did perform competently. Moreover, the specific deficit models were not confounded with general deficit predictions. There is no way that a general deficit model would predict either poor premorbid patients' equivalence to normal controls on the random-noise and cognitive masking conditions or the singular differences on the pattern-masking condition. Its a priori predictions covary with difficulty level, a complex interaction of SOA and mask type, not with mask type. In addition, the focus of the a priori hypotheses in this study was on the pattern of responses across conditions within groups rather than differences between groups.

Unfortunately, this study did not unequivocally implicate an STVM deficit. An alternative explanation for poor premorbid patients' sensitivity to a pattern mask in STVM was still reasonable. It was possible that they failed to identify rapidly the meaninglessness of the pattern mask and consequently allocated to it the processing capacity usually reserved only for meaningful stimuli. Such a failure could be accounted for by a Stage 1 sensory deficiency in processing the mask. A reality representation decision task was designed to test these opposing hypotheses (see Knight, 1992). A broad range of pictures that varied from meaningful to meaningless was presented, and the participant was required to judge as rapidly as possible whether the pictures represented a real object. It was hypothesized that if poor premorbid schizophrenia patients were slower in identifying meaningless pictures, a Stage 1 explanation would be corroborated. In contrast, if they were able to identify meaninglessness rapidly, this would disconfirm the alternative Stage 1 interpretation of the backward-masking picture study and thus would be more consistent with a Stage 2 STVM explanation. Meaningfulness in this reality representation study was operationalized empirically by having a large group of undergraduates rate the representativeness of a large spectrum of art work, covering the entire range from completely abstract to realistic. A Thurstone equal-appearing interval scale (see Mueller, 1986) was constructed by selecting a subset of pictures that narrowly measured each level of meaningfulness from definitely non-representational to definitely representational. The results of this study were clearly consistent with a Stage 2 deficit explanation and disconfirmed the Stage 1 hypothesis (see Knight, 1992). Poor premorbid schizophrenia patients judged there to be the same level of meaning in nonrepresentative stimuli as did other groups but less meaning in the most representative stimuli. All the control groups (normal participants, mood disordered patients, and good premorbid schizophrenia patients) significantly benefited from the presence of meaning, responding relatively more quickly to meaningful than meaningless stimuli. In contrast, poor premorbid patients' responses to meaningful pictures were slightly, but not significantly, slower than their responses to meaningless stimuli. Indeed, the latencies of their responses to meaningless stimuli did not differ from those of normal controls. These results were incompatible with the hypothesis that poor premorbid patients' performance in the backward-masking picture study is due to a failure to recognize rapidly the meaninglessness of the pattern mask. Instead, these results support the hypothesis that STVM is more likely the locus of poor premorbid schizophrenia patients' early processing deficiencies.

Distinguishing Allocation and Consolidation Deficits in STVM

Loftus et al. (1988) argued that the major function of STVM is essentially attentional. It allocates conceptual resources to process the perceptual representation, which is hypothesized to be the product of the preceding sensory store stage. This allocation leads inevitably to in-depth cognitive processing, which Potter (1976) labeled *consolidation*. Potter found that consolidation in STVM is necessary for subsequent long-term storage and stimulus recognition. Loftus et al. developed a double backward-masking paradigm that offered increased flexibility in studying masking deficiencies and provided a way to assess the relative contribution of allocation and consolidation functions to schizophrenia patient's processing deficiencies. In a picture-masking paradigm similar to the one used by Knight et al. (1985), Loftus et al. demonstrated that when a second pattern mask is presented within 50 ms of an initial primary cognitive mask, this second pattern mask cancels the cognitive mask's interruption of target processing in STVM. That is, it nullifies the effect of the first mask and "unmasks" the target. As the ISI between the second pattern mask and the initial cognitive mask increases, the effect of the second mask decreases until it no longer diminishes the masking effect of the original cognitive mask, and processing of the target is once again interrupted.

The failure to allocate conceptual resources appropriately in STVM leads to less differentiated stimulus processing, poorer consolidation of information, and weaker memory traces. In contrast, poor premorbid patients might properly allocate the appropriate resources to processing the perceptual representation, but their consolidation capabilities in STVM may be deficient and interference prone (i.e., susceptible to interference even by a pattern mask), thereby yielding weaker long-term memory traces. To test these competing hypotheses of allocation and consolidation deficiency in STVM, McMenamin, Waxman, Orne, and Knight (1994) created a double masking variant of Knight et al.'s (1985) picture-masking paradigm described earlier. They introduced conditions in which Loftus et al.'s (1988) second pattern mask was presented at various ISIs after the initial pattern or cognitive masks. Both deficit theories predict the initial inappropriate disruption of target processing in the single pattern-mask condition—the former because of inappropriate allocation of resources to the mask and the latter because of interruption of a weak ongoing consolidation process.

Dysfunctional allocation, however, predicts that the second pattern mask, presented within the visual masking range of the first mask, should block the first mask and prevent it from disrupting the allocation of cognitive capacity to the target, thereby allowing the schizophrenia patients, like controls, to process the target. Increasing the interval between the masks should once again free the initial mask to disrupt allocation. In contrast, if poor premorbid patients had allocated appropriate capacity to the target and the effect of the initial pattern mask at 200-ms SOA was to interfere with a weakly operating STVM consolidation process, which was overly sensitive to disruptive stimuli, the introduction of additional noise (i.e., a second mask) in this processing window, even at brief intermask ISIs, should not help and might even further hinder processing.

In the double pattern-masking condition in which an initial pattern mask presented at 200-ms SOA was followed by a second pattern mask at 250-ms SOA (i.e., 50 ms after the onset of the first mask), each group, including the poor premorbid schizophrenia patients, performed comparably with their no-mask baselines. As the ISI between the first and the second pattern mask increased, schizophrenia patients' pattern-masking deficit returned; but this increased delay between masks did not affect the performance of control groups. Thus, schizophrenia patient's masking deficit could be eliminated and reestablished by the presence and temporal patterning of the double mask.

Clearly, then, the results obtained support the a priori predictions of an allocation deficit rather than a consolidation deficit theory. Here, it is once again important to point out the presence of the hallmarks of the process-oriented approach—theory-driven, specific a priori predictions for competing models, demonstration of performance consistent with predictions for control groups, conditions in which poor premorbid patients are predicted to show and do show competence, and clear discrimination of specific and general deficit predictions. Indeed, the general deficit model would not predict that the introduction of a second mask improves a schizophrenia patient's performance at short ISIs and leads to poorer performance at longer ISIs.

Perceptual Organization and Automaticity

As we argued earlier, one of the hallmarks of the process-oriented approach is that it forces reseachers to compare opposing theoretical models. Because of its emphasis on converging lines of evidence across multiple paradigms, the approach encourages and indeed requires that researchers build testable, explanatory bridges to viable findings about related cognitive deficiencies identified in schizophrenia patients. Consequently, the theory generated from the studies we have just described that poor premorbid schizophrenia patients have intact sensory store processing and deficiencies in STVM needs to be integrated with the well-replicated finding that schizophrenia patients have an advantage in tasks that are facilitated by a deficit in perceptual organization. Perceptual organization refers to the ability to rapidly and automatically organize stimulus components into wholes, as first demonstrated by the gestalt psychologists (e.g., Koffka, 1935). A number of theories of human visual perception posit that perceptual organization functions to define automatically and preattentively objects in the visual field and that this is a prerequisite to attentional allocation and serial analysis of relevant objects in the visual field.

Place and Gilmore (1980) demonstrated that as the perceptual organization of sets of lines decreased—from a condition where all lines were oriented the same way to a condition that included lines of different orientations with no clear organization to the set—control participants' ability to count the lines in tachistoscopic presentations declined. This presumably occurred because controls' intact tendency to perform grouping operations and inability to perform serial analyses until these processes terminated interfered with counting the lines. That is, by the time serial processing began for the controls, the mental representation of the images was too degraded to allow for accurate numerosity determinations. Because schizophrenia patients apparently did not engage automatic grouping processes, however, their counting of lines proceeded unabated and their efficiency did not decrease with increasing organization. These results have been replicated by two other research teams (Orlowski, Keitzman, Dornbush, & Winnick, 1985; Wells & Leventhal, 1984).

Knight (1992, 1993) argued that schizophrenia patients' performance on the numerosity tasks could be reconciled with the cognitive backward-masking and reality representation decision results by considering the hypothesis of reduced top-down influences to the perceptual organization of schizophrenia patients. Substantial data now support the notion that with unfamiliar stimuli, perceptual organization develops over time with repeated exposure (Lassaline & Logan, 1993; Logan, 1990). Schizophrenia patients' apparent weaknesses in early perceptual organization could thus be secondary consequences of prior failures to develop memory templates for the stimuli. Such a failure would delay the processing of stimulus configurations as single units after varying amounts of repeated exposure and would instead lead to a continued reliance on a serial scanning strategy.

Rabinowicz, Opler, Owen, and Knight (1996) developed a task that assessed the degree to which inadequate memory representation formation was associated with abnormal perceptual organization. In this study, simple geometric forms, whose shapes were defined by an increasing number of dots, were presented (see Figure 1). Consequently, both numerosity and form judgments could be made for the same stimuli. The task was developed so that whereas increasing the number of dots enhanced formal structure and under conditions of brief exposure duration improved form judgments for normal controls, this increase in structure interfered with dot counting. This allowed for both an assessment of schizophrenia patients' ability to process formal structure and a replication of Place and Gilmore's (1980) numerosity effect. Moreover, Rabinowicz et al. introduced a response delay manipulation that directly assessed the persistence and operation of STVM. Thus, the experimental design made it possible to posit specific, theory-driven a priori hypotheses for competing models of schizophrenia patients' processing deficiencies.

This study yielded the following critical results. First, Place and Gilmore's (1980) differential effect of stimulus organization on the numerosity performance of schizophrenia patients and normal controls was replicated, with schizophrenia patients' accuracy in numerosity judgments again unaffected by the amount of formal structure. Second, like all other groups, schizophrenia patients increased the accuracy and decreased the latency of their form judgments as the number of dots (therefore the formal structure) increased, indicating that they responded to formal gestalts with the same patterns of performance across conditions as did the controls. The overall accuracy of schizophrenia patients' form judgments was however still lower, suggesting some overall weakness in their form processing. Third, in contrast to all other groups, response delay significantly reduced rather than enhanced schizophrenia patients' numerosity accuracy, indicating some differential deficiencies in their allocation of mnemonic resources in STVM. In general, the overall pattern of results was consistent with a primary STVM deficit in schizophrenia patients that contributed to the development of insufficient mnemonic traces and consequently led to deficiencies in the patients' perceptual organization. It is again important to point out that the pattern of results attained in this study, es-

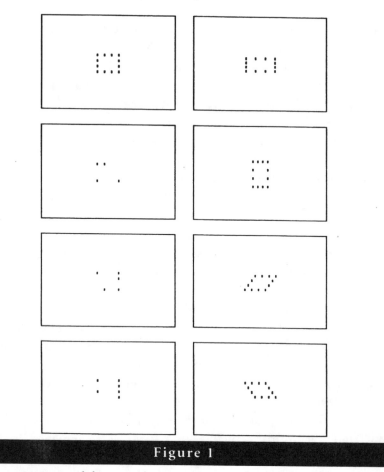

Figure 1

Square prototype and three sample square stimuli (left) and horizontal and vertical rectangle prototypes followed by right- and left-leaning rhombus prototypes (right). From Figure 1 of "Stimulus Configuration and Context Effects in Perceptual Organization in Schizophrenia," by S. M. Silverstein, R. A. Knight, S. B. Schwarzkopf, L. L. West, L. M. Osborn, and D. Kamin, *Journal of Abnormal Psychology, 105*, p. 412. Copyright 1996 by the American Psychological Association. Reprinted with permission.

pecially the superiority of schizophrenia patients in conditions in which formal structure interferes with counting in controls, is directly opposite to the predictions of a general deficit model.

Postperceptual and Configural Influences on Schizophrenia Patients' Perceptual Processing

The converging lines of evidence from the Rabinowicz et al. (1996) dot enumeration study, the reality representation decision task study, and the double-masking study provide considerable support for the hypothesis that reduced top-down influences, secondary to a failure to allocate sufficient cognitive resources in STVM, contribute to schizophrenia patients' early processing deficiencies. They further suggest that a strategy of examining various aspects of schizophrenia patients' perceptual organizational ability, especially their ability to generate top-down feedback to earlier perceptual processes, would help to further elucidate their deficiencies in perceptual organization. Consequently, we carried out a series of studies that explore these issues.

Target-detection studies. In two forced-choice target-detection studies, we (Silverstein, Knight, et al., 1996) again tested the hypothesis that poor premorbid schizophrenia patients tend to ignore global structure and to immediately process the individual elements of a configuration. We also wanted to determine whether a change in conditions that made the structure more salient, but without changing the stimuli themselves, would ameliorate poor premorbid patients' perceptual organizational difficulties. The five stimulus conditions used in the initial study are presented in Figure 2. In this task, a stimulus from one of

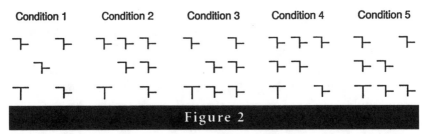

Figure 2

Examples of stimuli from the target-detection task study. From Figure 1 of "Dot Enumeration Perceptual Organization Task (DEPOT): Evidence for a Short-Term Visual Memory Deficit in Schizophrenia," by E. F. Rabinowicz, L. A. Opler, D. R. Owen, and R. A. Knight, 1996, *Journal of Abnormal Psychology, 105,* p. 339. Copyright 1996 by the American Psychological Association. Reprinted with permission.

the five conditions illustrated in the figure was briefly presented. The participant was then instructed to indicate by pressing the appropriate button whether the real letter in the display was a *T* or an *F* (the target could appear in any of the four corners, maintaining the relative positioning of target to noise elements). This task consists of two patterns that are diagnostic of normal grouping: Condition 2 is faster than Condition 1, and Condition 2 is faster than Conditions 3, 4, and especially 5. Superior performance in Condition 2 relative to Condition 1 indicates that organizational effects have overriden display size effects because even though Condition 1 has fewer elements, their arrangement in a symmetrical pattern facilitates grouping of the target with distractors and thus hinders rapid target identification (Banks & Prinzmetal, 1976). Superior performance in Condition 2 relative to Conditions 3–5 indicates that among displays with equivalent numbers of elements, the grouping of the target relative to distractors is the primary factor influencing task performance. These patterns were produced by good premorbid schizophrenia patients, poor premorbid schizophrenia outpatients, and nonschizophrenia psychotic controls. Only acutely psychotic poor premorbid schizophrenia patients demonstrated the abnormal patterns: Condition 1 faster than Condition 2 and Condition 2 equal to Conditions 3–5. The superiority of Condition 1 over Condition 2 for the poor premorbid inpatients suggested a sequential processing of individual items.

In the second study, only Conditions 1 and 2 were presented to highlight more clearly that the perceptually distinct single item in Condition 2 carried useful detection information. That is, we wanted to determine, by setting up the task so that the small group was the relevant information in 100% of the trials in which a large group and a small group appeared (i.e., Condition 2), whether schizophrenia patients would develop a processing strategy in which the elements were organized into two groups and the target was rapidly isolated and attended to. In this study, the poor premorbid patients normalized their performance and like the good premorbid patients and nonschizophrenic psychotic controls performed better in Condition 2 than Condition 1. This amelioration of the deficit under conditions of enhanced organizational salience supports the top-down nature of the deficit. These two studies also indicate that the perceptual organization dysfunction is relatively specific to poor premorbid schizophrenia patients in an acutely psychotic state (see also Silverstein, Raulin, Pristach, & Pomerantz, 1992).

Auditory suffix study. The schizophrenia patient's difficulty in using top-down feedback to modulate perceptual processes was also demonstrated using an auditory suffix task (Silverstein, Matteson, & Knight, 1996), adapted from Neath, Surprenant, and Crowder's (1993). On each trial, participants heard a tape-recorded male voice reading a list of nine numbers, followed by one other sound (i.e., the auditory suffix, see below). Their task was to recall the nine numbers. The five suffixes were (a) the male voice saying *moo*, (b) the male voice saying *woof* (i.e., a dog's bark), (c) the sound of a real cow mooing, (d) the sound of a real dog barking, and (e) the male voice saying the onomatopoetic word *baa*. Participants were initially told they would hear lists followed by suffixes that would be a male voice saying the sounds "moo," "woof," or "baa." Halfway through the experiment, participants were told that the baa sound was actually a real sheep.

For the remainder of the session, participants then heard the real cow and real dog suffixes in addition to the baa suffix. For normal controls, after the baa sound was reframed as an animal and presented in the context of other real animal sounds, the baa suffix interfered little with performance, no more than the other real animal sounds. These data indicate that the same physical stimulus produced varying degrees of interference with recall, depending on the context in which the sound was interpreted by the participant. When the participant categorized the suffix as originating from a different source than the previous material, the suffix was not included in the same perceptual stream and had little affect on recall. For schizophrenia patients, however, whereas the baa suffix continued to function as if spoken by the experimenter in the second half of the session, the real animal suffixes produced less interference than the experimenter-spoken suffixes. These data indicate an intact ability to group stimuli on the basis of physical characteristics but an impairment in generating contextually driven, top-down feedback to perceptual organizational processes.

Perceptual processing of symmetry. Symmetry is one of the fundamental principles of organization cited among gestaltists. It is a prepotent, early developing, and possibly innate organzational principle (Bornstein, Ferdinandsen, & Gross, 1981; Bornstein, Gross, & Wolf, 1978) that requires little experience for the development of automaticity and does not require contact with memory representations to occur (Peterson, 1994). Knight, Manoach, Elliott, and Hershenson (1998) compared performance on both physical and name match paradigms using two-letter combinations that were arranged in either symmetrical or asymmetrical configurations. To create response patterns that were not confounded with general deficit predictions, they made use of data that indicate that physical match of elements is inhibited by symmetry but that name match is facilitated (e.g., Fox, 1975; Mermelstein, Banks, & Prinzmetal, 1979). They found that symmetry interfered with the physical match for all groups equally, indicating that the poor premorbid schizophrenia patients like the normal controls automatically generated symmetrical organizations that interfered with their determination of physical match. In a name-matching task, the only difference among the groups was that the poor premorbid patients did not learn to use the vertical-axis-bilateral symmetry as a diagnostic to indicate that the two letters had the same name. Thus, the poor premorbid patients generated symmetrical representations automatically, but when top-down use of these organizations was required, they were not able to apply the strategy.

Directly Testing the Automaticity Deficit Hypothesis

A number of the studies reported above were consistent with, but did not directly test, the previously proposed hypothesis that schizophrenia patients can perceptually organize stimuli with strong configural properties but that they are deficient in their ability to use contextual information to organize weakly grouped stimuli. Silverstein, Bakshi, Chapman, and Nowlis (in press) developed a paradigm that directly tests this hypothesis. They created a pattern-recognition task in which participants viewed 600 briefly presented patterns, one on each trial, composed of six asterisks each. On each trial, their task was to indicate as quickly as possible by an appropriate button press whether they had seen the pattern before. Across the 600 trials, only two patterns repeated, 120 each of a "good" (symmetrical) and a "poor" (nonsymmetrical) form. The remaining 360 patterns were unique and were only presented once. Both schizophrenia patients and normal controls demonstrated evidence of improvement (i.e., increased frequency of correct judgments and systematically decreasing response latencies across blocks) in the good form condition, but only the controls demonstrated consistent improvement in the poor form condition. These data corroborate Knight's (1992, 1993) a priori hypothesis that poor premorbid schizophrenia patients have a deficit in their ability to automatize the processing of less prepotently organized stimuli.

Recent research on familiarity judgments for visual patterns in nonpatients is relevant to these pattern-recognition task data and suggest potential avenues to refine and broaden our model of schizophrenia patients' information-processing dysfunction. For instance, Chechile, Anderson, Krafczek, and Coley (1996) identified two types of encodings for visual objects. The first is an analogical–pictorial representation that corresponds to older concepts of sensory or iconic memory (Dick, 1974). The second and subsequent type of encoding is a propositional–syntactic representation that captures the relations among the stimulus components. In this model, the construction of a propositional–syntactic representation is considered a prerequisite for accessing acquired knowledge of the pattern and thus for deciding whether it had been previously seen. In several respects, the propositional–syntactic representation described in the model of Chechile et al. is similar to the earlier concept of STVM. The representation formed during this stage is not tied to spatial position and is invariant under transformations of the object's retinal size and relation location. The propositional–syntactic representation like STVM is hypothesized to be the point at which the transformation from a sensory representation to a conceptual representation occurs and to be the earliest linkage of the visual representation with linguistic information. Thus, the pattern-recognition task data are further evidence that early mnemonic processing, involving the transformation of sensory representations on the basis of past experience, is relevant to an understanding of the perceptual organization deficit and to schizophrenia patients' visual processing disturbances, as measured across a variety of paradigms.

New Models, Broadening Interpretations, and Future Specification Directions and Issues

The converging evidence of these studies has strongly supported the efficacy of the process-oriented approach in specifying the early mnemonic processing impairments that play a role in poor premorbid schizophrenia patients' processing dysfunction. The viability of the STVM and perceptual organization models in guiding theory development and paradigm selection is apparent. The full implications across all of these studies, however, once again require that as we have done in the past, we attempt to interpret all of the results in light of recent cognitive research and theoretical models that broaden and deepen the understanding of early perceptual–cognitive processing. In the last few years, the fields of cognitive psychology, cognitive neuroscience, and computational neuroscience have been replacing stage models with interactive models that emphasize parallel processing and complex feedback mechanisms. As a result, the two-stage models that guided the studies described above have now been replaced by more complex variants (e.g., Friedman-Hill & Wolfe, 1995; Kosslyn & Koening, 1992; W. A. Phillips & Singer, 1997), in which the outputs of various processes feedback on and interact with each other. Therefore, perhaps the most generative models for expanding the understanding of schizophrenia patient's processing deficiencies and giving direction to future specification research are those that move away from strictly stage notions and conceptualize early processing as more interactive and modular. As we argued earlier, this does not imply that the insights generated from past process-oriented work are no longer valid. On the contrary, they not only remain valid but also when integrated into more current frameworks suggest future directions for continued task refinement and further process specification.

W. A. Phillips and Singer (1997) have proposed a powerful new model that is relevant to our work. They have attempted to specify the mechanisms at both the cognitive and neurophysiological levels purportedly involved in the formation and processing of representations for visual stimuli. Singer (1995) proposed that perceptual objects are defined through the operation of two systems: (a) a system of feedforward connections that leads to the development of basic feature detectors, or receptive fields (RFs), and (b) linkages of these RFs based on their correlated activity into dynamic, functionally coherent cell assemblies, or contextual fields (CFs) that involve cortico–cortical connections and can represent the wide range of feature combinations corresponding to real-world objects. An important consideration here is that the formation of CFs can occur through bottom-up (i.e., stimulus driven) or top-down (e.g., attentional, strategic) mechanisms.

Humans develop a high sensitivity to gestalt properties, such as symmetry and collinearity, (Koffka, 1935), because these properties are continually experienced during development. This leads to the early strengthening of CFs that fire when the correlated and synchronized patterns of activity produced by the individual features are detected. Poor premorbid schizophrenia patients' sensitivity to strong configural properties such as symmetry (Knight, 1992; Silverstein, Bakshi, et al., in press) suggests an enduring responsivity to highly correlated and structured sensory input patterns and a normal development of feedforward connections (Crair & Malenka, 1995; K. D. Miller, Keller, & Stryker, 1989; Rauschecker & Singer, 1979). In contrast, the ability to use top-down influences to dynamically form new coherent cell assemblies is imparied in poor premorbid schizophrenia. Thus, poor premorbid schizophrenia patients can be characterized as having a deficiency in their ability to benefit from past experience and current context in detecting stimulus relations in complex environments and consequently in transforming sensory data into appropriate conceptual level representations and accurately assessing the behavioral significance of current stimuli. As we discuss below, this deficiency significantly affects adaptive functioning in poor premorbid schizophrenia patients.

The visual-processing mechanisms discussed by W. A. Phillips and

Singer (1997) are specific examples of what they view as a fundamental cortical processing algorithm. In their view, the cortex performs computational operations of a general nature that support functions such as perception, memory, language, and reasoning. The critical aspect of this algorithm is that processors and networks conform their activity to the statistical structure inherent in the external world by maximizing the transmission of information predictably related to the context in which it occurs. Schizophrenia could be characterized by a reduced effectiveness of this general cortical processing algorithm (see Silverstein & Schenkel, 1997). Potential manifestations of this impairment would include (a) a reduced grouping of stimulus components that tend to occur together but do not possess configural properties to which the visual system is predisposed to respond in early development (i.e., a reduced dynamic grouping based on experience and context as predicted by Knight, 1992, 1993, and demonstrated by Silverstein, Bakshi, et al., in press), and (b) a reduced influence of contextual information in the activation of relevant associations to perceived objects (i.e., reduced processing of meaning, as demonstrated in the reality representation and masking studies; Knight, 1992). The Phillips and Singer model thus provides a powerful framework from which our findings on perceptual organization and STVM may be integrated into a unified view: All of the impairments demonstrated by these studies reflect a reduced influence of past experience, current context, or some combination of the two on the formation of conceptual level visual representations.

It is the transformation of the sensory representation based on experience that signifies the end of sensory processing and the onset of conceptual processing or processing involving meaning, significance, and semantic structures. The data converge in suggesting that poor premorbid schizophrenia is characterized by an impairment in both the processes involved in this transformation and, subsequently, the top-down control of early visual information processing. It is a strength of the process-oriented approach that over 20 years of findings from various paradigms converge on similar conclusions and that these findings can be integrated better over time because of developments in related fields. The tasks that remain are clear. The nature and manifestations of these information transformation processes require further specification, and discriminating assessments that measure these deficient processes must be generated and validated so that they can be related to other aspects of schizophrenia.

GENERALIZATION OF THE PROCESS-ORIENTED STRATEGY: INTEGRATION WITH OTHER APPROACHES

Specification of core cognitive–perceptual processes deficient in schizophrenia patients is a central concern of the process-oriented strategy but not its sole or even its ultimate goal. The integration of the identified deficient process(es) into a unified theory of the etiology, macrobehavioral and symptom manifestations, and life course of the disorder is paramount. To date, most of the attempts to relate schizophrenia patients' cognitive deficiencies to biology or symptoms or to use these deficits as "markers" in high-risk or genetic studies have taken what has been called a *task-oriented* approach (Knight, 1984). Researchers have identified and developed sophisticated versions of tasks that have consistently demonstrated substantial discriminatory power between schizophrenia patients and various control groups. These tasks have then been administered to potential preschizophrenia individuals, schizophrenia patients, psychiatric controls, and normal controls, and the discriminative and predictive power of these tasks and their correlations with biological, behavioral, and symptom measures have been assessed. This task-oriented approach has yielded important data about the temporal stability, high-risk, and family–genetic aspects of cognitive deficiencies in schizophrenia (Cornblatt & Keilp, 1994; Nuechterlein et al., 1992). We suggest, however, that the benefits of this approach have reached an asymptote. Researchers must no longer be content with using generic, vaguely defined tasks to measure attention. Subsequent progress in mapping the cognitive developmental antecedents of schizophrenia, providing markers for genetic studies, relating cognitive deficits to symptoms, and identifying the biological mechanisms dysfunctional in schizophrenia requires the adoption of a process-oriented strategy.

Infusing Theoretical Meaning Into the Task-Oriented Approach

Performance on the tasks typically used in high-risk and family studies (e.g., the Continuous Performance Test [CPT], the Span of Apprehension Test [SPAN]) is determined by multiple cognitive processes whose nature, interaction, and relative contributions to task performance are poorly understood. Therefore, despite the significant contributions made by studies using these tasks, the lack of process specificity inherent in these measures limits the degree to which further progress can be made in understanding the nature of vulnerability to schizophrenia and in providing markers that maximize both sensitivity and specificity. The process-oriented strategy can contribute to high-risk and family studies in two ways.

First, it can suggest tasks that have more process specificity and that measure deficits that map directly onto specific deficit and neurophysiological models. Identifying such tasks involves more than simply lifting conditions from successful process-oriented cognitive studies, because as Embretson (1983) pointed out, information-processing paradigms have been designed to maximize task variability rather than individual differences. Developing a variant of a cognitive task so that it optimizes individual differences rather than task variability often requires substantial revamping of the task and considerable work validating the revised format of the task. Second, because the tasks that have traditionally been used in high-risk and family studies have amassed substantial data, it is important to determine which component processes contribute most to abnormal performance in these tasks. A process-oriented strategy to task decomposition can help to infuse greater process specificity into these tasks. In this section, we discuss two traditional tasks, the CPT and SPAN, to both illustrate the problems in interpreting what they measure and exemplify ways in which these tasks can be studied within a process-oriented framework.

The Continuous Performance Test

Although poor performance on the CPT appears to be a vulnerability marker for schizophrenia (Cornblatt & Keilp, 1994; Nuechterlein et al., 1992), it is still unclear what this test measures (Silverstein, Light, & Palumbo, in press; van den Bosch, Rombouts, & van Asma, 1996). Although many discussions of the CPT conceptualize it as a sustained attention or vigilance task, performance decrement over time is not always found in the context of overall poor performance; when found, it is often of small magnitude (van den Bosch et al., 1996). Moreover, participants often do poorly at the outset of a session, suggesting that poor performance is due to other factors. More important, recent event-related potential evidence does not support the hypothesis that vigilance decrement over time is associated with increasing difficulty in discriminating signals from nonsignals (Koelega et al., 1992). Even in cases where sensitivity (d' or A') declines with time, the discrimination of targets from nontargets, as reflected in event-related potential amplitudes, remains unchanged.

This raises the central issue of what the behaviorially defined measures of sensitivity really signify. In the vigilance literature in general, d' or A' has been hypothesized to indicate attentiveness, attention, attentional capacity, resources, alertness, discriminability, and perceptual accuracy. It has recently been suggested that sensitivity decrement over time reflects more of a decline in effort or resources allocated to the task than a change in perceptual ability or limitation in the perceptual system (Koelega et al., 1992). Findings that sensitivity and response bias indicators correlate with the same event-related potential measures (Koelega & Verbaten, 1991) raise further questions about the meaning of these indicators and their purported independence. In short, the disputed status of the primary behavioral indicators of performance on the CPT is a major barrier to clarifying both the meaning of abnormal task performance and its underlying mechanisms.

As noted above, some discussions (and most in the schizophrenia literature) conceptualize the CPT as an assessment of attentional capacity limitations. That is, for example, the parameters of the Degraded Stimulus CPT (DS-CPT) purportedly impose a high moment-to-moment degree of "processing load" on the participant; poor performance is seen as due to an inability to process as much information as normal controls can at any point in time (Nuechterlein, 1991). The problem of the lack of specificity in locus and cause in this explanatory model has been discussed elsewhere (Knight, 1993). In addition, the issue of limitations in attentional capacity is still controversial in the normal cognitive literature (van der Heijden, 1996), and even among proponents of the capacity limitation view, there are divergent theories about what conditions are necessary to produce capacity limitations (Sperling & Dosher, 1986). Moreover, methods for determining whether attentional capacity is limited or to what extent it is limited are quite different from any variant of the CPT ever used in schizophrenia research (Sperling & Dosher, 1986). In general, then, despite its many strengths, the CPT cannot be considered a strong measure of attentional capacity limitations. Indeed, other evidence suggests that the operative factors in schizophrenia patients' performance deficits on the two most widely used versions of the CPT, the DS-CPT (Nuechterlein, 1991) and the Identical Pairs CPT (CPT-IP; Cornblatt & Keilp, 1994), involve other factors.

Recent work has demonstrated that abnormal performance on tasks such as the CPT-IP and 3–7 CPT (Nuechterlein, Edell, Norris, & Dawson, 1986), where the target is defined on the basis of two consecutive stimuli meeting specific conditions, can be accounted for in terms of an impairment in context processing (Cohen & Servan-Schreiber, 1992). The context-processing model is quite powerful, in that it can account for data from a variety of information-processing paradigms (Cohen & Servan-Schreiber, 1992). In addition, recent models of context processing have demonstrated links between this process and specific neurophysiological mechanisms (Gray, Feldon, Rawlins, Hemsley, & Smith, 1991; O'Donnell & Grace, 1995, 1996; W. A. Phillips & Singer, 1997). Of equal importance, the context-processing model moves beyond older, global notions of attention and hypothesizes a specific cognitive process that can be tested without being confounded with the generalized deficit (Silverstein, Knight, et al., 1996). Future studies of vulnerability to schizophrenia could benefit greatly from using measures specifically designed to test this context-processing deficit (e.g., Silverstein, Matteson, et al., 1996).

A perceptual organization deficit might also contribute to schizophrenia patients' sensitivity to stimulus degradation on the DS-CPT because the patient is required to rapidly identify a blurred digit, which requires assembling the fragmented image. Wallace and Silverstein (1996), however, in a recent study in which 14 chronic schizophrenia patients completed both the DS-CPT and the perceptual organization task used in Silverstein, Knight, et al. (1996), found close to a zero correlation between the critical performance indexes. These data suggest that rapid target identification in the DS-CPT involves factors other than simple perceptual organization.

DS-CPT data are analyzed in terms of signal detection theory (SDT), but curiously the task has not been conceptualized from that perspective. From within SDT, the task can be seen not as one of attentional capacity but of decision. That is, in schizophrenia patients there can be assumed to be a greater overlap between the distributions corresponding to the internal representations of the noise (i.e., nontarget) trials and of the signal-plus-noise (i.e., target) trials than among normal controls. This makes it more difficult to decide whether a target is present. From within this model, the critical task is to determine why the representations in schizophrenia are "noisier" than among controls. This issue can be clarified by carrying out studies of DS-CPT that manipulate factors known to influence sensory processing or, more specially, to influence the activity of different visual pathways, like color, flicker rate, brightness, or spatial frequency (Lovegrove & Pepper, 1994).

In contrast to SDT models, which focus on the "finished product" of processing (i.e., the nature of the final signal vs. signal-plus-noise distributions), one could investigate the hypothesis that the lower d' or A' of schizophrenia patients reflects an abnormality in the way that information about the stimulus is accumulated or integrated over time to form the final percept. Because previous research suggests that schizophrenia patients are not characterized by a general slowness of processing (Knight, 1984, 1992), this raises the possibility that a normal integration of noisier information is occurring, that an abnormal in-

tegration of information is occurring (Schwartz, 1982), or some combination of the two. To the extent that these processes are operative, a
further consideration becomes whether these difficulties reflect sensory
integration or integration at later stages involving schematic persistence
(Irwin & Yeomans, 1991), STVM, or other hypothesized processes involving information accrual (Muise, LeBlanc, Lavoie, & Arsenault,
1991), where schizophrenia patients are known to have impairments.
Clarification of these issues will further the understanding of the nature
of schizophrenia patients' performance deficits on the DS-CPT and allow for an integration of methods and data between CPT and other
methodologies.

The DS-CPT may also be thought of as a template-matching task
because the participant has to match rapidly and briefly presented degraded numeric stimuli to a mental representation of what the target
(a degraded zero) looks like. Such template matching requires developing a memory representation for a relatively unstructured and degraded stimulus and maintaining this representation in working memory during task performance. This hypothesized mechanism is
consistent with our data, showing that schizophrenia patients are impaired in their ability to develop memory representations for unfamiliar
and unstructured stimuli (Knight, 1992; Silverstein, Bakshi, et al., in
press). If this hypothesis is valid, modifying the DS-CPT to place greater
demands on the development of memory representations for novel
stimuli might lead to a more sensitive measure of vulnerability. This
same strategy can be applied to the so-called *memory-load* CPTs, such
as the CPT-IP and the 3–7 CPT. These tasks have been used successfully
to discriminate schizophrenia patients from normal controls and other
psychiatric patients (Nuechterlein et al., 1992). Modifying these tasks
so that the stimuli monitored are not the ones that have been overlearned (i.e., are less familiar to participants) might lead to a much
more sensitive measure.

The Span of Apprehension Test

The SPAN is typically discussed as assessing the amount of information
that can be processed at one time, independent of short-term memory
or as a measure of attentional capacity (Asarnow, Granholm, & Sher-

man, 1991). Unfortunately, there are many unresolved issues regarding what performance on this task really measures. For example, in visual search tasks such as the SPAN, the critical issue is the extent to which decline in target-detection performance with increasing numbers of elements is due to a limitation of attention, to uncertainty in the decision processes, or to sensory factors (Sperling & Dosher, 1986). This important issue has not been adequately addressed in the schizophrenia literature. SDT again is useful here because it predicts a specific degree of decision-related decrement in performance whenever the participant is faced with a larger number of noise samples. Because it can be argued that decision factors are always involved in tasks such as this and that performance decrements can be interpreted as evidence of attentional capacity limitations only after accounting for the effects of decision uncertainty (Sperling & Dosher, 1986), the real issue becomes whether performance decline can be attributed to decision factors alone or exceeds that which would be predicted by a decision model and begins to approach a level that fits an attentional capacity limitation model. A process-oriented approach can systematically test competing hypotheses about the extent to which decision- versus attention-based models best fit the observed data (see Shaw, 1980).

The critical decisions in the SPAN involve determining at each spatial location where a letter occurs whether that character is a T or an F. From within SDT, the likelihood of making an error (i.e., of an internal representation of a nontarget character exceeding the threshold of either T-ness or F-ness) increases systematically as the number of elements are added to the display. Thus, schizophrenia patients' well-known performance decline relative to normal controls as the number of elements is increased may represent an impairment in (a) the ability to rapidly perform a series of decisions (a form of executive dysfunction), (b) the process of making each decision owing to noisy representations caused by sensory factors; (c) some other aspect of the decision-making process, or (d) some combination of the above. Mathematical models have been developed (Shaw, 1980) that can be applied to already collected data to determine whether schizophrenia patients' decline in performance with increasing display size fits what would be predicted from a pure decision model or whether the data fit other models that rely on the construct of attentional capacity to varying degrees. In addition, Palmer (1994a, 1994b; Palmer, Ames, & Lindsey, 1993) developed tasks that simultaneously control for sensory factors and allow for the determination of the extent to which task performance conforms to decisional versus attentional models. The SPAN could be modified to emulate these tasks and allow the same discriminations.

Whatever the critical process in SPAN performance turns out to be, another question about the task involves whether the operations are performed serially or in parallel and whether schizophrenia patients perform the task in the same way as other persons. Sperling and Dosher (1986) viewed tasks such as the SPAN as "compound" tasks, in that they involve the simultaneous performance of more than one task. On each trial, each element must be evaluated to determine whether it is a T (one task) or an F (another task). Research indicates that a stimulus element at one spatial position can be, but is not always, compared with a memory representation of a target at the same time that another item at another location is being compared with a representation of another target. The extent to which these decisions are made in parallel or serially depends on a number of factors (e.g., target familiarity, task automatization), which have not been investigated in the SPAN literature. Moreover, recent work has identified different variants of parallel and serial processes that are either limited or unlimited in attention capacity (Townsend, 1981, 1990). These distinctions have not been investigated in SPAN in the schizophrenia studies. Finally, it is known that the spatial distribution of attention can be altered by top-down factors (Sperling & Dosher, 1986) and that attentional strategies can mediate the effect of display size on visual search (Fisher, 1982). These are further issues needing clarification in the schizophrenia literature. Continued modification of the SPAN paradigm through a process-oriented approach has the potential to specify precisely the processing mechanisms involved in abnormal task performance and to produce a more sensitive vulnerability indicator.

Relating Processes and Symptoms

A decade ago a challenge was issued to researchers to abandon their complacent acceptance of a relation between performance on cognitive tasks and thought disorder symptoms and generate some hard empirical evidence (George & Neufeld, 1985; Knight, Elliott, Roff, & Watson, 1986; Neale, Oltmanns, & Harvey, 1985). Although some progress in relating performance on cognitive tasks to symptoms has been made and it appears that performance on several of the measures discussed above (e.g., CPTs) correlates in significant and meaningful ways with symptoms (e.g., Nuechterlein et al., 1992), to date discussion of these relationships has remained largely at a descriptive level, perhaps because the measures have been viewed more as vulnerability markers than as assessments of a specific process (Strauss, 1993). Significant methodological problems in relating processes to symptoms have been identified (Knight, 1987), but discussion of these is beyond the limits of this chapter. The field is still far from developing a cohesive, widely accepted strategy for addressing these problems, and no powerful model of the relations between cognitive deficits and either symptoms or behavior has emerged. Such methods and models must be developed if a comprehensive understanding of schizophrenia is to be achieved. Some preliminary data collected in our laboratories indicate some potentially important directions that might be pursued in formulating such a model.

One of the results of our process-oriented research programs has been the consistent finding that abnormal performance on measures of perceptual organization and STVM is found among schizophrenia patients with histories of poor premorbid social functioning but not among patients with good premorbid histories or with other psychotic disorders (Knight, 1992, 1993; Knight et al., 1985; Silverstein, Knight, et al., 1996). These data suggest that there may be a shared mechanism underlying poor social functioning during development and abnormal perceptual organization, as assessed after illness onset. The Silverstein, Knight, et al. study also indicates that this relationship is strongest in acutely psychotic patients. To determine specifically which symptoms are associated with perceptual organization dysfunction, we used the Positive and Negative Syndrome Scale (PANSS; Kay, Opler, & Fiszbein,

1987) to obtain symptom ratings on 33 chronic schizophrenia patients. In a series of hierarchical regression analyses, we determined the best predictors of the magnitude of the critical performance index in the Silverstein, Knight, et al. perceptual organization task (i.e., the relative difference in reaction times between Conditions 1 and 2). Using the original three factor PANSS solution, we found that only positive symptoms accounted for a significant proportion of variance ($R^2 = .15$, $p < .03$). When a recent five factor solution (Lindenmayer, Bernstein-Hyman, & Grochowski, 1994) was used, however, only the cognitive or disorganization factor (consisting of conceptual disorganization, mannerisms and posturing, disorientation, difficulty in abstract thinking, and poor attention) was a significant predictor ($R^2 = .14$, $p < .04$). These data were supported by a study in which the relations were determined between performance on the pattern-recognition task described earlier (Silverstein, Bakshi, et al., in press) and symptoms as rated by the PANSS. Correlation coefficients were calculated between PANSS factors and the good and poor form condition accuracy scores at Block 10 of the pattern-recognition task (the final block). These two variables represent the degree of recognition performance that could be achieved after maximal exposure to the visual patterns. Neither pattern-recognition task score was significantly correlated with the negative symptom or excitement factors. Only the positive and cognitive–disorganized symptom factors were significantly correlated with performance and only with accuracy in the poor form condition ($r = -.49$ and $-.58$, respectively, $p < .05$), which was hypothesized to be most sensitive to schizophrenia patients' context-mediated perceptual organization difficulties.

To explore further the relationships between abnormal perceptual organization and symptomatology, we obtained Thought Disorder Index (TDI; Solovay et al., 1986) scores from 21 acutely psychotic poor premorbid schizophrenia patients who completed Kahneman and Neisser's visual suffix task (reported in Kahneman, 1973). Specifically, we wanted to test our hypothesis that perceptual organization dysfunction is one manifestation of a broader disturbance in the adaptive organization of information based on context and experience. Therefore, we predicted that degree of perceptual organization disturbance would co-vary with the TDI scales indicating reduced thought organization (i.e., disorganized and associative thought disturbance). As shown in Table 1, these predictions were confirmed. There were significant correlations between these TDI scales and the magnitude of the indexes (in the first column), indicating perceptual grouping difficulty. The latter is mea-sured by poorer recall of the sixth digit in conditions where the irrel-evant suffix (0 or a # symbol) was grouped with the digit (Conditions 2, 4, and 6) compared with when the suffix formed its own group and could be easily segregated from the digit string, leading to less inter-ference (Conditions 3 and 5; see Figure 3). It is important to note that degrees of disorganized and associative thought disturbance were not associated with baseline, no suffix (Condition 1) performance, and de-gree of perceptual organization disturbance was not related to overall levels of thought disorder. It is also worth noting in both this acute sample and a second sample of chronic schizophrenia patients that degree of performance decline from baseline in Conditions 4 and 5, the conditions with the most information to be grouped, was significantly and inversely correlated with level of premorbid social functioning.

Table 1

Correlations Between Visual Suffix Task Baseline and Grouping Indexes and A Priori TDI Factors

Task	Associative	Combina-tory	Disorga-nized	Idiosyn-cratic	Total TDI
1 (baseline)	−.15	.03	−.23	.00	−.08
1 versus 2	.29	.13	.57**	−.14	.24
2 versus 3	.35	.13	.49**	−.13	.25
1 versus 4	.36	.15	.43*	−.15	.24
4 versus 5	.51**	.33	.37	−.01	.38

Note. TDI = Thought Disorder Index.

$^*p < .05.$ $^{**}p < .01.$

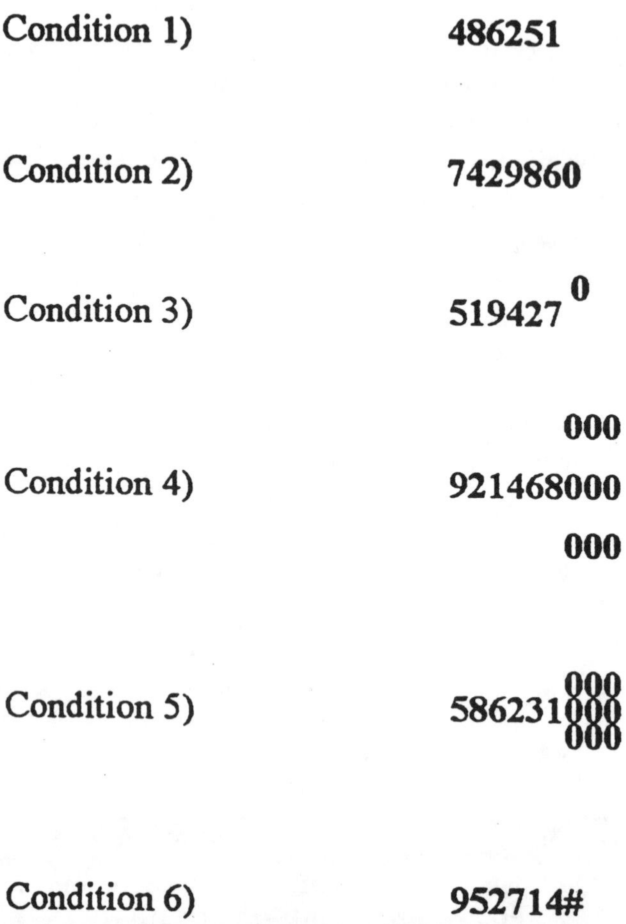

Condition 1)   486251

Condition 2)   7429860

Condition 3)   519427 ^{0}

                                    000
Condition 4)   921468000
                                    000

Condition 5)   586231 $\begin{matrix}000\\000\\000\end{matrix}$

Condition 6)   952714#

Figure 3

Examples of stimuli from the visual suffix task study.

These data and those reported above further indicate that perceptual organization dysfunction is specifically related to a reduced ability to evaluate context-related consistency in patterns of sensory input. They suggest that disorganized perception, verbal output, reduced sensitivity to social cues and poorer social competence, and positive and disorganized symptoms may reflect a generalized disruption of a cortical processing algorithm common to diverse cortical areas (Carr & Wale, 1986; Silverstein & Schenkel, 1997).

Interfacing Cognitive Deficits With Brain Functioning and Studying Neurodevelopment

The interface of psychological and biological models of schizophrenia patients' cognitive deficiencies is critical. Here, the role of psychological cognitive models, both as a guide to biological exploration and a bridge to macrobehavioral symptomatology, is essential. It is clear that any simple reductionism of psychological to biological explanations is not defensible on either empirical or theoretical grounds (G. A. Miller, 1996). As G. A. Miller convincingly argued, in studying psychopathology researchers need both the sophistication of valid cognitive psychological models to characterize the deficits in the implementation of psychological functions and the expertise of neuroscience to specify the biological mechanisms problematic in their implementation.

We would argue further for heuristic and practical reasons that the failure to use cognitive models to guide experimental design and task choice in biological studies will severely curtail progress in biological specification and leave studies vulnerable to many of the interpretative and methodological pitfalls discussed earlier. Studies that use brain-imaging techniques to assess function and structure during global tasks, like CPT (e.g., Buchsbaum et al., 1996) or eye tracking (e.g., Ross et al., 1995), which discriminate schizophrenia patients from controls but provide little specification of cognitive processing, do little to advance understanding and have reached the limits of their utility. Only when researchers have specific cognitive models and tasks that differentiate general from specific functioning can such techniques as the "O blood flow subtraction" method in positron emission tomography (Herron & Johnson, 1987) be effectively applied to provide greater neuroanatomical localization of cognitive functions. Without the guidance of better and more specific cognitive models, researchers will be condemned to the quagmire of confusing and sometimes contradictory findings that have plagued this literature.

Likewise neurodevelopmental research will profit from the incorporation of a process-oriented approach. Many developmental studies have used tasks that are not clearly tied to models of cognition or that have confounded multiple cognitive processes, making both the specification of deficits and the generation of an adequate theory of the development of schizophrenia difficult. Incorporating a process-oriented approach into a developmental framework will help to clarify the cognitive and behavioral aspects of both schizophrenia and other developmental disorders (Knight, 1987; Silverstein & Palumbo, 1995). Limited space in this chapter prohibits the unpacking of the complex issues involved in the interface of the process-oriented approach with both biological and neurodevelopmental research (see Silverstein & Knight, 1998, for further details on these issues).

CONCLUSION

When the process-oriented strategy was first introduced (Knight, 1984), it was argued that its cumulative record of advancement in the specification of the nature of schizophrenia patients' perceptual, attentional, and memory impairments and its finessing of apparently intractable methodological dilemmas justified its adoption as a strategy for studying cognitive deficits in schizophrenia. Now, with more than a decade of additional research guided by its precepts, the strategy's promise of continued progress toward specification remains. The studies we have reviewed continue to support the viability of the strategy in guiding perceptual–cognitive research in schizophrenia. Unfortunately, few researchers have heeded the methodological and theoretical concerns that this approach has endeavored to address; progress in identifying and specifying critical cognitive deficits in schizophrenia is still hampered by this failure.

We also attempted to indicate the potential of this strategy and the fruits of process specification for integrating cognitive and biological theories of schizophrenia, contributing specification and direction to neuroimaging studies, generating a unified theory of the cognitive symptoms of schizophrenia, and providing more sensitive measures for high-risk and genetic studies. Although the success of the process approach in these domains remains a promissory note, the stagnation and methodological conundrums of continued use of a task-oriented strategy leave little choice but to embrace a process-oriented approach.

REFERENCES

Asarnow, R. F., Granholm, E., & Sherman, T. (1991). Span of apprehension in schizophrenia. In S. R. Steinhauer, J. H. Gruzelier, & J. Zubin (Eds.), *Handbook of Schizophrenia. Vol. 5: Neuropsychology, psychophysiology, and information processing* (pp. 335–370). Amsterdam: Elsevier.

Balogh, D. W., & Merritt, R. D. (1987). Visual masking and the schizophrenia spectrum: Interfacing clinical and experimental methods. *Schizophrenia Bulletin, 13,* 679–698.

Banks, W. P., & Prinzmetal, W. (1976). Configural effects in visual information processing. *Perception and Psychophysics, 19,* 361–367.

Bornstein, M. H., Ferdinandsen, K., & Gross, C. G. (1981). Perception of symmetry in infancy. *Developmental Psychology, 17,* 82–86.

Bornstein, M. H., Gross, C. G., & Wolf, J. Z. (1978). Perceptual similarity of mirror images in infancy. *Cognition, 6,* 89–116

Breitmeyer, B. (1984). *Visual masking: An integrative approach.* New York: Oxford University Press.

Buchsbaum, M. S., Someya, T., Teng, C. Y., Abel, L., Chin, S., Najafi, A., Haier, R. J., Wu, J., & Bunney, W. E., Jr. (1996). PET and MRI of the thalamus in never-medicated patients with schizophrenia. *American Journal of Psychiatry, 153,* 191–199.

Carr, V., & Wale, J. (1986). Schizophrenia: An information processing model. *Australian and New Zealand Journal of Psychiatry, 20,* 136–155.

Chapman, L. J., & Chapman, J. P. (1973). *Disordered thought in schizophrenia.* New York: Appleton-Century-Crofts.

Chapman, L. J., & Chapman, J. P. (1978). The measurement of differential deficit. *Journal of Psychiatric Research, 14,* 303–311.

Chechile, R. A., Anderson, J. E., Krafczek, S. A., & Coley, S. L. (1996). A syntactic complexity effect with visual patterns: Evidence for the syntactic nature of the memory representation. *Journal of Experimental Psychology: Learning, Memory, and Cognition, 22,* 654–669.

Cohen, J. D., & Servan-Schreiber, D. (1992). Context, cortex, and dopamine:

A connectionist approach to behavior and biology in schizophrenia. *Psychological Review, 99,* 45–77.

Cornblatt, B. A., & Keilp, J. G. (1994). Impaired attention, genetics, and the pathophysiology of schizophrenia. *Schizophrenia Bulletin, 20,* 31–46.

Cowan, N. (1988). Evolving conceptions of memory storage, selective attention and their mutual constraints within the human information processing system. *Psychological Bulletin, 104,* 163–191.

Crair, M. C., & Malenka, R. C. (1995). A critical period for long-term potentiation at thalamocortical synapses. *Nature, 375,* 325–328.

Dick, A. O. (1974). Iconic memory and its relation to perceptual processing and other memory mechanisms. *Perception and Psychophysics, 16,* 575–596.

Embretson, S. (1983). Construct validity: Construct representation versus nomothetic span. *Psychological Bulletin, 93,* 179–197.

Eriksen, C. W., & Collins, J. F. (1967). Some temporal characteristics of visual pattern perception. *Journal of Experimental Psychology, 74,* 476–484.

Eriksen, C. W., & Collins, J. F. (1968). Sensory traces versus the psychological moment in the temporal organization of form. *Journal of Experimental Psychology, 77,* 376–382.

Farina, A., Garmezy, N., & Barry, H., III. (1963). Relationship of marital status to incidence and prognosis of schizophrenia. *Journal of Abnormal and Social Psychology, 67,* 624–630.

Fisher, D. L. (1982). Limited-channel models of automatic detection: Capacity and scanning in visual search. *Psychological Review, 89,* 662–692.

Fox, J. (1975). The use of structural diagnostics in recognition. *Journal of Experimental Psychology: Human Perception and Performance, 1,* 57–67.

Friedman-Hill, S., & Wolfe, J. M. (1995). Second-order parallel processing: Visual search for the odd item in a subset. *Journal of Experimental Psychology: Human Perception and Performance, 21,* 532–551.

George, L., & Neufeld, R. W. J. (1985). Cognition and symptomology in schizophrenia. *Psychological Bulletin, 93,* 57–72.

Gray, J. A., Feldon, J., Rawlins, J. N. P., Hemsley, D. R., & Smith, A. D. (1991). The neuropsychology of schizophrenia. *Behavioral and Brain Sciences, 14,* 1–84.

Herron, P., & Johnson, J. I. (1987). Organization of intracortical and commissural connections in somatosensory cortical areas I and II in the raccoon. *Journal of Comparative Neurology, 257,* 359–371.

Hulme, M. R., & Merikle, P. M. (1976). Processing time and memory for pictures. *Canadian Journal of Psychology, 30,* 31–38.

Irwin, D. E., & Yeomans, J. M. (1991). Duration of visible persistence in relation to stimulus complexity. *Perception and Psychophysics, 50,* 475–489.

Javitt, D. D., Strous, R., Grochowski, S., Ritter, W., & Cowan, N. (1997). Impaired precision, but normal retention, of auditory sensory ("echoic") memory information in schizophrenia. *Journal of Abnormal Psychology, 106,* 315–324.

Kahneman, D. (1973). *Attention and effort.* Englewood Cliffs, NJ: Prentice Hall.

Kay, S. R., Opler, L. A., & Fiszbein, A. (1987). The Positive and Negative Syndrome Scale (PANSS) for schizophrenia. *Schizophrenia Bulletin, 13,* 261–276.

Killian, G. A., Holzman, P. S., Davis, J. M., & Gibbons, R. (1984). Effects of psychotropic medication on selected cognitive and perceptual measures. *Journal of Abnormal Psychology, 93,* 58–70.

Knight, R. A. (1984). Converging models of cognitive deficit in schizophrenia. In W. D. Spaulding & J. K. Cole (Eds.), *Nebraska Symposium on Motivation, 1983: Theories of schizophrenia and psychosis* (pp. 93–156). Lincoln: University of Nebraska Press.

Knight, R. A. (1987). Relating cognitive processes to symptoms: A strategy to counter methodological difficulties. In P. D. Harvey & E. Walker (Eds.), *Positive and negative symptoms in schizophrenia* (pp. 1–29). Hillsdale, NJ: Erlbaum.

Knight, R. A. (1992). Specifying cognitive deficiencies in poor premorbid schizophrenics. In E. F. Walker, R. Dworkin, & B. Cornblatt (Eds.), *Progress in experimental psychology and psychopathology research* (Vol. 15, pp. 252–289). New York: Springer-Verlag.

Knight, R. A. (1993). Comparing cognitive models of schizophrenics' input dysfunction. In R. L. Cromwell & C. R. Snyder (Eds.), *Schizophrenia: Origins, processes, treatment, and outcome* (pp. 151–175). Oxford, England: Oxford University Press.

Knight, R. A., Elliott, D. S., & Freedman, E. G. (1985). Short-term visual memory in schizophrenics. *Journal of Abnormal Psychology, 4,* 427–442.

Knight, R. A., Elliott, D. S., Roff, J. D., & Watson, C. G. (1986). Concurrent and predictive validity of components of disordered thinking in schizophrenia. *Schizophrenia Bulletin, 12,* 427–446.

Knight, R. A., Manoach, D. S., Elliott, D. S., & Hershenson, M. (1998). *Perceptual organization in schizophrenia: The processing of symmetrical configurations.* Manuscript submitted for publication.

Knight, R. A., Sherer, M., Putchat, C., & Carter, G. (1978). A picture integration task for measuring iconic memory in schizophrenics. *Journal of Abnormal Psychology, 87,* 314–321.

Knight, R. A., Sherer, M., & Shapiro, J. (1977). Iconic imagery in overinclusive and nonoverinclusive schizophrenics. *Journal of Abnormal Psychology, 86,* 242–255.

Koelega, H. S., & Verbaten, M. N. (1991). Event related potentials and vigilance performance: Dissociations abound, a review. *Perceptual and Motor Skills, 72,* 971–982.

Koelega, H. S., Verbaten, M. N., van Leeuwen, T. H., Kenemans, J. H. K., Kemner, C., & Sjouw, W. (1992). Time effects on event-related potentials and vigilance performance. *Biological Psychology, 34,* 59–86.

Koffka, K. (1935). *Principles of gestalt psychology.* New York: Harcourt, Brace, & World.

Kosslyn, S. M., & Koening, O. (1992). *Wet mind: The new cognitive neuroscience.* New York: Free Press.

Kroll, J. F., & Hershenson, M. (1980). Two stages in visual matching. *Canadian Journal of Psychology, 34,* 49–61.

Lassaline, M. E., & Logan, G. D. (1993). Memory-based automaticity in the discrimination of visual numerosity. *Journal of Experimental Psychology, 19,* 561–581.

Lindenmayer, J.-P., Bernstein-Hyman, R., & Grochowski, S. (1994). A new five factor model of schizophrenia. *Psychiatric Quarterly, 65,* 299–322.

Loftus, G. R., Hanna, A. M., & Lester, L. (1988). Conceptual masking: How one picture captures attention from another picture. *Cognitive Psychology, 20,* 237–282.

Logan, G. D. (1990). Repetition priming and automaticity: Common underlying mechanisms? *Cognitive Psychology, 22,* 1–35.

Long, G. M. (1980). Iconic memory: A review and critique of the study of short-term visual storage. *Psychological Bulletin, 88,* 785–820.

Lovegrove, W., & Pepper, K. (1994). The influence of low-level processing in the global precedence effect. In S. Ballesteros (Ed.), *Cognitive approaches to human perception* (pp. 71–90). Hillsdale, NJ: Erlbaum.

McMenamin, S. D., Waxman, E., Orne, D. M., & Knight, R. A. (1994, September). *Using a double backward masking task to assess short-term visual memory deficits in schizophrenia.* Poster session presented at the ninth annual meeting of the Society for Research in Psychopathology, Coral Gables, FL.

Meehl, P. E. (1978). Theoretical risks and tabular asterisks: Sir Karl, Sir Ronald, and the slow progress of soft psychology. *Journal of Consulting and Clinical Psychology, 46,* 806–834.

Mermelstein, R., Banks, W., & Prinzmetal, W. (1979). Figural goodness effects in perception and memory. *Perception and Psychophysics, 26,* 472–480.

Miller, G. A. (1996). How we think about cognition, emotion, and biology in psychopathology. *Psychophysiology, 33,* 615–628.

Miller, K. D., Keller, J. B., & Stryker, M. P. (1989). Ocular dominance column development: Analysis and simulation. *Science, 245,* 605–615.

Mueller, D. J. (1986). *Measuring social attitudes: A handbook for researchers and practitioners.* New York: Teachers College Press.

Muise, J. G., LeBlanc, R. S., Lavoie, M. E., & Arsenault, A. S. (1991). Two-stage model of visual backward masking: Sensory transmission and accrual of effective information as a function of target intensity and similarity. *Perception and Psychophysics, 50,* 197–204.

Neale, J. M., Oltmanns, T. F., & Harvey, P. D. (1985). The need to relate cognitive deficits to specific behavioral referents of schizophrenia. *Schizophrenia Bulletin, 11,* 286–291.

Neath, I., Surprenant, A. M., & Crowder, R. G. (1993). The context-dependent stimulus suffix effect. *Journal of Experimental Psychology: Learning, Memory, and Cognition, 19,* 698–703.

Neisser, U. (1967). *Cognitive psychology.* New York: Appleton-Century-Crofts.

Nicewander, W. A., & Price, J. M. (1983). Reliability of measurement and the power of statistical tests: Some new results. *Psychological Bulletin, 94,* 524–533.

Nuechterlein, K. H. (1991). Vigilance in schizophrenia and related disorders.

In S. R. Steinhauer, J. H. Gruzelier, & J. Zubin (Eds.), *Handbook of schizophrenia. Vol. 5: Neuropsychology, psychophysiology, and information processing* (pp. 397–433). Amsterdam: Elsevier.

Nuechterlein, K. H., Dawson, M. E., Gitlin, M., Ventura, J., Goldstein, M. J., Snyder, K. S., Yee, C. M., & Mintz, J. (1992). Developmental processes in schizophrenic disorders: Longitudinal studies of vulnerability and stress. *Schizophrenia Bulletin, 18,* 387–424.

Nuechterlein, K. H., Edell, W. S., Norris, M., & Dawson, M. E. (1986). Attentional vulnerability indicators, thought disorder and negative symptoms in schizophrenia. *Schizophrenia Bulletin, 12,* 408–426.

O'Donnell, P., & Grace, A. A. (1995). Synaptic interactions among excitatory afferents to nucleus accumbens neurons: Hippocampal gating of prefrontal cortical input. *Journal of Neuroscience, 15,* 3622–3639.

O'Donnell, P., & Grace, A. A. (1996). Basic neurophysiology of antipsychotic drug action. In J. G. Csernansky (Ed.), *Handbook of experimental pharmacology: Antipsychotics* (pp. 164–202). Berlin, Germany: Springer-Verlag.

Orlowski, B., Keitzman, M. L., Dornbush, R. L., & Winnick, W. A. (1985, August). *Perceptual disorganization in schizophrenia.* Paper presented at the 93rd Annual Convention of the American Psychological Association, Los Angeles, CA.

Palmer, J. (1994a). Set-size effects in visual search: The effect of attention is independent of the stimulus for simple tasks. *Vision Research, 34,* 1703–1721.

Palmer, J. (1994b, June). *Visual search latency: The influence of target–distractor discriminability on the magnitude of set size effects.* Paper presented at the meeting of the Association for Research in Vision and Ophthalmology, Sarasota, FL.

Palmer, J., Ames, C. T., & Lindsey, D. T. (1993). Measuring the effect of attention on simple visual search. *Journal of Experimental Psychology: Human Perception and Performance, 19,* 108–130.

Peterson, M. (1994). Object recognition processes can and do operate before figure–ground organization. *Current Directions in Psychological Science, 3,* 105–111

Phillips, L. (1953). Case history data and prognosis in schizophrenia. *Journal of Nervous and Mental Disease, 117,* 515–525.

Phillips, W. A. (1974). On the distinction between sensory storage and short-term visual memory. *Perception and Psychophysics, 16,* 283–290.

Phillips, W. A., & Singer, W. (1997). In search of common foundations for cortical computation. *Behavioral and Brain Sciences, 20,* 657–683.

Place, E. J. S., & Gilmore, G. C. (1980). Perceptual organization in schizophrenia. *Journal of Abnormal Psychology, 89,* 409–418.

Popper, K. R. (1959). *The logic of scientific discovery.* New York: Basic Books.

Potter, M. C. (1976). Short-term conceptual memory for pictures. *Journal of Experimental Psychology: Human Learning and Memory, 2,* 509–522.

Rabinowicz, E. F., Opler, L. A., Owen, D. R., & Knight, R. A. (1996). Dot enumeration perceptual organization task (DEPOT): Evidence for a short-term visual memory deficit in schizophrenia. *Journal of Abnormal Psychology, 105,* 336–348.

Rauschecker, J. P., & Singer, W. (1979). Changes in the circuitry of the kitten visual cortex are gated by post-synaptic activity. *Nature, 280,* 58–60.

Rosen, K., & Hershenson, M. (1983). Test of a two-stage model of visual matching. *Perceptual and Motor Skills, 56,* 343–354.

Ross, D. E., Thaker, G. K., Holcomb, H. H., Cascella, N. G., Medoff, D. R., & Tamminga, C. A. (1995). Abnormal smooth pursuit eye movements in schizophrenic patients are associated with cerebral glucose metabolism in oculomotor regions. *Psychiatry Research, 58,* 53–67.

Saccuzzo, D. P., Hirt, M., & Spencer, T. J. (1974). Backward masking as a measure of attention in schizophrenia. *Journal of Abnormal Psychology, 83,* 512–522.

Schwartz, B. (1982). Early information processing in schizophrenia. *Psychiatric Medicine, 8,* 73–93.

Shaw, M. (1980). Identifying attentional and decision-making components in information processing. In R. S. Nickerson (Ed.), *Attention and performance VIII* (pp. 277–296). Hillsdale, NJ: Erlbaum.

Silverstein, S. M., Bakshi, S., Chapman, R. M., & Nowlis, G. (in press). Perceptual organization of configural and nonconfirgural visual patterns in schizophrenia: Effects of repeated exposure. *Cognitive Neuropsychiatry.*

Silverstein, S. M., & Knight, R. A. (1998). *The process-oriented approach: A paradigm for specifying neurobiological and neurodevelopmental factors in cognitive deficits in schizophrenia.* Manuscript in preparation.

Silverstein, S. M., Knight, R. A., Schwarzkopf, S. B., West, L. L., Osborn, L. M., & Kamin, D. (1996). Stimulus configuration and context effects in perceptual organization in schizophrenia. *Journal of Abnormal Psychology, 105,* 410–420.

Silverstein, S. M., Light, G. A., & Palumbo, D. R. (in press). The Sustained Attention Test: A brief measure of cognitive dysfunction. *Computers in Human Behavior.*

Silverstein, S. M., Matteson, S., & Knight, R. A. (1996). Reduced top-down influence in auditory perceptual organization. *Journal of Abnormal Psychology, 105,* 663–667.

Silverstein, S. M., & Palumbo, D. R. (1995). Nonverbal perceptual organization output disability and schizophrenia spectrum symptomatology. *Psychiatry, 66,* 66–81.

Silverstein, S. M., Raulin, M. L., Pristach, E. A., & Pomerantz, J. R. (1992). Perceptual organization and schizotypy. *Journal of Abnormal Psychology, 101,* 265–270.

Silverstein, S. M., & Schenkel, L. (1997). Schizophrenia as a model of context-deficient cortical computation [Commentary on Phillips and Singer]. *Behavioral and Brain Sciences, 20,* 696–697.

Singer, W. (1995). Development and plasticity of cortical processing architectures. *Science, 270,* 758–763.

Solovay, M. R., Shenton, M. E., Gasperetti, C., Coleman, M., Kestnbaum, E., Carpenter, J. T., & Holzman, P. S. (1986). Scoring manual for the Thought Disorder Index. *Schizophrenia Bulletin, 12,* 483–496.

Spaulding, W., Rosenzweig, L., Huntzinger, R., Cromwell, R. L., Briggs, D., & Hayes, T. (1980). Visual pattern integration in psychiatric patients. *Journal of Abnormal Psychology, 89,* 635–643.

Sperling, G. (1960). The information available in brief visual presentations. *Psychological Monographs, 74*(11, Whole No. 498).

Sperling, G., & Dosher, B. A. (1986). Strategy and optimization in human information processing. In K. R. Boff, L. Kaufman, & J. P. Thomas (Eds.), *Handbook of perception and human performance* (pp. 2-1–2-65). New York: Wiley.

Strauss, M. E. (1993). Relations of symptoms to cognitive deficits in schizophrenia. *Schizophrenia Bulletin, 19,* 215–231.

Townsend, J. T. (1981). Some characteristics of visual whole report behavior. *Acta Psychologica, 47,* 149–173.

Townsend, J. T. (1990). Serial vs. parallel processing: Sometimes they look like Tweedledum and Tweedledee but they can (and should) be distinguished. *Psychological Science, 1,* 46–54.

van den Bosch, R. J., Rombouts, R. P., & van Asma, M. J. O. (1996). What determines continuous performance task performance. *Schizophrenia Bulletin, 22,* 643–651.

van der Heijden, A. H. C. (1996). Two stages in visual information processing and visual perception? *Visual Cognition, 3,* 325–361

Wallace, C. J., & Silverstein, S. M. (1996). [Perceptual organization and Continuous Performance Test performance]. Unpublished raw data, University of California, Los Angeles.

Wells, D. S., & Leventhal, D. (1984). Perceptual grouping in schizophrenia: A replication of Place and Gilmore. *Journal of Abnormal Psychology, 93,* 231–234.

PART THREE

Approaches to Vulnerability

11

Neurocognitive Vulnerability Factors for Schizophrenia: Convergence Across Genetic Risk Studies and Longitudinal Trait–State Studies

Keith H. Nuechterlein, Robert F. Asarnow,
Kenneth L. Subotnik, David L. Fogelson,
Joseph Ventura, Richard D. Torquato,
and Michael E. Dawson

One prominent emphasis in attempts to understand the pathogenesis of schizophrenia involves the search for factors in genetic proneness or vulnerability to schizophrenia. Although the evidence for genetic factors in schizophrenia is overwhelming, the nature of heritable components to schizophrenia has remained elusive (Gottesman & Shields, 1982; Kendler & Diehl, 1993). Part of the problem may be that it is not schizophrenia itself that is heritable but that several underlying factors associated with vulnerability or liability to schizophrenia may be genetically transmitted. These vulnerability components may contribute to the varying forms of the clinical illness that we call schizophrenia but would also be expected to be present in other individuals

This research was supported by National Institute of Mental Health Grants MH37705, MH49716, MH45112, and MH30911. We thank our colleagues George Bartzokis, Michael Gitlin, Irving I. Gottesman, Michael Green, Sun Hwang, Kenneth Kendler, Robert Liberman, Charles MacLean, Jim Mintz, Michael Neale, and Cindy Yee-Bradbury for their many valuable contributions to the overall projects from which the described findings are drawn. We also thank the patients and family members who participated in these studies, without whose partnership in research it would be impossible to make progress in understanding the pathogenesis of schizophrenia.

who do not develop the clinical disorder because of the presence of protective factors or a lack of potentiating or triggering factors. Isolation of traitlike personal vulnerability factors, or *endophenotypes* (Gottesman & Shields, 1972; Holzman, 1994), might greatly aid the search for specific genes relevant to schizophrenia and may also further our understanding of the pathways between genes and the clinical disorder.

Two major strategies for isolating factors in vulnerability to schizophrenia are the identification of subtle anomalies in biological relatives of schizophrenia patients and the identification of traitlike abnormalities in schizophrenia patients that endure into clinically remitted periods (Asarnow & MacCrimmon, 1978; Garmezy & Streitman, 1974; Nuechterlein & Dawson, 1984a; Zubin & Spring, 1977). Both strategies serve to demonstrate that the anomaly is not simply a reflection of a current symptomatic state in schizophrenia but rather is likely to be an underlying component of ongoing proneness to develop the symptoms of schizophrenia. Studies of biological relatives can show that an anomaly is present to an increased degree in groups that would be expected to be characterized by increased genetic proneness to schizophrenia, even in individuals who have never had the disorder. Longitudinal studies of schizophrenia patients can distinguish further between enduring vulnerability factors that remain stable across remitted and symptomatic states and those that change with clinical state, thereby providing some clues to their relevance to symptom formation (Nuechterlein & Dawson, 1984a; Nuechterlein et al., 1992). Enduring vulnerability factors that remain stable across clinical states in schizophrenia patients are the prototypes of the genetically influenced traits typically called *genetic vulnerability markers* or endophenotypes (Gottesman, 1991; Holzman & Matthysse, 1990; Nuechterlein et al., 1992). However, it has been hypothesized that as shown in Figure 1, another type of vulnerability component, which has been labeled a *mediating vulnerability factor* (Nuechterlein & Dawson, 1984a), changes from being subtly abnormal during clinical remission to increasingly abnormal as the active symptomatic state approaches and occurs. The latter type of vulnerability factor may be genetically influenced like the more typical stable type. In addition, however, we infer from its increasing severity as symp-

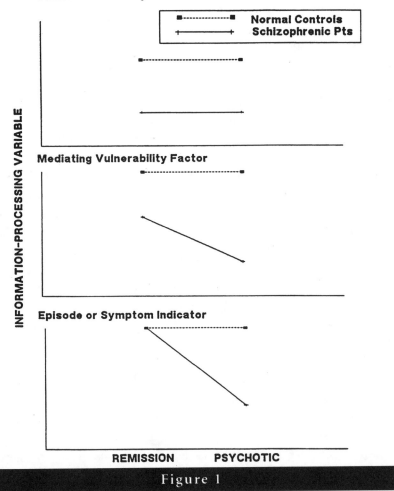

Figure 1

Characteristic patterns of information-processing performance across clinical states for stable vulnerability indicators, mediating vulnerability factors, and episode or symptom indicators. Pts = patients. From "Testing Vulnerability Models: Stability of Potential Vulnerability Indicators Across Clinical State" (p. 178), by K. H. Nuechterlein, M. E. Dawson, J. Ventura, D. Fogelson, M. Gitlin, and J. Mintz, 1991, in H. Häfner and W. F. Gattaz (Eds.), *Search for the Causes of Schizophrenia* (Vol. 2), Berlin: Springer-Verlag. Copyright 1991 by Springer-Verlag. Reprinted with permission.

tom onset occurs that it is closer in the causal pathway to symptom formation than is a stable vulnerability indicator and that it may be a mediating variable in certain forms of symptom formation (Nuechterlein et al., 1992).

The search for vulnerability factors for schizophrenia is underway at many differing levels of analysis, including basic neuroanatomical and neurochemical anomalies, intermediate levels such as cognitive processing abnormalities and associated networks of neuronal activity, and subjective experiences and overt behaviors that may be less severe variants of characteristic clinical symptoms of schizophrenia (Braff, 1993; Freedman et al., 1997; Moldin & Erlenmeyer-Kimling, 1994; Nuechterlein & Dawson, 1997; Weinberger, 1995). Subtle abnormalities in attentional, perceptual, and cognitive processes have been among the most prominent and promising vulnerability factors for schizophrenia (Braff, 1993; Cornblatt & Keilp, 1994; Kremen et al., 1994; Nuechterlein & Dawson, 1984b). The central role of such neurocognitive factors in research on vulnerability to schizophrenia derives from the prominence of attentional and cognitive abnormalities in the subjective experience of schizophrenia, the theoretical advantages of such variables as explanatory constructs between genes and the core symptoms and functional impairments of schizophrenia, and the consistency of objective experimental data documenting several forms of neurocognitive abnormalities in schizophrenia patients and their immediate biological relatives (Asarnow, Granholm, & Sherman, 1991; Braff, 1993; Frith, 1992; Green, 1996; Nuechterlein & Dawson, 1984b; Nuechterlein & Subotnik, 1998).

In this chapter, we describe studies that have used the strategies of genetic risk research and longitudinal trait–state research to examine neurocognitive deficits revealed by a forced-choice span of apprehension task and by versions of the Continuous Performance Test (CPT). We present converging evidence from studies of first-degree relatives and of remitted schizophrenia patients to support the hypothesis that both early perceptual processing abnormalities and working memory abnormalities are neurocognitive vulnerability factors for schizophrenia but may differ in their connection to clinical states in schizophrenia.

302

Before presenting data from our current studies with these measures, however, we first introduce the background of these two types of cognitive tasks.

SPAN OF APPREHENSION TASKS

Origins in Experimental Psychology

The span of apprehension task is a procedure with a long history of use in experimental psychology to examine the amount of information that can be processed when presented simultaneously (Asarnow et al., 1991; Sperling, 1960; van der Heijden, 1996). The question of how many items a person can process from a very briefly presented stimulus array is much more complex than it first seems. It turns out that the nature of the response required can fundamentally change the component of information processing measured.

As Sperling (1960) demonstrated, presenting visual arrays of letters very briefly and asking participants to report what they saw yielded quite different estimates of the number of items seen, depending on whether the instruction was to report the entire array or simply a part of the array. By cuing the participant, immediately after the array was presented, to report only a certain line of the letter array, Sperling was able to demonstrate that a temporary visual buffer storage (or icon) has a much larger capacity than is apparent when the instruction is to report the whole array. The requirement to report the whole visual array causes the performance to be a function of how many items can be quickly moved into immediate or short-term memory and then reported rather than a function primarily of the number of items that can be processed in the earlier sensory buffer storage.

A variant of Sperling's (1960) partial report span of apprehension procedure, called the *forced-choice span of apprehension,* was developed by Estes and Taylor (1964, 1966) to allow refined studies of a serial scanning process in very early perceptual processing. In this version, the participant is told beforehand to determine which of two target letters is present in an array of diverse letters, thereby allowing normal individuals to rapidly reject irrelevant letters in a covert scanning of the temporary visual buffer storage (or icon). The accuracy of detecting the target stimulus decreases as the array size increases, as is consistent with a serial scanning process. Through studies such as these, the forced-choice span of apprehension was established as an efficient procedure for measuring the effectiveness of an individual's early visual search processes, relatively free from the restrictive limits of immediate or short-term memory. Although we now know that parallel processing of stimuli in visual arrays is possible under conditions in which a single distinctive physical features can be used for discrimination of target stimuli (Treisman, 1988; Treisman & Gelade, 1980), typically the discriminations in forced-choice span of apprehension arrays are not of this type and at least partially reflect rapid serial processing of the stimuli in visual buffer storage.

Earlier Span of Apprehension Studies of Schizophrenia

A series of studies of schizophrenia patients have shown that symptomatic schizophrenia patients show lower target letter detection accuracy than normal participants in this forced-choice tachistoscopic task for arrays with large numbers of letters (e.g., 10 or 12) but not with a small number of letters (particularly if only 1; Asarnow et al., 1994; Asarnow & MacCrimmon, 1978; Granholm, Asarnow, & Marder, 1996; Neale, McIntyre, Fox, & Cromwell, 1969). Two studies have found that this deficit is not present when participants are asked to report all letters in a visual array presented at typical brief exposures (Asarnow & Sherman, 1984; Cash, Neale, & Cromwell, 1972). This pattern suggests that high perceptual processing loads pose a particular difficulty for the scanning of visual buffer storage by schizophrenia patients. Cross-sectional studies of schizophrenia outpatients also found that the impaired detection of target stimuli in large, briefly presented arrays also occurs during a relatively remitted, postpsychotic state (Asarnow & MacCrimmon, 1978, 1981), supporting the view that this deficit in early perceptual processing is a vulnerability factor rather than an episode indicator. Furthermore, short-term studies of chronic schizophrenic patients have indicated that these deficits are relatively stable over time (Asarnow & MacCrimmon, 1982; Asarnow, Marder, Mintz, Van Putten, & Zimmerman, 1988). These initial short-term, longitudinal studies did not contrast clinically remitted and psychotic states directly within the same patients, so additional research was needed to make the distinction between stable vulnerability indicators and mediating vulnerability factors.

Three prior studies have examined samples at genetic risk for schizophrenia, with inconsistent results. An initial study of children born to schizophrenic mothers revealed significant deficits in target identification in large letter arrays in a forced-choice span of apprehension task, relative to children born to mothers without psychiatric disorder (Asarnow, Steffy, MacCrimmon, & Cleghorn, 1977). However, Harvey, Weintraub, and Neale (1985) found no significant deficit in their version of this task in children of schizophrenic patients. More recently, Maier, Franke, Hain, Kopp, and Rist (1992) found that healthy siblings of schizophrenic patients processed significantly fewer letters in a large array in a forced-choice span of apprehension task than demographically matched normal comparison participants. Thus, two of three studies provide support for the sensitivity of the forced-choice span of apprehension task to a genetic vulnerability factor for schizophrenia, encouraging further attempts to examine this measure among biological relatives of schizophrenic patients.

CONTINUOUS PERFORMANCE TESTS

Origins in Vigilance and Neuropsychological Research

CPT refers to a class of neurocognitive tasks originally designed to examine sustained attention or vigilance in individuals with suspected brain damage (Rosvold, Mirsky, Sarason, Bransome, & Beck, 1956). *Vigilance* or *sustained attention* is the ability to maintain alertness and a focused readiness to detect and respond to changes in the environment over a prolonged time period. Vigilance tasks typically examine detection of target stimuli that occur relatively infrequently and randomly within a continuous series of stimuli over a period of 15 to 60 min (Davies & Parasuraman, 1982; See, Howe, Warm, & Dember, 1995).

Relative to typical vigilance tasks in cognitive psychology, the CPTs used in clinical research are rapidly paced tasks (typically 1 stimulus/ s), involve very brief individual stimulus durations (usually 30–100 ms), and require relatively short periods of vigilance (5–15 min; Nuechterlein, 1991). The individual stimuli are usually single visual letters or digits, although numbers with several digits (Cornblatt, Risch, Faris, Friedman, & Erlenmeyer-Kimling, 1988), nonsense shapes (Cornblatt et al., 1988), colors (Grunebaum, Weiss, Gallant, & Cohler, 1974), simple auditory stimuli (Mirsky, Yardley, Jones, Walsh, & Kendler, 1995; Sykes, Douglas, & Morgenstern, 1973), and other types of stimuli have been used. The participant's task is to monitor the continuous series of stimuli and to press a button each time that a target stimulus appears.

Within cognitive psychology, an important distinction has been made between vigilance tasks in which the discrimination of target and nontarget stimuli can be made on the basis of information in each stimulus (simultaneous discrimination tasks) and those in which a succession of stimuli must be examined to discriminate target and nontarget stimuli (successive discrimination tasks; Parasuraman & Davies, 1977). Simultaneous discrimination vigilance tasks require an analysis of the perceptual pattern of a given stimulus (e.g., whether the digit is a 0 or whether one line is longer than another one presented at the same time), whereas successive discrimination tasks require storage of prior stimuli in working memory (Baddeley, 1986) and a comparison of a sequence of stimuli (e.g., whether a 3 is immediately followed by a 7 or whether successive stimuli are identical). Thus, these two types of vigilance tasks differ markedly in the extent to which sustained demand for working memory plays a role in performance.

Initially, it was believed that only successive discrimination vigilance tasks with high event rates (rapid pacing) caused true declines in sustained attention (signal–noise discrimination) within the vigilance period in normal participants (Parasuraman & Davies, 1977). However, by burdening early perceptual encoding through substantial blurring of single digit stimuli, Nuechterlein (1983) and his colleagues (Nuechterlein, Parasuraman, & Jiang, 1983) were able to produce substantial signal–noise discrimination declines in a simultaneous discrimination task within 5–10 min, which is much faster than in traditional vigilance tasks. Nuechterlein et al. concluded that the perceptual degradation made the digit stimuli unfamiliar; therefore, perceptual encoding and analysis was much more effortful than for very familiar, clearly focused stimuli. Related to this finding, a recent meta-analysis concluded that a key dimension of vigilance tasks, beyond the presence or absence of a working memory load, is the extent to which the stimuli are highly familiar and well learned (See et al., 1995). The degree of sustained attention demand is increased by either sensory-perceptual load (degree of unfamiliarity) or working memory load.

Earlier CPT Research on Schizophrenia

Astute early clinical observations by Kraepelin (1913/1919) noted that a problem in maintaining focused attention appeared to be involved in the thinking disturbance in schizophrenia. CPT measures were applied to schizophrenia relatively shortly after their development (Orzack & Kornetsky, 1966) and have become one of the most popular and prominent measures in studies of neurocognitive deficits in schizophrenia (Cornblatt & Keilp, 1994; Nuechterlein, 1991). Deficits in ability to detect the target stimuli within the continuous series of very briefly presented stimuli have been found among symptomatic chronic schizophrenia patients in simple simultaneous discrimination as well as successive discrimination forms of the CPT (e.g., Bowen et al., 1994; Cornblatt, Lenzenweger, & Erlenmeyer-Kimling, 1989; Orzack & Kornetsky, 1966; Walker, 1981). Thus, even CPT versions without sustained working memory burdens and with relatively low overall processing resource demands can detect significant deficits in processing briefly presented stimuli in such symptomatic schizophrenia patients (Nuechterlein & Dawson, 1984b). These deficits are apparent in both target detection rates (Orzack & Kornetsky, 1966; Walker, 1981) and a sensitivity index from signal detection theory (Bowen et al., 1994; Cornblatt et al., 1989), indicating that they involve a genuine lower ability to discriminate target from nontarget stimuli rather than a response bias.

However, versions of the CPT with high-processing loads appear to be necessary to detect deficits among remitted schizophrenia patients and among biological relatives of schizophrenia patients. Relatively difficult versions with working memory loads and competing distracting stimuli (Asarnow & MacCrimmon, 1978; Wohlberg & Kornetsky, 1973) or with substantial perceptual loads (Nuechterlein et al., 1992) have shown an ability to detect processing deficits in clinically remitted schizophrenia patients, indicating that CPT target-detection abnormalities are not simply a reflection of concurrent clinical symptoms.

Among children of schizophrenia patients, Rutschmann, Cornblatt, and Erlenmeyer-Kimling (1977) first demonstrated a signal–noise discrimination deficit using a difficult successive discrimination CPT version. Using a factor score derived from five CPT versions with high perceptual discrimination or working memory loads, Nuechterlein (1983) showed that signal–noise discrimination of children of schizophrenia patients was poorer than that of normal control children from the same classrooms. Children of parents who had psychiatric disorders outside the schizophrenia spectrum did not show these CPT deficits (Nuechterlein, 1983). Another study demonstrated that children of parents with a major affective disorder do not share this CPT deficit (Rutschmann, Cornblatt, & Erlenmeyer-Kimling, 1986).

More recent studies have shown that this CPT abnormality is not limited to biological relatives who are children of a schizophrenia patient. Siblings and parents of schizophrenia patients have been found to show target-detection deficits on CPT versions with high perceptual discrimination loads (Grove et al., 1991; Maier et al., 1992) or high working memory loads (Finkelstein, Cannon, Gur, Gur, & Moberg, 1997; Mirsky et al., 1992) but not on CPT versions with low perceptual discrimination (Maier et al., 1992) and low working memory loads (Mirsky et al., 1992). Thus, available studies suggest that a deficit in rapid, sustained discrimination of very briefly presented stimuli under high processing load conditions is a very promising indicator of a vulnerability factor among first-degree relatives of schizophrenia patients.

The nature of the information-processing deficit being tapped by these various versions of the CPT is not well specified at this point. In cognitive psychology, the primary focus is on the vigilance decrement, or decline in performance within the vigilance session, as an index of sustained attention. However, studies of schizophrenia patients (Cornblatt et al., 1989) and children of schizophrenia patients (Nuechterlein, 1983) have generally found that it is the overall level of signal–noise discrimination, not the amount of decline within the vigilance period, that clearly distinguishes these groups from comparison participants. Thus, the neurocognitive processes underlying the CPT deficits associated with schizophrenia are apparently not primarily characterized by a differential linear decline over time but rather either (a) are linked to the sustained attention demand but are sporadic or (b) are relatively independent of the sustained attention demand and instead involve difficulties in the processing of briefly presented perceptual images (Nuechterlein, 1991). In addition, recent CPT work by Servan-Schreiber, Cohen, and Steingard (1996), involving the varying of demands on storage of contextual cues in working memory, supports the view that working memory deficits may be critical to schizophrenia patients' performance in some CPT conditions. Thus, further examination of the implications of differing types of vigilance tasks in needed to understand the nature of the information-processing deficits detected in schizophrenia patients and their biological relatives.

THE UCLA FAMILY MEMBERS STUDY

Overview of the Design

The UCLA Family Members Study is a large, ongoing family genetic study of two adult-onset disorders (adult-onset schizophrenia and bipolar affective disorder), two childhood-onset disorders (childhood-onset schizophrenia and attention deficit hyperactivity disorder), and two groups of community comparison probands matched demographically to the two samples of schizophrenia probands. Nuechterlein serves as the principal investigator for the adult-onset disorder component, Asarnow is the principal investigator for the childhood-onset disorder component, and Subotnik and Fogelson have been the key UCLA investigators since the project's inception. In addition, Kenneth Kendler, Michael Neale, and Charles MacLean of the Medical College of Virginia and Irving Gottesman of the University of Virginia serve as key collaborators.

The primary goals of this project are (a) to identify further the neurocognitive anomalies and subtle clinical symptoms and signs that index vulnerability factors for schizophrenia, (b) to determine the degree of familiality of these characteristics, (c) to determine whether one or several different dimensions of vulnerability are likely to be genetically transmitted, and (d) to assess whether adult-onset schizophrenia and childhood-onset schizophrenia differ with regard to prevalence of affected individuals and presence of vulnerability indicators in biological relatives. Direct structured diagnostic interviews with each available first-degree relative and family psychiatric history interviews are being conducted to assess a wide range of symptoms and signs. A forced-choice span of apprehension task and two versions of the CPT are among the neurocognitive measures obtained and are our focus here.

CPT and Span of Apprehension Abnormalities Among Schizophrenia Probands

The forced-choice span of apprehension task and the two CPT versions for this project were chosen to emphasize somewhat different aspects of information processing, whereas all are promising indicators of vulnerability factors relevant to schizophrenia. The specifications for these measures have been described in detail in Nuechterlein, Edell, Norris, and Dawson (1986) and are only briefly summarized here. As described earlier, the forced-choice span of apprehension task taps the ability to covertly scan the initial sensory buffer storage, relatively free from the constraints of short-term memory and working memory. Thus, it measures the effectiveness of early visual processing, particularly covert visual search, as a function of the number of items presented (Asarnow et al., 1991). Arrays with varying numbers of letters were presented at exposures of 70 ms. The task was to determine in each trial whether the array included a T or an F. The task was participant paced, with each trial initiated when the participant appeared ready for the next stimulus presentation. Here, we focus on the accuracy of the target letter discrimination in 10-letter arrays, which were typical of large arrays in prior studies (Asarnow et al., 1991).

One CPT version, the Degraded Stimulus CPT, is a simultaneous discrimination visual vigilance task that requires sustained difficult perceptual discriminations among highly blurred single digits over a period of 8 min (Nuechterlein et al., 1983, 1986). Participants were asked to respond each time that a 0 occurred in a quasirandom series of single digits, with individual exposures of 40 ms and an event rate of one per second. Thus, sustained early perceptual encoding and analysis processes were emphasized, without a working memory demand other than the need to remember and apply the initial task instructions. The signal detection index, d', was used to measure signal–noise discrimination free of response bias.

The second CPT version, the 3–7 CPT, is a successive discrimination visual vigilance task that requires sustained working memory processes in the context of easy perceptual discriminations. Specifically, the participants were asked to respond each time that a 3 was followed by a 7 in a series of quasirandom, clearly focused single digits. Exposure duration, event rate, and stimulus size were identical to the Degraded Stimulus CPT. This 3–7 CPT is a variant of the original A–X CPT (Rosvold et al., 1956), but the exposure duration was substantially shorter and additional partial targets (individual 3 and 7 stimuli) were added to increase difficulty level and to allow examination of the use of cues stored in working memory (Nuechterlein et al., 1986, 1992). Again, d' was the primary performance measure.

For the present interim report of a study in progress, all valid test data on these three primary test indexes from 75 adult-onset schizophrenia probands and their available parents were examined. These probands had a first onset of a schizophrenic psychosis within 2 years of the project contact and a diagnosis by the Research Diagnostic Criteria (RDC; Spitzer, Endicott, & Robins, 1978) of schizophrenia or schizoaffective disorder, mainly schizophrenic subtype. Full proband sample selection criteria are reported in Nuechterlein et al. (1992). Table 1

	Table 1						

Neurocognitive Performance of Schizophrenia Probands and Demographically Matched Normal Participants

	Schizophrenia probands			Matched normal participants			Effect size[a]
Measure	M	SD	n	M	SD	n	
Span correct identifications, 10-letter array	33.10	3.60	71	35.10*	3.20	53	0.59
Degraded Stimulus CPT d'	1.98	0.96	72	2.75*	0.84	54	0.86
3–7 CPT d'	3.84	0.93	71	4.56*	0.44	54	1.05

Note. CPT = Continuous Performance Test.
[a]Uses an unweighted mean standard deviation of the two groups.
*$p < .001$.

presents the performance of the schizophrenia probands on these neurocognitive tasks relative to normal comparison participants, matched for age, gender, race–ethnicity, and educational level. These data were for an assessment point at which these young schizophrenia patients with a recent initial onset of psychosis have been clinically stabilized on antipsychotic medication as outpatients rather than at an acutely ill inpatient point. It is evident that highly significant deficits were detected among these clinically stabilized schizophrenia patients on each of the three tasks, relative to matched normal comparison participants. Thus, these stabilized schizophrenia outpatients showed deficits in tasks emphasizing iconic visual search processes (span of apprehension), sustained early perceptual encoding and analysis (Degraded Stimulus CPT), and sustained working memory (3–7 CPT).

CPT and Scan of Apprehension Abnormalities Among Biological Parents of Schizophrenia Probands

To do a preliminary examination of whether these three neurocognitive measures are likely to detect vulnerability-linked anomalies in the first-degree relatives of the adult-onset schizophrenia patients as hypothesized, we examined the biological parents of schizophrenia probands in relationship to the individual normal participants who were demographically matched to the probands. Biological parents with a psychotic diagnosis were excluded from this analysis. A sample of community comparison families are currently being recruited and assessed within the UCLA Family Members Study and will later serve as a group of families who are demographically matched to the families of the schizophrenia probands. Thus, the current analyses must be viewed as preliminary and interpreted cautiously.

As can be seen in Table 2, the mean scores of the nonpsychotic biological parents of the schizophrenia probands are substantially lower than those of this preliminary normal comparison group on the forced-choice span of apprehension task, Degraded Stimulus CPT, and 3–7 CPT. Because these biological parents are much older ($M = 55$ years) than the normal comparison sample ($M = 24$ years) and scores on these

Table 2

Neurocognitive Performance of Nonpsychotic Biological Parents of Schizophrenia Probands and Normal Participants Demographically Matched to Probands

Measure	Parents of schizophrenia probands			Normal participants matched to probands			Effect size[a]
	M	SD	n	M	SD	n	
Span correct identifications, 10-letter array	30.30	3.50	87	35.10**	3.20	53	1.43
Degraded Stimulus CPT d'	2.04	1.07	89	2.75**	0.84	54	0.74
3–7 CPT d'	4.20	0.57	17[b]	4.56*	0.44	54	0.71

Note. CPT = Continuous Performance Test.
[a]Uses an unweighted mean standard deviation of the two groups. [b]Sample smaller because 3–7 CPT was added during the course of this study of biological relatives.
*$p < .01$. **$p < .001$.

measures appear to decrease somewhat with normal aging over this interval, we also compared these two groups after age effects were removed through polynomial regression on the basis of age effects in the siblings and parents of the schizophrenia probands. The group differences remained significant. Finally, because such regression procedures to remove age effects have significant limitations when applied to samples that do not overlap substantially on the regressed variable, we also contrasted the individual normal comparison group to the siblings of the schizophrenia probands. As will be presented in detail elsewhere, the siblings also had mean scores on the indexes of early perceptual processes from the span of apprehension and Degraded Stimulus CPT that were either significantly lower than those of the normal participants or neared statistical significance. As would be expected from most genetic transmission models for hypothesized liability factors, the mean differences were typically moderate in size after age effects were controlled, and there was substantial overlap between groups. Thus, although these results are preliminary and clearly in need of confirmation with a sample of demographically matched families, they are consistent with the hypothesis that anomalies in early perceptual discrimination processes and, at least for the parents, anomalies in sustained working memory processes are sensitive to genetic vulnerability factors relevant to schizophrenia.

DEVELOPMENTAL PROCESSES IN SCHIZOPHRENIC DISORDERS PROJECT

Overview of the Design

Findings regarding potential vulnerability factors that derive from biological relatives of schizophrenia patients become even more convincing when they converge with findings from studies of schizophrenia patients in clinical remission. Furthermore, as noted earlier, longitudinal studies of schizophrenia patients assessed in clinically remitted states and symptomatic states should help to clarify whether certain vulnerability factors might play a direct role in the development of various types of schizophrenic symptoms. Examination of these issues is one of the major goals of the Developmental Processes in Schizophrenic Disorders Project, which involves a series of longitudinal studies focusing on the initial years after the onset of schizophrenia (Nuechterlein et al., 1992).

During an initial phase with our first cohort of participants (Sample 1), this project included an examination of the neurocognitive functioning of recent-onset schizophrenia patients in a complete clinical remission or the best clinical recovery state achieved and, if it occurred, at a point at which psychotic symptoms returned. Both assessments were completed while the patients were being treated at the UCLA Aftercare Research Program with a combination of fluphenazine (Prolixin) decanoate, individual case management, supportive cognitive–behavioral group therapy, and family education. The forced-choice span of apprehension task, Degraded Stimulus CPT, and 3–7 CPT measures described above were administered at these points.

Trait–State Analyses

To provide the clearest comparison of performance across clinical states, we chose data from those patients who were assessed while in a clinical remission on all 18 traditional Brief Psychiatric Rating Scale items (Guy, 1976) and who were assessed in a psychotic state while on identical or nearly identical medication levels. The interim analyses discussed here represent the first 17 patients with RDC schizophrenia or schizoaffective disorder, mainly schizophrenic, whose data met these criteria (Nuechterlein et al., 1991, 1992). Normal comparison participants were individually matched to schizophrenia patients on age, gender, race–ethnicity, and educational level and were assessed at time intervals comparable with those of schizophrenia patients. Thirteen of the 17 pairs of participants had span of apprehension data available.

As shown in Figure 2, target letter detection in the forced-choice span of apprehension task for these recent-onset schizophrenia patients did not differ from that of normal participants for 1-letter arrays but was significantly impaired for 10-letter arrays. Even more important, the level of impairment in the 10-letter arrays remained stable across

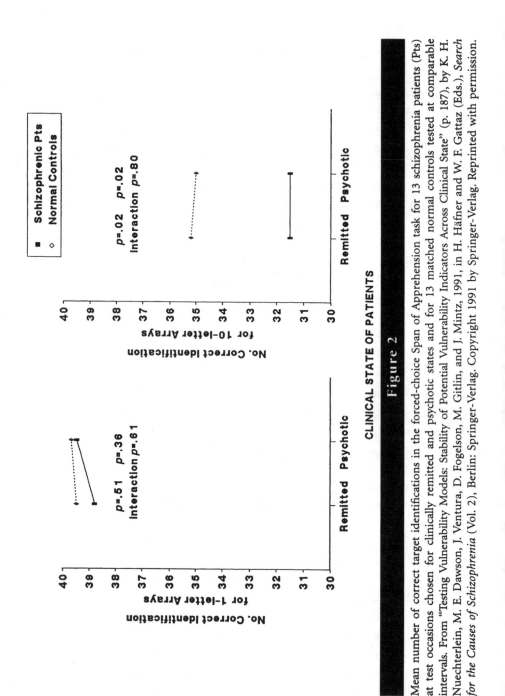

CLINICAL STATE OF PATIENTS

Figure 2

Mean number of correct target identifications in the forced-choice Span of Apprehension task for 13 schizophrenia patients (Pts) at test occasions chosen for clinically remitted and psychotic states and for 13 matched normal controls tested at comparable intervals. From "Testing Vulnerability Models: Stability of Potential Vulnerability Indicators Across Clinical State" (p. 187), by K. H. Nuechterlein, M. E. Dawson, J. Ventura, D. Fogelson, M. Gitlin, and J. Mintz, 1991, in H. Häfner and W. F. Gattaz (Eds.), *Search for the Causes of Schizophrenia* (Vol. 2), Berlin: Springer-Verlag. Copyright 1991 by Springer-Verlag. Reprinted with permission.

the clinically remitted and psychotic state, with no interaction of Diagnostic Group × Test Occasion. Thus, this early covert perceptual scanning of visual buffer storage remained stably impaired across clinical state, consistent with the pattern of a *stable vulnerability indicator* (Nuechterlein & Dawson, 1984a).

Figure 3 summarizes the data for d' within the Degraded Stimulus CPT. It is apparent that a highly significant deficit in signal–noise discrimination in this tachistoscopic vigilance task was present among the schizophrenia patients in both a clinically remitted state and a psychotic state. Furthermore, the magnitude of this deficit did not change significantly from the remitted state to the psychotic state. This performance pattern, like that of visual scanning of initial buffer storage in the span of apprehension task, is characteristic of a stable vulnerability indicator. Given that the information-processing demands of the Degraded Stimulus CPT emphasize initial perceptual encoding and analysis processes, the findings from the forced-choice span of apprehension and Degraded Stimulus CPT converge to suggest that early perceptual processes are abnormal in a rather stable fashion across clinical states in the early phase of schizophrenia. These analyses support the value of early perceptual abnormalities as schizophrenia-related endophenotypes that are not tightly tied to psychotic symptoms themselves.

In contrast to these remarkably stable levels of perceptual abnormality, signal–noise discrimination within the CPT that demands sustained working memory (but has low-perceptual discrimination requirements) shows a very different pattern. As summarized in Figure 4, d' within the 3–7 CPT is significantly abnormal, but relatively subtly so, during the patients' clinically remitted state. Ability to use working memory to guide one's choice of target stimulus (respond to 7 only if the preceding stimulus was a 3) was markedly poorer at the psychotic state assessment point and yielded a highly significant Diagnostic Group × Test Occasion interaction. Thus, this measure is characteristic of a potential mediating vulnerability factor (Nuechterlein & Dawson, 1984a). We would hypothesize on this basis that the deficits in sustained working memory tapped by the 3–7 CPT would be good candidates

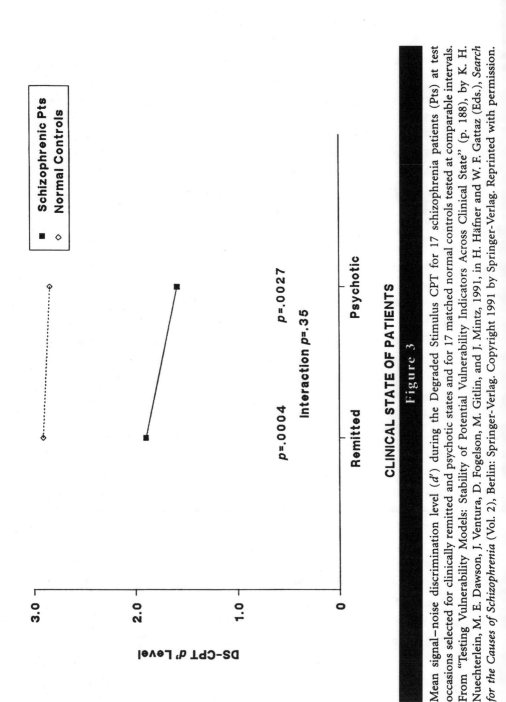

CLINICAL STATE OF PATIENTS

Figure 3

Mean signal–noise discrimination level (d') during the Degraded Stimulus CPT for 17 schizophrenia patients (Pts) at test occasions selected for clinically remitted and psychotic states and for 17 matched normal controls tested at comparable intervals. From "Testing Vulnerability Models: Stability of Potential Vulnerability Indicators Across Clinical State" (p. 188), by K. H. Nuechterlein, M. E. Dawson, J. Ventura, D. Fogelson, M. Gitlin, and J. Mintz, 1991, in H. Häfner and W. F. Gattaz (Eds.), *Search for the Causes of Schizophrenia* (Vol. 2), Berlin: Springer-Verlag. Copyright 1991 by Springer-Verlag. Reprinted with permission.

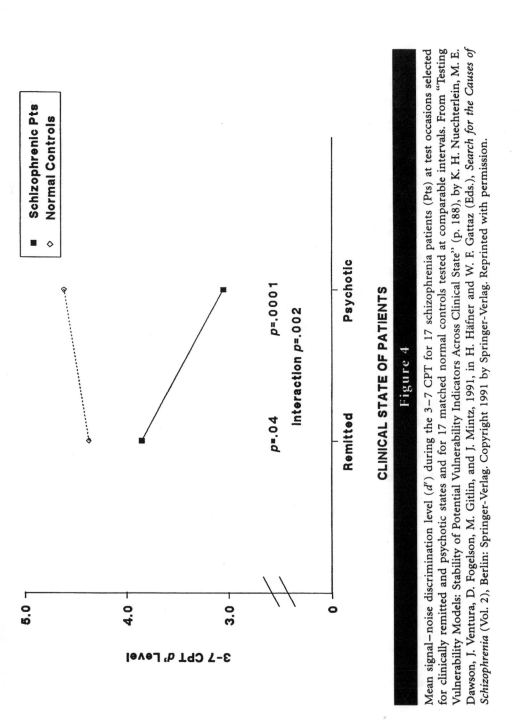

CLINICAL STATE OF PATIENTS

Figure 4

Mean signal–noise discrimination level (d') during the 3–7 CPT for 17 schizophrenia patients (Pts) at test occasions selected for clinically remitted and psychotic states and for 17 matched normal controls tested at comparable intervals. From "Testing Vulnerability Models: Stability of Potential Vulnerability Indicators Across Clinical State" (p. 188), by K. H. Nuechterlein, M. E. Dawson, J. Ventura, D. Fogelson, M. Gitlin, and J. Mintz, 1991, in H. Häfner and W. F. Gattaz (Eds.), *Search for the Causes of Schizophrenia* (Vol. 2), Berlin: Springer-Verlag. Copyright 1991 by Springer-Verlag. Reprinted with permission.

for attempts to link subtle changes in working memory processes within schizophrenia patients to subsequent changes in certain characteristic symptoms of schizophrenia. More fine-tuned study of such changes over time would be expected to yield a clearer understanding of the temporal ordering of such neurocognitive changes relative to the formation of positive or negative symptoms and could lead to development of more effective interventions as we come to understand the nature of presymptomatic states.

CONCLUSION

The analyses described here illustrate the complimentary contributions that can be made by genetic risk studies and longitudinal trait–state studies in the search for components of vulnerability to schizophrenia. Longitudinal studies of schizophrenia patients, even when they involve assessments of clinically remitted states, cannot rule out the possibility that observed abnormal processes are actually a consequence of having developed schizophrenia rather than a preexisting vulnerability factor. Studies of nonpsychotic biological relatives of schizophrenia patients can rule out this possibility. However, they are less effective in clarifying the extent to which vulnerability factors change over time with symptom development, in identifying the types of symptoms or functional outcomes that are affected by different vulnerability factors, and in isolating time relationships between changes in potential mediating vulnerability factors and subsequent symptom development. Thus, the combination of strategies is likely to have more impact than either one alone.

One working hypothesis that we are currently pursuing through further analyses and new studies is that deficits in early perceptual discrimination processes are separable from deficits in sustained working memory as vulnerability components of schizophrenia. Other recent studies using different measurement paradigms also support the role of early perceptual anomalies (e.g., Green, Nuechterlein, & Breitmeyer, 1997) and working memory anomalies (Park, Holzman, & Goldman-Rakic, 1995) as genetic vulnerability factors in relatives of schizophrenia patients, but their interrelationship remains relatively unexplored. On the basis of our work thus far, it appears that working memory abnormalities may be more closely linked to symptom formation processes during the course of schizophrenia, whereas some types of early perceptual abnormalities may be more distant from symptom formation but can serve as relatively stable traits that help to identify vulnerability factors for schizophrenia in genetic analyses.

REFERENCES

Asarnow, R. F., Asamen, J., Granholm, E., Sherman, T., Watkins, J. M., & Williams, M. E. (1994). Cognitive/neuropsychological studies of children with a schizophrenic disorder. *Schizophrenia Bulletin, 20,* 647–669.

Asarnow, R. F., Granholm, E., & Sherman, T. (1991). Span of apprehension in schizophrenia. In S. R. Steinhauer, J. H. Gruzelier, & J. Zubin (Eds.), *Handbook of schizophrenia. Vol. 5: Neuropsychology, psychophysiology, and information processing* (pp. 335–370). Amsterdam: Elsevier Science.

Asarnow, R. F., & MacCrimmon, D. J. (1978). Residual performance deficit in clinically remitted schizophrenics: A marker of schizophrenia? *Journal of Abnormal Psychology, 87,* 597–608.

Asarnow, R. F., & MacCrimmon, D. J. (1981). Span of apprehension deficits during postpsychotic stages of schizophrenia. *Archives of General Psychiatry, 38,* 1006–1011.

Asarnow, R. F., & MacCrimmon, D. J. (1982). Attention/information processing, neuropsychological functioning, and thought disorder during the acute and partial recovery phases of schizophrenia: A longitudinal study. *Psychiatry Research, 7,* 309–319.

Asarnow, R. F., Marder, S. R., Mintz, J., Van Putten, T., & Zimmerman, K. E. (1988). Differential effect of low and conventional doses of fluphenazine on schizophrenic outpatients with good or poor information-processing abilities. *Archives of General Psychiatry, 45,* 822–826.

Asarnow, R. F., & Sherman, T. (1984). Studies of visual information processing in schizophrenic children. *Child Development, 55,* 249–261.

Asarnow, R. F., Steffy, R. A., MacCrimmon, D. J., & Cleghorn, J. M. (1977). An attentional assessment of foster children at risk for schizophrenia. *Journal of Abnormal Psychology, 86,* 267–275.

Baddeley, A. D. (1986). *Working memory.* Oxford, England: Oxford University Press.

Bowen, L., Wallace, C. J., Glynn, S. M., Nuechterlein, K. H., Lutzker, J. R., & Kuehnel, T. G. (1994). Schizophrenic individuals' cognitive functioning and performance in interpersonal interactions and skills training procedures. *Journal of Psychiatric Research, 28,* 289–301.

Braff, D. (1993). Information processing and attention of dysfunctions in schizophrenia. *Schizophrenia Bulletin, 19,* 233–259.

Cash, T. F., Neale, J. M., & Cromwell, R. L. (1972). Span of apprehension in acute schizophrenics: Full-report technique. *Journal of Abnormal Psychology, 79,* 322–326.

Cornblatt, B. A., & Keilp, J. G. (1994). Impaired attention, genetics, and the pathophysiology of schizophrenia. *Schizophrenia Bulletin, 20,* 31–46.

Cornblatt, B. A., Lenzenweger, M. F., & Erlenmeyer-Kimling, L. (1989). The Continuous Performance Test, Identical Pairs version (CPT-IP): II. Contrasting attentional profiles in schizophrenic and depressed patients. *Psychiatry Research, 29,* 65–85.

Cornblatt, B. A., Risch, N. J., Faris, G., Friedman, D., & Erlenmeyer-Kimling, L. (1988). The Continuous Performance Test, Identical Pairs version (CPT-IP): I. New findings about sustained attention in normal families. *Psychiatry Research, 26,* 223–238.

Davies, D. R., & Parasuraman, R. (1982). *The psychology of vigilance.* New York: Academic Press.

Estes, W. K., & Taylor, H. A. (1964). A detection method and probabilistic models for assessing information processing from brief visual displays. *Proceedings of the National Academy of Sciences, 52,* 446–454.

Estes, W. K., & Taylor, H. A. (1966). Visual detection in relation to display size and redundancy of critical elements. *Perception and Psychophysics, 1,* 9–16.

Finkelstein, J. R. J., Cannon, T. D., Gur, R. E., Gur, R. C., & Moberg, P. (1997). Attentional dysfunctions in neuroleptic-naive and neuroleptic-withdrawn schizophrenic patients and their siblings. *Journal of Abnormal Psychology, 106,* 203–212.

Freedman, R., Coon, H., Myles-Worsley, M., Orr-Urtreger, A., Olincy, A., Davis, A., Polymeropoulos, M., Holik, J., Hopkins, J., Hoff, M., Rosenthal, J.,

Waldo, M. C., Reimherr, F., Wender, P., Yaw, J., Young, D. A., Breese, C. R., Adams, C., Patterson, D., Adler, L. E., Kruglyak, L., Leonard, S., & Byerley, W. (1997). Linkage of a neurophysiological deficit in schizophrenia to a chromosome 15 locus. *Proceedings of the National Academy of Sciences USA, 94,* 587–592.

Frith, C. D. (1992). *The cognitive neuropsychology of schizophrenia.* Hove, England: Erlbaum.

Garmezy, N., & Streitman, S. (1974). Children at risk: The search for the antecedents of schizophrenia. Part I. Conceptual models and research methods. *Schizophrenia Bulletin, 1* (Experimental issue no. 8), 14–90.

Gottesman, I. I. (1991). *Schizophrenia genesis: The origins of madness.* New York: Freeman.

Gottesman, I. I., & Shields, J. (1972). *Schizophrenia and genetics: A twin study vantage point.* New York: Academic Press.

Gottesman, I. I., & Shields, J. (1982). *Schizophrenia: The epigenetic puzzle.* Cambridge, England: Cambridge University Press.

Granholm, E., Asarnow, R. F., & Marder, S. R. (1996). Display angle and attentional scanpaths on the span of apprehension task in schizophrenia. *Journal of Abnormal Psychology, 105,* 17–24.

Green, M. F. (1996). What are the functional consequences of neurocognitive deficits in schizophrenia? *American Journal of Psychiatry, 153,* 321–330.

Green, M. F., Nuechterlein, K. H., & Breitmeyer, B. (1997). Backward masking performance in unaffected siblings of schizophrenic patients: Evidence for a vulnerability indicator. *Archives of General Psychiatry, 54,* 465–472.

Grove, W. M., Lebow, B. S., Clementz, B. A., Cerri, A., Medus, C., & Iacono, W. G. (1991). Familial prevalence and coaggregation of schizotypy indicators: A multitrait family study. *Journal of Abnormal Psychology, 100,* 115–121.

Grunebaum, H., Weiss, J. L., Gallant, D., & Cohler, B. J. (1974). Attention in young children of psychotic mothers. *American Journal of Psychiatry, 131,* 887–891.

Guy, W. (1976). *ECDEU assessment manual for psychopharmacology* (DHEW Publication No. ADM 76-338). Rockville, MD: National Institute of Mental Health.

Harvey, P. D., Weintraub, S., & Neale, J. M. (1985). Span of apprehension deficits in children vulnerable to schizophrenia: A failure to replicate. *Journal of Abnormal Psychology, 94,* 410–413.

Holzman, P. S. (1994). The role of psychological probes in genetic studies of schizophrenia. *Schizophrenia Research, 13,* 1–9.

Holzman, P. S., & Matthysse, S. (1990). The genetics of schizophrenia: A review. *Psychological Science, 1,* 279–286.

Kendler, K. S., & Diehl, S. R. (1993). The genetics of schizophrenia: A current, genetic–epidemiologic perspective. *Schizophrenia Bulletin, 19,* 261–285.

Kraepelin, E. (1919). *Dementia praecox and paraphrenia* (R. M. Barclay, Trans.). Edinburgh, Scotland: E. & S. Livingston. (Original work published 1913; reprinted by Krieger 1971).

Kremen, W. S., Seidman, L. J., Pepple, J. R., Lyons, M. J., Tsuang, M. T., & Faraone, S. V. (1994). Neuropsychological risk indicators for schizophrenia: A review of family studies. *Schizophrenia Bulletin, 20,* 103–119.

Maier, W., Franke, P., Hain, C., Kopp, B., & Rist, F. (1992). Neuropsychological indicators of the vulnerability to schizophrenia. *Progress in Neuro-Psychopharmacology and Biological Psychiatry, 16,* 703–715.

Mirsky, A. F., Lockhead, S. J., Jones, B. P., Kugelmass, S., Walsh, D., & Kendler, K. S. (1992). On familial factors in the attentional deficit in schizophrenia: A review and report of two new subject samples. *Journal of Psychiatric Research, 26,* 383–403.

Mirsky, A. F., Yardley, S. L., Jones, B. P., Walsh, D., & Kendler, K. S. (1995). Analysis of the attention deficit in schizophrenia: A study of patients and their relatives in Ireland. *Journal of Psychiatric Research, 29,* 23–42.

Moldin, S. O., & Erlenmeyer-Kimling, L. (1994). Measuring liability to schizophrenia: Progress report 1994: Editors' introduction. *Schizophrenia Bulletin, 20,* 25–29.

Neale, J. M., McIntyre, C. W., Fox, R., & Cromwell, R. L. (1969). Span of apprehension in acute schizophrenics. *Journal of Abnormal Psychology, 74,* 593–596.

Nuechterlein, K. H. (1983). Signal detection in vigilance tasks and behavioral attributes among offspring of schizophrenic mothers and among hyperactive children. *Journal of Abnormal Psychology, 92,* 4–28.

Nuechterlein, K. H. (1991). Vigilance in schizophrenia and related disorders. In S. R. Steinhauer, J. H. Gruzelier, & J. Zubin (Eds.), *Handbook of schizo-*

phrenia. Vol. 5: Neuropsychology, psychophysiology, and information processing (pp. 397–433). Amsterdam: Elsevier.

Nuechterlein, K. H., & Dawson, M. E. (1984a). A heuristic vulnerability/stress model of schizophrenic episodes. *Schizophrenia Bulletin, 10,* 300–312.

Nuechterlein, K. H., & Dawson, M. E. (1984b). Information processing and attentional functioning in the developmental course of schizophrenic disorders. *Schizophrenia Bulletin, 10,* 160–203.

Nuechterlein, K. H., & Dawson, M. E. (1997). Neurophysiological and psychophysiological approaches to schizophrenia and its pathogenesis. In S. J. Watson (Ed.), *Psychopharmacology: The fourth generation of progress* (CD/ ROM rev.). New York: Raven Press.

Nuechterlein, K. H., Dawson, M. E., Gitlin, M., Ventura, J., Goldstein, M. J., Snyder, K. S., Yee, C. M., & Mintz, J. (1992). Developmental Processes in Schizophrenic Disorders: Longitudinal studies of vulnerability and stress. *Schizophrenia Bulletin, 18,* 387–425.

Nuechterlein, K. H., Dawson, M. E., Ventura, J., Fogelson, D., Gitlin, M., & Mintz, J. (1991). Testing vulnerability models: Stability of potential vulnerability indicators across clinical state. In H. Häfner & W. F. Gattaz (Eds.), *Search for the causes of schizophrenia* (Vol. 2, pp. 177–191). Berlin, Germany: Springer-Verlag.

Nuechterlein, K. H., Edell, W. S., Norris, M., & Dawson, M. E. (1986). Attentional vulnerability indicators, thought disorder, and negative symptoms. *Schizophrenia Bulletin, 12,* 408–426.

Nuechterlein, K. H., Parasuraman, R., & Jiang, Q. (1983, April 15). Visual sustained attention: Image degradation produces rapid sensitivity decrement over time. *Science, 220,* 327–329.

Nuechterlein, K. H., & Subotnik, K. L. (1998). The cognitive origins of schizophrenia and prospects for intervention. In T. Wykes, N. Tarrier, & S. Lewis (Eds.), *Outcome and innovation in psychological treatment of schizophrenia* (pp. 17–41). Chichester, England: Wiley.

Orzack, M. H., & Kornetsky, C. (1966). Attention dysfunction in chronic schizophrenia. *Archives of General Psychiatry, 14,* 323–326.

Parasuraman, R., & Davies, D. R. (1977). A taxonomic analysis of vigilance performance. In R. R. Mackie (Ed.), *Vigilance: Theory, operational performance, and physiological correlates* (pp. 559–574). New York: Plenum.

Park, S., Holzman, P. S., & Goldman-Rakic, P. S. (1995). Spatial working memory deficits in the relatives of schizophrenic patients. *Archives of General Psychiatry, 52,* 821–828.

Rosvold, H. E., Mirsky, A., Sarason, I., Bransome, E. D., Jr., & Beck, L. H. (1956). A continuous performance test of brain damage. *Journal of Consulting Psychology, 20,* 343–350.

Rutschmann, J., Cornblatt, B., & Erlenmeyer-Kimling, L. (1977). Sustained attention in children at risk for schizophrenia: Report on a continuous performance test. *Archives of General Psychiatry, 34,* 571–575.

Rutschmann, J., Cornblatt, B., & Erlenmeyer-Kimling, L. (1986). Sustained attention in children at risk for schizophrenia: Findings with two visual continuous performance tests in a new sample. *Journal of Abnormal Child Psychology, 14,* 365–385.

See, J. E., Howe, S. R., Warm, J. S., & Dember, W. N. (1995). Meta-analysis of the sensitivity decrement in vigilance. *Psychological Bulletin, 117,* 230–249.

Servan-Schreiber, D., Cohen, J. D., & Steingard, S. (1996). Schizophrenic deficits in the processing of context: A test of a theoretical model. *Archives of General Psychiatry, 53,* 1105–1112.

Sperling, G. (1960). The information available in brief visual presentations. *Psychological Monographs, 74* (Whole No. 498).

Spitzer, R. L., Endicott, J., & Robins, E. (1978). Research Diagnostic Criteria: Rationale and reliability. *Archives of General Psychiatry, 35,* 773–782.

Sykes, D. H., Douglas, V. I., & Morgenstern, G. (1973). Sustained attention in hyperactive children. *Journal of Child Psychology and Psychiatry, 44,* 267–273.

Treisman, A. M. (1988). Features and objects: The fourteenth Bartlett memorial lecture. *Quarterly Journal of Experimental Psychology, 40A,* 201–237.

Treisman, A. M., & Gelade, G. (1980). A feature integration theory of attention. *Cognitive Psychology, 12,* 97–136.

van der Heijden, A. H. C. (1996). Visual attention. In O. Neumann & A. F. Sanders (Eds.), *Handbook of perception and action. Vol. 3: Attention* (pp. 5–42). London: Academic Press.

Walker, E. (1981). Attentional and neuromotor functions of schizophrenics, schizoaffectives, and patients with other affective disorders. *Archives of General Psychiatry, 38,* 1355–1358.

Weinberger, D. R. (1995). Neurodevelopmental perspectives on schizophrenia. In F. E. Bloom & D. J. Kupfer (Eds.), *Psychopharmacology: The fourth generation of progress* (pp. 1171–1183). New York: Raven Press.

Wohlberg, G. W., & Kornetsky, C. (1973). Sustained attention in remitted schizophrenia. *Archives of General Psychiatry, 28,* 533–537.

Zubin, J., & Spring, B. (1977). Vulnerability—A new view of schizophrenia. *Journal of Abnormal Psychology, 86,* 103–126.

12

Backward-Masking Performance in Schizophrenia

Michael F. Green and Keith H. Nuechterlein

Backward masking is a procedure to assess the earliest components of visual processing in which the identification of an initial stimulus (the target) is disrupted by a later stimulus (the mask). Schizophrenia patients show deficits in masking, meaning that they require a longer time interval between target and mask than controls to accurately identify the target. Backward masking involves the interactions of two types of visual channels (transient and sustained), which generate two types of masking mechanisms (integrative and interruptive). In addition, masking can be divided into an early component (e.g., up to about 60 ms), which reflects the involvement of sensory-perceptual processes, and a later component, which reflects susceptibility to attentional disengagement as the mask diverts processing away from the representation of the target.

In this chapter, we describe the backward-masking procedure, discuss its use in schizophrenia research, and consider how masking performance relates to the interactions of two types of visual channels (transient and sustained). We report on a series of studies from our

---

We thank Mary Jane Robertson and Kimmy Kee for help in preparing this chapter.

laboratory of backward masking with schizophrenia patients and their siblings. The findings are considered in terms of their relevance for understanding vulnerability to schizophrenia. Backward masking lends itself to a "parsing" approach of experimental reductivism in which the goals are to break a behavior (e.g., a performance deficit) into its smallest meaningful elements.

THE BASICS OF BACKWARD MASKING

While it is apparent that schizophrenia patients experience difficulties in a broad range of neurocognitive abilities, including basic perceptual processes, the etiology of these problems is rarely obvious. Deficits could reflect an underlying predisposition to the disorder or the disruptive influence of psychiatric symptoms. Specialized procedures, such as backward masking, help to determine the origins of neurocognitive deficits.

At its core, backward masking is fairly simple. There is a target, a brief interval, and a mask (see Figure 1). The duration of the target is usually brief (often 5–20 ms) and the interval between target and mask (interstimulus interval [ISI]) can range from a few milliseconds to hundreds of milliseconds. Duration of the mask is also usually brief but

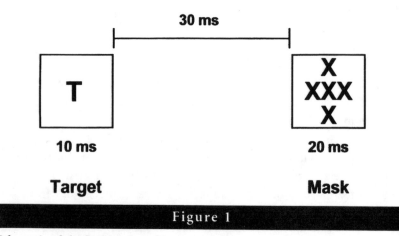

Figure 1

Schematic of the backward-masking procedure.

typically is longer than that of the target. The target can be almost any type of stimuli but frequently is a simple stimulus like a single letter. Composition of the mask is likewise variable but frequently is overlapping lines or letters. Note that there are only a finite number of parameters that can be manipulated in a backward-masking procedure: the intensity or duration of the target, the intensity or duration of the mask, the interval between the two, the structure of the target and mask stimuli, and their location in the visual field. Manipulation of this finite number of parameters yields an infinite number of combinations with rather substantial implications for performance.

The target is always presented at a duration so that it can be identified in the absence of the mask. Hence, if a target is shown alone, participants are able to identify it at some predetermined level of accuracy. But if a mask follows the target after a brief interval (e.g., 30 ms, as in Figure 1), participants might not be able to identify the target. In fact, they may not be aware that a target was presented at all. Because the mask appears to work backward in time (of course, it does not), this procedure is called *backward masking*.

Types of Masking Functions

Under most conditions, the performance of participants improves as the interval between the target and mask increases. This usually takes the form of a sigmoidal or monotonic function when accuracy is graphed along the y axis and the intervals are graphed along the x axis (see the top panel of Figure 2). However, under certain conditions (e.g., the mask does not spatially overlap the target or the duration of the mask is brief relative to that of the target), it is possible to achieve a non-monotonic function. Under optimal experimental conditions, a non-monotonic function could look U shaped, as in the bottom panel of Figure 2.

Until recently, the monotonic function was the only type of masking function achieved with schizophrenia patients. This has been a limitation for the field because, as we will see shortly, a non-monotonic function is much easier to interpret.

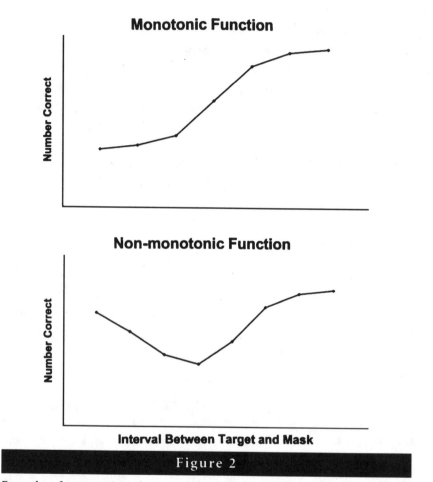

Figure 2

Examples of monotonic and non-monotonic masking functions.

Types of Visual Channels

According to a model proposed by Breitmeyer and Ganz (Breitmeyer, 1984; Breitmeyer & Ganz, 1976), backward masking is the result of a complex interaction of two types of visual channels. These channels differ in their anatomical distributions, their psychophysical characteristics, and the type of information they convey. Transient cells (also called *magnocellular* cells) derive from the Type A ganglion cells of the retina, project to the magnocellular layers of the lateral geniculate, and then project to layer 4C alpha of the primary visual area. Sustained (also called *parvocellular*) cells derive from the Type B ganglion cells of the retina, project to the parvocellular layers of the lateral geniculate, and project to layer 4C beta of the primary visual area. Transient cells have a rather rapid onset and a brief response. In contrast, sustained cells have a relatively long onset latency and maintain their response for a longer duration. More important for the studies that are described later, the cells differ in their sensitivity to spatial frequency; sustained cells are sensitive to high spatial frequency and transient cells are sensitive to low spatial frequency. Transient cells convey information on the onset, offset, and location of objects, but sustained cells are needed for a detailed scrutiny and identification of objects.

It should be noted that the psychophysical differences between the pathways are relative, not absolute. The distributions are overlapping, but it is fair to say that transient channels tend to be more sensitive to low spatial frequency, onset–offset, and location of stimuli compared with sustained channels.

Types of Masking Mechanisms

Transient and sustained channels of the target and mask can interact in a couple of different ways, which are displayed in Figure 3. The figure shows two masking intervals—one at a short ISI and one at a longer ISI. When a target is presented, it stimulates activity in the transient cells, followed by activity in sustained cells. Presentation of the mask does the same for its own transient and sustained channels. The figure also depicts two types of interactions. First, the sustained channels of the mask can sum, or integrate, with the sustained channels of the target. In this process, the icon (i.e., the internal representation) of the target would merge with the icon of the mask to yield a composite icon, similar to a double exposure; this process is called masking by *integration*. Alternatively, the transient cells of the mask can inhibit the sustained cells of the target, essentially terminating their activity too soon; this process is called masking by *interruption*.

Looking back at Figure 2, we can start to relate the mechanism to the shape of the masking function. In a monotonic function, mask-

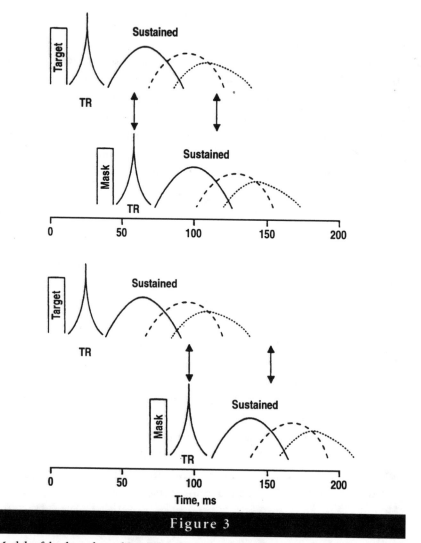

Figure 3

Model of backward masking. The diagram shows the proposed interactions of sustained and transient visual channels at two different interstimulus intervals. Transient activity is shown by the spike labeled TR, and the sustained activity is shown by three curves that represent increasing spatial frequency. Interactions between the visual channels are represented by the vertical arrows. From Figure 11 of "Implications of Sustained and Transient Channels for Theories of Visual Pattern Masking, Saccadic Suppression, and Information Processing," by B. G. Breitmeyer and L. Ganz, 1976, *Psychological Review*, *83*, p. 17. Copyright 1976 by the American Psychological Association. Adapted with permission.

ing occurs through both integration and interruption, with integration more pronounced at the early intervals. In the case of the non-monotonic functions, masking occurs mainly through interruption. Masking through integration always has its maximal effect at an ISI of 0 (maximal temporal overlap). However, maximal masking through interruption can occur at an ISI greater than 0 when the transient channels of the mask inhibit (interrupt) the sustained channels of the target. Note that we cannot directly view the interactions of the channels, so we infer the type of interaction from the shape of the masking function. Because a non-monotonic function indicates that masking is occurring through a single mechanism (interruption), the interpretation of results is more precise than with a monotonic masking function.

Early Versus Late Masking Components

Masking performance can be divided into two primary components, early and late. The early part of the masking function (i.e., ISIs roughly less than 60 ms) reflects *sensory-perceptual* processes; that is, performance at these short ISIs is determined primarily by the interaction of sustained and transient visual pathways. The later part of the masking function (roughly greater than 70 ms) relies on processes separate from interactions of sensory pathways. Instead, it reflects a susceptibility to *attentional disengagement*. Suppression of performance at these later intervals indicates that the mask has diverted attention away from the icon of the target. A model of the masking components is shown in Figure 4. Note that the two early components represent the two types of masking mechanisms (integration and interruption) described in the previous section. The later masking component is shown starting at the middle ISIs and would be expected to extend until performance returns to unmasked levels. The degree of masking due to attentional disengage can be estimated by the ascending slope of the masking function.

Overview

Visual masking offers a means to conduct a fine-grained analysis of specific processes that underlie visual perception. With manipulations of a limited number of parameters, we can begin to separate visual

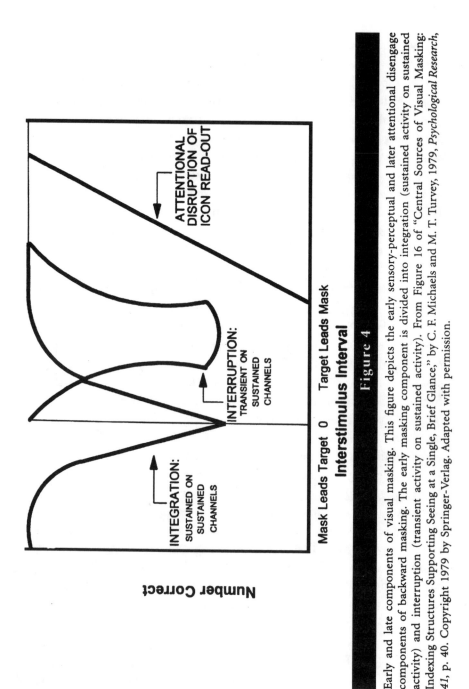

Figure 4

Early and late components of visual masking. This figure depicts the early sensory-perceptual and later attentional disengage components of backward masking. The early masking component is divided into integration (sustained activity on sustained activity) and interruption (transient activity on sustained activity). From Figure 16 of "Central Sources of Visual Masking: Indexing Structures Supporting Seeing at a Single, Brief Glance," by C. F. Michaels and M. T. Turvey, 1979, *Psychological Research*, 41, p. 40. Copyright 1979 by Springer-Verlag. Adapted with permission.

channels (transient vs. sustained), masking mechanisms (integration vs. interruption), and masking components (early sensory-perceptual vs. later attentional disengage). For the process of experimental reductivism in which the goal is to parse cognition into its smallest meaningful components (Holzman, 1994), visual masking is a sharp scalpel.

BACKWARD MASKING AND SCHIZOPHRENIA

The Notion of a Deficit

Schizophrenia patients are said to have a "masking deficit." While it is accurate to say that these patients have a performance abnormality, it is a misnomer to call it a masking deficit. The mask works just fine for schizophrenia patients, too well in fact. In schizophrenia, the masking is *overly* effective in preventing identification of the target. Excessive masking is reflected in the fact that schizophrenia patients consistently need a longer interval between the target and the mask to identify the target (Braff, 1981; Braff, Saccuzzo, & Geyer, 1991; Green & Walker, 1986; Knight, 1992; Saccuzzo & Braff, 1981; Schwartz, Winstead, & Adinoff, 1983; Weiss, Chapman, Strauss, & Gilmore, 1992). This finding was often interpreted descriptively to indicate that patients suffer from a slowing of early information processing.

Relationships of Performance to Clinical Variables and Diagnosis

What is the relationship between backward-masking performance and clinical factors in schizophrenia? Our initial studies in this area found that poor backward-masking performance was related to severity of negative but not psychotic symptoms (Green & Walker, 1984). This finding has now been replicated by others (Slaghuis & Bakker, 1995; Weiner, Opler, Kay, Merriam, & Papouchis, 1990). A study by Braff, Callaway, and Naylor (1989) offered indirect support for this finding, while presenting a slightly more complex picture. Braff et al. found that patients with negative symptoms (e.g., emotional blunting, motor retardation, poverty of speech) required a substantially longer stimulus duration to detect a target (i.e., critical stimulus duration) than both normal controls and patients with psychotic symptoms. Even with this difference in target duration, the patients with negative symptoms showed more pronounced deficits in masking performance than patients with psychotic symptoms, although the differences between the two subgroups of patients did not reach significance. In addition to negative symptoms, deficits in backward masking have been related to poor premorbid functioning (Knight, 1992; Knight, Elliot, & Freedman, 1985), poor prognosis (Saccuzzo & Braff, 1981), and greater chronicity (Rund, 1993). In a series of studies, Knight found a reliable relationship between premorbid history and masking performance, an effect attributed to deficiencies in short-term visual memory. Saccuzzo and Braff noted that good prognosis patients showed improvement with repeated administration while the poor prognosis patients showed a more stable deficit. Studies of negative symptoms, prognosis, and premorbid functioning may assess closely related constructs. The failure to find a close relationship between masking performance and psychotic symptoms across studies fits with the hypothesis that visual masking may not be merely related to the presence of symptoms but instead may be tapping a vulnerability factor for the disorder (Nuechterlein & Dawson, 1984; Zubin & Spring, 1977).

The performance deficit on backward masking in schizophrenia appears unlikely to be the result of neuroleptic medication, which, in fact, seems to reduce the deficit (Braff & Saccuzzo, 1982). In addition, normal older individuals demonstrate deficits on masking procedures, but these deficits are qualitatively different from those of schizophrenia patients (Brody, Saccuzzo, & Braff, 1980), suggesting that the masking problems in schizophrenia can be separated from a general processing deficit.

Although data have been inconsistent, it appears that performance deficits are not entirely specific to schizophrenia among major mental illnesses. One study reported that actively symptomatic patients with mood disorder showed deficits compared with normal controls (Saccuzzo & Braff, 1986), but another study did not find deficits in depressed and hypomanic patients with milder symptoms (Saccuzzo &

Braff, 1981). We found deficits in bipolar patients that were at least as large, and sometimes larger, than those of schizophrenia patients (Green, Nuechterlein, & Mintz, 1994a, 1994b). The bipolar patients in our studies were chronic inpatients but were not as symptomatic as the schizophrenia patients based on a psychiatric rating scale. These data argue against the notion that an overall visual backward-masking deficit is wholly specific to schizophrenia. However, we do not know if the deficits were present when the bipolar patients were stabilized in full remission. It remains entirely possible that masking performance deficits are nonspecific indicators of psychiatric (or psychotic) symptoms but specific indicators of vulnerability to schizophrenia.

Specifying a Mechanism for the Performance Deficit

In a program of research, we first set out to clarify the relevant masking mechanism for the performance deficit in schizophrenia (Green et al., 1994a). Because schizophrenia research had relied on masking procedures that yielded monotonic functions, reflecting contributions of both integrative and interruptive mechanisms, it was not entirely possible to interpret the processes that were responsible for the deficit. The performance deficit could be explained in two substantially different ways. If the masking occurred through integration, then schizophrenia patients may have deficits because they are not as good as controls at interpreting composite images or representations that would result from the integration of the target icon with the mask icon. Alternatively, if the masking occurred through interruption, then the deficit may reflect a type of slowing of information processing as the information from the target icon remains susceptible for longer periods of time. The latter theory of slowed processing was more generally accepted. In essence, the explanation was that schizophrenia patients have a clear (not composite) target icon, but they cannot move (extract or transform) the information fast enough to avoid the disruptive effects of the mask. As we will see later, neither explanation turned out to be fully accurate.

In our first study, we tried to separate the possible masking mechanisms (interruption vs. integration) by isolating interruption as the relevant mechanism. For all the studies in this series, the target was a

letter (either *O, Q, S,* or *C*) that appeared in one of four possible locations (up, down, left, or right) and was typically shown for 10 ms.
The mask consisted of overlapping Xs or adjacent Os and was presented
for 5 or 20 ms, depending on whether we wanted a high-energy or a
low-energy mask. The term *energy* refers to the intensity × duration
of stimulus. We obtained both monotonic and non-monotonic masking
functions by altering the relative durations of the target and mask. Figure 5 shows a non-monotonic N- or W-shaped function obtained with
a mask of overlapping Xs in which the schizophrenia patients performed significantly worse than normal controls at all intervals. Although patients and controls differed throughout the entire function,
the group differences at the middle ISIs (where interruptive processes
would be most influential) remained significant, even after the performance at the longest ISI served as a covariate. We were also able to

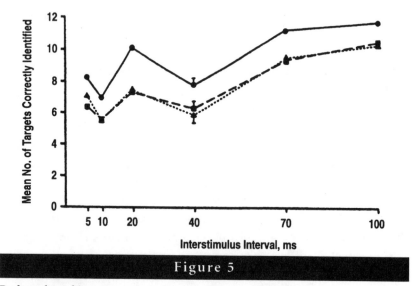

Figure 5

Backward masking on a non-monotonic function. Participants were administered
a low-energy backward-masking condition in which the energy of the mask was
set to one half that of controls. Squares indicate the performance of schizophrenia
patients; triangles, manic patients; and circles, normal controls. Mean *SE* bars are
shown at the 40-ms interstimulus interval.

obtain a more typical U-shaped masking function when we changed the mask from Xs to Os for a subgroup of normal controls and schizophrenia patients ($n = 10$ each). Patients differed significantly from controls on this purer U-shaped function, adding support to the conclusion that patients show abnormalities even when backward masking is largely limited to interruptive processes (as evidenced by the nonmonotonic functions).

Specifying Visual Channels for the Performance Deficit

Our second study in this series addressed another limitation in the masking literature in schizophrenia: Techniques had not allowed for the separation of sustained and transient visual channels (Green et al., 1994b). It has been variously suggested that processing abnormalities in schizophrenia can be explained by dysfunctional sustained channels (Schwartz & Winstead, 1988) or dysfunctional transient channels (Schuck & Lee, 1989). Our second experiment reduced substantially the role of sustained visual channels in two ways: by lowering spatial frequency of the target (through blurring) and by using a location task instead of an identification task. In both of these conditions (blurred target and location), schizophrenia patients showed deficits compared with controls. Hence, restricting the role of sustained visual channels (consequently increasing reliance on transient channels) did not eliminate the performance deficit. Nor did these conditions reduce the magnitude of the performance deficit when compared with conditions from our first study, which relied heavily on sustained channels. From these results, it appears that the performance deficit on masking procedures involves abnormalities at least in the transient channels.

Conclusions From Initial Studies

Some conclusions are warranted. First, the performance deficit in schizophrenia remained when masking was largely limited to interruption. Hence, the performance deficit involves at least interruptive mechanisms and cannot entirely be explained by patients' difficulty in interpreting composite representations. Second, the performance deficit was present and comparable (or larger) in magnitude when the role of transient channels was reduced. Hence, the masking performance deficit is likely to involve a deficit in transient channels. On the basis of the shape of the masking functions, we speculated that the transient channels might be overactive in schizophrenia. Third, schizophrenia patients showed deficits compared with controls across ISIs on both the early sensory-perceptual and the later attentional disengage masking components.

Can we conclude that schizophrenia patients are slower in their information processing?—not necessarily. The traditional explanation for the masking performance deficit in schizophrenia assumed that the problems began after the target icon was clearly formed and before it could be transferred to a more durable form of storage. However, such a formulation is inconsistent with current models in which the icon is not formed instantaneously but instead is the result of progressive waves of neural activity that are sensitive to increasingly higher spatial frequency information. This wavelike process of icon formation is interrupted in masking, and any explanation of the deficit in schizophrenia should take into account the progressive nature of icon formation. The masking performance deficit in schizophrenia could result from an unusually weak icon formation or an unusually strong mask. An analogy may help. Let us say that a heavy wind knocks down a wall that should have remained standing. Two factors could have contributed: The wall might have been unusually weak, or the wind might have been unusually strong. Likewise, if icon formation is disrupted for schizophrenia patients, it could be because their icon formation processes are unusually susceptible or that the mask is unusually disruptive. While both explanations are logically possible, the latter interpretation fits with the notion of overactive transient channels being overly disruptive to target processing. This latter explanation has little, if anything, to do with speed of processing.

BACKWARD MASKING AND VULNERABILITY TO SCHIZOPHRENIA

Suggestive Evidence for Vulnerability

Fundamental questions remain about the nature of masking performance deficits in schizophrenia. While masking performance deficits have been hypothesized to be indicators of vulnerability to schizophrenia, empirical support for this view is very limited. Typically, two types of designs are used as evidence for vulnerability indicators: studies of first-degree relatives of patients and studies of patients who are in symptomatic remission. One study (Miller, Saccuzzo, & Braff, 1979) reported masking performance deficits in 10 partially remitted patients compared with 10 matched controls, suggesting that masking performance might be an indicator of vulnerability to schizophrenia. The degree of remission for these patients was unclear because they were medicated and exhibiting poor social functioning.

If masking performance deficits indicate genetic vulnerability to schizophrenia, a disproportionate number of first-degree relatives of patients would be expected to show deficits compared with controls. This pattern could be true even if the relatives have no signs of illness because first-degree relatives are more likely to carry a genetic predisposition to the disorder than members of the general population. Only a minority of vulnerable individuals will actually develop the disorder, depending on their degree of vulnerability, their psychological coping mechanisms, and a range of protective biological and neurodevelopmental factors.

Performance of Unaffected Siblings

The aim of the third study in the series was to determine whether deficits on backward-masking procedures indicate hypothesized genetic vulnerability to schizophrenia that may be present in the absence of any clinical evidence of a schizophrenia spectrum disorder (Green, Nuechterlein, & Breitmeyer, 1997). We contrasted normal controls with siblings of schizophrenia patients on the four backward-masking conditions that were used in the previous studies (high-energy and low-energy mask conditions from the first study, blurred target and target location conditions from the second study). As mentioned previously, the blurred target and target location conditions differentially emphasize transient versus sustained visual channels. We considered whether the unaffected siblings of patients show masking abnormalities in one or both of the early versus late masking components.

We conducted three sets of analyses. First, normal controls were contrasted with all siblings of schizophrenia patients. Next, we repeated the analyses without siblings who received a diagnosis in the schizophrenia spectrum. Then, to test the possibility that observed group differences were due to the presence of other psychiatric disorders among the siblings, we conducted a third analysis in which we used even stricter selection criteria by excluding any sibling who would have been excluded from the normal control group (i.e., if they had a history of substance dependence, bipolar disorder, or recurrent depression). The results were essentially the same for all sets of analyses. The final, strictest selection procedure yielded a sample of 32 unaffected siblings of schizophrenia patients and 52 normal controls.

Across masking conditions, siblings performed more poorly than controls on the early part of the masking functions, but they returned to normal levels at the longer ISIs that reflect the later attentional disengage component of masking. The group differences tended to be larger on those masking conditions that emphasize transient channels. Figure 6 displays the data from one of the masking conditions. It appears that backward masking is a promising indicator of vulnerability to schizophrenia and that deficits on the early, sensory-perceptual masking components may be especially associated with vulnerability to schizophrenia (Zubin & Spring, 1977). The performance pattern of siblings differed from that of schizophrenia patients because the patients did not return to normal levels at the longer ISIs.

Preliminary analyses from the fourth study in this series offer converging evidence to support the theory that performance deficits on backward masking may indicate vulnerability to schizophrenia. In this study, we assessed recent-onset schizophrenia patients who had achieved psychotic remission and were in a period off medications. These unmedicated, remitted patients were compared with matched normal controls. The same four masking conditions were administered as in the previous studies. Consistent with the findings for the unaffected siblings of schizophrenia patients, these unmedicated patients in psychotic remission showed performance deficits across the masking conditions. The combination of data from both unaffected siblings

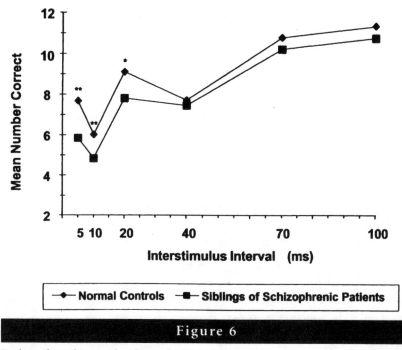

Figure 6

Backward masking with a blurred target. Data are from the unaffected siblings of schizophrenia patients and normal controls. The target was blurred to reduce reliance on sustained channels. Contrasts were performed at each interstimulus interval, and significant differences are indicated. $*p < .05$. $**p < .025$.

of patients and unmedicated, remitted patients implicate backward-masking performance deficits as an indicator of vulnerability to schizophrenia.

CONCLUSION

Masking procedures are useful for dissecting cognitive processes and lend themselves to a program of experimental reductivism, which attempts to identify the smallest meaningful units that make up a more complex behavior (Holzman, 1994). Our results suggest that the early, sensory-perceptual component of masking may be particularly relevant to genetic vulnerability to schizophrenia. Other neurocognitive measures such as the Span of Apprehension and the Continuous Performance Test have been linked to vulnerability to schizophrenia, and it is possible that these tests share components with backward masking that are central to the transmission of vulnerability to schizophrenia. Because backward-masking procedures are particularly suited for isolating subcomponents of neurocognitive processes, these types of procedures may enable us to develop more precise models of the nature of vulnerability to schizophrenia.

REFERENCES

Braff, D. L. (1981). Impaired speed of information processing in nonmedicated schizotypal patients. *Schizophrenia Bulletin, 7,* 499–508.

Braff, D. L., Callaway, E., & Naylor, H. (1989). Sensory input deficits and negative symptoms in schizophrenic patients. *American Journal of Psychiatry, 146,* 1006–1011.

Braff, D. L., & Saccuzzo, D. P. (1982). Effect of antipsychotic medication on speed of information processing in schizophrenic patients. *American Journal of Psychiatry, 139,* 1127–1130.

Braff, D. L., Saccuzzo, D. P., & Geyer, M. A. (1991). Information processing dysfunctions in schizophrenia: Studies of visual backward masking, sensorimotor gating, and habituation. In S. R. Steinhauer, J. H. Gruzelier, & J. Zubin (Eds.), *Handbook of schizophrenia* (Vol. 5, pp. 303–334). Amsterdam: Elsevier Science.

Breitmeyer, B. G. (1984). *Visual masking: An integrative approach.* New York: Oxford University Press.

Breitmeyer, B. G., & Ganz, L. (1976). Implications of sustained and transient channels for theories of visual pattern masking, saccadic suppression, and information processing. *Psychological Review, 83,* 1–36.

Brody, D., Saccuzzo, D. P., & Braff, D. L. (1980). Information processing for masked and unmasked stimuli in schizophrenia and old age. *Journal of Abnormal Psychology, 89,* 617–622.

Green, M. F., Nuechterlein, K. H., & Breitmeyer, B. (1997). Backward masking performance in unaffected siblings of schizophrenia patients: Evidence for a vulnerability indicator. *Archives of General Psychiatry, 54,* 465–472.

Green, M. F., Nuechterlein, K. H., & Mintz, J. (1994a). Backward masking in schizophrenia and mania: Specifying a mechanism. *Archives of General Psychiatry, 51,* 939–944.

Green, M. F., Nuechterlein, K. H., & Mintz, J. (1994b). Backward masking in schizophrenia and mania: Specifying the visual channels. *Archives of General Psychiatry, 51,* 945–951.

Green, M., & Walker, E. (1984). Susceptibility to backward masking in schizophrenic patients with positive and negative symptoms. *American Journal of Psychiatry, 141,* 1273–1275.

Green, M. F., & Walker, E. (1986). Symptom correlates of vulnerability to backward masking in schizophrenia. *American Journal of Psychiatry, 143,* 181–186.

Holzman, P. S. (1994). Parsing cognition: The power of psychology paradigms. *Archives of General Psychiatry, 51,* 952–954.

Knight, R. (1992). Specifying cognitive deficiencies in premorbid schizophrenics. *Progress in Experimental Personality and Psychopathology Research, 15,* 252–289.

Knight, R., Elliot, D. S., & Freedman, E. G. (1985). Short-term visual memory in schizophrenics. *Journal of Abnormal Psychology, 94,* 427–442.

Michaels, C. F., & Turvey, M. T. (1979). Central sources of visual masking: Indexing structures supporting seeing at a single, brief glance. *Psychological Research, 41,* 1–61.

Miller, S., Saccuzzo, D., & Braff, D. (1979). Information processing deficits in remitted schizophrenics. *Journal of Abnormal Psychology, 88,* 446–449.

Nuechterlein, K. H., & Dawson, M. E. (1984). A heuristic vulnerability/stress model of schizophrenic episodes. *Schizophrenia Bulletin, 10,* 300–312.

Rund, B. R. (1993). Backward-masking performance in chronic and nonchronic schizophrenics, affectively disturbed patients, and normal control subjects. *Journal of Abnormal Psychology, 102,* 74–81.

Saccuzzo, D. P., & Braff, D. L. (1981). Early information processing deficit in schizophrenia. *Archives of General Psychiatry, 38,* 175–179.

Saccuzzo, D. P., & Braff, D. L. (1986). Information-processing abnormalities. *Schizophrenia Bulletin, 12,* 447–459.

Schuck, J. R., & Lee, R. G. (1989). Backward masking, information processing, and schizophrenia. *Schizophrenia Bulletin, 15,* 491–500.

Schwartz, B. D., & Winstead, D. K. (1988). Visible persistence in paranoid schizophrenics. *Biological Psychiatry, 23,* 3–12.

Schwartz, B. D., Winstead, D. K., & Adinoff, B. (1983). Temporal integration deficit in visual information processing by chronic schizophrenics. *Biological Psychiatry, 18,* 1311–1320.

Slaghuis, W. L., & Bakker, V. J. (1995). Forward and backward visual masking of contour by light in positive and negative symptom schizophrenia. *Journal of Abnormal Psychology, 104,* 41–54.

Weiner, R. U., Opler, L. A., Kay, S. R., Merriam, A. E., & Papouchis, N. (1990). Visual information processing in positive, mixed, and negative schizophrenic syndromes. *Journal of Nervous and Mental Disease, 178,* 616–626.

Weiss, K. M., Chapman, H. A., Strauss, M. E., & Gilmore, G. C. (1992). Visual information decoding deficits in schizophrenia. *Psychiatry Research, 44,* 203–216.

Zubin, J., & Spring, B. (1977). Vulnerability: A new view of schizophrenia. *Journal of Abnormal Psychology, 86,* 103–126.

13

High-Risk Research in Schizophrenia: New Strategies, New Designs

Barbara A. Cornblatt, Michael Obuchowski,
Alyson Andreasen, and Christopher Smith

A major goal of schizophrenia high-risk research is the identification of developmental abnormalities that act as warning signals of future illness and therefore make intervention possible. Traditionally, the detection of subtle neurocognitive deficits in the young at-risk offspring of schizophrenic parents has been the focus of this search. The results of the first generation of high-risk studies (i.e., those begun in the 1960s and 1970s) have provided a foundation for intervention programs by suggesting a number of candidate predictors of illness. The function of such predictors or markers is to provide a feasible, accurate, and cost-effective means of identifying individuals in true need of intervention many years before the onset of illness. The expectation is that a proper intervention will prevent the disease from being clinically expressed or, at minimum, reduce its severity. Identification of markers that are useful as population screens is the necessary first step to initiating such intervention programs. However, even though the first generation of schizo-

This work was supported in part by United States Public Health Service Grant MH50203 and a research grant award from the Scottish Rite Schizophrenia Research Program, Northern Masonic Jurisdiction. We gratefully acknowledge the assistance of Tak Chun Chan and Uri Herzog in the preparation of this chapter.

phrenia high-risk studies pointed to a number of possibilities, none of the markers yet identified are sufficiently accurate for clinical application. As a result, high-risk research has not yet generated any type of successful primary intervention.

To overcome the problems preventing such intervention programs, the recently initiated Hillside Study of Risk and Early Detection in Schizophrenia (HSREDS) incorporated several new design features, including (a) a two-tiered sample that departs substantially from the traditional high-risk offspring design and (b) an expanded conceptualization of potential illness predictors.

In this chapter, we first provide an overview of the HSREDS high-risk paradigm. We then discuss Elmhurst Adolescent Project (EAP), which preceded the Hillside study. The EAP provided critical pilot data demonstrating the feasibility and advantages of targeting adolescents with schizophrenia as research probands. The EAP also introduced the notion that neurocognitive deficits and clinical symptoms were independent of each other and that both were likely to be separate predictors of illness. We close the chapter by presenting some very preliminary HSREDS findings indicating that schizophrenia-related symptoms can indeed be detected in the unaffected siblings of adolescent probands.

HILLSIDE STUDY OF RISK AND EARLY DETECTION: AN OVERVIEW

At-Risk Paradigm

Traditionally, schizophrenia high-risk studies have focused on the young, at-risk offspring of schizophrenic parents. The HSREDS has shifted this focus onto the young unaffected siblings of young schizophrenia patients. Although the risk for schizophrenia spectrum disorders in siblings of a schizophrenia patient is comparable with that in the children of a schizophrenic parent (Gottesman, 1991), young at-risk siblings have never been prospectively studied.

Probands

In contrast with most previous high-risk studies, the patient probands in the HSREDS are of particular interest in their own right. Although we include probands who range in age from 14 to 30, we are most actively recruiting adolescent schizophrenia patients between the ages of 14 and 20. On the basis of the results of the EAP, which are discussed in detail later in this chapter, we expect that the adolescent patient probands will be in the early stages of illness (often undergoing his or her first hospital admission for psychosis), providing many of the research benefits associated with a first episode sample. Furthermore, it can be assumed that young patients tend to have relatively young siblings, thus providing a sibling sample within the window of greatest risk for illness (i.e., siblings below age 26).

Advantages of the Design

The at-risk sibling design provides a number of advantages over the previous offspring studies. First, the early age of onset in the adolescent schizophrenia patients suggests a severe form of the illness and possibly a high genetic loading. This would be consistent with the patterns of other complex illnesses, such as breast cancer (e.g., Zimmermann et al., 1993; Spurr et al., 1993), Alzheimer's disease (e.g., Schellenberg et al., 1991), and maturity-onset diabetes of the young (e.g., Rothschild et al., 1993) in which the younger the age of onset, the more genetic the disorder. As a result, siblings of adolescent probands may have a particularly high risk of illness.

Second, the sibling design enables direct comparisons to be made between affected (proband) and at-risk (sibling) deficit profiles. This is not similarly possible in the traditional design because of the differences in age between affected parents and at-risk children and of a host of other confounds, such as chronic illness and long-term medication in the parents and generational differences between parents and offspring.

Third, previous research has indicated a similarity in age of onset for affected siblings (DeLisi, 1992). This suggests that if the siblings become ill, they will tend to do so at a fairly young age. This can be expected to reduce the length of follow-up necessary to evaluate outcome—an important consideration, given the difficulties of conducting long-term prospective research over a period of many years.

Predictors of Illness

A major goal of the HSREDS is to establish a profile of predictors that will provide the cornerstones of an intervention program. As mentioned above, considerable focus in previous high-risk studies has been directed at identifying subtle neurocognitive abnormalities during childhood—deficits assumed to be related to the biology of schizophrenia. Neurocognitive deficits such as attention, eye movements, and working memory are frequently referred to as *biobehavioral markers*— biobehavioral because the functions under study are assumed to be intermediate between basic brain operations ("bio") and more complex clinical characteristics. They are, therefore, functions that can be measured noninvasively on the "behavioral" (i.e., phenotypic) level, while providing a window to underlying brain pathology.

The "markers" part of the label refers to the notion that if valid, the deficits signal or "mark" the presence of a biological susceptibility to schizophrenia. That is, it is assumed that the presence of marker deficits reflects brain abnormalities that produce a vulnerability for schizophrenia. These basic biological abnormalities are thought most likely to be present at birth or very early in development and in many cases to have resulted from an abnormal gene or set of genes.

Biobehavioral markers are critical for carrying out preventive intervention programs because they provide the mechanism for identifying appropriate individuals (i.e., those at true risk) many years before the clinical illness emerges, when presumably intervention will be most effective. Premorbid neurocognitive deficits are only one category of markers, yet to date they appear to hold the most promise for primary prevention. However, as mentioned above, although there is now a range of candidate biobehavioral markers with potential to predict illness, a great deal of work remains to be done before they can be applied clinically. The long-range goal of the HSREDS, therefore, is to refine and validate the previously identified candidate risk markers and to transform them into an effective screen for use in primary intervention programs—expected to eventually be the most effective form of prevention. The candidate markers selected for assessment in the HSREDS study include impaired attention, eye-movement disorders (EMDs), and deficits in executive functioning and working memory.

The HSREDS also has a more immediate, short-term intervention goal: to identify a profile of prodromal clinical signs, which, when combined with our biobehavioral indicators, will generate secondary intervention programs. The prodromal risk factors are clinical signs and symptoms that appear prior to psychosis and signal impending illness. In contrast with the premorbid biobehavioral indicators, which are long-standing traits detectable during childhood, *prodromal* symptoms are risk factors that emerge much later in the process leading to illness. They consist of both general clinical disturbances such as reduced concentration, sleep disturbances, and increased anxiety and more specific attenuated psychotic features and schizotypal-like symptoms such as magical thinking and unusual perceptual experiences.

The starting strategy of the HSREDS, therefore, is to determine the combination of trait and state risk factors that will be most effective in predicting future schizophrenia during the nonpsychotic prodromal period. Although reliance on such prodromal indicators leads to secondary rather than primary prevention, because the clinical illness has already begun to emerge, we feel that there are considerable short-term advantages in this combined strategy. Intervention during the prodromal stage, although not fully preventive, may nevertheless reduce the impact of illness and possibly prevent the expression of full-blown psychosis. It has the added advantage of reducing the false-positive rate currently associated with the biobehavioral indicators now identified. Secondary intervention may therefore be a realistic first step, while research continues to work toward the longer range and more elusive goal of primary prevention.

However, prior to beginning this newly conceptualized approach to intervention, we considered it critical to assess the independence of the biobehavioral marker traits and clinical symptoms. It is necessary for these two domains to be essentially independent for the two types of indicators to incrementally contribute to the prediction of psychosis. The independence of the clinical–cognitive domains was therefore one of the major issues researched in the EAP, a 3-year pilot study leading to the larger HSREDS.

ELMHURST ADOLESCENT PROJECT

The EAP was designed to answer a number of questions supporting the structure of the subsequent HSREDS. Included were such issues as the demographic characteristics of adolescent schizophrenia patients, whether patients with such early onset represented a unique form of the disorder or were representative of schizophrenia patients in general, and as discussed above to evaluate the relationship between clinical symptoms and cognition in affected adolescents and adults. These issues are the focus of the next section of this chapter.

Sample

The EAP was conducted from 1992 to 1995 at Elmhurst Hospital Center, a New York City municipal hospital affiliated with Mount Sinai School of Medicine located in the borough of Queens (NY). A total of 58 adolescent and adult schizophrenia patients participated in the study. All patients were assigned a consensus diagnosis on the basis of either the Comprehensive Assessment of Symptoms and History; Andreasen, 1983) for adults over age 18 or the Schedule for Affective Disorder and Schizophrenia for School Age Children (K-SADS, Epidemiologic Version; Orvaschel & Puig-Antich, 1987) for adolescents. All study participants received a *DSM-III-R* (*Diagnostic and Statistical Manual of Mental Disorders*, 3rd ed., rev.; American Psychiatric Association [APA], 1987) diagnosis within the schizophrenia spectrum, including schizophrenia ($n = 49$), schizophreniform disorder ($n = 3$), and schizoaffective disorder ($n = 6$).

Patients were divided into those undergoing their first hospital admission for schizophrenia ($n = 34$) versus patients with a history of multiple hospitalizations ($n = 24$). First admissions were divided into two groups according to age at admission. The first hospitalization teenage (FHT) group consisted of 19 patients under the age of 18 who were recruited from the adolescent inpatient unit of Elmhurst; the first hospitalization adult (FHA) sample included 15 patients recruited from the adult inpatient research unit. The multiepisode adult (MEA) patient group consisted of 24 older, more chronic schizophrenia patients, also recruited from the inpatient research unit of Elmhurst.

Table 1 presents the demographic characteristics of the three groups. The mean age of admission was 15.42 years for the FHT group (age range of 13–17 years), 22.60 years for the FHA group (range of 18–36 years), and 35.38 years for the MEA group (range of 21–57 years). All three groups differed significantly in age. However, no differences between groups were found in gender, IQ, or ethnicity. There were slightly more male patients than female patients in all three groups, with the FHA group showing a somewhat larger, but nonsignificant, excess of male patients. All groups were quite similar in IQ and were in the low–normal range. In addition, there were no significant ethnic differences among the groups; overall, the sample was 31% Caucasian, 26% African American, 28% Hispanic, and 15% Asian.

The study design provides the following comparisons.

1. *FHT versus FHA:* Patients in both the FHT and FHA groups were comparable in phase of illness (i.e., are typically in their first year of illness). However, the two groups differed in age of onset (as approximated by age at first hospitalization). The FHT group had an unusually early onset—about age 15. In comparison, onset in the FHA group was consistent with the range reported most frequently in the literature (i.e., typically by age 21 in men and by age 27 in women; Gottesman, 1991). If patients in the FHT group were similar clinically and neurocognitively to the FHA patients, then it can be assumed that individuals with an adolescent age of onset do not constitute an atypical form of the illness.

Table 1

Sample Demographic Information

Demographic	All groups ($N = 58$)	FHT ($n = 19$)	FHA ($n = 15$)	MEA ($n = 24$)	Significant difference
Age at testing (in years)	25.53	15.42	22.60	35.38	$F(2, 55) = 43.46$
	(11.22)	(1.64)	(5.03)	(10.17)	$p < .001$
Gender (% female)	39.66	42.11	33.33	41.67	$\chi^2 = 0.34$
					$p = 0.84$
IQ	85.61	83.42	85.00	88.39	$F(2, 55) = 1.37$
	(8.26)	(6.95)	(5.65)	(10.54)	$p = .26$
Ethnicity (%)					
White	31	21	40	33	$\chi^2 = 7.67$
Black	26	21	13	38	$p = .26$
Hispanic	28	42	33	13	
Asian	15	16	14	16	

Note. FHT = first hospitalization teenagers; FHA = first hospitalization adults; MEA = multiepisode adults. Numbers in parentheses are standard deviations.

2. *FHA versus MEA:* The FHA and MEA groups were at different stages of illness (early vs. chronic) but were comparable in age of onset. The mean age of onset (i.e., first hospitalization) of the MEA patients was reported to be 24.17 ($SD = 6.33$), which is quite close to the average age of onset of 22.6 in the FHA patients. The two groups, therefore, differed in terms of chronicity, with the MEA group having a history of multiple hospitalizations (mean number of hospitalizations = 3.52) over a period of approximately 11 years. Cognitive traits that were more impaired in the MEA group than in the FHA group could be considered, at least preliminarily, to reflect a neurodegenerative process. Deficits that equally characterized all three groups, by contrast, were likely to be neurodevelopmental. It is the latter that we are most interested in because this suggests that the deficit under study is stable, appears early in development, and thus plausibly precedes the expression of illness. Comparability across the three patient groups therefore supports the selected deficits to be candidate predictors or markers of illness.

Study Design

Clinical and neurocognitive measures were administered twice, first shortly after admission (Time 1) and then again after all patients had been treated with standard neuroleptics for a minimum of 4 weeks (Time 2). At Time 1, patients were tested off medication. In the FHT and FHA groups, all patients were admitted drug free and nearly all were "medication naïve." Patients in the MEA group typically underwent a 2-week medication wash-out period prior to testing. In a previous report (Cornblatt, Obuchowski, Schnur, & O'Brien, 1998), the FHT and FHA groups were found to have similar clinical and neurocognitive characteristics when tested at Time 1, indicating the two groups to be comparable when acutely ill. In the current report, we focus on the characteristics measured at Time 2, just prior to discharge when all patients were considered to be clinically stable. (It should be noted that the current sample was somewhat larger than that included in the previous report because not all of the patients tested in this report at Time 2, when on medication, could be tested off medication at Time 1.)

Clinical State Ratings

Clinical state was evaluated for all patients at both Time 1 and Time 2 by trained psychiatrists and clinical psychologists using the Positive and Negative Syndrome Scale (PANSS; Kay, Opler, & Lindenmayer, 1989). The PANSS generates three scales, rating positive symptoms, negative symptoms, and general psychopathology. Table 2 presents the ratings for the three groups on positive and negative symptoms, which are the clinical focus of the current study, and mean medication levels per group at the time that ratings were made, expressed in chlorpromazine equivalents. Differences among patient groups were analyzed using separate analyses of variance (ANOVAs) for each of the two symptom scales (i.e., PANSS's Positive and Negative Scales) and for the chlorpromazine equivalent dose levels.

All patients were treated with standard neuroleptics, which in most cases was haloperidol. Average levels of medication needed to achieve clinical improvement were not significantly different among groups,

Table 2

Positive and Negative Syndrome Scale (PANSS) Ratings and Medication Level

Rating	FHT ($n = 19$)	FHA ($n = 15$)	MEA ($n = 24$)	F	p
PANSS Positive Syndrome Scale	13.53 (3.04)	12.13 (2.72)	14.25 (4.21)	1.68	.1959
PANSS Negative Syndrome Scale	16.21 (4.59)	15.07 (4.95)	15.79 (4.29)	0.27	.7677
Chlorpromazine equivalents	304.44 (181.50)	340.00 (233.15)	468.18 (280.11)	2.61	.0833

Note. FHT = first hospitalization teenagers; FHA = first hospitalization adults; MEA = multiepisode adults. Numbers in parentheses are standard deviations.

although as would be expected there was a trend for the MEA patients to receive the highest dosage of medication. Overall, medication levels were moderate, suggesting that even in the case of the more chronic MEA group, patients participating in this study were not among the most severely ill. No significant differences were found among groups in either positive or negative symptoms. As would be expected from the literature, positive symptoms were more responsive to treatment and generally lower than negative symptoms for all three groups. Therefore, with respect to clinical characteristics at discharge and dosage of medication necessary to reach clinical stability, the early onset FHT group did not differ from the more typical FHA or MEA patients.

Biobehavioral Measures

The EAP primarily focused on two biobehavioral domains as having the most promise for providing markers of schizophrenia: attention and eye tracking. (It should be noted that because the eye-tracking procedures were added to the test battery relatively late in the study, the number of patients tested was considerably smaller than for the attention, with the eye-tracking $n = 25$ and the size of the individual groups as follows: FHT = 10; FHA = 7; MEA = 8.)

Attention

Why selected. Impaired attention, especially as measured by some version of the CPT, is one of the most solidly established candidate biobehavioral markers of schizophrenia (Cornblatt & Keilp, 1994). Attentional deficits have been shown to characterize offspring of schizophrenia parents as young as 7 years old (Cornblatt & Erlenmeyer-Kimling, 1985; Nuechterlein, 1983; Orzack & Kornetsky, 1966; Wohlberg & Kornetsky, 1973) and, once detected, to be stable across premorbid development (Cornblatt, Winters, & Erlenmeyer-Kimling, 1989; Winters, Cornblatt, & Erlenmeyer-Kimling, 1991) and the early stages of illness (Cornblatt et al., 1997, 1998). Cornblatt, Risch, et al. (1988) also reported a substantial heritable component in both verbal and spatial attentional processing in normal families. Moreover, in participants free of psychosis, attentional impairments have been associated with schizotypal personality disorder and features considered genetically related to schizophrenia (Cornblatt et al., 1992; Lenzenweger, Cornblatt, & Putnick, 1991; Roitman et al., 1997). Thus, impaired attention appears to be a biologically based cognitive abnormality that precedes the clinical symptoms of schizophrenia by many years and is independent of psychotic state, thus fulfilling most criteria for a biobehavioral marker (see Cornblatt & Keilp, 1994, for a more detailed discussion).

Relationship between attention and clinical symptoms. Traditionally, it has been implicitly assumed that attentional disturbances run hand in hand with clinical symptoms. In fact, Andreasen (1982) included inattention as one of the five major scales of the Scale for Assessment of Negative Symptoms, along with affective flattening (diminished emotional expression and feeling), alogia (improverished thinking), avolition (lack of energy, drive, and interest), and anhedonia (inability to experience pleasure). However, of the substantial number of studies concerned with the role of attention in schizophrenia, only a handful have directly examined the association between impaired attention and clinical symptoms, with the findings reported inconsistent but tending to support no relationship. For example, in one of the earliest such studies, Nuechterlein, Edell, Norris, and Dawson (1986) found that attention, as measured on both the AX and degraded versions of the CPT, related primarily to negative symptoms, especially the anergia factor of the Brief Psychiatric Rating Scale (Overall & Gorham, 1962). However, the specific symptoms within the factor showing this relationship varied depending on whether attention was measured during an acute (inpatient) episode or after the patients were stabilized (outpatients). Some additional, more tentative relationships with thought disorder were also reported by these authors.

In contrast with Nuechterlein et al.'s (1986) findings, Strauss, Buchanan, and Hale (1993) did not find attention on the degraded CPT to relate to negative symptoms, although they did report a relationship with positive formal thought disorder, as did Pandurangi, Kenji, Pelonero, and Goldberg (1994) using the AX version of the CPT. Thus, where associations between attention and clinical symptoms have been found, the symptoms involved have varied from study to study. Moreover, many studies have found no relationship between impaired attention and clinical symptoms, as reported by Nestor, Faux, McCarley, Shenton, and Sands (1990) for the degraded CPT; by Cannon et al. (1994) and Finkelstein, Cannon, Gur, and Moberg (1997) using the Gordon diagnostics version of the AX CPT; or Cornblatt et al., 1997, 1998, for the considerably more difficult Continuous Performance Test–Identical Pairs version (CPT-IP). Thus, the literature has not provided a clear picture of an association, leaving the question of the independence of the two domains remaining to be more definitively resolved.

How measured. In the EAP, attention was measured using the CPT-IP, developed by Cornblatt and colleagues (e.g. Cornblatt, Lenzenweger, & Erlenmeyer-Kimling, 1989; Cornblatt, Risch, et al., 1988). The CPT-IP is a cognitively challenging version of the CPT that has previously been highly successful in detecting attentional deficits in young, unaffected at-risk offspring (e.g., Cornblatt, Winters, et al., 1989; Winters et al., 1991). It has been described in detail elsewhere (e.g., Cornblatt et al., 1988; Cornblatt, Winters, et al., 1989).

The CPT-IP consists of 12 conditions measuring a complex range of attentional processes. Of these, the 2 most difficult verbal conditions have been included in this report. Each of these 2 conditions consists of a series of 150 four-digit numbers that are rapidly flashed in sequence on a computer monitor. The four-digit numbers are considered verbal stimuli because they are read from left to right the way letters are and have no numerical properties. Digits are used in this task instead of letters because they avoid a variety of experimental confounds.

Stimuli are presented on-screen for 50 ms, followed by a 950-ms dark time (for a total intertrial interval of 1,000 ms). Participants are required to respond with a finger lift from a reaction time key whenever two identical stimuli appear in a row. Twenty percent of the trials are identical pairs (i.e., two in a row that are exactly alike), 20% are pairs that are almost alike but differ in one of the four digits (called *catch trials,* responses to which are false alarms), and the remaining 60% are filler trials that are not alike in any features. The baseline condition is referred to as numbers–no distraction (N-ND); the second condition is called numbers–distractions (N-D) because it is administered in the presence of both auditory and visual background distractions.

These 2 CPT-IP verbal conditions were selected for the current study because they represent difficult variants of the traditional X and AX CPTs most typically used in previous research and have been more widely studied than most of the other CPT-IP conditions. Overall task performance is measured using d', a signal detection index considered to be the purest measure of attentional capacity because it controls for response bias or the tendency to overrespond versus underrespond (see Cornblatt & Keilp, 1994; and Rutschmann, Cornblatt, & Erlenmeyer-Kimling, 1977). On the basis of the previous findings reported by Cornblatt et al. (1997) indicating no significant Group × Distraction interactions on the ND versus D tasks, we calculated a mean d' across the two conditions. The higher the d', the better the performance.

Eye-Movement Abnormalities

Why selected. Support for the marker potential of the second category of biobehaviors, EMDs, has largely been provided by family studies and investigations of first episode schizophrenia patients (e.g., Clementz & Sweeney, 1990; Holzman, 1987; Iacono, 1988); no research, to date, has been conducted assessing EMDs in young at-risk offspring. Thus, the data indicating that EMDs are likely to be predictors of future illness is indirect but nonetheless quite compelling.

Consistent with impaired attention, smooth pursuit EMDs are stable deficits that appear to reflect compromised capability (Iacono, 1988) and to have a strong heritable component (Iacono & Lykken, 1979). Researchers have consistently reported that eye-tracking abnormalities characterize between 50% and 80% of schizophrenia patients compared with only about 6–8% of the general population (Clementz, Grove, Iacono, & Sweeney, 1992; Holzman, Solomon, Levin, & Waternaux, 1984; Mialet & Pichot, 1981; Shagass, Amadeo, & Overton, 1974; Yee et al., 1987). They do not appear to be a product of such confounding factors as long-term medication or frequent hospitalizations because EMDs are clearly in evidence at the earliest stages of illness (Iacono, Moreau, Beiser, Fleming, & Lin, 1992; Lieberman et al., 1993; Sweeney, Haas, & Li, 1992). Furthermore, comparable abnormalities have been found to characterize patients with a range of schizophrenia-related disorders, including individuals from the general population with schizotypal personality disorders and features (Siever, Coursey, Alterman, Buchsbaum, & Murphy, 1984; Siever et al., 1989, 1990) and those whose responses on self-report inventories suggest they may have a predisposition for developing spectrum disorders (Simons & Katkin, 1985).

Although, as mentioned, there is no direct data available from at-risk youngsters, there are several lines of indirect support indicating EMDs have considerable marker potential. First, EMDs are displayed by approximately 50% of the older unaffected first-degree relatives of schizophrenia patients, compared with about 10% of the relatives of patients without schizophrenia (Clementz et al., 1990, 1992; Grove et al., 1991; Holzman et al., 1974, 1988; Kuechenmeister, Linton, Mueller, & White, 1977; Levy et al., 1983; Mather, 1985; Siegel, Waldo, Mizner, Adler, & Freedman, 1984). These findings indicate that EMDs are likely to be involved in the underlying biology of the illness rather than due to symptom expression, treatment, or long-term hospitalization.

Second, although not extensively studied, there is some evidence indicating that eye movements can be reliably measured in adolescents (Ross, Radant, & Hommer, 1993), thus enabling the detection of early dysfunctions. Third, some preliminary data have been reported suggesting that EMDs are not only detectable in adolescents but also in adolescents with schizophrenia and are comparable with those established to characterize affected adults (Cegalis & Sweeney, 1981; Obuchowski & Cornblatt, 1995a, 1995b; Schulz et al., 1992).

Thus, in summary, findings indicating that EMDs characterize affected patients across the full schizophrenia spectrum and at all stages of illness, can be reliably measured in adolescents, and are found in a substantial proportion of unaffected first-degree relatives of patients all strongly support our selection of these deficits as candidate biobehavioral markers of schizophrenia (see excellent reviews by Clementz & Sweeney, 1990; and Levy, Holzman, Matthysse, & Mendell, 1993, 1994, for more detailed discussions of this issue).

Relationship between EMDs and clinical symptoms. With respect to the relationship between EMDs and clinical symptoms, the state of the literature is comparable with that described for attention. Few studies have made direct comparisons; of those that have, there are widespread inconsistencies, both in the methodology used across studies and in the relationships reported. In terms of methodology, eye-tracking assessments differ from study to study in terms of target paradigms and focus on global accuracy versus specific quantitative measures of oculomotor abnormalities (Abel & Ziegler, 1988; Clementz, Sweeney, Hirt, & Haas, 1990). Cross-study comparisons are further complicated by major differences in clinical assessments used when examining relationships with EMDs. Measures of positive symptoms are particularly variable across studies, a difficulty further compounded by the use of specific symptoms in some studies and symptoms clusters in others.

Regardless of clinical instrument and nature of performance indexes, the majority of studies directly correlating eye-tracking performance with symptomatology have found no significant relationships between the two domains (e.g., Ebmeier et al., 1990; Friedman et al., 1995; Jacobsen et al., 1996; Kelly et al., 1990; Levy et al., 1983; Lieberman et al., 1993; Obuchowski et al., 1996; Rea, Sweeney, Solomon, Walsh, & Frances, 1989; Sweeney et al., 1992, 1994; Van den Bosch & Rozendaal, 1988). There are only a few exceptions to this general trend, for example, the study conducted by Katsanis and Iacono (1991) and those by Sweeney and colleagues (e.g., Sweeney et al., 1992, 1994). Thus, it appears possible that consistent with impaired attention, EMDs do not have a strong relationship with clinical symptoms and may, in fact, be independent of them.

How measured. An infrared scleral reflection technique is used to record eye movements. An infrared light source attached to glass frames specifically designed for this procedure (Applied Science Laboratories, Inc.) is aligned to within several millimeters of the iris–sclera border of each eye. Photodetectors situated laterally and medially to each infrared reflection light source detect the differential light reflectivity of these two regions as an electrical current change, providing an accurate representation of angular eye position. The resulting signal is digitized at 500 Hz using an AT-CODAS A/D board (Dataq Instruments, Inc., Akron, OH) and stored for off-line analysis. The target, a bright-red laser dot, is presented on a 90° matte-black circular arc 1 m away from the participant. To minimize head movement, we used chin, forehead, and head supports.

The eye-tracking procedure administered as part of the EAP battery consisted of several conditions, including a ramp task and a task with an oscillating target, each given at several different constant velocities. The ramp task requires a participant to track a target moving at a constant velocity but in unpredictable directions from a central fixation point. In this report, the data were limited to the ramp task presented at a constant velocity of 14°/s. Performance is expressed in terms of pursuit gain, which is a measure of the accuracy with which the eye is able to match the velocity of the target. Gain is considered the most effective single measure of the pursuit system (Clementz & Sweeney, 1990; Leigh & Zee, 1983).

Pursuit gain is calculated as the ratio of average pursuit eye movement velocity over target velocity. In this study, it was assessed by averaging point-to-point eye velocity after editing out saccades, blinks, pauses after anticipatory saccades, and periods of gross inattention using Rampskor software developed by Sweeney, Carl, and McCurtain (1995). In most normal participants, pursuit of slow-moving targets is close to 1 (Leigh & Zee, 1983), reflecting a close match of pursuit and target velocities. The extent to which gain drops below 1 is an indicator of the severity of eye-movement disturbance (Sweeney et al., 1992).

Table 3 presents CPT-IP and eye-tracking performance indexes by patient group. A repeated measures ANOVA was used to analyze d', the CPT-IP summary variable. The overall measure of eye tracking, pursuit gain, was evaluated using an one-way ANOVA (StatSoft, 1995). No differences were found among groups in either attention, as measured by d', or in EMDs, as indicated by the gain score.

It is important to note that although normal controls were not included in the EAP, population norms were available for purposes of comparison with the patient data. In both domains, patients were significantly impaired relative to normal controls (NCs), even though pa-

Table 3

Neurocognitive Performance by Patient Group

Performance measure	FHT	FHA	MEA	F	p
CPT-IP d'	1.25	1.03	0.95	1.25	.30
	(.69)	(.47)	(.72)		
Gain at 14°/s	0.67	0.71	0.64	0.40	.67
	(.15)	(.15)	(.20)		

Note. CPT-IP = Continuous Performance Test–Identical Pairs; FHT = first hospitalization teenagers; FHA = first hospitalization adults; MEA = multiepisode adults. Numbers in parentheses are standard deviations.

tients had shown considerable improvement clinically (see Cornblatt et al., 1997) and were not very symptomatic when tested at Time 2. In the case of the CPT-IP, this assessment was based on comparisons with mean performance levels provided by our normative databank. When we matched the performances of patients in the EAP with same-age participants in our databank, each of the three patient groups was found to be significantly impaired, as follows: FHT d' = 1.25 (SD = .69) versus NCs = 1.80 (.73), p = .002; FHA d' = 1.03 (.47) versus NCs = 2.16 (.79), p = .0001; MEA d' = 0.95 (.72) versus NCs = 1.87 (.79), p = .0001. For eye tracking, although less normative data was available, preliminary comparisons nevertheless strongly supported the patient performance levels presented in Table 3 to be deficient. Obuchowski, Chan, Sweeney, and Cornblatt (1997) reported that when the three groups of patients were combined, pursuit gain for patients (M = .79, SD = .14, n = 25) was significantly impaired relative to normal controls (M = .83, SD = .12, n = 27; p = .0002). Thus, the findings from the EAP suggest that in the case of both attention and eye tracking, clear deficits are detectable at the earliest stages of illness, regardless of age of onset, and appear to be independent of clinical state. Furthermore, in neither case do these deficits appear to deteriorate dramatically as the illness progresses. This finding supported the inclusion of both eye tracking and attention in the expanded HSREDS.

Table 4

Correlations Between Neurocognitive Measures and the Positive and Negative Syndrome Scales

Clinical measure	CPT-IP d'	Gain at 14°/s
Positive Syndrome Scale	−.16	−.29
	($p = .42$)	($p = .17$)
Negative Syndrome Scale	.03	.19
	($p = .86$)	($p = .31$)
Chlorpromazine equivalent dose	.01	.32
	($p = .98$)	($p = .14$)

Note. CPT-IP = Continuous Performance Test–Identical Pairs.

Relationship Between Clinical Symptoms and Neurocognitive Deficits

To directly evaluate the relationship between clinical and neurocognitive domains, we present correlations between attention deficits and EMDs versus positive and negative symptoms and medication levels in Table 4. Because there were no differences among the patient groups on clinical ratings, attention, or eye-tracking performance, the three groups were combined for the correlational analysis to obtain maximum statistical power. None of the correlations even approach significance. Thus, for affected schizophrenia patients across different phases of the illness, the neurocognitive deficits assessed in the EAP appear to be independent of clinical symptomatology. In addition, these deficits also appear to be independent of level of medication.

Conclusions From the EAP

The conclusions resulting from the EAP, based on the data presented here and in our previous reports (Cornblatt et al., 1997, 1998), formed the foundation for the HSREDS. These include the following:

1. Adolescent-onset patients do not appear to differ from patients with a more typical age of onset in clinical characteristics, neurocognitive

profiles, or response to medication. These findings validate the choice of patients with onset in early to middle teenage years as appropriate probands for a high-risk study.

2. Attention deficits and EMDs, both of which have been supported by considerable previous research to have a clear potential as candidate markers, are further validated by the EAP findings. In both cases, deficits characterizing affected adults are clearly in evidence in adolescents within the earliest stages of schizophrenia. This suggests that if valid, they will also be detectable in the young siblings of the affected adolescents who themselves have a biological susceptibility for future illness.

3. The candidate biobehavioral markers (attention deficits and EMDs) are independent of both positive and negative symptoms of schizophrenia after onset of illness. This suggests that the less pronounced prodromal clinical indicators may also be independent of neurocognitive deficit traits. We have therefore interpreted the EAP findings as encouraging our assumption that prodromal clinical features may provide a second category of psychosis predictors and have incorporated this notion into the strategy of the HSREDS.

HILLSIDE STUDY OF RISK AND EARLY DETECTION: PRELIMINARY FINDINGS

The HSREDS was launched in 1996 at Hillside Hospital of the Long Island Jewish Medical Center in Glen Oaks, New York. Many of the design features of the HSREDS were based on the EAP findings discussed above.

Sample

As of 1998, patient probands are being recruited from both the adolescent and adult inpatient units at Hillside Hospital. We accept probands who range from 14 to 30 years of age. Fourteen was established as the lower age limit because we are targeting a postpubertal schizophrenia sample. Although probands from 14 to 20 years of age are of primary interest, we accept older patients who have siblings within our age range of 12–26. Because we are only in the first half of the HSREDS study, we have only collected a portion of our projected sample and have thus far primarily concentrated on recruiting patients and their siblings.

Table 5 shows the number of schizophrenia probands and their siblings that have entered the study to date. Thirty patient probands have been recruited, of whom 24 have thus far received a consensus diagnosis of an Axis I schizophrenia spectrum disorder (schizophrenia = 19, schizoaffective = 5). The mean age of the probands is 19.11 years, with an age range of 14–26 years. Although there was a relatively even gender distribution among adolescent probands in the EAP, so far for the probands recruited at Hillside, a majority has been male patients (73%). Thirty siblings of the probands have also been entered into the study thus far. We are therefore, on average, recruiting one sibling per proband. The mean age of the siblings is 17.50 years, with ages ranging from 12 to 26 years and with gender split fairly evenly. While we have not made a strenuous effort to recruit normal controls as yet, 12 normal participants have nevertheless entered into the study. Normal controls range in age from 12–20 years of age, with the mean age at testing being 15.35 years.

Table 5

Hillside Study of Risk and Early Detection in Schizophrenia Sample Information

Statistic	Schizophrenia		Normal control
	Patient probands	Siblings	
N	30	30	12
Mean age	19.11	17.5	15.35
Age range (in years)	14–26	12–26	12–20
Female (%)	27	53	28

Assessment Procedures

Diagnostic Measures

All participants receive a consensus AXIS I diagnosis based on the Structured Clinical Interview for *DSM-IV* Axis I Disorders (SCID; First, Spitzer, Gibbon, & Williams, 1995) if over age 18 and the K-SADS if age 18 or younger. In addition, for adult probands, K-SADS modules have been added to the SCID to determine whether there is a past history of childhood attention deficit or conduct disorder. Siblings and normal controls additionally receive a range of AXIS II measures, including the Structured Interview for *DSM-IV* Personality Disorders (SID-P; Pfohl, Blum, & Zimmerman, 1995). Detection of schizophrenia spectrum personality disorders and schizophrenia-related features is emphasized throughout these assessments.

Biobehavioral Predictors

Consistent with the previous findings of the EAP (above and see Cornblatt et al., 1997, 1998), the two major biobehavioral domains included in the HSREDS are attention as measured by the CPT-IP and eye tracking using the infrared reflection procedure described earlier. However, we have also included a range of neuropsychological measures in the Hillside test battery. This is largely based on a number of findings recently emerging from the literature suggesting that a number of neuropsychological abnormalities may be involved in the etiology of schizophrenia (see Wolf & Cornblatt, 1996, for a review). It should be pointed out that in no case, however, is there direct evidence supporting any of these dysfunctions to be potential markers. For example, for the Wisconsin Card Sorting Test (WCST)—perhaps the most widely studied neuropsychological procedure—there is little evidence to suggest deficits can be detected prior to onset of illness. Furthermore, the question of whether the dysfunctions measured by the WCST and other neuropsychological procedures are stable traits independent of clinical state is still unresolved. In the case of the WCST, the relationship between errors on the task and clinical symptoms is far more complex than for either attention or eye-tracking procedures (e.g., Bilder, Mukherjee, Rieder, & Pandurangi, 1985; Hammer, Katsanis, & Iacono,

1995; Hoff, Riordan, O'Donnell, Morris, & DeLisi, 1992; Saykin et al., 1990, 1994). Nevertheless, on the basis of substantial indirect support, we have selected measures considered to tap executive functioning (i.e., WCST; Trailmaking Test, Part B [Spreen & Strauss, 1991]; Verbal Fluency [Benton & Hamsher, 1983]) and working memory (i.e., Letter–Number Span [Gold, Carpenter, Goldberg, & Weinberger, 1997]; Spatial Working Memory Test [Park, Holzman, & Goldman-Rakic, 1995]) as the two neuropsychological areas that currently appear most promising for identifying predictors of illness.

Prodromal Clinical Indicators

We included a variety of self-report assessments and structured interviews to evaluate potential clinical indicators, both categorically and dimensionally. Our emphasis, to start, is on the prodromal features most frequently found in the recent studies by McGorry and colleagues (Yung & McGorry, 1996; Yung et al., 1996). These include a variety of nonspecific prodromal features, such as reduced concentration, reduced drive and motivation, depressed mood, sleep disturbance, anxiety, social withdrawal, suspiciousness, deterioration in role functioning, and irritability. In addition, several features more specifically related to schizophrenia, mainly derived from the *DSM-III-R* description of the schizophrenia prodrome, are evaluated. These include markedly peculiar behavior; marked impairment in personal hygiene and grooming; blunted or inappropriate affect; digressive, vague, overelaborate, or circumstantial speech or poverty of speech or speech content; odd beliefs or magical thinking; and unusual perceptual experiences. These signs and symptoms are assumed to reflect the earliest manifestations of the disturbed clinical state.

Preliminary Clinical Findings

Even though we have not collected sufficient data from HSREDS participants to enable analysis of the biobehavioral measures, we do have some very preliminary clinical findings of interest. These are summarized in Figure 1.

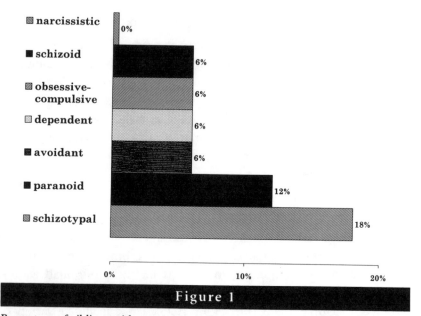

narcissistic   0%

schizoid   6%

obsessive-
compulsive   6%

dependent   6%

avoidant   6%

paranoid   12%

schizotypal   18%

0%   10%   20%

Figure 1

Percentage of siblings with two or more features within each AXIS II personality disorder, based on the Structured Interview for *DSM-IV* Personality Disorder. Note that one additional sibling had a diagnosis of schizotypal personality disorder.

Data about possible personality disorders and features in the siblings of the probands, as collected from the SID-P, was analyzed for 26 of the siblings of patient probands. None of the siblings displayed AXIS I schizophrenia spectrum disorders. One of the siblings received a diagnosis of AXIS II schizotypal personality disorder. None of the siblings met criteria for any other AXIS II disorder. However, a substantial number of siblings did display a variety of personality disorder features. Figure 1 displays the percentage of siblings with two or more features in each major personality disorder category selected for study. It should be noted that because there was a great deal of comorbidity, siblings often displayed two or more features for more than one disorder.

Virtually no siblings displayed narcissistic personality disorder features. Schizoid, obsessive–compulsive, dependent, and avoidant personality disorders were about equal in the percentage of siblings displaying two or more features, with 6% of the siblings falling into each category. A considerably higher proportion of siblings displayed features in the two disorders considered to be less severe genetic variants of schizophrenia: paranoid and schizotypal personality disorders. Twelve percent of the siblings displayed paranoid features, and 18% displayed two or more schizotypal features. These data, although preliminary, are consistent with the expectation that approximately 25% of the siblings may develop some type of schizophrenia-related disorder. These findings further suggest that it is likely that specific spectrum disorder features may appear prior to the emergence of full-blown psychosis. It should also be noted that the considerably lower rate of schizoid personality disorder features in the siblings is consistent with family studies suggesting that schizoid personality disorder is not genetically related to schizophrenia and should probably not be included in the schizophrenia spectrum. Our evidence that schizophrenia-related personality features can be detected in nonpsychotic at-risk siblings thus far supports our assumption that clinical predictors can be identified during the prodromal stage of illness.

CONCLUSION

The HSREDS is a newly initiated longitudinal project focusing on young (mostly adolescent) schizophrenia patients and their young at-risk siblings. The long-range goal of this study is to develop a cluster of biobehavioral deficits very early in development that will accurately identify individuals who carry a biological susceptibility to schizophrenia. These predictors will provide the means of intervening during childhood or early adolescence to prevent the clinical expression of schizophrenia-related illnesses. The candidate biobehavioral markers currently under study include attentional deficits, EMDs, and a range of neuropsychological abnormalities, especially those involving executive functioning and working memory.

The HSREDS is also concerned with a more immediate goal: to identify a profile of prodromal clinical indicators, which can be used in conjunction with the biobehavioral markers now developed to implement secondary intervention programs—a goal that we believe is attainable in the near future.

The prodromal stage of schizophrenia is considered to begin with the first noticeable change in behavior and to continue until the onset of psychosis. During this phase of the illness, a number of nonspecific clinical symptoms and attenuated psychotic behaviors are often in evidence. Pilot data collected during the EAP indicated that clinical symptoms are independent of the major neurocognitive marker traits (i.e., attention deficits and EMDs) and therefore have substantial potential to be independent predictors of illness. Our short-term goal, therefore, is to combine a profile of clinical indicators with the neurocognitive traits currently considered most likely to be biobehavioral markers. Individuals with this combination of indicators (prodromal symptoms and neurocognitive traits) will be considered to be at high risk for impending psychosis and in need of immediate intervention. Although this will lead to secondary intervention (because the clinical illness is already in evidence), if successful it can nevertheless be expected, at a minimum, to lessen the severity of the illness and, more optimistically, to block the emergence of full-blown psychosis. The clinical indicators selected for study at this time include nonspecific symptoms such as reduced concentration, reduced drive and motivation, depressed mood, sleep disturbance, anxiety, social withdrawal, suspiciousness, deterioration in role functioning, and irritability as well as a variety of more clearly schizophrenia-related features, such as peculiar behaviors, impairment in personal hygiene and grooming, blunted or inappropriate affect, digressive or vague speech, poverty of speech or speech content, odd beliefs or magical thinking, and unusual perceptual experiences. The preliminary data that has thus far emerged from the HSREDS suggests that such clinical indicators are clearly observable in the nonpsychotic at-risk siblings of schizophrenia patients. Identifying the prodromal symptoms that will be the most effective clinical predictors of psychosis and the relationship between these state indicators and neurocognitive marker traits is the focus of the HSREDS in the immediate future.

REFERENCES

Abel, L. A., & Ziegler, A. S. (1988). Smooth pursuit eye movements in schizophrenics—What constitutes quantitative assessments? *Biological Psychiatry, 24,* 747–762.

American Psychiatric Association. (1987). *Diagnostic and statistical manual of mental disorders* (3rd ed., rev.). Washington, DC: Author.

Andreasen, N. C. (1982). Negative symptoms in schizophrenia. *Archives of General Psychiatry 39,* 784–788.

Andreasen, N. C. (1983). *Comprehensive assessment of symptoms and history: CASH.* Iowa City: University of Iowa College of Medicine.

Benton, A. L., & Hamsher, K. (1983). Multilingual Aphasia Examination. Iowa City, IA: AJA Associates.

Bilder, R. M., Mukherjee, S., Rieder, R. O., & Pandurangi, A. K. (1985). Symptomatic and neuropsychological components of defect states. *Schizophrenia Bulletin, 11,* 409–419.

Cannon, T. D., Zorrilla, L. E., Shtasel, D., Gur, R. E., Gur, R. C., Marco, E. J., Moberg, P., & Price, A. (1994). Neuropsychological functioning in siblings discordant for schizophrenia and healthy volunteers. *Archives of General Psychiatry, 51,* 651–661.

Cegalis, J. A., & Sweeney, J. A. (1981). The effect of attention on smooth pursuit eye movements of schizophrenics. *Journal of Psychiatric Research, 16,* 145–161.

Clementz, B. A., Grove, W. M., Iacono, W. G., & Sweeney, J. A. (1992). Smooth-pursuit eye movement dysfunction and liability for schizophrenia: Implications for genetic modeling. *Journal of Abnormal Psychology, 101,* 117–129.

Clementz, B. A., & Sweeney, J. A (1990). Is eye movement dysfunction a biological marker for schizophrenia? A methodological review. *Psychological Bulletin, 108,* 77–92.

Clementz, B. A., Sweeney, J. A , Hirt, M., & Haas, G. (1990). Pursuit gain and saccadic intrusions in first-degree relatives of probands with schizophrenia. *Journal of Abnormal Psychology, 99,* 327–335.

Cornblatt, B., & Erlenmeyer-Kimling, L. (1985). Global attentional deviance as a marker of risk for schizophrenia: Specificity and predictive validity. *Journal of Abnormal Psychology, 94,* 470–485.

Cornblatt, B., & Keilp, J. (1994). Impaired attention, genetics, and the pathophysiology of schizophrenia. *Schizophrenia Bulletin, 20,* 31–46.

Cornblatt, B., Lenzenweger, M., Dworkin, R. H., & Erlenmeyer-Kimling, L. (1992). Childhood attentional dysfunctions predict social deficits in unaffected adults at risk for schizophrenia. *British Journal of Psychiatry, 161,* 59–64.

Cornblatt, B., Lenzenweger, M., & Erlenmeyer-Kimling, L. (1989). The Continuous Performance Test–Identical Pairs (CPT-IP): II. Contrasting profiles of attentional deficits in schizophrenic and depressed patients. *Psychiatry Research, 29,* 65–85.

Cornblatt, B., Obuchowski, M., Schnur, D., & O'Brien, J. D. (1997). Attention and clinical symptoms in schizophrenia. *Psychiatric Quarterly, 68*(4), 343–359.

Cornblatt, B., Obuchowski, M., Schnur, D., & O'Brien, J. D. (1998). The Hillside Study of Risk and Early Detection in Schizophrenia: An introduction. *British Journal of Psychiatry, 172*(Suppl. 33), 26–32.

Cornblatt, B., Risch, N., Faris, G., Friedman, D., & Erlenmeyer-Kimling, L. (1988). The Continuous Performance Test–Identical Pairs version (CPT-IP): I. New findings about sustained attention in normal families. *Psychiatry Research, 26,* 223–238.

Cornblatt, B., Winters, L., & Erlenmeyer-Kimling, L. (1989). Attentional markers of schizophrenia: Evidence from the New York High Risk Study. In S. C. Schulz & C. A. Tamminga (Ed.), *Schizophrenia: Scientific progress* (pp. 83–92). New York: Oxford University Press.

DeLisi, L. E. (1992). The significance of age of onset for schizophrenia. *Schizophrenia Bulletin, 18,* 209–216.

Ebmeier, K. P., Potter, D. D., Cochrane, R. H., Mackenzie, A. R., MacAllister, H., Besson, J. A., & Salzen, E. A. (1990). P300 and smooth eye pursuit: Concordance of abnormalities and relation to clinical features in *DSM-III* schizophrenia. *Acta Psychiatrica Scandinavia, 82*(4), 283–288.

Finkelstein, J. R., Cannon, T. D., Gur, R. E., & Moberg, P. (1997). Attentional dysfunctions in neuroleptic-naïve and neuroleptic-withdrawn schizophrenic patients and their siblings. *Journal of Abnormal Psychology, 106,* 203–212.

First, M. B., Spitzer, R. L., Gibbon, M., & Williams, J. B. W. (1995). *Structured*

Clinical Interview for DSM-IV *Axis I Disorders–Patient edition* (SCID-I/ P, Version 2.0). New York: New York State Psychiatric Institute, Biometrics Research Department.

Friedman, L., Jesberger, J., Cola, D., Findling, R., Kenny, J. T., Swales, T., & Schulz, S. C. (1995). Characterization of smooth pursuit performance in adolescent schizophrenics. *Schizophrenia Research, 15,* 176.

Gold, J. M., Carpenter, C., Goldberg, T. E., & Weinberger, D. R. (1997). Auditory working memory and Wisconsin Card Sorting Test performance in schizophrenia. *Archives of General Psychiatry, 54,* 159–165.

Gottesman, I. I. (1991). *Schizophrenia genesis: The origins of madness.* New York: Freeman.

Grove, W. M., Lebow, B. S., Clementz, B. A., Cerri, A., Medus, C., & Iacono, W. G. (1991). Familial prevalence and coaggregation of schizotypy indicators: A multitrait family study. *Journal of Abnormal Psychology, 100,* 115–121.

Hammer, M. A., Katsanis, J., & Iacono, W. G. (1995). The relationship between negative symptoms and neuropsychological performance. *Biological Psychiatry, 37*(11), 828–830.

Hoff, A. L., Riordan, H., O'Donnell, D. W., Morris, L., & DeLisi, L. E. (1992). Neuropsychological functioning in first episode schizophreniform patients. *American Journal of Psychiatry, 149,* 898–903.

Holzman, P. S. (1987). Recent studies of psychophysiology in schizophrenia. *Schizophrenia Bulletin, 13,* 49–75.

Holzman, P. S., Kringlen, E., Matthysse, S., Flanagan, S. D., Lipton, R. B., Cramer, G., Levin, S., Lange, K., & Levy, D. L. (1988). A single dominant gene can account for eye tracking dysfunctions and schizophrenia in offspring of discordant twins. *Archives of General Psychiatry, 45,* 641–647.

Holzman, P. S., Proctor, L. R., Levy, D. L., Yasillo, N. J., Meltzer, H. Y., & Hurt, S. W. (1974). Eye tracking dysfunctions in schizophrenic patients and their relatives. *Archives of General Psychiatry, 31,* 143–151.

Holzman, P. S., Solomon, C. M., Levin, S., & Waternaux, C. S. (1984). Pursuit eye movement dysfunctions in schizophrenic patients and their relatives. *Archives of General Psychiatry, 45,* 1140–1141.

Iacono, W. G. (1988). Eye movement abnormalities in schizophrenic and affective disorders. In C. W. Johnston & F. J. Pirozzolo (Eds.), *Neuropsychology of eye movements* (pp. 115–145). Hillsdale, NJ: Erlbaum.

Iacono, W. G., & Lykken, D. T. (1979). Eye tracking and psychopathology: New procedures applied to a sample of monozygotic twins. *Archives of General Psychiatry, 36,* 1361–1369.

Iacono, W. G., Moreau, M., Beiser, M., Fleming, J. A. E., & Lin, T. (1992). Smooth-pursuit eye tracking in first-episode psychotic patients and their relatives. *Journal of Abnormal Psychology, 101,* 104–116.

Jacobsen, L. K., Hong, W. L., Hommer, D. W., Hamburger, S. D., Castellanos, F. X., Frazier, J. A., Giedd, J. N., Gordon, C. T., Karp, B. I., McKenna, K., & Rapoport, J. L. (1996). Smooth pursuit eye movements in childhood-onset schizophrenia: Comparison with attention-deficit hyperactivity disorder and normal controls. *Biological Psychiatry, 40,* 1144–1154.

Katsanis, J., & Iacono, W. G. (1991). Clinical, neuropsychological, and brain structural correlates of smooth-pursuit eye tracking performance in chronic schizophrenia. *Journal of Abnormal Psychology, 100,* 526–534.

Kay, S. R., Opler, L. A., & Lindenmayer, J.-P. (1989). The Positive and Negative Syndrome Scale (PANSS): Rationale and standardization. *British Journal of Psychiatry, 155,* 59–65.

Kelly, P., Rennie, C., Gordon, E., Anderson, J., Howson, A., & Meares, R. (1990). Smooth pursuit eye tracking dysfunction and negative symptoms in schizophrenia. *Psychiatry Research, 34,* 89–97.

Kuechenmeister, C. A., Linton, P. H., Mueller, T. V., & White, H. B. (1977). Eye tracking in relation to age, sex, and illness. *Archives of General Psychiatry, 34,* 578–599.

Leigh, R. J., & Zee, D. S. (1983). *The neurology of eye movements.* Philadelphia: Davis.

Lenzenweger, M. F., Cornblatt, B. A., & Putnick, M. (1991). Schizotypy and sustained attention. *Journal of Abnormal Psychology, 100,* 84–49.

Levy, D. L., Holzman, P. S., Matthysse, S., & Mendell, N. R. (1993). Eye tracking dysfunction and schizophrenia: A critical perspective. *Schizophrenia Bulletin, 19,* 461–536.

Levy, D. L., Holzman, P. S., Matthysse, S., & Mendell, N. R. (1994). Eye tracking and schizophrenia: A selective review. *Schizophrenia Bulletin, 20,* 47–62.

Levy, D. L., Yasillo, N. J., Dorus, E., Shaughnesssy, R., Gibbons, R. D., Peterson,

J., Janicak, P. G., Gaviria, M., & Davis, J. M. (1983). Relatives of unipolar and bipolar patients have normal pursuit. *Psychiatry Research, 10,* 285–293.

Lieberman, J., Jody, D., Geisler, S., Alvir, J., Loebel, A., Szymanski, S., Woerner, M., & Borenstein, M. (1993). Time course and biologic correlates of treatment response in first-episode schizophrenia. *Archives of General Psychiatry, 50,* 369–376.

Mather, J. A. (1985). Eye movements of teenage children of schizophrenics: A possible inherited marker of susceptibility to the disease. *Journal of Psychiatric Research, 19,* 523–532.

Mialet, J. P., & Pichot, P. (1981). Eye-tracking patterns in schizophrenia: An analysis based on the incidence of saccades. *Archives of General Psychiatry, 38,* 183–186.

Nestor, P. G., Faux, S. F., McCarley, R. W., Shenton, M. E., & Sands, S. F. (1990). Measurement of visual sustained attention in schizophrenia using signal detection analysis and a newly developed computerized CPT task. *Schizophrenia Research, 3,* 329–332.

Nuechterlein, K. H. (1983). Signal detection in vigilance tasks and behavioral attributes among offspring of schizophrenic mothers and among hyperactive children. *Journal of Abnormal Psychology, 92,* 4–28.

Nuechterlein, K. H., Edell, W. S., Norris, M., & Dawson, M. E. (1986). Attentional vulnerability indicators, thought disorder and negative symptoms. *Schizophrenia Bulletin, 12,* 408–426.

Obuchowski, M., Chan, T., Sweeney, J. A., & Cornblatt, B. (1997). Attention, frontal functioning and eye movements dysfunctions in schizophrenia. *Schizophrenia Research, 24*(1, 2), 244.

Obuchowski, M., Chan, T., Sweeney, J. A., Schnur, D., O'Brien, J. D., & Cornblatt, B. (1996). Attentional and eye movement dysfunctions in schizophrenia. *Biological Psychiatry, 39,* 572.

Obuchowski, M., & Cornblatt, B. (1995a). Eye-movement dysfunctions and the neurodevelopmental view off schizophrenia. *Schizophrenia Research, 15,* 182.

Obuchowski, M., & Cornblatt, B. (1995b). Eye-movement dysfunctions in schizophrenia: State or trait? *Biological Psychiatry, 37*(Suppl.), 670.

Orvaschel, H., & Puig-Antich, J. (1987). *Schedule for Affective Disorder and*

Schizophrenia for School Age Children (Epidemiologic version). Philadelphia: Medical College of Pennsylvania.

Orzack, M. H., & Kornetsky, C. (1966). Attention dysfunction in chronic schizophrenia. *Archives of General Psychiatry, 14,* 323–326.

Overall, J. E., & Gorham, D. R. (1962). The Brief Psychiatric Rating Scale. *Psychological Reports, 10,* 799–812.

Pandurangi, A. K., Kenji, W. S., Pelonero, A. L., & Goldberg, S. C. (1994). Sustained attention and positive formal thought disorder in schizophrenia. *Schizophrenia Research, 13,* 109–116.

Park, S., Holzman, P. S., & Goldman-Rakic, P. S. (1995). Spatial working memory deficits in the relatives of schizophrenic patients. *Archives of General Psychiatry, 52,* 821–828.

Pfohl, B., Blum, N., & Zimmerman, M. (1995). *Structured Interview for* DSM-IV *Personality (SIDP-IV)*. Iowa City: University of Iowa, College of Medicine.

Rea, M. M., Sweeney, J. A., Solomon, C. M., Walsh, V., & Frances, A. (1989). Changes in eye tracking during clinical stabilization in schizophrenia. *Psychiatry Research, 28,* 31–39.

Roitman, S. E. L., Cornblatt, B. A., Bergman, A., Obuchowski, M., Mitropoulou, V., Keefe, R. S. E., Silverman, J. M., & Siever, L. J. (1997). Attentional functioning in schizotypal personality disorder. *American Journal of Psychiatry, 154*(5), 655–660.

Ross, R. G., Radant, A. D., & Hommer, D. W. (1993). A developmental study of smooth pursuit eye movements in normal children from 7 to 15 years of age. *Journal of the American Academy Child and Adolescent Psychiatry, 32*(4), 783–791.

Rothschild, C. B., Akots, G., Hayworth, R., Pettenati, M. J., Rao, P. N., Wood, P., Stolz, F. M., Hansmann, I., Serino, K., Keith, T. P., Fajans, S. S., & Bowden, D. W. (1993). A genetic map of chromosome 20q12-q13.1: Multiple highly polymorphic microsatellite and RFLP markers linked to the maturity-onset diabetes of the young (MODY) locus. *American Journal of Human Genetics, 52,* 110–123.

Rutschmann, J., Cornblatt, B., & Erlenmeyer-Kimling, L. (1977). Sustained attention in children at risk for schizophrenia. *Archives of General Psychiatry, 34,* 571–575.

Saykin, A. J., Gur, R. C., Gur, R. E., Mozley, L. H., Resnick, S. E., Kester, D. B.,

& Stafiniak, P. (1990). Characterization of neuropsychological dysfunction in schizophrenia: Relation to clinical subtypes and positive and negative features. *Archives of Clinical Neuropsychology, 5,* 211.

Saykin, A. J., Shtasel, D. L., Gur, R. E., Kester, D. B., Mozley, L. H., Stafiniak, P., & Gur, R. C. (1994). Neuropsychological deficits in neuroleptic naive, first-episode schizophrenia. *Archives of General Psychiatry, 51,* 124–131.

Schellenberg, G. D., Pericak-Vance, M. A., Wiijsman, E. M., Moore, D. K., Gaskell, P. C., Yamaoka, L. A., Bebout, J. L., Anderson, L., Welsh, K. A., Clark, C. M., Martin, G. M., Roses, A. D., & Bird, T. D. (1991). Linkage analysis of familial Alzheimer disease, using chromosome 21 markers. *American Journal of Human Genetics, 48,* 563–583.

Schulz, S. C., Goyer, P., Kenney, J., Freidman, L., Semple, W., & Low-Beer, J. (1992, December). *Brain imaging, neuropsychological, and eye-tracking assessments of adolescents with psychosis.* Presented at the annual meeting of the American College of Neuropsychopharmacology, San Juan, PR.

Shagass, C., Amadeo, M., & Overton, D. A. (1974). Eye-tracking performance in psychiatric patients. *Biological Psychiatry, 9,* 245–260.

Siegel, C., Waldo, M., Mizner, G., Adler, L. E., & Freedman, R. (1984). Deficits in sensory gating in schizophrenic patients and their relatives: Evidence obtained with auditory evoked responses. *Archives of General Psychiatry, 41,* 607–612.

Siever, L. J., Coursey, R. D., Alterman, I. S., Buchsbaum, M. S., & Murphy, D. L. (1984). Impaired smooth pursuit eye movement: Vulnerability marker for schizotypal personality disorder in a normal volunteer population. *American Journal of Psychiatry, 141,* 1560–1566.

Siever, L. J., Coursey, R., Alterman, I., Zahn, T., Brody, L., Bernad, P., Buchsbaum, M., Lake, C., & Murphy, D. (1989). Clinical, psychophysiological, and neurological characteristics of volunteers with impaired smooth pursuit eye movements. *Biological Psychiatry, 26,* 35–51.

Siever, L. J., Keefe, R., Bernstein, D. P., Coccaro, E. F., Klar, H. M., Zemishlany, Z., Peterson, A. E., Davidson, M., Mahon, T., Horvath, T., & Mohs, R. (1990). Eye tracking impairment in clinically identified patients with schizotypal personality disorder. *American Journal of Psychiatry, 147,* 740–745.

Simons, R. F., & Katkin, W. (1985). Smooth pursuit eye movements in subjects reporting physical anhedonia and perceptual aberrations. *Psychiatry Research, 14,* 275–289.

Spreen, O., & Strauss, E. (1991). *A compendium of neuropsychological tests.* New York: Oxford University Press.

Spurr, N. K., Kelsell, D. P., Black, D. M., Murday, V. A., Turner, G., Crockford, G. P., Solomon, E., Cartwright, R. A., & Bishop, D. T. (1993). Linkage analysis of early-onset breast and ovarian cancer families, with markers on the long arm of chromosome 17. *American Journal of Human Genetics, 52,* 777–785.

StatSoft. (1995). *STATISTICA for Windows* [Computer program manual]. Tulsa, OK: Author.

Strauss, M. E., Buchanan, R. W., & Hale, J. (1993). Relations between attentional deficits and clinical symptoms in schizophrenic outpatients. *Psychiatry Research, 74,* 205–213.

Sweeney, J. A., Carl, J. R., & McCurtain, B. J. (1995). *Rampskor 1.0.* Pittsburgh, PA: University of Pittsburgh, School of Medicine.

Sweeney, J. A., Clementz, B. A., Haas, G. L., Escobar, M. D., Drake, K., & Frances, A. J. (1994). Eye tracking dysfunction in schizophrenia: Characterization of component eye movement abnormalities, diagnostic specificity, and the role of attention. *Journal of Abnormal Psychology, 103,* 222–230.

Sweeney, J. A., Haas, G. L., & Li, S. (1992). Neuropsychological and eye movement abnormalities in first-episode and chronic schizophrenia. *Schizophrenia Bulletin, 18,* 283–293.

Van den Bosch, R. J., & Rozendaal, N. (1988). Subjective cognitive dysfunction, eye tracking, and slow brain potentials in schizophrenic and schizoaffective patients. *Biological Psychiatry, 24,* 741–746.

Winters, L., Cornblatt, B. A., & Erlenmeyer-Kimling, L. (1991). The prediction of psychiatric disorders in late adolescence. In E. Walker (Ed.), *Schizophrenia: A life-course developmental perspective* (pp. 124–139). New York: Academic Press.

Wohlberg, G. W., & Kornetsky, C. (1973). Sustained attention in remitted schizophrenics. *Archives of General Psychiatry, 28,* 533–537.

Wolf, L. E., & Cornblatt, B. A. (1996). Neuropsychological functioning in children at risk for schizophrenia. In C. Pantelis, H. E. Nelson, & T. R. E.

Barnes (Eds.), *Schizophrenia: A neuropsychological perspective* (pp. 161–179). New York: Wiley.

Yee, R. D., Balogh, R. W., Marder, S. R., Levy, D. L., Sakala, S. M., & Honrubia, V. (1987). Eye movements in schizophrenia. *Investigative Ophthalmology and Vision Science, 28,* 366–374.

Yung, A. R., & McGorry, P. D. (1996). The prodromal phase of first-episode psychosis: Past and current conceptualizations. *Schizophrenia Bulletin, 22,* 353–370.

Yung, A. R., McGorry, P. D., McFarlane, C. A., Jackson, H. J., Patton, G. C., & Rakkar, A. (1996). Monitoring and care of young people at incipient risk of psychosis. *Schizophrenia Bulletin, 22,* 283–303.

Zimmermann, W., Bender, E., Rohde, K., Reis, A., Wiseman, R., Futreal, A., Krause, H., Prokoph, H., Werner, S., & Scherneck, S. (1993). Linkage analysis in German breast cancer families with early-onset of the disease, using highly polymorphic markers from the chromosome 17q11-q24 region. *American Journal of Human Genetics, 52,* 789–791.

14

Affective Expression and Affective Experience in Schizophrenia

Robert H. Dworkin, Harriet Oster, Scott C. Clark, and Stephanie R. White

> The study of the causes of things must be preceded
> by the study of things caused.—
> *attributed to Hughlings Jackson by Beveridge (1950, p. 10)*

THE STUDY OF THE CAUSES OF THINGS

Affective deficits have long been considered a prominent feature of schizophrenia (Bleuler, 1911/1950; Kraepelin, 1919; Strauss, Carpenter, & Bartko, 1974). Included among these deficits are *flat affect* (i.e., an absent or diminished expression of emotion) and *anhedonia* (i.e., an absent or diminished capacity to experience pleasure), which have played a central role in theory and research on negative symptoms (Andreasen, 1982; Crow, 1985; McGlashan & Fenton, 1992). Flat affect (also referred to as *affective flattening* or *blunting*) is the only symptom included in every major negative symptom rating scale (Fenton &

This chapter and a portion of the research it summarizes were supported, in part, by National Institute of Mental Health Grant MH-51791.

McGlashan, 1992), and in a recent follow-up study of inpatients with schizophrenia (Fenton & McGlashan, 1991), flat affect and anhedonia were the only negative symptoms that predicted long-term outcome independently of premorbid functioning and severity of positive symptoms. The importance of affective deficits in schizophrenia is further supported by the finding that negative symptoms, including affective flattening, are associated with frontal lobe dysfunction in research using single-photon emission computed tomography (e.g., Andreasen et al., 1992) and positron emission tomography (e.g., Wolkin et al., 1992). On the basis of their review of research addressing the validity of the distinction between positive and negative symptoms, McGlashan and Fenton proposed that flat affect should be one of the criteria for a diagnosis of schizophrenia.

It is beyond the scope of this chapter to comprehensively review the extensive literature on affective deficits in schizophrenia. Fortunately, two excellent reviews of this literature are available (Knight & Roff, 1985; Knight & Valner, 1993). The first author's research on affective deficits in schizophrenia began with analyses of twin data in which genetic influences on positive and negative symptoms, including affective flattening, were examined (Dworkin & Lenzenweger, 1984; Dworkin, Lenzenweger, Moldin, Skillings, & Levick, 1988). It was concluded from these analyses that negative symptoms were more closely associated with the genetic predisposition to develop schizophrenia than were positive symptoms. This conclusion was further supported by a series of studies in which positive and negative symptoms and social competence in the offspring of parents with schizophrenia and mood disorder were examined (e.g., Dworkin et al., 1991; Dworkin, Cornblatt, et al., 1993). In these studies, two negative symptoms—affective flattening and poverty of speech—were examined, and the results indicated that the adolescent offspring of parents with schizophrenia had significantly greater affective flattening (and poverty of speech) than the adolescent offspring of parents with mood disorder and of normal comparison parents. The belief that negative symptoms—and affective deficits in particular—provide important information about individuals with schizophrenia was further strengthened by the results of a series of studies in which the underlying structure of schizophrenic symptoms was examined (Lenzenweger & Dworkin, 1996; Lenzenweger, Dworkin, & Wethington, 1989, 1991). In these studies, negative symptoms were consistently found to represent a dimension of schizophrenic symptomatology independent of both positive symptoms and social functioning.

The results of these studies and of research conducted by other investigators suggest that it is important to include assessments of affective deficits in research on the psychopathology and pathogenesis of schizophrenia. Support for this conclusion is provided by the results of several recent family studies in which negative symptoms (Kendler, McGuire, Gruenberg, & Walsh, 1995b) and affective deficits such as flat affect (Tsuang, 1993; Tsuang, Gilbertson, & Faraone, 1991) and anhedonia (Clementz, Grove, Katsanis, & Iacono, 1991; Franke, Maier, Hardt, & Hain, 1993; Grove et al., 1991; Katsanis, Iacono, & Beiser, 1990; Kendler, Thacker, & Walsh, 1996) were found to discriminate the relatives of patients with schizophrenia from other groups. Consistent with the results of the twin analyses discussed above, the results of other studies have provided suggestive evidence that more prominent negative symptoms in individuals with schizophrenia may predict greater risk of the disorder in their relatives (Berenbaum, Oltmanns, & Gottesman, 1990; Cannon, Mednick, & Parnas, 1990; Gottesman, McGuffin, & Farmer, 1987; Kendler, McGuire, Gruenberg, & Walsh, 1994; McGuffin, Farmer, & Gottesman, 1987; cf. Baron, Gruen, & Romo-Gruen, 1992) and that the correlations between individuals with schizophrenia and their first-degree relatives may be greater for negative symptoms than for positive symptoms (Tsuang, 1993; cf. Kendler et al., 1997). In addition, a number of twin and family studies have found evidence of genetic influences on affective deficits and other negative symptoms in normal participants and in individuals with schizophrenia, further supporting the relevance of these symptoms for the pathogenesis of schizophrenia (e.g., Berenbaum & McGrew, 1993; Berenbaum et al., 1990; Dworkin & Saczynski, 1984; Kendler & Hewitt, 1992; Kendler et al., 1991). Finally, the results of two recent studies of adolescents with elevated levels of anhedonia indicated that these individuals appear to be at greater risk of psychotic illnesses and schizotypal symptoms at a follow-up assessment 10 years later (Chapman, Chapman, Kwapil, Eckblad, & Zinser, 1994; Kwapil, Miller, Zinser, Chapman, & Chapman, 1997).

It has been suggested that continued progress in research on the etiology of schizophrenia is dependent on improved measures of the schizophrenia phenotype and of putative markers of the schizophrenia genotype (e.g., Matthysse et al., 1992; Matthysse & Parnas, 1992). The data collected to date provide considerable support for Tsuang's (1993) conclusion that "a growing body of evidence ... points to the significance of negative symptoms as indicators of the genetic and neurobiological underpinnings of schizophrenia" (p. 305). However, it must be emphasized that an appreciable number of biobehavioral measures have the potential to serve as such indicators (Holzman, 1992). It is therefore very likely that the role played by affective deficits—and other single indicators—will be as one constituent of a multidimensional characterization of the schizophrenia phenotype and of individuals with the predisposition to develop the disorder (Dworkin & Cornblatt, 1995; Matthysse & Parnas, 1992).

In the remainder of this chapter, we review recent studies in which the nature of affective responses in individuals with schizophrenia has been examined. First, however, we discuss several issues regarding the nature of emotional responding in normal individuals that we believe have important implications for research on the nature of affective deficits in individuals with schizophrenia.

THE STUDY OF THINGS CAUSED

There is a clear potential for affective deficits to be *candidate symptoms* in schizophrenia, that is, clinical features strongly associated with etiologic processes (Tsuang, 1993). Unfortunately, only limited attention has been paid to systematically characterizing the nature of these deficits. Indeed, counter to the recommendation of the epigraph of this chapter, the study of the causes of affective deficits in schizophrenia has largely preceded the study of the affective deficits themselves.

The Nature of Emotional Responding

Research on emotional functioning in normal individuals can help to formulate hypotheses about emotional deficits in individuals with schizophrenia and can suggest paradigms and research measures for systematic studies within and between diagnostic groups (Knight & Valner, 1993). At the same time, detailed behavioral studies of affective deficits in individuals with schizophrenia may be able to provide insights into the nature of normal emotional functioning. One obstacle, however, has been a continuing lack of agreement on the definition of *emotion* (Buck, 1984; Ekman, 1993; Frijda, 1986; Oatley & Jenkins, 1996). There is a continuing debate about the relative importance and temporal primacy of the different components of emotion and about the way in which the component processes are interrelated. In particular, emotion theorists have disagreed about the validity of categorical versus dimensional representations of emotion, the role of cognitive processes in the elicitation of emotion, the nature of the appraisal process, the extent to which facial and vocal expressions reflect the subjective experience of emotion, and the nature of the subjective experience of emotion (for recent views, see Buck, 1984; Ekman, 1993; Fridlund, 1994; Frijda, 1986; Lazarus, 1991; Oatley & Jenkins, 1996; Ortony & Turner, 1990; Plutchik, 1980; Russell, 1994; and Zajonc, 1984).

Despite their differences, most emotion theorists today acknowledge that emotion is a complex biobehavioral phenomenon involving multiple, interrelated component processes, including attention, sensory and perceptual processing of external and internal stimuli, evocation of memories and associations, conscious and unconscious appraisal of the eliciting event, physiological arousal, activation of neuromotor programs for generating expressive behavior (spontaneous and voluntary) and instrumental responses, and subjective feeling states—not necessarily occurring in this sequence. Although we are not concerned with the perception of emotion in schizophrenia (cf. Kerr & Neale, 1993) in this chapter, it should be noted that the identification of emotional expressions would involve many of the same component processes, including physiological responses and overt and covert expressive behavior (e.g., Cacioppo, Bush, & Tassinary, 1992).

Most theorists also acknowledge that emotion is not elicited by stimulation per se but by the meaning of an external or internal stimulus or event for the individual at a particular time within a particular context (Lazarus, 1991). The emotional meaning of an event (if any) is believed to come not only from characteristics of the stimulus but also from its relevance to what Frijda (1986) called the individual's *concerns*, that is, its relevance to survival and well-being and its relation to the individual's motivational state, expectations, goals, wishes, and relationships with others at the particular moment in time when the event occurred. In other words, unless the individual is "touched" in some way by an event, unless the event is perceived as relevant to the individual's life, it may not evoke an emotional response. Similarly, unless there is at least the potential for normal social engagement, the communicative functions of emotional expression may be disrupted.

Although the appraisal of an eliciting event is determined by many factors, the initial appraisal process can be rapid, automatic, and entirely outside of conscious awareness. As Frijda (1986) noted, people are generally aware of having a particular emotion, but they are usually not aware of the reasons, at least not initially. However, because of cultural and individual variability in the appraisal of emotion elicitors, there is no reason to expect invariant relations between specific eliciting stimuli and emotional responses (Ekman, 1972). At the same time, there is evidence for similarities across cultures in the general categories of events that evoke particular emotions, suggesting the existence of biologically based, universal meaning structures (Boucher & Brandt, 1981; Ekman, 1993; Frijda, 1986; Oatley & Jenkins, 1996; Plutchik, 1980). For example, contact with decaying, noxious, or disliked substances or practices is widely seen as an elicitor of disgust (Rozin, Haidt, & McCauley, 1993); potentially dangerous, life-threatening events or objects are seen as elicitors of fear; the death of a loved one or loss of a valued object is universally identified as an elicitor of sadness; obstacles to desired goals are seen as producing anger; and pleasurable sensory stimulation and attainment of desired goals are seen as elicitors of joy. Such shared meanings form the basis for examining possible deviations from normative or expected affective responses in psychiatric populations.

The picture is further complicated by the fact that conscious and unconscious regulatory mechanisms can operate at every stage in the processing of emotion-eliciting events, not just at the final "output" stage of attempting to modulate, inhibit, or feign overt expressions of emotion (Frijda, 1986). Thus, the experience and expression of emotion are affected by characteristic modes of regulating attention, arousal, and behavioral responsiveness (Rothbart, Posner, & Rosicky, 1994), by biases in the appraisal of events, and by awareness of both one's own responses to the event and the responses of others. Disturbances in emotional functioning can occur at any stage in the process of responding to an emotional stimulus, and a disruption or disturbance in one aspect of emotional processing can influence other aspects.

From this perspective, symptoms of schizophrenia, such as avolition and social disengagement and disorders of attention, memory, and thought, may be integral components of affective deficits. The challenge, therefore, is to discover the specific ways in which deficits in these other domains may contribute to deficits in emotional functioning and vice versa. In summarizing the research results discussed in their review of the literature, Knight and Valner (1993) concluded that although empirical studies have confirmed the existence of disturbances in some aspects of the emotional response system in some individuals with schizophrenia, the concept of affective flattening has often been too imprecisely defined to be useful.[1] The key conceptual and methodological issues delineated by Knight and Valner are still pertinent to any effort to understand the precise nature and possible underlying mechanisms of affective deficits in schizophrenia. Many questions remain about the specific nature of affective deficits in schizophrenia and their possible sources—questions that can only be answered by detailed de-

---

[1]Most investigators of affective deficits in schizophrenia, including us, have used the terms *affect* and *emotion* interchangeably in discussing their research.

scriptions of emotional responding in schizophrenia patients and comparison participants in a variety of settings.

A detailed description of emotional responding in schizophrenia would address the different domains of emotional functioning (e.g., appraisal, physiological responses, subjective experience, expressive behavior, emotion regulation, action tendencies), the modalities of emotional communication (e.g., decoding vs. encoding), and, within each of these two modalities, the specific "channels" of affective communication (facial expressions, gaze, body movements, vocal–prosodic expressions, lexical expression). When examining these different domains, modalities, and channels of affective communication, it would be important to determine whether there are deficits in both spontaneous and deliberate expressions and whether positive and negative emotions are differentially affected.

Clearly, a comprehensive examination of all of these facets of emotional functioning would be beyond the scope of any single study. Most studies of affective deficits in schizophrenia have focused on expressive behavior (in most cases, facial expression and prosody), ratings of emotional experience, and (to a lesser degree) psychophysiological responses. Few investigations have examined more than one of these response systems, and only one (Kring & Neale, 1996) has examined all three. Within each of these domains, most investigators have examined a single communication channel (facial or vocal expression; but see Borod et al., 1990; and Kring, Alpert, Neale, & Harvey, 1994) and have studied either spontaneous or posed expression. Certain aspects of emotional functioning have received very little attention (e.g., lexical expressions of emotion and understanding of the causes and consequences of emotions). Other component processes (e.g., appraisal, emotion regulation, and action tendencies) have been largely ignored in existing studies, although distortions or disturbances in these processes could contribute to the deficits in emotional expression observed in schizophrenia.

In the remainder of this chapter, we selectively review recent studies of affective deficits in schizophrenia, pointing out gaps in current knowledge and suggesting avenues for future research. Two central questions are emphasized in the following discussion: (a) Are deficits in one domain of affective functioning associated with deficits in other domains? and (b) Does affective flattening reflect affective processes and not just other deficits prevalent in schizophrenia, specifically neuro-motor or social skills abnormalities?

The Relationship Between Deficits in Affective Expression and Affective Experience

Few studies of affective deficits in schizophrenia have examined whether deficits in one domain of affective functioning are associated with deficits in other domains. One important aspect of this question involves the nature of the relationship between deficits in observed affective *expression* (what is rated in existing measures of flat affect) and deficits in subjective affective *experience*. Although both Bleuler (1911/1950) and Kraepelin (1919) suggested that there was a dissociation between patients' reports of their subjective emotional experience and their outward expressions of emotion, it has often been assumed that the observed flattening of affect in schizophrenia reflects a corresponding blunting of affective experience in individuals with the disorder, for example, that diminished smiling is a consequence of a diminished ability to experience pleasure (i.e., anhedonia). Only recently, however, has research on affective deficits in schizophrenia explicitly examined the relationship between expressed and experienced affect, and the results of three recent studies of this relationship have important implications for future research on affective deficits.

Berenbaum and Oltmanns (1992) examined affective expression and experience in response to positive and negative affect-evoking film clips and drinks. Four groups of participants were compared: schizophrenia patients with blunted affect, schizophrenia patients with non-blunted affect, patients with major depression, and normal controls. As would be expected, schizophrenia patients with blunted affect exhibited significantly fewer positive facial expressions to the positive stimuli and negative facial expressions to the negative stimuli than did normal controls. However, there were no significant group differences in affective experience; that is, schizophrenia patients with blunted affect did not differ significantly from the nonblunted patients or from the patients with major depression and normal controls in their ratings of how happy or disgusted the positive and negative film clips and drinks made them feel. These data therefore suggest that patients with schizophrenia can exhibit a flattening of affective expression in the absence of a corresponding reduction in subjective affective experience.

A second study in which facial expressions and self-reported responses to positive and negative affect-evoking film clips were examined in patients with schizophrenia and normal controls was then reported by Kring, Kerr, Smith, and Neale (1993). An important feature of this study was the examination of patients who had been withdrawn from all neuroleptic medication for at least 2 weeks. The title of Kring et al.'s article—"Flat Affect in Schizophrenia Does Not Reflect Diminished Subjective Experience of Emotion"—provides a succinct summary of their results, which were very similar to the principal findings reported by Berenbaum and Oltmanns (1992). In this study, patients with schizophrenia exhibited diminished facial expressiveness in response to the film clips but reported experiencing as much positive and negative emotion as the normal controls.

Kring and Neale (1996) went on to replicate this pattern of findings in a third study, in which unmedicated patients with schizophrenia again were found to differ significantly from normal controls in their expression of emotion but not in their self-reported emotional experience in response to affect-evoking film clips. On the basis of the results of their studies, Kring and Neale suggested that there is a "disjunction" between expressed and experienced affect in schizophrenia and that the "flat affect typical of some patients ... misrepresents the underlying emotional experience" (p. 256). They concluded that it cannot be assumed that "diminished expressivity reflects diminished subjective experience of emotion when, in fact, this may not be true" (p. 256).

That three studies of affective expression and experience in schizophrenia all reached the same conclusion is notewothy in a field where failures to replicate are not uncommon. Each of these three studies reached this conclusion on the basis of an examination of group differences; that is, patients were, on average, significantly flatter in affective expression than normal controls, but patients and controls did not differ in their reports of subjective affective experience. However, instead of the conclusion that a dissociation between affective expression and experience accounts for these group differences in expression but not in experience, an alternative explanation can be proposed. It is possible that this pattern of group differences simply demonstrates that there is a reduction in affective expression in patients with schizophrenia compared with normal controls but that despite this overall flattening, affective expression still accurately reflects affective experience *within* patients. Indeed, such a pattern has been reported in patients with neurological diseases (e.g., Ross & Mesulam, 1979).

Consistency between emotional expression and subjective emotional experience—what we term *affective congruence*—has been demonstrated in normal populations in studies that have used within-subjects designs. These studies have examined the association between expression and experience within individuals across multiple stimuli or affective episodes (e.g., Ekman, Friesen, & Ancoli, 1980; Kleck et al., 1976; Rosenberg & Ekman, 1994; Ruch, 1995). To provide evidence of a dissociation between expression and experience in schizophrenia (or other disorders; e.g., see Brown, 1981, 1982), investigators would need to demonstrate that patients are less likely than comparison participants to show facial expressions of a particular emotion when they report experiencing that particular emotion and are less likely to report experiencing a particular emotion when they show that emotion in their face. Similarly, it would also be necessary to demonstrate that moment-to-moment variations in the intensity of expressed emotion are less likely to match moment-to-moment variations in emotional experience in patients compared with comparison participants. Thus, within-subjects designs are needed to determine the congruence between affective expression and experience.

To provide a preliminary examination of affective congruence in schizophrenia, we examined the extent to which affective expression reflected affective experience across a standard set of stimuli in schizophrenia inpatients and control participants.

Method

Participants. Twenty-seven patients with *Diagnostic and Statistical Manual of Mental Disorders* (3rd ed., rev.; American Psychiatric Association, 1987) diagnoses of schizophrenia or schizoaffective disorder were recruited from the Schizophrenia Research Unit inpatient ward at the New York State Psychiatric Institute (New York, NY).[2] Individuals are not admitted to this ward if they are younger than 18 years of age, do not speak English well enough to consent to research procedures, or have a current serious medical illness or a clear history of suicidal or homicidal behavior; individuals are also excluded if they have a history of substance abuse within the past 6 months or any history of substance abuse sufficient to obscure the diagnosis of schizophrenia.

Diagnoses were based on the consensus among the patient's treating psychiatrist, an expert diagnostician, and either one of two trained and reliable master's level clinicians who administered the Diagnostic Interview for Genetic Studies (Nurnberger et al., 1994). The two raters were trained by the developers of this instrument and achieved 100% diagnostic agreement on 15 cases prior to rating patients independently of the other rater.

A nonpsychiatric control sample of 22 individuals was recruited by means of posters soliciting participation distributed throughout Columbia–Presbyterian Medical Center. This method of recruiting control participants provided a heterogeneous sample with respect to age, sex, race, and education. Three of these participants were receiving psychotropic medication as part of an ongoing psychiatric treatment and were therefore excluded from the following data analyses, which were based on the remaining 19 control participants.

Procedure. The patients in this study underwent rigorous diagnostic and historical assessment shortly after their admission to the research unit. During their hospital stay, they entered a standardized antipsychotic medication treatment phase that lasted approximately 6

---

[2]The results of a recent study (Kendler, McGuire, Gruenberg, & Walsh, 1995a) suggest that patients with schizoaffective disorder have a high liability for schizophrenia (as well as affective disorder).

weeks. Patients were placed on haloperidol, receiving 5 mg per day for the 1st week, 5 mg twice daily for the 2nd week, and 5 mg three times daily for the final 4 weeks of this phase. Benztropine (1 or 2 mg) was given to patients for prophylaxis of extrapyramidal symptoms.

In addition to this standardized antipsychotic medication treatment phase, many patients were tapered off all neuroleptic medications and kept drug free for up to 4 weeks. Nonpharmacological approaches were used to help maintain patients during this phase of their admission. Eighteen of the 27 patients tested while receiving haloperidol were also tested during this medication-free phase. Thirteen of these patients had been withdrawn from all neuroleptic medication for at least 14 days, and three patients had been withdrawn for 8, 9, and 10 days ($M = 19.9$ days, $SD = 7.9$, $n = 16$). One patient had never received neuroleptic medication. One patient was tested after being withdrawn from neuroleptic medication for only 2 days, and the data for this testing session were excluded from the following analyses. Two of the patients received as-needed doses of 0.5–3.0 mg of lorazepam during the period when they had been withdrawn from neuroleptics, including the day of testing. Patients were administered the following measures during the standardized medication phase and after being withdrawn from all neuroleptic medication.

Self and Observer Affect Rating Scale. It has been noted that various biases are likely to play a role in current approaches to the clinical assessment of affective flattening. For example, Lewine and Sommers (1985) have argued that differences among interviewers (e.g., in sociodemographic characteristics and affective expression) may exert an important influence on a patient's affective expression; Kitamura, Kahn, and Kumar (1984) have reported that the content of patients' speech during interviews appears to bias ratings of observed affective flattening (their raters had been instructed to evaluate only observed behavior and to ignore speech content); and Alpert, Pouget, Sison, Yahia, and Allan (1995) have found that clinical ratings of negative symptoms are influenced by global impressions at least as much as they are by the discrete behaviors being rated. In addition, although ratings of affective flattening are often based on structured interviews, this struc-

ture typically provides minimal assistance in rating, for example, reduced facial expressiveness or poor eye contact. For these reasons, we
developed a structured approach to the assessment of affective expression and experience that can be easily administered and scored but that
is not based on an interview.

Meehl (1990) has suggested that blunted affect in schizophrenia is
more readily observed in the domain of positive emotions. Consistent
with this suggestion, the results of several studies have found greater
evidence of affective flattening in emotions in this domain when compared with emotions such as sadness and anger (e.g., Gottheil, Paredes,
Exline, & Winkelmayer, 1970; Kayton & Koh, 1975; Krause, Steimer,
Sänger-Alt, & Wagner, 1989). In addition, it has been reported that
patients with schizophrenia and depression smiled less during an admission interview than normal controls but that only in the patients
with schizophrenia did this deficit persist after clinical improvement
(Jones & Pansa, 1979). Given these results, humorous stimuli were used
in developing a structured approach to the assessment of affective expression and experience.

The Self and Observer Affect Rating Scale (SOARS; Dworkin, Clark,
Amador, & Gorman, 1996; Dworkin, Clark, et al., 1993) was developed
based on these considerations. This measure consists of 16 single-panel
cartoons that are presented to a participant using a large-screen slide
viewer. The cartoons were drawn from samples of cartoons used in
research on humor (e.g., Donoghue, McCarrey, & Clement, 1983; Gavanski, 1986; Masten, 1986, 1989) and from published collections of
cartoons (e.g., Gross & Charlton, 1991; Moore, 1989). In the development of this measure, pilot testing of these cartoons was conducted
with a heterogeneous sample of volunteers recruited in laundromats in
Greenwich Village, a New York City neighborhood very diverse in respect to socioeconomic status, race, and ethnicity. The cartoons vary in
content and were chosen so that half of them have primarily social
content and half have primarily nonsocial content. Because the experimenter administering the SOARS sits alongside of the slide viewer, it
is apparent that he or she cannot see the cartoons; the participant therefore does not expect the experimenter to respond to the cartoons.

As each of the patient and control participants in the present investigation were administered the SOARS cartoons, their facial and vocal responses were rated by the experimenter using a 4-point scale (0 = *no response*, 1 = *mild smile*, 2 = *broad smile*, 3 = *audible laughter*) that was based on similar rating scales of mirth responses used by Gavanski (1986) and by Masten (1986, 1989). After the presentation of each cartoon, participants were asked to rate how funny the cartoon was to them using a modification of a scale developed by Gavanski to assess the person's emotional experience of humor. The means of these two sets of ratings for each person provide a measure of overall observer-rated affective expression and a measure of overall self-reported affective experience. In addition, these observer ratings of affective expression and self-reports of affective experience were correlated across the 16 cartoons for each participant. This correlation reflects each participant's affective congruence, that is, the extent to which the participant's observed affective expressions and self-reports of affective experience in response to the 16 cartoons are associated. These correlations were transformed to z scores for all data analyses and then converted back to correlation coefficients for presentation and discussion of the results.

Blunted affect. The blunted affect rating from the Positive and Negative Syndrome Scale (PANSS; Kay, Fiszbein, & Opler, 1987), a widely used measure based on a clinical interview, was rated for all patients.

Neuromotor dysfunction. A brief structured clinical examination of nonlocalizing neurological signs (Clark, Malaspina, Hasan, Koeppel, & Gorman, 1993; Dworkin et al., 1996) was administered to all patients. Based on this examination, a summary measure of neuromotor dysfunction (that included, e.g., ratings of rapid alternating movements and tandem walk) was derived.

The PANSS ratings were conducted by trained master's level and above clinicians independently and without knowledge of the ratings of neurological signs, which were also conducted by trained master's level and above clinicians. The SOARS ratings of affective expression were conducted by a trained research assistant independently and without knowledge of the other ratings. The intraclass correlation coefficient interrater reliabilities and coefficient alpha internal consistency reliabilities of these measures were presented in a previous article (Dworkin et al., 1996).

Results

Figure 1 presents the results of the analyses of affective congruence using the SOARS. As can be seen from the figure, patients with schizophrenia had lower affective congruence than control participants. The z-transformed mean correlation between affective expression and affec-

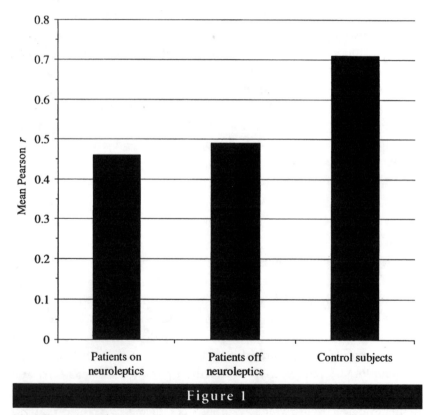

Figure 1

Mean Pearson product–moment correlation coefficients between Self and Observer Affect Rating Scale (SOARS) ratings of affective expression and affective experience as a function of group.

tive experience in patients taking neuroleptic medication, $r = .46$, $F(1, 25) = 6.71$, $p < .05$, was significantly lower, $t(44) = 3.00$, $p < .01$, than the z-transformed mean correlation for the control participants, $r = .71$, $F(1, 17) = 17.28$, $p < .001$. The z-transformed mean correlation for the patients withdrawn from all neuroleptic medication, $r = .49$, $F(1, 15) = 4.74$, $p < .05$, was also significantly lower, $t(34) = 2.42$, $p < .05$, than the mean correlation for the control participants.

It is possible that the group differences in these correlations reflect a restricted range of affective expression in the patients with schizophrenia. Hierarchical regression analyses were conducted to address this possibility. In these analyses, presented in Table 1, the means and variances of participants' affective expression ratings were entered in the first step of the analysis. Each participant's group (patient vs. control) was then entered to determine whether there were significant group differences in affective congruence, controlling for differences in overall affective expression and variability in affective expression. As can be seen from the table, affective congruence in the patients taking neuroleptic medication and in the patients withdrawn from all neuroleptics remains significantly reduced compared with control participants in these regression analyses.

Discussion

Three aspects of these analyses of affective congruence are noteworthy. The first is that the results for our sample of control participants provide a clear demonstration that the expression of positive affect and the subjective experience of positive affect are closely associated in normal individuals when examined across a standard set of stimuli using a within-subjects design. Such consistency between expressed and experienced emotion has been demonstrated in relatively few previous studies of normal participants (e.g., Ekman et al., 1980; Kleck et al., 1976; Rosenberg & Ekman, 1994; see a recent review by Ruch, 1995). Because the present findings are based on different eliciting stimuli, experimental tasks, and analytic methods than those used in previous studies, they provide important additional evidence of the coherence of emotional expression and experience in normal individuals.

The second important aspect of these results is the finding that

		Table 1		

Summary of Hierarchical Regression Analyses Predicting Affective Congruence

Variable	B	SE B	β
Patients on neuroleptic medication			
Step 1			
SOARS affective expression	.46	.16	.45***
SOARS affective expression variance	.28	.25	.18
Step 2			
SOARS affective expression	.31	.18	.29
SOARS affective expression variance	.39	.25	.24
Group (Patients vs. controls)	.25	.13	.27*
Patients withdrawn from all neuroleptic medication			
Step 1			
SOARS affective expression	.38	.17	.44**
SOARS affective expression variance	−.16	.16	−.19
Step 2			
SOARS affective expression	.20	.18	.24
SOARS affective expression variance	.12	.19	.14
Group (Patients vs. controls)	.40	.17	.45**

Note. SOARS = Self and Observer Affect Rating Scale.
$*p < .06.$ $**p < .05.$ $***p < .01.$

there was a significantly reduced level of affective congruence in patients with schizophrenia when taking neuroleptic medication and after withdrawal from all neuroleptics. The third, and perhaps most important, aspect of these results was that even though the strength of the association between affective expression and affective experience was reduced in the patients with schizophrenia, it was still statistically significant; that is, patients' affective expressions of smiling and laughter were significantly associated with their affective experiences of amusement in response to the humorous stimuli. These data therefore provide evidence that affective expression does reflect affective experience in individuals with schizophrenia and that there is only a partial dissociation between expression and experience in this disorder.

Buck, Easton, and Goldman (1995) have provided a preliminary report of a recent study in which a similar pattern of results was found. Participants were videotaped while they viewed emotionally evocative slides and rated their responses to each slide on separate scales of emotional response (happy, sad, fear, anger, surprise, and pleasant vs. unpleasant; see Buck, 1984, for a general description of this slide-viewing paradigm). Videotapes of their facial expressions were judged by observers, who were asked to guess which slide category the participant was viewing and to rate the participant's emotional response on the same scales as those used by the participants. The facial expressions of the patients with schizophrenia were judged significantly less accurately than those of the normal controls, in terms of both the judges' slide categorizations and the correlations between self-reported and judged emotions. For both groups, the correlations between observer-rated and self-reported emotional responses were generally modest and positive. However, the correlations were significantly higher in the control group for three of the ratings: happy, fear, surprise. As found in our data, these results suggest that the congruence between self-reported and expressed emotion is less in patients with schizophrenia than in normal controls.

Although the results of these analyses of affective congruence indicate that the dissociation between affective expression and experience in patients with schizophrenia is not complete, they also indicate that the expression of affect does not reflect affective experience in individuals with this disorder as closely as it does in normal individuals. It is necessary, therefore, to account for this partial dissociation between affective expression and experience in schizophrenia.

Several explanations have been suggested, with different implications for the nature of the disturbance in emotional functioning in schizophrenia. The most straightforward interpretation of the findings of the studies of affective expression and experience in schizophrenia is that affective deficits are limited primarily to the outward display of emotion and that the subjective, experiential component of emotion is relatively intact. In this view, the flat affect shown by individuals with schizophrenia is a misleading indicator of their inner emotional life. However, before this conclusion can be accepted, it is necessary to have more evidence than is presently available that the experience of emotion—not just the participant's self-report of emotional experience—is in fact normal in patients with schizophrenia.

The measures of emotional experience used in most of the reported studies have been based on global rating scales for positive and negative emotions or ratings on separate emotion scales that have been collapsed into global positive and negative scores. Such ratings are indirect measures of experienced emotion, involving complex perceptual and cognitive information-processing skills: the translation of a felt experience into a rating on a numeric scale. The fact that patients with schizophrenia and normal controls do not differ in rating their emotional responses to emotion-eliciting stimuli suggests that they process the stimuli in similar ways. However, we cannot be sure that such ratings reflect their subjective experience of emotion rather than cognitive assessments of the hedonic valence of the stimuli. For this reason, it will be crucial in future research to use methods of assessing emotional experience in schizophrenia that do not rely solely on the participant's self-report (e.g., Lang, 1995).

Kring and her associates (Kring et al., 1993; Kring & Neale, 1996) have proposed that individuals with schizophrenia may inhibit the outward expression of emotion, either consciously or unconsciously. Research on the internalizing–externalizing distinction in normal populations (Buck, 1980; Fridlund, Ekman, & Oster, 1987) has found that individuals who are less facially expressive tend to show greater physiological responses (and presumably more intense emotional experience) than those who are more facially expressive. The negative correlation between facial expressiveness and physiological reactivity revealed in between-subjects designs has been interpreted as evidence that the outer display of emotion discharges physiological arousal, whereas the inhibition of overt facial expression is accompanied by an increase in physiological reactivity. If overt facial expression is habitually inhibited in schizophrenia, it could be expected that there would be a larger negative correlation between facial expression and both physiological arousal and self-reported emotion in patients with schizophrenia than in comparison normal participants. Such patterns of negative correlations have generally not been found in studies of affective deficits in schizophrenia (e.g., Dworkin et al., 1996; Kring et al., 1993).

The available data suggest not only that individuals with schizophrenia are less expressive overall than normal controls but also that their expressions are less likely to accurately reflect their feelings when they express emotion. A lack of coherence between expression and experience of this nature could indicate a disruption of the biologically based neural "programs" thought to underlie the generation of coordinated patterns of emotional responding across multiple response systems. According to evolutionary theories of emotion (e.g., Buck, 1984; Ekman, 1972; Frijda, 1986; Izard, 1977), different emotions are characterized by distinctive patterns of coordinated expressive, experiential, physiological, and behavioral responding that enable the organism to respond rapidly and adaptively in a wide variety of circumstances. Thus, a lack of congruence between expression and subjective experience would interfere with the communicative and adaptive functions of emotion. An abnormality of this nature would be indicative of more pervasive pathology than just a reduction in facial expressiveness by itself or a tendency to inhibit overt expressions of emotion.

Affective, Social, or Motor Deficits?

One possible explanation of the partial dissociation between affective expression and experience may be found in the reliance of existing measures of affective expression on motor behaviors during an interview or other interpersonal situation. The specific behaviors included in these measures, for example, facial expressiveness, vocal inflection, eye contact, are all social behaviors that facilitate communication. It is certainly possible that a schizophrenia patient's interpersonal behavior lacks these qualities because he or she suffers from an affective deficit. But it is just as plausible that the patient has, for example, diminished facial expressiveness or vocal inflections because he or she suffers from social (Dworkin, 1992) or neuromotor (Berenbaum & Rotter, 1992; Dworkin, 1992; Knight & Valner, 1993) deficits.

Indeed, in recent research on social deficits in schizophrenia, the very same behaviors used to measure affective flattening have been considered components of social skill (e.g., eye contact or facial expressiveness; Liberman et al., 1986; Lindsay, 1982; Morrison & Wixted, 1989); not surprisingly, affective flattening has been found to be associated with social skills deficits in patients with schizophrenia (Bellack, Morrison, Wixted, & Mueser, 1990; Jackson et al., 1989; Mueser, Bellack, Morrison, & Wixted, 1990). Moreover, the results of several studies have suggested that affective flattening is associated with neuromotor deficits in individuals with schizophrenia (Butler et al., 1992; Manschreck, Maher, Rucklos, & Vereen, 1982; Manschreck, Maher, Waller, Ames, & Latham, 1985), and Dworkin, Cornblatt, et al. (1993) have found that neuromotor dysfunction in childhood predicts affective flattening in adolescents at risk for schizophrenia. Based on these findings, it seems likely that deficits in such behaviors as facial expressiveness and vocal inflection may reflect, at least in part, social or neuromotor abnormalities rather than affective deficits in individuals with schizophrenia.

To test the hypothesis that affective flattening in schizophrenia reflects, in part, the neuromotor dysfunction found in individuals with this disorder, we examined the sample of patients withdrawn from neuroleptic medication described above (a more detailed discussion of these analyses can be found in Dworkin et al., 1996). Because the results of studies with normal participants suggest that there can be significant relationships between the facial expression of emotion and subjective emotional experience, as discussed above, we hypothesized that neuromotor dysfunction and affective deficit both contribute to the flattening of affective expression characteristic of individuals with schizophrenia. We examined whether the SOARS measure of overall affective expression and the PANSS blunted affect rating were each correlated with both a measure of neuromotor dysfunction and a measure of affective deficit that does not involve the expression of affect (the SOARS measure of overall affective experience).

Table 2 presents the Pearson product–moment correlation coefficients between the two measures of affective flattening and the measures of neuromotor dysfunction and affective experience. Because it had been predicted that positive correlations would be found among these measures, one-tailed tests were used in evaluating statistical significance. As can be seen from the first column of the table, the SOARS measure of affective expression was significantly correlated with both neuromotor dysfunction and the SOARS measure of affective experience. As can be seen from the third column of the table, the PANSS measure of blunted affect was, as predicted, positively correlated (although not at a conventional level of statistical significance) with the measure of neuromotor dysfunction and significantly correlated with the SOARS measure of affective experience.

These results suggest that measures of affective flattening or blunting in schizophrenia reflect not only affective deficits but also the neuromotor abnormalities prevalent in individuals with this disorder (e.g.,

Table 2

Correlations Between Measures of Affective Flattening and Measures of Neuromotor Dysfunction and Affective Experience

Measure	Diminished affective expression (SOARS)		Blunted affect (PANSS)	
	r^a	N	r^a	N
Neuromotor dysfunction[b]	.65**	12	.41*	12
Diminished affective experience (SOARS)	.42**	17	.44**	17

Note. SOARS = Self and Observer Affect Rating Scale; PANSS = Positive and Negative Syndrome Scale. The SOARS measures of affective expression and affective experience have been reversed in sign to reflect diminished affective expression and experience. Data from Dworkin et al. (1996). [a]Pearson product–moment correlation coefficients. [b]Five patients were not administered the neurological signs examination.
*$p < .10$.   **$p < .05$.

Manschreck, 1989, 1993; Walker, 1994). It may therefore be that the significantly reduced affective congruence we found in patients with schizophrenia occurs because the motoric expression of their emotions is compromised, not because their experience of emotions is diminished.

The measure of neuromotor dysfunction that we used in this study did not involve facial motor abnormalities, and a stronger test of this hypothesis would examine the relationship between facial motor deficits and facial emotional expression. In one of the few such studies, Braun, Bernier, Proulx, and Cohen (1991) examined three kinds of voluntary facial movements in schizophrenia patients and normal controls: facial expressions of emotion cued by verbal command, facial expressions cued by slides of prototypical facial expressions, and complex nonemotional bucco-facial behaviors (e.g., cheeks puffed with brows down) cued by examples shown in slides. The patients were impaired overall compared with the controls, but they showed relatively greater deficits on the emotional facial expressions than on the nonemotional facial behaviors, suggesting that the deficit in facial expression in schizophrenia involves not only a deficit in voluntary facial motor control but also a deficit in the processing of affective information. However, the difference between emotional and nonemotional facial movements was significant only for the speech-cued expressions. Because there was no speech-cued nonemotional facial movement task, it is possible that the deficit in the patients with schizophrenia was related to the verbal aspects of the speech-cued condition, not to its emotional component.

The role of neuromotor deficits in the production of facial expressions could be further clarified by systematic comparisons of spontaneous as well as deliberate emotional and nonemotional facial movements—an extension of the strategy used by Borod, Lorch, Koff, and Nicholas (1987) in comparing patients with left- and right-brain damage. Several types of spontaneous nonemotional facial movements occur in everyday interactions: conversational markers (e.g., brow raising and lowering), facial movements occurring during visual search (e.g., brow raising while looking up and brow lowering while looking down), mobility of the lips and midface while articulating speech, wiping the lips with the tongue, and even reflex behaviors like yawning and sneezing. There have been no systematic studies of such behavior, even in normal individuals.

It will also be important in future research to examine the specific facial actions that are reduced in individuals with schizophrenia. Based on the existing literature, it is unclear whether there are qualitative differences in the emotional expressions shown by individuals with schizophrenia versus those with other disorders and normal participants, or whether the group differences are solely in the overall amount or intensity of affective expression. Such research would make it possible to determine whether specific types of facial expressions of emotion occur less frequently in schizophrenia (e.g., Duchenne smiles of enjoyment; Ekman, 1992; Ekman, Davidson, & Friesen, 1990). Recent studies have found that patients with schizophrenia show decreased upper face actions during social interaction relative to patients with depression and other patient groups (Krause et al., 1989; Steimer-Krause, Krause, & Wagner, 1990; cf. Mattes, Schneider, Heimann, & Birbaumer, 1995). These findings suggest that there may be reductions in Duchenne smiles, conversational facial movements, or both in schizophrenia. Conversational facial movements share an interpersonal, communicative function with emotional facial expressions, and both are diminished in Parkinson's disease (Rinn, 1984). Such movements could be examined not only in comparison to facial expressions of emotion but also in comparison to nonemotional, noncommunicative facial movements, for example, brow movements accompanying instrumental activities like visually tracking an object above or below the line of sight.

The data presented in this section indicate the importance of examining more precise measures of facial expression, affective experience, and neuromotor functioning in research on schizophrenia. The interpretation of existing measures of affective flattening (based on global measures of affective expression) is rendered ambiguous by their association with neuromotor dysfunction. The difficulty of clearly distinguishing affective flattening from both social skills and neuromotor deficits has important implications for research on the role of affective flattening in the diagnosis, etiology, and treatment of schizophrenia (Dworkin, 1992). Indeed, it can be argued that given the confounding among these variables, it is currently not possible to make a compelling argument that affective flattening characterizes patients with schizophrenia; it would be just as valid to consider the phenomena presented as evidence of affective flattening as evidence of social deficits, motor deficits, or both. Because the conceptual and measurement overlap among these variables has not been recognized, approaches to affective flattening in schizophrenia that take into account the contribution of social and neuromotor processes must be developed. More sensitive measures of diminished affective experience—reflecting, for example, anhedonia (Rado, 1953) and analgesia (Dworkin, 1994)—may help to tease apart the various component processes responsible for the clinical presentation of affective deficits in individuals with schizophrenia. The validity of such measures in research on schizophrenia may be greater than that of measures of affective expression in which social and neuromotor influences are not considered.

CONCLUSIONS

The results of the studies reviewed in this chapter suggest that affective deficits play an important role in the pathogenesis and psychopathology of schizophrenia. However, these studies also call to mind the suggestion that research should be conducted on the pathophysiological and psychological processes underlying the symptoms of schizophrenia (Carpenter, 1992; Carpenter & Buchanan, 1989; Neale, Oltmanns, & Harvey, 1985; Strauss et al., 1974). As we have suggested throughout this chapter, one of the goals of such research should be to determine which specific aspects of affective functioning are abnormal in individuals with schizophrenia in which situations, that is, to "parse" affective deficits as a function of their context.

Few studies of affective deficits in schizophrenia have examined the role of the different contexts in which emotional behavior may be observed—or not observed. The theoretical importance of studying context-related differences is that the relative invariance versus variability of affective deficits may reveal whether the deficits are a matter of "competence" versus "performance." In other words, are there any circumstances in which emotional expressions in individuals with schizophrenia can be observed that are normal in appearance and intensity? If this were found, it would not be consistent with the argument that neuromotor deficits are a major source of the affective flattening observed in individuals with schizophrenia. Such studies might also be able to elucidate the mechanisms underlying emotional responsivity versus nonresponsivity in these individuals. For example, is there a threshold for activation that must be exceeded for overt facial expressions to be displayed? Conversely, are overt expressions more likely to occur in less threatening or less highly arousing contexts (which might be less likely to activate inhibitory and other regulatory mechanisms)? Likewise, is affective expression greater in social interactions with peers than in clinical interviews with mental health professionals?

Related to the question of the context in which affective deficits occur is the nature of the appraisal processes involved in emotional responding in individuals with schizophrenia. The finding that patients with schizophrenia do not differ from normal controls in rating their experience of emotion in response to emotionally arousing stimuli (Berenbaum & Oltmanns, 1992; Kring et al., 1993; Kring & Neale, 1996) suggests that their appraisal of these stimuli does not differ from normative appraisals. However, as discussed above, these studies examined only global positive and negative responses. The specific patterns of appraisal in response to affect-eliciting stimuli have not been examined. In recent years, extensive cross-cultural research has been conducted on the structure of these cognitive appraisals in normal individuals (Roseman, Wiest, & Swartz, 1994; Scherer, Wallbott, & Summerfield, 1986), and the paradigms developed by these researchers could be used to examine appraisal processes in individuals with schizophrenia and other disorders.

Experimental emotion elicitors such as cartoons, tastes, and films have the advantage of evoking emotions that arise in everyday life and that could potentially be included in structured clinical assessments. In addition, unlike paradigms based on the recall of emotion-eliciting events, such elicitors do not rely on memory. However, responses to eliciting stimuli presented in controlled laboratory situations and vicarious emotional responses to events seen in films might not be representative of a participant's ordinary mode of appraising and responding to emotionally charged events. Therefore, studies of emotional responses to stimuli or events in real-life situations that have some direct and immediate relevance to the life of the individual with schizophrenia are needed (e.g., Walker, Grimes, Davis, & Smith's, 1993, creative study of home movies).

If the appraisal and emotional experience systems are in fact intact in individuals with schizophrenia, as the data from film-viewing studies suggest, it would be expected that individuals with schizophrenia would report appropriate emotional responses to events that are of immediate concern to them. Of course, one problem of studying affect in inpatient populations is that much of the environment may be devoid of relevance to patients' concerns, which may in part account for discrepancies between the results found with measures of emotional experience derived from affect-eliciting films (see above) and those derived from clinical interviews or ward observation (e.g., Brown, Sweeney, & Schwartz, 1979).

Throughout this chapter, we have discussed affective deficits in schizophrenia as if these deficits were characteristic of all individuals with the disorder. Of course, as is true of all schizophrenic symptoms, not all patients with the disorder have prominent affective flattening or anhedonia. It is very likely that deficits in emotional responsivity are greatest in patients with the deficit syndrome (Carpenter, 1992; Carpenter & Buchanan, 1989), and it can be hypothesized that these patients are characterized by both flat affect and diminished affective experiences, including anhedonia. Because this may reflect not only a greater degree of emotional dysfunction in individuals with the deficit syndrome but also their lack of investment in personal relationships and goal-directed activities, relationships between avolition and affective deficits should be examined (Knight & Valner, 1993). Although it will be important to study deficit syndrome patients in future research on affective expression and experience in schizophrenia patients, it must be emphasized that dimensional approaches to affective deficits and the other symptoms of schizophrenia continue to have great merit and allow all individuals with the disorder to be investigated.

We have not discussed the effects of neuroleptic medication and other treatments on affective deficits in individuals with schizophrenia—topics well beyond the scope of this chapter. We would like to conclude, however, by briefly indicating several issues about neuroleptic medication and affective deficits that we believe are important to consider in future studies. Associations between extrapyramidal symptoms and ratings of flat affect (Mayer, Alpert, Stastny, Perlick, & Empfield, 1985) and negative symptoms (Prosser et al., 1987) have been reported, and it has been recognized that neuroleptic medication is a potential confound in studies of affective deficits in individuals with schizophrenia (Earnst et al., 1996; Knight & Valner, 1993). But it has also been reported that neuroleptic medication may lead to an amelioration of affective flattening due to clinical improvement and that if "neuroleptically induced reduction in facial activity is confounded by an increase in facial activity during improvement, two opposing tendencies would exist" (Schneider et al., 1992, p. 238). Such opposing tendencies on affective expression would make it more difficult to assess the consequences of neuroleptic medication on affective deficits in schizophrenia patients. Recent reports, however, suggest that treatment with atypical antipsychotic medications not only may be associated with fewer extrapyramidal symptoms than typical neuroleptics but also may lead to significantly greater improvement in affective flattening and other negative symptoms (e.g., Tollefson et al., 1997; Tollefson & Sanger, 1997). These data suggest that future studies of affective deficits in individuals with schizophrenia should examine two groups of patients: those treated with atypical neuroleptics and those treated with typical neuroleptics. Such studies may make it possible to address the issues discussed in this chapter more directly than would studies of patients treated with only one of these types of medication.

REFERENCES

Alpert, M., Pouget, E. R., Sison, C., Yahia, M., & Allan, E. (1995). Clinical and acoustic measures of the negative syndrome. *Psychopharmacology Bulletin, 31,* 321–326.

American Psychiatric Association. (1987). *Diagnostic and statistical manual of mental disorders* (3rd ed., rev.). Washington, DC: Author.

Andreasen, N. C. (1982). Negative symptoms in schizophrenia: Definition and reliability. *Archives of General Psychiatry, 39,* 784–788.

Andreasen, N. C., Rezai, K., Alliger, R., Swayze, V. W., II, Flaum, M., Kirchner, P., Cohen, G., & O'Leary, D. S. (1992). Hypofrontality in neuroleptic-naive patients and in patients with chronic schizophrenia. *Archives of General Psychiatry, 49,* 943–958.

Baron, M., Gruen, R. S., & Romo-Gruen, J. M. (1992). Positive and negative symptoms: Relation to familial transmission of schizophrenia. *British Journal of Psychiatry, 161,* 610–614.

Bellack, A. S., Morrison, R. L., Wixted, J. T., & Mueser, K. T. (1990). An analysis of social competence in schizophrenia. *British Journal of Psychiatry, 156,* 809–818.

Berenbaum, H., & McGrew, J. (1993). Familial resemblance of schizotypic traits. *Psychological Medicine, 23,* 327–333.

Berenbaum, H., & Oltmanns, T. F. (1992). Emotional experience and expression in schizophrenia and depression. *Journal of Abnormal Psychology, 101,* 37–44.

Berenbaum, H., Oltmanns, T. F., & Gottesman, I. I. (1990). Hedonic capacity in schizophrenics and their twins. *Psychological Medicine, 20,* 367–374.

Berenbaum, H., & Rotter, A. (1992). The relationship between spontaneous facial expressions of emotion and voluntary control of facial muscles. *Journal of Nonverbal Behavior, 16,* 179–190.

Beveridge, W. I. B. (1950). *The art of scientific investigation.* New York: Norton.

Bleuler, E. (1950). *Dementia praecox or the group of schizophrenias* (J. Zinkin, Trans.). New York: International Universities Press. (Original work published 1911)

Borod, J. C., Lorch, M. P., Koff, E., & Nicholas, M. (1987). Effect of emotional context on bucco-facial apraxia. *Journal of Clinical and Experimental Neuropsychology, 9,* 155–161.

Borod, J., Welkowitz, J., Alpert, M., Brozgold, A. Z., Martin, C., Peselow, E., & Diller, L. (1990). Parameters of emotional processing in neuropsychiatric disorders: Conceptual issues and a battery of tests. *Journal of Communication Disorders, 23,* 247–271.

Boucher, J. D., & Brandt, M. E. (1981). Judgment of emotion: American and Malay antecedents. *Journal of Cross-Cultural Psychology, 12,* 272–283.

Braun, C., Bernier, S., Proulx, R., & Cohen, H. (1991). A deficit of primary affective facial expression independent of bucco-facial dyspraxia in chronic schizophrenics. *Cognition and Emotion, 5,* 147–159.

Brown, S. (1981). Dissociation of pleasure in psychopathology. *Journal of Nervous and Mental Disease, 169,* 3–17.

Brown, S. (1982). The relationship between expressed and experienced emotion in depression. *International Journal of Psychiatry in Medicine, 12,* 29–41.

Brown, S., Sweeney, D. R., & Schwartz, G. E. (1979). Differences between self-reported and observed pleasure in depression and schizophrenia. *Journal of Nervous and Mental Disease, 167,* 410–415.

Buck, R. (1980). Nonverbal behavior and the theory of emotion: The facial feedback hypothesis. *Journal of Personality and Social Psychology, 38,* 811–824.

Buck, R. (1984). *The communication of emotion.* New York: Guilford Press.

Buck, R., Easton, C., & Goldman, C. (1995). A developmental-interactionist theory of motivation, emotion, and cognition: Implications for understanding psychopathology. *Japanese Journal of Research on Emotion, 3,* 1–16.

Butler, S. A., Juhasz, J. A., Purcell, D. W., Horner, A. I. W., Brookshire, R. J., Caudle, J., Risch, S. C., & Lewine, R. R. J. (1992, November). *Use of neuropsychological performance to subtype schizophrenia.* Paper presented at the meeting of the Society for Research in Psychopathology, Palm Springs, CA.

Cacioppo, J. T., Bush, L. K., & Tassinary, L. G. (1992). Microexpressive facial actions as a function of affective stimuli: Replication and extension. *Personality and Social Psychology Bulletin, 18,* 515–526.

Cannon, T. D., Mednick, S. A., & Parnas, J. (1990). Antecedents of predominantly negative- and predominantly positive-symptom schizophrenia in a high-risk population. *Archives of General Psychiatry, 47,* 622–632.

Carpenter, W. T., Jr. (1992). The negative symptom challenge. *Archives of General Psychiatry, 49,* 236–237.

Carpenter, W. T., Jr., & Buchanan, R. W. (1989). Domains of psychopathology relevant to the study of etiology and treatment in schizophrenia. In S. C. Schulz & C. A. Tamminga (Eds.), *Schizophrenia: Scientific progress* (pp. 13–22). New York: Oxford University Press.

Chapman, L. J., Chapman, J. P., Kwapil, T. R., Eckblad, M., & Zinser, M. C. (1994). Putatively psychosis-prone subjects 10 years later. *Journal of Abnormal Psychology, 103,* 171–183.

Clark, S. C., Malaspina, D., Hasan, A., Koeppel, C., & Gorman, J. M. (1993). Non-localizing neurological abnormalities in schizopohrenia. *Schizophrenia Research, 9,* 96.

Clementz, B. A., Grove, W. M., Katsanis, J., & Iacono, W. G. (1991). Psychometric detection of schizotypy: Perceptual aberration and physical anhedonia in relatives of schizophrenics. *Journal of Abnormal Psychology, 100,* 607–612.

Crow, T. J. (1985). The two-syndrome concept: Origins and current status. *Schizophrenia Bulletin, 11,* 471–486.

Donoghue, E. E., McCarrey, M. W., & Clement, R. (1983). Humour appreciation as a function of canned laughter, a mirthful companion, and field dependence: Facilitation and inhibitory effects. *Canadian Journal of Behavioral Science, 15,* 150–162.

Dworkin, R. H. (1992). Affective deficits and social deficits in schizophrenia: What's what? *Schizophrenia Bulletin, 18,* 59–64.

Dworkin, R. H. (1994). Pain insensitivity in schizophrenia: A neglected phenomenon and some implications. *Schizophrenia Bulletin, 20,* 235–248.

Dworkin, R. H., Bernstein, G., Kaplansky, L. M., Lipsitz, J. D., Rinaldi, A., Slater, S. L., Cornblatt, B. A., & Erlenmeyer-Kimling, L. (1991). Social competence and positive and negative symptoms: A longitudinal study of children and adolescents at risk for schizophrenia and affective disorder. *American Journal of Psychiatry, 148,* 1182–1188.

Dworkin, R. H., Clark, S. C., Amador, X. F., & Gorman, J. M. (1996). Does affective blunting in schizophrenia reflect affective deficit or neuromotor dysfunction? *Schizophrenia Research, 20,* 301–306.

Dworkin, R. H., Clark, W. C., Lipsitz, J. D., Amador, X. F., Kaufmann, C. A., Opler, L. A., White, S. R., & Gorman, J. M. (1993). Affective deficits and pain insensitivity in schizophrenia. *Motivation and Emotion, 17,* 245–276.

Dworkin, R. H., & Cornblatt, B. A. (1995). Predicting schizophrenia. *Lancet,* *345,* 139–140.

Dworkin, R. H., Cornblatt, B. A., Friedmann, R., Kaplansky, L. M., Lewis, J. A., Rinaldi, A., Shilliday, C., & Erlenmeyer-Kimling, L. (1993). Childhood precursors of affective vs. social deficits in adolescents at risk for schizophrenia. *Schizophrenia Bulletin, 19,* 563–577.

Dworkin, R. H., & Lenzenweger, M. F. (1984). Symptoms and the genetics of schizophrenia: Implications for diagnosis. *American Journal of Psychiatry, 141,* 1541–1546.

Dworkin, R. H., Lenzenweger, M. F., Moldin, S. O., Skillings, G. F., & Levick, S. E. (1988). A multidimensional approach to the genetics of schizophrenia. *American Journal of Psychiatry, 145,* 1077–1083.

Dworkin, R. H., & Saczynski, K. (1984). Individual differences in hedonic capacity. *Journal of Personality Assessment, 48,* 620–626.

Earnst, K. S., Kring, A. M., Kadar, M. A., Salem, J. E., Shepard, D. A., Loosen, P. T. (1996). Facial expression in schizophrenia. *Biological Psychiatry, 40,* 556–558.

Ekman, P. (1972). Universals and cultural differences in facial expressions of emotion. *Nebraska Symposium on Motivation, 19,* 207–283.

Ekman, P. (1992). Facial expressions of emotion: New findings, new questions. *Psychological Science, 3,* 34–38.

Ekman, P. (1993). Facial expression and emotion. *American Psychologist, 48,* 384–392.

Ekman, P., Davidson, R. J., & Friesen, W. V. (1990). The Duchenne smile: Emotional expression and brain physiology: II. *Journal of Personality and Social Psychology, 58,* 342–353.

Ekman, P., Friesen, W. V., & Ancoli, S. (1980). Facial signs of emotional experience. *Journal of Personality and Social Psychology, 39,* 1125–1134.

Fenton, W. S., & McGlashan, T. H. (1991). Natural history of schizophrenia subtypes: II. Positive and negative symptoms and long-term course. *Archives of General Psychiatry, 48,* 978–986.

Fenton, W. S., & McGlashan, T. H. (1992). Testing systems for assessment of negative symptoms in schizophrenia. *Archives of General Psychiatry, 49,* 179–184.

Franke, P., Maier, W., Hardt, J., & Hain, C. (1993). Cognitive functioning and anhedonia in subjects at risk for schizophrenia. *Schizophrenia Research, 10,* 77–84.

Fridlund, A. (1994). *Human facial expression: An evolutionary view.* San Diego, CA: Academic Press.

Fridlund, A., Ekman, P., & Oster, H. (1987). Facial expressions of emotion: Review of literature. In A. W. Siegman & S. Feldstein (Eds.), *Nonverbal behavior and communication* (2nd ed., pp. 143–224). Hillsdale, NJ: Erlbaum.

Frijda, N. (1986). *The emotions.* New York: Cambridge University Press.

Gavanski, I. (1986). Differential sensitivity of humor ratings and mirth responses to cognitive and affective components of the humor response. *Journal of Personality and Social Psychology, 51,* 209–214.

Gottesman, I. I., McGuffin, P., & Farmer, A. (1987). Clinical genetics as clues to the "real" genetics of schizophrenia (a decade of modest gains while playing for time). *Schizophrenia Bulletin, 13,* 23–47.

Gottheil, E., Paredes, A., Exline, R. V., & Winkelmayer, R. (1970). Communication of affect in schizophrenia. *Archives of General Psychiatry, 22,* 439–444.

Gross, S., & Charlton, J. (Eds.). (1991). *Play ball! An all-star lineup of baseball cartoons.* New York: Harper.

Grove, W. M., Lebow, B. S., Clementz, B. A., Cerri, A., Medus, C., & Iacono, W. G. (1991). Familial prevalence and coaggregation of schizotypy indicators: A multitrait family study. *Journal of Abnormal Psychology, 100,* 115–121.

Holzman, P. S. (1992). Behavioral markers of schizophrenia useful for genetic studies. *Journal of Psychiatric Research, 26,* 427–445.

Izard, C. E. (1977). *Human emotions.* New York: Plenum.

Jackson, H. J., Minas, I. H., Burgess, P. M., Joshua, S. D., Charisiou, J., & Campbell, I. M. (1989). Negative symptoms and social skills performance in schizophrenia. *Schizophrenia Research, 2,* 457–463.

Jones, I. H., & Pansa, M. (1979). Some nonverbal aspects of depression and schizophrenia occurring during the interview. *Journal of Nervous and Mental Disease, 167,* 402–409.

Katsanis, J., Iacono, W. G., & Beiser, M. (1990). Anhedonia and perceptual aberration in first-episode psychotic patients and their relatives. *Journal of Abnormal Psychology, 99,* 202–206.

Kay, S. R., Fiszbein, A., & Opler, L. A. (1987). The Positive and Negative Syndrome Scale (PANSS) for schizophrenia. *Schizophrenia Bulletin, 13,* 261–276.

Kayton, L., & Koh, S. D. (1975). Hypohedonia in schizophrenia. *Journal of Nervous and Mental Disease, 161,* 412–420.

Kendler, K. S., & Hewitt, J. (1992). The structure of self-report schizotypy in twins. *Journal of Personality Disorders, 6,* 1–17.

Kendler, K. S., Karkowski-Shuman, L., O'Neill, F. A., Straub, R. E., MacLean, C. J., & Walsh, D. (1997). Resemblance of psychotic symptoms and syndromes in affected sibling pairs from the Irish Study of High-Density Schizophrenia Families: Evidence for possible etiologic heterogeneity. *American Journal of Psychiatry, 154,* 191–198.

Kendler, K. S., McGuire, M., Gruenberg, A. M., & Walsh, D. (1994). Clinical heterogeneity in schizophrenia and the pattern of psychopathology in relatives: Results from an epidemiologically-based family study. *Acta Psychiatrica Scandinavica, 89,* 294–300.

Kendler, K. S., McGuire, M., Gruenberg, A. M., & Walsh, D. (1995a). Examining the validity of *DSM-III-R* schizoaffective disorder and its putative subtypes in the Roscommon Family Study. *American Journal of Psychiatry, 152,* 755–764.

Kendler, K. S., McGuire, M., Gruenberg, A. M., & Walsh, D. (1995b). Schizotypal symptoms and signs in the Roscommon Family Study: Their factor structure and familial relationship with psychotic and affective disorders. *Archives of General Psychiatry, 52,* 296–303.

Kendler, K. S., Ochs, A. L., Gorman, A. M., Hewitt, J. K., Ross, D. E., & Mirsky, A. F. (1991). The structure of schizotypy: A pilot multitrait twin study. *Psychiatry Research, 36,* 19–36.

Kendler, K. S., Thacker, L., & Walsh, D. (1996). Self-report measures of schizotypy as indices of familial vulnerability to schizophrenia. *Schizophrenia Bulletin, 22,* 511–520.

Kerr, S. L., & Neale, J. M. (1993). Emotion perception in schizophrenia: Specific deficit or further evidence of generalized poor performance? *Journal of Abnormal Psychology, 102,* 312–318.

Kitamura, T., Kahn, A., & Kumar, R. (1984). Reliability of clinical assessment of blunted affect. *Acta Psychiatrica Scandinavica, 69,* 242–249.

Kleck, R. E., Vaughan, R. C., Cartwright-Smith, J., Vaughan, K. B., Colby,

C. Z., & Lanzetta, J. T. (1976). Effects of being observed on expressive, subjective, and physiological responses to painful stimuli. *Journal of Personality and Social Psychology, 34,* 1211–1218.

Knight, R. A., & Roff, J. D. (1985). Affectivity in schizophrenia. In M. Alpert (Ed.), *Controversies in schizophrenia: Changes and constancies* (pp. 280–316). New York: Guilford.

Knight, R. A., & Valner, J. B. (1993). Affective deficits in schizophrenia. In C. G. Costello (Ed.), *Symptoms of schizophrenia* (pp. 145–200). New York: Wiley.

Kraepelin, E. (1919). *Dementia praecox and paraphrenia* (R. M. Barclay, Trans.). Edinburgh, Scotland: Livingstone.

Krause, R., Steimer, E., Sänger-Alt, C., & Wagner, G. (1989). Facial expression of schizophrenic patients and their interaction partners. *Psychiatry, 52,* 1–12.

Kring, A. M., Alpert, M., Neale, J. M., & Harvey, P. D. (1994). A multimethod, multichannel assessment of affective flattening in schizophrenia. *Psychiatry Research, 54,* 211–222.

Kring, A. M., Kerr, S. L., Smith, D. A., & Neale, J. M. (1993). Flat affect in schizophrenia does not reflect diminished subjective experience of emotion. *Journal of Abnormal Psychology, 102,* 507–517.

Kring, A. M., & Neale, J. M. (1996). Do schizophrenic patients show a disjunctive relationship among expressive, experiential, and psychophysiological components of emotion? *Journal of Abnormal Psychology, 105,* 249–257.

Kwapil, T. R., Miller, M. B., Zinser, M. C., Chapman, J., & Chapman, L. J. (1997). Magical ideation and social anhedonia as predictors of psychosis proneness: A partial replication. *Journal of Abnormal Psychology, 106,* 491–495.

Lang, P. (1995). The emotion probe: Studies of motivation and attention. *American Psychologist, 50,* 372–385.

Lazarus, R. S. (1991). *Emotion and adaptation.* New York: Oxford University Press.

Lenzenweger, M. F., & Dworkin, R. H. (1996). The dimensions of schizophrenia phenomenology? Not one or two, at least three, perhaps four. *British Journal of Psychiatry, 168,* 432–440.

Lenzenweger, M. F., Dworkin, R. H., & Wethington, E. (1989). Models of positive and negative symptoms in schizophrenia: An empirical evaluation of latent structures. *Journal of Abnormal Psychology, 98,* 62–70.

Lenzenweger, M. F., Dworkin, R. H., & Wethington, E. (1991). Examining the underlying structure of schizophrenic phenomenology: Evidence for a three-process model. *Schizophrenia Bulletin, 17,* 515–524.

Lewine, R. J., & Sommers, A. A. (1985). Clinical definition of negative symptoms as a reflection of theory and methodology. In M. Alpert (Ed.), *Controversies in schizophrenia: Changes and constancies* (pp. 267–279). New York: Guilford.

Liberman, R. P., Mueser, K. T., Wallace, C. J., Jacobs, H. E., Eckman, T., & Massel, H. K. (1986). Training skills in the psychiatrically disabled: Learning coping and competence. *Schizophrenia Bulletin, 12,* 631–647.

Lindsay, W. R. (1982). The effects of labeling: Blind and nonblind ratings of social skills in schizophrenic and nonschizophrenic control subjects. *American Journal of Psychiatry, 139,* 216–219.

Manschreck, T. C. (1989). Motor abnormalities and the psychopathology of schizophrenia. In B. Kirkcaldy (Ed.), *Normalities and abnormalities in human movement* (pp. 100–127). Basel, Switzerland: Karger.

Manschreck, T. C. (1993). Psychomotor abnormalities. In C. G. Costello (Ed.), *Symptoms of schizophrenia* (pp. 261–290). New York: Wiley.

Manschreck, T. C., Maher, B. A., Rucklos, M. E., & Vereen, D. R. (1982). Disturbed voluntary motor activity in schizophrenic disorder. *Psychological Medicine, 12,* 73–84.

Manschreck, T. C., Maher, B. A., Waller, N. G., Ames, D., & Latham, C. A. (1985). Deficient motor synchrony in schizophrenic disorders: Clinical correlates. *Biological Psychiatry, 20,* 990–1002.

Masten, A. S. (1986). Humor and competence in school-aged children. *Child Development, 57,* 461–473.

Masten, A. S. (1989). Humor appreciation in children: Individual differences and response sets. *Humor, 2–4,* 365–384.

Mattes, R. M., Schneider, F., Heimann, H., & Birbaumer, N. (1995). Reduced emotional response of schizophrenic patients in remission during social interaction. *Schizophrenia Research, 17,* 249–255.

Matthysse, S., Levy, D. L., Kinney, D., Deutsch, C., Lajonchere, C., Yurgelun-Todd, D., Woods, B., & Holzman, P. S. (1992). Gene expession in mental illness: A navigation chart to future progress. *Journal of Psychiatric Research, 26,* 461–473.

Matthysse, S., & Parnas, J. (1992). Extending the phenotype of schizophrenia: Implications for linkage analysis. *Journal of Psychiatric Research, 26,* 329–344.

Mayer, M., Alpert, M., Stastny, P., Perlick, D., & Empfield, M. (1985). Multiple contributions to clinical presentation of flat affect in schizophrenia. *Schizophrenia Bulletin, 11,* 420–426.

McGlashan, T. H., & Fenton, W. S. (1992). The positive–negative distinction in schizophrenia: Review of natural history validators. *Archives of General Psychiatry, 49,* 63–72.

McGuffin, P., Farmer, A., & Gottesman, I. I. (1987). Is there really a split in schizophrenia? The genetic evidence. *British Journal of Psychiatry, 150,* 581–592.

Meehl, P. E. (1990). Toward an integrated theory of schizotaxia, schizotypy, and schizophrenia. *Journal of Personality Disorders, 4,* 1–99.

Moore, S. (1989). *Born in the bleachers.* New York: Collier Books.

Morrison, R. L., & Wixted, J. T. (1989). Social skills training. In A. S. Bellack (Ed.), *A clinical guide for the treatment of schizophrenia* (pp. 237–261). New York: Plenum.

Mueser, K. T., Bellack, A. S., Morrison, R. L., & Wixted, J. T. (1990). Social competence in schizophrenia: Premorbid adjustment, social skill, and domains of functioning. *Journal of Psychiatric Research, 24,* 51–63.

Neale, J. M., Oltmanns, T. F., & Harvey, P. D. (1985). The need to relate cognitive deficits to specific behavioral referents of schizophrenia. *Schizophrenia Bulletin, 11,* 286–291.

Nurnberger, J. I., Blehar, M. C., Kaufmann, C. A., York-Cooler, C., Simpson, S. G., Harkavy-Friedman, J., Severe, J. B., Malaspina, D., Reich, T., & collaborators from the NIMH Genetics Initiative. (1994). Diagnostic interview for genetic studies: Rationale, unique features, and training. *Archives of General Psychiatry, 51,* 849–859.

Oatley, K., & Jenkins, J. M. (1996). *Understanding emotions.* Cambridge, MA: Blackwell.

Ortony, A., & Turner, T. J. (1990). What's basic about basic emotions? *Psychological Review, 97,* 315–331.

Plutchik, R. (1980). *Emotion: A psychoevolutionary synthesis.* New York: Harper & Row.

Prosser, E. S., Csernansky, J. G., Kaplan, J., Thiemann, S., Becker, T. J., & Hollister, L. E. (1987). Depression, parkinsonian symptoms, and negative symptoms in schizophrenics treated with neuroleptics. *Journal of Nervous and Mental Disease, 175,* 100–105.

Rado, S. (1953). Dynamics and classification of disordered behavior. *American Journal of Psychiatry, 110,* 406–416.

Rinn, W. E. (1984). The neuropsychology of facial expression: A review of the neurological and psychological mechanisms for producing facial expressions. *Psychological Bulletin, 95,* 52–77.

Roseman, I. J., Wiest, C., & Swartz, T. S. (1994). Phenomenology, behaviors, and goals differentiate discrete emotions. *Journal of Personality and Social Psychology, 67,* 206–221.

Rosenberg, E. L., & Ekman, P. (1994). Coherence between expressive and experiential systems in emotion. *Cognition and Emotion, 8,* 201–229.

Ross, E. D., & Mesulam, M. (1979). Dominant language functions of the right hemisphere? Prosody and emotional gesturing. *Archives of Neurology, 36,* 144–148.

Rothbart, M. K., Posner, M. I., & Rosicky, J. (1994). Orienting in normal and pathological development. *Development and Psychopathology, 6,* 635–652.

Rozin, P., Haidt, J., & McCauley, C. R. (1993). Disgust. In M. Lewis & J. M. Haviland (Eds.), *Handbook of emotions* (pp. 575–594). New York: Guilford.

Ruch, W. (1995). Will the real relationship between facial expression and affective experience please stand up: The case of exhilaration. *Cognition and Emotion, 9,* 33–58.

Russell, J. A. (1994). Is there universal recognition of emotion from facial expression? A review of cross-cultural studies. *Psychological Bulletin, 115,* 102–141.

Scherer, K., Wallbott, H., & Summerfield, A. (1986). *Experiencing emotion: A cross-cultural study.* New York: Cambridge University Press.

Schneider, F., Ellgring, H., Friedrich, J., Fus, I., Beyer, T., Heimann, H., & Himer, W. (1992). The effects of neuroleptics on facial action in schizophrenic patients. *Pharmacopsychiatry, 25,* 233–239.

Steimer-Krause, E., Krause, R., & Wagner, G. (1990). Interaction regulations used by schizophrenic and psychsomatic patients: Studies on facial behavior in dyadic interactions. *Psychiatry, 53*, 209–228.

Strauss, J. S., Carpenter, W. T., Jr., & Bartko, J. J. (1974). The diagnosis and understanding of schizophrenia: Part III. Speculations on the processes that underlie schizophrenic symptoms and signs. *Schizophrenia Bulletin, 1*, 61–69.

Tollefson, G. D., Beasley, C. M., Jr., Tran, P. V., Street, J. S., Krueger, J. A., Tamura, R. N., Graffeo, K. A., & Thieme, M. E. (1997). Olanzapine versus haloperidol in the treatment of schizophrenia and schizoaffective and schizophreniform disorders: Results of an international collaborative trial. *American Journal of Psychiatry, 154*, 457–465.

Tollefson, G. D., & Sanger, T. M. (1997). Negative symptoms: A path analytic approach to a double-blind, placebo- and haloperidol-controlled clinical trial with olanzapine. *American Journal of Psychiatry, 154*, 466–474.

Tsuang, M. T. (1993). Genotypes, phenotypes, and the brain: A search for connections in schizophrenia. *British Journal of Psychiatry, 163*, 299–307.

Tsuang, M. T., Gilbertson, M. W., & Faraone, S. V. (1991). Genetic transmission of negative and positive symptoms in the biological relatives of schizophrenics. In A. Marneros, N. C. Andreasen, & M. T. Tsuang (Eds.), *Negative versus positive schiozophrenia* (pp. 265–291). Berlin, Germany: Springer-Verlag.

Walker, E. F. (1994). Developmentally moderated expressions of the neuropathology underlying schizophrenia. *Schizophrenia Bulletin, 20*, 453–480.

Walker, E. F., Grimes, K. E., Davis, D. M., & Smith, A. J. (1993). Childhood precursors of schizophrenia: Facial expressions of emotion. *American Journal of Psychiatry, 150*, 1654–1660.

Wolkin, A., Sanfilipo, M., Wolf, A. P., Angrist, B., Brodie, J. D., & Rotrosen, J. (1992). Negative symptoms and hypofrontality in chronic schizophrenia. *Archives of General Psychiatry, 49*, 959–965.

Zajonc, R. B. (1984). On the primacy of affect. *American Psychologist, 39*, 117–123.

PART FOUR

Developmental Processes, Course, and Outcome

Prediction From Longitudinal Assessments of High-Risk Children

L. Erlenmeyer-Kimling, Simone A. Roberts,
Donald Rock, Ulla Hildoff Adamo,
Barbara Maminski Shapiro, and Sky Pape

The New York High-Risk Project (NYHRP; Erlenmeyer-Kimling & Cornblatt, 1987b; Erlenmeyer-Kimling et al., 1984, 1995) is a multitrait, multimeasurement prospective study, in which two independent samples of offspring of schizophrenic, affectively ill (those with major depression or bipolar 1 disorder), and psychiatrically normal parents have been followed from mid-childhood to midadulthood. Started in 1971, the NYHRP was one of several investigations (Watt, Anthony, Wynne, & Rolf, 1984) that began in the 1960s and early 1970s with the intention—as had been suggested in the first formal proposal of the high-risk research paradigm (Pearson & Kley, 1957)—of carrying out longitudinal assessments of children at increased statistical risk for developing schizophrenia, compared with a general population risk of about 1%.

The goal was to identify variables that might predict the development of schizophrenia as the children reached adulthood. These studies

The project was supported in part by a MERIT award from the National Institute of Mental Health (Grant R37 MH19560-25), by the Office of Mental Health of the State of New York, and by Clinical Research Center Grant MH20906.

of high-risk offspring, as well as later studies using different approaches to search for early precursors, cast a wide net and appear from the recent literature to have collected a large haul of characteristics putatively associated either with high-risk status or with later schizophrenia itself, among them, for example, (a) separation from the affected parent (e.g., Mednick, Cudeck, Griffith, Talovic, & Schulsinger, 1984) and other aspects of family relationships and communication patterns (e.g., Watt, 1984); (b) maternal influenza during pregnancy (e.g., Mednick, Huttunen, & Machon, 1994; Sham et al., 1992) and other perinatal complications (e.g., McNeil, 1987; O'Callaghan et al., 1992); (c) social and school behavior, particularly during young adolescence (Dworkin, Lewis, Cornblatt, & Erlenmeyer-Kimling, 1994; Jones, Rodgers, Murray, & Marmot, 1994; Olin et al., 1997); and (d) a number of biobehavioral domains of functioning (e.g., Erlenmeyer-Kimling & Cornblatt, 1987a; Holzman, 1992; Nuechterlein & Dawson, 1984; Watt et al., 1984).

Little attempt has been made, however, to distinguish between precursors that interact with or potentiate (Meehl, 1962) the genetic liability to schizophrenia, such as those in categories a and b above, and variables that are probably expressions of the liability itself, for example, categories c and d. Interactive or potentiating variables usually have been found to explain only a small percentage of the increase in risk of actually developing schizophrenia. This is to be expected as many models of schizophrenia currently suggest that there are few (if any) specific, but many nonspecific and idiosyncratic, environmental factors implicated in the development of schizophrenia (e.g., Erlenmeyer-Kimling et al., 1984; Gottesman & Shields, 1972; Woolf, 1997). Moreover, as Erlenmeyer-Kimling et al. (1984) noted, the usefulness of family interaction and most other types of environmental data collected on offspring living with their schizophrenic parents is questionable because it cannot be generalized to the backgrounds of the majority of schizophrenia patients, most of whom did not have an affected parent. They have argued, therefore, that high-risk studies need to focus on early biobehavioral traits, which may reflect premorbid effects of the genes underlying the illness. The emphasis in the NYHRP, accordingly, has been on several such variables. We summarize some of the recent findings below.

DESCRIPTION OF THE NYHRP (1971-1996)

The NYHRP includes two samples of individuals followed prospectively since the ages of 7 to 12. Sample A was recruited in 1971–1972 and Sample B in 1977–1979. Both samples consist of offspring of schizophrenic, affectively ill, and psychiatrically normal parents (HRSz, HRAff, and NC groups, respectively). Offspring in both samples and all groups were free of psychiatric disorders at the time of entry into the study. Both samples have been followed continuously since recruitment, with six rounds of tests and assessments at intervals of approximately 2.5 years apart and telephone interviews conducted at least once every year.

Details of the inclusion criteria for the children and parents and descriptions of the diagnostic procedures for the parents have been reported previously (Erlenmeyer-Kimling & Cornblatt, 1987b; Erlenmeyer-Kimling et al., 1995). Measures assessed at the various testing rounds have been described in a number of articles (e.g., Cornblatt & Erlenmeyer-Kimling, 1985; Erlenmeyer-Kimling & Cornblatt, 1992; Erlenmeyer-Kimling, Golden, & Cornblatt, 1989) as well as in the articles summarized below regarding the relationship between performance on specific measures in early test rounds and adulthood diagnoses of schizophrenia-related psychoses and other disorders.

Of the 206 individuals originally recruited in Sample A and 150 in Sample B, 188 and 132, respectively, were followed and assessed with diagnostic interviews in adulthood. They are 54 HRSz, 41 HRAff, and 93 NC participants in Sample A (86%, 95%, and 93% of the original groups) and 39, 32, and 61, respectively, in Sample B (85%, 82%, and 94% of the original groups). Details were described for the diagnostic assessments for Sample A offspring (Erlenmeyer-Kimling et al., 1995) using the Schedule for Affective Disorders and Schizophrenia–Lifetime version (SADS-L; Spitzer & Endicott, 1978) interviews to obtain Axis I diagnoses according to the Research Diagnostic Criteria (RDC; Spitzer, Endicott, & Robins, 1978) and Personality Disorder Examination (PDE; Loranger, Susman, Oldham, & Russakoff, 1987) interviews for the *Diagnostic and Statistical Manual of Mental Disorders* (3rd ed., rev. [*DSM-III-R*]; American Psychiatric Association [APA], 1987) Axis II diagnoses. The same interviews were also administered to Sample B according to the procedures described for Sample A. The latest evaluation of Axis I diagnoses, used for the present report, was effective at a mean age of 31.1 years for Sample A and 27.1 years for Sample B, as of Autumn 1995.

PREVALENCE OF ADULTHOOD PSYCHIATRIC DISORDERS IN NYHRP PARTICIPANTS

Prevalence rates have been reported for psychotic disorders for Sample A participants alone in Erlenmeyer-Kimling et al. (1995) and for all Axis I disorders for the same participants and their (mostly older) siblings in a later article (Erlenmeyer-Kimling et al., 1997). Table 1 presents prevalence rates (not age corrected) for (a) schizophrenia-related psychoses (schizophrenia, mainly schizophrenic schizoaffective disorder according to the RDC distinction, and unspecified psychosis), (b) major affective disorders in total and subdivided into psychotic and nonpsychotic disorders (bipolar I or II disorder and unipolar major depression), (c) anxiety disorders (phobic disorders, generalized anxiety disorder, and panic disorder), and (d) substance abuse (alcohol and drug abuse). The proportions of participants in each risk group with no Axis I disorder and with two or more Axis I disorders are also shown in Table 1.

In both samples, schizophrenia-related psychoses occurred with greatest frequency in the HRSz group, as expected, and, especially for Sample A, are consistent with rates reported for offspring of schizophrenic parents in the earlier literature and in other current samples (see Erlenmeyer-Kimling et al., 1995). The frequency of major affective disorders did not differ significantly among the groups in either sample but tended to be lower in the NC group, particularly in Sample B. Psychotic affective disorders also did not differ significantly but, again, tended to occur with lower frequency in the NC group. Anxiety disorders, which tended to be most common in the HRAff group and least common in the HRSz group in Sample A, showed remarkably little difference across Sample B's three groups. The NC group had a greater percentage of participants with no Axis I disorder and a smaller per-

Table 1

Prevalence (Not Age Corrected) of Selected Axis I Disorders in Each Sample

Variable	Sample A			Sample B		
	HRSz	HRAff	NC	HRSz	HRAff	NC
N	54	41	93	39	32	61
No Axis I disorders (%)	33.3	26.8	40.9	33.3	28.1	42.6
Less than 2 Axis I disorders (%)	35.2[a]	56.1[cc]	29.0	46.2[b]	46.9[c]	23.0
Schizophrenia-related psychosis (%)	18.5[bb]	9.8[c]	1.1	7.7	0.0	0.0
Major affective disorders (%)	37.0[1]	48.8	31.2	41.0[1]	40.6	24.6
Psychotic	3.7	4.9	0.0	7.7	6.3	1.6
Nonpsychotic	35.2	43.9	31.2	35.9	34.4	23.0
Anxiety disorders (%)	16.7	29.3	20.4	12.8	12.5	11.5
Substance abuse (%)	29.6	39.0	33.3	43.6	46.9	39.3

Note. Mean age at last diagnostic information (Autumn 1995) was 31.1 ± 1.83 years (Sample A) and 27.1 ± 2.23 years (Sample B). Schizophrenia-related psychosis = schizophrenia, mainly schizophrenic schizoaffective disorder, unspecified psychosis; major affective disorders = bipolar I, bipolar II, unipolar disorder; HRSz = high risk for schizophrenic disorders group; HRAff = high risk for affective disorders group; NC = normal comparison group. *p* values for group contrasts: HRSz vs. HRAff: [a]*p* ≤ .05; HRSz vs. NC: [b] *p* ≤ .05, [bb]*p* ≤ .01; HRAff vs. NC: [c]*p* ≤ .05, [cc]*p* ≤ .01.
[1]One participant was comorbid for psychotic and nonpsychotic major affective disorders.

centage with two or more Axis I disorders in both samples compared with the HRSz and HRAff groups (Erlenmeyer-Kimling et al., 1997). Although we expect to see few further cases of schizophrenia-related psychoses in Sample A, we estimated on the basis of the current ages of the Sample B participants and the age-at-onset pattern demonstrated in Sample A that the total prevalence rate for these disorders in Sample B may increase substantially. Analyses of prediction to schizophrenia-related psychoses in adulthood may, therefore, be premature for this sample and may eventually yield stronger results than those reported below.

Reports on Axis II disorders for Sample A participants in several articles (e.g., Squires-Wheeler et al., 1993; Squires-Wheeler, Skodol, & Erlenmeyer-Kimling, 1992) have shown (a) higher rates of most of the personality disorders in both high-risk groups (HRSz and HRAff) than in the NC group, as would be expected, but (b) no difference in rates of schizotypal personality disorder (STPD) in the HRSz and HRAff groups. Rates of the several personality disorders are similar in Sample B to those reported in Sample A, again, with no difference in STPD between the HRSz and HRAff groups. Erlenmeyer-Kimling et al. (1995) noted that several other research teams (e.g., Kety et al., 1994; Lyons, Toomey, Faraone, & Tsuang, 1994; Maier, Lichtermann, Minges, & Heun, 1994) have also reported finding little difference in the prevalence of STPD between relatives of schizophrenia and affectively ill probands. Some authors have pointed out, however, that the disorder observed in families of affective disorder probands may not actually be the same entity as the one associated with familial risk for schizophrenia (Lyons et al, 1994; Siever, Keefe, & Bernstein, 1991) and that efforts need to be made to identify particular features that distinguish between the relatives of the two types of probands (Squires-Wheeler et al., 1992; Torgersen, Onstad, Skre, Edvarsen, & Kringlen, 1993). Squires-Wheeler et al., for example, have shown that schizotypal features in adolescence predict different Axis I disorders at a later assessment in offspring of schizophrenic versus affectively ill parents, just as other researchers (Lyons et al., 1994) have found that different comorbid disorders are associated with STPD in relatives of affectively ill and schizophrenia probands.

432

Other evidence, too, has been elucidated in the NYHRP that suggests that the *DSM-III* (APA, 1980) and *DSM-III-R* (APA, 1987) criteria for Cluster A (STPD, schizoid, paranoid) personality disorders may not be the best for identifying conditions with a familial relationship to schizophrenia. For example, latent structure analyses of the *DSM-III-R*-based PDE data on the NC families indicated that STPD and paranoid personality disorder are not discrete personality variants (Moldin, Rice, Erlenmeyer-Kimling, & Squires-Wheeler, 1994). By contrast, the Minnesota Multiphasic Personality Inventory yielded a distinct cluster of personality aberrations that clearly differentiates the HRSz group from both of the other groups (Moldin, Gottesman, Erlenmeyer-Kimling, & Cornblatt, 1990). Thus, attempts are being made to categorize the NYHRP participants according to other classifications of personality features. These include ratings of social competence based on videotaped interviews at various ages (Dworkin et al., 1994), evaluations of negative and positive dimensions of STPD (Squires-Wheeler et al., 1997), and factor analyses of the PDE scales. The latter analyses have yielded a social isolation factor (Cornblatt, Lenzenweger, Dworkin, & Erlenmeyer-Kimling, 1992; Erlenmeyer-Kimling et al., 1993) as well as factors indicating lack of empathy and social insecurity (Freedman, Rock, Roberts, Cornblatt, & Erlenmeyer-Kimling, 1998), all of which relate to HRSz group membership but not to membership in either of the other two groups.

BETWEEN-GROUP DIFFERENCES IN CHILDHOOD MEASURES

Prospective high-risk studies are usually obliged to follow their participants for several years before deviant psychiatric outcomes become apparent. Thus, in studies which begin by examining possible predictor variables in childhood or even earlier (e.g., Fish, 1984; McNeil, 1987), there is necessarily a long wait until hypothesized associations between such variables and later indexes of psychopathology can be verified. In the NYHRP, in which the participants were on average 9.0 to 9.5 years old at the first examination, we have had to hold our questions about predictive relations in abeyance for a number of years and, instead, to focus initially on a search for differences between the HRSz and the other two groups.

Establishment of differences between risk groups with respect to neurobehavioral or other variables does not answer questions about prediction to schizophrenia or other psychiatric outcomes. However, identification of variables that are more frequently dysfunctional in off-spring and other relatives of schizophrenia probands than in controls is useful because it (a) helps to pinpoint variables that may be an ex-pression of the genetic liability and (b) narrows down the search for variables that may be strongly associated with later outcomes of interest. Within the group at risk for schizophrenia, however, not all variables that are expressions of the genetic liability are strongly correlated with the development of schizophrenia as an outcome because some indi-viduals with the liability may exhibit deviance in certain neurobehaviors without later developing the disorder. Thus, merely demonstrating that a variable is significantly more often deviant in individuals at risk for schizophrenia does not indicate that the variable will predict which members of the high-risk group will develop the disorder.

In the NYHRP, we have found abundant evidence of differences in cognitive and other variables between the HRSz and the other two groups. For example, we have observed significant differences between the HRSz and NC groups (and in many instances between the HRSz and HRAff groups as well) with respect to (a) deviance on a battery of attentional tests administered in childhood (e.g., Erlenmeyer-Kimling & Cornblatt, 1992); (b) membership in a composite of attentional, IQ, and neuromotor measures that identifies a taxon of participants within the HRSz group (Erlenmeyer-Kimling et al., 1989); (c) relatively im-paired performance on gross neuromotor measures (Erlenmeyer-Kimling et al., 1998); (d) poor verbal working memory (Erlenmeyer-Kimling et al., 1998); (e) behavior in school during adolescence (Watt, Grubb, & Erlenmeyer-Kimling, 1984); (f) a factor representing a com-posite of childhood behavior problems (i.e., discipline problems, fight-ing, poor sibling and peer relationships, temper tantrums, and eating problems; Amminger et al., 1998); (g) lower IQ scores; and (h) IQ subtest scatter (Ott et al., in press). In all instances, differences between the HRSz and NC groups (or HRSz and HRAff groups) were in the direction of poorer performance or more deviant behavior among the individuals at risk for schizophrenia.

Recently, we have also been able to evaluate between-group differences in tests administered in adulthood. Although adulthood measures cannot be considered to be predictors of psychopathology, their correlation with risk group membership is of interest. We have observed significant differences between the HRSz group and the other groups in the following measures administered in adulthood: (a) eye-tracking performance (Rosenberg, Sweeney, Squires-Wheeler, Cornblatt, & Erlenmeyer-Kimling, 1997), (b) visual fixation (Amador, Amodt, Gassaway, Roberts, & Erlenmeyer-Kimling, 1998), (c) performance on the Wisconsin Card Sorting Test (Wolf, Cornblatt, Roberts, Shapiro, & Erlenmeyer-Kimling, 1998), and (d) the Thought Disorder Index (Coleman et al., 1998).

PREDICTION OF GLOBAL ADJUSTMENT, CLUSTER A PERSONALITY FEATURES, AND SOCIAL FUNCTIONING

It has been shown in a number of earlier reports with a focus on attentional deviance (summarized in Erlenmeyer-Kimling & Cornblatt, 1992) that poor performance on attentional measures administered in childhood (between ages 7 and 12) not only occurred more frequently in the HRSz children of both samples than in the HRAff or NC children but also was associated with poor global adjustment in adolescence among the HRSz participants. A similar relationship between the childhood measures of attention and adolescent measures of global adjustment, however, was not seen in the other two groups.

Similarly, childhood attentional deviance is associated with measures of later social adjustment in HRSz participants but not in members of the HRAff or NC groups. Cornblatt et al. (1992) have hypothesized that early problems in attentional functioning may underlie a gradual development of difficulties in forming social connectedness.

Thus, in HRSz participants, poor attentional performance at the mean age of 9.0–9.5 has been found to be associated with both adolescent measures of lack of social competence, as evidenced in a videotaped interview (Dworkin et al., 1993), and physical anhedonia (Erlenmeyer-Kimling et al., 1993; Freedman et al., 1998) and early adulthood measures of social isolation (Cornblatt et al., 1992) as well as lack of empathy and social insecurity (Freedman et al., 1998).

Links between other aspects of childhood behavior and social or personality functioning at later ages have also been noted in the HRSz participants. For example, Amminger et al. (1998) have demonstrated that the childhood problem behavior factor described above not only occurs most commonly in the HRSz group but also has different predictive relationships in the different groups. In the HRSz participants, this factor, assessed at a mean age of 9, is linked with the later development of Cluster A personality disorders, whereas in HRAff and NC participants the childhood behavior factor is associated with the development of substance abuse disorders rather than Cluster A disorders.

Squires-Wheeler et al. (1997) have shown a differential pattern of correlations between cognitive measures obtained in childhood and adolescence and dimensions of STPD in adulthood. Specifically, in HRSz participants, negative symptom features of STPD (based on the PDE) were related to poor childhood performance on the Digit Span subtest of the Wechsler IQ Scale for Children and amplitude reduction in the P3 component of the event-related potentials assessed in adolescence. Similar relationships were not found in the other two groups of the NYHRP or between cognitive measures and positive symptom features in any of the three groups under study.

PREDICTION OF SCHIZOPHRENIA-RELATED PSYCHOSES

Mean differences between groups, which are often based chiefly on a subset of performance outliers, typically begin to be examined in childhood in high-risk research. Relationships between early deviance on neurobehavioral measures and personality traits or other global signs of psychopathological adjustments that emerge in adolescence, too, can be identified well before the participants reach the peak risk period for schizophrenia. Evaluation of the effectiveness of measures examined in childhood or young adolescence in predicting schizophrenia or related psychoses, however, requires waiting until the individuals have completed their 20s, at least. Thus, in the NYHRP, it has only recently become possible to carry out such analyses.

We have recently considered prediction for three neurobehavioral measures that had shown a significant difference between the HRSz and NC groups in the first round of testing (at ages 7–12). We used the following measures: (a) the Attention Deviance Index (ADI), a composite measure of deviance on attentional tests, as summarized in Erlenmeyer-Kimling and Cornblatt (1992); (b) verbal working memory, a factor extracted by factor analysis from the same attentional tests (Erlenmeyer-Kimling et al., 1997, 1998); and (c) Gross Motor Dysfunction, a subscale based on selected items from the Lincoln–Oseretsky Test of Motor Impairment (Erlenmeyer-Kimling et al., 1998). These analyses, conducted in both samples separately and combined, have shown similar relationships in the two samples. However, because of the younger age of Sample B and the strong possibility, mentioned earlier, that the rate of schizophrenia-related psychoses can be expected to increase in this sample, we summarize here the findings on Sample A only.

As shown in Table 2, the verbal working memory factor shows a remarkably high rate of prediction (sensitivity) to schizophrenia-related psychoses in the HRSz group; that is, 88.9% of the HRSz participants who developed these disorders had shown impairment on the factor in childhood. Gross Motor Dysfunction is also a good predictor. The composite ADI, although it related to global measures of poor adjustment and poor social outcomes in the HRSz group (see previous section), is not a good predictor of schizophrenia-related psychoses. All three measures, however, showed substantial specificity in their relationship to the HRSz group as a whole, with virtually none of the NC participants exhibiting gross motor dysfunction or verbal working memory impairment and very few manifesting poor ADI scores; similarly, significantly

Table 2

Prediction of Schizophrenia-Related Psychoses on the Basis of Childhood (ages 7–12) Measures in Sample A

| Childhood measures | Percentage of participants deviant on childhood measure | | | | | | | | |
| | HRSz | | | HRAff | | | NC | | |
	All	SRP	NOSRP	All	SRP	NOSRP	All	SRP	NOSRP
N	51	10	41	36	4	32	89	1	88
ADI ≥ 4	27.5	10.0	31.7	8.3	25.0	6.3	4.5	0.0	4.5
Gross motor dysfunction	47.1	80.0	39.0	14.6	50.0	10.8	0.0	0.0	0.0
Verbal working memory	50.0	88.9	41.0	22.9	50.0	19.4	0.0	0.0	0.0

Note. HRSz = high risk for schizophrenic disorders group; HRAff = high risk for affective disorders group; NC = normal comparison group; SRP = schizophrenia-related psychoses (schizophrenia, mainly schizophrenic schizoaffective disorder, unspecified psychosis); NOSRP = no schizophrenia-related psychoses. Childhood measures: ADI ≥ 4 = Composite of Attention Deviance Index: 4 or more response indexes; gross motor dysfunction = dysfunction on a gross motor subscale of the Lincoln–Oseretsky test of motor impairment; verbal working memory = verbal working memory factor derived from attentional tests.

fewer HRAff than HRSz participants were deviant on any of the three measures. The false-positive rates for each of the measures, however, were moderately large in the HRSz group. False positives are the individuals who show deviance on a given childhood measure but have not developed a schizophrenia-related psychosis. A possible explanation is that many of the false positives are individuals who have the genetic liability to schizophrenia but fail to develop the full clinical syndrome. If we think of schizophrenia as a complex genetic disorder in which several, probably fungible (capable of being used in place of another), genes play a part in reaching a threshold at which the disorder is manifested, then it can be envisaged how different dysfunctions may be expressed singly in some at-risk individuals without reaching the critical threshold for the disorder itself. The task remaining in the NYHRP is to examine interrelations among the many early signs and potentiators of deviance and their collective impact on different behavioral, social, and adulthood psychiatric outcomes.

CONCLUSIONS

As a group, the offspring of schizophrenic parents in the NYHRP exhibited a number of differences in neurobehavioral characteristics and social behavior in childhood and adolescence compared with the groups with affectively ill or psychiatrically normal parents. Likewise, a number of relationships between disturbances in childhood performance on cognitive measures and later assessments of both nonspecific adjustment and specific personality dysfunctions emerged in the HRSz group but not in the other two groups. Childhood measures of verbal working memory impairment and gross motor impairment had predictive associations with schizophrenia-related psychoses in the HRSz participants. The strong and specific predictive associations of verbal working memory, both with group membership (HRSz) and schizophrenia-related psychoses, suggested that the gene(s) underlying this factor may be a necessary constant in an otherwise fungible set of genes implicated in the susceptibility to schizophrenia.

REFERENCES

Amador, X. F., Amodt, I., Gassaway, S., Roberts, S. A., & Erlenmeyer-Kimling, L. (1998). *Visual fixation abnormalities in the offspring from the New York High-Risk Project*. Manuscript under review.

American Psychiatric Association. (1980). *Diagnostic and statistical manual for mental disorders* (3rd ed.). Washington, DC: Author.

American Psychiatric Association. (1987). *Diagnostic and statistical manual for mental disorders* (3rd ed., rev.). Washington, DC: Author.

Amminger, G. P., Squires-Wheeler, E., Ott, S. L., Roberts, S., Kestenbaum, C., Pape, S., Rende, R., Rock, D., & Erlenmeyer-Kimling, L. (1998). *Behavior problems in childhood: A prospective analysis of different links to adulthood psychopathology in the subjects of the New York High-Risk Project*. Manuscript under review.

Coleman, M. J., Shenton, M. E., Levy, D. L., Shapiro, B. M., Holzman, P., & Erlenmeyer-Kimling, L. (1998). *Thought disorder in offspring of schizophrenic parents in the New York High-Risk Project*. Manuscript in preparation, Harvard University.

Cornblatt, B., & Erlenmeyer-Kimling, L. (1985). Global attentional deviance in children at risk for schizophrenia: Specificity and predictive validity. *Journal of Abnormal Psychology, 94*, 470–486.

Cornblatt, B. A., Lenzenweger, M. F., Dworkin, R. H., & Erlenmeyer-Kimling, L. (1992). Childhood attentional dysfunctions predict social deficits in unaffected adults at risk for schizophrenia. *British Journal of Psychiatry, 161*(Suppl. 18), 59–64.

Dworkin, R. H., Cornblatt, B., Friedman, R., Kaplansky, L. M., Lewis, J. A., Rinaldi, A., Shilliday, C., & Erlenmeyer-Kimling, L. (1993). Childhood precursors of affective versus social deficits in adolescents at risk for schizophrenia. *Schizophrenia Bulletin, 19*, 563–577.

Dworkin, R. H., Lewis, J. A., Cornblatt, B., & Erlenmeyer-Kimling, L. (1994). Social competence deficits in adolescents at risk for schizophrenia. *Journal of Nervous and Mental Disorders, 182*, 103–108.

Erlenmeyer-Kimling, L., & Cornblatt, B. (1987a). High-risk research in schizophrenia: A summary of what has been learned. *Journal of Psychiatric Research, 21*, 401–411.

Erlenmeyer-Kimling, L., & Cornblatt, B. (1987b). The New York High-Risk Project: A follow-up report. *Schizophrenia Bulletin, 13,* 451–463.

Erlenmeyer-Kimling, L., & Cornblatt, B. (1992). A summary of attentional findings in the New York High-Risk Project. *Journal of Psychiatric Research, 26,* 405–426.

Erlenmeyer-Kimling, L., Cornblatt, B. A., Rock, D., Roberts, S., Bell, M., & West, A. (1993). The New York High-Risk Project: Anhedonia, attentional deviance, and psychopathology. *Schizophrenia Bulletin, 19,* 141–153.

Erlenmeyer-Kimling, L., Golden, R., & Cornblatt, B. (1989). A taxometric analysis of cognitive and neuromotor variables in children at risk for schizophrenia. *Journal of Abnormal Psychology, 98,* 203–208.

Erlenmeyer-Kimling, L., Hilldoff Adamo, U., Rock, D., Roberts, S. A., Bassett, A. S., Squires-Wheeler, E., Cornblatt, B. A., Endicott, J., Pape, S., & Gottesman, I. I. (1997). The New York High-Risk Project: Prevalence and comorbidity of Axis I disorders in offspring of schizophrenic parents at 25 years of follow-up. *Archives of General Psychiatry, 54,* 1096–1102.

Erlenmeyer-Kimling, L., Marcuse, Y., Cornblatt, B., Friedman, D., Rainer, J. D., & Rutschmann, J. (1984). The New York High-Risk Project. In N. Watt, E. J. Anthony, L. Wynne, & J. Rolf (Eds.), *Children at risk for schizophrenia: A longitudinal perspective* (pp. 169–189). New York: Cambridge University Press.

Erlenmeyer-Kimling, L., Squires-Wheeler, E., Adamo, U. H., Bassett, A., Cornblatt, B., Kestenbaum, C. J., Rock, D., Roberts, S. A., & Gottesman, I. I. (1995). The New York High-Risk Project: Lifetime diagnoses of psychoses and cluster A personality disorders in the offspring of schizophrenic parents at 23 years of follow-up. *Archives of General Psychiatry, 52,* 857–865.

Erlenmeyer-Kimling, L., Rock, D., Janal, M., Amminger, G. P., Squires-Wheeler, E., Ott, S., Cornblatt, B., Roberts, S., & Pape, S. (1997, April). *Evaluation of the effectiveness of early predictors of schizophrenia spectrum disorders in the New York High-Risk Project.* Poster session at the International Congress on Schizophrenia Research, Colorado Springs, CO.

Erlenmeyer-Kimling, L., Rock, D., Roberts, S., Janal, M., Cornblatt, B., & Greenhalgh, J. (1998). *The New York High-Risk Project: Specific predictors from childhood neurobehavioral performance to schizophrenia-related psychoses in adulthood.* Manuscript in preparation, Columbia University.

Fish, B. (1984). Characteristics and sequelae of the neurointegrative disorder in infants at risk for schizophrenia: 1952–1982. In N. F. Watt, E. J. Anthony, L. C. Wynne, & J. Rolf (Eds.), *Children at risk for schizophrenia: A longitudinal perspective* (pp. 423–439). New York: Cambridge University Press.

Freedman, L. R., Rock, D., Roberts, S. A., Cornblatt, B. A., & Erlenmeyer-Kimling, L. (1998). The New York High-Risk Project: Attention, anhedonia, and social outcome. *Schizophrenia Research, 30,* 1–9.

Gottesman, I. I., & Shields, J. (1972). *Schizophrenia and genetics: A twin study vantage point.* New York: Academic Press.

Holzman, P. S. (1992). Behavioral markers of schizophrenia useful for genetic studies. *Journal of Psychiatric Research, 26,* 427–445.

Jones, P., Rodgers, B., Murray, R., & Marmot, M. (1994). Child development risk factors for adult schizophrenia in the British 1946 birth cohort. *Lancet, 344,* 1398–1402.

Kety, S. S., Wender, P. H., Jacobsen, B., Ingraham, L. J., Jansson, L., Faber, B., & Kinney, D. (1994). Mental illness in the biological and adoptive relatives of schizophrenic adoptees: Replication of the Copenhagen study in the rest of Denmark. *Archives of General Psychiatry, 51,* 442–455.

Loranger, A. W., Susman, V. L., Oldham, J. M., & Russakoff, L. M. (1987). The Personality Disorder Examination: A preliminary report. *Journal of Personality Disorders, 1,* 1–13.

Lyons, M. J., Toomey, R., Faraone, S. V., & Tsuang, M. T. (1994). Comparison of schizotypal relatives of schizophrenia versus affective probands. *American Journal of Medical Genetics, 54,* 279–285.

Maier, W., Lichtermann, D., Minges, J., & Heun, R. (1994). Personality disorders among relatives of schizophrenic patients. *Schizophrenia Bulletin, 20,* 481–493.

McNeil, T. F. (1987). Perinatal influences in the development of schizophrenia. In H. Helmchen & F. A. Henn (Eds.), *Biological perspectives of schizophrenia* (pp. 125–138). Chichester, England: Wiley.

Mednick, S. A., Cudeck, R., Griffith, J. J., Talovic, S. A., & Schulsinger, F. (1984). The Danish High-Risk Project: Recent methods and findings. In N. F. Watt,

J. Anthony, L. C. Wynne, & J. E. Rolf (Eds.), *Children at risk for schizophrenia: A longitudinal perspective* (pp. 21–42). London: Cambridge University Press.

Mednick, S. A., Huttunen, M. O., & Machon, R. A. (1994). Prenatal influenza infections and adult schizophrenia. *Schizophrenia Bulletin, 20,* 263–267.

Meehl, P. E. (1962). Schizotaxia, schizotypy, schizophrenia. *American Psychologist, 17,* 827–838.

Moldin, S. O., Gottesman, I. I., Erlenmeyer-Kimling, L., & Cornblatt, B. (1990). Psychometric deviance in offspring at risk for schizophrenia: I. Initial delineation of a distinct subgroup. *Psychiatry Research, 32,* 297–310.

Moldin, S. O., Rice, J., Erlenmeyer-Kimling, L., & Squires-Wheeler, E. (1994). Latent structure of *DSM-III-R* Axis II psychopathology in a normal sample. *Journal of Abnormal Psychology, 103,* 259–266.

Nuechterlein, K., & Dawson, M. (1984). Information processing and attentional functioning in the developmental course of schizophrenic disorders. *Schizophrenia Bulletin, 10,* 160–203.

O'Callaghan, E., Gibson, T., Colohan, H., Buckley, P., Walshe, D. G., Larkin, C., & Waddington, J. L. (1992). Risk of schizophrenia in adults born after obstetric complications and their association with early onset of illness: A controlled study. *British Medical Journal, 305,* 1256–1259.

Olin, S. S., Raine, A., Cannon, T. D., Parnas, J., Schulsinger, F., & Mednick, S. A. (1997). Childhood behavior precursors of schizotypal personality disorders. *Schizophrenia Bulletin, 23,* 93–103.

Ott, S. L., Spinelli, S., Rock, D., Roberts, S., Amminger, G. P., & Erlenmeyer-Kimling, L. (in press). The New York High-Risk Project: The development of social intelligence in relation to general intelligence in children with parental risk or before onset of schizophrenia. *Schizophrenia Research.*

Pearson, J. S., & Kley, I. B. (1957). On the application of genetic expectancies as age-specific base rates in the study of human behavior disorder. *Psychological Bulletin, 54,* 406–420.

Rosenberg, D., Sweeney, J., Squires-Wheeler, E., Cornblatt, B., & Erlenmeyer-Kimling, L. (1997). Eye-tracking dysfunction in offspring from the New York High-Risk Project: Diagnostic specificity and the role of attention. *Psychiatry Research, 66,* 121–130.

Sham, P. C., O'Callaghan, E., Takei, N., Murray, G. K., Hare, E. H., & Murray,

R. M. (1992). Schizophrenia following pre-natal exposure to influenza epidemics between 1939 and 1960. *British Journal of Psychiatry, 160,* 461–466.

Siever, L. J., Keefe, R., & Bernstein, D. P. (1991). Dr. Siever and colleagues reply. *American Journal of Psychiatry, 148,* 1097.

Spitzer, R. L., & Endicott, J. (1978). *Schedule for Affective Disorders and Schizophrenia—Lifetime Version* (3rd ed.). New York: New York State Psychiatric Institute, Biometrics Unit.

Spitzer, R. L., Endicott, J., & Robins, E. (1978). *Research Diagnostic Criteria.* New York: New York State Psychiatric Institute, Biometrics Department.

Squires-Wheeler, E., Friedman, D., Amminger, G. P., Skodol, A., Looser-Ott, S., Roberts, S., & Erlenmeyer-Kimling, L. (1997). Negative and positive dimensions of schizotypal personality disorder. *Journal of Personality Disorders, 11,* 285–300.

Squires-Wheeler, E., Skodol, A. E., Adamo, U. H., Bassett, A. S., Gewirtz, G. R., Honer, W. G., Cornblatt, B. A., Roberts, S. A., & Erlenmeyer-Kimling, L. (1993). Personality features and disorder in the subjects in the New York High-Risk Project. *Journal of Psychiatric Research, 27,* 379–393.

Squires-Wheeler, E., Skodol, A. E., & Erlenmeyer-Kimling, L. (1992). The assessment of schizotypal features over two points in time. *Schizophrenia Research, 6,* 75–85.

Torgersen, S., Onstad, S., Skre, I., Edvarsen, J., & Kringlen, E. (1993). "True" schizotypal personality disorder: A study of co-twins and relatives of schizophrenic probands. *American Journal of Psychiatry, 150,* 1661–1667.

Watt, N. (1984). In a nutshell: The first two decades of high-risk research in schizophrenia. In N. F. Watt, E. J. Athony, L. Wynne, & J. Rolf (Eds.), *Children at risk for schizophrenia: A longitudinal perspective* (pp. 572–595). New York: Cambridge University Press.

Watt, N., Anthony, E. J., Wynne, L., & Rolf, J. (1984). *Children at risk for schizophrenia: A longitudinal perspective.* New York: Cambridge University Press.

Watt, N., Grubb, T., & Erlenmeyer-Kimling, L. (1984). Social, emotional and intellectual functioning at school among New York City children at high risk for schizophrenia. In N. Watt, E. J. Anthony, L. Wynne, & J. Rolf

(Eds.), *Children at risk for schizophrenia: A longitudinal perspective* (pp. 212–226). New York: Cambridge University Press.

Wolf, L., Cornblatt, B., Roberts, S., Shapiro, B., & Erlenmeyer-Kimling, L. (1998). *Wisconsin Card Sorting deficits in the offspring of schizophrenics in the New York High-Risk Project*. Manuscript under review.

Woolf, C. M. (1997). Does the genotype for schizophrenia often remain unexpressed because of canalization and stochastic events during development? *Psychological Medicine, 27,* 1–10.

16

Expressed Emotion and the Pathogenesis of Relapse in Schizophrenia

Jill M. Hooley and Jordan B. Hiller

Forty years have now elapsed since Brown, Carstairs, and Topping (1958) published the first report of a link between clinical outcome and the living environment into which schizophrenia patients were discharged after a period of hospitalization. Within this span of 4 decades, the construct of expressed emotion (EE) has been developed, refined, empirically tested, and scientifically validated. Research efforts have generated a large and consistent body of evidence documenting the association between family environment and the course of schizophrenia and have produced family-based treatments with considerable promise for reducing or delaying schizophrenic relapse. EE research has stood the test of time, flourishing even within a prevailing climate that has emphasized biological rather than psychosocial pathways to the understanding of severe mental disorders.

Yet, a backward glance at the tradition of EE research highlights just how traditional EE research has become. The conventional paradigm—measuring EE in family members of psychiatric patients during a period of hospitalization and then correlating this with subsequent relapse—has now been used in dozens of studies, in many countries, and with patients having a wide range of diagnoses. These studies have, without question, established that EE is a robust predictor of psychiatric relapse. What these studies have told us almost nothing about, however, is why EE and relapse are related.

In this chapter, we cast a critical eye on EE research in an effort to examine its strengths and document its limitations. We highlight a number of conceptual and methodological problems that we believe impede the development of EE research and that will, in all probability, limit its future if left unchecked. Finally, we suggest places to begin the search, not only for solutions to the problems we raise but also for the successor to the EE construct itself. We begin, however, with a consideration of what is good, or what has been good, about the tradition of EE research in psychopathology.

THE HISTORY OF THE EE CONSTRUCT

In 1958, George Brown et al. observed that the clinical course of schizophrenia following a hospitalization depended to a great degree on patients' living arrangements after discharge. More specifically, patients returning to live with parents or spouses had higher relapse rates compared with those living alone or with siblings. Brown et al. reasoned that highly emotional family environments might be stressful to patients. This was an unusual insight at the time. As Brown (1985) remembered, "in 1956 there was little hint in the literature of British psychiatry that the core symptoms of schizophrenia might be importantly influenced by social experience" (p. 10). Nonetheless, Brown continued to explore this hypothesis and went on to develop a measure of the kinds of emotional attitudes that might be particularly important in this regard. The result was the EE index, which, as time has proven, was quite well suited for this original purpose.

Perhaps the most essential feature of EE measurement is its assessment within an individual interview format. Brown (e.g., see 1985) was concerned that relatives might not be willing to admit to critical or hostile attitudes toward a patient in a questionnaire or on direct questioning. Because of this, he allowed relatives to talk about patients in a relatively open-ended fashion. The hope here was that in the course of describing the patient's history and symptoms, relatives would reveal their attitudes in a manner that might be extracted reliably.

The Camberwell Family Interview (CFI) was the result of Brown's collaborations with Michael Rutter (Brown & Rutter, 1966; Rutter & Brown, 1966). Named after the area of London where its developers worked, the CFI (revised further by Vaughn & Leff, 1976) is the measure of choice in EE research. The CFI takes between 1 and 2 hr to administer and essentially provides the relative with the opportunity to describe the events in the home in the months leading up to the patient's hospitalization. The interview is always audiotaped for later coding by trained raters. EE is operationalized by counting the frequency of critical remarks, degree of hostility, and extent of emotional overinvolvement (EOI) expressed while the relative is speaking about the patient. If the relative makes more than a threshold number of critical remarks about the patient, or expresses any evidence of either hostility or marked EOI, the relative is classified as *high in EE*. If the relative makes fewer than the specified number of critical remarks and shows no evidence of hostility or marked EOI, he or she is classified as *low in EE*. More information about EE measurement as well as examples of critical, hostile, or EOI comments can be found in Hooley, Rosen, and Richters (1995) or Leff and Vaughn (1985).

THE PREDICTIVE VALIDITY OF EE
IN SCHIZOPHRENIA

The great strength of the EE construct is undoubtedly its validity as a predictor of psychiatric relapse. When measured during a period of crisis (i.e., during a psychiatric hospitalization), family levels of EE show a highly reliable association with symptom relapse. Patients who return home to live with relatives classified as high in EE are significantly more likely to relapse within the next 9–12 months than are patients who return home to live with relatives classified as low in EE. More specifically, relapse rates for patients living in high EE families are in the region of 50–65% while those for patients living with low EE families are around 23–35% (see Butzlaff & Hooley, in press; and Kavanagh, 1992).

Some indication of just how robust the EE–relapse link is comes from a recent meta-analysis. Butzlaff and Hooley (in press) examined 26 published studies of EE and relapse in schizophrenia patients. These studies included investigations conducted in many different parts of the world, including North America, Europe, India, and Australia. All of the studies followed the traditional EE–relapse paradigm of using the CFI to measure EE and using a postdischarge follow-up period of 9–12 months. The meta-analytic effect size of the EE–relapse association was in the region of .30 (Pearson r), with 95% confidence limits between .24 and .38. Moreover, the calculation of the file-drawer statistic (Rosenthal, 1991) revealed that over 1,000 studies averaging null results would be required to reduce the effect size to just barely significant (p = .05). In short, the EE–relapse link in schizophrenia is real, robust, and remarkably resilient.

ARE FAMILY VARIABLES OF CAUSAL IMPORTANCE IN THE RELAPSE PROCESS?

In many respects, the future direction of EE research hinges critically on the answer to this question. Certainly, EE predicts patient relapse in schizophrenia. But correlation, as everyone knows, is not causation. Although many clinicians and researchers have implicitly assumed that family EE levels influence patients' risk of relapse, alternative explanations for the association are also tenable. Quite possibly, the EE–relapse correlation reflects nothing more than the fact that patients who are relapse prone are likely to draw criticism from those closest to them. If this is the case, EE is important only to the extent that it might usefully point the way to the real variable or variables of interest.

In the last decade, the issue of causality has generated a great deal of heated debate, and an adequate discussion of this topic is clearly beyond the scope of this chapter. However, a detailed evaluation of the various competing models capable of explaining the EE–relapse link was recently provided by Hooley et al. (1995). After a review of the existing literature, two main conclusions were drawn. First, EE may, to some extent, be a reaction of the relatives to the functioning deficits of the patients. Second, EE in all likelihood plays a causal role in the relapse process. A similar conclusion was also reached by Nuechterlein, Snyder, and Mintz (1992) on the basis of a path analysis of relapse data obtained from recent-onset schizophrenia patients.

The results of family-based interventions provide further support for the notion that EE is causally related to relapse (Leff & Vaughn, 1985). In the typical intervention study, families were offered some form of psychosocial treatment in addition to case management and pharmacotherapy. This may be delivered in an individual family format (e.g., Falloon et al., 1982; Leff, Kuipers, Berkowitz, Eberlein-Fries, & Sturgeon, 1982; Leff et al., 1988) or in multifamily groups (McFarlane, Link, Dushay, Marchal, & Crilly, 1995; McFarlane, Lukens, et al., 1995). In contrast, families assigned to the control group received only general case management and pharmacotherapy. A growing number of reports have now demonstrated that family-based treatments do reduce patients' relapse rates relative to controls. Moreover, when EE levels decrease, the prognosis for patients invariably improves. Definite conclusions about causality cannot be drawn, however. This is because all treatment studies, for good ethical reasons, do not include the condition that would allow causality to be appropriately demonstrated. Quite obviously, low EE families cannot be assigned to an experimental manipulation designed to increase EE levels with the purpose of examining if this leads to a corresponding increase in patients' relapse rates. Because of this, statements about the causal significance of EE must necessarily remain tentative. However, it is becoming clear that the accumulation of evidence is consistent with the idea that EE does play a causal role in the relapse process.

WHAT BEHAVIOR IS EE INDEXING?

If EE is causally related to relapse, the next question of interest is What do high and low EE relatives do when they are with the patients? Efforts to address this question are informed by research that began in the early 1980s and was designed to demonstrate the concurrent validity of EE. Of specific concern at this time was whether relatives who criticized patients during an interview with a researcher were also critical of patients during a face-to-face interaction. Interactionally based data soon revealed that this was the case, both for schizophrenia (Miklowitz, Goldstein, Falloon, & Doane, 1984; Valone, Norton, Goldstein, & Doane, 1983) and depression (Hooley, 1986). Recognizing the limitations of simply analyzing base rates of behaviors, researchers subsequently extended their efforts to include examinations of the transactional processes related to EE. Sequential analysis of behavioral data revealed differences in the patterning of high versus low EE relative–patient interactions. In samples with schizophrenia and depression, high EE dyads were found to be much more likely to engage in protracted sequences of negative escalation than were low EE dyads (Hahlweg et al., 1989; Hooley, 1990). Competition for control was also characteristic of interactions involving high EE families of bipolar and schizophrenia patients (Wuerker, 1994).

High and low EE relatives also differ in their cognitive appraisals of undesirable events. Specifically, the spontaneous attributions that high EE relatives make about the causes of patients' problems are more likely to invoke factors that are internal, controllable, and personal to patients than are the spontaneous causal attributions that characterize low EE relatives (Barrowclough, Johnston, & Tarrier, 1994; Brewin, MacCarthy, Duda, & Vaughn, 1991; Hooley & Licht, 1997). Moreover, Hooley (in press) recently demonstrated that consistent with the emphasis high EE relatives place on controllability, high levels of criticism reflect a tendency toward a more internally based locus of control. Whether this finding is related to the role of culture in understanding EE (Jenkins & Karno, 1992) is interesting to speculate. Certainly, the ratio of high EE to low EE relatives is lower in India (Leff et al., 1987) and in relatives of Mexican descent (Karno et al., 1987) than it is in British or Anglo American samples. Whether this relates to cross-cultural differences in beliefs about personal control or the controllability of psychiatric symptoms has yet to be examined.

THE PITFALL OF STUDYING EE

What is valuable about these studies is their focus on the interpersonal and psychological correlates of high and low levels of EE. To understand

EE, it is necessary and obvious that we must first understand what high and low EE relatives (and patients who interact with them) actually think and do. Inherent in such an approach, however, is a potential danger: Research that examines the correlates of EE results inevitably in a tendency toward reification of the EE construct. Moreover, when we reify EE, we think of it as an explanation of relapse rather than a construct to explain. As a consequence, we forget to conduct the most necessary and most informative analyses of our data. More specifically, we forget to explore the mechanism of the EE–relapse relationship.

These problems are exemplified in the approach taken by Hooley (1986). In her examination of the face-to-face behavior of high and low EE spouses of patients with depression, Hooley presented a series of results describing differences in the behavior of high versus low EE spouses and the patients who interacted with them. High EE spouses were reported to be more critical, to disagree with patients more, and to be more nonverbally negative than were their low EE counterparts.

As support for the concurrent validity of EE, these are obviously interesting and important findings. However, they tell us nothing about the mechanism of the EE–relapse link. Although behavioral correlates of EE are identified, conspicuous by their absence are correlations exploring the links between these behavioral variables and patient relapse. The focus of interest in this study is solely on EE. Forgotten is the fact that EE is only of importance because of its predictive validity with respect to relapse. With the benefit of hindsight, it is clear that what should also have formed an integral part of Hooley's (1986) data analysis was an examination of the extent to which the behavioral correlates of EE might be the "active ingredients" of the construct that are predictive of relapse. In short, in this study (as in many others), emphasis on EE as an independent variable results in a lack of consideration of relapse as a dependent variable.

These problems are also implicit in approaches designed to find alternative ways of measuring EE. In the past 10 years, efforts have been made to simplify EE assessment, either by reducing the time the relative talks to the interviewer (e.g., the Five Minute Speech Sample; Magaña et al., 1986) or by using self-report instruments (Cole & Kazarian, 1988;

Docherty, Serper, & Harvey, 1990). Almost invariably, the alternative measures are then validated against EE assessed using the CFI. However, as Hooley and Richters (1991) have noted, this is hardly the appropriate criterion variable. What is needed are not better measures of EE but better predictors of relapse. Again, the problem of reification of EE puts us in danger of losing sight of what it is we really want to know.

HOW IS EE ASSOCIATED WITH RELAPSE?

Most researchers who study psychosocial factors in schizophrenia do so within the conceptual framework of the diathesis–stress model (Nuechterlein & Dawson, 1984; Zubin & Spring, 1977). In this context, high EE is viewed as a stressor that can result in another episode of illness being triggered in a vulnerable patient.[1] Negative life events, which have also been shown to precipitate relapse in some patients, are conceptualized in a similar manner (Leff & Vaughn, 1985; Ventura, Nuechterlein, Lukoff, & Hardesty, 1989).

When viewed within the context of the diathesis–stress framework, what becomes striking is just how remarkable the EE–relapse association truly is. EE is a measure of the attitude of a family member that is expressed privately to a researcher during an interview conducted when the patient is hospitalized. Relapse is a clinical event expressed in the behavior and social functioning of a patient months after the EE interview is finished. Whatever is indexed through EE is hardly proximal to the cascade of events that culminates in a psychiatric relapse. How, then, can this psychosocial variable be of such importance to the relapse process?

This, we believe, is the most pressing question on the EE research

---

[1] Whether high EE in reality is a risk factor for relapse or low EE functions more as a protective factor is clearly an important issue here. Not infrequently, risk and protective factors are simply viewed as two sides of the same coin. However, as Goldstein (1990) noted, protective factors should ideally serve to modify the outcome for an individual known to be at risk. Given that high EE is more normative than low EE in the families of schizophrenia patients (at least in most developed countries), it is perhaps more appropriate to view low EE as protective because it is more unusual and associated with decreased risk for relapse. To avoid confusion and to remain consistent with the traditional conceptualization of EE, however, we adopt the high-EE-as-stressor approach in the discussion that follows.

agenda. If EE research is truly to fulfill its potential, the nature of EE research now needs to change direction. If those interested in the construct remain satisfied with it as it currently stands and if they continue to use the construct in traditional ways, the future of EE research cannot be considered promising. EE is now fully established as a measure of something important. But the important variable is relapse, not EE. The way forward must be through more clearly articulated ideas about the mechanisms through which EE and relapse might be related. There are numerous intervening variables that necessarily lie between EE and relapse. It is to these variables that researchers interested in this question need to turn.

WHAT VARIABLES LIE BETWEEN EE
AND RELAPSE?

Figure 1 highlights some of the domains of inquiry that in all probability lie along the pathway between EE and relapse.[2] This is not the first time that a "boxological approach" has been offered in EE research. However, rather than being a formal model of relapse (see Kavanagh, 1992; and Nuechterlein, Dawson, et al., 1992), our figure simply attempts to highlight the domains of inquiry that we believe are both necessary and important as a guide to future research endeavors. For example, it is expected that high EE attitudes on the part of relatives are translated into specific modes of behavior toward the patients. Moreover, the precise nature of these behaviors is also likely to reflect and be influenced by relatives' perceptions and beliefs about the patients. In turn, these perceptions are likely to be colored by contextual factors, which might include culture, religion, personality, and mood as well as a host of other possible variables. Thus, if we wish to understand EE, these are the domains of inquiry that should be examined.

---

[2] Although we use the global term *relapse* in the figure and in our discussion to describe the recrudescence of schizophrenia symptoms, we recognize that it may ultimately be necessary to differentiate the roles of different types of symptoms. For example, it may be the case that negative symptoms tend to elicit the expression of critical attitudes from relatives, whereas positive symptoms would increase as a result of the patient's exposure to criticism.

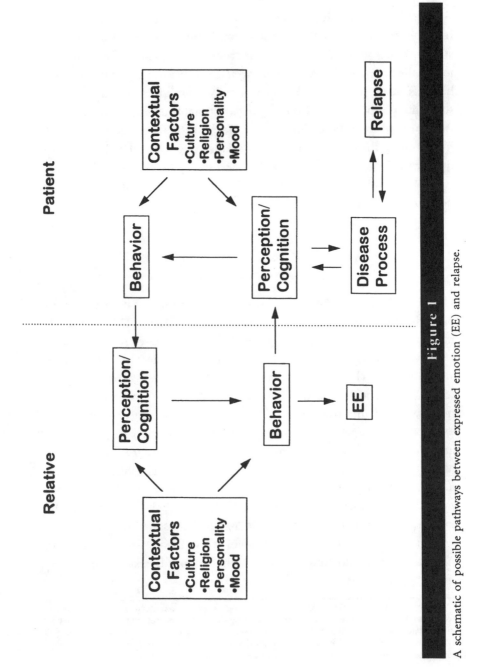

Figure 1

A schematic of possible pathways between expressed emotion (EE) and relapse.

In contrast, if researchers wish to address the issue of relapse, different areas of our schematic figure should begin to command attention. More specifically, researchers would do well not only to focus on the process by which familial attitudes are translated into behavior but also to attend to how relatives' behavior is perceived by vulnerable patients. It would be beneficial to examine the psychophysiological and neurobiological correlates of these perceptions and the behaviors that result from them as well as learning as much as possible about the factors that influence the nature of the perceptions themselves. In short, if researchers wish to understand relapse, they should focus more on the experiences of patients and less on the experiences of relatives.

EE FROM THE PERSPECTIVE OF PATIENTS

What do we know about patients' experiences of the family emotional climate? With the exception of the relapse variable, the majority of EE research has focused on domains of inquiry that fall more to the left than the right side of our schematic figure. Nonetheless, there are a number of things that we already know.

First, we know that part of the behavioral experience of patients who live in high EE homes is one of conflict. As discussed earlier, patients with high EE relatives are exposed to more negative interpersonal behavior than are patients who live with low EE relatives. However, it is also the case that the patients themselves may play a role in this process. Strachan, Feingold, Goldstein, Miklowitz, and Nuechterlein (1989) examined the behavior of schizophrenia patients who were involved in face-to-face discussions with their relatives. Compared with patients interacting with low EE relatives, patients interacting with high EE relatives criticized their relatives more. Patients with high EE relatives also made fewer statements indicating that they intended to solve a problem themselves (autonomous statements).

Similar findings were also reported by Mueser et al. (1993), who based their study on family problem solving. When discussing areas of conflict, patients living with critical family members were more likely to direct nonconstructive criticisms toward their relatives and to make more demands and commands. Their critical relatives were more inclined to engage in these behaviors. Again, these data echo those of Hahlweg et al. (1989), concerning the tendency of patients and high EE family members to engage in protracted sequences of negative behavioral exchanges. Although we can currently say little about who is reacting to whom, it is clear that high EE family environments are more affectively negative than are low EE family environments.

Second, there is evidence that patients who experience their family environment as more negative and critical are at elevated risk for relapse. In married patients with depression, for example, it has been demonstrated that both the patients' ratings of the marital relationship (assessed using the Dyadic Adjustment Scale; Spanier, 1976) and patients' rating of their spouses' criticality were significantly predictive of later relapse (Hooley & Teasdale, 1989). Patients who reported more marital difficulties or who perceived their spouses to be more critical of them fared worse clinically in the 9 months after they left the hospital than did patients who considered their relationships to be happier or who rated their spouses as low in criticism. It is interesting to note that the findings concerning relationship quality have recently been replicated by Lebell et al. (1993) in a sample of schizophrenia patients. In addition, patients' ratings of their current feelings toward their relatives using a 5-point Likert-type scale (mostly strong negative thoughts to mostly strong positive thoughts) also predicted psychotic exacerbation over a 1-year follow-up.

Increases in patients' unusual thinking have also been shown to occur immediately after being criticized by a family member. In an interesting and potentially important study, Rosenfarb, Goldstein, Mintz, and Nuechterlein (1995) examined the behavior of schizophrenia patients and their high and low EE relatives. They found that high EE families were more likely than low EE families to respond with criticism after hearing the patient make an unusual remark (e.g., "If that kid bites you, you'll get rabies."). Moreover, when criticism occurred, patients were more likely to make another remark that was unusual in content. Although it is possible that this study simply demonstrates that patients who make one unusual remark are likely to make another, the data from Rosenfarb et al. are certainly intriguing. They are also, to our knowledge, the first to suggest that there may be a temporal association between negative affective behavior on the part of the relatives and increases in unusual thinking on the part of the patients.

How might patients' experiences of their relationships be related to relapse? One possibility is that this association is mediated by psychophysiologic change. Investigations that have measured electrodermal activity are consistent with the notion that interactions with high EE relatives are stressful for schizophrenia patients. Although more work in this area needs to be conducted, several investigators have reported that higher levels of autonomic arousal characterize patients who have high versus low EE relatives. In one study, the entry of a relative into the testing room resulted in an increase in the patient's electrodermal activity and heart rate. These responses soon decreased for patients who were in the presence of a low EE relative. In the group of patients with high EE relatives, however, the increase in autonomic arousal persisted (Tarrier, Vaughn, Lader, & Leff, 1979). In another investigation, patients with high EE relatives showed higher baseline levels of autonomic arousal compared with patients with low EE relatives (Sturgeon, Turpin, Kuipers, Berkowitz, & Leff, 1984).

Interpreting the data concerning autonomic hyperarousal and EE in schizophrenia is complicated, no less because the findings seem to differ according to whether patients are studied in an acute phase of the illness or in remission. However, as Tarrier and Turpin (1992) pointed out, higher levels of electrodermal arousal do appear to characterize patients with high EE relatives. Life events may also be associated with elevated electrodermal arousal (Nuechterlein, Goldstein, Ventura, Dawson, & Doane, 1989). Perhaps most important, there is some preliminary evidence that elevated levels of electrodermal arousal, particularly in the presence of high EE, are associated with relapse. Therefore, within the context of trying to understand the EE–relapse association, these psychophysiological findings clearly have considerable promise.

The dangers of reifying electrodermal arousal are as great as the dangers of reifying EE, however. We need to keep in mind that electrodermal arousal is more akin to a behavior than to a mechanism. How autonomic hyperarousal might lead to the reappearance of psychotic symptoms is far from clear. In all likelihood, increased arousal is an indicator of neural processes involved in the perception of negative attitudes. No doubt our future research efforts will be informed by a fuller understanding of the neural correlates of emotional regulation.

FUTURE RESEARCH DIRECTIONS

Where might researchers go from here to further the understanding of the pathogenesis of relapse? One possibility is to begin at the beginning and ask relatives what they have observed about the participants and the early signs of relapse in their diagnosed family member. The experiences of relatives are often ignored. As experts on the patients with whom they live, however, they may prove to be a rich and valuable source of ideas that could be translated into testable research hypotheses.

Implicit in this suggestion is a point that needs repeating. Rather than striving to develop alternative measures of EE, researchers must develop more valid predictors of relapse that are based on patients' experiences. The EE measure, although historically useful, focuses on the wrong unit of analysis. Researchers need to move toward measures that more accurately reflect the experiences of the patient. At the very least, these assessments will be necessarily more proximal to relapse than an EE assessment obtained from a relative.

This having been said, what else might researchers do? Quite obviously, researchers need to study low EE families. Although they may not be present in large numbers, these families warrant serious attention. So, too, do the families of all nonrelapsing patients, more generally. Moreover, in addition to examining what they do *not do* (e.g., criticize patients or engage in other negative behaviors), researchers need to examine what these families *are doing* that might be helpful to patients. One problem is that available coding systems often tend to note more negative than positive behaviors. The way forward may require the development of new systems of coding that have a different emphasis.

Researchers might also consider turning the diathesis–stress model around and using EE as a means to explore the issue of vulnerability to poor outcome more generally. The conventional focus of EE researchers on relapse obscures the fact that the course of illness in patients exposed to high family levels of EE is quite varied. Certainly, a significant number of patients living in high EE homes go into remission and then relapse again. However, in other cases and despite being discharged from the hospital, some patients fail to enter a period of clinically significant remission. In short, these patients never recover enough to relapse. In yet other cases, patients have a very favorable course of illness and remain well throughout the follow-up period, despite being exposed to high levels of psychosocial stress (i.e., high EE).

These observations raise two important questions. Specifically, (1) what factors are associated with patients staying well even in the face of a known psychosocial stressor; conversely, (2) what characteristics identify patients who are unable even to attain clinical remission within a high EE family environment? Do the differences lie in characteristics of the family or are the differences more appropriately explained by clinical or other characteristics of the patients themselves? In addition to using EE as a vehicle to facilitate understanding about relapse, it may also be the case that researchers can use EE to reveal more about the patient factors associated with underlying vulnerability to relapse.

This could be done through analyses that compare patients who live with high EE relatives yet who have different clinical outcomes. Careful examination of the ways patients who remain well, relapse, or fail to show any significant clinical improvement differ in their clinical presentation and clinical history may shed some much needed light on the patient characteristics that signal differential vulnerability to the stress of a high EE home environment. In short, we may be able to use what we know about EE as a stressor to learn more about diathesis.

What kind of variables might be worthy of specific attention here? Certainly, researchers should consider factors that might influence how criticism from a family member is perceived. For example, how important is the warmth of the family member in determining how upsetting negative remarks are for the patient? Because of its lack of predictive validity in the early studies (Brown, Birley, & Wing, 1972), the role of warmth has been largely neglected in EE research. However, the possibility that warmth does have a relation to relapse (albeit not a linear one) should be considered. A benefit might also come from considering clinical or characterological variables in patients that might influence how they interpret the behavior of the relative. The possibility that patients who are high on suspiciousness will do worse in high EE environments, for example, is certainly very plausible.

Relatedly, there is now a literature documenting that schizophrenia patients are impaired in their abilities to identify emotion from facial expressions (Mandal & Palchoudhury, 1989; Walker, Marwit, & Emory, 1980). However, no research to date has attempted to relate patients' abilities to detect emotional expression in others to their risk of relapse in the context of a high EE home environment. If high EE environments are perceived as stressful, however, patients must be able to detect the negative cues to which they are exposed. The extent to which patients who are better at doing this are at higher risk for relapse is an intriguing possibility and one that warrants further exploration.

Implicit in all of this is that researchers in this area should develop hypotheses that might help to understand why patients relapse. Wherever possible, researchers will benefit most from research designs that provide a carefully articulated mechanism through which EE and relapse might be related. What this means is that researchers should study known vulnerability markers or variables that can be conceptualized to either confer risk or protection in the face of a high EE environment. The literature on candidate vulnerability markers in schizophrenia, such as backward masking (Green & Nuechterlein, chapter 12, this volume), impaired eye tracking (Levy et al., chapter 7, this volume), or poor performance on the Continuous Performance Task (Nuechterlein et al., chapter 11, this volume), continues to grow. Rather than simply paying lip service to notions of diathesis–stress, the time may now be right for thoughtful collaborations between researchers who study vulnerability and researchers who study stress.

Finally, we would note that in our efforts to understand the EE–relapse link in schizophrenia, we owe a considerable debt to the researchers who have explored the psychophysiological correlates of EE in patient samples. Yet sadly, little research in this area has been conducted of late. Far from being a research area of historical interest, the way forward is now through studies that will enhance our understanding of the psychophysiological, neurobiological, and neurochemical correlates of high levels of family stress. The changes in technology that have occurred over the last decade have been enormous. Brain imaging techniques such as positron emission tomography are now being used to study emotion (George et al., 1995; Pardo, Pardo, & Raichle, 1993). If researchers want to know what is happening to patients when they are subjected to psychosocial stress, they now have the technology to examine these issues more directly.

CONCLUDING COMMENTS

In closing, we believe that this is a critical juncture for psychosocial research in general and EE research in particular. Although EE has been demonstrated to be a reliable and robust predictor of relapse in schizophrenia, the future contribution of the construct will be determined by the extent to which those who study it can use it as a launching pad to the understanding of relapse. When correlates of EE are identified, these variables should form part of a focused effort to shed light on the pathogenesis of relapse. Of particular interest is the extent to which the correlates of EE are capable of outpredicting EE with respect to explaining relapse variance.

But researchers are now ready to do even more. In the EE construct, we have a known and well-studied psychosocial stressor. By using it more creatively and studying it in the context of vulnerability markers, researchers may be able to come to a greater understanding of the factors that place patients at higher or lower risk of poor clinical outcomes. As the chapters in this book demonstrate, there are researchers who study stress and there are researchers who study vulnerability. In addition to paying lip service to the diathesis–stress explanations of major mental disorders, perhaps researchers are now ready to begin to translate this formulation into new and more collaborative research approaches.

REFERENCES

Barrowclough, C., Johnston, M., & Tarrier, N. (1994). Attributions, expressed emotion, and patient relapse: An attributional model of relatives' response to schizophrenic illness. *Behavior Therapy, 25,* 67–88.

Brewin, C. R., MacCarthy, B., Duda, K., & Vaughn, C. E. (1991). Attribution and expressed emotion in the relatives of patients with schizophrenia. *Journal of Abnormal Psychology, 100,* 546–554.

Brown, G. W. (1985). The discovery of expressed emotion: Induction or deduction? In J. Leff & C. Vaughn (Eds.), *Expressed emotion in families* (pp. 7–25). New York: Guilford Press.

Brown, G. W., Birley, J. L. T., & Wing, J. K. (1972). Influence of family life on the course of schizophrenic disorders: A replication. *British Journal of Psychiatry, 121,* 241–258.

Brown, G. W., Carstairs, G. M., & Topping, G. (1958). Post hospital adjustment of chronic mental patients. *Lancet, 2,* 685–689.

Brown, G. W., & Rutter, M. L. (1966). The measurement of family activities and relationships. *Human Relations, 19,* 241–263.

Butzlaff, R. L., & Hooley, J. M. (in press). Expressed emotion and psychiatric relapse: A meta-analysis. *Archives of General Psychiatry.*

Cole, J. D., & Kazarian, S. S. (1988). The level of expressed emotion scale: A new measure of expressed emotion. *Journal of Clinical Psychology, 44,* 392–397.

Docherty, N. M., Serper, M. R., & Harvey, P. D. (1990). Development and preliminary validation of a questionnaire assessment of expressed emotion. *Psychological Reports, 67,* 279–287.

Falloon, I. R. H., Boyd, J. L., McGill, C. W., Ranzani, J., Moss, H. B., & Gilderman, A. M. (1982). Family management in the prevention of exacerbation of schizophrenia: A controlled study. *New England Journal of Medicine, 306,* 1437–1440.

George, M. S., Ketter, T. A., Parekh, P. I., Horwitz, B., Herscovitch, P., & Post, R. M. (1995). Brain activity during transient sadness and happiness in healthy women. *American Journal of Psychiatry, 152,* 341–351.

Goldstein, M. J. (1990). Risk factors and prevention in schizophrenia. In A. Kales, C. N. Stefanis, & J. Talbot (Eds.), *Recent advances in schizophrenia* (pp. 191–212). New York: Springer-Verlag.

Hahlweg, K., Goldstein, M. J., Nuechterlein, K. H., Magaña, A. B., Mintz, J., Doane, J. A., Miklowitz, D. J., & Snyder, K. S. (1989). Expressed emotion and patient–relative interaction in families of recent onset schizophrenics. *Journal of Consulting and Clinical Psychology, 57,* 11–18.

Hooley, J. M. (1986). Expressed emotion and depression: Interactions between patients and high- versus low-expressed-emotion spouses. *Journal of Abnormal Psychology, 95,* 237–246.

Hooley, J. M. (1990). Expressed emotion and depression. In G. I. Keitner (Ed.), *Depression and families: Impact and treatment* (pp. 57–83). Washington, DC: American Psychiatric Press.

Hooley, J. M. (in press). Expressed emotion and locus of control. *Journal of Nervous and Mental Disease.*

Hooley, J. M., & Licht, D. M. (1997). Expressed emotion and causal attributions in the spouses of depressed patients. *Journal of Abnormal Psychology, 106,* 298–306.

Hooley, J. M., & Richters, J. E. (1991). Alternative measures of expressed emotion: A methodological and cautionary note. *Journal of Abnormal Psychology, 100,* 94–97.

Hooley, J. M., Rosen, L. R., & Richters, J. E. (1995). Expressed emotion: Toward clarification of a critical construct. In G. Miller (Ed.), *The behavioral high-risk paradigm in psychopathology* (pp. 88–120). New York: Springer-Verlag.

Hooley, J. M., & Teasdale, J. D. (1989). Predictors of relapse in unipolar depressives: Expressed emotion, marital distress, and perceived criticism. *Journal of Abnormal Psychology, 98,* 229–235.

Jenkins, J. H., & Karno, M. (1992). The meaning of expressed emotion: Theoretical issues raised by cross-cultural research. *American Journal of Psychiatry, 149,* 9–21.

Karno, M., Jenkins, J. H., de la Selva, A., Santana, F., Telles, C., Lopez, S., & Mintz, J. (1987). Expressed emotion and schizophrenic outcome among Mexican-American families. *Journal of Nervous and Mental Disease, 175,* 143–151.

Kavanagh, D. J. (1992). Recent developments in expressed emotion and schizophrenia. *British Journal of Psychiatry, 160,* 601–620.

Lebell, M. B., Marder, S. R., Mintz, J., Mintz, L. I., Tompson, M., Wirshing, W., Johnston-Cronk, K., & McKenzie, J. (1993). Patients' perceptions of family emotional climate and outcome in schizophrenia. *British Journal of Psychiatry, 162,* 751–754.

Leff, J. P., Berkowitz, R., Shavit, N., Strachan, A., Glass, I., & Vaughn, C. (1988). A trial of family therapy v. a relatives group for schizophrenia. *British Journal of Psychiatry, 153,* 58–66.

Leff, J. P., Kuipers, L., Berkowitz, R., Eberlein-Fries, R., & Sturgeon, D. (1982). A controlled trial of social intervention in schizophrenia families. *British Journal of Psychiatry, 141,* 121–134.

Leff, J., & Vaughn, C. (1985). *Expressed emotion in families.* New York: Guilford Press.

Leff, J., Wig, N. N., Ghosh, A., Bedi, H., Menon, D. K., Kuipers, L., Korten, A., Ernberg, G., Day, R., Sartorius, N., & Jablensky, A. (1987). Influence of relatives' expressed emotion on the course of schizophrenia in Chandigarh. *British Journal of Psychiatry, 151,* 166–173.

Magaña, A. B., Goldstein, M. J., Karno, M., Miklowitz, D. J., Jenkins, J., & Falloon, I. R. H. (1986). A brief method for assessing expressed emotion in relatives of psychiatric patients. *Psychiatry Research, 17,* 203–212.

Mandal, M. K., & Palchoudhury, S. (1989). Identifying the components of facial emotion and schizophrenia. *Psychopathology, 22,* 295–300.

McFarlane, W. R., Link, B., Dushay, R., Marchal, J., & Crilly, J. (1995). Psychoeducational multiple family groups: Four-year relapse outcome in schizophrenia. *Family Process, 34,* 127–144.

McFarlane, W. R., Lukens, E., Link, B., Dushay, R., Deakins, S. A., Newmark, M., Dunne, E. J., Horen, B., & Toran, J. (1995). Multiple-family groups and psychoeducation in the treatment of schizophrenia. *Archives of General Psychiatry, 52,* 679–687.

Miklowitz, D. J., Goldstein, M. J., Falloon, I. R., & Doane, J. A. (1984). Interactional correlates of expressed emotion in the families of schizophrenics. *British Journal of Psychiatry, 144,* 482–487.

Mueser, K. T., Bellack, A. S., Wade, J. H., Sayers, S. L., Tierney, A., & Haas, G. (1993). Expressed emotion, social skill, and response to negative affect in schizophrenia. *Journal of Abnormal Psychology, 102,* 339–351.

Nuechterlein, K. H., & Dawson, M. E. (1984). A heuristic vulnerability/stress model of schizophrenic episodes. *Schizophrenia Bulletin, 10,* 300–312.

Nuechterlein, K. H., Dawson, M. E., Gitlin, M., Ventura, J., Goldstein, M. J.,

Snyder, K. S., Yee, C. M., & Mintz, J. (1992). Developmental processes in schizophrenic disorders: Longitudinal studies of vulnerability and stress. *Schizophrenia Bulletin, 18*, 387–425.

Nuechterlein, K. H., Goldstein, M. J., Ventura, J., Dawson, M. E., & Doane, J. A. (1989). Patient–environment relationships in schizophrenia: Information processing, communication deviance, autonomic arousal and stressful life events. *British Journal of Psychiatry, 155*(Suppl. 5), 84–89.

Nuechterlein, K. H., Snyder, K. S., & Mintz, J. (1992). Paths to relapse: Possible transactional processes connecting patient illness onset, expressed emotion, and psychotic relapse. *British Journal of Psychiatry, 161*(Suppl. 18), 88–96.

Pardo, J. V., Pardo, P. J., & Raichle, M. E. (1993). Neural correlates of self-induced dysphoria. *American Journal of Psychiatry, 150*, 713–719.

Rosenfarb, I. S., Goldstein, M. J., Mintz, J., & Nuechterlein, K. H. (1995). Expressed emotion and subclinical psychopathology observable within the transactions between schizophrenic patients and their family members. *Journal of Abnormal Psychology, 104*, 259–267.

Rosenthal, R. (1991). *Meta-analytic procedures for social research* (rev. ed.) Newbury Park, CA: Sage.

Rutter, M. L., & Brown, G. W. (1966). The reliability and validity of measures of family life and relationships in families containing a psychiatric patient. *Social Psychiatry, 1*, 38–53.

Spanier, G. B. (1976). Measuring dyadic adjustment: New scales for assessing the quality of marriage and similar dyads. *Journal of Marriage and the Family, 38*, 15–28.

Strachan, A. M., Feingold, D., Goldstein, M. J., Miklowitz, D. J., & Nuechterlein, K. H. (1989). Is expressed emotion an index of a transactional process? II. Patent's coping style. *Family Process, 28*, 169–181.

Sturgeon, D., Turpin, G., Kuipers, L., Berkowitz, R., & Leff, J. (1984). Psychophysiological responses of schizophrenic patients to high and low expressed emotion relatives: A follow-up study. *British Journal of Psychiatry, 145*, 62–69.

Tarrier, N., & Turpin, G. (1992). Psychosocial factors, arousal and schizophrenic relapse: The psychophysiological data. *British Journal of Psychiatry, 161*, 3–11.

Tarrier, N., Vaughn, C., Lader, M. H., & Leff, J. P. (1979). Bodily reactions to people and events in schizophrenics. *Archives of General Psychiatry, 36,* 311–315.

Valone, K., Norton, J. P., Goldstein, M. J., & Doane, J. A. (1983). Parental expressed emotion and affective style in an adolescent sample at risk for schizophrenia spectrum disorders. *Journal of Abnormal Psychology, 92,* 399–407.

Vaughn, C., & Leff, J. (1976). The measurement of expressed emotion in the families of psychiatric patients. *British Journal of Social and Clinical Psychology, 15,* 157–165.

Ventura, J., Nuechterlein, K. H., Lukoff, D., & Hardesty, J. P. (1989). A prospective study of stressful life events and schizophrenic relapse. *Journal of Abnormal Psychology, 98,* 407–411.

Walker, E., Marwit, S., & Emory, S. (1980). A cross-sectional study of emotion recognition in schizophrenics. *Journal of Abnormal Psychology, 89,* 428–436.

Wuerker, A. M. (1994). Relational control patterns and expressed emotion in families with schizophrenia and bipolar disorder. *Family Process, 33,* 389–407.

Zubin, J., & Spring, B. J. (1977). Vulnerability: A new view of schizophrenia. *Journal of Abnormal Psychology, 86,* 103–126.

17

Developmental Changes in the Behavioral Expression of Vulnerability for Schizophrenia

Elaine F. Walker, Kym M. Baum, and Donald Diforio

Implicit in contemporary models of the etiology of schizophrenia is the assumption that the behavioral expression of the diathesis is moderated by various exogenous and endogenous factors (Cannon et al., 1994; Fowles, 1992; Walker & Diforio, 1997; Zubin & Spring, 1977). The identification of these moderators has been of primary interest to many investigators in the field. Among the exogenous factors that have been the focus of research attention are psychosocial stress and obstetrical insults. Potential endogenous moderating factors include cognitive abilities and central nervous system maturation.

It has been shown that the onset of schizophrenia is often preceded by childhood adjustment problems and that the severity of these problems increases with age (Neumann, Grimes, Walker, & Baum, 1995). It has long been assumed that the prodromal phase begins in adolescence for many patients; the above studies document a particularly marked increase in interpersonal deficits and ideational abnormalities with the onset of puberty. These findings are consistent with the assumption that the behavioral expression of the diathesis is moderated by maturational processes.

In this chapter, we focus on the developmental trajectory of behavioral deficits in adolescents who meet diagnostic criteria for schizotypal personality disorder (SPD). Our longitudinal study of adolescents with SPD was intended to test several hypotheses generated by a "neural diathesis–stress" model, described below. We used data from the initial assessment of these adolescents to address three questions here. First, is SPD preceded by escalating behavioral problems similar to those shown by individuals who are diagnosed with schizophrenia in adulthood? Second, is SPD associated with a heightened biological stress response (i.e., heightened cortisol release)? Third, is the magnitude of this stress response linked with behavioral deficits?

DIATHESIS–STRESS MODELS

Diathesis–stress models have dominated the literature on the etiology of schizophrenia for decades, and as typically conceptualized (Rosenthal, 1970; Zubin & Spring, 1977), these models emphasize the impact of exogenous factors on the vulnerable individual. They assume that exposure to stressful events increases the likelihood that the clinical syndrome of schizophrenia will be manifested. Behavioral evidence of stress sensitivity in schizophrenia is provided by several lines of investigation (for reviews, see Norman & Malla, 1993a, 1993b, 1994). For example, retrospective and prospective studies indicate that exposure to stressful events is associated with exacerbation of symptoms and increased likelihood of relapse in schizophrenia patients (Malla & Norman, 1992). Similarly, studies of participants at high risk for schizophrenia have shown that behavioral problems and psychiatric symptoms are increased by exposure to dysfunctional family environments (Tienari, 1991; Walker, Downey, & Bergman, 1989). To date, however, the biological mediators of stress sensitivity in schizophrenia have received relatively less attention from investigators. In a recent article, Walker and Diforio (1997) reviewed research findings on both the behavioral and biological aspects of stress responsivity in schizophrenia and presented a diathesis–stress model that incorporates biological elements. This neural diathesis–stress model and the empirical literature on which it was based are briefly described here.

Walker and Diforio (1997) pointed out the substantive parallels between the literatures on psychosocial stress and biological stress sensitivity in schizophrenia. Both bodies of literature suggest that stress exacerbates schizophrenia symptoms and that individuals who are at risk for schizophrenia are characterized by heightened sensitivity to stress. At the biological level, the hypothalamic-pituitary-adrenal (HPA) axis—one of the primary neural systems mediating the biological response to stress—appears to be dysregulated in some schizophrenia patients. One index of HPA activity is the release of cortisol, a glucocorticoid for which there are receptors throughout the brain, particularly the hippocampus. These receptors are presumed to play an important role in the provision of "negative feedback" to the HPA axis, thus serving to dampen its response. The release of cortisol is one component of a cascade of events that follows stress exposure. In response to stress, the periventricular nucleus of the hypothalamus releases corticotropin releasing hormone (CRH), which triggers the release of ACTH from the pituitary. Pituitary ACTH, in turn, stimulates cortisol release from the adrenal gland. If there is a persistent elevation in cortisol release because of chronic stress exposure, hippocampal damage can ensue. Because the hippocampus contains a high concentration of glucocorticoid receptors, this can result in a dysregulation of the HPA axis, presumably because the feedback system that typically dampens its activity is impaired. (For a detailed review of stress and the HPA axis, see Sapolsky, 1992.)

A review and meta-analysis of the research findings led Walker and Diforio (1997) to the following conclusions. Schizophrenia patients showed elevated cortisol release both at baseline and in response to certain pharmacological challenges, most notably the Dexamethasone Suppression Test (Kraus, Grof, & Brown, 1988). Furthermore, symptom severity was correlated with cortisol levels in plasma and saliva, and antipsychotic medications reduced cortisol levels. Although only two studies have examined the longitudinal relation between cortisol release and symptom changes (Franzen, 1971; Sachar, Kanter, Buie, Engle, & Mehlman, 1970), both revealed that symptom exacerbations were preceded by increased cortisol release.

Of course, hypercortisolemia is also observed in patients with other psychiatric disorders, so it is not unique to schizophrenia. We are therefore confronted with the question of what specific role the HPA axis might play in the neuropathophysiology of schizophrenia. It is likely that in schizophrenia activation of the HPA axis serves to potentiate the expression of abnormalities in other neural systems.

In this connection, the dopaminergic (DA) system is a plausible candidate. It is well established that stress exposure is associated with changes in DA activity as well as cortisol (for reviews, see Benes, 1994; Deutch & Young, 1995; and Walker & Diforio, 1997). Recent findings, reviewed in detail by Walker and Diforio, suggest that this is at least partially due to the augmenting effects of cortisol on DA. Both animal and human research has shown that administration of glucocorticoids leads to an increase in DA activity. In rodents, maternal stress exposure during pregnancy results in heightened cortisol release, increased subcortical DA D_2 receptor densities, and greater behavioral sensitivity to DA agonists. Similar results are yielded by studies of nonhuman primates. Of course, DA has continued to play a major role in theories of the neuropathophysiology of schizophrenia, and extensive data from clinical and preclinical studies indicate that overactivation of DA mesolimbic pathways is involved in at least some cases of schizophrenia (Benes, 1994; Walker, 1994).

On the basis of these and other findings from a variety of sources, Walker and Diforio (1997) proposed that stress exposure exacerbates schizophrenia symptoms through its effects on the HPA axis. More specifically, it is hypothesized that the HPA axis moderates the expression of the organic liability for schizophrenia, such that cortisol release worsens symptoms through its augmenting effect on DA activity. This neural diathesis–stress model thus offers a biological mechanism for the worsening of psychotic symptoms by psychosocial stress. Furthermore, as pointed out by Walker and Diforio, the model is compatible with several key findings in the literature on schizophrenia. First, schizophrenia patients show hippocampal volumetric reductions and cellular abnormalities—this is noteworthy given that the hippocampus is a critical source of negative feedback to the HPA axis and acts to dampen its activity. In medical patients, reductions in hippocampal volume are associated with heightened cortisol release (Starkman, Gebarski, Berent, & Schteingart, 1992). The fact that hippocampal volumetric reductions have been found to be the most distinguishing aspect of brain morphology in comparisons of discordant monozygotic twins is consistent with the assumption that prenatally acquired hippocampal damage potentiates the expression of the liability for schizophrenia (Suddath, Christison, Torrey, Casanova, & Weinberger, 1990). Second, as noted, it has been shown that both typical and atypical antipsychotics reduce cortisol levels in schizophrenia patients and normal participants. Third, there is evidence of a relation between the length of untreated psychotic episodes and illness prognosis, such that the longer the duration of the nonmedicated psychosis, the worse the long-term prognosis. This may reflect an irreversible effect of persistently elevated cortisol on hippocampal function. Finally, Walker and Diforio pointed out the striking parallels between the obstetrical complications that have been found to be linked with schizophrenia and the pre- and postnatal factors that have been shown to be associated with hippocampal and HPA abnormalities in animals. These include prenatal maternal stress exposure, prenatal nutritional deficiency, hypoxia, and viral infection.

It should be noted that stress exposure and HPA activation are also associated with changes in other neurotransmitters, most notably, norepinephrine and serotonin. Compared with the DA system, however, the mechanisms of stress effects on these other systems are less well elucidated. Also, the role of these other neurotransmitter systems in the clinical course and psychopharmacological treatment of schizophrenia are not yet well documented. In contrast, the clinical consequences of DA agonism and antagonism are well established.

MATURATIONAL FACTORS

One of the many aspects of schizophrenia that has challenged investigators is the appearance of the "prodromal" phase in adolescence and the modal age-at-onset of clinical symptoms in late adolescence–early adulthood. Some investigators have proposed that within the diathesis–

stress model, this developmental period is characterized by significantly increased risk for onset because it is associated with increased exposure to stressful events. Exogenous factors are, therefore, posited as the determinant of developmental changes in risk for onset.

Although a plausible hypothesis, there has been little empirical data to support this notion. There is striking cross-cultural consistency in the age at onset for schizophrenia, despite dramatic cross-cultural differences in the life-status changes associated with late adolescence and early adulthood (Jablensky et al., 1992). These findings are not easily reconciled with the notion that increased exogenous stressors trigger illness onset. Thus, endogenous factors, specifically developmental changes in the central nervous system, may be more plausible candidates in moderating the expression of the diathesis for schizophrenia.

Several potential "biological triggers" have been proposed to account for the modal age-at-onset of schizophrenia. Included among these are the pruning of neuronal synapses (Feinberg, 1982–1983), the increase in DA activity (Weinberger, 1987), and the myelination of limbic pathways (Benes, 1994). Taken together, these and other neural processes are presumed to be among the maturational events that give rise to the emergence of the higher level cognitive abilities, which are subserved by frontal and limbic cortices (Walker, 1994).

Developmental changes in observable behavior may provide important clues regarding the central nervous system maturational processes that play a role in moderating the expression of the liability for schizophrenia. In studies of the precursors of schizophrenia, Neumann et al. (1995) obtained retrospective parental reports of childhood behavior problems in participants who were diagnosed with schizophrenia in adulthood. A modified version of the Achenbach Child Behavior Checklist (CBCL; Achenbach, 1977, 1991; Achenbach & Edelbrock, 1979) was completed by parents. Ratings were made for four age periods: birth–4, 4–8, 8–12, and 12–16 years. The developmental trajectories of the preschizophrenia participants were compared with their healthy siblings. Using Achenbach's empirically derived behavior scales, the preschizophrenia participants showed a higher rate of Internalizing and Externalizing behavior problems as well as higher ratings on the Social Problems, Thought Problems, and Attention Problems scales. The predominant developmental trend was one in which the magnitude of the group differences increased with age. Noteworthy, however, were some differences among the CBCL scales in the patterns of age-related changes. For example, Social Problems scores were significantly elevated in the preschizophrenia participants at all age periods. Attention problems scores significantly differentiated the two groups as early as the first age period, birth–4 years, and then became much more pronounced in the 12–16 year period. In contrast, Thought problems scores emerged in the 4–8 year period and then showed a dramatic increase in the 12–16 year period.

A pattern of gradually escalating behavior problems across childhood has been detected in previous studies of schizophrenia patients. The fact that similar age-related increases have been documented in prospective (Watt, Grubb, & Erlenmeyer-Kimling, 1982) and archival (Watt & Saiz, 1991) studies of preschizophrenia children suggests that this is not an artifact of retrospective reports.

Using the developmental trajectory for behavior problems as a template, we are posed with the challenge of identifying a neurodevelopmental process that follows a similar trajectory; namely, gradual increases throughout childhood. Recent findings on normal developmental changes in cortisol release suggest that the HPA axis may be a candidate as a moderating system in the epigenesis of schizophrenia. It has been shown that there is a gradual rise in levels of saliva cortisol through childhood, with a marked escalation in adolescence that corresponds with stages of pubertal maturation (Kiess et al., 1995). Thus, HPA activity shows a rapid rise during puberty, the same period when the prodromal signs of impending schizophrenia typically emerge. Within a diathesis–stress framework, this is consistent with the assumption that adolescence–early adulthood is associated with an augmentation of the biological stress response. The HPA axis may, therefore, play a role in moderating the expression of the prodromal signs of schizophrenia and in triggering the initial expression of clinical symptoms.

A Prospective Study of Schizotypal Adolescents

Exploring the role of the HPA axis in triggering the behavioral expression of the diathesis in vulnerable individuals requires prospective, longitudinal studies of at-risk samples. Individuals who meet diagnostic criteria for SPD constitute such a population. Behavioral genetic research as well as studies of the prodromal phase in schizophrenia indicate that SPD is part of the "schizophrenia spectrum" and is associated with a heightened risk for the subsequent development of schizophrenia. The study of SPD has the additional advantage of eliminating the confounding effects of antipsychotic medication, given that most who meet diagnostic criteria for this disorder (but not an Axis I disorder) have not received pharmacological treatment.

We have recently undertaken research aimed at elucidating the biological stress response in individuals who manifest SPD, with the ultimate objective of determining the longitudinal relation of cortisol release with the emergence of clinical symptoms. The research focuses on preadolescent–adolescent participants, with the assumption that they are in a critical developmental period for the onset and progression of the prodromal phase of schizophrenia. In this chapter, we present findings from the initial assessment of the participants. The goals are threefold. First, we compare the developmental trajectories of childhood behavior problems in adolescent SPD participants with those of both normal and psychiatric controls. Our intent is to determine whether SPD participants manifest a pattern of increasing behavioral problems similar to that shown by schizophrenia patients. Second, we test the hypothesis that SPD participants will show heightened cortisol levels. Third, we examine the relation between cortisol release and childhood behavior problems, with the aim of identifying links between specific behavioral dimensions and elevated cortisol.

Participants

There were 65 participants in this study, 42 male adolescents and 23 female adolescents who ranged in age from 11 to 19 years. Recruitment of participants was through a published announcement directed at parents. Twenty (12 male adolescents) met diagnostic criteria for SPD, 20

(13 male adolescents) met diagnostic criteria for one or more other personality disorders or conduct disorders (other personality disorder [OPD]), and 26 (17 male adolescents) did not meet the criteria for any *Diagnostic and Statistical Manual of Mental Disorders* (4th ed. [*DSM-IV*]; American Psychiatric Association, 1994) diagnosis (normal control [NC]). Mean ages for the SPD, OPD, and NC groups were 14.2 ($SD =$ 1.2), 14.7 ($SD =$ 2.2) and 13.9 ($SD =$ 1.6), respectively. None of the participants met diagnostic criteria for an Axis I disorder.

The assessment included the following: (a) the Structured Clinical Interview for *DSM-IV* Personality Disorders (SCID-II) questionnaire (Spitzer, Williams, Gibbon, & First, 1990), (b) the SCID-II interview, and (c) the SCID-P psychotic screen (all administered by an advanced graduate student in clinical psychology). Interrater reliability for *DSM* diagnoses was established at .80 in preliminary training with all interviewers. In addition, saliva samples were obtained for measurement of cortisol (ng/ml) at predetermined points throughout the assessment (one/hr from 12 to 4 p.m.; cortisol was assayed using materials and procedures provided by Incstar Corp., Stillwater, MN).

As expected, there was a high rate of comorbidity, such that many of the participants met criteria for more than one disorder. Thus, some participants in the SPD group also met criteria for another Axis II disorder (avoidant, $n = 4$; obsessive–compulsive, $n = 1$; paranoid, $n = 4$; dependent, $n = 1$; borderline, $n = 3$; conduct disorder, $n = 1$). The OPD group's other diagnoses were dependent, $n = 1$; obsessive–compulsive, $n = 4$; paranoid, $n = 3$ schizoid, $n = 3$; borderline, $n = 1$; conduct disorder, $n = 6$; and not otherwise specified, $n = 7$. (The total diagnoses exceed the number of participants in the OPD group because of comorbidity.) There was no difference among the groups in race or sex composition; however, there was a significant group difference in age. The OPD group was significantly older than the NC group, therefore, age was included as a covariate in the analyses of group differences described below.

Parental Reports of Behavior Problems

The same retrospective version of the CBCL used in the Neumann et al. (1995) study of schizophrenia patients was completed by the parents of the participants in this prospective study. As noted, the modified CBCL and was found to be highly sensitive to diagnostic group differences in premorbid behavior (Baum & Walker, 1995). Use of this retrospective CBCL allows for the exploration of early childhood behavioral antecedents as well as the comparison of the developmental trajectories of the SPD participants with those of patients having schizophrenia.

The CBCL questions were modified such that parents rated their offspring on 123 "problem behavior" items within five age levels (birth–3 years, 4–7 years, 8–11 years, 12–15 years, and 16–18 years). Because most ($n = 46$) participants in the sample were age 15 or younger, their ratings only extended through the fourth age period. For each problem behavior item at each age period, parents rated all of their children on a 3-point scale (0 = *not true of the child,* 1 = *sometimes true of the child,* 2 = *often true of the child*).

CBCL behavior items yield scores for the following factor scales: Withdrawal, Somatic Complaints, Anxiety/Depression, Social Problems, Thought Problems, Attention Problems, Delinquency, and Aggression (Achenbach & Edelbrock, 1981). The first three scales load on a second-order factor labeled *Internalizing,* and the last two factors load on a second-order factor labeled *Externalizing.* These two second-order factors are examined in addition to the separate Social Problems, Thought Problems, and Attention Problems scales.

Following standard scoring procedures for the CBCL, an Internalizing score (Withdrawn, Somatic Complaints, and Anxious/Depressed scales), and an Externalizing score (Delinquent Behavior and Aggressive Behavior scales) were derived for each participant by summing his or her CBCL ratings on the items comprising these two scales. Also following Achenbach's (1991) procedures, scores were derived for the Social Problems, Thought Problems, and Attention Problems scales. Data on childhood behaviors were obtained for 54 participants: 14 SPD, 17 OPD, and 23 NC. Of these, 8 were over 16 years old at the time of the assessment, so ratings of their current behavior problems were based on the 16+ age period.

Diagnostic Group Differences in Current
Behavior Problems

Diagnostic groups were compared on the mean ratings for the CBCL scales for the participant's current age period. For most of the participants, this is the 12–16 year period. The scores from the scales on the CBCL were standardized using all of the participants in the sample. To test the hypothesis that the SPD group is characterized by significantly more behavior problems than controls, we conducted a multivariate analysis of covariance (MANCOVA). The scores from the CBCL behavior problem scales (Internalizing, Externalizing, Social Problems, Thought Problems, Attention Problems) were the dependent variables, whereas the independent variables were diagnostic status (SPD, OPD, NC) and sex. Because age was found to differ significantly among the diagnostic groups, it was used as a covariate in the analysis.

MANCOVAs revealed a significant main effect for diagnostic status, $F(16, 78) = 2.89$, $p < .01$. The main effect for sex was not significant, nor was the Diagnostic Status × Sex interaction effect. Univariate tests, conducted to determine which behavior scales differentiated the groups, were consistent with predictions. Results showed that diagnostic groups differed on CBCL Internalizing behaviors, Social Problems, Thought Problems, and Attention Problems. Diagnostic groups did not differ on CBCL Externalizing ratings.

Planned post hoc comparisons were conducted to determine the nature of the diagnostic group differences. When compared with OPD participants, SPD participants were rated by their parents as exhibiting more Internalizing behavior problems ($t = 2.47$, $p < .01$), more Social Problems ($t = 4.13$, $p < .01$), more Thought Problems ($t = 2.07$, $p < .05$), and more Attention Problems ($t = 2.56$, $p < .01$). Similarly, when compared with the NC group, the SPD group was rated by their parents as exhibiting more Internalizing behavior problems ($t = 2.82$, $p < .01$), more Social Problems ($t = 4.65$, $p < .01$), more Thought Problems ($t = 3.83$, $p < .01$), and more Attention Problems ($t = 3.95$, $p < .01$).

Similar to previous reports (e.g., Asarnow & Ben-Meir, 1988; Nagy & Szatmari, 1986; Wolff, 1991), these results indicate that adolescents with SPD have more behavioral deficits than normal control adolescents as well as adolescents with other psychiatric disorders.

CROSS-TEMPORAL STABILITY OF CHILDHOOD CHARACTERISTICS AND DIAGNOSTIC GROUP DIFFERENCES IN BEHAVIOR PROBLEMS

The retrospective data obtained on the CBCL allow for an exploration of the development of social and behavioral difficulties over time. Correlational analyses revealed significant positive intercorrelations across age periods within each CBCL behavior problem scale. (All p values were less than .05.) These results suggest longitudinal stability of the ratings.

To determine if the diagnostic groups differed significantly in behavioral adjustment over the first four age periods, we conducted a repeated measures MANOVA for each behavior problem scale. The scores for the CBCL factors at each age period were the dependent variables and diagnostic status, sex, and age (birth–3, 4–7, 8–11, and 12–15 years) were the independent variables. Results revealed significant Diagnostic Status × Age interactions for Internalizing behavior, $F(6, 74) = 4.00$, $p < .01$; Externalizing behavior, $F(6, 70) = 2.35$, $p < .05$; Thought Problems, $F(6, 70) = 2.44$, $p < .05$; Attention Problems, $F(6, 80) = 3.43$, $p < .01$; and Social Problems, $F(6, 78) = 3.90$, $p < .01$. (The degrees of freedom vary due to missing data on some scales.) There were no significant Sex × Age × Diagnostic Status interactions nor any Sex × Age interaction for any behavior problem scale. To determine the nature of the Diagnostic Status × Age interactions, we conducted univariate analyses of variance and compared the diagnostic groups at each age level for each CBCL behavior problem scale. The scale scores are presented in each figure by age period and diagnostic group.

As shown in Figure 1, there were no statistically significant diagnostic group differences in parental ratings on the Internalizing behavior factor at the first three age periods, although there was a trend toward significance in the second age period. At the fourth age period,

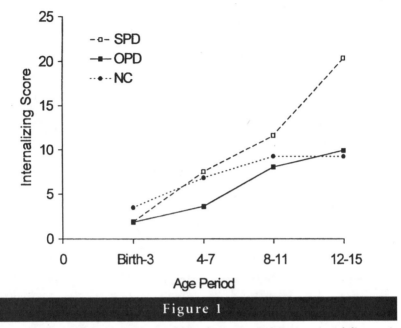

Figure 1

Ratings for Internalizing behavior problems by age period (in years) and diagnostic group. SPD = schizotypal personality disorder; OPD = other personality disorder; NC = normal control.

however, there was a statistically significant difference among diagnostic groups, such that SPD participants were characterized by significantly more Internalizing behaviors relative to both OPD ($t = 3.19$, $p < .01$) and NC ($t = 3.63$, $p < .01$) participants.

Similar results were obtained for Externalizing behaviors (Figure 2). Statistically significant diagnostic group differences were found for the fourth age period only. SPD adolescents were rated as having more Externalizing problems than NC participants ($t = 2.14$, $p < .05$). The OPD participants did not differ from either of the other groups.

For Thought Problems (Figure 3), no statistically significant difference in parental ratings were found in the first three age periods, although there was a trend toward significance in the first age period. Again, in the fourth age period, SPD adolescents were rated as having more Thought Problems than NC adolescents ($t = 2.94$, $p < .01$), with

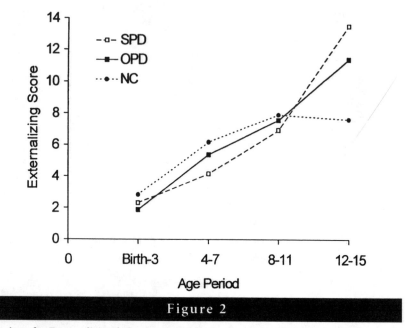

Figure 2

Ratings for Externalizing behavior problems by age period (in years) and diagnostic group. SPD = schizotypal personality disorder; OPD = other personality disorder; NC = normal control.

a trend toward more problems than OPD adolescents ($t = 1.55$, $p = .06$).

Analysis of the Attention Problems scores revealed statistically significant differences among the diagnostic groups in the first and fourth age periods (Figure 4). At the first age period, SPD participants were rated as showing more Attention Problems than both OPD ($t = 2.22$, $p < .05$) and NC ($t = 1.70$, $p < .01$) participants. At the fourth age period, SPD participants were rated as exhibiting more Attention Problems than both OPD ($t = 1.66$, $p < .05$) and NC ($t = 3.59$, $p < .01$) participants.

For the Social Problems scale, there were statistically significant differences among the diagnostic groups at each of the four age periods (Figure 5). At all four age periods, SPD participants were rated as exhibiting more Social Problems than OPD participants ($t = 3.23$, $p <$

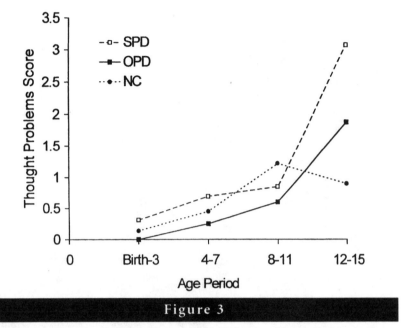

Figure 3

Ratings for Thought Problems by age period (in years) and diagnostic group. SPD = schizotypal personality disorder; OPD = other personality disorder; NC = normal control.

.01; $t = 3.14$, $p < .01$; $t = 2.39$, $p < .01$; $t = 4.11$, p $< .01$, respectively) and NC participants ($t = 1.93$, $p < .05$; $t = 1.71$, $p < .05$; $t = 2.05$, $p < .05$; $t = 5.07$, $p < .01$, respectively).

Diagnostic Group Differences in Cortisol

Cortisol data were obtained for all participants. For each participant, the mean of four cortisol measures was computed. Comparisons revealed that the SPD group showed higher cortisol release when compared with the NC participants ($t = 1.90$, $p = .03$) but not the OPD group ($t = 1.27$, $p = .21$). Means for the SPD, OPD, and NC groups were 3.2 ($SD = 1.1$), 2.7 ($SD = 1.1$), and 2.4 ($SD = 0.8$) ng/ml, respectively. There was no difference between the OPD and NC group. When age was included as a covariate, the same pattern of group differences was obtained.

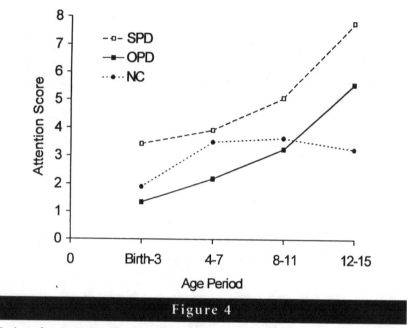

Figure 4

Ratings for Attention Problems by age period (in years) and diagnostic group. SPD = schizotypal personality disorder; OPD = other personality disorder; NC = normal control.

The Relation Between Cortisol Release and Behavior Problems

To determine whether cortisol levels were linked with current behavior problems, we conducted a regression analysis. The Behavior Problem scale scores were the predictor variables, and mean cortisol level was the criterion variable. In these analyses, age was entered first as a co-variate, then the Internalizing, Externalizing, and other behavior scores were entered as a block. Stepwise entry was used with the second block to reduce problems with multicollinearity. Participants from all three diagnostic groups were included in the analysis.

The results indicated that age was a significant predictor of cortisol level, $R^2 = .18$, $F(1, 48) = 9.84$, $p < .01$; as expected, there was a rise in cortisol level with increasing age ($r = .41$). The addition of the Internalizing and Externalizing behavior problems scores resulted in a

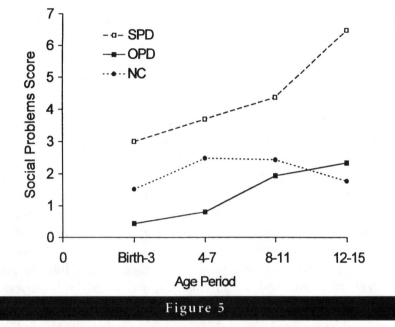

Figure 5

Ratings for Social Problems by age period (in years) and diagnostic group. SPD = schizotypal personality disorder; OPD = other personality disorder; NC = normal control.

significant increase in R^2, $R^2 = .32$; $F(3, 46) = 7.18$, $p < .001$. The Betas associated with the individual predictors indicated that Internalizing behavior problems ($\beta = .37$) were linked with higher cortisol, whereas Externalizing behavior problems ($\beta = -.37$) were associated with lower cortisol levels.

DISCUSSION

In this chapter, we have described our reformulation of the diathesis–stress model and presented preliminary findings from a recently initiated study aimed at testing some predictions generated by the model. The primary goals of this research were to elucidate the developmental course of SPD and, ultimately, to identify potential moderating factors in the onset of schizophrenia. As presented here, the results from the first assessment suggest developmental parallels between schizophrenia and SPD; they also support the hypothesis that SPD is associated with abnormalities in the HPA axis.

The Nature and Developmental Course of Behavior Problems in SPD

We found that adolescents with SPD showed a pattern of gradually escalating behavior problems similar to what we have observed in our research on the precursors of schizophrenia. As with the preschizophrenia children, this gradual increase was apparent for all of the behavior problem scales, although more pronounced for some, and involved a marked rise in adolescence (12–16 years old). Furthermore, it is noteworthy that the same developmental trajectory was not observed in the group of participants with other disorders. An examination of Figures 1–5 reveals that the OPD group is readily distinguishable from the SPD participants on the Internalizing and Social Problem scales where the OPD group does not show the adolescent (12–16 years) rise manifested by the SPD group. However, it is clear that the OPD group generally falls between the SPD and NC group in behavior problems rating on all of the scales in the 12–16 year range. We must await follow-up assessments of the samples to determine whether the subsequent group trends are toward divergence or convergence.

It is also intriguing that the SPD participants showed developmental patterns on the Attention, Social, and Thought Problems scales that are similar to those observed in preschizophrenia children (Neumann et al., 1995). Like the preschizophrenia participants, the SPD group showed an early (birth–4 years) divergence from the NC and OPD groups on the Attention Problems scale. This is consistent with the assumption that attentional dysfunction is a stable characteristic of individuals at risk for schizophrenia and spectrum disorders (Cornblatt & Keilp, 1994; Cornblatt, Lenzenweger, Dworkin, & Erlenmeyer-Kimling, 1992). Also noteworthy, like the preschizophrenia children, the SPD group was characterized by an early and persistent manifestation of high scores on the Social Problems scale. Finally, Thought Problems scores, although somewhat apparent earlier, showed the most marked increase in adolescence.

The Relation of Cortisol Level With Diagnostic Status and Behavior Problems

Consistent with evidence from studies of schizophrenia patients, we found that the SPD group manifested a higher cortisol level than the normal group. Again, the OPD group fell midway between. This is consistent with the hypothesis that schizophrenia spectrum disorders are associated with abnormalities of the HPA axis and biological hypersensitivity to stress.

We also found that heightened cortisol was associated with a higher rate of current Internalizing behavior problems and fewer Externalizing behavior problems in the total sample. In an interpretation of this cross-sectional finding, it is important to note that the OPD comparison group in the present study was composed of adolescents who showed relatively high rates of conduct problems but little depression. Thus, not all symptoms or syndromes were represented in the total sample. The association between behavior problems and cortisol observed here may be unique to this sample and its clinical characteristics and may not be generalizable to randomly selected samples. It will be of particular interest to explore longitudinal relations and to determine whether the subsequent development of behavior problems is associated with cortisol levels as measured in the initial assessment.

Consistent with findings from previous studies of normals, a positive correlation between age and cortisol level was observed. Thus, it appears that during adolescence, the maturational process is associated with increments in HPA activity. In this sense, adolescence may be aptly described as a period of increased stress sensitivity.

Ultimately, the issue of greatest interest is how cortisol release is related with behavioral and diagnostic outcomes. In particular, are those individuals with SPD who show the highest cortisol levels at greatest risk for developing Axis I disorders, especially schizophrenia? We must await the results of follow-up assessments to answer this question.

SUMMARY

The research described here uses a behavioral high-risk paradigm to shed light on developmental processes in schizophrenia. Of course, in addition to being a putative risk factor for schizophrenia, SPD is of interest in its own right as a disorder that impairs interpersonal functioning. The SPD participants in this research had experienced significant distress. It is therefore of value to understand the origins of SPD, independent of its links with schizophrenia.

The data presented here provide further support for the links between schizophrenia and SPD. They indicate striking developmental parallels between the two and indicate the importance of prospective, longitudinal research on adolescents with SPD. Our findings also provide support for the neural diathesis–stress model proposed by Walker and Diforio (1997). Specifically, the results are consistent with the hypothesis that SPD is linked with heightened activity of the HPA axis and that the HPA axis may play a role in moderating the expression of prodromal features and symptoms of schizophrenia.

REFERENCES

Achenbach, T. M. (1977). *Child Behavior Checklist.* Bethesda, MD: National Institute of Mental Health.

Achenbach, T. M. (1991). *Manual for the Child Behavior Checklist.* Burlington, VT: University of Vermont, Department of Psychiatry.

Achenbach, T. M., & Edelbrock, C. S. (1979). The Child Behavior Profile: II. Boys aged 12–16 and girls aged 6–11 and 12–16. *Journal of Consulting and Clinical Psychology, 47,* 223–233.

Achenbach, T. M., & Edelbrock, C. S. (1981). Behavioral problems and competencies reported by parents of normal and disturbed children aged four through sixteen. *Monograph of the Society for Research in Child Development, 46*(1), 1–82.

American Psychiatric Association. (1994). *Diagnostic and statistical manual of mental disorders* (4th ed.). Washington, DC: Author.

Asarnow, J. R., & Ben-Meir, S. (1988). Children with schizophrenia spectrum and depressive disorders: A comparative study of premorbid adjustment, onset pattern and severity of impairment. *Journal of Child Psychology and Psychiatry and Allied Disciplines, 29,* 477–488.

Baum, K., & Walker, E. (1995). The relation between childhood behavior problems and clinical symptoms in adult-onset schizophrenia. *Schizophrenia Research, 16,* 111–120.

Benes, F. M. (1994). Developmental changes in stress adaptation in relation to psychopathology. *Development and Psychopathology, 6,* 723–739.

Cannon, M., Byrne, M., Cotter, D., Sham, P., Larkin, C., & O'Callaghan, E. (1994). Further evidence for anomalies in the hand-prints of patients with schizophrenia: A study of secondary creases. *Schizophrenia Research, 13,* 179–184.

Cornblatt, B. A., & Keilp, J. G. (1994). Impaired attention, genetics and the pathophysiology of schizophrenia. *Schizophrenia Bulletin, 20,* 31–46.

Cornblatt, B. A., Lenzenweger, M. F., Dworkin, R. H., & Erlenmeyer-Kimling, L. (1992). Childhood attentional dysfunctions predict social deficits in unaffected adults at risk for schizophrenia. *British Journal of Psychiatry, 16*(Suppl. 18), 59–64.

Deutch, A. Y., & Young, C. D. (1995). A model of the stress-induced activation of the prefrontal cortical dopamine systems. In M. J. Friedman, D. S. Charney, & A. Y. Deutch (Eds.), *Neurobiological and clinical consequences of stress* (pp. 163–175). Philadelphia: Lippencott–Raven.

Feinberg, I. (1982–1983). Schizophrenia: Caused by a fault in programmed synaptic elimination during adolescence? *Journal of Psychiatric Research, 17,* 319–334.

Fowles, D. C. (1992). Schizophrenia: Diathesis–stress revisited. *Annual Review of Psychology, 43,* 303–336.

Franzen, G. (1971). Serum cortisol in chronic schizophrenia. *Psychiatrica Clinica, 4,* 237–246.

Jablensky, A., Sartorius, N., Ernberg, G., Anker, M., Korten, A., Cooper, J., Day, R., & Bertelsen, A. (1992). Schizophrenia: Manifestations, incidence and course in different cultures: A World Health Organization ten-country study. *Psychological Medicine, 22*(Monograph Suppl. 20), 1–97.

Kiess, W., Meidert, A., Dressendorfer, R. A., Schriever, K., Kessler, U., Konig, A., Schwarz, H. P., & Srasburger, C. J. (1995). Salivary cortisol levels throughout childhood and adolescence: Relation with age, pubertal stage and weight. *Pediatric Research, 37,* 502–506.

Kraus, R., Grof, P., & Brown, G. M. (1988). Drugs and the DST: Need for reappraisal. *American Journal of Psychiatry, 145,* 666–674.

Malla, A. K., & Norman, R. M. (1992). Relationship of major life events and daily stressors to symptomatology in schizophrenia. *Journal of Nervous and Mental Disease, 180*, 664–667.

Nagy, J., & Szatmari, P. (1986). A chart review of schizotypal personality disorders in children. *Journal of Autism and Developmental Disorders, 16*, 351–367.

Neumann, C. S., Grimes, K., Walker, E. F., & Baum, K. (1995). Developmental pathways to schizophrenia: Behavioral subtypes. *Journal of Abnormal Psychology, 104*, 558–566.

Norman, R. M., & Malla, A. K. (1993a). Stressful life events and schizophrenia. I: A review of the research. *British Journal of Psychiatry, 162*, 161–166.

Norman, R. M., & Malla, A. K. (1993b). Stressful life events and schizophrenia. II: Conceptual and methodological issues. *British Journal of Psychiatry, 162*, 166–174.

Norman, R. M., & Malla, A. K. (1994). A prospective study of daily stressors and symptomatology in schizophrenic patients. *Social Psychiatry and Psychiatric Epidemiology, 29*, 244–259.

Rosenthal, D. (1970). *Genetic theory and abnormal behavior.* New York: McGraw-Hill.

Sachar, E. J., Kanter, S. S., Buie, D., Engle, R., & Mehlman, R. (1970). Psychoendocrinology of ego disintegration. *American Journal of Psychiatry, 126*, 1068–1078.

Sapolsky, R. (1992). *Stress, the aging brain, and the mechanisms of neuronal death.* Cambridge, MA: MIT Press.

Spitzer, R. L., Williams, J. B., Gibbon, M., & First, M. B. (1990). *Structured Clinical Interview for* DSM-III-R *Personality Disorders.* Washington, DC: American Psychiatric Association Press.

Starkman, M. N., Gebarski, S. S., Berent, S., & Schteingart, D. E. (1992). Hippocampal formation volume, memory dysfunction, and cortisol levels in patients with Cushing's syndrome. *Biological Psychiatry, 32*, 756–765.

Suddath, R. L., Christison, G. W., Torrey, E. F., Casanova, M. F., & Weinberger, D. R. (1990). Anatomical abnormalities in the brains of monozygotic twins discordant for schizophrenia. *New England Journal of Medicine, 322*, 789–794.

Tienari, P. (1991). Interaction between genetic vulnerability and family environment. *Acta Psychiatrica Scandanavica, 84,* 460–465.

Walker, E. (1994). Developmentally moderated expression of the neuropathology underlying schizophrenia. *Schizophrenia Bulletin, 20,* 453–480.

Walker, E., & Diforio, D. (1997). Schizophrenia: A neural diathesis–stress model. *Psychological Review, 104,* 667–685.

Walker, E., Downey, G., & Bergman, A. (1989). The effects of parental psychopathology and maltreatment on child behavior: A test of the diathesis–stress model. *Child Development, 60,* 15–24.

Watt, N. F., Grubb, T. W., & Erlenmeyer-Kimling, L. (1982). Social, emotional, and intellectual behavior at school among children at high risk for schizophrenia. *Journal of Consulting and Clinical Psychology, 50,* 171–181.

Watt, N. F., & Saiz, C. (1991). Longitudinal studies of premorbid development of adult schizophrenics. In E. F. Walker (Ed.), *Schizophrenia: A life-course developmental perspective* (pp. 158–192). San Diego, CA: Academic Press.

Weinberger, D. (1987). Implications of normal brain development for the pathogenesis of schizophrenia. *Archives of General Psychiatry, 44,* 660–669.

Wolff, S. (1991). 'Schizoid' personality in childhood and adult life. III: The childhood picture. *British Journal of Psychiatry, 159,* 629–635.

Zubin, J., & Spring, B. (1977). Vulnerability: A new view of schizophrenia. *Journal of Abnormal Psychology, 88,* 103–126.

Epilogue: Comments on the Origins and Development of Schizophrenia

Richard R. J. Lewine

The preceding chapters represent an excellent cross-section of contemporary psychological research in schizophrenia. The strong biological orientation of much of this work is reflected in the chapters on genetics (Cannon, chapter 3, this volume; Gottesman & Moldin, chapter 1, this volume), obstetric and birth complications (Mednick et al., chapter 2, this volume), neural circuitry (Grace & Moore, chapter 5, this volume), and neurodevelopmental theory (Cannon, chapter 3, this volume; Walker et al., chapter 17, this volume). The "biologizing" of psychiatric disorders has been widespread and readily accepted, with good reason. I would like, however, to raise some epistemological and methodological concerns about the role of psychosocial inquiry and explanation in the understanding of schizophrenia. I complete these cautionary words with a review of what researchers (myself included) do and do not know about schizophrenia and a suggestion for the psychological study of schizophrenia.

I would like to thank Mark Lenzenweger and Bob Dworkin for their helpful critiques of an earlier draft of this chapter. In particular, I very much appreciate the support and suggestions from Greg Miller for undertaking this chapter at all.

THE BIOLOGIZING OF SCHIZOPHRENIA

Some historical context for my comments is appropriate. Two decades ago, the University of Rochester School of Medicine was host to an international conference on schizophrenia, which was remarkable for its acceptance of a biological perspective (Wynne, Cromwell, & Matthysse, 1978). The "decade of the brain" had not yet been declared, and psychosocial theories predominated in the speculations about schizophrenia's etiology; to suggest at that time that schizophrenia might have its roots in genetic or constitutional processes was not a popular position. Researchers have, in the succeeding 20 years, made considerable progress in their understanding of the biological bases of psychological constructs such as emotion and cognition. Similarly, the study of schizophrenia has yielded substantial information about the biological correlates of disordered psychological functions, such as impaired working memory and various aspects of attention. My concern is that such study has been more limited in its yield for the understanding of schizophrenia than for the understanding of circumscribed behavioral functions (see Lewine, 1990, for a discussion of psychological functions). I am pleased that some of my observations have been presaged by Gregory Miller (1996) in his scholarly 1995 presidential address to the Society of Psychophysiological Research. I refer to his discussion where appropriate, while focusing my attention on the conceptualization of schizophrenia and the technology that seems to drive some of the research.

The convergence of political action by families, major advances in biological technology, and the limited results of 6 decades of largely psychological, social, and psychoanalytic study has led to the decade of the brain (Keith, Regier, & Judd, 1988). The entrance of the "hard" sciences into psychopathology has allowed researchers to believe that they are accumulating hard evidence about the nature (particularly the etiology) of schizophrenia. However, what is known about schizophrenia *qua* disorder or syndrome is limited compared with what is not known about it. I want to make clear that I do believe a considerable body of knowledge about genetics, brain development, circumscribed behavioral systems, and treatment of psychotic disorders has been accumulated. I wonder, however, what has been learned about schizophrenia.

Consider, for example, that several investigators increasingly report findings that are not specific to schizophrenia, and, if anything, the cumulative data lend greater and greater credence to the "general vulnerability" model of psychosis (Zubin & Spring, 1977). Mednick et al. (chapter 2, this volume) have found that many of the obstetric and birth factors, in particular, 2nd-trimester exposure to influenza virus, originally thought to be specific antecedents of schizophrenia, are associated with a very broad range of disordered behaviors (e.g., affective disorders, antisocial behavior, and impaired cognition). Similarly, Cornblatt et al. (chapter 13, this volume) propose that the well-documented attentional deficits associated with schizophrenia may have little to do with the clinical presentation of the disorder. In short, it appears that what researchers have learned tends paradoxically to be narrowly circumscribed in behavioral terms yet broadly applicable to psychopathology.

TECHNOLOGY AND THE STUDY OF SCHIZOPHRENIA

A more serious problem in the study of the schizophrenias is an uncritical reliance on the utility of technology for the direction of research and on extreme reductionism as a primary epistemological model. By *extreme reductionism*, I mean the assumption that certain domains of explanation, such as the biochemical, "underlie" and therefore have epistemological dominance over other domains of explanation, such as the behavioral. I refer you to Miller's article (1996) regarding the logical fallacies in attempting to explain all behavioral (or psychological) phenomena with molecular biological units. The spirit of this argument is partially captured by the distinction he makes between the understanding of time and the understanding of how a clock works. Theories about time do not require an understanding of how the gears of a clock work to move the hands around its face. Clocks and time intersect; they are not the same. Similarly, one can understand the nature of abnormal eye movements (Holzman et al., chapter 6, this volume; Levy et al., chapter 7, this volume) and anomalies of backward masking (Green & Nuechterlein, chapter 12, this volume) without necessarily understanding any more about schizophrenia.

I appreciate Gottesman's reference to Stromgren's warning about the "tyranny of methodology" (personal communication, November 1996). Psychologists like nothing better than using sophisticated research design and technology to address psychological questions. In an eagerness to join the hard sciences with technology, however, it is important that the use of behavioral explanation not be relinquished. It appears to me sometimes that researchers are undergoing a crisis of faith in psychological approaches to schizophrenia with which they cope by showing a brain picture as a way of legitimizing and validating the behavior. This view is directly tied to the assumptions about the relationships among different domains of observation and explanation (*supra vide*).

I would propose that seduction by simple biological theory and technological machinery hampers genuine breakthroughs in the understanding of schizophrenia. More specifically, many research technologies may be prematurely applied to the study of schizophrenia. As a grant reviewer, I have far too often been impressed with how frequently methodology seems to be in search of a disorder to study, a common rationale being that "it has not been tried before." The mere availability of a procedure should not dictate its use.

THE COSTS OF HIGH TECHNOLOGY

Consider, as one example, neuroimaging and, more specifically, positron emission tomography (PET) imaging, an extraordinarily powerful technique to see the brain "at work." The use of color representations to reflect brain activity may be a particularly misleading data presentation strategy. Color maps, which psychologists evaluate perceptually, may cause them to see larger differences in activity level between brain regions than they would from presentation of the actual quantitative data. This belies the extraordinarily complex statistical problems of rendering PET data into comprehensible fashion (Andreasen, 1989; see

Tufte, 1983, 1990, for elegant discussions of the impact of data presentation on interpretation). A recent article about brain and behavior reviewed some brain-imaging studies of veterans with and without posttraumatic stress disorder (PTSD).

> The key color, however, is white. White shows brain areas that the healthy vets were using as they watched the slide show and the unhealthy vets were hardly using at all; in Bremmer's computer print-out, there is a huge white blob in the front of every non-PTSD scan. (Gladwell, 1997, p. 146)

The "huge white blob" has assumed a reality far more convincing, and large, than the numbers underlying it. A simple study to ascertain the differences in the interpretation of data as a function of their presentation as color maps versus numbers would be straightforward and illuminating. For example, what degree of confidence does one assign findings expressed as numbers versus color codes? How more likely is one to recall color differences versus numerical differences? To what extent is the recalled magnitude of differences exaggerated with color coding versus numerical data? In short, how much does the use of color coding distort differences in brain activity from that expressed in the numbers?

High-technology procedures are often so financially costly, time consuming, and complicated that sample sizes are quite restricted. I continue to find little discussion in the literature, however, about the sample biases created by eliminating from study those individuals who cannot tolerate IVs, find lying in a scanner intolerable, are too paranoid to consent to complicated procedures, or who find exposure to ionizing radiation unacceptable.

Finally, the extremely rapid technological advances in the imaging field guarantee hardware and software obsolescence over very short time periods, also lending to the small sample sizes of any given study. Yet, researchers lend such studies rather considerable weight. It is as if the expense and sophistication of the assessment override the usual concerns about power, generalizability, and standardization of assessment technique. It would be very informative to conduct a rigorous review of high-technology schizophrenia studies with the specific goal of addressing the issues of power, generalizability, and validity and to hold such studies to the high standards used for test development.

Misuse of technology is not, of course, limited to either brain-imaging or biological procedures. Anyone with a computer and the appropriate software can conduct complicated statistical analyses that yield meaningless results; thoughtless use of neuropsychological testing and interviews can impede one's progress as much as the inappropriate application of imaging techniques. In all such cases, it is the narrowness of perspective that is the obstacle: "A man who owns only a hammer sees all the world as a nail."

THE FACTS ABOUT SCHIZOPHRENIA

There are few "facts" about schizophrenia that are not contested by one psychopathologist or another. Nevertheless, many would agree on the following: (a) The disorder runs in families and tends to have its onset in adolescence, especially among men; (b) attentional and eye-tracking impairments or anomalies may be markers of vulnerability to schizophrenia; (c) a wide variety of brain abnormalities have been reported even at schizophrenia's onset and prior to significant medication treatment; (d) individuals with schizophrenia perform poorly on most tests of neuropsychological function, suggesting a general performance deficit; and (e) antipsychotic medications are generally effective in treating the acute symptoms of schizophrenia, and structured psychosocial environments enhance the individual's ability to cope with the stresses of daily living.

Although this is not a minor list, it is disconcerting to realize that some version of these facts (other than those relating to antipsychotic medications) have been known since the beginning of this century (e.g., E. Bleuler, 1911/1950; Kraepelin, 1917). It can be legitimately argued that psychologists have far more detail about each fact than ever before; they have, as Gottesman said, "put some meat on the bones" (personal communication, November, 1996). Save for the details, however, there has been only modest discovery.

The facts are, furthermore, constricted by the ever ubiquitous heterogeneity of schizophrenia. For example, there is no brain abnormality in schizophrenia that characterizes more than 20–33% of any given sample. The brains of the majority of individuals with schizophrenia are normal as far as researchers can tell at present. Despite the limited generalizability of such findings, there is no lack of discussion of schizophrenia as a brain disease, with enthusiastic claims for the amygdala, frontal lobes, hippocampus, and, most recently, the cerebellum as the seat of schizophrenia's etiology. Similarly, recall Dworkin et al.'s (chapter 14, this volume) question to Knight and Silverstein (chapter 10, this volume) regarding the complete absence of cognitive-processing deficits in good premorbid schizophrenia patients. That is, although psychologists legitimately focus on the subgroup that demonstrates the "deficit" in any given study, they are faced with the presence of a substantial number of individuals with schizophrenia who do not exhibit the deficit in question.

Although psychologists frequently allude to schizophrenia's heterogeneity, the vast majority of discussion sections I have read assume that schizophrenia is homogeneous. However, there is rather considerable within-diagnosis variability. That not all individuals exhibit all symptoms and signs has been addressed with such taxonomic concepts as "fuzzy sets." However this may be adequate with respect to diagnosis, it may not be adequate when trying to explain behavior. That is, even though paranoid and disorganized schizophrenia patients may belong to the same diagnostic category, they are functioning in often extremely different ways, for example, with respect to their attention. Consequently, studies of attention in schizophrenia may be largely studies of disorganization in schizophrenia, not necessarily about whatever psychologists mean when they say that paranoid and disorganized patients belong to the same diagnostic category.

Furthermore, diagnostic categories are subject to substantial variation as a function of different sets of operational criteria for schizophrenia, thereby creating considerable between-diagnosis variability. Add to this diagnostic heterogeneity the fact that researchers rarely generate sample sizes large enough (Bellak, 1994, has suggested at least 500) to address adequately subtype analyses and that they are faced with a sobering reminder of the sample specificity of many of research results. In summary, it is hazardous to talk about schizophrenia's etiology.

WHAT RESEARCHERS DO NOT KNOW ABOUT SCHIZOPHRENIA

I would like to emphasize a distinction I made earlier between schizophrenia and the behaviors emitted by those with schizophrenia. There is little argument that researchers have learned a great deal about attention, information processing, eye movement, and numerous other circumscribed behavioral functions. None, however, is synonymous with schizophrenia or unambiguously linked with the clinical processes that lead to its diagnosis.

Researchers Do Not Know What the Core Disorder of Schizophrenia Is

There was an attempt by *Schizophrenia Bulletin* some years ago to invite recognized schizophrenia researchers at the time to answer the question, "What is schizophrenia?" (Strauss, Bowers, & Keith, 1982). Two things struck me about that short-lived effort. First, there was no unanimous agreement on a set of core features of schizophrenia: "The plain fact is that we just don't know what schizophrenia is" (Rifkin, 1984, p. 367). Second, almost all of the contributors (10 medical doctors and 2 doctors of psychology) represented the traditional medical model. I am optimistic that clinicians could ultimately agree on the essence of schizophrenia but that they would have to restrict themselves to psychological constructs such as *ego boundary* and *reality testing*. Although I do not suggest a return to untested speculation about the unconscious, I do suggest that schizophrenia has been oversimplified in the adoption of a simple medical-illness model. Consider Stern and Silbersweig's (chapter 9, this volume) discussion of hallucinations. They point to the occurrence of hallucinations in various conditions but emphasize that what distinguishes schizophrenia from other conditions is the lack of reality testing in schizophrenia. Their studies of the brain imaging of hallucinations are, therefore, more correctly viewed as studies of hallucinations, not studies of schizophrenia.

Researchers Do Not Know Why the Age of Schizophrenia Onset Is So Remarkably Consistent

Consider that many psychiatric–psychological disorders, such as depression, can emerge anywhere in the life span. Yet, schizophrenia occurs with regularity at the cusp of adulthood. Increasingly, psychologists use concepts such as *maturation* and *coming on-line* to incorporate this fact about schizophrenia's timing into their theories of etiology. However, such theories are not theories about schizophrenia's cause but rather about its timing. I believe this is valuable and of potentially significant practical utility, but it tells nothing about why or how people think the TV is sending them personal messages.

Researchers Do Not Know the Source of the Ubiquitous Heterogeneity of Schizophrenia

Despite Herculean efforts to reduce the schizophrenias into empirical or clinical subtypes, the standard deviations remain large relative to the typical comparison groups.

THE "REPSYCHOLOGIZING" OF SCHIZOPHRENIA

How then should psychologists proceed into the next century of schizophrenia research? There are two strategies. First, they can become increasingly focused on circumscribed functions. This is a valuable avenue for research and is most likely to live up to the promise of the decade of the brain. This strategy, however, appears to take researchers further and further from schizophrenia specific processes, as illustrated so clearly in Mednick et al.'s (chapter 2, this volume) studies of 2nd-trimester exposure to the influenza virus and Cornblatt et al.'s (chapter 13, this volume) studies of attention. Second, and not mutually exclusive of the first strategy, researchers can reconceptualize schizophrenia as a psychological construct. The conceptual model I would suggest is that of intelligence. Like intelligence, schizophrenia is made up of multiple components; psychologists "know" what intelligence is but have difficulty agreeing on its core.

There are significant implications in this shift.

1. Psychologists could develop a complex and thorough psychological theory, using various levels of molar and molecular conceptual units (see Miller's, 1996, discussion of cognitive theories as an example).
2. Schizophrenia could be conceptualized as a lifelong process, which takes on protean forms during various developmental stages.
3. Whereas psychologists could acknowledge a significant genetic contribution to schizophrenia, they would not have to ascertain the "locus" of the genetic defect for all forms of schizophrenia (see below).
4. Psychologists could, however, study various factors affecting its development and severity, including neurodevelopment, enrichment strategies, and treatment.

There may exist an extreme subgroup of schizophrenia that is linked to traditional brain disorder, for example, as in the case of extreme mental retardation and phenylketonuria. All other forms of schizophrenia could be conceptualized as complex interactions between brain parameters and the full range of environmental influences, in much the same way that personality and personality disorders are conceptualized.

Let me anticipate those who might read this chapter as evidence of my pessimism. I am extremely enthusiastic and confident about psychologists' ability to learn about increasingly complex relationships between the brain and behavior. Some of this knowledge comes from the study of schizophrenia. I am, however, more sober about efforts to understand the disorder of schizophrenia. It appears to me that the seduction of technology has directed efforts to cope with the frustrations in understanding and treating this problem (cf. M. Bleuler, 1978). I do not believe that psychologists must follow one scientific path to the exclusion of the other; after all there are many ways out of the forest. That both biological and psychological research, however, are equally scientific should go without saying.

REFERENCES

Andreasen, N. (Ed.). (1989). *Brain imaging applications in psychiatry.* Washington, DC: American Psychiatric Press.

Bellak, L. (1994). The schizophrenic syndrome and attention deficit disorder: Thesis, antithesis, and synthesis. *American Psychologist, 49,* 25–29.

Bleuler, E. (1950). *Dementia praecox or the group of schizophrenias* (J. Zukin, Trans.). New York: International Universities Press. (Original printed work in 1911)

Bleuler, M. (1978). *The schizophrenic disorders: Long-term patient and family studies.* New Haven, CT: Yale University Press.

Gladwell, M. (1997). Damaged. *The New Yorker,* February 24 and March 3, pp. 132–147.

Keith, S., Regier, D., & Judd, L. (Eds.). (1988). *A national plan for schizophrenia research.* Rockville, MD: National Institute of Mental Health.

Kraepelin, E. (1917). *Lectures on clinical psychiatry.* New York: Wood.

Lewine, R. (1990). Psychological evaluation. In S. Levy & P. Ninan (Eds.), *Schizophrenia: Treatment of acute psychotic episodes* (pp. 45–60). Washington, DC: American Psychiatric Association.

Miller, G. (1996). Presidential address: How we think about cognition, emotion, and biology in psychopathology. *Psychophysiology, 33,* 615–628.

Rifkin, A. (1984). A comment on Strauss and Carpenter's definitions of "What is Schizophrenia?" *Schizophrenia Bulletin, 10,* 367–368.

Strauss, J., Bowers, M., & Keith, S. (Eds.). (1982). What is Schizophrenia? *Schizophrenia Bulletin, 8,* 433–437.

Tufte, E. (1983). *The visual display of quantitative information.* Cheshire, CT: Graphics Press.

Tufte, E. (1990). *Envisioning information.* Cheshire, CT: Graphics Press.

Wynne, L., Cromwell, R., & Matthysse, S. (1978). *The nature of schizophrenia: New approaches to research and treatment.* New York: Wiley.

Zubin, J., & Spring, B. (1977). Vulnerability: A new view of schizophrenia. *Journal of Abnormal Psychology, 86,* 103–126.

Author Index

Numbers in italics refer to listings in reference sections.

Abebe, T., 71, *87*
Abel, L., 165, *180,* 287, 364, *375*
Achenbach, T. M., 474, 478, *488*
Ackenheil, M., *21, 25*
Adami, H., 189, *210*
Adamo, U. H., *441, 444*
Adams, C., *323*
Adams, H. E., *119*
Adams, W., 38, *60*
Adinoff, B., 337, *347*
Adinolphi, M., 51, 53, *61, 65*
Adler, L. E., 58, *61, 323,* 363, *381*
Aggleton, J., 139, *148, 151, 155*
Agid, Y., 190, *209*
Akbarian, S., 58, *61,* 71, *84,* 126, 146, *148*
Akots, G., *380*
Albert, M. S., 242, *245*
Albus, M., *21, 25*
Alexander, G. E., 126, *148*
Alheid, F. G., 130, *157*
Alheid, G. F., 127, *151*
Allan, E., 397, *414*
Alliger, R., *414*
Aloia, M. S., 240, *246*
Alpert, M., xxvi, *xxvii,* 115, 392, 397, 413, *414, 415,* 420, *421, 422*
Alpert, N. M., *182,* 242, *245*
Alphs, L. D., *156*
Alsterberg, G., 240, *243*
Alterman, I., 363, *381*
Altman, J., 127, *148*
Altshuler, L. L., 126, *148*
Alvir, J., *87, 379*
Amadeo, M., 161, *183,* 362, *381*

Amador, X. F., 398, *416,* 435, *440*
Amaral, D. G., 130, *148*
American Psychiatric Association, *61,* 95, *115, 180,* 197, *207,* 354, *375,* 396, *414,* 433, *440, 488*
Ames, C. T., 280
Ames, D., 406, *421*
Amminger, G. P., 434, 436, *440, 441, 443, 444*
Amodt, I., 435, *440*
Anand, A., *87*
Ancoli, S., 395, *417*
Anderson, J., *378*
Anderson, J. E., 269, *287*
Anderson, L., *381*
Anderson, M. J., 221, *231*
Anderson, S., 82, *89*
Andreasen, N., 30, *61,* 75, *84,* 124, 125, 130, *148,* 354, 360, *375,* 385, 386, *414,* 424, 496, *503*
Angrist, B., 123, 140, *148, 149,* 424
Anker, M., *489*
Annett, M., 212, *231*
Anthony, E. J., xxvi, *xxvii,* 427, *441, 442, 444*
Anthony, J., *443*
Antonarakis, S., 13, *20, 22, 24*
Aravagiri, M., *153*
Archer, T., *153*
Arndt, S., *148*
Arnold, S. E., 71, *84,* 126, 146, *149*
Arolt, V., *23*
Arsenault, A. S., 278, *291*
Asamen, J., *321*
Asarnow, J. R., 479, *488*

Asarnow, R. F., 278, *287*, 300, 302, 303, 304, 305, 308, 309, 310, 311, *321, 323*
Aschauer, H. N., *23*
Ashburner, J., *246*
Ashburner, M., 48, *64, 65*
Asherson, P., 8, *23, 26*
Ashtari, M., *87*
Austin, R., 71, *87*

Babb, R., *20, 24*
Bachus, S. E., 123, *149*
Baddeley, A., 240, *243*, 306, *322*
Bakker, V. J., 337, *347*
Bakshi, S., 268, 271, 272, 278, 282, *293*
Ballard, L., 75, *89*
Ballesteros, S., *291*
Balogh, D. W., *287*
Balogh, R. W., *383*
Baloh, R. W., *210*
Banks, W., 266, 268, *287, 291*
Barchas, Jack D., 93
Barclay, R. M., *xxvii, 118, 420*
Barker, D. J. P., 50, *61*
Barker, G. J., 126, *153*
Barlow, H. B., 169, *183*
Barnes, T. R. E., *382*
Baron, M., 387, *414*
Barr, C. E., 38, 46, 58, *61, 64, 86*
Barraclough, B., *25*
Barron, S. A., 75, *85*
Barrowclough, C., 452, *464*
Barry, H., III, 254, *288*
Bartko, J. J., 385, *424*
Bassett, A., *441, 444*
Battaglia, M., 102, *115*
Baum, K., 469, 478, *488, 490*
Bearden, C. E., 69, 81, *86*
Beart, P. M., 127, *150*
Beasley, C. M., Jr., *424*
Beaudette, S., 214, *233*
Bebout, J. L., *381*
Beck, L. H., 305, *326*
Becker, T. J., *423*

Beckmann, H., 71, 72, *85, 88, 89*
Bedi, H., *466*
Beech, A. R., 103, *115*
Beidermann, J. A., *63*
Beiser, M., 75, *91*, 362, *378*, 387, *418*
Bell, M., *441*
Bellack, A. S., 406, *414*, 422, *466*
Bellak, L., 499, *503*
Bellodi, L., *115*
Ben Ari, Y., 53, *61*
Bender, E., *383*
Benes, F. M., 71, 72, *85*, 92, 209, 240, *243*, 472, 474, *489*
Ben-Meir, S., 479, *488*
Benton, A. L., 371, *375*
Berenbaum, H., 102, *115*, 387, 393, 394, 406, 411, *414*
Berendse, H. W., *151*
Berent, S., 473, *490*
Bergman, A., *380*, 470, *491*
Berkowitz, R., 451, 459, *466, 467*
Berman, K. F., 103, *121*, 124, 125, 136, 137, *149, 150, 151, 157*, 240, *246*
Bernad, P., *381*
Bernier, S., 408, *415*
Bernstein, D. P., 109, *121, 381*, 432, *444*
Bernstein, G., *416*
Bernstein-Hyman, R., 282, *290*
Bertelsen, A., 6, *21*, 76, *88*, 114, *117, 489*
Besson, J. A., *376*
Beveridge, W. I. B., *414*
Beyer, T., *423*
Bhugra, D., 9, *20, 22*
Bigelow, L. B., 75, *90, 150*
Bilder, R. M., *87*, 370, *375*
Birbaumer, N., 409, *421*
Bird, E. D., 71, 72, *85*, 240, *243*
Bird, T. D., *381*
Birley, J. L. T., 462, *464*
Bishop, D. T., *382*
Black, D. M., *382*

Blackwood, D., *21, 23*
Blamire, A. M., 192, *209*
Blehar, M. C., *422*
Bleuler, E., xx, *xxvii*, 67, *85*, 94, 95, 99, *115*, 385, 393, *414*, 498, *503*
Bleuler, M., 502, *503*
Bloch, B., 130, *152*
Bloom, F. E., *151, 327*
Bloom, R., *209*
Blouin, J. L., *20, 24*
Blum, N., 370, *380*
Blyler, C. R., 214, *231*
Boccio, A., *87*
Bodis-Wollner, I., *183*
Boff, K. R., *294*
Bogerts, B., 71, 72, *85, 87, 88*, 124, 125, 126, 130, *149*
Bolton, 16, *25*
Bonnet, D., 38, *64*
Boodeau-Pean, S., *21*
Booth, J. D., 72, *87*
Borenstein, M., 268, *287, 379*
Borod, J., 392, 408, *414, 415*
Boronow, J. J., 140, *156*
Borrmann, M., *25*
Boucher, J. D., 390, *415*
Bowden, D. W., *380*
Bowen, L., 307, *322*
Bowers, M., 500, *503*
Bowler, A. E., 38, *61*
Boyd, J. L., *464*
Bracha, H. S., *150*
Braff, D., 57, *61*, 302, *322*, 343, 337, 338, 339, *346, 347*
Brandt, M. E., 390, *415*
Brann, A. W., 31, *62*
Bransome, E. D., Jr., 305, *326*
Braun, A. R., *149*
Braun, C., 408, *415*
Breese, C. R., *323*
Breier, A., 125, *149*
Breitmeyer, B., 204, *207, 287*, 320, *323*, 332, 334, 343, *346*
Brennan, P., 57, *63*

Brewin, C. R., 452, *464*
Briggs, D., *294*
Brodie, J. D., *424*
Brody, D., 338, *346*
Brody, L., *381*
Brookshire, R. J., *415*
Brown, A. S., 38, *65*
Brown, G., 448
Brown, G. M., 471, *489*
Brown, G. W., 447, 449, 462, *464, 467*
Brown, R., 72, *85*
Brown, S., 395, 412, *415*
Brownstein, J., *209*
Brozgold, A. Z., *415*
Brynjolfsson, J., *21, 25*
Buchanan, R., 125, *149, 152, 156*, 360, *382*, 410, 412, *416*
Buchsbaum, M., 124, *150*, 285, 287, 363, *381*
Buchtel, H. A., 189, *208*
Buck, R., 389, 403, 404, 405, *415*
Buckley, P., *443*
Bui, M.-T., *23*
Buie, D., 471, *490*
Buijs, R. M., 127, *157*
Buka, S. L., 69, 70, *86*
Bunney, B. S., 127, *155*
Bunney, W. E., Jr., 58, *61*, 71, *84*, 148, *150*, 287
Burgess, P. M., *418*
Burke, J., *22, 25*
Burnet, P. W., 126, *150*
Bush, L. K., 390, *415*
Butcher, J. N., *120*
Butler, R., *21*
Butler, S. A., 406, *415*
Butzlaff, R. L., 449, 450, *464*
Byerley, W., *20, 23, 24, 26, 323*
Byrne, M., *489*

Cacioppo, J. T., 390, *415*
Cador, M., 127, *155*
Cahill, C., *244, 245, 246*
Callaway, E., 337, *346*
Campbell, I. M., *418*

Campion, D., *21*
Cannon, M., 469, *489*
Cannon, T., v, 28, 32, 34, 36, 57,
    62, 63, 64, 69, 70, 73, 74, 76,
    77, 78, 80, 81, *86, 88,* 308,
    322, 361, *375, 376,* 387, *415,*
    443, 493
Card, J. P., 130, *154*
Cardon, L., *20*
Carey, A., *20*
Carl, J. R., 365, *382*
Carlsson, A., 123, 141, *150*
Carlsson, M., 141, *150*
Carmichael, S. T., 130, *148*
Carney, M. W. P., 124, *152*
Carpenter, C., 371, *377*
Carpenter, J. T., *294*
Carpenter, W. T., Jr., *156,* 385, 410,
    412, *415, 416, 424*
Carr, V., *287*
Carroll, B., *117*
Carstairs, G. M., 447, *464*
Carter, G., 255, *290*
Cartwright, R. A., *382*
Cartwright-Smith, J., *419*
Casacchia, M., *155*
Casanova, M. F., 71, 78, *86, 91,*
    125, 156, 473, *490*
Cascella, N. G., *293*
Casey, D. E., 75, *89*
Cash, T. F., 304, *322*
Cassady, S., 189, *210*
Castellanos, F. X., *378*
Caudle, J., *415*
Cazzullo, C. L., 75, *91*
Cegalis, J. A., 363, *375*
Cerri, A., *117, 323, 377, 418*
Chan, T., 366, *379*
Chapman, H. A., 337, *347*
Chapman, J. P., 100, 101, 103, 112,
    115, 116, 118, 248, 249, 251,
    287, 388, *416, 420*
Chapman, L. J., 100, 101, 103, 112,
    115, 116, 118, 248, 249, 251,
    287, 388, *416, 420*

Chapman, R. M., 268, *293*
Chapman, S., 75, *90*
Charisiou, J., *418*
Charlton, J., 398, *418*
Charney, D. S., *489*
Chase, T. N., *156*
Chechile, R. A., 269, *287*
Chen, A. H.-S., *21*
Chen, H., *24*
Chen, Y., 171, 173, 177, *180*
Chiba, T., 103, *117, 207, 208*
Chin, S., *287*
Cho, A. K., *149, 152*
Choi, D. W., 70, *87*
Christie, M. J., 127, *150*
Christison, G. W., 78, *91,* 125, *156,*
    473, *490*
Chua, S. E., *245*
Cizadlo, T., *148*
Claridge, G. S., 103, *115*
Clark, C. M., *381*
Clark, J., *245*
Clark, S. C., 398, 399, *416*
Clark, W. C., *416*
Cleghorn, J. M., 305, *321*
Clement, R., 398, *416*
Clementz, B. A., *117,* 176, *180,*
    187, 188, 189, 190, *207, 323,*
    362, 363, 364, 365, *375, 377,*
    382, 387, *416, 418*
Clifford, C. A., 77, *91*
Cloninger, C. R., *21*
Coccaro, E. F., *381*
Cochrane, R. H., *376*
Cohen, B., *183*
Cohen, B. D., *153*
Cohen, G., *414*
Cohen, H., 408, *415*
Cohen, J. D., 276, *287,* 309, *326*
Cohler, B. J., 306, *323*
Cola, D., *377*
Colby, C. Z., *419*
Cole, J. D., 453, *464*
Cole, J. K., *289*

Coleman, M., *91*, 93, 106, *116, 294*, 435, *440*
Coley, S. L., 269, *287*
Collier, D., *20, 26*
Collins, F., *25*
Collins, J. F., 255, *288*
Colohan, H., *443*
Colter, N., *85*, 226, *231*
Comazzi, M., *20*
Commenges, D., *23*
Connell, P. H., 123, *150*
Conrad, A., 126, *148*
Conrad, A. J., 71, *87*
Coon, H., 13, *20, 24, 26, 322*
Cooper, J., *489*
Cooper, J. E., 29, *66*, 94, *116*, 235, 246
Copeland, J. R. M., *116*
Coppola, R., *150*
Core, L., *155*
Coren, S., 226, *231*
Cornblatt, B., xxv, 80, *88*, 93, 103, 104, 112, *116, 119*, 273, 275, 276, *288, 289*, 302, 306, 307, 308, 309, 322, *326*, 357, 359, 360, 361, 362, 363, 366, 367, 370, *375, 376, 378, 379, 380, 382*, 386, 388, 406, *416, 417*, 427, 428, 429, 433, 434, 435, 436, *440, 441, 442, 443, 444, 445*, 486, *489*, 495, 501
Corsellis, J. A. N., *85*
Costello, C. G., *420, 421*
Cotter, D., *64, 489*
Couch, F. H., 187, *207*
Coursey, R., 363, *381*
Cowan, N., 251, 256, *288, 289*
Crair, M. C., 271, *288*
Cramer, G., *117, 377*
Craufurd, D., 9, *26*
Crawford, T. J., 187, 188, 189, 190, 191, *207*
Creutzfeldt, O. D., 136, *155*
Crilly, J., 451, *466*
Crockford, G. P., *382*

Cromwell, R., xxvi, *xxvii, 289, 294*, 304, *322, 324*, 494, *503*
Cronbach, L. J., 102, *117*
Crow, T., *21, 24*, 38, *62*, 67, 71, *85*, 87, 88, 89, 124, *152*, 226, *231, 232*, 385, *416*
Crowder, R. G., 267, *291*
Crowe, R. R., 15, *20, 21, 23*
Csernansky, J. G., 240, *243, 292*, 423
Cudeck, R., 36, *65*, 428, *442*
Cunningham, R., *24*
Curtis, D., *21*

Dagg, B. M., 72, *87*
Dalvati, A., 75, *89*
Damasio, A. R., 71, *84*, 126, *149*
d'Amato, T., *21*
Dambska, M., 146, *150*
Daniel, D. G., 140, *150*
Danion, J.-M., 136, *155*
Dann, J., *20*
David, A. S., *244*
Davidson, B., 71, *85*
Davidson, M., *381*
Davidson, R. J., 409, *417*
Davies, D. R., 305, 306, *322, 325*
Davis, A., *322*
Davis, D. M., 412, *424*
Davis, H. R., *121*
Davis, J. M., 161, *181, 182*, 248, *289, 379*
Davis, Z. T., 221, *231*
Dawson, M., 104, *120*, 276, *292*, 300, 301, 302, 307, 310, 316, 317, *325*, 338, *347*, 360, *379*, 428, *443*, 454, 455, 459, *466*, 467
Day, R., *466, 489*
Deakins, S. A., *466*
Degreef, S. R., 75, *87*
de la Selva, A., *465*
DeLisi, L., *20*, 75, 77, *87, 92*, 227, *232*, 351, 371, *376, 377*
DeLong, M. R., 126, *148*

Dember, W. N., 305, *326*
Den Boer, J. A., *156*
Dennert, J. W., 75, *84*
Der, G., *20*
Descarries, L., 131, *150*
Detera-Wadleigh, S., *26*
de Trincheria, I., 104, *120*
Deutch, A. Y., 127, *155*, 472, *489*
Deutsch, C., *421*
Deutsch, S. I., 188, *210*
Devinsky, O., 125, *150*
de Vries, 16, *20*
Diaferia, G., *115*
Dick, A. O., 269, *288*
Diefendorf, A. R., 187, *207*
Diehl, S. R., 22, *26*, 76, *87*, *89*, 299, *324*
Diforio, D., 469, 470, 471, 472, 473, 488, *491*
Diller, L., *415*
Di Michele, V., *155*
Doane, J. A., 452, 459, *465*, *466*, *467*, *468*
Dobbs, M., *25*
Dobie, D. J., *153*
Docherty, N. M., 454, *464*
Dodge, R., 187, *207*
Dolan, R. J., 72, *87*, *244*
Dombroski, B., *20*
Domenech, E., 104, *120*
Domesick, V. B., 127, *152*
Domino, E. F., *153*
Done, D. J., 38, *62*, 70, *87*, 187, *207*, *226*, *231*
Donis-Keller, H., *21*
Donoghue, E. E., 398, *416*
Dornbush, R. L., 262, *292*
Dorogusker, B., *182*
Dorsa, D. M., *153*
Dorus, E., *181*, *378*
Dosher, B. A., 276, 279, 280, *294*
Doucet, G., 131, *150*
Douglas, R. M., 189, *208*
Douglas, V. I., 306, *326*
Downey, G., 470, *491*

Drake, K., *382*
Dressendorfer, R. A., *489*
Duda, K., 452, *464*
Dudleston, K., *25*
Duffy, D. L., *26*
Duivenvoorden, H. J., *20*
Duke, F., 22, *25*
Dunne, E. J., *466*
Dursteler, M. R., 169, 180, *182*, *183*
Dushay, R., 451, *466*
Duster, T., *24*
Dworkin, R., xxv, 112, *116*, *289*, *376*, 386, 387, 388, 398, 399, 400, 405, 406, 407, 410, *416*, *417*, 420, 421, 428, 433, 436, *440*, 486, *489*, *499*

Earnst, K. S., 413, *417*
Easter, S. M., *22*
Easton, C., 403, *415*
Eastwood, S. L., 126, *150*
Eaves, L. J., 10, *22*
Eberlein-Fries, R., 451, *466*
Ebmeier, K. P., 364, *376*
Ebstein, R. P., *21*, *25*
Eckblad, M., 112, *116*, 388, *416*
Eckman, T., *421*
Eckstein, G. N., *25*
Edelbrock, C. S., 474, 478, *488*
Edell, W. S., 100, 103, *116*, *117*, 276, *292*, 310, *325*, 360, *379*
Edvarsen, J., 432, *444*
Ekman, P., 389, 390, 395, 401, 404, 405, 409, *417*, *418*, *423*
Elkashef, A., *149*
Ellgring, H., *423*
Elliot, D. S., 338, *347*
Elliott, D. S., 257, 268, 281, 289, *290*
Embretson, S., 248, 274, *288*
Emmi, A., 145, *150*
Emory, S., 462, *468*
Empfield, M., 413, *422*
Endicott, J., 23, 29, *62*, *65*, 95, *121*, 213, *233*, 311, *326*, 429, 441, *444*

Engle, R., 471, *490*
Enquist, L. W., 130, *154*
Eriksen, C. W., 255, *288*
Erlenmeyer-Kimling, L., xxv, 38, 65, 80, *88*, 104, 112, *116*, 302, 306, 307, 308, *322, 324, 326*, 359, 361, 362, *375, 376, 380, 382, 416, 417*, 427, 428, 429, 430, 432, 433, 434, 435, 436, 437, *440, 441, 442, 443, 444, 445*, 475, 486, *489, 491*
Ernberg, G., *466, 489*
Ernst, S. T., *85*
Ertl, M. A., *25*
Escobar, M. D., *382*
Estes, W. K., 303, *322*
Everitt, B. J., 127, 139, *148, 150, 155*
Ewens, W. J., 16, *25*
Exline, R. V., 398, *418*
Eyler Zorilla, L. T., 78, *88*

Faber, B., *442*
Fahy, T. A., *22*, 38, *62*
Fajans, S. S., *380*
Falkai, P., 71, 72, *85, 88*
Falloon, I. R., 451, 452, *464, 466*
Faraone, S. V., *324*, 387, *424*, 432, *442*
Farber, N. B., 240, *245*
Farde, L., 123, 124, *155*
Farina, A., 254, *288*
Faris, G., 104, *116*, 306, *322, 376*
Farmer, A., 8, *23*, 76, *88*, 387, *418, 422*
Faustman, W. O., 240, *243*
Faux, S. F., 361
Feinberg, I., 82, *88*, 474, *489*
Feingold, D., 457, *467*
Feldman, P. M., *90*
Feldon, J., 276, *288*
Feldstein, S., *418*
Fenton, W. S., 214, *231*, 385, 386, *417, 422*
Ferdinandsen, K., 268, *287*

Fey, E. T., 125, *151*
Filloux, F. M., *153*
Findling, R., *377*
Fine, B., *24*
Finer, D. L., *232*
Finkelstein, J. R., 308, *322*, 361, *376*
First, M., 171, *183*, 198, *210*
First, M. B., 370, *376, 477, 490*
Fischer, B., 204, *207*
Fischer, M., 76, *88*
Fish, B., 433, *442*
Fisher, D. L., 280, *288*
Fiszbein, A., 281, *289*, 399, *418*
Flanagan, S. D., *117, 377*
Flaum, M., *148, 414*
Flechtner, M., 187, *209*
Fleming, J. A. E., 362–363, *378*
Fletcher, P., 236, *244*
Fletcher, W. A., 190, *207*
Fog, R., *231*
Fogelson, D., 301, 309, 316, *325*
Folstein, S. E., 190, *208*
Forsythe, S., 71, *87*
Fournier, E., 190, *209*
Fournier, M. C., 130, *152*
Fowlerm, R. C., 124, *154*
Fowles, D., *118*, 469, *489*
Fox, J., 268, *288*
Fox, J. C., 187, *207*
Fox, P. T., 192, *209*
Fox, R., 304, *324*
Frackowiak, R., *152*, 236, 240, 241, 242, *243, 244, 245, 246*
Frances, A., 364, *380, 382*
Franke, P., 305, *324*, 387, *417*
Frankenburg, F. R., *92*
Franks, R., *61*
Franz, B. R., 71, *84, 149*
Franzen, G., 471, *489*
Frazier, J. A., *378*
Freedman, E. G., 257, *289*, 338, 347
Freedman, J. D., *62*
Freedman, L. R., 433, 436, *442*

Freedman, R., 21, 61, 302, 322, 363, 381
Fridlund, A., 389, 404, 418
Friedman, D., 104, 116, 306, 322, 376, 441, 444
Friedman, L., 165, 180, 364, 377, 381
Friedman, M. J., 489
Friedman, R., 440
Friedman-Hill, S., 270, 288
Friedmann, R., 417
Friedrich, J., 423
Friesen, W. V., 395, 409, 417
Frijda, N., 389, 390, 391, 405, 418
Friston, K., 241, 244
Friston, K. J., 152, 236, 240, 242, 243, 244
Frith, C., 67, 85, 87, 89, 124, 152, 187, 207, 226, 231, 236, 237, 240, 241, 242, 243, 244, 245, 246, 302, 323
Fuhrmann, M., 62
Fukushima, J., 103, 117, 187, 188, 189, 190, 207, 208
Fukushima, K., 103, 117, 187, 188, 189, 190, 207, 208
Fuller, B., 24
Fus, I., 423
Futreal, A., 383

Galderisi, S., 75, 89
Gallant, D., 306, 323
Gallucci, M., 155
Gangestad, S. W., 17, 26
Ganz, L., 332, 334, 346
Garcia, S., 131, 150
Garcia-Domingo, M., 104, 120
Garcia-Rill, E., 63
Garmezy, N., 254, 288, 300, 323
Garner, C., 14, 20
Gaskell, P. C., 381
Gasperetti, C., 294
Gasperini, M., 115
Gassaway, S., 435, 440
Gattaz, W. F., 22, 301, 316, 325

Gavanski, I., 398, 399, 418
Gaviria, M., 181, 379
Gaymard, B., 190, 209
Gebarski, S. S., 473, 490
Geiger, B., 72, 88
Geisler, S., 379
Gelade, G., 304, 326
Gelernter, J., 15, 20
Gellad, R., 149
Gelsema, K., 20
George, L., 281, 288
George, M. S., 463, 464
Gerlach, J., 231
Gershon, E., 21, 24, 26, 87
Gershon, S., 140, 149
Gewirtz, G. R., 444
Geyer, M. A., 337, 346
Ghosh, A., 466
Gibbon, M., 95, 121, 171, 183, 198, 210, 370, 376, 477, 490
Gibbons, R., 248, 289
Gibbons, R. D., 181, 378
Gibson, T., 443
Giedd, J. N., 378
Gilbertson, M. W., 387, 424
Gilderman, A. M., 464
Gill, M., 13, 20, 26
Gilmore, G. C., 262, 263, 293, 337, 347
Gilvarry, C., 22
Gitlin, M., 292, 301, 316, 325, 466
Gladwell, M., 497, 503
Glass, I., 466
Glautier, S., 148
Gloor, H., 48, 49, 62
Glover, G., 38, 64, 65
Glynn, S. M., 322
Gold, J. M., 105, 117, 125, 151, 371, 377
Goldberg, E., 211, 232
Goldberg, S. C., 360, 380
Goldberg, T. E., 125, 137, 150, 151, 240, 246, 371, 377
Golden, R., 110, 120, 429, 441
Goldin, L., 21, 24, 26, 87

Golding, J., *87*
Goldman, C., 403, *415*
Goldman, D., 15, *20*
Goldman-Rakic, P. S., 72, *91,* 105, *117,* 240, *244,* 320, *326,* 371, *380*
Goldstein, M. J., *292, 325,* 452, 457, 458, 459, *464, 465, 466, 467, 468*
Gooddale, M. A., *183*
Gordon, C. T., *378*
Gordon, E., *378*
Gorham, D. R., 197, *209,* 360, *380*
Gorman, A. M., *118, 419*
Gorman, J. M., 398, 399, *416*
Gottesman, I. I., xix, xxii, *xxvii,* 5, 6, 7, 8, 9, 10, 12, 17, *21, 22, 23, 24,* 76, *88,* 100, 110, 114, *117,* 299, 300, *323,* 350, 355, *377, 387, 414, 418, 422, 428,* 433, *441, 442, 443,* 493, 496, 498
Gottheil, E., 398, *418*
Gottlieb, J. S., *153*
Gould, L. N., 238, *244*
Goyer, P., *381*
Grace, A., xxvii, 108, 115, *117,* 127, 130, 131, 132, 135, 139, 141, 143, 144, 146, *151, 152, 153, 154,* 276, *292,* 493
Graffeo, K. A., *424*
Grange, D., 136, *155*
Granholm, E., 278, *287,* 302, 304, *321, 323*
Gray, J. A., 276, *288*
Green, M., xxv, *21,* 192, *208,* 251, 252, 302, 320, *323,* 337, 339, 343, *346, 347,* 462, 496
Greenhalgh, J., *441*
Gregson, A., 51, *65*
Greve, B., *85*
Griffith, J. J., 428, *442*
Grimes, K., 469, *490*
Grimes, K. E., 412, *424*
Grimson, R., *87*

Grochowski, S., 251, 282, *289, 290*
Groenewegen, H. J., 127, 131, *151, 153*
Grof, P., 471, *489*
Grootoonk, S., *245*
Gross, C. G., 268, *287*
Gross, S., 398, *418*
Grove, W. M., 104, *117,* 308, *323,* 362, 363, *375, 377,* 387, *416, 418*
Grubb, T., 434, *444*
Grubb, T. W., 475, *491*
Gruen, R. S., 387, *414*
Gruenberg, A. M., *118,* 387, *419*
Gruetter, R., 192, *209*
Grunebaum, H., 306, *323*
Gruzelier, J. H., 211, *232, 287,* 292, *321, 324, 346*
Guitton, D., 189, 190, *208*
Gupta, S. M., *87*
Gur, R. C., *149,* 308, *322, 375, 380, 381*
Gur, R. E., 74, *88,* 126, *149,* 211, *232,* 308, *322,* 361, *375, 376, 380, 381*
Gurland, B. J., *116*
Gurling, H., 11, 14, *21*
Gurling, H. M. D., *25*
Gutkind, D., 36, *62*
Guy, W., 315, *323*
Guze, S., 102, *121*

Haas, G., 363, 364, *375, 382,* 466
Haber, S. N., *151*
Haberman, S., 162, *180, 181*
Haddad, R., 146, *150*
Hadley, T., 69, 81, *86*
Haegar, B., 187, *207*
Häfner, H., *22,* 301, 316, *325*
Hagman, J. O., *61, 84*
Hahlweg, K., 452, 458, *465*
Haidt, J., 390, *423*
Haier, R. J., *150, 287*
Hain, B., 305
Hain, C., *324,* 387, *417*
Hain, T. C., 190, *208*

Haines, T., *181*
Hale, F., 37, *63*
Hale, J., 360, *382*
Hallett, P. E., 190, *208*
Halley, D. J., *20*
Hallmayer, J., *21, 25*
Halthore, S. N., *87*
Hamburger, S. D., *378*
Hammer, M. A., 370, *377*
Hamovit, J. R., *87*
Hamsher, K., 371, *375*
Handel, S., *150*
Hanin, I., *151*
Hanna, A. M., 256, *290*
Hansmann, I., *380*
Hanson, D. R., 100, *117*
Hardesty, J. P., 454, *468*
Hardt, J., 387, *417*
Hare, E. H., 38, *60, 443*
Hare, H., *65*
Harkavy-Friedman, J., *422*
Harris, G., *148*
Harris, T., *20*
Harrison, P. J., 126, *150*
Harvey, P., *232*
Harvey, P. D., 105, *117,* 281, *289,*
    291, 305, *323,* 392, 410, *420,*
    422, 454, *464*
Hasan, A., 399, *416*
Hassan-Govroff, B., *63*
Haupts, M., *85*
Haviland, J. M., *423*
Haviland, M. B., 5, *25*
Havsteen, B., *23*
Hayes, T., *294*
Hayward, N. K., *21*
Hayworth, R., *380*
He, L., *21*
Heath, A. C., *22*
Heckers, S., 72, *88, 89*
Heilman, K., 211, *232*
Heimann, H., 409, *421, 423*
Heimer, L., 127, 130, *151, 157*
Heinsen, H., 72, *88, 89*
Heinsen, Y., 72, *89*

Heinzmann, U., *85*
Helgason, T., *23*
Helmchen, H., *442*
Hemmingsen, R., *231*
Hemsley, D. R., 136, 146, *151,* 276,
    288
Henderson, L., 187, *207*
Henn, F. A., *87, 442*
Henter, I., xix, *xxvii,* 7, *26*
Herold, S., *244*
Herron, P., 285, *288*
Herscovitch, P., *464*
Hershenson, M., 256, 268, *290, 293*
Hertel, P., 124, *151*
Hetti, G., *23*
Heun, R., 432, *442*
Hewitt, J., 387, *419*
Hewitt, J. K., *118, 419*
Hichwa, R. D., *148*
Higashima, M., *152*
Higgins, N., 242, *244*
Hilldoff Adamo, U., *441*
Hiller, J. B., xxv
Hilwig, M., *20*
Himer, W., *423*
Hirsch, S. R., *88, 152,* 242, *244*
Hirt, M., 255, *293,* 364, *375*
Hisada, K., *152*
Hoff, A. L., *87, 232,* 371, *377*
Hoff, M., 20, 24, *322*
Hoffman, W. F., 75, *89*
Hokama, H., *91*
Holan, V., *87*
Holcomb, H. H., *293*
Holik, J., 20, 24, *322*
Hollister, J. M., 51, 53, 57, *63, 64,*
    69, 70, 81, *86*
Hollister, L. E., *423*
Holmans, P., *20*
Holmes, A., *245*
Holzman, P., xxiv, 93, 103, 106,
    110, 115, *116, 117, 118, 119,*
    120, 121, 161, 162, 167, 168,
    180, 181, 182, 187, 188, 190,
    191, 192, 205, 206, *208, 209,*

210, 248, 251, *289, 294*, 300,
320, *324, 326*, 337, 345, *347*,
362, 363, 371, *377, 378, 380*,
388, *418, 421*, 428, *440, 442*,
496
Hommer, D. W., 363, *378, 380*
Honer, W. G., *444*
Honey, C. R., 141, *151*
Hong, W. L., *378*
Honig, S., *25*
Honrubia, V., *210, 383*
Hooley, J. M., xxv, 449, 450, 452,
453, 454, 458, *464, 465*
Hoover, T. M., 229, *232*
Hopkins, J., *322*
Horen, B., *466*
Horner, A. I. W., *415*
Horvath, T., *381*
Horwitz, B., *464*
Hossein, B., *20*
Housman, D., *20, 22, 24*
Howe, S. R., 305, *326*
Howson, A., *378*
Hudson, K., *24*
Hughes, D. W., 161, *181*
Hulme, M. R., 257, *289*
Huntington's Disease Collaborative
Research Group, 17, *21*
Huntzinger, R., *294*
Hurt, S. W., *377*
Husain, M. M., *63*
Husband, J., 67, *89*
Hutchinson, G., 9, *22*
Huttenlocher, P. R., 71, *89*
Huttunen, M., 38, 46, 58, *63, 64*,
80, *86*, 428, *443*
Hwu, H.-G., *21, 23*
Hyman, B. T., 71, *84*, 126, 146, *149*
Hynd, G. W., 71, *89*

Iacono, W., 75, *91, 117*, 161, 167,
181, 187, *208, 323*, 362, 364,
370, *375, 377, 378*, 387, *416,
418*
Ichikawa, M., *151*

Iijima, T., 134, *151*
Ingraham, L. J., *442*
Irving, W. L., 51, *63*
Irwin, D. E., 278, *289*
Iurlo, M., *151*
Ivarsson, O., *23*
Izard, C. E., 405, *418*

Jaber, M., 130, *152*
Jablensky, A., *466*, 474, *489*
Jackson, H. J., *383*, 406, *418*
Jackson, J. H., 167
Jacobs, H. E., *421*
Jacobs, L., 75, *85*
Jacobsen, B., *64, 442*
Jacobsen, L. K., 364, *378*
Jacoby, C. G., 75, *90*
Jagoe, R., *85*
Jakob, H., 71, *85*
Jakob, J., *89*
James, L. B., 127, *150*
Janal, M., *441*
Jang, K., *23*
Janicak, P. G., 181, *379*
Jansson, L., *442*
Janzarik, W., *22*
Jaskiw, G. E., 144, *149, 153*
Javitt, D. C., 141, *152*
Javitt, D. D., 251, *289*
Jay, M., *21*
Jenkins, J., *466*
Jenkins, J. H., 452, *465*
Jenkins, J. M., 389, 390, *422*
Jenkins, T., 14, *24*
Jensen, B. A., 190, *208*
Jerabek, P. A., *150*
Jesberger, J., *377*
Jesberger, J. A., 165, *180*
Jeste, D. V., *63*, 71, *89*
Jiang, Q., 306, *325*
Jody, D., *379*
Jody, D. N., *87*
Johnson, J. I., 285, *288*
Johnson, R. A., 167, *181*, 187, *208*
Johnston, C. W., *378*
Johnston, M., 452, *464*

Johnston, M. H., 103, *118*
Johnston-Cronk, K., *465*
Johnstone, E. C., 38, *62*, 67, 73, *85, 87, 89*, 124, 130, *152*, 226, *231*
Jolesz, R. A., *91*
Jones, A., 167, *181*, 187, *208*
Jones, B., *207*
Jones, B. P., 306, *324*
Jones, D. L., 127, *153*
Jones, D. W., *150*
Jones, E. G., *61, 84*, 148, 245
Jones, I. H., 398, *418*
Jones, P., 81, *89*, 428, *442*
Jones, P. B., 38, *62*
Jones, T., *152, 244, 245, 246*
Jonsson, G., *153*
Jorritsma-Byham, B., 127, *157*
Joshua, S. D., *418*
Joslyn, G., *20*
Judd, L., 494, *503*
Judd, L. L., 124, *154*
Juhasz, J. A., *415*
Juliano, D. M., 75, *90*

Kadar, M. A., *417*
Kagan, J., *209*
Kahn, A., 397, *419*
Kahn, M. J. E., *24*
Kahneman, D., 282, *289*
Kajiwara, R., *151*
Kales, A., *464*
Kaleva, M., *26*
Kalivas, P. C., *151*
Kalivas, P. W., 145, *152*
Kalsi, G., *21*
Kamin, D., *156*, 264, *294*
Kanter, S. S., 471, *490*
Kaplan, H. I., *22, 23*
Kaplan, J., *423*
Kaplansky, L. M., *416, 417, 440*
Kaprio, J., 80, *86*
Karayiorgou, M., *22, 24*
Karkowski-Shuman, L., *419*
Karno, M., 452, *465, 466*

Karp, B. I., *378*
Karson, C. N., 58, *63*
Kasch, L., *20, 22, 24*
Katkin, W., 363, *381*
Kato, M., *207*
Katsanis, J., 364, 370, *377, 378*, 387, *416, 418*
Katschnig, H., 6, *22*
Katz, M., *150*
Kaufman, L., *294*
Kaufmann, C., 12, *26, 76, 91, 416, 422*
Kavanagh, D. J., 449, 455, *465*
Kawasaki, Y., 136, *152*
Kay, S. R., 281, *289*, 337, *347*, 358, *378, 399, 418*
Kayton, L., 398, *419*
Kazarian, S. S., 453, *464*
Kazazian, H., *20, 22, 24*
Keefe, R., *381, 432, 444*
Keefe, R. S. E., *380*
Keilp, J., 103, *116*, 273, 275, 276, *288*, 302, 307, *322*, 359, 360, 362, *376*, 486, 489
Keith, S., 494, 500, *503*
Keith, T. P., *380*
Keitner, G. I., *465*
Keitzman, M. L., 262, *292*
Keller, J. B., 271, *291*
Kelley, A. E., 127, *152*
Kelly, M., *20*
Kelly, P., 364, *378*
Kelsell, D. P., *382*
Kemali, D., 75, *89*
Kemner, C., *290*
Kemp, I. W., 38, 58, *63*
Kendall, P. C., *120*
Kendell, R. E., 38, 58, *60, 63, 116*
Kendler, K. S., 10, 13, 14, *20, 22, 25, 26, 76, 87, 89*, 95, 99, 100, 110, *118*, 198, *208*, 299, 306, *324*, 387, *419*
Kenemans, J. H. K., *290*
Kenji, W. S., 360, *380*
Kennard, C., 187, *207*

Kennedy, J. L., *23*
Kenney, J., *381*
Kenny, J. T., *377*
Kerr, S. L., 389, 394, *419, 420*
Keshavan, M. S., 82, *89*
Kessler, R. C., *22*
Kessler, U., *489*
Kestenbaum, C., *440, 441*
Kester, D. B., *380, 381*
Kestnbaum, E., *294*
Ketter, T. A., *464*
Kety, S. S., xxvi, *xxvii*, 95, *118*, 432, *442*
Kiba, K., *152*
Kidd, K. K., 15, *22, 23*
Kiess, W., 475, *489*
Kikinis, R., *91*
Killian, G. A., 248, *289*
Kim, J. J., *61, 84, 148*
Kim, S. Y., 188, *210*
Kimberland, M., *24*
King, M.-C., *24*
Kinkel, W. R., 75, *85*
Kinney, D., *421, 442*
Kipps, B. R., *26*
Kirchner, P., *414*
Kirkcaldy, B., *421*
Kirkpatrick, B., 125, *149, 152, 156*
Kitamura, T., 397, *419*
Klar, H. M., *381*
Kleck, R. E., 395, 401, *419*
Kleinman, J. E., 71, *86*, 123, *149, 150*
Kley, I. B., 427, *443*
Knight, J. G., 51, *63*
Knight, R., xxiv, *156,* 249, 250, 253, 254, 255, 256, 257, 258, 259, 260, 262, 264, 265, 267, 268, 269, 271, 272, 273, 276, 277, 278, 281, 282, 286, *289, 290, 291, 293, 294,* 337, 338, *347,* 386, 389, 391, 406, 412, 413, *420,* 499
Koelega, H. S., 275, *290*
Koening, O., 270, *290*

Koeppel, C., 399, *416*
Koff, E., 408, *414*
Koffka, K., 261, 271, *290*
Koh, S. D., 398, *419*
Kolachana, B. S., *149*
Komatsu, H., 180, *183*
Konig, A., *489*
Kopp, B., *324*
Kopp, C., 305
Korfine, L., 93, 99, 105, 111, *118, 119*
Kornetsky, C., 307, 308, *325, 327,* 359, *380, 382*
Korten, A., *466, 489*
Koskenvuo, M., 80, *86*
Kosslyn, S. M., 270, *290*
Kovelman, J. A., 71, *90, 91,* 126, *148*
Kozlowski, P. B., 146, *150*
Kraepelin, E., xx, *xxvii,* 67, 82, *90,* 93, 94, 95, *118,* 307, *324,* 385, 393, *420,* 498, *503*
Krafczek, S. A., 269, *287*
Kraus, R., 471, *489*
Krause, H., *383*
Krause, R., 398, 409, *420, 424*
Krauzlist, R. G., 169, *182*
Kreel, L., 67, *89*
Kremen, W. S., 302, *324*
Kring, A. M., 392, 394, 404, 405, 411, *417, 420*
Kringlen, E., *117,* 162, *180, 181, 377,* 432, *444*
Kristbjarnarson, H., *21, 23*
Kroll, J. F., 256, *290*
Kronenberg, S., *88*
Krueger, J. A., *424*
Kruglyak, L., 12, 13, *22, 323*
Kuczenski, R., 124, *152*
Kuechenmeister, C. A., 363, *378*
Kuehnel, T. G., *322*
Kugelmass, S., *324*
Kuipers, L., 451, 459, *466, 467*
Kulkarni, M. V., *90*
Kumar, R., 397, *419*

Kunugi, H., 38, 58, *63*
Kupfer, D. J., *151, 327*
Kurtz, D., *87*
Kushner, M., *87, 232*
Kwapil, T. R., 100, 112, *115, 116,*
388, 416, 420

Lader, M. H., 459, *468*
Lahti, I., *26*
Laing, P., 51, *63*
Lajonchere, C., *182, 421*
Lake, C., *381*
Laksy, K., *26*
Lander, E., 12, 13, *22*
Lang, P., 404, *420*
Lange, K., 110, *117, 119, 377*
Lanzetta, J. T., *420*
Larkin, C., *64, 443, 489*
Lasker, A. G., 190, *208*
Lassaline, M. E., 262, *290*
Lasseter, V. K., 13, *20, 22, 24*
Latham, C., 168, *181*
Latham, C. A., 406, *421*
Laurent, C., *21*
LaVancher, C. A., *209*
Lavin, A., 127, 130, *152, 154*
Lavoie, M. E., 278, *291*
Lazarus, R. S., 389, 390, *420*
Leary, M. C., xix, *xxvii,* 7, *26*
Lebell, M. B., 458, *465*
LeBlanc, R. S., 278, *291*
Lebow, B. S., *117, 323, 377, 418*
LeDoux, J. E., 136, 139, *152, 155*
LeDuc, C., *20*
Lee, G., *87*
Lee, M. H., 146, *150*
Lee, R. G., 341, *347*
Lee, S., *182*
Lee, V. M., 126, *149*
Leff, J., *20, 22,* 449, 451, 454, 459,
464, 466, 467, 468
Lehner, T., 12, *26,* 76, *91*
Leigh, R. J., 165, *181,* 190, *208,*
365, *378*
LeMay, M., *91*

Lencz, T., *115*
Lennon, D. P., *23*
Lenzenweger, M., xxiii, 99, 100,
102, 103, 104, 105, 106, 111,
112, *116, 118, 119, 120, 121,*
307, *322,* 360, 361, *376, 378,*
386, 387, *417, 420, 421,* 433,
440, 486, *489*
Leonard, S., *323*
Lerer, B., *21, 25*
Lester, L., 256, *290*
Leventhal, D., 262, *295*
Levick, S. E., 386, *417*
Levin, S., 105, *117, 119,* 165, 167,
168, 176, *181, 182,* 187, *208,*
362, *377*
Levinson, D. F., *21*
Levy, D., xxiv, 93, 103, 106, *116,*
117, 119, 161, 162, 165, 168,
179, *180, 181, 182,* 187, 188,
189, 190, 191, *208, 209, 210,*
363, 364, *377, 378, 383, 421,*
440, 462, 496
Levy, S., *503*
Lew, R., 8, *24*
Lewine, R., xxvi, 397, *415, 421, 503*
Lewis, J. A., *417,* 428, *440*
Lewis, M., *423*
Lewis, S., *325*
Lewis, S. W., *207*
Li, S., 363, *382*
Liberman, R. P., 406, *421*
Licht, D. M., 452, *465*
Lichter, J., *20*
Lichtermann, D., *25,* 432, *442*
Liddle, P. F., 124, 125, 126, *152,*
236, 241, 242, *244*
Lieberman, J., *87,* 99, *118, 182,*
363, 364, *379*
Liebowitz, S., 51, *65*
Light, G. A., 272, 275, *294*
Lim, L. C., *26*
Lin, S. P., 38, *65*
Lin, T., 363, *378*
Lindenmayer, J. D., 358

Lindenmayer, J.-P., 282, *290, 378*
Lindqvist, M., 123, *150*
Lindsay, W. R., 406, *421*
Lindsey, D. T., 280
Link, B., 451, *466*
Linton, P. H., 363, *378*
Lipsitt, L. P., 69, *86*
Lipsitz, J. D., *416*
Lipska, B. K., 125, 144, *153, 157*
Lipton, R. B., *117*, 161, 167, 168,
    181, 182, 187, *208, 377*
Lisberger, S. G., 169, *182*
Lishman, W. A., 212, *232*
Liu, X., *21, 23*
Livesley, W. J., *23*
Ljungberg, T., 124, *156*
Lo, Y., *209*
Lockhead, S. J., *324*
Loebel, A., *379*
Lofthouse, R., *20–21*
Loftus, G. R., 256, 259, 260, *290*
Loftus, J., *20*
Logan, G. D., 262, *290, 291*
Logan, T. P., *90*
Lohmann, A. H. M., *151*
Lohr, J., *150*
Lohr, J. B., *63*, 71, *89*
Long, G. M., 256, *291*
Lönnqvist, J., 80, *86*
Loosen, P. T., *417*
Looser-Ott, S., *444*
Lopez, S., *465*
Loranger, A., 30, *63*, 93, 99, 102,
    103, *119*, 429, *442*
Loranger, P. E., 95
Lorch, M. P., 408, *414*
Lottenberg, S., *150*
Lovegrove, W., 277, *291*
Low-Beer, J., *381*
Luby, E. D., *153*
Luchins, D. J., 212, *232*
Luebke, A., *181*
Lukens, E., 451, *466*
Lukoff, D., 454, *468*
Lumey, L. H., 38, *65*

Lutzker, J. R., *322*
Lykken, D. T., 161, *181*, 362, *378*
Lyon, M., *86, 324*, 432, *442*

MacAllister, H., *376*
MacCarthy, B., 452, *464*
Macciardi, F., *23*
MacCrimmon, D. J., 300, 304, 305,
    308, *321*
MacDonald, J. F., 141, *151*
Machon, R. A., 38, 40, 41, 46, 53,
    62, 63, 64, 428, *443*
Mackenzie, A. R., *376*
Mackert, A., 187, *209*
Mackie, R. R., *325*
MacLean, C., *20, 22, 25, 26*, 419
Maeda, Y., *152*
Magaña, A. B., 453, *465, 466*
Maguire, S., *21*
Maher, B. A., xxiv, 213, 214, 219,
    222, 229, *231, 232, 233*, 406,
    421
Mahon, T., *381*
Maier, M., 126, *153*
Maier, W., *21, 25*, 305, 308, *324*,
    387, *417*, 432, *442*
Maj, M., 75, *89*
Malaspina, D., 399, *416, 422*
Malenka, R. C., 271, *288*
Malki, A., 165, *180*
Malla, A. K., 470, *490*
Mallet, J., *21*
Mallett, R., *20, 22*
Mancini, F., *155*
Mandal, M. K., 462, *466*
Manoach, D. S., 213, 226, *233*, 268,
    290
Manschreck, T., xxiv, 168, *181*, 213,
    214, 216, 219, 226, 229, *231,
    232, 233*, 406, 408, *421*
Mansfield, R. J. W., *183*
Marceau, H., *20*
Marchal, J., 451, *466*
Marchbanks, R. M., *23*
Marco, E., 78, *86*

Marco, E. J., *375*
Marcuse, Y., *441*
Marder, S. R., *210*, 304, 305, *321*, *323*, *383*, *465*
Markou, A., *148*
Markow, T. A., 17, *22*
Marmot, M., 81, *89*, 428, *442*
Marneros, A., *424*
Marsh, L., *85*, 242, *244*
Martin, C., *415*
Martin, G. M., *381*
Martin, J., *91*
Marwit, S., 462, *468*
Massel, H. K., *421*
Masten, A. S., 398, 399, *421*
Mathe, A. A., *151*
Mathe, J. M., *151*
Mather, J. A., 187, *209*, 363, *379*
Mathew, R. J., 75, *90*
Matsuda, H., *152*
Matsumoto, G., *151*
Mattei, P., *155*
Mattes, R. M., 409, *421*
Matteson, S., 267, 277, *294*
Matthysse, S., xxvi, *xxvii*, 93, 103, 108, 110, 115, *117*, *119*, 120, 161, *180*, *182*, 192, *209*, 300, *324*, 363, *377*, *378*, 388, *421*, *422*, 494, *503*
Maxwell, E., *87*
Mayer, M., 413, *422*
McCalley-Whitters, M., 75, *90*
McCarley, R. W., *91*, 361, *379*
McCarrey, M. W., 398, *416*
McCarthy, G., 192, *209*
McCauley, C. R., 390, *423*
McClearn, G. E., *21*
McClelland, J., *87*
McClure, W. O., 37, *64*
McCurtain, B. J., 365, *382*
McDonald, A. J., 127, *153*
McDowell, J. E., 176, *180*, 187, *207*
McFarlane, C. A., *383*
McFarlane, W. R., 451, *466*
McGill, C. W., *464*

McGinnis, R. E., 16, *25*
McGlashan, T. H., 385, 386, *417*, 422
McGorry, P. D., 371, *383*
McGrath, J. J., 38, *66*
McGrew, J., 102, *115*, 387, *414*
McGue, M., 7, 8, 10, *23*
McGuffin, P., 8, 11, *20*, *23*, *26*, 76, 88, 387, *418*, *422*
McGuire, M., *118*, 387, *419*
McGuire, P. K., 238, 241, *244*, *245*
McIntyre, C. W., 304, *324*
McKenna, K., *378*
McKenna, P., *245*
McKenzie, J., *465*
McLardy, T., 71, *90*
McLaughlin, J. E., 72, *87*
McMeekan, E. R. L., 212, *232*
McMenamin, S. D., 260, *291*
McNeil, T. F., 53, *64*, 68, 69, *90*, 428, 433, *442*
McSparren, J., 71, *85*, *92*
McWilliam, J., 103, *115*
Meares, R., *378*
Mednick, B., *62*
Mednick, S., xxiii, 28, 32, 36, 38, 40, 41, 46, 51, 53, 57, 58, *61*, *62*, *63*, *64*, *65*, 86, 88, *90*, *115*, 387, *415*, 428, *442*, *443*, 493, 495, 501
Medoff, D. R., *293*
Medus, C., *117*, *323*, *377*, *418*
Meehl, P., 6, *23*, 93, 95, 96, 97, 99, 100, 101, 102, 109, 110, 111, 114, *117*, 120, 250, *291*, 398, *422*, 428, *443*
Meertz, E., 72, *85*, 125, *149*
Mehlman, R., 471, *490*
Meidert, A., *489*
Meltzer, H. Y., 165, *180*, *377*
Mendell, N., 161, *182*, *209*, 363, *378*
Mendell, R., 103, *119*
Menon, D. K., *466*
Merchant, K. M., 130, *153*

Meredith, G., 131, *153*
Meredith, G. E., *151*
Merikangas, K., 16, *24*
Merikle, P. M., 257, *289*
Mermelstein, R., 268, *291*
Merriam, A. E., 337, *347*
Merrigan, W. H., 169, *183*
Merrin, E. L., 167, *181*, 187, *208*
Merritt, R. D., *287*
Mesulam, M., 395, *423*
Mesulam, M. M., 236, *245*
Metcalf, D., *91*
Meyers, D., 22, *24*
Mialet, J. P., 362, *379*
Michaels, C. F., 336, *347*
Mikami, A., 169, *182*
Miklowitz, D. J., 452, 457, *465,*
    466, 467
Milici, N., 75, *89*
Miljovic, Z., 141, *151*
Millar, K., 221, *233*
Miller, C., 214, *233*
Miller, G., 214, 217, 222, *233, 465,*
    494, 495, 502, *503*
Miller, G. A., *117*, 285, *291*
Miller, K. D., 271, *291*
Miller, M. B., 388, *420*
Miller, S., 343, *347*
Minas, I. H., *418*
Minges, J., 432, *442*
Minor, B. G., *153*
Mintun, M., 192, *209*
Mintz, J., 192, *208*, 292, 301, 305,
    316, *321, 325,* 339, *346, 347,*
    451, 458, *465, 467*
Mintz, L. I., *465*
Mirsky, A., *118*, 305, 306, 308, *324,*
    326, 419
Mishkin, M., 180, *183*
Mitchell, H. K., 48, *64*
Mitropoulou, V., *380*
Miyasaka, K., 187, *207*
Mizner, G., 363, *381*
Moberg, P., 308, *322,* 361, *375, 376*
Moberg, P. J., *149*

Mogenson, G., 127, *153*
Mogudi-Carter, M., 14, *24*
Mohammed, A. K., 146, *153*
Mohkamsing, S., *20*
Mohs, R., *23, 381*
Moises, H. W., 13, 14, *21, 23*
Mojtahedi, S., 71, *89*
Mol, E., *20*
Moldin, S. O., xxii, 7, 8, 12, *23,*
    302, *324,* 386, *417,* 433, *443,*
    493, 496
Moore, D. K., *381*
Moore, H., v, 108, 115, 139, 146,
    153, 493
Moore, S., 398, *422*
Moran, M., 189, *210*
Moran, P., 22
Moreau, M., 362, *378*
Morgenstern, G., 306, *326*
Moring, J., 26
Morita, N., 187, 188, 189, 190, *207,*
    208
Morrell, M. J., 125, *150*
Morris, L., 371, *377*
Morris, M., 38, *64*
Morrison, R. L., 406, *414, 422*
Morton, N. E., 8, 16, *23, 24*
Moss, H. B., *464*
Movshon, A., 169, *182*
Mowry, B. J., 14, *21, 23*
Mozley, L. H., *380, 381*
Mrak, R. E., *63*
Mueller, D. J., 258, *291*
Mueller, T. V., 363, *378*
Mueser, K. T., 406, *414, 421, 422,*
    457, *466*
Muir, W., *21*
Muise, J. G., 278, *291*
Mukherjee, S., 370, *375*
Mulley, J. C., 16, *26*
Munk-Jorgensen, P., 38, *60, 61*
Munson, R. C., *149*
Murday, V. A., *382*
Murphy, B., 22, *25*
Murphy, D., 363, *381*

Murphy, G. M., 240, *243*
Murphy, P., *21*, 24
Murray, G. K., *65*, *443*
Murray, R., *20*, 38, *64*, 81, *89*, 428, 442
Murray, R. M., *22*, *26*, 38, *62*, *65*, 77, *91*, 244, 245, *443*
Myles-Worsley, M., *20*, 322

Naarala, M., *26*
Nagy, J., 479, *490*
Najafi, A., *287*
Nakayama, K., 169, *180*, *182*, *183*
Nancarrow, D. J., *21*, 23
Nance, M. A., 17, *24*
Nanko, S., *20*, *26*, 38, *63*
Napier, T. C., *151*
Nasrallah, H. A., 75, *90*, 124, *154*
Naylor, H., 337, *346*
Neale, J. M., 281, *291*, 304, 305, *322*, *323*, *324*, 389, 392, 394, 404, 410, 411, *419*, *420*, *422*
Neale, M. C., *22*
Neath, I., 267, *291*
Neehall, J., *20*
Neisser, U., 255, 282, *291*
Nelson, H. E., *382*
Neophytides, A. N., 77, *92*
Nestadt, G., *20*, *22*, *24*
Nestor, P. G., 361, *379*
Neufeld, R. W. J., 281, *288*
Neumann, C. S., 469, 477, 486, *490*
Neumann, O., *326*
Newman, S. A., 190, *208*
Newmark, M., *466*
Newsome, W. T., 169, *182*
Nguyen, J. A., 188, *210*
Nicewander, W. A., 249, *291*
Nicholas, M., 408, *414*
Nickerson, R. S., *293*
Niermeijer, M. F., *20*
Nijran, K., *207*
Ninan, P., *503*
Ninchoji, T., *233*
Nishizawa, S., *233*

Niskanen, P., 58, *63*
Nomikos, G. G., *151*
Nopoulos, P., *148*
Norman, R. M., 470, *490*
Norris, M., 276, *292*, 310, *325*, 360, *379*
Norton, J. P., 452, *468*
Nowlis, G., 268, *293*
Nuechterlein, K., xxiv, xxv, 6, 104, *120*, *150*, 192, *208*, 251, 252, 273, 275, 276, 278, 281, *291*, *292*, 300, 301, 302, 306, 307, 308, 309, 310, 311, 315, 316, 317, 320, *322*, *323*, *324*, *325*, 338, 339, 343, *346*, *347*, 359, 360, *379*, 428, *443*, 451, 454, 455, 457, 458, 459, 462, *465*, *466*, *467*, *468*, 496
Nurnberger, J. I., 396, *422*
Nutt, D., *148*

Oatley, K., 389, 390, *422*
Obiols, J. E., 104, *120*
O'Brian, C., 162, *181*
O'Brien, J. D., 357, *376*, *379*
Obuchowski, M., 357, 363, 364, 366, *376*, *379*, *380*
O'Callaghan, E., 38, 58, *64*, *65*, 428, *443*, *489*
Ochs, A. L., *118*, *419*
O'Donnell, D. W., 371, *377*
O'Donnell, P., 130, 131, 132, 135, 141, 143, 144, *154*, 276, *292*
O'Donovan, M. C., 76, *90*
O'Driscoll, G., 93, 106, *120*, 167, *182*
O'Hare, A., *118*
Oldfield, R. C., 212, *233*
Oldham, J. M., *63*, 429, *442*
Oldman, J. M., 30
O'Leary, D. S., *148*, *414*
Olin, S. S., 428, *443*
Olincy, A., *322*
Olney, J. W., 240, *245*
Olsen, S. A., 75, *84*

Olsen, S. C., 75, *90*
Oltmanns, T. F., 281, *291*, 387, 393, 394, 410, 411, *414, 422*
O'Neill, A., *22*
O'Neill, F. A., *25, 26, 419*
Onn, S.-P., 130, *154*
Onstad, S., 432, *444*
Oostra, B. A., *20*
Opler, L. A., 262, 265, 281, *289, 293*, 337, *347*, 358, *378*, 399, *416, 418*
Oretti, R., *148*
Orlowski, B., 262, *292*
Orne, D. M., 260, *291*
O'Rourke, D. H., 8, 10, *24*
OrrUrtreger, A., *322*
Ortony, A., 389, *422*
Orvaschel, H., 354, *379*
Orzack, M. H., 307, *325*, 359, *380*
Osborn, L. M., *156*, 264, *294*
Oster, H., 404, *418*
Ott, J., 11, 12, *24, 26*, 76, *91*
Ott, S., *441*
Ott, S. L., 435, *440, 443*
Overall, J. E., 197, *209*, 360, *380*
Overton, D., 161, *183*
Overton, D. A., 362, *381*
Owen, D. R., 262, 265, *293*
Owen, M., 8, *20, 23, 26*
Owen, M. J., 76, *90*
Owens, D. G. C., 226, *231*

Pachtman, E., *61*
Pakkenberg, B., 72, *90*, 130, *154*
Pakstis, A. J., *23*
Palafox, G., 171, *180, 183*
Palchoudhury, S., 462, *466*
Palmer, J., 280, *292*
Palmstierna, T., 124, *154*
Palumbo, D. R., 275, 286, *294*
Pandurangi, A. K., 360, 370, *375, 380*
Pandy, G. N., *181*
Pandya, D. N., 242, *245*
Pansa, M., 398, *418*

Pantelis, C., *382*
Pape, S., *440, 441*
Papouchis, N., 337, *347*
Parasuraman, R., 305, 306, *322, 325*
Pardo, J. V., 463, *467*
Pardo, P. J., 463, *467*
Pare, E. B., 169, *182*
Paredes, A., 398, *418*
Parekh, P. I., *464*
Park, S., 93, 103, 106, *120, 121*, 320, *326*, 371, *380*
Parnas, J., 28, 29, 30, 36, *62, 64*, 78, *86, 88, 90*, 115, *120*, 387, 388, *415, 422, 443*
Partain, C. L., *90*
Pasternak, T., 169, *183*
Patterson, D., *323*
Patton, G. C., *383*
Paulesu, E., 240, *245*
Paux, S. F., *379*
Pearlson, G. D., 74, *88*
Pearson, J. S., 427, *443*
Pecevich, M., *61*
Pelonero, A. L., 360, *380*
Pemberton, M. R., 38, *66*
Pennartz, C., 131, *153*
Pepper, K., 277, *291*
Pepple, J. R., *324*
Pericak-Vance, M. A., *381*
Perlick, D., 413, *422*
Peroutka, S. J., 123, *154*
Peselow, E., *415*
Peters, A., *245*
Peters, J., 124, *157*
Peters, M., 229, *233*
Petersen, N. S., 48, *64*
Petersen, S. E., 192, *209*
Peterson, A. E., *381*
Peterson, J., *378*
Peterson, M., 268, *292*
Pettegrew, J. W., 82, *89*
Pettenati, M. J., *380*
Petursson, H., *21, 25*
Pfohl, B., 370, *380*

Phillips, G. D., *148*
Phillips, L., 254, *292*
Phillips, R. G., 136, *155*
Phillips, W. A., 256, 270, 271, 272, 276, *293*
Pichot, P., 362, *379*
Pierrot-Deseilligny, C., 190, *209*
Pillon, B., 190, *209*
Pillowsky, B., 75, *90*
Pirozzolo, F. J., *378*
Pitkanen, A., 130, *148*
Place, E. J. S., 262, 263, *293*
Plant, G. T., 169, *183*
Pliskin, N. H., 137, *151*
Plomin, R., *21*
Plutchik, R., 389, 390, *423*
Podd, M. H., 137, *151*
Pollack, S. D., *91*
Polymeropoulos, M., 20, *322*
Polymeropoulos, M. H., 13, *24*
Pomerantz, J. R., 267, *294*
Ponto, L. L. B., *148*
Pope, H. G., *92*
Popper, K. R., 250, *293*
Posner, M. I., 192, *209*, 391, *423*
Post, R. M., *464*
Potkin, S., *61, 84, 148, 150*
Potter, D. D., *376*
Potter, M., *25*
Potter, M. C., 256, 257, 259, *293*
Pouget, E. R., 397, *414*
Powell, T., 103, *115*
Praestholm, J., *62, 86, 88*
Prescott, C. A., *24*
Price, A., *375*
Price, J. L., 130, *148, 155*
Price, J. M., 249, *291*
Price, J. S., 124, *152*
Prinzmetal, W., 266, 268, *287, 291*
Pristach, E. A., 267, *294*
Proctor, L. R., 161, 168, *181, 182, 377*
Prokoph, H., *383*
Prosser, E. S., *423*
Proulx, R., 408, *415*

Puig-Antich, J., 354, *379*
Pulver, A. E., 13, 14, 20, *20, 22, 24*
Purcell, D. W., *415*
Puri, B. K., *207*
Püschel, J., 106, *121*
Putchat, C., 187, *209*, 255, *290*
Putnick, M., 360, *378*
Putnick, M. E., 104, *119*

Rabinowicz, E. F., 262, 263, 265, *293*
Radant, A. D., 363, *380*
Rado, S., 100, *121*, 410, *423*
Raichle, M. E., 192, *209*, 463, *467*
Raine, A., *115, 443*
Rainer, J. D., *441*
Rajabi, H., 145, *150*
Rajagopalan, S., 14, *24*
Rajkowska, G., 72, *91*
Rakash, R., *90*
Rakkar, A., *383*
Ranzani, J., *464*
Rao, D. C., 8, *22, 24*
Rao, P. N., *380*
Rapoport, J. L., *378*
Rashbass, C., 165, 166, 175, *183*
Rauch, S. L., 182, 242, *245*
Raulin, M. L., 101, *116*, 267, *294*
Rauschecker, J. P., 271, *293*
Rawlins, J. N. P., 276, *288*
Ray, J. P., 130, *155*
Raz, N., 75, *90*
Raz, S., 75, *90*
Rea, M. M., 364, *380*
Read, C. M., *21*
Read, T., *21*
Redmond, D. A., 214, *233*
Regier, D., 494, *503*
Reich, T., 8, *24, 422*
Reilly, S. L., 5, *25*
Reimherr, F., 20, *323*
Reis, A., *383*
Rende, R., *440*
Rennie, C., *378*
Resnick, S. E., *380*

Reveley, A. M., 77, *91*
Reveley, M. A., 77, *91,* 187, *207*
Reynolds, C., *150*
Reynolds, G., 125, *155*
Rezai, K., *148, 414*
Ribera-Jullien, I., *63*
Rice, J., 433, *443*
Rice, J. P., 8, *24*
Richters, J. E., 449, 454, *465*
Rick, J. T., 51, *65*
Rieder, R. O., 370, *375*
Rifkin, A., 500, *503*
Riley, B. P., 14, *24*
Rinaldi, A., *416, 417, 440*
Rinn, W. E., 409, *423*
Riordan, H., *87,* 371, *377*
Risch, N., *25,* 359, 361, *376*
Risch, N. J., 8, 15, 16, *20, 24,* 104, *116,* 306, *322*
Risch, S. C., *415*
Rist, F., 305, *324*
Ritter, W., 251, *289*
Rivaud, S., 190, *209*
Rizzo, L., 136, *155*
Robbins, T. W., 127, 139, *148, 150, 155*
Roberts, G. W., 71, *88,* 146, *155*
Roberts, S., 433, 435, *440, 441, 442, 443, 444, 445*
Robertson, G. M., *xxvii,* 118
Robins, E., 102, *121,* 311, *326,* 429, *444*
Robins, L., *62*
Robinson, D. R., *181*
Robson, J. G., 169, *183*
Rock, D., 433, *440, 441, 442, 443*
Rodgers, B., 81, *89,* 428, *442*
Roff, J. D., 281, *290,* 386, *420*
Rohde, K., *383*
Roitman, S. E. L., 360, *380*
Rolf, J., xxvi, *xxvii,* 427, *441, 442, 443, 444*
Romano, J., xxvi, *xxvii*
Rombouts, R. P., 275, *295*
Romo-Gruen, J. M., 387, *414*

Ron, M. A., 126, *153*
Roseman, I. J., 411, *423*
Rosen, K., 256, *293*
Rosen, L. R., 449, *465*
Rosenbaum, G., *153*
Rosenberg, D., 435, *443*
Rosenberg, E. L., 395, 401, *423*
Rosenfarb, I. S., 458, 459, *467*
Rosenthal, D., xxvi, *xxvii,* 95, *118,* 470, *490*
Rosenthal, J., *322*
Rosenthal, R., 450, *467*
Rosenzweig, L., *294*
Roses, A. D., *381*
Rosicky, J., 391, *423*
Ross, D. E., *118,* 189, *210,* 285, *293, 419*
Ross, E. D., 395, *423*
Ross, L. E., 191, *210*
Ross, R. G., 363, *380*
Ross, S. M., 191, *210*
Rosse, R. B., 188, 190, *210*
Rossi, A., 125, *155*
Rosvold, H. E., 305, 311, *326*
Roth, R. H., 127, *155*
Rothbart, M. K., 391, *423*
Rothenberg, K., 19, *24*
Rothenberg, S. J., 167, *181,* 187, *208*
Rothman, D. L., 192, *209*
Rothman, S. M., 70, *87*
Rothschild, C. B., 351, *380*
Rothstein, M., *24*
Rotrosen, J., 140, *149, 424*
Rotter, A., 406, *414*
Rozendaal, N., 364, *382*
Rozin, P., 390, *423*
Rozumek, M., 72, *88*
Rubenstein, J., *24*
Ruch, W., 395, 401, *423*
Rucklos, M. E., 213, *232,* 406, *421*
Rund, B. R., 338, *347*
Russakoff, L. M., 30, *63,* 429, *442*
Russell, J. A., 389, *423*

Rutschmann, J., 308, *326,* 362, *380,*
    441
Rutter, M., 16, 25, *62,* 440, 449,
    464, 467
Ryu, H., *233*

Saarento, O., *26*
Sacchetti, E., 75, *91*
Saccuzzo, D., 57, *61,* 255, *293,* 337,
    338, 343, *346, 347*
Sachar, E. J., 471, *490*
Sacker, A., 226, *231*
Saczynski, K., 387, *417*
Sadock, B. J., *22, 23*
Saiz, C., 475, *491*
Sakala, S. M., *210, 383*
Sakuma, M., *87, 232*
Salem, J. E., *417*
Salzen, E. A., *376*
Salzmann, E., 135, 136, *155*
Sanders, A. F., *326*
Sandkuijl, L. A., *20, 23*
Sandman, C. A., *61*
Sandman, E. A., *84*
Sands, S. F., 361, *379*
Sanfilipo, M., *424*
Sanger, T. M., 413, *424*
Sänger-Alt, C., 398, *420*
San Giovanni, J. P., 71, *85,* 240,
    243
Santana, F., *465*
Sapolsky, R., 471, *490*
Sarason, I., 305, *326*
Sargeant, M., *23*
Sartorius, N., 29, *66,* 235, *246, 466,*
    489
Saslow, K., 191, *210*
Savage, C. R., 242, *245*
Sayers, S. L., *466*
Saykin, A. J., 371, *380, 381*
Schacter, D. L., 242, *245*
Scheel-Kruger, J., *151*
Scheibel, A., 126, *148*
Scheibel, A. B., 71, *87, 90, 91*
Schellenberg, G. D., 351, *381*

Schenkel, L., 272, *294*
Scher, S. C., *121*
Scherer, K., 411, *423*
Scherillo, P., *115*
Scherneck, S., *383*
Schizophrenia Linkage Collabora-
    tive Group for Chromosones
    3, 6 and 8, 14, *25*
Schlesinger, M. J., 48, *64, 65*
Schneider, F., 409, 413, *421, 423*
Schnorr, L., *245, 246*
Schnur, D., 357, *376, 379*
Schonfeldt-Bausch, R., 72, 125, *149*
Schriever, K., *489*
Schteingart, D. E., 473, *490*
Schuck, J. R., 341, *347*
Schuckit, M. A., 124, *155*
Schulsinger, F., 36, *62, 64, 65, 86,*
    90, 95, 118, 428, *442, 443*
Schulsinger, H., *64, 90*
Schulz, S. C., 363, *376, 377, 381,*
    416
Schwab, S. G., 13, 14, *25*
Schwartz, B., 278, *293*
Schwartz, B. D., 337, 341, *347*
Schwartz, B. L., 188, *210*
Schwartz, G. E., 412, *415*
Schwartz, J. E., *87*
Schwarz, H. P., *489*
Schwarzkopf, S. B., *156,* 264, 272,
    294
Schwinger, E., *23*
Sciuto, G., *115*
Seaward, J., *245*
Sedvall, G., 123, 124, *155*
See, J. E., 305, *326*
Seeman, P., 123, *155*
Segal, D. S., 124, *149, 152*
Seidman, L. J., 211, *232, 324*
Selemon, L. D., 72, *91*
Selfridge, J., 214, 217, 222, *233*
Selten, J. P., 38, *65*
Semple, W., *381*
Semrud-Clikeman, M., 71, *89*

Sen, A., 222, *233*
Sereno, A. B., 188, 190, 191, 205, 206, *210*
Serino, K., *380*
Serper, M. R., 454, *464*
Servan-Schreiber, D., 276, *287*, 309, *326*
Sesack, S. R., 127, *155*
Severe, J. B., *422*
Sexton, R. H., *149*
Shagass, C., 161, *183*, 362, *381*
Shakow, D., xxvi
Sham, P., *20, 22, 26, 64, 65, 489*
Sham, P. C., 38, 58, 62, *65*, 428, *443*
Shapiro, B., 435, *445*
Shapiro, B. M., *440*
Shapiro, J., 254, *290*
Shapiro, R. M., 125, *149, 156*
Sharma, N. K., 222, *233*
Sharma, T., 11, *21*
Sharp, T., 124, *156*
Sharpe, J. A., 190, *207*
Sharpe, L., *23, 116*
Shaughnessy, R., *181, 378*
Shavit, N., *466*
Shaw, M., 279, *293*
Shedlack, K., *87*
Shek, J., 146, *150*
Shenton, M. E., 74, *91, 294*, 361, *379, 440*
Shepard, D. A., *417*
Shepherd, P. M., *87*
Sher, K. J., 98, *121*
Sherer, M., 254, 255, *290*
Sherman, T., 278, *287*, 302, 304, *321*
Sherrington, R., 11, *25*
Shields, G., *20*
Shields, G. W., *87*
Shields, J., 5, 6, 8, *21*, 299, 300, *323*, 428, *442*
Shilliday, C., *417, 440*
Shimoyama, I., *233*
Shinkwin, R., *22, 25*

Shonfeldt-Bausch, R., *85*
Shtasel, D., *375*
Shtasel, D. L., *381*
Shulman, R. G., 192, *209*
Siegel, C., 363, *381*
Siegman, A. W., *418*
Siever, L. J., *23*, 109, *121*, 363, *380, 381*, 432, *444*
Sigmundson, T., *21*
Silbersweig, D., xxiv, 236, 237, 238, 239, 241, 242, *244, 245, 246,* 500
Silverman, J. M., *21, 23*, 109, *121, 380*
Silverstein, S. M., xxiv, 136, *156,* 264, 265, 267, 268, 271, 272, 275, 276, 277, 278, 281, 282, 286, *293, 294, 295*, 499
Silverton, L., 40, *64*
Simon, R., *116*
Simonoff, 16, *25*
Simons, R. F., 363, *381*
Simpson, J. C., *64, 90*
Simpson, S. G., *422*
Sing, C. F., 5, 6, *25*
Singer, H. S., 190, *208*
Singer, W., 270, 271, 272, 276, *293, 294*
Sison, C., 397, *414*
Sjogren, B., *23*
Sjouw, W., *290*
Skillings, G. F., 386, *417*
Skinner, R. D., *63*
Skodol, A., 432, *444*
Skovengaard, J., 222, *233*
Skre, I., 432, *444*
Slaets, J. P., 38, *65*
Slaghuis, W. L., 337, *347*
Slater, A., 54, *65*
Slater, S. L., *416*
Smith, A. D., 276, *288*
Smith, A. J., 412, *424*
Smith, A. M., *20, 24, 87*
Smith, D. A., 394, *420*
Smith, M. R., 75, *84*

Snyder, C. R., *289*
Snyder, K. S., *292, 325,* 451, *465,* 467
Snyder, S. H., 123, *154*
Soderberg, U., *153*
Solomon, C. M., 362, 364, *377, 380*
Solomon, E., *382*
Solovay, M. R., 282, *294*
Someya, T., *287*
Sommers, A. A., 397, *421*
Sorensen, I., 72, *85*
Sorri, A., *26*
Spanier, G. B., 458, *467*
Spaulding, W., 255, 256, *289, 294*
Spellman, M., *118*
Spencer, T. J., 255, *293*
Sperling, G., 254, 255, 276, 279, 280, *294,* 303, *326*
Spielman, R. S., 15, *25*
Spinelli, S., *443*
Spinks, T., *245*
Spitzer, R., 29, *62,* 95, 109, *121,* 171, *183,* 198, 210, 213, *233,* 311, *326,* 370, *376,* 429, *444,* 477, *490*
Sponheim, S. R., 75, *91*
Spreen, O., 371, *382*
Spring, B., 300, *327,* 338, 344, *347,* 469, 470, *491,* 495, *503*
Spring, B. J., 454, *468*
Spurr, N. K., 351, *382*
Squire, L., 136, *156*
Squires-Wheeler, E., 12, *26, 76, 91,* 432, 433, 435, 436, *440, 441,* 443, 444
Srasburger, C. J., *489*
St. Clair, D., *21*
Stafiniak, P., *381*
Stark, L., 167, *181,* 187, *208*
Starkman, M. N., 473, *490*
Stastny, P., 413, *422*
StatSoft, 365, *382*
Stefanis, C. N., *464*
Steffy, R. A., 305, *321*
Steimer, E., 398, *420*

Steimer-Krause, E., 409, *424*
Steingard, S., 309, *326*
Steinhauer, S. R., 232, 287, 292, *321,* 324, *346*
Stern, E., xxiv, 236, 237, 242, *245,* 246, *500*
Stevens, J. R., 71, *86*
Stevens, M., *89*
Stewart, J., 145, *150*
Stolz, F. M., *380*
Strachan, A., *466*
Strachan, A. M., 457, *467*
Strakowski, S. M., *182*
Stratta, P., *155*
Straub, R. E., 13, 14, *20, 22, 25, 26,* 419
Strauss, E., 371, *382*
Strauss, J., 500, *503*
Strauss, J. S., 385, 410, *424*
Strauss, M. E., 281, *294,* 337, *347,* 360, *382*
Street, J. S., *424*
Streitman, S., 300, *323*
Strick, P. L., 126, *148*
Stritzke, P., *87*
Strohman, R. C., 6, *26*
Stromgren, 496
Strous, R., 251, *289*
Stryker, M. P., 271, *291*
Sturgeon, D., 451, 459, *466, 467*
Styles, B. C., 221, *233*
Suarez, B. K., 8, *24*
Subotnik, K. L., 302, 309, *325*
Suddath, R., 78, *91,* 125, *156, 157,* 242, 244, 473, *490*
Sugarman, P. A., 9, *26*
Summerfield, A., 411, *423*
Sun, C.-E., *26*
Sundstrom, E., *153*
Surprenant, A. M., 267, *291*
Susman, V. L., 30, *63,* 429, *442*
Susser, E., 38, *65*
Sutherland, 16, *26*
Sutker, P. B., *119*
Suzuki, M., *152*

Svensson, T. H., *151*
Swales, T., *377*
Swartz, T. S., 411, *423*
Swayze, V., *148*
Swayze, V. W., II, *414*
Sweeney, D. R., 412, *415*
Sweeney, J., 435, *443*
Sweeney, J. A., 362, 363, 364, 365, 366, *375, 379, 380, 382*
Swergold, G., *24*
Sykes, D. H., 306, *326*
Syzmanski, S., *182*
Szatmari, P., 479, *490*
Szymanski, S., *379*

Tafalla, R., *150*
Takei, N., 22, 38, *62, 63, 64, 65, 443*
Talbot, J., *464*
Talovic, S. A., 428, *442*
Tamminga, C. A., 124, 125, 130, 156, 188, *210, 293, 376, 416*
Tamura, R. N., *424*
Tanaka, S., 103, *117, 207, 208*
Tao, L., *21*
Tapernon-Franz, U., *85*
Taravath, S., 71, *89*
Tarrier, N., *325, 452, 459, 464, 467, 468*
Tartaglini, A., *182*
Tassinary, L. G., 390, *415*
Taylor, E., xix, *xxvii, 7, 26*
Taylor, H. A., 303, *322*
Taylor, J. R., 127, *155*
Teasdale, J. D., 458, *465*
Teasdale, T. W., *90*
Telles, C., *465*
Teng, C. Y., *287*
Tew, W., *87*
Thacker, L., 387, *419*
Thaker, G. K., 156, *188, 189, 190, 210, 293*
Thiemann, S., *423*
Thieme, M. E., *424*
Thomas, J. P., *294*

Tibben, A., *20*
Tidmarsh, S., *23*
Tienari, P., 9, *26, 470, 491*
Tierney, A., *466*
Tison, F., 130, *152*
Tissieres, A., 48, *64, 65*
Tofts, P. S., 126, *153*
Tole, J., 168, *181*
Tollefson, G. D., 413, *424*
Tominaga, T., *151*
Tompson, M., *465*
Toomey, R., 432, *442*
Topping, G., 447, *464*
Toran, J., *466*
Torgersen, S., 432, *444*
Torrey, E. F., 38, *61, 78, 91*, 125, *156, 157, 473, 490*
Totzke, M., *153*
Townsend, J. T., 280, *295*
Tran, P. V., *424*
Treisman, A. M., 304, *326*
Trenary, M., *150*
Trojanowski, J. Q., 71, *84*, 126, *149*
Trull, T. J., 98, *121*
Tsuang, M. T., *64, 69, 90*, 219, *233, 324, 387, 388, 424, 432, 442, 865*
Tuason, V. B., 167, *181, 187, 208*
Tufte, E., 497, *503*
Turner, E. H., 75, *89*
Turner, G., *382*
Turner, T. J., 389, *422*
Turpin, G., 459, *467*
Turvey, M. T., 336, *347*

Uemura, K., *233*
Ungerleider, L. F., 180, *183*
Ungerstedt, U., *156*
Urata, K., *152*
US–UK Cross National Project, 94
Uylings, H. B., 130, *156*

Valenstein, E., 211, *232*
Vallada, H., *20*
Vallada, H. P., 13, *26*

Valner, J. B., 386, 389, 391, 406, 412, 413, *420*
Valone, K., 452, *468*
Valvassori, G., 75, *91*
van Asma, M. J. O., 275, *295*
van den Bosch, R., 136, *156*, 275, *295*, 364, *382*
van den Ouweland, A. M., *20*
van der Heijden, A. H. C., 276, *295*, 303, *326*
Van Der Linden, M., 136, *155*
Van Dijk, C., 127, *157*
van Eden, C. G., 130, *156*
Van Eyl, O., *87*
Van Hoesen, G. W., 71, *84*, 126, *149*
van Kammen, D. P., 124, 140, *156*, *157*
van Kammen, W. B., 124, *157*
van Leeuwen, T. H., *290*
van Praag, H. M., *156*
Van Putten, T., 305, *321*
van Rijn, M., *20*
Vaughan, K. B., *419*
Vaughan, R. C., *419*
Vaughn, C., 449, 451, 454, 459, *464*, *466*, *468*
Vaughn, C. E., 452, *464*
Venables, P., 57, *65*, 211, *232*
Ventura, J., *292*, 301, 316, *325*, 454, 459, *466*, *467*, *468*
Verbaten, M. N., 275, *290*
Vereen, D. R., 406, *421*
Vestergaard, A., *62*, *86*, *88*
Vidyasagar, T. R., 135, *155*
Vincent, S. L., 71, *85*, 240, *243*
Vinuela, A., 58, *61*, 71, *84*, *148*
Vita, A., *20*, 75, *91*
Vladar, K., *149*
Vogt, B. A., 125, *150*
Voorn, P., 127, *151*, *157*
Vourlis, S., *24*

Waddington, J. L., 38, *64*, *65*, *443*
Wade, J. H., *466*

Wagner, G., 398, 409, *420*, *424*
Wahlberg, K. E., *26*
Walczak, C. A., *26*
Waldo, M., *20*, 363, *381*
Waldo, M. C., *323*
Waldo, M. D., *61*
Wale, J., *287*
Walker, E., 36, *65*, 80, *91*, *232*, *289*, 307, *326*, 337, *347*, *382*, 408, 412, *424*, 462, *468*, 469, 470, 471, 472, 473, 474, 478, 488, *488*, *490*, *491*, 493
Wallace, C. J., 277, *295*, 322, *421*
Wallbott, H., 411, *423*
Waller, N. G., 406, *421*
Walsh, D., *20*, *22*, *25*, *26*, *64*, 99, *118*, 306, 324, 387, *419*
Walsh, V., 364, *380*
Walshe, D. G., *443*
Walters, E. E., *22*
Wang, S., 13, 14, *26*
Warkany, J., 37, *66*
Warm, J. S., 305, *326*
Warner, R., 70, *91*
Wasmuth, J., *25*
Wastell, D. G., 221, *233*
Waternaux, C., 162, *181*, 362, *377*
Watkins, G. L., *148*
Watkins, J. M., *321*
Watson, A. B., 169, *183*
Watson, C. G., 281, *290*
Watson, S. J., *325*
Watt, N., xxvi, *xxvii*, 427, 428, 434, *441*, *442*, *444*, 475, *491*
Waxman, E., 260, *291*
Webb, B. T., *22*, *25*
Wechsler, D., 197, *210*
Weeks, D. E., 12, *26*, 76, *91*
Weinberger, D., 75, 77, 78, 82, *88*, 90, *91*, *92*, 103, 105, *121*, 124, 125, 136, 137, 144, *149*, *150*, *151*, 153, *156*, *157*, 212, *232*, 240, 242, *244*, *246*, 302, *327*, 371, *377*, 473, 474, *490*, *491*

Weiner, R. U., 337, *347*
Weintraub, S., 305, *323*
Weiss, J. L., 306, *323*
Weiss, K. M., 337, *347*
Weissenbach, J., *23*
Weisstein, C. C., 229, *232*
Welham, J. L., 38, *66*
Welkowitz, J., *415*
Wells, D. S., 262, *295*
Welsh, K. A., *381*
Wender, P., 20, 95, *118, 323, 442*
Werner, S., *383*
West, A., *441*
West, L. L., *156*, 264, *294*
Westenberg, H. G. M., *156*
Wethington, E., *420, 421*
Wetterberg, L., *23*
Whatley, S., *23*
White, H. B., 363, *378*
White, S. R., *416*
Wible, C. G., *91*
Wiese, C., *21, 23*
Wiest, C., 411, *423*
Wig, N. N., *466*
Wigal, S. B., *61, 84*
Wiijsman, E. M., *381*
Wildenauer, D. B., *21, 25*
Williams, J., 171, *183*, 198, *210*
Williams, J. B., 370, *376*, 477, *490*
Williams, M. E., *321*
Williamson, R., 14, *24*
Willner, P., *151*
Wilson, J. G., *66*
Wilson, W. H., *90*
Wing, J. K., 29, *66*, 235, *246*, 462, *464*
Winkelmayer, R., 398, *418*
Winnick, W. A., 262, *292*
Winstead, D. K., 337, 341, *347*
Winters, L., 359, 361, *376, 382*
Wirshing, W., *465*
Wiseman, R., *383*
Wistedt, B., 124, *154*
Witter, M. P., *151*
Wixted, J. T., 406, *414, 422*

Woerner, M., *379*
Wohlberg, G. W., 308, *327*, 359, *382*
Wolf, A. P., *424*
Wolf, J. Z., 268, *287*
Wolf, L., 435, *445*
Wolf, L. E., 370, *382*
Wolfe, J. M., 270, *288*
Wolff, S., 479, *491*
Wolkin, A., 386, *424*
Wolters, J. G., *151*
Wolyniec, P., *20, 24*
Wolyniec, P. S., *22, 24*
Wood, P., *380*
Woods, B., *421*
Woods, B. T., 75, *92*, 219, *233*
Woolf, C., 6, 18, *26*
Woolf, C. M., 428, *445*
Wright, I., 238, *244, 245*
Wright, P., 51, *63*
Wu, J., *150, 287*
Wuerker, A. M., 452, *468*
Wurtz, R. H., 169, 180, *182, 183*
Wyatt, N. F., *xix*
Wyatt, R. J., *xxvii*, 7, *26*, 77, *92*, 212, *232*
Wykes, T., *325*
Wynne, L., xxvi, *xxvii, 26*, 427, *441, 442, 443, 444, 494, 503*

Xie, S., *87*

Yahia, M., 397, *414*
Yamaguchi, N., *152*
Yamaoka, L. A., *381*
Yamasaki, D. S. G., 180, *183*
Yamashita, I., 187, *207, 208*
Yang, L., *21, 23*
Yardley, S. L., 306, *324*
Yasillo, N. J., *181, 377, 378*
Yaw, J., *323*
Yee, C. M., 292, 325, *467*
Yee, R. D., 188, *210, 362, 383*
Yeo, R. A., 17, *26*
Yeomans, J. M., 278, *289*

Yeterian, E. H., 242, *245*
Yim, C. Y., 127, *153*
Yokoyama, T., *233*
Yonce, L. J., 110, *120*
Yonce, Leslie J., 93
York-Cooler, C., *422*
Young, C. D., 472, *489*
Young, D. A., *323*
Young, W. S., III, 130, *157*
Yu, M.-H., *23*
Yung, A. R., 371, *383*
Yurgelun-Todd, D., *92, 209,* 219, *233, 421*

Zahn, T., *381*
Zajonc, R. B., 389, *424*
Zamacola, A., *63*
Zec, R. F., 103, *121,* 124, *149*
Zee, D., *181*
Zee, D. S., 165, *181,* 190, *208,* 365, *378*
Zeki, S. M., 180, *183*
Zemishlany, Z., *381*

Zerba, K. E., 5, *25*
Zetterstrom, T., 124, *156*
Zhang, J., *22, 25*
Ziegle, J. S., *26*
Ziegler, A., 165, *180*
Ziegler, A. S., 364, *375*
Zigun, J. R., *150*
Zimmerman, K. E., 305, *321*
Zimmerman, M., 370, *380*
Zimmermann, W., 351, *383*
Zinkin, J., *115, 414*
Zinser, M. C., 112, *116,* 388, *416, 420*
Zisook, S., 187, *207*
Zitner, R., *182*
Zoega, T., *23*
Zorilla, L. E., *375*
Zubin, J., xxvi, *232,* 287, *292,* 300, *321, 324, 327,* 338, 344, *346, 347, 454, 468,* 469, 470, *491,* 495, *503*
Zukin, S. R., 141, *152*

Subject Index

ADI. *See* Attention Deviance Index

Adolescence
neurodevelopmental changes in, 82
onset of clinical symptoms in, 473
onset of schizophrenia in, 498
prediction of schizophrenia in, 437,
438
'prodromal' phase in, 473–474
and vulnerability to schizophrenia,
469

Adolescents, 354
See also Elmhurst Adolescent Project
behavioral deficits in, 470
EMDs in, 363
parental reports of behavior problems in, 477–479
with SPD, 486

Adolescents, schizotypal
behavior problems of, 479–480
prospective study of, 476

Adulthood, neurodevelopmental
changes in, 82

Affect, expression of positive, 401

Affective congruence, 395, 400–403

Affective deficits, 385
behavioral studies of, 389
as candidate symptoms, 388
expression and experience, 393
studies of, 392–393

Affective disorders
and maternal influenza, 46
in NYHRP, 430, 431
and reflexive saccade errors, 189

Affective experience

and affective expression, 395
measures of, 410
research in, 413

Affective expression, 393
and affective experience, 403
measures of, 405
research in, 413
SOARS, measure of, 407
SOARS, ratings of, 399–400

Affective flattening, 360, 385, 386
clinical assessment of, 397
defined, 391
measures of, 407, 409
ratings of, 397–399
and social skills, 406

Affective processes, involvement of
nucleus accumbens in, 127

African Caribbean community, schizophrenia in, 9

Aftercare Research Program, UCLA,
315

Age, and cortisol level, 487

Age of onset
and extent of amplified region, 17
for schizophrenia, 474, 501

Alcoholism, 74

Allan, E., 397

Allocation deficits, in STVM, 259–261

Alogia, 360

Alpert, M., 397

Alzheimer's disease, 74, 189

Amadeo, M., 161

Amphetamine
increase in dopaminergic transmission caused by, 147

Amphetamine (*continued*)
  psychosis induced by, 123, 124
  psychotic symptoms derived from,
    143–144
Amplification, progressive, 16
Amygdala
  and developmental disruption of
    limbic circuit formation, 146–
    147
  effect on accumbens cells of, 147
  effect on PFC activity of, 138
  in pathological changes, 125
  and diminished smiling, 393
Anderson, J. E., 269
Anderson, M. J., 221
Andreasen, N. C., 360
Anhedonia, 360, 385
Animal studies
  of amygdala stimulation, 139
  of limbic cortical–basal ganglia cir-
    cuit, 130–131
  of MAM exposure, 146
  of PCP, 141
  of PFC, 145
Annett Scale, 212, 215, 219
Anoxia, 32
Antipsychotic drugs, 130
  efficacy of, 124
  treatment with, 396–397
Antisaccade performance, xxiv
  cognitive demands of, 190
  correct, 187
  disinhibition in, 202–206
  experimental latencies for, 200–202
  experimental tasks for, 192–196
  and frontal lobe pathology, 206
  increased inhibition in, 202–206
  latency of, 189
  measurement of error in, 187, 188
  parsing strategy for, 192
  participants in experiments on,
    197–198
  rationale for examining, 189–192
  recording eye movement in, 196

reflexive saccade tasks in, 196
  in schizotypic patients, 106–108,
    113
  statistical methods for experiments
    on, 198
Antisaccades, defined, 185
Anxiety disorders
  in NYHRP, 430, 431
  and reflexive saccade errors, 189
Articulatory/phonological loop, 240
Asarnow, R. F., 309
Ascertainment, methodological differ-
    ences in, 15
Association studies, 15–16
Associative processes, in schizophrenia
    patients, 136
Attention, impaired
  and clinical symptoms, 360–362
  in EAP, 359–362
  in HSREDS, 353
Attention, studies of, 499
Attentional disengagement, suscepti-
    bility to, 335
Attentional factors, and performance
    measures, 229
Attentional measures, in NYHRP, 435
Attention deficits, 125, 495
  as candidate markers, 368
  and emotional functioning, 391
  in schizotypes, 104, 113
Attention Deviance Index (ADI), 437
Attention Problems Scale, 475, 478,
    479, 484, 486
Auditory-linguistic stimuli, 242
Auditory suffix study, 267–268
Autoantibodies, maternal, and fetal
    brain, 51, 54
Automaticity, in process-oriented ap-
    proach, 261–265
Automaticity deficit hypothesis, 268–
    270
Autopsy studies, 68, 71–73
Avolition
  defined, 360

and emotional functioning, 391
Axis II personality disorder, diagnostic
    criteria for, 99

Backward masking, 255, 462
    basics of, 330–337
    defined, 329
    early vs. late components in, 335
    functions in, 331, 332
    mechanisms for, 333–335
    model of, 334, 336
    notion of deficit in, 337
    performance and clinical factors in,
        337–339
    performance deficit in, 339–340
    procedure for, 330
    visual channels for, 332–333, 341
    and vulnerability to schizophrenia,
        342–345
Bakshi, S., 268, 272
Barker, D. J. P., 50
Barry, H., III, 254
Battaglia, M., 102
Bayesian analysis, 108
Beaudette, S. M., 214
Behavioral disorders, and teratogenic
    action, 50
Behaviors, schizophrenic
    emotional significance of, 147
    released from context, 147
Berenbaum, H., 102, 393, 394
Biobehavioral markers, 352, 360
    and clinical symptomatology, 368
    in HSREDS, 370–371
Biological orientation, of schizophre-
    nia research, 493, 494–495
Biological stress response, 475
"Biological triggers," 474
Bipolar disorders, in NYHRP, 430, 431
Bipolar patients, 339
Birth weights, 31
Bleuler, E., ii, 94, 95, 393
Blunted affect
    frontal lobe pathology and, 125

ratings of, 399
Blunting
    measures of, 407
    in symptom rating scale, 385
Blyler, C. R., 214
Body image, in schizotypy, 100–101
Bonnet, D., 38
Braff, D. L., 338
Brain abnormalities
    See also Frontal lobe dysfunction
        in adulthood, 82
    evidence for, 79
    lack of progression for, 74–76
    in schizophrenic patients, 78
    in unaffected relatives, 76–78, 79
Brain damage, and poor lateralization,
    227
Brain development
    and disruption of limbic circuit
        formation, 147
    and hypoxic–ischemic neuronal in-
        jury, 70
    and teratogenic action, 50
    and visual habituation, 57–58
Brain development, fetal, 47–48
    effect of obstetric events on, 67
    and maternal influenza, 54
    and schizophrenic risk, 60
    and visual attention habituation, 54
    window of vulnerability in, 58–59
Brain-imaging studies, 73–80
Breitmeyer, B. G., 332
Bremmer, 497
Brief Psychiatric Rating Scale, 197,
    315, 360
British families, 11
Brown, G., 448, 449
Buchanan, R. W., 360
Buck, R., 403

CAG repeats, 17
California, University of, at Los Ange-
    les, family members study at,
    309–314

Camberwell Family Interview (CFI), 449
Cannabis abuse, 9
Cannon, T. D., xxiii, 77
Catch trials, 361
CBCL. *See* Child Behavior Checklist
Cell assemblies, functionally coherent, 271
Cell death, in normal aging, 75
Cell migration, prenatal disturbances of, 71
Cerebrospinal fluid volume, increase in, 78
CFI. *See* Camberwell Family Interview
CGG trinucleotide, 16
Chapman, J. P., 101, 248, 249
Chapman, L. J., 101, 248, 249
Chapman, R. M., 268
Chechile, R. A., 269
Child Behavior Checklist (CBCL), 474, 477–478, 479, 480
Childhood
  adjustment problems of, 469
  measures, false positives in, 439
  prediction of schizophrenia in, 437, 438
Child rearing, nonoptimal early, 28
Children
  with preschizophrenia, 475
  of schizophrenia patients, signal–noise discrimination of, 308, 309
  See also Relatives
China Earthquake Project, 58–59
Chromosomal regions, for schizophrenia, 13
Chromosome
  5, DNA polymorphisms on, 11
  8, evidence for linkage to, 14
  6, for schizophrenia, 13–14
Cingulate gyrus, correlated with hallucinations, 239
Classical view, of schizophrenia, 83
Clifford, C. A., 77

Closed–loop gain, in eye tracking, 164–165
Cognition, biological basis of, 494
Cognitive ability, and teratogenic action, 50
Cognitive deficits
  differential deficit strategy for, 248
  and maternal influenza, 60
  study of, 247
Cognitive dysfunction, 68
Cognitive functioning
  prospective studies of, 80–83
  in Tangshan study, 59
Cognitive psychology
  process-oriented strategy in, 249–273
  task-oriented approach in, 250–252
Cohen, J. D., 309
Cohen's *d*, 104, 107
Cohort analytic study, 34
Coley, S. L., 269
Collinearity, processing of, 271
Columbia–Presbyterian Medical Center, 396
Communication deviance, in adoptive parents, 9
Communicative functions, of emotional expression, 390
Comprehensive Assessment of Symptoms and History, 354
Computerized tomography (CT)
  in Copenhagen Project, 30
  early studies, 67
  of frontal lobe dysfunction, 386
Consistency tests, in process-oriented strategy, 250
Consolidation, and integration, xxi, xxii
Consolidation deficits, in STVM, 259–261
Construct validation, question of, 248
Context, and schizophrenic behavior, 147

Continuous Performance Test (CPT), 104, 274, 275–278, 302
Degraded Stimulus version (CPT-DS), 275–276, 311, 312, 313, 314, 315, 317, 318
in Developmental processes in Schizophrenic Disorders Project, 315–317
in earlier research on schizophrenia, 307–309
Identical Pairs version (CPT-IP), 361–362, 366
origins of, 305–307
in UCLA family members study, 310–314
3–7 version, 311, 312, 313, 314, 315, 317, 319, 320
and vulnerability to schizophrenia, 345–346
Control, delusions of, 240
Controllability, and expressed emotion, 452
Copenhagen Habituation Project, 27, 54–55
Copenhagen High-Risk Project, 27, 28–36
cortical anomalies in, 33–35
CPT. See Continuous Performance Test
CPT-IP. See Continuous Performance Test Identical Pairs version
CPT-DS. See Continuous Performance Test Degraded Stimulus version
CT. See Computerized tomography
CT scan procedures in, 30
delivery complications score in, 30–31
diagnostic methods in, 29–30
genetic–environmental interaction in, 31–32
methods in, 34, 36

results in, 32, 34, 36
unstable rearing circumstances in, 35–36, 60
Cornblatt, B., xxv, 104, 112, 308, 361, 495, 501
Cornell–Harvard Schizotypy Study, 106–109
Cornell University, laboratory studies in schizotypy at, 103
Corollary discharge, 240
Correlational research, causative interpretation in, 229
Corrigan Mental Health Center (Fall River, RI), 224
Cortical anomalies
in Copenhagen High-Risk Project, 32
and SPD, 33–35
Cortical development, disruptions of, 126
Corticoaccumbens system, DA regulation of, 145
Corticotropin releasing hormone (CRH), 471
Cortisol level, and diagnostic status, 182
Cortisol release, 475
and behavioral outcomes, 487
and behavior problems, 484–485
measurement of, 483
Cowan, N., 251
Craufurd, D., 9
CRH. See Corticotropin releasing hormone
Criminal activity, and exposure to maternal influenza, 47
Criticality, and psychiatric relapse, 458
Criticism, and expressed emotion, 452
Cromwell, R. L., xxvi
Crow, T. J., 226
Crowder, R. G., 267
CSF. See Cerebrospinal fluid, volume, increase in

CSF–brain ratio, 35
  sulcal, 45–46
  ventricular, 46

DA. *See* Dopamine
Danish Adoption Study, 95
Danish Birth Cohort Project, 27
  methods, 52
  results, 52–53
  Rh incompatibility in, 51
Dawson, M. E., 310, 360
DCs. *See* Delivery complications
Deficit theory, 253–254
Degenerative changes, slow-
    progressing, 82
Delayed response task, in schizotypic
    patients, 106–108, 113
DeLisi, L. E., 77
Delivery complications (DCs), 28, 31
  in Copenhagen Project, 30
  and schizophrenic risk, 60
Dementing disorders, 67, 84
Derailment, and hand preference, 213
de Trincheria, I., 104
Developmental instability, indicators
    of, 17
Developmental processes in
    Schizophrenic Disorders
    Project, 314–320
  design of, 314–315
  trait–state analyses in, 315–320
Dexamethasone Suppression Test, 471
Diagnosis of schizophrenia
  clinical indicators in, 374
  methodological differences in, 15
  by Research Diagnostic Criteria
    (RDC), 311
  value of, xx
*Diagnostic and Statistical Manual of
    Mental Disorders* (*DSM*), xix
  2nd ed., 95
  3rd ed., 29, 30, 95, 171, 197, 354,
    371, 396, 429, 433
  SPD diagnosis in, 109
  4th ed., 28, 96, 99, 477

Diagnostic Interview for Genetic
    Studies, 396
Diathesis–stress model, 454, 463,
    470–475, 485, 488
Diforio, D., 471, 472, 473, 488
Domenech, E., 104
Dopamine agonists, pathological
    change induced by, 140
Dopamine (DA) system, 123, 472
  and hippocampal lesions, 145–146
  increase in activity of, 474
  and schizophrenic symptomatology,
    124
Dosher, B. A., 280
Drosophila
  effect of teratogens on, 48–49
  heat shock in, 48–49
  larval development in, 49, 50
Drug addiction, involvement of nu-
    cleus accumbens in, 127
DSM. See *Diagnostic and Statistical
    Manual of Mental Disorders*
Duchenne smiles, 409
Dworkin, R. H., xxv, 112, 499
Dyadic Adjustment Scale, 458
Dyslexia, 71
DZ (dyzygotic). *See* Twin studies,
    MZ:DZ ratio in

EAP. *See* Elmhurst Adolescent Pro-
    gram
Easton, C., 403
Echoic memory functioning, 251
Edell, W. S., 310, 360
Edinburgh Inventory, 212
EE. *See* Expressed emotion
Ego boundary, 500
Electrodermal arousal, and expressed
    emotion, 459–460
Elliott, D. S., 268
Elmhurst Adolescent Project (EAP),
    350
  biobehavioral measures in, 359–366
  clinical state ratings in, 358–359

conclusions from, 367–368
demographic information for, 356
sample for, 354–357
study design for, 357–358
symtomatology in, 374
Embretson, S., 248, 274
EMDs. *See* Eye-movement disorders
Emotion
biological basis of, 494
evolutionary theories of, 405
expression of, 392
nature of, 389–390
processing of, 391
Emotion, expressed
behavior indexed by, 451–454
and competition for control, 452
construct of, 447, 448–449
patients' perspective of, 457–460
predictive validity of, 440–450
as predictor of psychiatric relapse, 449
and psychiatric relapse, 454–457
research in, 463
studying, 452–454
Emotional behavior, observation of, 410–412
Emotional functioning, in normal individuals, 389
Emotional overinvolvement (EOI), 449
Emotional response, scales of, 403
Endophenotypes, 300
Entorhinal cortex, in etiology of schizophrenia, 125, 126
Environmental factors
focus on, xx
and schizophrenic risk, 60
studies on, 428
EOI. *See* Emotional overinvolvement
Epidemiological studies, viral, 38–39
See also Influenza virus
Epidemiology, genetic, 7, 18
Epigenetic approach, 5–6
Epilepsy

and prenatal structural ectopias, 71
seizure foci of patients with, 241
Epistasis, 17
EPSPs. *See* Excitatory postsynaptic potentials
Erlenmeyer-Kimling, L., xxv, 112, 308, 430
Estes, W. K., 303
ETD. *See* Eye-tracking dysfunction
Ethical issues, 19
Etiology of schizophrenia
and developmental factors, 144
diathesis–stress models in, 470–475
heterogeneity of, 5
neuropathology studies of, 71–73
obstetric complications and, 68–70, 83
and pathological changes, 125
two-hit working model of, 27–28, 60
Excitatory postsynaptic potentials (EPSPs)
within accumbens neurons, 135
in nucleus accumbens, 131, 132
Executive functioning
in HSREDS, 353
of psychometrically identified schizotypes, 103, 105–106, 113
Experience, 393
See also Affective experience
and schizophrenic behavior, 147
and sensory processing, 272
Experience, emotional, measures of, 404
See also Affective experience
Experimental psychology, Span of Apprehension task in, 303–304
Expressed emotion (EE) index, 448
See also Emotion
Externalizing behavior, of adolescents, 480–482
Externalizing behavior problems, scores for, 482

Extrapyramidal limbic cortical–basal ganglia circuits, 128–130
Extrapyramidal symptoms, and flat affect, 413
Eye-movement disorders (EMDs)
    as candidate markers, 368
    and clinical symptoms, 364–366
    in EAP, 362–366
    in HSREDS, 353
Eye movements, recording of, 196.
    See also Neurocognitive deficits
Eye-movement tasks, 185, 186.
    See also Antisaccade performance
Eye tracking, in schizotypic patients, 106–108, 113
Eye-tracking dysfunction (ETD), xxiv
    essential abnormality in, 167
    and motion discrimination, 168–179
    roots of, 163–168
    in schizophrenia, 161–162
    twin concordance for, 162
Eye-tracking performance, in NYHRP, 435
Eye-tracking procedure, 364–365

Facial expression
    in affective deficit, 394
    deficit in, 408
    and physiological reactivity, 404–405
Facial movements
    emotional vs. nonemotional, 408
    study of, 408–409
Familial attitudes, and behavior, 457
Familial risk
    and Fetal Viral Infection Project, 42
    genetic predisposition, 43
Family members study, UCLA
    CPT in, 310–314
    design overview for, 309–310
    parents of schizophrenia probands in, 312–314
    Span of Apprehension in, 310–314

Family studies, 7, 8
    affective deficits in, 387
    expressed emotion in, 457–458
    process-oriented strategy for, 274
    psychiatric relapse in, 450–451, 460–461
Farina, A., 254
Feed-forward connections, system of, 271
Feingold, D., 457
Fenton, W. S., 214
Fetal Viral Infection Project, 27, 36–51
    genetic predisposition in, 43
    influenza infection in, 39–40
    methods, 39–40, 40–42, 45
    results, 40, 41, 42, 44–45, 45–46
    and teratogenicity, 37–39, 43
Fight or flight response, 140
Finland. See Fetal Viral Infection Project
Finnish Adoptive Study, 9
Flat affect, 385, 386
    See also Affective flattening
Fogelson, D., 309
Follow-up study, of psychometrically identified schizotypes, 112
Form judgments, 263
Form processing, weakness in, 263
Fragile X disorder, 16
Frijda, N., 390
Frontal lobe dysfunction
    and affective deficits, 386
    and antisaccade performance, 190
Frontal lobe pathology
    and antisaccade performance, 206
    in schizophrenia patients, 124
Fronto-temporal interactions, PET studies of, 236–237
Fruit fly. See Drosophila
Functional connectivity, 239–240

Gangestad, S. W., 17
Ganz, L., 332

Gap paradigm in antisaccade performance, 191, 193–196, 205–206
Garcia-Domingo, M., 104
Garmezy, N., 254
Gavanski, I., 399
Gene–environment interaction, 8–10
Gene expression
  and heat shock, 48
  and teratogenic action, 50
Genes, nonpolymorphic, 16
Genetic developmental pathology, and poor lateralization, 227
Genetic influences
  on affective deficits, 386
  non-Mendelizing, 16–18
Genetic predisposition
  and brain abnormalities, 68
  and defective habituation, 57
  and familial incidence, 43
  and maternal influenza, 41–45
  and obstetric complications, 79
Genetic privacy, model laws for, 19
Genetic research
  future for, 18–20
  and liability for schizophrenia, 115
Genetic risk
  See also Risk for schizophrenia
  defining, 43
  and familial incidence, 44
  studies, 320
  and unaffected relatives, 76
Genetics, 493
  and age of onset, 351
  molecular, 18
  role of, xxii
Genetic vulnerability markers, 300
Genome, human, systematic screening of, 12
Genotypic risk, markers of, 76
Genotyping
  and association analysis, 16
  methodological differences in, 15

Gestation, critical periods during, 37
Gilmore, G. C., 262, 263
Glial scarring, 83
Gliosis, 72
Gloor, H., 48, 49
Glutamatergic N-methyl-D-asparate receptor system, 70
Goldberg, S. C., 360
Goldman, C., 403
Goldstein, M. J., 457, 458
Gonadal mosaicism, 16
Gottesman, I. I., xxii, 6, 17, 310, 496, 498
Grace, A. A., xxiii, 132, 139
Green, M. F., xxv
Grochowski, S., 251
Gross motor dysfunction, and prediction of schizophrenia, 438
Gross Motor Dysfunction Scale, 437
Gross motor impairment, childhood measures of, 439
Grove, W. M., 104
Guze, S., 102

Hahlweg, K., 458
Hale, F., 37
Hale, J., 360
Hallucinations, xxiv, 500
  neural substrates of, 239
  pathogenesis of, 243
  predisposition for, 238
  words generated during, 237–238
Hallucinations, schizophrenic
  auditory-linguistic form of, 235
PET studies of, 236–237
Hand preference, 212
  See also Lateral performance
  and lateralization, 226
  vs. lateral performance, 216–224
  and thought disorder, 213–214
Harvard University, 106
Heat shock
  in Drosophila development, 49, 50
  as teratogen, 48

Heat-shock protein response, 49–50
Helsinki, 1957 epidemic findings in, 39, 40
Helsinki Habituation Project, 27, 54–55, 56–58
Hemispheric asymmetry, development of, 227
Hemispheric dominance, anomalies of, 226–227
Hemispheric lesions, eye-tracking dysfunction in, 165
Hemolytic disease, and schizophrenic risk, 52–54
Heritability of schizophrenia, 299
    See also Genetic predisposition
    degree of, 76
    models of, 8
Hershenson, M., 268
Heterogeneity
    diagnostic, 499
    etiological, 5, 12
Heterozygosity, genetic, 17
Hierarchical approach, 5–6
High-risk studies, xx
    See also New York High-Risk Project
    major goal of, 349
    and neurobehavioral measures, 436–437
    process-oriented strategy for, 274
High-technology procedures, costs of, 497
Hiller, J. B., xxv
Hillside Study of Risk and Early Detection in Schizophrenia (HSREDS), 350
    assessment procedures in, 370–371
    design of, 351–352
    goals of, 373–374
    predictors of illness in, 352–354
    preliminary clinical findings, 371–373
    probands for, 351
    sample in, 368–369

Hippocampus
    correlated with hallucinations, 239
    and developmental disruption of limbic circuit formation, 146–147
    effect on accumbens cells of, 147
    in etiology of schizophrenia, 125, 126
    information flow through accumbens controlled by, 135
    neonatal lesions of, 145
    prenatally acquired damage to, 472–473
    in schizophrenic patients, 137
Hollister, J. M., 51, 53
Holzman, P. S., xxiv, 106, 161, 191, 205, 206
Homozygosity, genetic, 17
Hooley, J. M., xxv
Hormonal changes, and neurodevelopment, 82
Hospitalization, and hand preference, 212
HPA. See Hypothalamic-pituitary-adrenal
HSREDS. See Hillside Study of Risk and Early Detection in Schizophrenia
Hughes, D. W., 161
Hulme, M. R., 257
Huntington's disease, 17
    antisaccade performance in, 189
    pathological changes associated with, 127
Hutchinson, G., 9
Huttenen, M. O., 38
Hyperbilirubinemia, 53
Hypercortisolemia, 472
Hypokrisia, 96
Hypothalamic-pituitary-adrenal (HPA) axis, 471, 472, 475, 488
Hypoxia
    fetal, 53, 67
    perinatal, 31, 81, 83

prenatal, 473
and schizophrenic risk, 69–70

Iacono, W. G., 161
Icelandic families, 11
Iconic image, defined, 255
Illogical thinking, and hand preference, 213
See also Thought disorder
Imagery
vs. hallucinations, 238
inner speech/auditory-verbal,
241
Imprinting, genomic, 16, 17
Influenza, maternal, 40
and brain abnormalities, 46
criminal activity and, 47
and fetal brain development, 47
and genetic risk, 41–45
and schizophrenic risk, 60
2nd trimester, 41, 42, 46, 53, 501
and visual attention habituation,
55, 57–58
Influenza epidemic
in Helsinki, 56
as methodological tool, 37
1957, 41, 42, 43
and rate of schizophrenia, 38
Influenza teratogen, 35
Influenza virus
and placental barrier, 51
and schizophrenia risk, 39–40
Information, poverty of, and hand
preference, 213
Information processing
models of, 255
in schizophrenia patients, 342
and vulnerability to schizophrenia,
301
Information-processing deficit, in
CPT research, 308–309
Information-processing disturbances
and dysfunctions, 192, 254

Inheritability
in Copenhagen High-Risk
Project, 32
See also Heritability
Inheritance, single locus, 10–11
Institute for Psychiatric Demography
(Danish), 52
Integration, and consolidation, xxi,
xxii
Intelligence, nature of, 502
Internalizing behavior, of adolescents,
480–482
Internalizing behavior problems,
scores for, 481
Intervention programs
and HSREDS, 353, 374
IQ scores, in NYHRP, 434
Irish schizophrenia pedigrees, 13

Jackson, John Hughlings, 167
Jaundice, 53
Javitt, D. D., 251

Kahn, A., 397
Kahneman, D., 282
Katschnig, H., 6
Kendler, K. S., 10, 14
Kendler, Kenneth, 310
Kenji, W. S., 360
Kety, S. S., xxvi
Kitamura, T., 397
Knight, R. A., xxiv, 259, 260, 262, 268,
269, 272, 277, 281, 282, 391,
499
Korfine, L., 111
Kraepelin, E., xx, 67, 84, 93, 94, 95,
307, 393
Krafczek, S. A., 269
Kring, A. M., 394, 404
Kruglyak, L., 12, 13
K-SADS. See Schedule for Affective
Disorders and Schizophrenia
for School Age Children
Kumar, R., 397

Laboratory, in schizophrenia research,
xxii
See also Technology
Labor times, 31
See also Delivery complications
Lack of progression, evidence for, 74–
76
Lander, E., 12, 13
Language
and hemispheric dominance, 227
and laterality, 228–230
Latent liability for schizophrenia, and
PAS scores, 114
See also Liability for schizophrenia
Latent trait model, of schizotypy, 110
Laterality
assessment of, 212
distribution of, 212, 215–216
and language, 228–230
measures of, 216–224
and memory, 224–227
Lateralization
anomalous, 211
and hand preference, 227
Lateral performance
See also Hand preference
line drawing, 215–216
measurement of, 214
vs. preference, 216–224
and repetitiousness, 230
and short-term recall, 230
L-DOPA, 123
See also Dopamine system
Learning
contextual, 135
and hippocampal damage, 136
Lebell, M. B., 458
Left-handedness. *See* Hand preference
Lenzenweger, M. F., xxiii, 102, 103,
104, 111, 112
Levin, S., 165
Levy, D., xxiv, 161, 189
Lewine, R. J., xxvi, 397
Liability for schizophrenia

See also Vulnerability to schizophrenia
and CNS maturational processes,
474
early views of, 94–95
environmental contributions to, 8–
9
environmental factors, 10
genetic, 27
genetic transmission of, 299
Meehl's model for, 96–98
and PAS scores, 111
and prenatally acquired damage,
473
schizotypy and, 94
studies of, 428
underlying, 94
Life events, and psychiatric relapse,
459
Limbic cortical–basal ganglia circuit,
dysfunction in, 130
Limbic pathways, myelination of, 474
Limbic system, impact of neonatal
hippocampal lesions on, 144–
145
Lincoln–Oseretsky Test of Motor Impairment, 437
Line drawing
measurement of performance by,
215–216
measures based on, 214
Linkage studies, 10–15
Lishman, W. A., 212
Lithium, ETD produced by, 162
Lod score, 11, 12
Loftus, G. R., 259, 260
Long Island Jewish Medical Center
(Glen Oaks, NY), 368
Longitudinal studies, of vulnerability
factors, 300
Longitudinal trait–state studies, 320
Loranger, A., 102, 103
Low-risk rates, calculating, 43
See also Risk for schizophrenia

Luchins, D. J., 212
Lykken, D. T., 161

Machon, R. A., 38
MacLean, Charles, 310
Magnetic resonance imaging (MRI), 243
Magnetoencephalographic methods, 243
Maher, B. A., xxiv, 214
MAM. *See* Methylazoxymethanol acetate
Manoach, D. S., 268
Manschreck, T. C., xxiv, 214, 216
Markow, T. A., 17
Masking deficiencies, 259
   See also Backward masking
Masking function, Type A, 255
Masking stimulus, 255
Masten, A. S., 399
Matthysse, S., xxvi, 161
MAXCOV procedure, 111
McGrew, J., 102
McGuffin, P., 11
McLean Hospital (Belmont, NY), 106
McMeekan, E. R. L., 212
McMenamin, S. D., 260
Meaning, emotional, 390
Mednick, S. A., xxiii, 38, 53, 495, 501
Meehl, P. E., 6, 95, 96, 97, 101,
   109–110, 111, 114, 398
Memory
   See also Working memory
   diurnal variations in, 221–224
   and hippocampal damage, 136
   laterality and, 224–227
   laterality and context-aided, 216–224
Memory disorders, and emotional functioning, 391
Mendelian
   diseases, 11
   principles, 16
Mendell, N. R., 161

Mental disorders, genetic analysis of, 15
Mental retardation, 502
Merikangas, K., 16
Merikle, P. M., 257
Methylazoxymethanol acetate (MAM), 146
Miklowitz, D. J., 457
Millar, K., 221
Miller, C., 214
Miller, G., 214, 495
Miller, G. A., 285
Miller, Gregory, 494
Miller–Selfridge Test, 217, 218, 220
Minnesota Multiphasic Personality Inventory (MMPI), in psychometrically defined schizotypes, 104–105, 113
Mintz, J., 458
Mitochondrial inheritance, 16
Mitotoxin methylazoxymethanol acetate, 139
MMPI. *See* Minnesota Multiphasic Personality Inventory
Moldin, S. O., xxii, 496
Monitoring, perinatal and prenatal, 70
Monozygotic (MZ) concordance rate, 7–8
Moore, H., xxiii, 139
Moral issues, 19
Mother
   "schizophrenic," xxii
   See also Relatives of schizophrenia patients
Motion
   and contrast sensitivity, 169, 170, 171
   and ETD, 173–179
   perception of, 168–169
   and speed discrimination, 169, 170
   tasks for perception of, 170
Motion detection
   and maintenance of pursuit, 177–179

Motion detection (*continued*)
and onset of pursuit, 175–177
Motor deficits, vs. affective deficits,
405–410
Motor development, delayed, 80
Motor performance, impaired, and
anomalous language, 230
Mount Sinai School of Medicine, 354
MRI. *See* Magnetic resonance imaging
Mueser, K. T., 457
Multiepidemic studies, 38
Multifactorial diseases, 7
Multilocus model, 8
Murray, R. M., 77
MZ. *See* Monozygotic, concordance
rate

National Collaborative Perinatal Pro-
ject, 69, 81
Neale, J. M., 394
Neale, Michael, 310
Neath, I., 267
Neisser, U., 255, 282
Neonate, damage to hippocampus in,
145
See also Hippocampus
Neophytides, A. N., 77
Neuchterlein, K. H., xxv, 309
Neural diathesis–stress model, 470
See also Diathesis–stress model
Neural mechanisms, distributed na-
ture of, 236
Neuroanatomical changes, in psycho-
sis, 68
Neurobehavioral functioning, prospec-
tive studies of, 80
Neurocognitive deficits
backward masking in, 330
as biobehavioral markers, 352
and clinical symptoms, 350, 367
CPT measures for, 307
in HSREDS, 353
in young at-risk offspring, 349
Neurocognitive processes, xxiii, 309
Neurodegeneration

changes of, 74
signs of, 79
Neurodevelopment
and adult onset, 82–83
schizophrenia as disorder of, 84
Neurodevelopmental model
brain-imaging studies in, 73–80
cognitive functioning in, 80–83
neuropathology studies in, 71–73
obstetric complications, 68–70, 73
Neurodevelopmental pathways, 19
Neurodevelopmental research
process-oriented approach in, 285–
286
theory, 493
Neurofibrillary tangles, 71
Neuroimaging studies, 74–75, 83
Neuroimaging technologies, 236
Neuroleptic medication
and affective congruence, 402
and affective deficits, 413
in EAP, 358
Neuromotor dysfunction, 399
and facial expression, 408
measures of, 407, 408
Neuromotor impairment, 68
Neuromotor measures, in NYHRP,
434
Neuronal synapses, pruning of, 474
Neurons, heterotopic displacement of,
68
Neuropathology studies,
postmortem, 68, 71–73
Neuropsychological measures, 370
New York High-Risk Project
(NYHRP), xxv, 427
childhood measures in, 433–435
description of, 429–430
participants in, 430–433, 430
New York State Psychiatric Institute
(New York, NY), 396
Nicewander, W. A., 249

No-gap/no-overlap paradigm, in antisaccade performance, 193–196, 205–206
Norris, M., 310, 360
Nowlis, G., 268
Nucleus accumbens
    afferent inputs to, 130–134
    excitatory transmission from amygdala to, 137–140
    functional implications of hippocampal gating, 135–137
    hippocampal modulation of PFC throughout in, 134–135
    input from hippocampus to, 134
    limbic inputs to, 142–143
    medium spiny neuron in, 131
    relevance of, 126–130
    role of hippocampally driven bistable state in, 132, 133
    subregion of, 130
Nuechterlein, K. H., xxiv, 6, 307, 308, 310, 360, 457, 458
Numerosity judgments, in perceptual organization, 263
Nutritional deficiency, prenatal, 473
NYHRP. See New York High-Risk Project
Nystagmus, in schizophrenic patients, 168

Obiols, J. E., 104
Obstetrical insults, 469
Obstetric complications, and schizophrenic risk, 68–70, 83
    See also Delivery complications
O'Donnell, P., 132
O'Driscoll, G. A., 167
Oltmanns, T. F., 393, 394
Open-loop gain, in eye tracking, 165, 175, 176, 178
Opler, L. A., 262
Orne, D. M., 260
Overlap paradigm, in antisaccade performance, 193–196, 205–206

Overton, D., 161
Owen, D. R., 262

Palafox, German, 171
Palmer, J., 280
Pandurangi, A. K., 360
Panic disorders, in NYHRP, 430, 431
PANSS. See Positive and Negative Syndrome Scale
Parahippocampal cortex, in etiology of schizophrenia, 125, 126
Parallelism, processing of, 271
Paranoid personality disorders, in HSREDS, 373
Paranoid subtypes, and maternal influenza, 53
Parent–offspring analyses, environmental variance in, 18
Parents of schizophrenia patients, neurocognitive studies in, 312–314
    See also Relatives of schizophrenia patients
Parkinson's disease, 409
    eye-tracking dysfunction in, 165
    pathological changes associated with, 127
Parsimony, in laterality measurement, 219
Parsing approach
    for antisaccade performance, 192
    to backward masking, 330
PAS. See Perceptual Aberration Scale
Passivity, 240
Pathological changes, 125
Pathophysiology, 123
Patients, preschizophrenic, 81
    See also Schizophrenia patients
Pattern-recognition task, 268–269
Pattern-recognition test, 282
PCP. See Phencyclidine (phenylcyclohexyl-piperidine)
PDE. See Personality Disorder Examination

Pelonero, A. L., 360
Perceptual aberrations, in schizotypy, 100–101
Perceptual Aberration Scale (PAS), 101
  and latent liability for schizophrenia, 114
  latent structure of, 110
Perceptual-cognitive research, 286
Perceptual discrimination deficits
  and vulnerability to schizophrenia, 320–321
Perceptual organization
  abnormal, 263
  abnormal performance on, 281
  and automaticity deficit hypothesis, 268–269
  deficit in, 277
  defined, 261
  dysfunction in, 267
  and insufficient mnemonic traces, 263
  in process-oriented approach, 261–265
  and thought disorder, 283
Perceptual processing, configural influences on, 265–268
Performance, in process-oriented strategy, 250
Performance measures
  diurnal variation in, 224
  variables affecting, 220
Periventricular damage, 28
Perseveration, and role of hippocampus, 137
Personality, and teratogenic action, 50
Personality Disorder Examination (PDE), 429
  in Copenhagen High-Risk Project, 30
  and SPD symptoms, 103, 104–105
Personality disorders, in HSREDS, 372–373

Personality tests, in Tangshan study, 59
PET. See Positron emission tomography
Peters, M., 229
PFC. See Prefontal cortex
Pharmaceutical industry, 19
Phencyclidine (phenyl-cyclohexyl-piperidine [PCP])
  decrease in glutamatergic transmission by, 147
  pharmacology of, 141
  psychotic symptoms derived from, 143–144
  and schizophrenic symptoms, 140–141
Phenomenology, xx
Phenotype, schizophrenia, schizotype as valid extension of, 113–114
Phenylketonuria, 502
Phillips, L., 254
Phillips, W. A., 256, 271, 272
Pituitary ACTH, 471
Place, E. J. S., 262, 263
Polygenic multifactorial threshold model of schizotypy, 110
Polygenic (multilocus) model, 8
Population screens, and intervention programs, 349
Positive and Negative Syndrome Scale (PANSS), 281–282, 358
  blunted affect measured by, 406
  blunted affect rating from, 399
Positron emission tomography (PET), 236, 496
  of eye-tracking dysfunction, 167
  of frontal lobe dysfunction, 386
  in hallucinations, 237
Postmortem analysis, 68, 71–73
Postpregnancy stressors, 35
Posttraumatic stress disorder (PTSD), 497
Potter, M. C., 259
Pouget, E. R., 397

Prefrontal cortex (PFC)
and amygdala stimulation, 137–139
effect on accumbens cells of, 147
failure to activate, 124
hippocampal modulation of, 134–135
lesions of, 124
and nucleus accumbens, 127
Premorbid factors, identification of, 29
Present State Examination (PSE), 29–30
Preventive intervention programs, biobehavioral markers in, 352–353
Price, J. M., 249
Processing strategy, development of, 266
Process-oriented approach
hallmarks of, 261
Process-oriented strategy
in cognitive psychology, 249–273
efficacy of, 270, 286
example of, 257
generalization of, 273–286
specification progress using, 254–273
successful implementation of, 253
Process specification, 248
Proctor, L. R., 161
Prodromal indicators, 353
Prodromal phase, 476
Prognosis, long-term, 473
Prominent deficit syndrome, 124
Propositional-syntactic representation, 269
Protein synthesis, and heat shock, 48
PSE. See Present State Examination
Psychiatric disorders, biological bases of, 127
Psychoanalytic theory, xx
Psychological cognitive models, 285
Psychopathologists, xix
Psychopathology
and developmental instability, 17
experimental, xxi
schizotypic, xxiii, 111
Psychopathology scales, 29
Psychophysiological Research, Society of, 494
Psychoses
amphetamine, 140
in NYHRP, 430, 431
prediction of schizophrenia-related, 436–439
Psychosocial factors, as environmental risk, 10
Psychosocial inquiry, 493
Psychosocial stress, 469
Psychotomimetics, DA-related, 143
Psychotropic medications, 198
PTSD. See Posttraumatic stress disorder
Puberty, HPA activity during, 475
See also Adolescence

Rabinowicz, E. F., 262, 263, 265
Rashbass, C., 165, 166, 175
Raulin, M. L., 101
Raven Progressive Matrices, 59
RDC. See Research Diagnostic Criteria
Reality testing, 500
Rearing, unstable circumstances in, 35–36, 60
Recall
and hand lateralization, 230
and hand preference, 214
Redmond, D. A., 214
Reflexive saccades
behavioral parsing approach to, 192
cognitive demands of, 190
correction of errors in, 188
defined, 185
disinhibition in, 202–206
experimental latencies for, 199–200
and gap paradigm, 191
increased inhibition in, 202–206
latency in, 187–188
normal range for, 187

Reflexive saccade task, correct performance on, 186
Relapse, psychiatric
 and expressed emotion, 454–457
 and family variables, 450–451
 pathogenesis of, 460
 predictors of, 449
Relapse-triggering role, xxv
Relatives of schizophrenia patients.
 See also Family members study
 and affective deficits, 387
 antisaccade performance in, 189
 CPT for, 308
 EMDs in, 363
 and expressed emotion, 449
 information-processing deficits detected in, 309
 and masking performance, 343–345
 perception of, 455
 in Span of Apprehension Test studies, 305
 subtle anomalies in, 300
 vulnerability studies of, 320
Repetitiousness
 and hand lateralization, 230
 and thought disorder, 229
Research, schizophrenia
 future of, xxii
 history of, xx
 recent development in, xxi
Research Diagnostic Criteria (RDC), 429
Reveley, A. M., 77
Reveley, M. A., 77
Reward learning, involvement of nucleus accumbens in, 127
Rh. *See* Rhesus, compatibility
Rhesus (Rh) compatibility, 51
Risch, N. J., 16
Risk factors, 35
 in Copenhagen project, 28–36
 environmental, 9–10

genetic, 10
 teratogenic disturbance, 36
Risk for schizophrenia
 average sulcul CSF–brain ratio in, 33
 and intellectual functioning, 81
 and obstetrical complications, 67–68
 and Rh incompatibility, 51, 52–53, 52–54
 SPD as, 499
 and ventricular size, 77
Ritter, W., 251
Robins, E., 102
Rochester, University of, international conference on schizophrenia at, 494
Rosenfarb, I. S., 458, 459
Rosenthal, D., xxvi
Rubella infection, prenatal, 9
Rutschmann, J., 308
Rutter, M., 440

Saccade latency, defined, 197
Saccadic eye movements, 162–163, 167
Saccuzzo, D. P., 338
SADS. *See* Schedule for Affective Disorders and Schizophrenia
SADS-L. *See* Schedule for Affective Disorders and Schizophrenia–Lifetime version
Samples, study, and high technology, 497
SCA1. *See* Spinocerebellar ataxia Type 1
Schedule for Affective Disorders and Schizophrenia for School Age Children (K-SADS, Epidemiological version), 354, 370
Schedule for Affective Disorders and

Schizophrenia–Lifetime
version (SADS–L), 29, 429
Schedule for Affective Disorders and
Schizophrenia (SADS), 213
SCID. *See* Structured Clinical Interview for *DSM-IV* Axis I Disorders
SCID-II. *See* Structured Clinical Interview for *DSM-IV* Personality
Disorders
Schizoaffective disorder
in Developmental processes in
Schizophrenic Disorders Project, 315
in NYHRP, 430, 431
Schizoaffective patients, hand preference in, 212
Schizophrenia
costs associated with, 7
in Developmental processes in
Schizophrenic Disorders Project, 315
development of, 6
diagnostic criteria for, 94
incidence of, xix, 7
"latent," 94
pathogenesis of, xix
schizotypic psychopathology and,
96–98, 99
standards for, 94
teratogen-related, 41
Schizophrenia patients
in clinical remission, 314, 315
frontal lobe pathology in, 124
lateralization in, 211
with structural abnormalities, 78
Schizotaxia, 96
Schizotypal personality disorder
(SPD), 33–35, 95, 432
and abnormalities in HPA axis, 486
in adolescents, 470
behavior problems in, 486
in EAP, 359–360
EMDs associated with, 363

in HSREDS, 373
and obstetrical complications,
77–78
schizophrenia and, 488
study of, 476
Schizotypes, 96
biological relatives of, 102
description of, 99
detection of, 99–100
deviance displayed by, 103–109
"genotypic," 100
long-term follow-up of, 112
multiple laboratory tasks for, 106–
108
psychometric, 114
relatives of schizophrenia patients,
100
symptoms associated with, 102–
103, 113
Schizotypy, 96
body image in, 100
defined, 98
developmental model for, 96–98
latent structure of, 109–112
measures of, 100
modal study of, 106
perceptual aberrations in, 100
prevalence of, 114
psychometric approach to, 110
taxometric exploration of, 110–112
Schwab, S. G., 14
SDT. *See* Signal detection theory
Search-coil method, for recording eye
movements, 165
Self and Observer Affect Rating Scale
(SOARS)
affective expression measured by,
406–408
explained, 398–399
Selfridge, J., 214
Senile plaques, 71
Sensitivity, measures of, 27
Sereno, A. B., 191, 205, 206
Servan-Schreiber, D., 309

Shagass, C., 161
Shakow, David, xxvi
Shields, J., 6
Short-term visual memory (STVM).
    See also Memory
    abnormal performance on, 281
    allocation and consolidation deficits
        in, 259–261
    discriminating sensory store from,
        256–259
Siblings of schizophrenia patients,
    350, 372–373
    See also Relatives of schizophrenia
    patients
SID-P. *See* Structured Interview for
    DSM-IV Personality Disorders
Signal detection theory (SDT), 277,
    307
Silbersweig, D. A., xxiv, 500
Silverstein, S. M., xxiv, 268, 272, 277,
    281, 282, 499
Sine wave target, in motion discrimi-
    nation studies, 173
Singer, W., 271, 272
Single locus model, 10
Sison, C., 397
Slater Hospital (Providence, RI), 224
Smooth pursuit eye movements
    (SPEM), 162–163
    complex organization of, 167–168
    of normal control, 164
    perceptual aspects of, 168
SOARS. *See* Self and Observer Affect
    Rating Scale
SOAs. See Stimulus onset asynchron-
    ies
Social adjustment, and childhood at-
    tentional deviance, 435
Social competence, lack of, 31
Social deficits, vs. affective deficits,
    405–410
Social disengagement, and emotional
    functioning, 391

Social functioning, and schizophrenic
    symptomatology, 387
Social isolation, measures of, 436
Social problems
    of adolescents, 480
    scores for, 485
Social Problems Scale, 475, 478, 479,
    486
Social situations, inability to respond
    to, 125
Sommers, A. A., 397
SPAN. *See* Span of Apprehension Test
Span of Apprehension Test (SPAN),
    278–280
    in high-risk and family studies, 274
    and vulnerability to schizophrenia,
        345–346
    studies
        earlier, 304–305
        in experimental psychology, 303–
            304
        forced-choice task in, 303–304,
            305, 310, 315–317
    tasks
        in Developmental processes in
            schizophrenic disorders pro-
            ject, 315–317
        in UCLA family members study,
            310–314
Spatial negative priming, in schizo-
    typic patients, 106–108, 113
Spaulding, W., 256
SPD. *See* Schizotypal personality dis-
    order
Speech, poverty of, 386
SPEM. See Smooth pursuit eye move-
    ments
Sperling, G., 254, 255, 280, 303
Sperling iconic imagery model,
    254–256
Spinocerebellar ataxia Type 1 (SCA1),
    14
Spitzer, R. L., 109

SPM. *See* Statistical parametric mapping, techniques
Statistical parametric mapping (SPM) techniques, 237
Steingard, S., 309
Step-ramp target
  in eye tracking, 165–167, 175
  in motion discrimination studies, 173
Stern, E., xxiv, 500
Stimulus onset asynchronies (SOAs), 257
Stochastic processes, 17
Strachan, 457
Strauss, M. E., 360
Stress
  childhood, 28
  and HPA axis, 471
  and neurodevelopment, 82
  prenatal, 473
  and schizophrenia symptoms, 472
Stress, maternal, and fetal development, 58–59
Stress, prenatal, and schizophrenic risk, 60
Striatum, functional subdivisions of, 126–127
Stromgren, 496
Stroop effect, and antisaccade performance, 190–191
Strous, R., 251
Structured Clinical Interview, for *DSM-III-R*–Patient Edition, 198
Structured Clinical Interview for *DSM-IV* Axis I Disorders (SCID), 370
Structured Clinical Interview for *DSM-IV* Personality Disorders (SCID-II), 477
Structured interview, for schizotypal symptoms, 198
Structured Interview for *DSM-IV* Personality Disorders (SID-P), 370
STVM. See Short-term visual memory
Styles, B. C., 221
Subcortical structures, correlated with hallucinations, 239
Subotnik, K. L., 309
Subpsychotic symptoms, risk for, 76
Substance abuse, 396
  and childhood problem behavior, 436
  in NYHRP, 430, 431
Successive parsing, 192
Sugarman, P. A., 9
Supranuclear palsy
  antisaccade performance in, 189
  eye-tracking dysfunction in, 165
Surprenant, A. M., 267
Susceptibility, disease, 15
Sustained attention, in CPT, 305
Sustained attentional functioning, in psychometrically defined schizotypes, 103, 104–105, 113
Symmetry
  perceptual processing of, 268
  sensitivity to, 271
Symptom formation, 241
  and mediating vulnerability factor, 300–302, 305
  and working memory abnormalities, 321
Symptoms, Scale for Assessment of Negative, 30, 360
Symptoms, Scale for Assessment of Positive, 30
Symptoms of schizophrenia
  affective deficits, 385–387
  and biobehavioral markers, 368
  eye-movement disorders, 364–366
  impaired attention, 360–362
  negative, 337–338
  and neurocognitive deficits, 367
  and PCP, 140–144
  prodromal, 371

Symptoms of schizophrenia
(*continued*)
and stress exposure, 472

Tangshan study, 58–59
Target-detection studies, 265–267
Target letter detection
accuracy, 304
in forced-choice span of apprehension task, 315–317
Tarrier, 459
Task decomposition strategy, vs. process-oriented strategy, 251, 252
Task-oriented approach
to cognitive deficiencies, 273
vs. process-oriented strategy, 250–252
theoretical meaning of, 274–280
Taylor, H. A., 303
TDI. *See* Thought Disorder Index
TDT. *See* Transmission disequilibrium tests
Technology
costs of high, 497
misuse of, 498
and study of schizophrenia, 495–496
Temperament, and teratogenic action, 50
Temporal cortex, abnormal development of, 126
Temporal lobe volumes, reduced, 74
Teratogenicity, early studies of, 37–39
Teratogenic risk, in Fetal Viral Infection Project, 43
Teratogens
adventitious, 27, 28
chemical, 49
and fetal brain development, 47
fetal virus as, 38–40
and genetic risk, 41–45
heat shock, 48
influenza, 35
Teratology, mammalian, 37
Thalamic region, 130
Thalamus, and hallucinations, 239

Thalidomide, 50
Theory, schizophrenia, developments in, xix
Thought disorder
and cognitive tasks, 281
and emotional functioning, 391
and hand preference, 213–214
and perceptual organization, 283
repetitiousness, 229
in schizotypic patients, 106–108, 113
Thought Disorder Index (TDI), 106
in NYHRP, 435
in process-oriented strategy, 282–283
Thought problems
of adolescents, 480–482
scores for, 483
Thought Problems Scale, 475, 478, 479, 486
Thurstone equal-appearing interval scale, 258
Time of day (TOD) measurement, 214, 221
and laterality and memory correlation, 224–227
and memory, 221–224
as significant artifact, 230
Tone-discrimination study, 251
TOD. *See* Time of day
Trait studies, 236
Transient channels, in masking performance deficit, 342
Transmission disequilibrium tests (TDT), 16
Triplet repeat mutations, implications of, 17
Tupin, 459
Twins
concordance rates, 76
longitudinal assessment of, 10
offspring of, 6
schizophrenia in, 144
and schizophrenic risk, 7–8

Twin studies
affective deficits in, 387
MZ:DZ ratio in, 8
neuroanatomical markers in, 78
nonadditive genetic variance in, 18
Two-hit model, xxiii, 27, 60
first hit, 27–28
second hit, 28

UCLA. See University of California,
Los Angeles, family member
study at
University of California, Los Angeles
(UCLA), family members
study at, 309–314
Understandability, and hand prefer-
ence, 213
US–UK Cross National Project, 94

Valner, J. B., 391
Velocity discrimination experiments,
171–173
Venables, P., 57
Ventral limbic cortical–basal ganglia
circuits, 128–130
Ventral striatum, correlated with hal-
lucinations, 239
Ventricular abnormalities, in
Copenhagen High-Risk
Project, 32, 33–35
Ventricular enlargement, 74
and genetic risk, 77
in schizophrenic patients, 73–74
Vigilance research
CPT in, 305
simultaneous discrimination tasks
in, 306–307
Viral infection, prenatal, 473
Viral studies, 38–39
See also Influenza virus
Vision Sciences Laboratory, at Har-
vard University, 171
Visual arrays, parallel processing of
stimuli in, 304

Visual attention habituation
in Copenhagen project, 54–55
in Helsinki project, 57–58
measurement of, 55
Visual fixation, in NYHRP, 435
Visual masking
See also Backward masking
explained, 335, 336
and vulnerability to schizophrenia,
338, 339
Visual processing, backward masking
for, 329
Visual signals, processing of, 169
Visual suffix task study, 283–284
Vulnerability factors, xxiv
Vulnerability to schizophrenia, 79
and adolescence, 469
and backward masking, 342–345
and CPT, 345–346
and CPT research, 308
creation of, 28
vs. development of, 320
diathesis–stress models of, 470–
475
genetic transmission of, 299–301
and information-processing performance, 301
markers of, 462, 498
mediating vulnerability factor, 300–
302, 305
and memory processes, 314
and perceptual discrimination processes, 314
and Span of Apprehension Tests,
345–346
stable indicators of, 305, 317
studies of, 276–277

Walker, E., 471, 472, 473, 488
Wallace, C. J., 277
Wang, S., 13, 14
Warkany, J., 37
Wastell, D. G., 221
Waxman, E., 260

WCST. *See* Wisconsin Card Sorting
Test
Wechsler Adult Intelligence Scale–
Revised, 197
Wedding Feast, The (Breughel), 228
Weinberger, D. R., 77, 82, 212
Wernicke's area, and hallucinations,
239
Wilcoxon Signed-Rank Test, 198
Wisconsin Card Sorting Test (WCST),
125, 190, 191, 370
and antisaccade performance, 190–
191
in NYHRP, 435
in schizophrenia patients, 136
and SPD symptoms, 105–106, 107
Word generation experiments, 241
Working memory
See also Memory; Neurocognitive
deficits

childhood measures of, 439
in HSREDS, 353
in NYHRP, 434
and prediction of schizophrenia,
437
in schizotypic patients, 106–108,
113
Working memory deficits
in CPT research, 309
and vulnerability to schizophrenia,
320–321
World Health Organization studies, 9
Wyatt, R. J., 77, 212
Wynne, L. C., xxvi

X chromosome, FMR-1 gene on, 16

Yahia, M., 397
Yeo, R. A., 17

Zubin, Joseph, xxvi

About the Editors

Mark F. Lenzenweger, PhD, is an associate professor of psychology in the Department of Psychology at Harvard University. Before moving on to Harvard, he was a faculty member at Cornell University in Ithaca, New York, and the Cornell University Medical College in New York City, New York. He received his BA from Cornell University and his PhD in clinical psychology from Yeshiva University (New York City), completing his internship training at the New York Hospital Cornell Medical Center, Westchester Division. Dr. Lenzenweger currently conducts two programs of experimental psychopathology research: One focuses on the nature and structure of schizotypy in relation to schizophrenia, and the other involves the prospective longitudinal study of personality disorders, personality, and temperament.

Robert H. Dworkin, PhD, is a professor of anethesiology and psychiatry at the University of Rochester. He received his BA from the University of Pennsylvania and his PhD from Harvard University. He was a faculty member at both Cornell University and Columbia University before moving to the University of Rochester. His current research involves two different areas: affective deficits in individuals with schizophrenia and their first-degree relatives and the pathogenesis of chronic pain (in individuals with herpes zoster and patients following a mastectomy).